WHEN THE
MUSIC STOPS . . .

Norman Lebrecht is music columnist for the *Daily Telegraph* and author of eight books that have been translated into many languages, from Chinese to modern Hebrew. His most recent books include the international bestseller *The Maestro Myth* (1991) and *The Companion to 20th Century Music* (1993). He has made many television and radio documentaries for the BBC and lectures extensively around the world. He is also the founder-editor of a major series of composer biographies.

Born in London in 1948, Norman Lebrecht studied sociology and psychology and covered world events as a television news producer before becoming a full-time writer at the age of thirty. He is married to the food writer and archivist Elbie Lebrecht and lives in central London with their three daughters.

ALSO BY NORMAN LEBRECHT

The Maestro Myth
The Companion to 20th Century Music

WHEN THE
MUSIC STOPS . . .

MANAGERS, MAESTROS AND
THE CORPORATE MURDER OF CLASSICAL MUSIC

NORMAN LEBRECHT

POCKET
B O O K S

LONDON · SYDNEY · NEW YORK · TOKYO · SINGAPORE · TORONTO

First published in Great Britain by Simon & Schuster Ltd, 1996
This edition published by Pocket Books,
an imprint of Simon & Schuster Ltd, 1997
A Viacom company

Simon & Schuster Ltd
West Garden Place
Kendal Street
London W2 2AQ

Simon & Schuster Australia
Sydney

A CIP catalogue record for this book is available from the British Library

ISBN 0-671-01025-5

Printed and bound in Great Britain by Caledonian International Book
Manufacturing, Glasgow

music business *n*. 1. the commercial exploitation of musical works and artists by means of publishing, performing, recording, touring, &c. 2. collective term for companies engaged in the above. 3. the ever-hidden link between music and mammon.

Usage: late 20th century. *Sources/References*: scarce.

Contents

INTRODUCTION TO
THE PAPERBACK EDITION

> This is the way the world ends
> Not with a bang, but with a whimper.[1]

Nothing in this world ever comes to a complete halt. Nor would a responsible commentator seriously predict the abrupt cessation of an activity that has flourished for two centuries and continues to be widely enjoyed. Why, even bare-knuckle boxing and the riding of penny-farthing bicycles retain a circle of adherents long after the march of civilisation has rendered them apparently obsolete.

So if anything can be confidently predicted in the ever-receding horizons of the information revolution it is that the public performance of classical music will endure in some form or other, great or small. It is equally certain, however, that the nightly enactment of music and opera will, in the very foreseeable future, cease to be as central and essential a feature of metropolitan life as it has been for the past two and a half centuries.

The grounds for this assertion are multiple and mutually unrelated. Across

[1] T. S. Eliot, *Journey of the Magi*

the world, music audiences are being eroded by an array of domestic electronic attractions. Habitual concertgoers fear to venture into the inner city after dark, or get deterred by traffic jams and parking restrictions. A new generation raised on television soundbites and instant hamburgers has been jaggedly desensitised to the stately magniloquence of an hour-long symphony. The sharing of music within families has been blighted by the decline of the nuclear family. Music teaching, insofar as it is still provided in public school systems, has been rendered almost worthless by a politically correct tendency to treat all musics as equal – the primitive with the refined, the commercial with the spiritual.

The box-office consequences of dwindling audiences and educational dereliction are serious enough, without the art having to suffer parallel disasters of a drop in state and business subsidies, an acute reduction of recording activities and rampaging greed on the part of star musicians and their managements. Together, they spell financial and structural ruin.

These issues have been widely acknowledged within the music world, but until this book was written they were never publicly addressed. Industry leaders, fearing to face the future, hoped it would go away if no one talked about it. Trapped on a carousel that books dates and casts recordings three or four years in advance, they were like officers on a ship who saw coral reefs ahead but were unable to swerve or reverse fast enough to avoid them. No matter how complacent or negligent they had been in the past, you had to feel a smidgeon of sympathy for those well-meaning professionals who were doing their best to keep music afloat, as danger loomed and sharks circled lazily in the waters below.

It was clearly a struggle for survival, and those performing and recording companies that responded quickly and decisively were the ones likeliest to outlast the millennium. Vision and boldness usually find their reward; inaction is always risky, never more so than in mortal peril. An art that entered the epoch of instant communications in a state of managerial stasis, moral decay and fiscal unreality would appear to be flirting with a death-wish. That, in a nutshell, was my assessment of the state of classical music at the close of the twentieth century. It is not a revolutionary hypothesis, but a prudent, admonitory analysis.

Yet when this book first appeared in June 1995, the music industry reacted as if my sole purpose was to pronounce and accelerate the incipient death of classical music. Instead of facing up to the perplexity of their problems, the tight little world of classical music turned upon the messenger with uninhibited bile. A leading orchestral manager attacked me for being 'knowingly destructive'[2] – which seemed to mean that I knew the situation

___

[2] *Classical Music* magazine, 3.viii.1996, p. 11

all too well and was making it worse by open debate. Classical record chiefs issued a press briefing denying a state of crisis, while frantically covering up their most savage cuts since the Great Depression. Agents who tutored artists in avarice accused anyone who raised a moral dimension in classical music of being motivated by pecuniary gain.

Panic-stricken outbursts from music critics, retailers, managers and all manner of hangers-on who relied for their livelihood on the work of musicians helped turn this book into an unexpected bestseller. A bestseller, that is, on the modest scales of classical music, where a new recording can top the charts on sales of a few hundred copies and famous orchestras play to halls that are habitually half-empty. Classical music was becoming 'exclusive' in the most perjorative sense. In the space of a decade it had all but vanished from the terrestrial television schedules. Its foremost living composers were known to a handful of aficionados and its middle-aged stars displayed none of the conscience of rock celebrities who dropped everything to rally for famine relief in Ethiopia, or flew in to lift the spirits in besieged Sarajevo.

Classical music was out of touch with the real world and out of tune with the concerns of millions of people who found spiritual uplift in other musical forms. Classical music was losing out on every front. These truths may be unpleasant, but they are equally indisputable. While some music bosses disputed my interpretation of events, not one of my facts was contested, let alone refuted.

Once the immediate furore abated, I found myself being discreetly thanked by senior figures in the music world for having set the picture in a broad historical context and given some options for regeneration. Eminent conductors called up to ask what they could do personally to help revive the music economy. 'If there are scandals, it's better to know about them,' said György Ligeti, doyen of contemporary composers. 'There is mean, ugly manipulation, not only with finances but with having to accept people you don't want because you're blackmailed in a power game.'[3]

There were even some agents who welcomed the airing of soiled linen in the interest of constructive discussion. These were, it should be stressed, a high-minded minority. The major agencies remained mercenary as ever. When a gifted and popular conductor fell seriously ill, he was visited by his agent with flowers, a pile of books – and the news that, in view of the maestro's reduced workload, the agency was increasing its commission from 15 to 20 per cent . . .

In the year since publication, the signs are that the gentle decline of classical music has begun to spin dizzyingly out of control. Concert audiences

---

[3] Comments on *When the Music Stops* in interview with Martin Hoyle, *Time Out* magazine, 4–12.xii. 1996

are not so much subsiding as collapsing. In my home city, London, orchestral concerts at the Royal Festival Hall and Barbican Centre played in 1995/6 to paying audiences of 61 and 62 per cent respectively, a bleak statistic averring that one seat in three was permanently unoccupied. But the reality was even worse. Orchestras, facing the prospect of vast empty spaces, have secretly been giving away thousands of tickets, in an under-the-table process known as 'papering', around medical and clerical workplaces. To get into the best concerts for nothing, all you had to do was phone the kitchens of University College Hospital and ask for an open-handed chef called Frank.

Top conductors like Sir Georg Solti and Sir Simon Rattle were thus devalued by the organisers of their concerts, along with the entire classical economy. People who got in for nothing would never pay for another ticket; those who paid and found themselves sitting next to freeloaders were doubly discouraged. The market for classical music was being undercut before our very eyes, while the industry begged us to believe in its vitality, its glamour and eternal appeal to a discriminating elite.

London with its glut of orchestras was an emergency case in the general ward of classical ailments, but there was no denying the emptying of halls wherever music was played. In Berlin, opera attendances dropped to 70 per cent, one orchestra was abolished and three others were forcibly merged. Even the Salzburg Festival had trouble marketing its prestigious opera nights. Sales were down 10 per cent in two successive summers – and opera, in general, was in a much healthier state than orchestral music.

In the record industry, classical producers received final orders from their corporate masters: make a profit within two years or we'll shut the studios and reissue the backlist. Deutsche Grammophon, the market leader, laid off one third of its headquarters staff and searched despairingly for a maestro who could inspire public confidence as Herbert von Karajan once did. EMI, last of the large independents, halved its classical operations over five years and closed down its German office. As the company slimmed down for sale, its American executive director, Jim Fifield, took home a £6.5 million salary[4] – and the biggest classical promotion for Christmas 1996 was not for a new opera recording but for a figure-flattering price cut.

The few records that sold in viable quantities were archival compilations of 'the greatest music ever' and aria albums from heart-throb opera stars. The full-length symphony was becoming defunct as a commercial proposition and staple concert repertoire was ruled out of studio plans, bringing to a whimpering end the interpretative tradition on record.

[4] *Daily Telegraph* magazine, 9.xi.96, p52

The compact disc, an emblem of prosperity for the record industry during the 1980s, was given away for nothing in national newspapers and on the covers of software magazines. As soon as consumers were able to record music from the Internet on personal computers, the packaged recording would face sudden death. 'The compact disc as a carrier of music is on its last legs,' said an official of the International Federation of Phonographic Industries at a gloomy public forum in Amsterdam.[5] A survey conducted by the IFPI's German wing suggested that revenue from all vendable sound carriers was drying up and the industry's only hope lay in licensing deals with media owners.[6] There was not much prospect of people going into shops and purchasing the latest releases.

In the land where it began, classical recording was brought to an end as Decca withdrew from the Cleveland Orchestra, Philips from Boston, EMI from Philadelphia and Deutsche Grammophon from the Metropolitan Opera. Label chiefs explained that the cost of making recordings in America had become prohibitive and the discs were not selling nearly enough copies to cover their outlay in seven years. Executives brandished evidence from this book to prove their point.

Devastated by the loss of a recording contract that stretched back to Leopold Stokowski's heyday at the end of the First World War, musicians in the Philadelphia Orchestra went on strike for two months. A wave of orchestral unrest spread across the United States, from Atlanta to San Francisco, where players handed out protest cards for their audiences to wave. In September 1996, the Sacramento Symphony Orchestra struck itself out of existence. Weeks later, the music library of the San Diego Symphony Orchestra was put up for sale by liquidators.

In Europe, orchestras clung on by their fingertips as governments which could no longer afford proper care for sick and elderly citizens began cutting the luxuries of arts subsidy – starting with the electorally unrewarding area of classical music. Regional ensembles in Germany and France suffered stringent cuts. Italian opera houses were paralysed by strikes as one *sovrintendente* after another went searching for private money and freelance deals to replace state subsidy and unionised security.

Classical music could not be protected from social factors and corporate demands. When public service positions were casualised, permanent jobs in orchestras became anomalous. When Hollywood sneezed, serious music caught pneumonia. For each decimal point of royalties that Michael Jackson's

---

[5] Rob Edwards, Amsterdam, 21.xi.96
[6] See 'Nichtkäufer Motivation' in *Süddeutsche Zeitung*, 29.vi.96

lawyers packed into his Sony deal — he earned 42 per cent of the sale price of each CD, seven times as much as most artists — the label had less to invest in slower-moving classical music; if Jackson flopped, Beethoven got buried. An increasing dependence on general entertainment trends was one of the gravest aspects of the classical crisis.

The few profit turners within the classical industry were quick to adopt a profit-first orientation. One of the saddest phenomena was the cancellation by Roberto Alagna and Angela Gheorghiu of weeks of opera dates on grounds of exhaustion. The newly weds had spent much of the summer of 1996 singing opera pops in public parks, capitalising on an opera-stage romance that made world headlines. Alagna, the finest lyric tenor for a generation, seemed drawn to the fame as a butterfly to a flame, jettisoning his classical agent to join the same management as crooner Charles Aznavour.

All the while the Three Tenors were touring the world for a million bucks a night. Musicians in the orchestra that accompanied them took home a hundred and twenty dollars and a rain-soaked t-shirt.

Nevertheless, viewed against the historical background outlined in *When the Music Stops . . .*, all was not forlorn. The pace of post-modern life with its plethora of fast foods and plastic objects had intensified, rather than attenuated, may people's need for spiritual comfort. The masses were satisfied with synthetic cults and arts; but millions who sought the genuine article found meaning and refuge in uncorrupted corners of classical music. Interest kept growing in medieval music and Gregorian chant. The inner voices of chamber music found a revivified audience. And, for the first time since 1945, there was a surgent demand for contemporary music: the living composer had become a celebrated oracle of these uncertain times. The music business snapped up ink-wet scores; a cerebral figure like Ligeti had his entire life's work recorded, and several labels went in hot pursuit of crossover composers who mixed rock and classics in an appealing cocktail.

There were not unhopeful prospects on which classical music might rebuild its future once the detritus of a mercenary star system had been washed away and economic sanity restored. It was not going to be a quick or easy rebirth but, having closely observed the classical patient over a period of decline, I would confidently assert that the ailment is critical rather than terminal. With a dash of managerial ingenuity and artistic genius, there is no telling how much can be retrieved — providing past corruptions are avoided, along with the quack remedies of star-mongers and show doctors.

Speaking personally, I could not bear to spend my life writing about an art that might not exist when my children have grown up. Far from declaring the death of classical music, I have tried to define the parameters of an unfolding, man-made disaster and look beyond them to a fitter, healthier future.

Norman Lebrecht, St John's Wood,
London, New Year's Day 1997

I

WHEN THE MUSIC STOPS . . .

CHAPTER I

SEX, LIES
AND VIDEODISCS

The history of music is usually studied from its creative aspect – how masterpieces of western culture came into being, how composers advanced the state of the art, how major works were received. The underside is rarely discussed: who paid for the music, who profited, who organised it, and why. The history of the music business is a half-glimpsed enigma, unknown to modern managers and undiscussed in polite society. The term itself is impolite, invoking images of fat, ash-flecked agents in loud suits. The truth is necessarily more complex. Some of the more successful operators practised an almost saintly devotion to artists and their art. Others were outright villains, in it for what they could get. Both types took the greatest care to cover their traces. The music business imposes a stringent vow of silence that is designed to protect a myth of the immaculate artist.

That myth is now under siege from the information society. It is no longer a secret, for instance, that some tenors spend more time singing in sports arenas than on the opera stage; that 'unprofessional behaviour' was the reason given by the Metropolitan Opera for dismissing a top soprano; that half the orchestras in Britain are facing bankruptcy; that Russian soloists who resisted communism cheered on the brutal invasion of Chechnya; that a well-known conductor ran off with his stepmother; that almost everything in music is up for sale to the highest bidder. Greed and fear have become the leading motives of an art in crisis. There are few secrets left in music, and little shame. While a handful of high performers grow rich and distant, unpushy artists go hungry and concerts halls are increasingly half empty. Even the big names fail to sell out, amid a widening yawn of ennui. The music business was only ever as potent as the brightest of its stars. If the stars fall, there is little the music business can do to save music.

'It's not our fault,' say the artist agents, the record chiefs, the orchestra managers and festival directors who populate the business – and there is some validity to their denial. But looking back over two and a half centuries of organised musical activity, it was they who invented the temptations that have brought music to its present turmoil. If you want to know why classical music is in trouble, why it plays a smaller role in middle-class life than at any time since Beethoven's death, you will need to take a closer look at the camera-shy figures who control its organisation and assets. People like the superagent who holds eight hundred careers in the palm of his hand (see pp. 140–190). People like the sports king who has never seen *The Marriage of Figaro* but wants to change the way opera is run (pp. 343–365). People like the press agent who runs a record conglomerate, and the Japanese industrialist who owns it (pp. 366–393). People like the great conductor who wrecked the economic balance of musical performance (pp. 167–172). People like the sponsor broker, the take-over tailor, the disc undercutter. It is often said that the music business is a people business, requiring a talent for managing other people's talents. It is a measure of the current star-drought that some of the operators seem more interesting than the opera.

It may be a minor heresy on my part, but in a dozen years of close attention to this cloistered world I have come to believe that music is more than the sum of its composers and performers. Its concert fixers and ticket sellers, its publishers and promoters, its agents and impresarios, its acousticians, accountants, sound engineers and interior decorators – yea, even unto the critic that pisseth upon the performance – all play a greater role, for better or worse, than has been publicly acknowledged. No musician ever made it on talent alone. Tchaikovsky would have looked fairly *pathétique* without the backing of his publisher, Jürgenson. Stravinsky owed his career to the balletmaster Diaghilev. The philharmonic traditions of Vienna and Berlin were founded on the foresight of two unsung entrepreneurs (pp. 58–68). Orchestras exist in America thanks to a pair of piano makers and a radio mogul (pp. 53–56).

The record industry owes its professional standards to an EMI embezzler and a conductor thief (pp. 295–311). Music publishing flourished by making composers sell their birthright for a mess of promises (pp. 322–330). Such methods and motives were not necessarily admirable, but they were formative in establishing serious music as a base necessity of civilised life.

The misdeeds of founding fathers of the music business have been overlooked or pardoned by scholarly historians who, regrettably, extend the same generosity to living malefactors. The existence of the main power-brokers in classical music is delicately ignored by major reference works like *The New Grove Dictionary of Music and Musicians* and *Die Musik in Geschichte und Gegenwart* – a reticence which, it seems to me, impedes any constructive understanding of the musical crisis. Unless old crimes are exposed, new ones will go unpunished. If we cannot acknowledge, for example, the unpleasant fact that the map of music publishing was permanently redrawn by Adolf Hitler (pp. 330–1, 335–6), we are unlikely to grasp the creative plight of present-day composers. And unless we accept that the record industry is now wholly in the hands of hardware and armaments manufacturers (pp. 394–5), we will not appreciate why the ideals that governed recording have become irrelevant and outmoded. If music, in concert or on record, does not thrill you the way it once did, there must be a reason for it – and there is, take my word for it, there is.

Most serious thinkers about musical affairs (and there are rarely more than a handful) admit, privately at least, that their world has overturned in the period since – for want of a better date – the Black Monday stock market crash of October 1987. Ticket sales have tumbled, record revenue has shrivelled, major players have lost their independence, state and business funds have dried up and artists who might formerly have looked forward to an independent solo career have gone begging for wage packets in the ranks of orchestras, themselves threatened with extinction.

This contraction cannot be attributed to recessionary pressures alone. It bears no comparison, for example, to the Crash of 1929 when, after two or three jittery years, musical activity boomed again on a burgeoning radio and record industry and the public's need for spiritual sustenance as war clouds rolled in. This time, the habit of concert going has been attenuated by rival attractions – computer games, TV sport, second homes in the country – and by the night fears that stalk great cities. Mature citizens who were the mainstay of live music are frightened to venture downtown after dark. For younger listeners, the passing impulse to buy a record has been dulled by stars who have lost their shine. Agents called it 'a problem of presenter decline'. Outsiders saw it as divine retribution upon a music business that tried, for want of real genius, to fool us with overpaid fakes and under-age fiddlers. When those big guns failed to fire, the entire army was imperilled.

Meanwhile, the few genuine stars were induced to flog their precious gifts to the point of exhaustion. The genial Russian violinist Nathan Milstein once told me he would never play more than thirty dates a year. 'There were always other things in my life – books, people, conversation,' he said,[1] and people queued to hear Milstein well into his eighties, knowing that each performance would be enriched by fresh experience and insight.

Latterly, the outstanding Israeli violinist, Itzhak Perlman, gave no fewer than one hundred concerts in his fiftieth birthday year. 'Some evenings it's more difficult than others,' he sighed, when asked how he motivated himself to play hackneyed concertos às if new.[2] Perlman, whose name was once guaranteed to sell five thousand seats at London's Royal Albert Hall, was left looking at empty rows in the half-sized Royal Festival Hall. Famous conductors and orchestras faced similar embarrassments. The Vienna Philharmonic, touring European capitals with Seiji Ozawa, Riccardo Muti and James Levine, achieved neither the seat prices nor the sell-outs for which they budgeted. The Berlin Philharmonic found itself, for the first time in a century, having to cancel scheduled concerts for want of public interest. Small wonder, perhaps, in an age when jetlagged musicians played spaced-out works with tedium engraved on their countenances. Offended by a plethora of ersatz music-making, the public defected in droves. You can fool all of the people most of the time, said Abraham Lincoln; but concert audiences know instinctively when the music fails to move them and do not return for more.

The only soloists who could invariably expect a full house were semi-reclusives like Carlos Kleiber and Arturo Benedetti Michelangeli. Other performers, overworked and often under-involved, paid the price of over-exposure. The more they played, the more they earned – and the less anyone wanted to hear them. The magic of stardom, like the aura of majesty once attached to royal personages, was dispelled by excessive familiarity – and everyone knows what familiarity breeds. In desperate bids to sell half-empty halls and please their promoters, the stars frittered what remained of their mystery in publicity tours and back-to-back interviews. Arts pages were stuffed weekly with the same handful of star faces flogging the same old story.

But that was still less than half the story. The half that stayed untold were the bits the music business did not want anyone to know: *the money, the lies, the illegal sex*. These last taboos lay chokingly close to the heart of the crisis.

Remuneration was no longer much of a secret; on the contrary, it was now fashionable for agents to brandish their stars' fees as a kind of virility symbol. But how and where the money was paid was kept quiet. Record labels, for example, no longer signed contracts with their stars. The document was made out to a shell company set up by the artist's agent in the Dutch Antilles, or some similar haven. By such dodges, and others more contorted, artists avoided paying their contribution to the societies that bred and fed them. If the music they play lacks personal or indigenous character, it may have something to do with the fact that the contracted performer is not a live individual but a distant corporation.

Behind these arrangements lies a larger conspiracy. The agents who represent musicians are understandably coy about their finances. The balance sheet of the biggest agency has never been glimpsed by an outsider, or even by half of its board of directors. Artist managements are private firms, and nobody's business but their own. There is, however, a compelling reason for their exceptional shyness. Music agencies make most of their money from public-funded institutions: opera houses and orchestras that rely heavily on state and corporate donations. Agents owe their living to this largesse. If the public only knew what these middlemen were making and how, there would be an outcry. Their profits *per se* are not necessarily excessive; we shall examine them shortly. But what is unhealthy is the wholly unpoliced relationship between private agents and public-funded institutions, an arrangement that gives rise to quotidion collusion and occasional corruption.

This is how it works: a state opera house, in order to engage a good tenor, makes a deal with this agent to take on a dud conductor and soprano. An orchestra, to keep its music director, agrees to book most of its soloists from the maestro's agent. For the prize of a world tour, it may have to accept a dreary conductor. For everything it pays high over the odds.

Evidence of arm-twisting is ubiquitous. We have heard maestros at the Met who did not know the score, singers at the Bastille who could not reach the notes and soloists at the Musikverein who were certainly not engaged for the purity of their tone. The public is not stupid. It knows when it is being conned and does not come back for seconds. Critics are not stupid either; but the larger picture of collaboration between the music business and music institutions is largely ignored. There is too much bad music about, and no one seems to ask who is to blame. If the music business were to come clean on its finances and give up on fixes it might help clear the air and refill the halls – but then the business could not operate quite so influentially. If merit alone were rewarded, who would need agents?

Leaders in the music business like to pretend it is very small, essentially a cottage industry that provides personal care to delicate artistic plants. 'Nobody gets rich in this business,' said the biggest agent of all. 'The people who just come for money leave, because there is not that much money in it.'[3] Since few firms publish end-of-year results, there is no easy way of assessing size; but a trawl through institutional statistics suggests that there is enough money involved in the business to make agenting extremely worth while.

In 1991, orchestras in America spent close to seven hundred million dollars, of which just over half (fifty-one per cent, $355.8 million) went on soloists and guest conductors.[4] Music directors cost an extra forty million. American opera houses in 1992 paid $52.4 million to soloists and conductors.[5] With US agencies taking a twenty-per-cent commission, there was around ninety million dollars to be earned by agents from major public institutions – just for the price of picking up the phone. And more still from recitals at venues like Carnegie Hall, as well as commission on artists' broadcast and recording royalties. Most of the nine-digit loot was collared by three US-based international agencies (see chapter 6). Nice work, for some.

The profits in Europe were smaller and more diffuse. A London orchestra in 1992–3 spent nine hundred and two thousand of its five-million-pound budget on soloists and conductors.[6] There were four parallel bands in the capital, half a dozen more on smaller budgets around the country and four low-fee BBC orchestras. In all, UK agents taking ten to fifteen per cent were earning around a million pounds a year in concert commissions, and about as much again on opera and recitals, mostly sustained by state subsidy.

The picture varied across Europe, where the agents' net was cast over hundreds of institutions. A regional Dutch orchestra spent just over a million guilders (four hundred thousand pounds) of its eleven-million 1992 budget on artists, of which agents took a modest tithe. But there were half a dozen good orchestras for agents to service in little Holland and 150 more across the German border. In Italy, every small town had a state-funded opera house. The French and Swiss authorities paid fool's gold to attract big names to inferior orchestras.

Taken together, the agency sector earned slightly more in Europe than it did in the United States. And there were rich pickings for agents of every nationality to be made from touring their artists in the high-income halls of Japan. A conservative assessment, therefore, would put the global take of the music agency business somewhere in excess of *quarter of a billion dollars*, which is not, by any reckoning, peanuts. Early in 1995, the second largest international artists management company reported an annual turnover in the region of one hundred million dollars.[7] A proportion of this money came from extraneous arena concerts, but the bulk was earned from public-funded institutions.

The cosiness of this commerce between public bodies and private agencies is cynically admitted on both sides. There is, however, one shaming truth that neither can afford to admit – namely, that the commodities they exchange are no longer worth the price.

In Hollywood, a movie actor who makes eighteen million dollars for a six-week film will earn back the money in two months at the box-office. When Elton John receives a forty-one-million-dollar advance on his next four albums, Warner/Chappell who signed the cheque expect to recoup full value, knowing that the pop singer/writer clears twenty-seven million dollars a year in royalties. A soccer club that buys a striker for five million pounds will regain it in gate money and sponsorships, especially if the new recruit helps win a trophy.

Classical artists are, by comparison, an uneconomic embarrassment. While Caruso and Heifetz justified their high fees by leaving some profit in the till, today's stars are judged by how much of a loss they are going to rack up for the companies that engage them. Unless they sing in a ballpark and sell ten million discs, the big modern names are massive loss-leaders.

Every opera, concert and major recording loses pots of money, largely because the artists who get top billing are grotesquely overpaid and their agents are in on the take. Caruso and Heifetz also had agents, but stars in those days earned every cent of their hire and no one got conned. Today, with music on a life support of subsidy, charity and sponsorship, it seems slightly offensive for stars and their agents to milk the donors so remorselessly.

There is, of course, a simple route for live performance to stand again on its own two feet. If star fees were halved, other costs would fall commensurately, tickets could be made cheaper and audiences would increase. This is not an agenda that the music business wishes to contemplate. Stars and their managers have got used to living off the fat of the public purse.

To protect this set up, the music business has erected a screen of lies that would earn the envy of a Baron Munchausen. Half the English language has had to be rewritten to furnish excuses for an industry where double-booking is more prevalent than on airlines. 'Indisposed' means overbooked; 'unwell' means overworked; 'invited to conduct' means begged for a date; and 'a committed performance' means played, for once, as if the musicians still loved music.

These are the white lies, almost amusing in their transparency. The dirty ones, the whoppers, cover up criminal acts. It is widely known on the classical circuit that a certain top conductor has a compulsion for sex with under-age boys. He has been arrested more than once and was banned for many years from a major capital. His agent, instead of sending the sick musician for counselling, ignores his perversion until it threatens to reach print – when he leaps in with the best lawyers money can buy and covers up with a trail of libel threats, glossy interviews and fake mistresses. Many people within the upper echelons of classical music are party to the deceit. The corruption of youth and truth would be tolerated in no other sector of the entertainment industry; even Hollywood retched when Michael Jackson was accused of child molesting. Yet the classical music business condones child-sex and forgives the maestro. Should his vice ever come to light (as it doubtless must), the damage to music will be incalculable. But the music business is not overly bothered by the health and welfare of music.

In any other area of public service the activities of the twilight zone where the music business meets public institutions would provoke parliamentary questions. Here is a sampling of current affairs that crossed my desk in the space of a few months:

– The head of a major European festival inserts his male lover, without public tender, as the company's press director.

– The director of Berlin's Deutsche Oper, Götz Friedrich, is savaged by critics for casting his soprano wife, Karan Armstrong, in the much-coveted role of the Marschallin in *Der Rosenkavalier*. She is not, apparently, asked to sing the role elsewhere.

– The tenor Placido Domingo, artistic director of the Washington Opera, hires his wife and son to direct operas for him in Spain.

– José Carreras breaks a Covent Garden contract to sing *Stiffelio* because he prefers singing outdoor concerts in Germany and Scotland.

– The head of the Bastille Opéra defies a court order to allow the music director to enter the house. He ends up paying the conductor a million dollars of public money to go away.

– A stage manager sues the Metropolitan Opera for prejudicing her career, alleging jobs backstage are reserved for homosexuals.

– A conductor in Belgium uses his state-salaried orchestra to make unpaid recordings for his own label; players who object or ask for royalties are warned they could lose their jobs.

– English National Opera appoints a composer-in-residence whose publisher is the ENO managing director's wife.

– The business manager of a top German orchestra allows a record company to pay his secretary-girlfriend's salary.

Enough? There's plenty more. Anywhere else in public life an official who awards contracts to a relative or lover is obliged to declare the interest, or face the sack. A civil servant who uses public resources for private gain is prosecuted. A performer who breaks his contract is sued. In music, abuses of public trust are everyday occurrences, the common vernacular of transactions between public servants and private agents. So close is their contact that roles are readily interchangeable. A singers' agent, Ion Holender, becomes head of the Vienna State Opera. The outgoing Met chief, Rudolf Bing, joins the board of CAMI, the agency that until recently supplied most of his singers. The former Covent Garden chairman, Sir Claus Moser, is recruited by the Harold Holt agency.

Music, like the prison service, is a law unto itself. What goes on behind bars and after lights out is concealed from the public gaze, in full confidence that the public does not want its illusions of security or stardom shattered. The public is invariably the loser, for the result of unscrutinised collusion is an inferior level of performance, on stage and backstage.

The immediate victims are often musicians, who have no recourse to appeal against unseen deals and have scant protection from physical and artistic rape by maestros and stage directors. Many good singers have been shut out of opera because they would not lie down on the casting couch. A British counter-tenor, popular in Europe, has been absent for nine years from Covent Garden because, he believes, he refused the sexual advances of a director. Others, summarily replaced at the whim of a powerful artist or agent, are warned that their careers will be throttled if they seek legal or public redress.

The saddest victims are the youngest, their shining ideals shattered by callous exploitation. A former music student wrote to me from Florida recalling the summer he spent in the company of a celebrated conductor who surrounded himself with admiring teenagers and habitually abused them:

> The adoration and subservience is a little hard for me to describe . . . One evening, one of the girls was walking past 'Jack' (a pseudonym), who was sitting in his usual reclining chair. Without discussing it, 'Jack' stopped her next to his chair, with his hand, slowly reached up and pulled her panties down, and stroked her legs up to her crotch. She didn't protest, and neither did anyone else. Such was his power. And he didn't want to have a sexual relationship with her. One of the reasons why she left – she saw no future with 'Jack'.

Another night the conductor ordered my informant, then seventeen, to strip naked and engage in mutual masturbation. The boy, a virgin, was still mortified twenty years later by his subsequent rejection.

I think 'Jack' really was just interested in the sex, and was interested in relationships only to the extent that they served him . . . It's bad when your God dumps on you, hurts you on purpose and will not discuss or negotiate the subject . . . I was so subservient that I accepted abuse from him. He continued till I broke down and cried. No one ever hurt me except him. I can think of no description of that evening other than physical abuse. 'Jack' said that in a way his relationships with me and the others 'saved us all from a first divorce'. Yet that was exactly what his relationship was – without alimony, social support, or anything else.

His tormentor occupies a prominent position at a major opera house. He is, so far as I am aware, an unreformed character – and there are more like him. The music authorities and the music business cover up for star abuses and give them ample opportunity to wreck more lives. Misconduct cannot be stopped, but it should certainly not be fostered by an art that aspires to spiritual values.

The trouble is, classical music has become so polluted by the unregulated intercourse of private pushers and public servants that it cannot distinguish principle from expedience. Unless some light is shed on shady dealings and some probity restored, more young lives will be blighted and careers choked off. This book is not primarily an exercise in whistle-blowing, but I make no apologies for breaking the silence. It would be easier, and legally safer, for me to discuss the issues in the kind of anonymous generalities I have used until now. But enough's enough. From here on, I shall name names and call witnesses. The future of musical performance hangs in the balance at the close of the twentieth century. Orchestras and opera houses are in peril and musicians tremble for their livelihoods. It would be irresponsible on my part to employ euphemisms in order to spare the blushes of those who wield authority over a wilting art. If music lovers can see behind the curtains of collusion, it may help them differentiate between harmony and hype, art and lies. It may also help rebuild a measure of public faith in the integrity of the art itself.

There will be no more sex and lies in this chapter. All that remains to be discussed is the videodisc dimension, the last-ditch resort of an art in retreat. The gleam of high technology has rescued music many times in the past. Stereo in the 1950s buttered the bread of major orchestras; compact disc in the early Eighties put jam on the loaf. In the gloom of Black Monday, as live music faced recession, a posse of white knights appeared on the trading screen bearing good tidings for the faltering record industry. CBS and RCA, the American parents of classical recording, were bought in quick succession by

Sony of Japan and Bertelsmann of Germany. Philips of Holland consolidated its control of the PolyGram grouping of Deutsche Grammophon, Decca-London and Philips Classics. Thorn, an electronics conglomerate, corporatised the senior British label, EMI. The world's six big classical labels changed hands or line-control in the space of two years, and the new owners were bullish about budgets and prospects.

Classical music was not necessarily the principal motive for their moves, but it was not an insignificant element. Sony's two-billion-dollar acquisition of CBS was driven by Norio Ohga, a classically trained baritone and close friend of the conductor Herbert von Karajan. Bertelsmann, a book conglomerate, followed its RCA swoop with a raid on Ricordi, publishers of Verdi and Puccini. PolyGram, which headed into Hollywood with such hits as *Four Weddings and a Funeral*, strategised its classical labels as resource centres for movie sound-tracks and computer software. When Thorn-EMI was readied for demerger in 1995, its classical archive was listed among the company's prime attractions. In a world where movies, broadcasting, computers, telephones and home entertainment were hurriedly interfacing, no major player could afford to be without a classical music component, which it could reproduce in all forms and media.

The monetary value of classical recording was not a large factor in this equation, but it was fairly substantial. In 1992, the world value of record sales was $28.7 billion (in plain English, eighteen thousand million pounds), having surprisingly doubled in six years of world recession.[8] The classical share of this amount was around seven per cent, or two billion dollars; its value had doubled in a decade. Of this amount, roughly ten per cent – two hundred million dollars – was paid out as artist and orchestra royalties, and one-tenth of that went back to artist agents, a small matter of twenty million dollars. These sums were vital infusions into a nervous musical economy. Without them many institutions and individuals would have gone under. The music establishment was touchingly grateful to the new masters of the record business for their support. But how long that support would be sustained, and what direction it might take, turned uncertain within seven years.

The alarm bells began ringing late in 1994 when Sony slashed budgets after writing off losses of $3.2 billion in Hollywood and an untold amount at its Hamburg-based classical label (see pp. 380–2). Decca, which had dominated the classical charts through the 1990s, turned in a 1993 net loss of a hundred and forty-two thousand pounds, small but shocking. If Decca had a bad year, others had a nightmare from which they awoke in sheer panic. In a blether of self-doubt, market leader Deutsche Grammophon launched quick-shot chart-busters called 'Top Gear Classics' and 'Classic Relaxation' and put out a disco-beat album with the London Symphony Orchestra. EMI, once the proud carrier of Furtwängler and Beecham recordings, blew its promotions budget on a pubescent violinist, Vanessa-Mae, who played rocked-up Bach and paraded in a see-through swimsuit. Sony Classical plastered a dread-locked would-be conductor, Bobby McFerrin, on Manhattan bus shelters and buses.

These were not the sort of reactions normally expected from a thoughtful, cultured industry that had weathered a century of storms without sacrificing its highbrow image. Rather, these were the snap decisions you got from corporate salarymen whose careers were on the line if they stayed more than a couple of years in the red. Across the spectrum of classical recording an historic sense of purpose was being weakened by executives whose main concern was to please the corporate parent.

In these seven years, the record industry lost its last autonomy. Labels that were once owned by music-loving businessmen and run by musicians were reduced to a cog within a conglomerate. If a multimedia boss in Tokyo or Hollywood decreed that videodiscs were to be the next household gadget, classical music would be retuned to fit the format. If markets responded better to CD–ROM or CD–I, classics would meekly supply the software. The glorious history of western art music was reduced to the status of a servile database. The continuity of musical creation and interpretation held a priority so low it was almost invisible.

Any classical record that did not sell a thousand copies a year was deleted by computer regardless of its artistic significance. Any fad that caught the fleeting imagination was proclaimed 'classical' and ruthlessly promoted. Recordings that were truly classic were disdained as old hat or recycled notelessly in bargain bins.

In the hands of multinational electronics giants and armament manufac-turers, symphonies were no more meaningful than bytes and bullets. The recording factor that had underpinned musical life for a hundred years had fallen into alien hands and was unable to save music in its hour of need. In the maelstrom of the market-place, classical music was an art held hostage by business interests. This book charts the course of its capitulation.

St John's Wood, London, March 1996

NOTES

1 author's interview, November 1983
2 author's interview, May 1995
3 Ronald Wilford, author's interview
4 source: ASOL–92, and personal clarification
5 source: *Opera America*
6 private information
7 information from John Webber, IMG
8 source: HM Government, Monopolies and Mergers Commission: 'The supply of recorded music', presented to Parliament, June 1994

C H A P T E R   I I

THE DAY
THE MUSIC DIED

Vienna, 11 a.m., New Year's Day 2001: the first morning of a
millennium. It is billed as *The Concert To End All Concerts*. The oak-
and-ochre Musikvereinsaal is packed with notables, many of whom have
occupied the same family seats since Franz Joseph was emperor and Gustav
Mahler chief conductor. For once, local dignitaries are outshone by a krug of
celebrities flown in by the Austrian republic to celebrate its accession to the
presidency of the European Union. The outgoing president, Professor
Umberto Eco of Italy, shares a box with premiers of four member states.
Prince Edward, the British theatrical royal, has contributed a benign
introduction to the gilted programme. Laser-sharp coiffures belonging to
Yevgeny Yevtushenko, Steffi Graf, Sonia Gandhi and Arnold Schwarzenegger
can be seen bobbing above and among the settling attendance. The United
States is represented by ambassador at large Barbra Streisand, Japan by its
heir to the throne. Outside, in the freezing sleet, paparazzi and scalpers stave
off hypothermia with thoughts of rich pickings, while two thousand onlookers
shiver at the thrill of proximity. Never have so many stars gathered for an
orchestral concert – and that is just the audience.

On stage, the Vienna Philharmonic plays Strauss waltzes under the baton of Carlos Kleiber, whose podium appearances have become as rare as zoo-born pandas. Luciano Berio, doyen of living composers, comes on to conduct a world première – his orchestration of a youthful violin sonata by Richard Strauss, each movement played by a different soloist: Midori, Itzhak Perlman, Anne-Sophie Mutter. After the interval Lorin Maazel, described as 'the world's top-paid conductor', conducts the great Spanish tenor, Placido Domingo, in a farewell performance of favourite arias, ending with the climax of Verdi's *Otello*, the indestructible Kiri Te Kanawa enfolded in his arms.

It has been hotly reported, and half-heartedly denied, that the mountainous Italian, Luciano Pavarotti, will emerge from Modenese retirement to partner Domingo in a *Barber of Seville* duet that they never dared to record together in their prime. 'It will all be over if the fat man sings,' quips a columnist, but the King of the High Cs and his surefire publicists cannot steal more than two tabloid headlines from this 'all-time dream team of classical music'.

One hundred million people around the world will watch the concert on television, where it is timed to follow the women's final of the Australian Open tennis championship. A million or more will buy the recording, issued exclusively on Sony's new solid-state soundcard – two hours of music on a laminated sliver of plastic the size of a personal credit card. Only the crabbiest of critics will cavil at the antediluvian musical content, in which all the waltzes and arias are Victorian hits and even the so-called world première is a reworking of a piece of 1880s romanticism. It is as if the twentieth century has been expunged as too disturbing, too redolent of conflict and unpleasantness. 'People go to concerts to enjoy themselves,' says the promoter, 'not to be reminded of things they came here to get away from.'

Escapism, entertainment and a televised shuffle of familiar faces – is this the deadly future of an art that sold its soul? Fantasy concerts of this kind are increasingly being touted around the media circuit, stealing valuable resources and airtime from the meaningful performance of full symphonies and operas. In a soundbite society, they represent all the viewing public are presumed to want to know about their musical heritage. The presumption, by media bosses, is repugnant. But it reflects starkly on a reality in which state schools are cutting music hours (even in Germany, land of Bach, of Brahms) and a generation is growing up devoid of inspiring musical experience.

Television is only a medium, not the message, but its priorities are generally those of society at large. Organised sport replaced organised music as the most popular form of mass entertainment, as surely as soap operas displaced parlour games. Classical music struggled masterfully in the television era to retain its regular audience but at the close of the millennium found itself on the cusp of calamity, with institutions that had survived since Bach's day cracking under financial, political and social pressures. The Gewandhaus Orchestra in Leipzig, Bach's town, could not afford to renew its instruments. Less fortunate towns in east and west Germany lost their long-standing orchestras, or saw them forcibly merged with the local theatre. Berlin's seven symphony orchestras would eventually be whittled down to four in the slow process of post-Wall unification.

German ensembles were the most protected in Europe and the damage there was relatively containable. Everywhere else, a firestorm raged through musical infrastructures. Radio ensembles were abolished in Belgium, Italy and The Netherlands. Regional funding was slashed in France. Two of London's top orchestras were saved from bankruptcy only by a last-minute loan from the Musicians Union. Most British orchestras were deep in debt and playing on borrowed time. The BBC tried to demerge its northernmost band, leaving just one symphonic ensemble in the whole of Scotland, a nation of five million bereft of concert options.

Music in Poland lost seventy per cent of its state funding. The best orchestras of the former Soviet Union embarked on endless hard-currency tours, eking their players' five dollars a day to cook tinned food over bunsen burners in double-occupancy motel rooms. The pavements of Jerusalem were clogged with mendicants who once played in the Bolshoi. The Toronto Symphony, Canada's largest, was saved only by its players taking a fifteen per cent pay cut.

In the United States, Congress's proposed abolition of the National Endowment for the Arts pushed middle-budget orchestras to the brink of an abyss. New Orleans lost its orchestra. Honolulu cancelled half its concert season. The Louisville Orchestra laid off half its musicians. Seven not-for-profit theatres shut in 1992 alone. Dallas decimated the operating budget of its spanking new concert hall. *Musical America*, the last US journal devoted to classical music, ceased publication. 'No matter how great the worldly success it may enjoy, no matter how high the hype that can be purchased, no matter how large the paying audience can be made to seem, classical music today is in deep trouble,' wrote the conservative commentator Samuel Lipman.[1]

There had been crises before, but none so severe or intractable. Wherever you looked, audiences were collapsing, state funding was begrudged, corporate sponsorship was dwindling. Society was shifting its resources to new needs – AIDS research, old-age care, showpiece buildings – and music was left to fend for itself in a pool of open-market ideologies and mass-media promoters. The core of its existence, the nightly live performance of western masterpieces, was being mercilessly eroded as the public pursued less taxing and cheaper diversions. Dire warnings went unheeded. 'All over the world,' said the St Petersburg conductor Mariss Jansons, 'politicians do not take enough care about art. There has been technological progress, but the harmony between spiritual and material things has been stretched. The spiritual life of the world has been degraded, with wars and narcotics, because people's souls are empty. Cutting art creates tragedy.'[2]

For the average politician, though, there were few votes in saving a symphony orchestra, and more kudos to be gained from getting photographed with Pavarotti in the park. Governments were concerned with bread and circuses, and disdainful of essential heritage. When orchestras and opera houses extended the begging bowl, they were told to make themselves more popular and – buzzword – accessible. That meant ruling out any repertoire that might challenge the median intelligence and delegating the production of classic profundities to whizzkid directors and sexpot soloists. The alternative was to lose subsidy and risk getting supplanted by promoters who dispensed decontextualised arias and symphonic snippets. The traditional three-course concert was fading fast. Symphony halls began reducing their commitment. London's key venue, the Royal Festival Hall, seeing its average concert audience slump to fifty-five per cent in the early 1990s, threw open its doors to a rainbow coalition of pop and ethnic promoters.

Students and young couples who once discovered music by sitting nightly in the Gods were deterred by price, presentation and ambience from forming a concert-going habit. Instead of savouring a range of symphonies in the flesh, they were reduced to listening to records, losing the intimacy and combustion of live performance – the thrill of being there when Klemperer conducted Mahler and taking away a memory to save for future grandchildren. Live music was losing its constituency and the direct communication between musicians and listeners stood in imminent danger of severance.

As in most sagas of decline and fall, the rot set in at the moment of greatest triumph and, *pace* Gibbon, in the heart of the eternal city. One summer's night in 1990, three tenors in Rome wearied of watching a goal-starved soccer World Cup and went to sing an operatic medley at the Baths of Caracalla. Their sideshow, globally televised, turned a sporting famine into a feast of music, scoring more heavily in cash and kind than any of the soccer teams. The concert diverted world attention from hooliganism on the terraces and cynicism on the pitch. It turned the '*vincerò! vincerò!*' cry of Puccini's 'Nessun dorma' aria into a football chant and the Three Tenors into a pop phenomenon. Their first disc topped the charts for more than a year; their reunion at the 1994 World Cup in Los Angeles repeated the feat.

Ringmasters the world over sat up and took note. José Carreras was booked by the Barcelona Olympics to stage musical galas at the opening and closing ceremonies. Rugby Football recruited Kiri Te Kanawa to decorate its mudcaked World Cup with an anthem that strongly resembled a theme from Holst's *Planets*. Mark H. McCormack, agent to many of the world's top sportsmen, organised quayside classical concerts for the American Cup yacht race and an orchestral prelude to the Nobel prize-giving ceremony. Sports apart, McCormack's International Management Group (IMG) represented Miss World, the Mayo Clinic and the Pope's overseas tours. When his Holiness travelled, the heavenly voices belonged to IMG.

McCormack spotted 'a tremendous parallel between sports and music'[3] and bought his way by stages into the music business. 'I couldn't tell a good violinist from a bad one,' he declared, but he knew how to achieve high returns for star performers by hiking up their fees and plastering product logos on their shirts and hats. If he could not make musicians rich in the concert hall, he would put them on before thirty thousand picnickers in the great outdoors. Along with the lesson of the Three Tenors, the lure of McCormack prompted many classical artists to refocus their careers away from regular concert and opera performances to arena recitals and so-called 'special events'. Some tenors wound up singing more nights in amplified arenas than in the opera house. 'Carreras fans will be disappointed yet again [by his absence from opera] and seek consolation in the now rather boringly predictable pop concerts that seem to fill the ex-opera singer's calendar,' wrote a disgruntled fan.[4] Luciano Pavarotti spent the evening of his years in converted car-parks and exhibition centres. Placido Domingo, who devoted four-fifths of his year to opera, vigorously defended the arena concept. 'How many Covent Garden performances do I have to give to reach such a crowd? Do they want us to be completely unknown, hardly making a living? In some of these performances we can make real money, because in opera we don't.'[5]

No one begrudged the stars their fortune and fame, but coming at a moment of unparalleled pressure on orchestras and opera houses, it accentuated the widening gulf between a handful of household names and the rest of the musical profession. Stars, from the soaring of their comet in the mid-nineteenth century, had always been a law unto themselves, hogging the limelight and imposing outrageous whims on their promoters and collaborators. But the *star system* that governed their activities was firmly affixed to the musical mainstream. While Enrico Caruso sang Neapolitan ditties and Fritz Kreisler played Viennese sweetmeats, their loyalties lay in the opera house and concert hall, and their priority was the performance of full works, not bleeding chunks.

What happened in the Nineties is that these links were loosened by the vastly inflated temptations proffered by media conglomerates. The three tenors shared sixteen million dollars of Time-Warner-Toshiba money at their Los Angeles concert, with more to come in royalties. After that, the inducement to sing a whole opera at the Met or Covent Garden for a maximum fee of twenty thousand dollars was understandably weakened. 'Why am I doing this?' muttered a star soprano as she walked on stage for a Barbican concert in London. Why bother to learn a difficult lieder-cycle for two thousand people and ten thousand pounds before tax, when she could be singing pops for seventy thousand lawn-sitters and an offshore fortune?

The distance had never been greater between the stars and their humble accompanists. And when the musical world turned in distress to its celebrities and prime assets, the star system committed an irreparable betrayal. Where great performers in the recent past were satisfied with slightly more than their nearest rival, today's performers and their agents could break an orchestra's budget. Ten per cent more than the next fiddler was plenty for Fritz Kreisler and Jascha Heifetz; but agents for Itzhak Perlman and Anne-Sophie Mutter exacted a nightly fee that was double the annual income of most players in the orchestra. Instead of boosting the box-office, the stars added new headaches to a reddening balance sheet. Unless a sponsor could be lined up to pay their monstrous fee, they would vanish from the concert hall and confine themselves to the stellar stratosphere occupied by newscasters, footballers, errant actors and politicians' mistresses. It is from this exalted company that bigtime fixers pick their 'dream team' for a putative Concert To End All Concerts.

The economics of such events are more straightforward than those of a subscription symphony concert. To ensure a top-drawer crowd with a spangle of royalty, the performers are required to donate their fees to a children's hospital. This leaves no gap in their wallets since broadcast and record royalties will earn them ten times as much. The orchestra is paid for by sponsors – a German car manufacturer, Japanese computer maker and Swiss confectioner – who are rewarded with a halo of good citizenship, two rows of seats and prestige beyond the price of advertising. Their beneficence, which will not be forgotten at contract time, enables European leaders to look cultured and the Austrian government to claim credit for an event that has not cost its taxpayers one pfennig. The politicians are grateful, the artists appear generous and hoteliers all along the Kärntnerstrasse are positively beaming. Happiest of all is the concert promoter who earns ten per cent on every transaction – the artists' fees, the television contract, the sponsorship, ticket sales, full-page advertisements in the concert brochure, even the ovatory bouquets of flowers that are presented to the performers.

So what's the harm, if everyone has a good time and a hard-working organiser is rewarded for his initiative? No damage to the social fabric. No risk, either, to public probity (although there are areas of back-scratching that would not withstand scrutiny). The only loser is music. For when music is reduced to synthetic soundbites it sacrifices something of its integrity and, in shows like this, gains no active followers. And when top musicians are brought together by a motive no higher than monetary gain and social glitz, theirs truly will be The Concert To End All Concerts.

Against the crumbling of concert life and traditional values, a parallel myth proliferated that classical music had never been so popular. Record sales trebled in Britain and many other markets during the 1980s,[6] boosted by compact disc and a mounting disillusion with the mindless rap that passed for rock music. Ex-Beatle fans tuned in to the Kronos Quartet. Grateful Deadheads followed their band into symphonic explorations. Contemporary classics invaded the pop charts. Henryk Mikolai Górecki's meditative third symphony sold seven hundred thousand copies. Three-quarters of a million people crowded New York's Central Park to hear Domingo sing; one hundred thousand braved torrential rain to see Pavarotti in Hyde Park.

It became chic to whistle Verdi in the trading rooms of Wall Street and Cheapside. Hard-headed finance houses invested in opera, aware of its social cachet and the exclusive opportunities it afforded for corporate hospitality. New money slushed around the crush bars, but none of it went into any kind of rainy-day contingency and, when the largesse evanesced after Black Monday, there was no fat in reserve. The only companies that could plan ahead with confidence were a few state showpieces in France and Germany and the plutocratic playgrounds of Glyndebourne and the Metropolitan Opera.

The Met faced a forty-million-dollar deficit in 1992, more than the entire budget of the next-biggest US opera house; happily it had enough friends to pay the debt. Covent Garden, that year, went three and a half million pounds into the red and was threatened with closure. The New York Philharmonic spent fourteen and a half million dollars on orchestral operations, covered by its wealthy board; the Boston Symphony Orchestra relied on private donations and endowments for half its budget. The London Philharmonic and Philharmonia orchestras, with smaller costs, had to cut their players' wages to stay alive. Life was not fair; inequality was rife.

Feudalism returned with a vengeance. Interventionist arts ministers like Jack Lang in France and David Mellor in Britain showered pet ensembles with largesse. 'A piece of art is not a normal product,' said Lang. 'We consider it to be morally unacceptable that art and culture belong to a commercial agreement. For psychological, intellectual and moral arguments, we refuse this idea.'[7] Selective generosity, however, turned a blind eye to regional institutions while the Bastille and London's South Bank were allowed to squander millions in payroll costs. Where private money was ventured, it was often with strings attached. A Texan widow, Mrs Donald D. Harrington, pledged a fortune to the Met, provided it could be spent by her favourite director, the extravagant Franco Zeffirelli. A British widow gave a million pounds to Covent Garden to be used only for 'traditional' productions. Industrial patrons summoned symphony orchestras to play at their weddings, unheard, unpaid and, in one instance known to me, unfed. Music was overwhelmingly dependent on state, corporate and individual charity, sacrificing all pride, as players and directors went grovelling for charity to financiers and brokers. The concert hall became, for them, an after-hours extension of the trading floor, a secluded club where contacts were made and deals struck. It was, in the words of the French *penseur* and ex-banker Jacques Attali, a 'place used by the élite to convince itself that it is not as cold, inhuman and conservative as it is accused of being'.[8] Their presence, for the ordinary concert goer, was an additional deterrent. As the top seats filled with freeloaders, the balconies continued to empty.

Was it not ever thus? Did music not always rely on patronage of some kind? Not until recently. After the passing of feudalism and through the two centuries of its greatest fertility, music was a popular art, popularly funded for the most part. Orchestras were formed by players and sustained by ticket sales. Concerts were open to all and affordable to all but the indigent.

Opera, a far costlier proposition, was run by state officials, or in America by boards of wealthy socialites. Richard Wagner could not have staged the *Ring* without financial help from King Ludwig of Bavaria; Giuseppe Verdi made his name in publicly funded theatres. But their works, once successful, toured the world as paying propositions. *Lohengrin* and *La Traviata* were box-office hits that could bankroll an entire season. Gounod's *Faust* made a fortune. Puccini wrote for everyman. Richard Strauss built a villa with the profits of *Salome*'s strip-tease and could have retired at fifty on the proceeds of *Rosenkavalier*. In 1928–9, the Metropolitan Opera produced a surplus of $90,937 and had two million dollars on deposit in the bank,[9] equivalent to over a hundred million dollars today.

As recently as the late 1940s, Covent Garden ran its season on a state grant of twenty-five thousand pounds and the London Symphony Orchestra got by on just two thousand pounds. Today Covent Garden cannot manage on twenty million pounds and the LSO needs two and a half million pounds to stay alive. The cost of live performance has shot up one thousandfold in two generations, at least forty times in excess of the rate of inflation.

In the United States, a typical big-city orchestra gave one hundred concerts in 1946 and broke even. Twenty years later, it played a hundred and fifty dates and lost forty thousand dollars. In 1991, it put on two hundred concerts and shed seven hundred and thirty-five thousand dollars.[10] At this rate, the orchestra would not exist by the end of the century. 'The five biggest orchestras are protected by large endowments, but many of our municipal orchestras are simply not going to survive,' warned Deborah Borda, executive director of the New York Philharmonic.[11]

When New York's finest played a free concert in Central Park, sceptics quipped, 'why don't they give away admission to Lincoln Center, when they lose sixteen dollars on every ticket sold?' A symphony concert at London's Royal Festival Hall was budgeted to lose thirty thousand pounds, more if tickets sold badly. The cost of live performance had gone through the roof. The only way orchestras could save money was to stop playing. Organised music had taken leave of its financial senses.

There were many causes for the crunch, but its core was a star system that had been allowed to run amok. Covent Garden, under the tightest fiscal restraints after Black Monday, more than doubled its payments to artists in the half-decade from 1987 to 1992[12] – an increase of a hundred and twenty-five per cent, against inflation of thirty per cent. American orchestras spent $253.4 million in 1986 on soloists and guest conductors, and half as much again five years later.[13] As a direct consequence, the orchestral community posted a deficit of twenty-three million dollars in 1991. Any other industry would have imposed a freeze on artistic fees, the largest single outlay. But stars and their agents had performing institutions by the throat and firmly believed that someone would always come forward to pay the bills. So far, they have generally been proved right. But orchestras have started to fold across Europe and America and the classical world is holding its breath for the crash of a major company. Some illustrious houses have actually come to within hours of closure.

To save their jobs, low-waged orchestral players are having to take pay cuts to subsidise the high fees of conductors and soloists, and their agents' commission. The players are caught in a cleft stick. Unless well-known performers are engaged, the public will not attend and the orchestra will go bust; but each star costs a fee that drives the orchestra closer to extinction.

The difficulty is acknowledged by some sensitive conductors, but they are notable exceptions. Leonard Slatkin, music director of the National Symphony Orchestra in Washington, DC, actually instructed his agent to reduce his standard fee. 'I decided to cut back,' he explained, 'because I want to be around in twenty years and I want to have orchestras around then to conduct. If we carry on like this, there won't be any left.'[14]

The effect of high fees on seat prices cannot be overstated. In the 1950s it cost the equivalent of two beers to sit in the upper galleries at Covent Garden, and the price of a hardback novel to occupy the grand tier – two shillings and six pence at the top or a pound in the stalls.[15] Today, there is standing room at eight pounds, 'cheap' tickets at thirty-five pounds and the best seats at anything from a hundred and twenty to two hundred and thirty-five pounds. The picture is much the same at many European houses. For young wage earners, going regularly to concerts or the opera is becoming unaffordable. Opera on the grand scale with the finest living singers has become an enclave of privilege to which rich insiders and their friends can always get a ticket, outsiders never. Want to hear Pavarotti? Who do you know who can get you in?

In the concert hall, the central rows are reserved for corporate guests, while young music lovers can afford only the remoter regions, leaving them feeling less involved, less enraptured and less likely to return. Prime seats cost up to eighty pounds in London, two hundred and fifty pounds in Tokyo. The moral foundation of music – the inherent democracy of a lovely noise that can be admired by all, regardless of status or education – has been thoughtlessly abandoned. The Concert To End All Concerts is almost upon us.

NOTES

1 Lipman, p. 25
2 interview with the author, December 1993
3 interview with the author, June 1991
4 *Opera Now*, August 1995, p. 15; letter from D. Eaves of Preston
5 author's interview, August 1991
6 source: BPI market information bulletin, 26 February 1993
7 *Interview for No Money, No Music*, BBC World Service, 1994
8 Attali, p. 118
9 HOR, p. 150
10 ASOL–92, A1–A9
11 author's interview, 1992
12 *Classical Music*, 13 March 1993, p. 3
13 ASOL–92, pp. 11–13; Mayer, The Met, p. 335; *Opera News*, October 1992, p. 4
14 author's interview, June 1992
15 White, p. 204

II

MANAGERS

CHAPTER III

A STAR SYSTEM IS BORN

B ach had no agent, Handel no manager. The classical masters, liberated from feudal serfdom, launched music on its evolutionary course with a clear sense of its monetary worth. Johann Sebastian Bach, a cantor on the payroll of the Leipzig town hall, composed to order for sacred and official occasions under his terms of employment. But on Friday nights he loosened his wig and struck up orchestral suites, harpsichord concertos and secular choruses with a 'collegium musicum' in a suburban coffee house. His famous *Coffee Cantata* of 1735 was a tribute to the café owner, who charged admission when music was played and gave Bach a share of the takings. The café collegium grew in the course of a decade into the Gewandhaus concerts, the world's earliest form of organised orchestral activity. Servile as he seemed, Bach sensed the commercial potential of music and helped establish a market.

The history of music is traced by its creative growth. With Bach and Handel, one senses the start of an alternative history, as social and economic stirrings brought great music into general circulation. George Frideric Handel, a doughtier figure than Bach, fled his post at the house of Hanover, swearing that no ducal whim would govern his music. He moved to London, an investor's heaven in the grip of the South Sea Bubble, and raised venture capital to stage his operas. He formed companies, hired singers and orchestras, directed performances from the keyboard and crashed

29

spectacularly when a capricious nobility boycotted his productions for inferior Italian operas.

Handel, adaptably, pursued a new audience of middle-class Jews and Christian nonconformists with heroic Old Testament oratorios – *Saul*, *Solomon*, *Jephtha*, *Judas Maccabaeus* – achieving a momentous apotheosis in *Messiah*, whose score he donated to a charity for foundling children. Throughout his vicissitudes, Handel avoided bankruptcy.

His secretary, John Christopher Smith, 'regulated the expenses of his public performance and filled the office of treasurer',[1] but business decisions, great or small, were taken by Handel. He was a shrewd investor on the stock exchange and held a personal account at the Bank of England. 'The money he used to take to his carriage of a night . . . in gold and silver, [would] weigh him down and throw him into a fever,' reports an eyewitness.[2] He valued freedom of enterprise as greatly as freedom of expression and, on his death in April 1759, left more than twenty thousand pounds to friends and charities. Newspapers remarked on the size of his estate, because Handel was the first composer ever to achieve self-sufficiency.

Three years after Handel's death Bach's youngest son, Johann Christian, set up in London. Dubbed 'the London Bach', he devised a subscription series of some fifteen concerts with co-director Carl Friedrich Abel. They acquired premises at Hanover Square and came unstuck when competitive concerts were set up at the Pantheon on Oxford Street (nowadays a Marks & Spencer store). Bach died aged forty-six with debts of four thousand pounds; he is remembered as the musician who invented the seasonal subscription and, with it, the framework for concert organisation.

Concerts Spirituels were started meanwhile in Paris by the composer Anne-Danican Philidor, playing instrumental music on religious festivals when the opera was shut. They were run from 1725 until the Great Terror of 1791 by various musicians – 'not as mere speculators, but as true artists' – among them Jean-Joseph Mouret, Jean-Féry Rebel and Pierre-Montan Berton, 'the best composers and leaders of the orchestra that the Académie can show.'[3] These concerts were the core of Parisian musical life.

The focus on a visiting celebrity can be credited to a German-born violinist in the Covent Garden orchestra, Johann Peter Salomon. In 1790, while visiting Cologne to audition singers, Salomon heard that Joseph Haydn had been left unemployed on the death of his patron, Prince Nicolaus of Esterhazy. He set off for Vienna, announcing to the indigent kapellmeister: 'I am Salomon of London and have come to fetch you. Tomorrow we will arrange an accord.' Haydn, almost sixty, had never left his native land and was warned grimly by Mozart of the risks involved. Two trips and twelve symphonies later, he returned home in triumph with a solid pension and a continental reputation, a doctorate from Oxford, a compliment from King George III and a roar of public adulation. Salomon played first violin at his concerts, enjoying a dual satisfaction as player and promoter, having made the London season revolve upon his resident composer. He invited Mozart for a season, but mortality sadly intervened.

Haydn's London presence outshone all rivals, prompting the pianist-composer Muzio Clementi to announce his retirement and set up in partnership with a piano maker and publisher, John Longman. As a virtuoso, Clementi had 'invented and elaborated, at one stroke and in its final shape, the new piano style destined henceforth to replace the old harpsichord style'.[4] As a businessman, he was as conscientious as profit permitted, mitigating an obligatory obsequiousness with a flare of artistic integrity. 'I have aimed at perfection,' he told one customer, '*comparative* perfection, I mean, for I do not need to inform YOU that *absolute* perfection is unattainable by *man*.'[5] His warehouse burned down in March 1807 with forty thousand pounds' worth of pianos going up in flames.

The following month in Vienna he signed a contract with Ludwig van Beethoven, reporting the deal to his London partner with an engaging mixture of musical and mercantile glee:

> By a little management and without committing myself, I have at last made a compleat conquest of that *haughty beauty*, Beethoven . . . Imagine the ecstasy of such a meeting! I took pretty good care to improve it to our *house*'s advantage, therefore, as soon as decency would allow, after praising very handsomely some of his compositions: 'Are you engaged with any publisher in London?'
> 'No,' says he.
> 'Suppose, then, that you prefer *me*?'
> 'With all my heart.'
> 'Done. What have you ready?'
> 'I'll bring you a list.'[6]

Beethoven sold him three string quartets, a symphony, an overture, a piano concerto and his violin concerto, which he promised to 'adapt for the pianoforte with and without additional keys'. On Clementi's return to Vienna three years later, he found that Beethoven had not been paid. 'A most shabby figure you have made me cut in this affair!' he upbraided his partner, ' – and that with one of the first composers of the day! Don't lose a moment and send me word what you have received from him that I may settle with him.'[7] In 1813, Clementi was among the founders of the Philharmonic Society, which invited Beethoven to London and commissioned him to compose his ninth symphony, bringing temporary relief to his endemic indigence. 'If only I were in London, how many works would I compose for the Philharmonic Society!' he exclaimed.

The Society, which regulated London's musical life for much of the nineteenth century, was formed by musicians – Salomon, Clementi, the pianist-publisher John B. Cramer and his violinist brother Franz, the conductor Sir George Smart, the composer-publisher Vincent Novello and the fiery violinist, Giovanni Battista Viotti, among others – to promote their professional interests. The directors of the Society constituted its performing ensemble, Salomon leading the inaugural concert from the violin, with Clementi at the keyboard. Eight concerts were given each year and offered to the public for an eight-guinea subscription. Music lovers could become Associates of the Philharmonic Society, but only musicians were electable as Members.

With aristocratic patronage looking uncertain in the post-Napoleonic period, musicians took increasing control of concert activity. A Société des Concerts du Conservatoire was convened in Paris by the conductor François-Antoine Habeneck; an independent Gesellschaft der Musikfreunde was formed in Vienna by Beethoven's librettist, Joseph von Sonnleithner. From 1842, players at the Habsburg Court Opera regrouped on their free nights as the self-governing Vienna Philharmonic Orchestra. New York, that year, saw the birth of a Philharmonic Society whose members were required to 'be an efficient performer on some instrument'. The upshot of these initiatives was a thorough professionalisation of public concerts. Part-timers were expelled from the bands and musicians shed their medieval status as vagrant entertainers, adopting a new vocation as servants and apostles of the great composers. 'My duty, and that of anyone who finds himself in my position, is to present the heavenly creations of Beethoven before the public as well as possible with the means at hand, and at the very least with the innermost love and enthusiasm,' declared Otto Nicolai, preparing the Vienna Philharmonic for its inaugural performances.[8]

As orchestras shook off chains of serfdom and courted the new urban middle class, solo instrumentalists began to contemplate international careers instead of itinerant wanderings. Their trail was blazed by Niccolò Paganini, the cadaverous violinist of Genoa, whose fiendish finger skills aroused feminine hysteria and accusations of devilment. Paganini was forty-five years old before he ventured abroad in 1828, having acquired a torrid Italian reputation which credited him with seducing Napoleon's sister and serving time for murder (the former more likely than the latter). It was said that the fourth string on his fiddle was made from the intestine of a mistress he had killed. The publication of his twenty-four Caprices for unaccompanied violin in 1820 earned him a call to the imperial court in Vienna, but Paganini was in no hurry to travel. When he eventually packed his fiddle and headed north, Schubert talked of 'hearing an Angel sing' and Schumann sensed a 'turning point' in the art of public performance.[9] Paganini proceeded through Prague and Berlin to Paris and London. 'There is something in his playing that drives one to distraction,' said the doyen of French violinists, Pierre Baillot,[10] sensing that musical virtuosity would never be the same again.

For two whole months, Viennese newspapers reported daily on his progress. Restaurants, snuff-boxes, billiard-canes were named after him. No musician had ever commanded such intensity of attention and Paganini adjusted his ticket prices accordingly. For fifteen London concerts he collected the huge sum of ten thousand pounds. In Paris he took a hundred and sixty-five thousand francs at twelve concerts. When he played during the 1832 cholera epidemic, 'all pain and sadness was suspended; one forgot both death and the fear that is worse than death'.[11]

People of all classes flocked to hear him; the poorer elements in London rioted when tickets soared out of their reach. Paganini was his own promoter, assisted only by his mistress, Antonia Bianchi, and after her defection, by their small son, Achille. He booked the halls, fixed the programmes, hired accompanists and checked the takings, keeping a beady eye on the box-office and moving on to the next venue the moment sales began to flag. He kept two-thirds of the proceeds of a full house, reckoned by the *Harmonicon* to reach £2,260 'for about an hour's fiddling'. He accepted engagements from local entrepreneurs, but on his own terms. He charged Oxford one thousand pounds for an appearance; when the hall manager tried to haggle, he struck out 'pounds' and substituted 'guineas'. Yet he was not without sympathy for brother-promoters. When his partner in an 1834 English tour overreached himself and was jailed for debt, the compassionate Paganini bailed him out and gave a benefit concert on behalf of his sixteen-year-old daughter.

His solicitude, it seems, was misinterpreted: the girl followed him to France and her father sued for abduction. The harassed violinist fled home to Genoa with the remnants of his fortune and briefly assembled a ducal orchestra in Parma. He returned to Paris and opened a casino but, denied a gambling licence, departed with losses of one hundred thousand francs. Stricken with tuberculosis, he took his son to the south of France, where he set up as a dealer in fine instruments. At his death in May 1840 Paganini owned seven Stradivari and four Guarneri violins among a stock of twenty-six Cremona treasures. He was refused a Christian burial by the Bishop of Nice on grounds of his proven atheism and alleged demonism, and five years passed before the Grand Duchess of Parma retrieved his coffin from a cellar and arranged a quiet funeral. By this time Paganini had entered the realms of legend, leaving behind an exploitable myth and the makings of a soloist's profession. The demand for virtuosity and sensation was primed and ready. All that was needed was a durable product to be marketed and distributed.

That is where Franz Liszt came in. The young Hungarian, blessed with cherubic looks and the kiss of Beethoven, was twenty-one years old and the toast of *jeune Paris* when Paganini's cholera concert produced a 'blinding flash' that changed his life in music. 'What a man! what a violin! what an artist! Heavens, what sufferings, what misery, what tortures in those four strings!' he cried.[12] And from that night on young Liszt resolved to become, in his own words, 'the Paganini of the piano'. Within weeks he composed a finger-flying *Clochette* fantasy on the bell-like 'Campanella' theme from Paganini's B-minor violin concerto, followed by six fearsome Etudes on the Campanella and transcriptions of five of Paganini's twenty-four Caprices for unaccompanied violin. These pieces, and the way Liszt played them, marked a breakthrough in what human hands were believed capable of co-ordinating on a keyboard. He raised the pianoforte out of the genteel salon and, one night in December 1837 before three thousand listeners, thundered its percussive power through the grand auditorium of La Scala, Milan. 'Never before has a piano created such an effect,' he told his piano maker, Pierre Erard.[13] Liszt then took Beethoven's symphonies and arranged them for keyboard solo, declaring that there was no effect in the whole of music that could not be reproduced on the piano.

Like Paganini, Liszt cultivated an aura of Romantic fatality. He conceived three children out of wedlock, with the French literary countess Marie d'Agoult, consorted with the temptress Lola Montez and (chastely, it is said) escorted the courtesan Marie Duplessis who became Alexandre Dumas's consumptive heroine in *La Dame aux Camélias*. Alongside his amorous complications, he exuded a priestly sanctity that, late in life, led to ordination in Rome as the Abbé Liszt. Sinner or saint, his triple personation of the musical, the erotic and the sacerdotal inflamed the public imagination.

In straitlaced Leipzig, 'half the people stood on their chairs'[14] when he played his own arrangement of Schubert's diabolical 'Erlkönig'. Hans Christian Andersen found 'something demoniac about him . . . as he played, his face changed and his eyes flashed'. 'We were like men in love, like men obsessed,' wrote the Russian critic Vladimir Stasov. 'We had never heard anything like it before, never been confronted by such a passionate, demoniac genius.'[15] Women came tearing at his hair and scrabbling for his cigar butts, secreting them between their heaving breasts. Heinrich Heine, a clinical observer, diagnosed these reactions as 'Lisztomania' – which, by dictionary definition, can mean a 'mental derangement characterised by hallucinations' or a 'vehement passion or desire'. Heine sensed, however, that the response was not instinctual. The public was being somehow whipped up into an artificial commotion:

> How powerful was the effect merely of his appearance! How violent the applause that greeted him! Bouquets were thrown at his feet. It was impressive to observe how tranquilly this conqueror allowed the bouquets to rain down on him; how graciously he smiled as he placed a red camelia, which he had plucked from one of them, in his lapel . . . Frenzy unparalleled in the history of frenzy! What was the real explanation? . . . It sometimes seemed to me that the whole enchantment is to be traced to the fact that no one in the world knows how to organise 'successes' as well as Franz Liszt or, better, how to stage them. In that art he is a genius. The most eminent persons are his accomplices and his hired enthusiasts are admirably trained.[16]

'Eminent accomplices and hired enthusiasts' – Heine hinted at what he dared not write: that Lisztomania was a man-made eruption, a demagogic manipulation of masses and media. That the 'mania' was manufactured is obvious in retrospect. Liszt had been giving concerts for almost twenty years before the swoonings and mobbings began. The change in his reception can be dated fairly accurately to 1841, when the pianist decided that his life needed organising. He had become discontented with the way musicians were running musical life – not at the Gewandhaus (where his reviewer was Robert Schumann), nor at the Philharmonic Society in London where, contrary to all precedent, he dismissed the orchestra and devised the concept of a solo recital. But while touring the provinces he would find his piano all too frequently untuned, his advertisements unposted and his tickets unsold. The best intentions of local musicians and musician-impresarios, like the composer Louis Lavenu who ran his 1840 England tour, were no longer adequate for a performer of his ambition. What Liszt needed was a personal agent but the occupation had not yet been invented and he was forced to improvise.

He employed a fellow-Hungarian as his secretary but sacked him for incompetence. He then engaged a trusted former pupil, who absconded with three thousand francs. In February 1841 Marie d'Agoult suggested that he take a music copyist, Gaetano Belloni, on his next tour as a travel companion and factotum. Liszt offered Belloni a job and the Italian defined it. Over the next six years he organised and accompanied Liszt's *années de pèlerinage*, the most extensive and lucrative concert tours ever undertaken – from Lisbon and Limerick at the western edge of Europe, to Constantinople and Elisavetgrad in the east. In one week in Moscow he earned enough to buy a house. By the time he returned to Paris, Liszt had a quarter of a million francs on deposit with Rothschilds. He was rich, famous and widely adored, and he owed much of it to the shadowy, self-effacing Belloni.

Rewriting his Will some years later, Liszt paid tribute to Belloni, whom 'I ought to put in the forefront [of my friends]. He was my secretary during the period of my concerts in Europe from 1841 to 1847 and remained my faithful and devoted servant and friend . . . Whether he likes it or not, he is part of the New German School through his great attachment to me – as also through his recent participation in the concerts of Berlioz and Wagner.' This was praise indeed. For an unknown music copyist to be ranked among the great revolutionaries in music suggests that Liszt was keenly aware of the innovations Belloni was working on his behalf.

Ignoring confusions of status ('servant and friend') and nation (the New German School contained a Hungarian, a Frenchman and an Italian), Liszt needed to acknowledge that Belloni had changed the way that concerts were perceived and promoted. Exactly how he did this is unclear, since Belloni was the soul of discretion and, alone among Liszt's circle, left not a single letter or diary leaf unburned. Piecing together their relationship from fragmentary glimpses, it is abundantly clear that Belloni was never a servant awaiting his master's orders nor a supine companion. A Weimar historian, chronicling their voyages, writes that 'Liszt gave a concert almost every evening and travelled both day and night . . . His secretary Belloni was *always ahead of him*, seeing to and arranging everything'.[17]

In advance of Liszt's arrival in any town, Belloni either went ahead or sent ahead to prime the local press of the hysteria aroused at his previous engagements. By the time Liszt turned up in a carriage drawn by six white horses, the town would be agog and the concert sold out. Belloni seemed to know intuitively that people were seeking novelty, that sensation fed upon itself and that a bandwagon, once rolling, accelerates on its own momentum. He anticipated the methods and shared the scruples of a latter-day pop publicist. One well-placed advance story, true or false, of a female admirer who collected Liszt's coffee dregs in a glass phial belted beneath her stays, would guarantee a crush of hyper-ventilating ladies at his next appearance. In the last hours of human innocence, before telegraph and telephones could carry information faster than word of mouth, Belloni invented the rules of star promotion and thought control, the matrix of Hitler heiling and Beatle screamers. Liszt might have flourished as a pianist and composer without such methods but, enjoying their rewards, he became a willing accomplice in their exploitation.

The only man to sense anything nefarious in Belloni's furtive ubiquity was Heinrich Heine, who accused him of hiring old-fashioned claqueurs to fake ecstatic applause at Liszt's concerts. 'Stories of popping champagne bottles and the most prodigal generosity are loudly trumpeted,' rumbled the poet. Poor Heine. He had spotted the malefactor but misread his function, identifying Belloni only as 'Liszt's poodle' and blaming his master for manipulating public emotions. He could not have been more mistaken. Affable, corpulent and sly, Belloni strategised Liszt's elevation from salon pianist to superpriest. Where Paganini toured just four countries and bore a taint of disreputability – a sleazy spoor of sex, drugs and underworld connections – Liszt conquered all of Europe and was courted by church and crown. Prudish Queen Victoria invited him to Buckingham Palace. When they met at the unveiling of a Beethoven memorial in Bonn, Liszt was so dismayed at the state of her furniture that he offered to lend her his own gilt chairs. At the ceremony he refused to play until the assembled monarchs stopped chattering. Sitting at the keyboard, he was king of all he beheld – and behind his coronation lurked the mysterious cleverness of Gaetano Belloni. To be idolised by commoners and kings, pursued by popes and patronesses, was the most a star could demand from a publicist. Liszt can safely be regarded as the first concert star, and Belloni as the inventor of the star system.

In addition to this function, Belloni held the purse strings on Liszt's tours. He cashed the takings and paid for the halls. The only surviving letter with his signature finds him negotiating with piano firms, deciding which one Liszt should favour.[18] There is a memoir of him standing in the wings of one of Liszt's recitals, counting the heads of the paying public against the night's box-office receipts. That anecdote spoke so meaningfully from one entertainment industry to another that it earned Belloni a cameo appearance in Charles Vidor's Hollywood biopic of Liszt's life.

Their relationship came to an end in 1848, when Liszt set up home in Weimar with Countess von Sayn-Wittgenstein – who described her triumph as 'Belloni's Austerlitz' – but the Italian remained eternally at his service. Liszt turned to him ('Dear Bell') when his hot-headed friend Richard Wagner fled Germany with the police at his heels; Belloni helped Wagner gain political asylum and employment in Paris. He brought Liszt's aged mother to visit him in Weimar and ferried the children over to their father after his bitter custody battle with Marie d'Agoult. Belloni was the soul of discretion, outliving Liszt in a village on the outskirts of Paris, where he was traced in 1887 by Rothschild executors after making no claim on his master's estate. He had made Liszt the biggest name in Europe; probably, he made Liszt. Unknowingly, he also made the method by which stars would be manufactured in more efficient times.

The scale of Liszt's success was bound to attract a less bashful type of promoter. In 1855, Phineas T. Barnum, 'the Greatest Showman on Earth', let it be known that he was offering Liszt half a million dollars to play an American tour. Barnum, the self-proclaimed 'Prince of Humbug', made his fortune parading 'real' mermaids, a wool-coated horse, a Swiss bearded lady, a human ape and other freaks and frauds before a credulous continent. He introduced the midget 'General' Tom Thumb at the court of Queen Victoria and stole Jumbo the elephant from London Zoo. He was a child of an expansionist age, 'a great Bible thumper who lies in his advertisements with the pure, tranquil conscience of a Quaker, and who is always ready to lift up to God his innocent hands, filthy from lucre taken at the box-office'.[19] He is supposed to have said 'there's a sucker born every minute', though he denied the utterance. 'I myself relished a higher grade of amusement,' he averred in a colourful memoir, 'and I was a frequent attendant at the opera, first-class concerts, lectures and the like.'[20]

First-class or fifth, his pretensions cut no ice with Liszt, who assured friends he would never leave Europe. Barnum, for his part, was unmoved by Liszt's refusal, having already launched a world sensation upon musical America. In 1850, hearing that Jenny Lind was renouncing opera to apply her divine voice to sacred and pure songs, Barnum sent an emissary to the Swedish Nightingale. For a thousand dollars a night, he proposed, she could sing whatever she liked in America. He would additionally guarantee first-class travel for herself, three servants and a lady companion, plus a twenty-per-cent share of profits on one hundred and fifty concerts. Her music director, Julius Benedict, would get a hundred and sixty dollars a night and her baritone duettist, Giovanni Belletti, half as much. All moneys to be paid in advance through Baring Brothers in London. It was a proposal to tempt a saint, a fee out of all proportion to any previous musical offering – about ten times as much per night as the prima donna earned in any Italian opera house. It amounted, said Lind's daughter, to 'the fulfilment of her dreams of charitable enterprises and immunity from financial anxieties'.[21] The diva was not unnaturally greedy, but she knew her own worth and she went through her Barnum contract with a fine-tooth comb before appending her signature. At her pre-embarkation concert in Liverpool tickets sold for ten shillings each. One hundred years later the costliest concert seat in Liverpool was eight shillings and sixpence, still well below the Lind ceiling.

Boarding her steamship as it entered the port of New York on 1 September 1850, Barnum confessed that he had never heard her sing. 'I risked it on your reputation,' he said, to her instant gratification. He had stoked up a busy press campaign in advance of her arrival, playing down her musical virtues and focusing on the fortune Barnum was paying her and on the acts of piety that, he calculated, would most appeal to a mass American following. 'Since her début in England,' he averred with unusual veracity, 'she has given to the poor more than the whole amount which I have engaged to pay her.'[22] Barnum relied on her generosity striking a chord in open American hearts. 'Without this peculiarity in her disposition,' he would later admit, 'I would never have dared make the engagement which I did.'[23] Jenny Lind was brought to America not as a singer, but as a pre-ordained saint. Nevertheless, as a musical proposition the timing of her arrival could not have been bettered. America had come alive in the 1840s to the sound of music, borne from town to town by small bands and theatre troupes on the new railroads that criss-crossed the prospering north-eastern states. An orchestra had assembled in New York and Boston had a busy concert life. All that was needed was the grace of a great star to give this expanding number of musical performances the semblance of a tradition and a structure.

Barnum had primed the nation for Lind's arrival with a Welcome-to-America song contest, putting up a two-hundred-dollar prize and the chance to hear Jenny sing the ode at her opening concert. Thirty thousand people turned out to meet her ship and twenty thousand more thronged outside her hotel. At midnight, the fire brigade band and two hundred members of the Musical Fund Society turned up at the head of a torchlight parade. 'Reputation was manufactured for her by wholesale,' reported a theatre manager, 'not merely made by the inch but prepared by the cartload.'[24]

Mobbed wherever she went, Lind begged her manager to keep her movements secret. Barnum, pledging her his confidentiality, slipped advance notice of her movements to the newspapers. He admitted in his memoirs that 'the interests of the enterprise depended in a great degree upon these excitements.'[25] He whipped up a storm of so-called 'Lindomania' and worked it for all it was worth. Instead of selling tickets to her first Boston concert, he auctioned them off to the highest bidder. A local singer, Ossian E.

Dodge by name, won the first seat for six hundred and twenty-five dollars, anticipating that the publicity he gained would advance his own career.

Some halls were dangerously oversold and there were riots in the aisles. The pianist had to be bundled over the audience's heads because all stage entrances were jammed with spectators. When Lind's veil fell into the stalls one night it was ripped to shreds by relic hunters. She sang thirty-five concerts in New York, of which the first six earned back fully half Barnum's outlay. To augment his profit he stuffed twenty-eight-page concert programmes with paid advertisements and sold them at twenty-five cents each. When Lind objected to his avarice, he told her to tear up her contract and write another with improved terms. He was not mean. So long as he kept her happy, she would make his fortune.

But Jenny was not a woman who stayed happy for very long. Stern, sexless and relentlessly self-critical, she turned petulant, moody and loudly intolerant of alien races and religions. Barnum made sure the public saw only her most beatific countenance. They sailed together to Havana, where the dock was so crowded that she feared to disembark. Barnum threw a cloth over his own daughter's head and took her through as a decoy, returning for the Nightingale when the mob had safely dispersed. After nine months and ninety-five concerts, she told Barnum 'I am not a horse' and asked to be released from the remainder of her contract. Her earnings had reached $176, 675.09. Barnum had grossed half a million. He freed her without demur, thinking she would head straight back home to Europe. Instead, she continued the tour under her own steam, broodily marrying a straitlaced pianist nine years her junior, Otto Goldschmidt, and pressing his feeble talents on dwindling audiences. Barnum turned up from time to time to hear her. 'People cheat me and swindle me very much,' she told him. 'She looked as stingy as a hive of wasps and as black as a thundercloud, and all because the house was not crowded,' reported a Philadelphia paper.[26] When she finally left for Europe in May 1852 on the steamship *Atlantic* that had brought her to America, barely two thousand turned up to bid her farewell.

Barnum offered her a return tour, which she declined. Their partnership entered posterity as a fairy-tale, Beauty and the Beast. But, given Barnum's probity and Lind's abuse, the natural roles were reversed. Barnum preserved friendly relations with her for many years, which cannot have been easy. Otherwise, he showed no interest in music, apart from his approach to Liszt and a vainglorious attempt to unite the choral societies of several cities at the Crystal Palace exhibition in New York.

For the world of music, however, Barnum's venture was a turning point. Before Lind, no European artist of any consequence was prepared to risk the discomfort of transatlantic travel and the dangers of a wild west. Once they heard how much Lind was getting and how she was faring, musicians set off on an American gold-rush, especially towards the end of their careers. The fading divas Henrietta Sontag and Marietta Alboni arrived within months of Lind's departure. Sigismond Thalberg, a former rival of Liszt's, gave three hundred concerts in eighteen months across the United States and Canada. The Norwegian violinist, Ole Bull, invested his concert fees in 11,144 undeveloped acres of Pennsylvania, planning a settlement for his countrymen. Henri Herz arrived from Paris, to play the pianos he manufactured. Louis Moreau Gottschalk, a New Orleans virtuoso living in Paris, returned in 1853 to a hero's welcome. After Lind, America became part of the musical world.

Its accession was not uniformly welcomed, as one immediate effect was to force up artists' fees in Europe. A diva's ransom in Italy after the Barnum–Lind breakthrough became ten times what the incomparable Giuditta Pasta and Maria Malibran had commanded in the pre-travelling 1830s. If Italy wanted to keep top singers, it now had to reward them on an American scale.

Some starry-eyed historians have asserted that Barnum and Lind set an unbeatable record in real terms for what a singer could earn in a single night. That is a romantic untruth. Adelina Patti, the sweetest songbird of the Victorian era, serenely quintupled Lind's rates. Today's divas, taking into account their media increments, earn far more per concert than the equivalent value of Barnum's copper-bottomed Baring cheques to his stony-hearted Jenny.

One record the unlikely pair did establish, however, was the demarcation line between stars and all other performers. For singing Violetta in the 1870s, Patti would earn five thousand dollars; while in any small town in Italy the prima donna in La Traviata was paid approximately two dollars. Nellie Melba made sixteen hundred dollars a night as prima donna assoluta at the Metropolitan Opera in 1896; the mezzo who sang with her was paid forty-eight dollars.[27] This discrepancy, stemming from Barnum and Lind, was the economic basis of a star system that prevails, essentially unchanged, to the present day in which the stars name their own price and the rest live in financial uncertainty. By bringing Jenny to the world's first democracy, Barnum had unwittingly instituted a new artistic serfdom.

Barnum's other enduring legacy was his marketing method, the blaze of hype that brought the Nightingale's name into every American homestead. He was the first promoter to sell a singer as something other than a singer. The impresarios who followed him for the next half-century failed to grasp this principle and were unable to arouse the same fever for Patti, Christine

Nilsson or Melba, who were promoted purely as great voices. Barnum recognised that serious music is inimical to mass taste. It could be marketed to the masses, but only by removing it from any artistic context.

It took almost a century and a half for his formula to be repeated. Television schedulers, searching for a prime-time filler for an international football contest, alighted on three tenors in a Roman bath and broadcast their concert to every corner of the globe. What the three tenors sang was unimportant and, apart from Puccini's 'Nessun dorma' which became a football anthem, soon forgotten. But what the Three Tenors Concert and its many spin-offs demonstrated was that there was a mint to be made out of music, provided it was not presented as music. Just as Jenny Lind had been projected as an angel who gave twenty-dollar bills to lady beggars, so the three tenors were not refined artists but three football fans on a night off. Their mountainous profits brought relief and revelation to a hard-pressed music industry, which sought salvation in further such ruses. No one gave much thought to the wasteland that awaited, should the stars ever lose their shine.

These immodest beginnings – a Belloni here, a Barnum there – marked the birth of the classical business around the midpoint of the nineteenth century. From the outset there were obvious distinctions between the practice of music management on opposite sides of the Atlantic. European agents tended to follow Belloni's discreet interventionism, while Americans copied Barnum's breezy marketeering. Setting aside personality factors, there were strong cultural grounds for this divergence. Musical life in northern Europe was rooted in the Church and concert hall; in America, it was an optional, after-hours distraction. The symphonic tradition in Europe commanded a social and intellectual allegiance; in the US it had to sell itself afresh. A classical artist in the Old World was revered as the bearer of a sacred tradition; in the New, he was just another greenhorn trying to earn a buck. What both continents had in common was that they discovered simultaneously within the decade of Liszt and Lind that the organisation of music was too complex and important to be left in the hands of musicians.

A professional operator was needed to make sure that artist and audience arrived at the same place and time; that one was properly rewarded and the other aurally satisfied; that talent was noted and nurtured, and that appetites were whetted to applaud it. The art of music was in need of sound management, and there was no shortage of businessmen willing to provide that service. 'The very call-boys in the theatres were ambitious of becoming Barnums. Not a hungry teacher of the piano, nor a theatrical check-taker, but had a longing to try his hand at the great game of sowing nothing and reaping dollars,'[28] wrote one of the first agents, Max Maretzek.

Four music managers had set up in New York shortly before Lind's arrival and were quick to capitalise on her popularity. They consisted of Maretzek, a Brno-born conductor who arrived in 1848 after losing his London podium; his two cousins Maurice and Max Strakosch, pianists from Lemberg who left Europe in the year of revolutions; and Bernard Ullmann, a Budapest émigré. All four shared a Jewish background in central Europe. Maretzek and Maurice Strakosch had achieved some success as performers, while Ullmann and Max Strakosch were salesmen. All lived within a couple of fashionable blocks of one another and formed alternate alliances and feuds. All but one married for money. Ullmann, a lifelong bachelor, was probably gay.

Maretzek was the best established, managing a succession of New York theatres and a string of European singers. He particularly despised Ullmann – not for having been sacked by Henri Herz and defrauding Henrietta Sontag, but for committing the unforgivable offence of publishing, albeit in Spanish, a whistle-blowing book about the music business. Maretzek may have conspired with and against his competitors to rack up ticket prices and promote fake sensations, but he did not want word of their tricks to get about. He was, however, candid enough to admit to a friend, the British composer Michael William Balfe that it was impossible to overestimate 'the various rascalities of the American musical agent'[29] who, he intimated, robbed public and performers with indiscriminate greed. Ullmann, for his part, described his occupation frankly as 'financial music'.

Maurice Strakosch was the luckiest of the breed, and the biggest liar. He claimed to have spent three whole years beside Lake Como, learning from the legendary Pasta all there was to know about the singing voice. Research suggests that he spent a few weeks with Pasta, some months at most. On his voyage to New York in 1848, Strakosch befriended a Sicilian *tenore robusto*, Salvatore Patti, who was preparing to sing and manage Italian opera at a new theatre on Astor Place. Opera, he discovered, was all the rage. Introduced to America in 1825 by the singing family Garcia, with *The Barber of Seville* that Rossini wrote for them, it was taken up by the exiled Lorenzo Da Ponte, Mozart's librettist, who organised a staging of *Don Giovanni*, 'the best opera in the world'.[30] Within a decade there were four theatres playing opera in New York. Astor Place was built in 1847 by 'the richest man in America', John Jacob Astor, along with a hundred and fifty citizens 'of social prominence'. The financial risk of performance, however, was borne by promoter-managers who booked the theatre for short runs. Their role models were the robber-barons of Italian opera, *impresarii* like Domenico Barbaja and Domenico Merelli who held imperial licences to run the great theatres of Naples, Rome and Milan. The *impresarii* nurtured Rossini and Verdi and ran a racket in singers. They were clued in to creative sources and owned rights in the masterpieces they commissioned. Their imitators in America lacked the same authority.

Salvatore Patti opened Astor Place and went bust before its inaugural season was out. With eight children to feed, he was relieved when Maurice Strakosch engaged his entire family for an independent opera festival. Strakosch, twenty-three years old, was smitten by Patti's twelve-year-old daughter, Amalia. Over her mother's objections, he married her two years later. Amalia was a good soprano, but her kid sister was something else.

No one remembered when sweet Adelina first gave voice; 'I think I was trilling when I came into the world,' she said. Strakosch claimed to have been her 'first and only master', but Adelina credited her half-brother, Ettore Barili, and others said her technique was God-given. Jenny Lind, said a pianist who accompanied both divas, achieved success 'through study and hard work; [but] Patti had genius and her voice was of more exquisite timbre'.[31] In 1850 Patti's father took her, aged seven, to the next Astor Place manager, Max Maretzek, who allotted her two numbers in a small-hall recital. The moment Adelina walked on stage she seemed to possess it. 'The beauty of her fresh young voice was thrilling enough, but the brilliancy of her execution was something the like of which people had never heard from the lips of a girl before; and the combination simply took their breath away,' reported a lady ear-witness. 'We left the hall with the feeling that Mr Maretzek had discovered the greatest vocal prodigy of the age.'[32]

Strakosch was not going to let his cousin M run away with his own sister-in-law. He induced Salvatore to let him tour Adelina to every state in America, a five-year trawl of three hundred concerts. Initial uptake was slow, so he booked Ole Bull as supporting act. When the novelty faded in 1855, he announced Adelina's retirement for the duration of her puberty.

He had, by now, formed an agency in partnership with Bernard Ullmann, who was touring the celebrated Sigismond Thalberg with a mixture of populism and snobbery. Ullmann said he would only sell tickets to customers from a good address; when the democratic press protested, he took his pianist to play in an inner-city school. The Strakosch–Ullmann agency tried to foist Marietta Piccolmini on the New York public as a putative second Lind. When she quit in disarray to marry an Italian count, Strakosch had Adelina Patti in waiting.

New York's newest opera house, the Academy of Music, had passed from

Maretzek's hands into Strakosch's and Ullmann's and it was there, on the night of 24 November 1859, aged sweet sixteen, that Patti went chillingly mad as *Lucia di Lammermoor*. Strakosch produced her in fourteen more operas that season and toured her tirelessly across America as the first home-grown diva. One night her sleeve caught fire on the footlights. She tore it off without missing a beat. Adelina was born for the opera stage.

Strakosch composed her cadenzas, conducted the orchestra, sang her lines when she did not feel like rehearsing and, reputedly, stole her virginity. He also took her money. At the Academy of Music, he registered Patti's fee as one hundred dollars a night. But, under his five-year contract with Salvatore, he was entitled to employ her 'at a much lower rate, and thus insured himself a handsome margin of profit'.[33] By pocketing the difference, he defrauded both Patti and his partner, Ullmann.

He was never much of a musician. Rossini, hearing Patti sing his arias with her manager's efflorescent embellishments, groaned 'Ce sont des Strakoschonneries!' – a savage pun, implying a porcine regard for the finer points of music. Yet Strakosch was kind to Patti in his crooked way. He was always there when she needed to let off steam, weathering the force of her tantrums without flinching and allowing her to slap and abuse him in public without retaliation. He protected her from importuners and showed her only the warmest reviews. He loved her as a brother-in-law should, and sometimes more.

The rest of his singers he treated with outright contempt, telling Ullmann to pay seventy-five per cent of their salary the first week, sixty the next and so on, like the parsimonious peasant who trained his donkey to get by on progressively less hay. One day as Ullmann was counting the cash, he was grabbed by the neck by an infuriated *basso*, reduced to the point of starvation. 'You have here the money – either you pay me all or I kill you,' snarled his assailant. 'Help! murder! thieves!' squeaked the agent in his natural high falsetto. His partner burst into the room. 'Your donkey kicks, Mr Strakosch,' whined Ullmann. 'He wants all the oats he sees before him.'[34] Knowing when he was beaten, Strakosch told the man to release Ullmann and paid his salary in full – but he warned the *basso* not to utter a word of this to his colleagues.

Strakosch, said a rival, was 'remarkable for the suavity of his manners'[35] – a well-dressed swindler, who once declared that ten people in a thousand might laugh at his hype, but the rest would buy tickets. Ullmann, on the other hand was sober, long-suffering and something of a dreamer, casting next year's operas when there was no cash to pay for tonight's. In 1861, losing money in New York and sniffing the cordite of civil war, Maurice

Strakosch took Patti to Europe and Ullmann followed soon after, as manager of Patti's other sister, Carlotta. Max Strakosch stayed behind to wage a 'Battle of the Maxes' with Maretzek for operatic paramountcy in New York.

Patti conquered Europe in a trice. Charles Dickens was entranced at Covent Garden. Kaiser Wilhelm led the ovations in Berlin and Napoleon III came backstage in Paris. Verdi, asked to name three favourite divas, listed: 'Adelina, Adelina, Adelina.' Even Jenny Lind was moved to declare: 'There is only one Niagara Falls, there is only one Patti.'[36] The Reign of Patti had begun. It was an absolute monarchy that lasted longer than any other diva's: an unbroken run at Covent Garden that stretched from 1861 to 1895.

Strakosch was constantly at her side in the early years, quitting only in 1868 when she married the Marquis de Caux, an empty-headed sportsman eighteen years her senior. 'The joys of the domestic hearth,' Strakosch warned her, 'are not always for artists; family life is rarely suited to those idols of the public whose existence is passed in an imaginary world.' But Patti ignored him and, though the Marquis asked Strakosch to stay on, 'these offers, however advantageous and honourable . . . were refused.'[37] Strakosch knew he could not cheat a husband the way he milched the star. He left her (or so he said) with engagements worth three hundred thousand dollars for the next three years. He also installed as her long-serving secretary one of his own assistants, an Italian called Franchi, who promptly doubled her fees, making Patti the highest-paid singer on earth. Franchi drew no salary; he lived entirely on commission.

Bereft of his star, Strakosch settled down with Amalia and old Salvatore in Paris, where he produced an opera season in 1873. Another year, he and brother Max ran the Teatro Apollo in Rome. When the Marquis sequestrated Adelina's French accounts after her affaire with a tenor, Strakosch eased her need by organising an 1878 Italian tour with her beloved Ernesto Nicolini, culminating in ten consecutive *Aida*s at La Scala. The lovebirds were ecstatic and the public, apprised by Strakosch of their romance, enthralled. In return for a divorce, the Marquis took half her money. Beside this blue-blooded chiseler, her brother-in-law seemed almost altruistic, a principled swindler. Promoting an American soprano named Emma Thursby, Strakosch (with a nod to Barnum) underlined 'the high personal character of the young singer and especially her great "purity", vowing that acquaintance with her, hardened old sinner that he was, had made him a better man'.[38] He was, wrote a Patti biographer, 'not a bad sort',[39] and among the agents of his time Maurice Strakosch was not exceptionally crooked – though in any better regulated era he would never have stayed out of jail.

He enjoyed one final brush with glory, a last-gasp discovery who was, mercifully, spared the worst of his attentions. Strakosch had heard Nellie Melba sing in a Paris salon in 1887, when she was twenty-six and totally unknown. 'I want that voice,' he said, signing her to an exclusive ten-year contract. When the Monnaie theatre in Brussels approached the young Australian to sing Gilda in *Rigoletto*, Strakosch rushed up five flights to her atelier, waving an outsized walking stick in her face. 'But your contract with me? What of that? Is that nothing?' he expostulated. Melba fled to Brussels where, entering the theatre to begin rehearsals, she was served with a court order obtained by Strakosch, forbidding her to sing anywhere except under his management. 'I was in the depth of despair,' she recalled. Stressed to breaking point by anxiety and insomnia, she continued to rehearse. In the dawn of a restless night, she answered a violent knocking at her door. It was the director of the Monnaie. '*Strakosch est mort!*' exclaimed the happy Belgian. '*Il est mort hier soir, dans un cirque* – he died last night at a circus.'[40] Later that week, Melba's star soared unhindered into the international firmament.

Back in 1861, Strakosch's first point of contact in Europe when he came over with Adelina had been a like-minded Englishman who ran London's first music agency in the Haymarket. James Henry Mapleson, a violinist at Her Majesty's Theatre during the Jenny Lind seasons, had his voice trained at La Scala by Alberto Mazzucatto, the orchestral concertmaster. His reappearance at Drury Lane as Alphonso in Auber's *Masaniello*, under the assumed name of Enrico Mariani, was disastrous. 'The unfortunate debutant was exposed to a fire of irony and laughter,' reported the *Morning Post*. Dodging the rotten eggs, Mapleson opted for a quieter life as an agent. Supplying singers to theatres during an opera boom required no great ingenuity. 'As I was well known in Italy,' he noted, 'numbers of artists inscribed their names on my books. I did a good business and was making a large income.'[41]

He made enough to run an Italian opera season with E. T. Smith, manager of the Drury Lane Theatre. Supplying singers to his own shows gave him a cut on both sides of the curtain. When Strakosch walked Patti into his office singing 'Home Sweet Home', Mapleson realised he 'had secured a diamond of the first water'. The two managers struck a deal – forty pounds a week according to Mapleson, four hundred pounds a month in Strakosch's version – and Mapleson raced off to France to hire a cast. He arrived home to find that Strakosch had sold Patti to Frederick Gye at Covent Garden. 'Maurice Strakosch told me that, as their last five-pound note had been spent, he had been obliged to borrow fifty pounds off Gye,' reports Mapleson. 'And after a deal of difficulty I ascertained that he had signed a receipt for the said loan in a form which really constituted an engagement for the Royal Italian Opera, Covent Garden. In short, I found myself manager of the Lyceum Theatre, with an expensive company, and with Mlle. Patti opposed to me in the immediate vicinity at Covent Garden.'[42]

Neither man, needless to say, was telling the truth. Mapleson tricked Strakosch into thinking he had a theatre, when he knew that Smith had vanished and was secretly selling out to Gye. Strakosch, as soon as Mapleson was gone, flogged Patti to the highest bidder – for a hundred and fifty pounds a month, rising to four hundred pounds after five years. Mapleson, though, did not give up. His shows at Her Majesty's ate into Gye's takings and they eventually joined forces in 'coalition seasons' at Covent Garden, splitting a two-year yield of twenty-four thousand pounds. From 1878 to 1886, Mapleson shipped part of Her Majesty's company to New York and seven other cities, simultaneously running opera seasons on both sides of the Atlantic.

A strapping man, whose brother was music librarian to the Queen, Mapleson flourished a military pair of moustaches and liked to be called 'Colonel'. Cynics said he showed greatest valour at the mess-table of his suburban, part-time regiment. If music is the food of love, said the Colonel, I shall be the caterer. Twice he retrieved French delicacies from Parisian rejection, turning Gounod's *Faust* and Bizet's *Carmen* into London hits by packing the house with noisy claqueurs. In 1882, he leased Her Majesty's to the German company that gave the first British performance of Wagner's *Ring*. He campaigned loudly for a national opera house on the Thames Embankment. For these triumphs of daring and imagination, Mapleson has been warmly praised by operatic historians. He died destitute in 1901, his funeral arranged by two cleaners from Her Majesty's Theatre and his son, in a letter to *The Times*, upbraided 'the many artists and musicians whose fortunes he made [who] have entirely forgotten their indebtedness to him'.[43]

The truth was less flattering. When Mapleson went broke, it was his artists who suffered. His loyal conductor, Luigi Arditi, was owed three hundred pounds at one bankruptcy, of which he recovered just three pounds and six shillings from the liquidators. Patti knew the Colonel well enough never to go on stage without first being paid. Even she had to send debt-collectors after him when he defaulted on her advances for an American tour (Mapleson issued counter-writs against her husband, Nicolini). In order to get paid Lilli Lehmann, the august German soprano, would waylay Mapleson at his office on Patti nights, knowing that if she caught him with bulging pockets he could hardly withhold her wages.

He would be seen mingling with the upper classes between acts of an opera, 'borrowing fivers from the patrons in front with which to satisfy the choristers and artistes to finish the second act'.[44] To save a few pounds, he would ship an Italian chorus to Dublin on a rickety, filthy coal freighter. When Arditi collapsed in Chicago, Mapleson abandoned him; the first his wife heard of his illness was a telegram from the solicitous Patti. In his memoirs, Mapleson refers to that episode bluffly as 'Arditi's Remains'. A scrounger, miser and snob, he got by on sang-froid, a stiff upper lip and the languid charm of a Raffles. 'I have known *prime donne* enter his office infuriatedly,' noted Arditi, 'vowing they would not depart from his presence without "a little cheque" or hard cash, and these same irate ladies would sally forth, after waiting his leisure for some considerable time, with their angry looks transformed to absolute serenity, and actually feeling, to all appearance, as though Mapleson were conferring a considerable favour upon them by continuing to owe them their hard-earned salaries. His manner was quite irresistible; there never lived the man whose suave, gentle art in calming the irrepressible creditor was more conspicuous or effective . . .

'This was an art in itself; but a fact of far greater importance is that Mapleson was, unlike E. T. Smith, a Musician.'[45]

This was, in fact, Mapleson's ultimate deception: the appeal to a shared ideal that, when he hit rock-bottom, persuaded many artists including Patti herself to stage benefit concerts on his behalf as a fellow-musician in difficulties. Yet Mapleson was insensate to their welfare, obsessed by greed and self-importance. He blamed his failures on the public, the artists and the stars – although neither he, nor any other promoter, ever lost a penny on Patti.

Mapleson and, to a lesser extent, the Strakosch brothers are numbered by musicologists among the masterminds of the *belle époque*, men who shaped the world of opera and nurtured its great voices. In reality, they were predators who squeezed talent for their own pecuniary ends and ran the opera industry as a den of thieves. If Patti and Melba demanded preposterous pay and conditions, they did so not simply out of personal vanity but to protect themselves from leeching managers. The public, unaware of these pressures, blamed the singers for high prices and high-and-mighty airs – which the managers coolly advertised as a stellar prerogative. The diva-as-bitch was their invention, bred of defensive necessity.

If Barnum had not said 'there's another fool born every minute', Mapleson would have done so. His operas consisted of a supine star, surrounded by unrehearsed ancillaries on a cheap set. Patti, in his productions, would kick off her shoes and settle comfortably on a specially-provided divan to deliver her death aria in *Aida*. The dramatic power of opera meant nothing to the agent-managers.

They ruled unhindered for twenty years until, in 1888, Mapleson was outfaced in London by the high-minded Augustus Harris, his sometime trainee. Harris milked subsidies from duchesses, replaced Patti with Melba, diversified the Covent Garden Italian season with grand French and German operas and – being of independent means – broke the vice-like grip of the rapacious agent-manager by conscientiously taking no cut for himself. He died, aged forty-four, of aggravated workaholism. His friend Carl Rosa, who reformed touring opera in Britain with comparable dedication, expired at forty-seven. Theirs was a Golden Age of glorious voices, growing repertoires and a dawning sense of professional duty among those who aspired to run national opera houses.

The cleansing moment in New York was the opening of the Metropolitan Opera House in 1883. Funded by *nouveau riche* brokers who felt uncomfortable in the Academy of Music, it was run by a 'Knickerbocker Aristocracy' who barred Jews from holding shares in the company. Mapleson saw the Met as a mortal threat, called it 'the new yellow brewery on Broadway' and tried to spend it out of existence with an all-star season topped by Patti, who was back home, sweet home, for the first time in twenty years. But the Met had a bottomless purse for stars and could keep going in adversity with star-free German operas whose conductor, Walter Damrosch, vowed 'to sweep away forever the artificial and shallow operas of the old Italian school with which Mapleson, Max Strakosch and others had until then principally fed our public'.[46] The Met's sets and costumes were lavish and the house possessed a magnificent ambience. Its image as a solid institution, not a bawdy house to be hired by any procurer, delivered the killer blow to murky impresarios and Mapleson retreated from America muttering, 'You can't fight Wall Street.'[47]

The Met's board of businessmen kept a beady eye on the managers they licensed. The first was Sarah Bernhardt's agent, Henry Abbey, assisted by an operetta impresario Maurice Grau, whose uncle, Jacob Grau, had once worked for Strakosch. After an interlude of Damrosch leadership, Maurice Grau ran the Met until his retirement in 1903; for three seasons after Harris's death, he concurrently ran Covent Garden. Grau, said Damrosch who owed him no favours, 'was honourable in his dealings with the artists and in a grudging way (which operatic artists often have) they liked him, although they tortured him incessantly. He used to sit in his office like a spider from morning until night, working out repertoires, quarrelling with the singers or placating them, and altogether having no interests in life beyond that.' His only known vice was playing poker.

When, in failing health, he failed to show a profit in 1902, Grau was replaced by a low-caste operetta producer, Heinrich Conried, who announced that he could run the Met more economically without the magnificence of Nellie Melba, whose 'scintillating bubbles of sound' had brought the house down every season since 1893. Conried's cost-conscious-ness appealed mightily to the self-made millionaires who sustained the company. Little could they know that Conried would cream off three hundred thousand dollars in five seasons on top of his twenty-thousand-dollar salary; he made a little extra giving acting lessons in his brocaded office. Musically ignorant and socially uncouth, he once told G Mahler to use a tenor when no bass could be found. He provoked the first orchestral strike in Met history by cutting musicians' wages and was sustained only by the fidelity of the fabulous Enrico Caruso, whose contract he inherited from Grau. Every time Caruso sang outside the Met, whether at a rich man's home or in concert, Conried took a cut of his fee. He belonged spiritually to the brigand breed of Strakosch and Mapleson and was finally sacked for 'grievous and irreparable faults', having lost the best French operas and most of Puccini's hits to a rival opera house.

In France, too, dodgy *impresarii* gave way to professional managers, many of them former musicians with a fervour for art. The sonorous bass Pierre Gailhard cut short a fine singing career to rejuvenate the Paris Opéra; the stagewise Albert Carré at the Opéra-Comique trumped him with Debussy's *Pelléas et Mélisande*, Charpentier's monstrously popular *Louise* and operas by Dukas, Fauré and Ravel. In Italy and Germany the opera palaces of defunct princedoms, formerly licensed to freewheeling *impresarii*, were taken over by public authorities and vested with subsidy. When Milan failed to meet its financial obligations in 1898, a committee of citizens liberated La Scala, installing the thirty-year-old Giulio Gatti-Casazza of Ferrara as Sovrinten-dente and his contemporary Arturo Toscanini as chief conductor. Power in opera was shifting towards the podium.

The showdown between outmoded avarice and aspirational art came to a head in Hamburg where the piratical Bernhard Pollini hired Gustav Mahler as chief conductor in 1891. Pollini (born Baruch Pohl) paid big money to his stars and kept the rest of the cast on subsistence wages, forcing them to sing four nights a week. He was among the first to stage Tchaikovsky operas and a *Ring* cycle, which he shipped to London. He is described in *New Grove* as 'an Intendant of international stature'.[48] He was a slave-driver and swindler.

Pollini managed the Hamburg theatre under licence from city hall, taking two and a half per cent of the proceeds. This arrangement was known locally as 'mono-pollini'. He had promised Mahler the title of artistic director but allowed him no say in casting or staging. Mahler accused Pollini of 'shabby tricks' and fought to protect his singers from vocal damage. He scrubbed his hands red each night as he came home from the theatre, cleansing his pores of

Pollini's pollution. He escaped only when Pollini was too sick with cancer to stop his going.

Mahler's five seasons of anguish were not, however, wasted. When Vienna appointed him chief conductor in 1897, he tore into the Court Opera like an avenging angel, evicting slackers and spongers and declaring the supremacy of a music director in the management of an opera house. He re-energised stage design and choreography, encouraged the company to dream of perfection and demanded probity in all commercial dealings. Most important of all, he impressed upon the public the notion that the art of opera transcended the abilities of performers and the desires of organisers. The art was an end in itself and Vienna under Mahler's ten-year rule signified its apogee. Toscanini, over the same decade, terrorised La Scala with fanatical purism. Both proceeded to stamp their standards on the Met in the opening decade of the twentieth century.

In London and Paris, the conductor-composer André Messager became manager successively of Covent Garden, the Opéra and the Opéra-Comique. Applied at key power points, the authority of musicians evicted money grabbers from the temples of opera – not immediately, nor entirely, but sufficiently to ensure their lasting defeat.

The final charge of the buccaneers came from Oscar Hammerstein, inventor of a cigar-making machine who, rebuffed by the Met, built a Manhattan Opera House in 1906 on West 34th Street, with Melba as queen bee, Luisa Tetrazzini as rising luminary and the US premières of Pelléas, Louise and Strauss's Elektra – all turned down by the incompetent Conried. Hammerstein paid his four top singers a quarter of a million dollars a season, and cleared as much again for himself. He built a second house in Philadelphia and another in London in 1911. The Met responded by sacking Conried and outspending Oscar. Caruso, crucially, pledged his troth to the Met. Told to name his own terms, he froze his fee at two thousand five hundred dollars a night, half of what Hammerstein offered him and one-sixth of his going rate in South America. The chairman, Otto H. Kahn, was so moved by his consideration that he decided to converse ever after with the tenor in his native tongue, studying Italian each morning as he drove to the office with Caruso's secretary, Bruno Zirato.

Hammerstein had deep pockets and parcels of real estate planted all over the east coast. He held out until 1910, when Kahn bought him out for a million dollars; Covent Garden crushed his London house three years later. With the elimination of Oscar, the operatic establishment closed ranks, tamped down fees and clamped down on interlopers. Toscanini's partner, Giulio Gatti-Casazza – lofty, libidinous but institutionally loyal – ran the Met for twenty-three years and kept it in surplus. He saw the house through the Depression by cutting all wages, including his own.

Retiring on Kahn's death in 1934, Gatti-Casazza handed over to hand-reared successors and the century was half over before his influence waned. During that time the Met set a scale of fees that became a litmus test for international opera. The pickings grew slim on the lyric stage, and agents were obliged to look elsewhere – to the wide-open spaces of the under-plundered concert hall and its electrifying virtuosi.

The initial promoters of commercial concerts were a light-fingered lot, makers and pushers of keyboard instruments, the heavy industrial heirs of Muzio Clementi. 'The piano is an American invention,' claims Steinway's historian, 'in America, iron entered the piano.'[49] Two firms fought for dominance – Chickering and Sons of Boston (founded 1823) and Steinway of New York, established in 1853 by a German cabinet-maker, Heinrich Engelhard Steinweg, and four of his sons. Both built eponymous concert halls in the 1860s to promote their wares as prices dropped after the Civil War and domestic models became affordable. In the next decade, both produced upright pianos for the drawing-room. Together they persuaded the public that no American home was properly furnished without a piano in the parlour. The problem was how to convince purchasers to buy a brand-name piano, when cheap clones were being sold all over the West under such rubrics as 'Steinmay' and 'Shumway'.

William Steinway, crown prince of an industrial estate that occupied four hundred acres of Long Island, reckoned that he could imprint his name on customers' minds if a famous pianist came over and endorsed his product right across America. The virtuoso he chose was Anton Rubinstein, a Russian of Jewish birth, whose square skull and leonine mane bore so close a resemblance to Beethoven's that he was rumoured to be the Master's natural son. The agent Jacob Grau had long-sightedly placed the Lion of St Petersburg under contract and when Steinway made his request in 1872 it was this former Strakosch aide who brought Rubinstein to America. He set up an eight-month tour of two hundred and fifteen concerts, accompanied by the moody Polish violinist Henryk Wieniawski, two singers and a chamber ensemble, sometimes playing two or three towns a day. 'Rubi' as the Russian was popularly dubbed, was paid eighty thousand dollars in gold coins, 'Wine-and-whisky' got half as much. The pair squabbled incessantly. Jacob Grau cried off sick and delegated the tour to his twenty-four-year-old nephew, Maurice. 'I was under the entire control of the manager,' wailed Rubinstein in his memoirs. 'May Heaven preserve us from such slavery! Under these conditions there is no chance for art – one grows into an automaton, simply performing mechanical work; no dignity remains to the artist, he is lost . . .'[50] Given the pianist's seniority and the manager's inexperience, Rubi's encomium says as much for Grau's precocious authority as it does for his own discomfort.

For Steinway, however, the tour was an unqualified triumph. Their pianos survived heavy pounding and bore a large Steinway hoarding at all concerts. Steinway Hall was packed to the rafters to hear Rubinstein play his own D minor concerto with an orchestra formed by Theodore Thomas, a serial founder of American orchestras. Rubinstein insisted on giving solo recitals, confounding Grau's fear that people would not pay good money to hear one man play. He played seven Beethoven sonatas one evening, and an all-Schumann recital the next, to an ecstatic reception. The American public had become more sophisticated since Strakosch's time.

Over in Boston, Chickering smarted at Steinway's success. In 1875 they struck back with the German pianist Hans von Bülow, former son-in-law of Liszt, whose life fell apart when his wife, Cosima, set up home with Wagner. Bülow begged friends to find him a manager who would take him far from the scene of his marital disaster. They led him to Bernard Ullmann, Strakosch's former partner, restored to prosperity in Europe and keen to reconquer America. Ullmann sent Bülow on a Russian tour, where he discovered music by Peter Ilyich Tchaikovsky. He then sold him to Chickering, who bragged that 'Rubinstein's remarkable tour through the States [had] served only to increase the popular desire to see and hear von Bülow.' This was no small coup for the Chickerings. The choleric Bülow had previously only played pianos that were crafted by his Berlin friend, Carl Bechstein. He twice rebuffed Steinway.

On 18 November 1875, Hans von Bülow made his US début in the Chickerings' home town of Boston, playing a Beethoven concerto with an orchestra assembled by Leopold Damrosch. A week later he gave the world première of Tchaikovsky's B-flat minor piano concerto, a thunderous score the composer had dispatched to him after Nikolai Rubinstein, Anton's brother, dismissed it as 'worthless and unplayable'. In Bülow's hands, the concerto brought the house down and he had to repeat the finale.

Then the tour fell apart. Bülow, in a newspaper interview, spoke abusively about the beer-swilling Germans he met in the new world. He kicked the Chickering placard on his piano and told the audience, 'I am not a travelling advertisement.' Febrile and tendentious, he teetered on the verge of mental collapse. He left America with a quarter of his dates unfulfilled, but the tour was a success, selling thousands of pianos and confirming the public appreciation of late Beethoven. Every piano maker worth his pedals now rushed into concert promotion. Bechstein built halls in Berlin and London, Pleyel one in Paris, Steinway another in London.

Pianists pounded out their praises on an ever-widening US concert circuit, confusing consumers by switching periodically from one make to another. Rubinstein, back in Europe, endorsed a Bechstein. Bülow returned to the US in 1888 playing a Knabe. Tchaikovsky, three years later, opened Carnegie Hall on a Knabe, then switched to a Steinway. Patti, who could barely play, endorsed a Kimball. Paderewski and Rachmaninov were Steinway men. Chickering went bust. There was a clear correlation between the calibre of a piano maker's concert artists and the state of his market.

Piano production peaked at the turn of the twentieth century, then spiralled downwards as gramophones and radio brought music less effortfully into the home. Piano manufacturers, like organ-grinders and castrati, virtually disappeared. Their principal legacy was the establishment of a regular and reasonably well-regulated cycle of concert activity across America. Thanks to the Steinways and Chickerings, the country was opened to a superior class of soloist and new orchestras flowered wherever they appeared. Theodore Thomas started symphony orchestras in New York, Brooklyn, Cincinnati and Chicago. Major Henry Lee Higginson, a Civil War hero with a family bank, set up the Boston Symphony Orchestra in 1881 and brought over the inspirational Arthur Nikisch from Leipzig to professionalise it. St Louis started an orchestra in 1893, Philadelphia and Dallas in 1900, Minneapolis and Seattle in 1903, San Francisco in 1911. By the First World War, no self-respecting city was without one.

A shoal of middlemen swam into play, supplying the orchestras with soloists and conductors. This clutch of concert agents, flourishing codes of discretion and notarised contracts, could not possibly be confused with their disgraceful predecessors, the rapscallion purveyors of operatic entertainments – although in many cases the concert agent was merely an opera shark who had changed his velvet jacket for a business suit.

Hans von Bülow, a hard man to please, wrote to his ex-wife about Bernard Ullmann in the following terms: 'I have on the whole found him entirely satisfactory up till now; his politeness and sincerity certainly deserve mention.'[51] This cannot surely have been the same Ullmann who once ripped off Henrietta Sontag with a $6,701.32 bill 'to cover his advertising costs'. Jacques Offenbach, brought to America by Maurice Grau, remarked upon his agent's 'incessant work, cares of every kind, extraordinary activity; preoccupations every hour of the day have aged him before his time'.[52] There could be no better model of selfless dedication to art. Even Maurice Strakosch was heard talking of himself in Paris as a 'reformed character'. It looked for all the world as if the music business, now well established, was in danger of going straight.

NOTES

1 Hogwood, p. 70
2 Charles Burney, quoted in Hogwood, p. 230
3 Gustave Chouquet in *Grove's* Dictionary of Music and Musicians, 1st edition, London (Macmillan) 1889
4 Wyzewa, Introduction to the Sénart edition of Clementi's sonatas
5 Letter to Miss Penny of Weymouth, offered for sale at Sotheby's, 28 May 1993
6 *Atheneum* magazine, 26 July 1902
7 Elliot Forbes (ed.), *Thayer's Life of Beethoven* (Princeton University Press, Princeton N.J.) 1969, pp. 468–9
8 Clemens Hellsberg, *Demokratie der Könige* (Schweizer Verlagshaus, Zürich) 1992, p. 11
9 Schwarz, p. 181
10 Jeffrey Pulver, *Paganini, the Romantic Virtuoso* (Herbert Joseph, London) 1936, p. 217
11 G. I. C. de Courcey, *Paganini the Genoese* (University of Oklahoma Press, Norman) 1957, vol. II, p. 101
12 Walker, vol. I, p. 174
13 Walker, vol. I, p. 316
14 Hiller, p. 165
15 Laszlo, p. 94
16 Frederic Ewen (ed./transl.) *Heinrich Heine: Self-Portrait and Other Prose Writings* (The Citadel Press, Syracuse, N.J.) 1948, pp. 386–7
17 Adelheid von Schorn
18 Walker, vol. II, pp. 4–5
19 Barbey d'Aurevilly, quoted in Saxon, p. 2
20 Barnum, p. 135
21 Mrs Rayond Maude, *Jenny Lind* (Cassell, London) 1926, p. 141
22 Maretzek, p. 121
23 Barnum memoirs, np
24 Maretzek, p. 121
25 Barnum, pp. 301–2
26 Goldin, p. 39
27 Roselli, p. 138
28 Maretzek, p. 184
29 Maretzek, p. 180
30 Da Ponte, p. 448
31 Ganz, p. 75
32 Klein, pp. 21, 29
33 Klein, p. 47
34 Maretzek, *Sharps*, p. 44
35 Maretzek, *Sharps*, p. 36
36 Klein, p. 381
37 Strakosch, p. 55
38 Damrosch, p. 75
39 Klein, p. 242
40 Melba, pp. 26–7
41 Mapleson, p. 16

42 Mapleson, p. 30
43 Mapleson, p. 10
44 Glover, p. 124
45 Arditi, p. 89
46 Damrosch, pp. 52–3
47 *Golden Horseshoe*, p. 26
48 see *New Grove* entry 'Hamburg'
49 Ratcliffe, p. 5
50 Rubinstein, p. 115
51 letter to Cosima Wagner
52 *Orpheus in America: Offenbach's diary of his journey to the New World*, transl. Lander MacClintock (Hamish Hamilton, London) 1958, p. 82

CHAPTER IV

THE COMPANY OF WOLFF'S

It was a fair exchange. Europe gave America the gift of music and America, in return, gave Europe the music business. In 1875, just as Hans von Bülow was crossing the Atlantic in Bernard Ullmann's care, Albert Gutmann set up as a concert agent beneath the stone arches of the Vienna Court Opera, where no musician could pass him by. A year later, while Offenbach was being promoted in America by Maurice Grau, Alfred Schulz-Curtius founded an agency in London to organise a Richard Wagner festival. Around the same time in Berlin, a weary Anton Rubinstein walked into the Bote & Bock music shop and unloaded his woes on to the sympathetic proprietor 'I travel the world to earn money for my family, and I need someone who can organise the concerts and protect my personal needs,' he sighed. 'I have just the man for you,' said Bock, calling out from behind the counter a busy clerk named Hermann Wolff. Bock knew that Wolff's restless entrepreneurship could not be confined to a humble music shop. He could not have foreseen that, within two decades, Wolff would become the Kaiser of musical Germany.

Berlin was a cultural backwater, however, compared to Vienna, where Gutmann got off to a flying start. During a welcome party for Richard Wagner the agent got friendly with Vienna Philharmonic players and arranged to sell concert tickets in his shop. He soon collected enough subscribers to fill the Musikvereinsaal twice over, enabling the orchestra to repeat concerts without extra rehearsal. He was asked to help engage soloists and, when stars came to Vienna, persuaded them to stay an extra night and appear in his chamber music and vocal recitals. His were the only independent promotions advertised in Vienna Philharmonic programmes. He procured a Habsburg warrant and styled himself 'Albert Gutmann, k. und k. Hofmusikalienhandlung' – the royal and imperial Court's supplier of musical commodities. 'Almost unchallenged,' said an unhappy violinist, 'he dominated Vienna's concert world.'[1]

As his prosperity grew Gutmann began to publish music. He printed études by the seventeen-year-old Ferruccio Busoni on receiving a testimonial from Johannes Brahms, but turned down Hugo Wolf. His one notable intervention in the artistic process came in 1884 when, impressed by a crested dedication to Archduke Max Emanuel of Bavaria, he issued a quintet by the mature but obscure Anton Bruckner. The composer, peripheralised by powerful pro-Brahmsian critics, was experiencing an upturn in his fortunes. Arthur Nikisch, reading his seventh symphony, said 'there has been nothing to approach it since Beethoven' and gave a magnificent première in Leipzig. Hermann Levi conducted the score in Munich and Bruckner then approached Gutmann, who agreed to publish the symphony – provided he paid one thousand guilders to cover printing costs. Levi organised a whip-round and, on the eve of Bruckner's sixtieth birthday, presented the composer with his first published symphony. After an interval of five years the composer offered Gutmann his fourth symphony. Although the Vienna Philharmonic had performed the work successfully, the terms were unchanged – a thousand guilders sponsorship, or no edition. A subsidy was raised again, but on this occasion Gutmann committed the cardinal sin of violating the composer's wishes and savagely editing the score. Conductors and scholars are still struggling to piece together Bruckner's original intentions.

With his Philharmonic links, his sheet-music business and a thriving piano store on the Gateway-to-Heaven Street, Gutmann greatly expanded musical activity in the city of Schubert and the Strausses. His booking office beneath the opera arches was a premier assignation point for musicians – Liszt, when he visited Vienna, demanded to stay 'near Gutmann's' – and his recitals set many a young soloist on the celestial path. Yet few noticed when, in 1907, he sold up, suffered a nervous breakdown and died.[2]

Gutmann's success was founded on his friendly relations with the Vienna Philharmonic. The only challenge to his influence came with the rise of an ulterior family interest within the orchestra. In 1881, a seventeen-year-old Jewish boy from the Romanian town of Iasi gave a sensational performance of the freshly minted violin concerto by Karl Goldmark. Despite his youth,

Arnold Rosé was voted into the concertmaster's seat. 'The purity of his intonation was proverbial,' commented the violinist Carl Flesch. 'On the interpretative side, the highest praise was due to his power of phrasing, the absolute certainty with which he always found the right kind of dynamic and agogical expression. An ideal orchestral leader, irresistibly carrying the others with him, [he was] an infallible sight-reader, an unfailing support to the conductor.'[3] Rosé held sway in the orchestra for fifty-seven years, until his merciless eviction by Nazi colleagues.

A combative, lascivious, uncerebral man, Rosé aroused affection and animus in equal measure, sentiments that intensified when Gustav Mahler was appointed chief conductor in 1897. Rosé was Mahler's double brother-in-law. His brother, Eduard, a cellist, married Mahler's sister Emma in 1898, and Arnold himself wed Mahler's favourite sibling, Justine, four years later. During Mahler's decade in Vienna, Rosé became a tinpot tyrant. 'He was seized with a sort of Caesar-like madness and ruled in the orchestra with brutal and narrow-minded arbitrariness,'[4] wrote the composer Franz Schmidt, a cellist in the Philharmonic.

Rosé had an elder brother, Alexander, who, lacking the same zest, set up in Vienna as a music publisher and agent. In the former capacity, he produced reams of sentimental piano trash, composed and paid for by aristocratic dilettantes. As an agent, he had an ear for young violinists and discovered both Fritz Kreisler and Jan Kubelík. Kreisler dubbed him the '*celebrissima e illustrissima impresa dei più grandi e conosciuti artisti del vecchio e nuovo mondo*',[5] but Alexander was never solvent for very long and needed his famous brother to pull strings on his behalf. His concerts were neither as glamorous nor as well-patronised as Gutmann's, and his artists were usually unknowns. He had to get in with the Vienna Philharmonic if he was to grab a share of Gutmann's action.

In 1900, Alexander Rosé came up with the brilliant idea that the orchestra could serve as a cultural ambassador for the crumbling empire, camouflaging its national fissures beneath the glories of a common musical heritage. He formed a committee of prominent citizens and raised a subvention to send the orchestra to Paris for the International Exposition. The musicians were thrilled, but his brother – whether for form's sake or out of fraternal anxiety – vociferously opposed the venture. At an orchestral meeting, Arnold argued that Paris would be too hot in June and too expensive, the hotels uncomfortable and the public unappreciative.[6] He was hugely outvoted and the voyage went ahead. It brought a breakthrough in bilateral relations, exciting fevered admiration from the rising politicians Paul Picquart and Georges Clemenceau. It was also a financial disaster. Half-way through the visit, unable to afford the rail fare home, the players sent Mahler to Baron

Albert Rothschild, head of the family bank, to beg for twenty thousand francs.

The following winter Alexander Rosé staged on Mahler's behalf the world première of his juvenile cantata, *Das Klagende Lied*. It was poorly sung and caustically received, one racialist critic crudely underlining the blood ties between Mahler and 'his brother-in-law, the impresario and music merchant, Alexander Rosé'.[7] In a Viennese context, this taint of shared semitism was more damaging than accusations of nepotism. Alexander, lacking Mahler's resilience, cracked under a combination of musical and domestic pressures. His wife, a stage-struck English spinster, had mistaken him during courtship for the celebrated Arnold and made their home a frigid misery on discovering his artistic inadequacy. After their divorce, Alexander went into decline and his concert advertisements took on a forlorn appearance. His soloists, Kreisler and Kubelík among them, switched allegiance to Gutmann. By 1911, the year of his early death (and Mahler's), his concert agency was earning less than his sheet-music distribution and score-rental businesses. On 5 November that year the Philharmonic played Beethoven's fifth symphony in Rosé's memory, repaying a debt of honour to the man who established its continental status. Future histories of the orchestra would suggest that it created itself *ab nihilo* by the will of its player-members and the magic of its conductors, ignoring the formative interventions by Gutmann and Rosé. But when the Austrian empire crashed in 1918 and its glittering capital was reduced to provinciality, it was the subscription system devised by Gutmann that saved the Vienna Philharmonic from starvation and the touring plans generated by Rosé that kept its fame alive.

Hermann Wolff learned his vocation the hard way. Trundling with Anton Rubinstein across a snow-covered terrain from Silesia to Herzegovina was tough enough, without having to cope with the pianist's dietary peculiarities and concupiscent proclivities. Rubi stormed out of any restaurant that failed to cook his meal '*au naturel*' and led him on fifty-mile dirt-track detours in search of feminine company. Hans von Bülow, his second client, was violently misanthropic and suicidally depressed. Upper-floor windows had to be nailed shut to prevent auto-defenestration.

If Wolff carried a musical dictionary around with him for reference, he could scarcely have found within it two more truculent personalities. When both stayed in the same small London hotel, he was at his wits' end to keep one from sighting the other. Yet, by protecting them from shocks and discomforts, Wolff earned their undying trust. '*M. Wolff, mon agent, est un homme charmant, instruit, aimable, honnête, sachant vivre et amusant,*[8] said Bülow, a testimonial warmer than he gave to any other living soul.

It took all of Wolff's charm, knowledge, amiability, *savoir-faire* and wit to keep his artists playing. He gave and wrote press interviews on their behalf, handled their finances with discretion and flair and made connections wherever he travelled. While in Barcelona with Rubinstein, he sighted an opening for an orchestral conductor and signed the contract for an unwitting Rhineland composer, Ferdinand Hiller. By the time he returned to Berlin in 1880, Wolff was known to concert givers all over the continent. Aged thirty-five, he set up Konzertdirektion Hermann Wolff with an artists' list that included, in addition to Rubinstein and Bülow, the sagacious violinist Joseph Joachim and his soprano wife Amalie; the French composer Camille Saint-Saëns whom he met on a Rubi-run around Paris; the Belgian tenor Ernest van Dyck; the pianists Eugène d'Albert and Emil Sauer; and a dozen lesser others. Wolff also held a scouting post as European representative for Abbey, Schoeffel and Grau of the Metropolitan Opera, and as booking agent for orchestras from London, Paris and Copenhagen.

For Berlin, he had bigger ideas. In January 1882 he brought Bülow to the German capital with his Meiningen ensemble of forty-eight hand-picked musicians and Johannes Brahms at the keyboard playing his B-flat major piano concerto. The response to their performances was a mixture of ecstasy and embarrassment.

A decade after the declaration of the German Empire, Berlin's population had grown to half a million but its culture was sparse. The musical fare consisted of an opera house run by aristocrats and a court orchestra led by the entrepreneurial Benjamin Bilse, who had beer and coffee served while Beethoven was played. Berlin needed something better and Bülow's visiting orchestra hinted at what that might be.

It so happened that most of Bilse's band walked out some weeks later, when he underpaid them for a Polish tour and supplied fourth-class railway tickets, instead of third. The fifty-four musicians regrouped into an orchestra they called the Berlin Philharmonic and went to Hermann Wolff for practical advice. He found them a roller-skating rink to perform in and, after a promising début, persuaded two business friends to convert it into a concert hall. Two series of subscription concerts were announced under local conductors, Ludwig von Brenner and Karl Klindworth. Joachim, head of the Hochschule für Musik, stepped into the podium whenever help was needed, and need was never greater than when the Philharmonic lost all its instruments in a fire at the Scheveningen Casino in Holland in September 1886. Joachim kept up the players' spirits by conducting most of the next season. Berlin's wealthiest houses, led by the Mendelssohn and Siemens families, contributed handsomely to an appeal fund. But it was Wolff who saved the orchestra by offering to manage its concerts entirely at his own risk. There was one condition: he would appoint Hans von Bülow as chief conductor.

Haunted by the loss of his first wife to Richard Wagner, Bülow lived in Hamburg with a docile second spouse, Marie, and conducted a concert series that Wolff organised for him there. At fifty-seven, with Wagner dead, Brahms estranged and all ambition spent, he was not easily enticed to Berlin. But Wolff promised him complete freedom of programming, as much rehearsal as he needed and a chance to become a national figurehead. The last option proved decisive.

Bülow entered Berlin with a concert of unprecedented severity – three symphonies by Mozart, Haydn and Beethoven, no concerto, no sweetmeats. The orchestra played as men possessed and the critics marvelled at an occasion that removed all frippery from music-making. 'I will no longer promote bad music,'[9] said Bülow. His energies were reserved for the highest causes of German art and his concerts took on a character of near-sanctity; beer and coffee were banished from the rinkside. By the close of his first season, the Berlin Philharmonic was the benchmark orchestra of greater Germany.

Bülow's concerts were electrifying and unpredictable. He would lock the doors and play Beethoven's ninth symphony over again if he felt the audience had not shown proper appreciation. He relied on Wolff for all practicalities including the choice of soloists, allowing the manager to showcase his own artists. The pianist for Moscheles's E-flat major concerto in February 1889 was a twelve-year-old Berlin wunderkind, Bruno Walter Schlesinger. Witnessing Bülow's 'glow of inspiration and concentration of energy', the boy 'recognised what I had been born for'[10] and decided to become a conductor. Bruno Walter would grow into a pillar of the Berlin Philharmonic.

For five years Bülow was the talk of the town, whether for his performances or his outbursts. His whiplash tongue spared no one – neither players, nor public, nor the Kaiser himself. He fell out with Joachim, abused the Jews, reminded the Royal Opera House that it was an arts institute not an army barracks, recited bawdy verses, addressed Prussian junkers in fluent French and turned the Philharmonie hall into a forum for democratic debate. He wore black gloves to conduct Beethoven's *Eroica* and dedicated his valedictory concert to the sacked Bismarck – a public snub to the young Kaiser.

Such liberties would not be permitted in Wilhelminian Berlin, but Bülow had already resigned. His letter to Wolff complained of monotony; he told his wife he was unable to raise standards any higher. The players begged him to return but, after giving a benefit concert for the musicians' pension fund, he went on a recuperative visit to Egypt and died on arrival. His memorials are a great orchestra and an epithet for his profession: 'Conduct with the score in your head, not your head in the score.'

Bereft of Bülow, the orchestra asked Wolff for a successor, and after trying out the young Richard Strauss and Felix Weingartner, accepted his first nomination, Arthur Nikisch. Nikisch was a Hungarian with deepset eyes and an almost motionless baton. Where Bülow jangled every nerve in the band, Nikisch exuded a noble authority that could, at will, crescend in a massive expression of musical power. Where his predecessor would stop a rehearsal to fret over imperfections, Nikisch played through an entire work with apparent satisfaction, adjusting any errors afterwards in a quiet, jocular word with the players concerned. If a passage sounded too loud, he would adjust the rest of the symphony to make transient misdemeanour sound like inspired intention. The Philharmonie hall was renamed 'Viel Harmonie' and resounded under Nikisch with human and musical concord.

He introduced Tchaikovsky and Bruckner, broadening the orchestra's capacities and spreading its wings on tours, organised by Wolff, to France, Russia, Austria, Italy, Spain and Portugal. The Berlin Philharmonic became the first widely travelled orchestra and Nikisch's delicate mannerisms were imitated by maestros the world over. They were the most celebrated concert partnership of a world that Kaiser Wilhelm would destroy in 1914, expressing the rampant confidence of Germany reawakened. Wolff was honoured at court and respected wherever music was performed.

Not everyone was thrilled at his achievement. Strauss complained that the orchestra was 'in the gift of the agent Hermann Wolff',[11] and any musician wanting to get a hearing in the capital needed Wolff as his manager. Weingartner was equally displeased. Wolff, anxious to avoid unpleasantness, offered Strauss the podium of the Metropolitan Opera House at three times his German wage; rebuffed, he procured him a professorship in Berlin, which the composer sulkily refused. It was unwise, though, for a composer, even one as important as Strauss, to fall out with the ringleader of German music and their relations settled into a wary amicability.

Wolff opened possibilities for a world career through his polyglot connections and his contract with the Met. A promising début in Berlin could launch an artist on a Wolff world tour, from Stavanger to San Francisco. Fritz Kreisler, who thoughtfully arranged for half his Berlin début tickets to be bought by a benefactor, was sent off around Scandinavia and the Mediterranean, before reaching America, where he earned two thousand five hundred dollars in his début season – five times the average German income. Tchaikovsky, introduced to Wolff by Nikisch and Bülow, was despatched to open Carnegie Hall in 1891; Busoni was bundled off for an unhappy year in Boston, where Nikisch was conductor. Wolff was a world coloniser, as expansionist in outlook as the most bellicose of Wilhelm's generals. When the Kaiser went to Russia to visit his cousin the Tsar, Wolff packed off the Berlin opera company with celebrity reinforcements to entertain them. Back in Berlin, Wilhelm would drop in unannounced for family tea at the Wolffs'.

No concert agent before him, or for many years after, forged such heavyweight connections. Wolff's motives were suspected by many who feared that political and commercial considerations, rather than a musical imperative, controlled the national art. 'The development of German concert life under his influence during the next fifty years was in no way due to any artistic or social need,' charged the high-minded Carl Flesch.

It was the outcome of Wolff's idea of the politico-economic correspondance between artistic performances and agricultural or industrial products. Why shouldn't a virtuoso be 'ordered' or 'despatched' in the same way as wheat or steel? It was simply a question of organisation; the concert-giving societies had to become accustomed to 'ordering' their artists through a central agency. Supply and demand were to fix the artist's fee just as stocks and shares were priced on the exchange . . . Wolff's theory must be regarded as entirely novel. He was, moreover, regarded as a connoisseur whom you could not influence.[12]

Wolff was presumed to hold powers of life and death over musical careers. He was a mover and a shaker, a manipulator and a builder. Unlike previous agents, he did not merely supply musicians to satisfy a pre-existing demand. He identified gaps and plugged them with products, anticipated shifts in public taste and groomed his artists to respond to them. He was a barometer of musical tastes, telling artists that 'there were cycles when temperamental players have success, and cycles when impersonal musicians please the public; at some periods the taste for the extra-musical prevails, at others mechanical accuracy is most admired . . . There came an era when pianists were all the rage and another when violinists were the stars; eras of prodigies, and times when no one would listen to children's playing.'[13] Come rain or shine, Wolff made sure he was well covered, a man for all seasons.

Artists gave him ten per cent of their earnings, a commission that he established as standard in Europe. His terms were unnegotiable and firmly enforced. Musicians summoned to Wolff's office were faced by an admonitory portrait of a well-known singer stripped to her underwear. The caption noted that Miss X had regrettably failed to reimburse Herr Wolff for the costs of her concert.

He begrudged favours to any but the most illustrious, provoking the composer Max Bruch to attack Wolff's 'pigsty at the Philharmonie' when he was denied access to general rehearsals of his own works. Yet even antagonists admitted that Wolff's musical judgement was impeccable. His only lapses in taste were dictated by his greater love of money. Plenty of musicians, then as now, were prepared to pay for their own concerts, and so were young composers who had no other way of getting heard. Wolff took their money and did nothing. If he reckoned a concert was worthless, he barely bothered to announce it. Gustav Mahler found the hall unsold when he conducted the Berlin Philharmonic in the world première of his second symphony. Like Strauss, Mahler dared not object to the big, bad Wolff.

Very few musicians ever thwarted him, the most prominent being Ignace Jan Paderewski, the heart-throb pianist with a flowing red mane who became the first prime minister of independent Poland. As a young unknown, Paderewski beseeched Wolff for admission to a Rubinstein recital and was rudely refused. Soon after he approached Wolff for a recital and, lacking visible means, was ejected. His Warsaw publisher, meanwhile, persuaded Bülow to conduct Paderewski's piano concerto in Berlin with the composer as soloist. A tremendous ovation brought Wolff running to Padererwski's green room. 'I am sincerely overjoyed at your success,' said the agent, 'and I now propose to you that under my management you will have similar success everywhere, not only in Germany, but in every country in the world. I am sure of it.' Paderewski replied that Wolff had turned him down only months before and that he had now found a compatible manager, a London impresario called Daniel Mayer.

'That is business, my dear sir – business!' exclaimed Wolff. 'Don't regard it so seriously. Join me now and you will be very glad you have done it.' Paderewski demurred. 'Well,' said Wolff, 'it seems impossible but if No is your answer, I must tell you very frankly that you will regret it.'[14]

The following night the orchestra sabotaged his concerto with abominable playing. Bülow jumped up and ran off the stage while Paderewski was playing his encore solos, unsettling the audience and wrecking the atmosphere. 'Was he in league with Wolff?' wondered the pianist, swearing never to return to Berlin.

A dozen years later, on Mayer's retirement, Paderewski found that his German management had fallen mysteriously into Wolff's hands. Passing through Berlin, he was summoned to the agent's home and found him on his deathbed. 'He was very ill and weak, but he managed to tell me that he appreciated my visit more than he could express and wanted me to know that he regretted deeply whatever wrong he had done me in the past. Poor man! He hoped that I would forgive him.'[15]

Paderewski declined gracelessly, but there are enough discrepancies in his story to suggest that anti-German rancour overcame accuracy in his memoirs. Growled at by a Berlin cabbie to get a haircut, the proud Pole blew a commonplace incident into an international insult for which Wolff, with all his tact, was unable to atone. This, it seems, was the cause of his walk-out. But he soon discovered that concert stars could ill afford to leave Berlin off their itinerary.

Wolff's daughter records that Paderewski was a regular visitor at their home throughout her childhood and wrote a cheery dedication in her autograph album in February 1898, seven years after his 'lifelong' boycott. Wolff, whatever his faults, was a worshipper of musical talent. He may have resented Paderewski's recalcitrance but he did not sabotage artists – even those, like Flesch, who left him for another agent. A rotund, bearded man with a winning smile, he liked nothing more than lunching among the living greats after the Sunday morning general rehearsal at the Philharmonic. To his groaning table he invited fledgelings and encouraged them to strut their stuff before the lions of the concert platform. He helped them find affordable lodgings and held open house for hungry newcomers. His business was, in many respects, an extension of his family life. His wife Louise, a sometime actress from Vienna, ruled the office with an iron hand in his absence. His brother Charles came in as a partner and learned the ropes by touring with the pianists Josef Hofmann and Eugène d'Albert. His daughters, Edith and Lilli, started working in the agency as schoolgirls.

Late in 1901, while building a new Beethovensaal, Wolff was stricken with an intestinal disorder. An international congress of surgeons was being held in Berlin and senior specialists were called out to operate on him. He never recovered from their ministrations and died on 3 February 1902, aged fifty-six. The Berlin Philharmonic Orchestra under Nikisch and the Philharmonic Choir under Siegfried Ochs performed the final musical rites for a pioneer who, in the assessment of the periodical *Die Musik*, 'created a monopoly in concert giving and artist engagements in Berlin and attained a sphere of activity beyond the reach of any of his competitors'.[16] His only malice, it was reported, was an impish tendency to inform débutants that Busoni or Joachim was in the hall, causing the beginner's blood to freeze in his or her veins.

By the turn of the century every city had a concert agency of some consequence. There was Gutmann in Vienna, Wolff in Berlin, Lionel Powell in London, the Wolfsohn Bureau in New York – 'my gang of thieves',[17] as they were designated by the Belgian virtuoso, Eugène Ysaÿe. A soloist like Ysaÿe played a hundred concerts a year at two to three thousand francs each, making a mint in those pre-tax times of well over fifty thousand dollars per annum, perhaps two million in modern terms. With ten Ysaÿes on his books, an agent would earn as much as Ysaÿe himself without suffering a moment of stagefright.

'A manager it is necessary to have,' advised the New York critic Henry T. Finck in 1891. 'Some agents are honest, some are not; inquiry among musicians is advisable. A good concert agent knows the condition of the musical market in all the cities and towns of the country; he gets demands for artists and sends circulars to inquirers and others. Of course he is, at best, in this business not to help singers or pianists but to make money.'[18]

The pianist Mark Hambourg recognised three types of agent: the old-fashioned personal representative, the would-be impresario and the professional concert manager. The antiquated first category was personified by Emil Ledner, a Berliner who saved Caruso from abuse by a former teacher. 'A gent from head to foot', Ledner was 'a world-travelled man with a global command of languages'.[19] He took twenty per cent from Caruso and an under-the-table retainer of five per cent on all north European singers who appeared at the Met – a pay-off for the Caruso contract. His advice was not always helpful. On his last German tour in 1913, the tenor asked Ledner to cash in his securities. Ledner allayed his fears and left his savings on deposit. Unable to touch the money during the war, Caruso lost a million Marks – equivalent to a quarter of a million dollars – in the 1918 crash.

The paragon of professional concert management was Wolff's, bequeathed in Hermann's Will to his brother Charles but commandeered by the widow, Louise. Ten years younger than her spouse, Queen Louise (as she was crowned by musicians) concentrated on what she knew – the smooth running of concert life in Berlin and northern Germany. Foreign ventures were run down and eventually cut off by war but the Berlin Philharmonic prospered, becoming the first orchestra to make a full symphonic recording and displacing the Viennese in prominence and proficiency. The magic of Nikisch and management of Wolff created an instrument with which every ambitious soloist and conductor needed to appear. And each successful début added another star to the Wolff list – Artur Schnabel in 1903, Pablo Casals in 1908, Mischa Elman in 1910, Jascha Heifetz in 1912.

When Germany surrendered and revolution broke out on the streets of Berlin, Louise Wolff kept the orchestra alive and occupied until a febrile stability was restored. When inflation destroyed the German currency she revived her foreign exchanges and packed her artists off abroad – Nikisch with his pianist son to Argentina, Walter, Schnabel and Otto Klemperer to Soviet Russia, the Philharmonic with Wilhelm Furtwängler around northern Europe and annually to England. Tea with the Kaiser gave way to lunches with Gustav Stresemann and leaders of the Republic. The state financed three opera houses and several other orchestras, but the Philharmonic remained autonomous and received little subsidy. Any conductor could buy the orchestra for a night – and many did. For its artistic integrity, the orchestra depended on Queen Louise and she never let them down.

Behind a chaotic desk, her ample frame wrapped in countless scarves and shawls, she received each caller with a glare of suspicion. 'Now show me the bad ones,' she told a young pianist who flourished a sheaf of glowing reviews.

'But, madame, they are all good,' stuttered the soloist.

'You'd better find another manager,' said the icy Queen.

Square of jaw and sharp of tongue, she curried favour with no one. 'She was not liked much,' said Elena Gerhardt, Nikisch's lover, 'by those she did not like. She was very candid to young artists . . . if she could not see a chance of success, she would refuse unhesitatingly to add their names to her list.'[20]

A comic verse, sung to the tragic theme of Tchaikovsky's *Pathétique*, was circulated about her: 'What have you done for art/Louise?' She would muscle into green rooms after a concert and, in place of the usual emollients, deflate performers with a pointedly ambiguous compliment: '*Noch nicht dagewesen wie Sie gespielt haben* – I have never heard playing like yours.' (The phrase could also be taken to mean, 'I had not yet arrived while you were playing.')

She took on two partners – the heavy-jowled Hermann Fernow and Erich Simon, owner of the Philharmonie hall – and took over the smaller agency of Jules Sachs, changing the letterheads to 'Wolff und Sachs'. Sunday lunch she held open house to a mixture of celebrities and nonentities. Strauss and Caruso regularly attended Rankestrasse 13, next door to a busy fire station, excited at the prospect of whom they might meet.

Her son, Werner, a staff conductor at the Hamburg Opera, sent along his most promising students, whom she fed, housed and gave free access to her box at the Philharmonie. The young composer Berthold Goldschmidt met

Nikisch, Walter, Furtwängler and Otto Klemperer over lunch at Queen Louise's, 'the room blue with smoke'. Goldschmidt helped Erich Kleiber prepare the world première of *Wozzeck*, a performance regarded as the birth of modern opera. Experience of this nature was priceless to an emergent composer; it could never have been acquired without the entrée granted him, and others like him, by the redoubtable Louise Wolff. She brushed aside thanks and showed no concession to sentiment. Though any amateur maestro with a fistful of hard currency could hire the Philharmonic by the hour, she refused to allow her son, Werner, 'a good musician but a bad conductor', ever to conduct in Berlin.

Louise was a woman of principle, a beacon of rectitude in a business that appealed to card-sharpers. Lesser fry in Berlin, scrabbling for leftovers, were reduced to perjury and extortion. In 1926, Otto Klemperer was threatened with a lawsuit by the Berlin agent Norbert Salter, who claimed a commission on his début with the New York Symphony Society. Salter, an old-timer who had been involved in Gustav Mahler's American transfer back in 1907, claimed that he had 'recommended' Klemperer to the Society's president, Walter Damrosch. 'It is true that he mentioned your name,' wrote Damrosch in an angry affidavit, '[but] I am not in the habit of taking recommendations of musical agents very seriously, as their objects are commercial, and I therefore gain my information regarding artists either through hearing them personally or through the testimony of colleagues or music lovers whose opinion I respect and whose judgement is not warped by financial interests . . . Mr Salter did not enter into the situation.'[21]

Louise Wolff was well aware of the seamy side of her profession and strove to set her firm above controversy, as an institution devoted to the best interests of music. One wall of her private sitting-room was dominated by a life-sized portrait of Anton Rubinstein, patron saint of the Wolff enterprise. It was here she repaired in moments of crisis, none more testing than the night of 23 January 1922, when word arrived of Nikisch's death at the age of sixty-six and the summit of his serenity. Philharmonic players wept openly, knowing they would not see his like again. Louise faced a delicate dilemma. She managed the best conductors in the land, all of whom coveted the Berlin podium and some of whom believed it was theirs by divine right. Strauss, Kleiber and Felix Weingartner threw their hats in the ring; Willem Mengelberg, the Amsterdam conductor, was a favoured outsider. Bruno Walter resigned from the state opera in Munich, telling friends, 'It's between Furtwängler and me.' As a native Berliner and a Wolff favourite, he felt 'the orchestra is unanimously behind me and Louise Wolff wants it.'[22]

Furtwängler, however, had other ideas. He hared off to Leipzig to give a memorial concert with the Gewandhaus, Nikisch's other orchestra. Back in Berlin, he burst into Louise's office and told her he wanted the Philharmonic. Was he not satisfied with a state salary at the Staatsoper? she inquired. Furtwängler shook his elliptical head. He would give up anything for the Philharmonic. Louise had never known him so decisive. Unlike her late husband, she was not a musician and could not assess the two leading candidates on artistic grounds. Yet she alone would have to take one of the pivotal decisions of musical succession. As she withdrew to the sanctum she was determined to be guided by instinct and principle rather than personal preference and potential profit. Walter, she knew, was a marvellous conductor, popular with players and large sections of the public and susceptible to her guidance. He never gave an unsatisfactory concert and, at forty-eight, was an interpreter of high maturity. Furtwängler, twelve years his junior, was a diffident intellectual with no public following and a wavery baton that few players could follow. He had but to mount the rostrum, though, and an aura of reverence descended upon the congregation. The character of his performance was dictated by what he felt at that moment and, perhaps, by divine intimation. He was unique and inimitable as Nikisch and Bülow had been before him.

The Queen did what she had to do. Acting against commercial prudence and her own best interests, she engaged Furtwängler to conduct the Nikisch memorial concert in Berlin, opening with the Brahms chorus, 'O world I must leave you'. Privately, she advised the players to elect him as chief conductor and, before their votes were counted, arranged for Furtwängler to be crowned in Leipzig as Nikisch's heir. For his rival, crestfallen and betrayed, she financed a series of Bruno Walter Concerts with the Philharmonic. In retrospect, she could hardly have done better.

Furtwängler elevated the Philharmonic to new levels of national importance. In jazz-age Berlin, with its licentious cabarets and nefarious politics, it struck a reasoned balance between conservatism and modernism. In the night terrors of the Third Reich it represented a bastion of security and tradition. Accused of supporting the Nazis by remaining in their capital, Furtwängler argued that the Berlin Philharmonic stood for the real Germany and it was his moral and national duty to lead it.

For the Wolffs his appointment was bad business. Alarmed by the exercise of Louise's power, the players formed a limited liability company (GmbH) and exercised greater independence. Furtwängler picked his own soloists and his personal assistant, Berta Geissmar, set out to marginalise Louise. 'The firm and the family came first with her,' wrote Geissmar, 'and this view was gradually becoming incompatible with public interests. While an orchestra like the Berlin Philharmonic had to count on public support, it was in the long run impossible that seventy-five per cent of the profit of the great concerts should go into the pocket of private enterprise.'[23]

Geissmar's figures are uncorroborated and her motive was personal. A profoundly unattractive woman of exceptional intelligence and efficiency, Berta became besotted with Furtwängler in her teens and, knowing she could not attract him, set out to possess him in all other ways. The conductor, who hated taking any kind of decision, let her run the most intimate particulars of his life. She chose his first wife's wedding ring and lined up women to gratify his insatiable libido, calling them the following morning for a report on his prowess. Taking control of his career, she extricated him from unglamorous Leipzig and slapped his hand down as he was about to shake on an agreement with the Vienna State Opera. When the Concertgebouw invited him to conduct, Berta negotiated the terms, violating Wolff's exclusive contract.

Louise asked Berta round for a glass of cherry brandy and quietly conceded defeat. From that day on, gloated Geissmar, 'Furtwängler never used any intermediary other than myself when possible, and I was dubbed *Louise II*, after Louise Wolff.'[24] Other musicians, seeing Furtwängler's liberation, drifted away from Wolff's in increasing numbers as Nazi propaganda smeared the agency as a conduit for Jewish control of German music. Six weeks after Hitler came to power the telephone rang at Louise's home shortly before midnight. It was Bruno Walter, saying the Nazis were planning to blockade his Gewandhaus concerts. Louise got Richard Strauss to replace him, but contacts within the old civil service warned her that Walter was in physical danger. She told him to leave the country 'this very day'. On 7 April 1933 the Nazis banned Jews from all state institutions. Many of Louise's artists, headed by Schnabel, Kreisler and Bronislaw Hubermann, decided to emigrate.

At seventy-eight years of age, Louise Wolff made a final effort to save her kingdom. She dismissed her Jewish partners, Erich Sachs and Erich Simon (one fled to Palestine, the other to Paris), and restored the original name of Hermann Wolff Konzertdirektion. She was herself born Christian and her daughters were Jewish only by paternity and not yet outlawed by the Nuremberg Laws. Aryanisation, however, could not save the firm from avaricious Nazis. A crony of Hermann Goering's, Rudolf Vedder, set his sights on the company. Vedder had been secretary to the pianist Edwin Fischer and violinist Georg Kulenkampff, both Wolff artists, before a spell at the piano firm Steinway's ended with his dismissal in 1927 for embezzling ten thousand Marks in artists' fees. There was no prosecution; Vedder promised to repay the money and was released with a neutral testimonial. He begged

Furtwängler for a job and, rebuffed, set up as a concert agent. Furtwängler put him on an orchestral blacklist after one of Vedder's sopranos missed a *Matthew Passion* rehearsal in Berlin because the agent had found her a higher-paid engagement elsewhere.

Vedder was not blessed with a forgiving nature. Once the Nazis were in power he targeted Wolff's and Furtwängler. Using high-placed friends in the rampant SS, he compiled a dossier on Wolff's from government sources which revealed that the firm was late in paying taxes and had, unsurprisingly, suffered a four-thousand-mark loss in the financial year ending 1 July 1933. Vedder persuaded the Nazi general manager of the Berlin Philharmonic to suspend contracts with Wolff's until its half-Jewish directors were removed. He then approached Louise to blackmail her into yielding him the company.

The old Queen put up a flutter of resistance. She offered to let Vedder take over the firm, provided he kept her daughters on the payroll. Vedder laughed, and left. Weeks later he was appointed commercial director of the concert division of the Reichsmusikkammer, which governed all musical activity in Nazi Germany by the simple method of restricting work permits to racially and politically acceptable artists. Any racially acceptable artist who wanted to play in the Reich had to register with the Chamber and pay a commission to Vedder. When the Spanish cellist Gaspar Cassado asked to be released from Vedder's list, he was warned that he might find it difficult to obtain a performing licence in future. Vedder did not believe in concealing his considerable power.

Nothing was left for Louise Wolff but to liquidate and die. On her eightieth birthday she sent a sad note to all artists and agencies abroad announcing the closure of the firm after fifty-five years. Weeks later, on 25 June 1935, she expired at home and was buried in Dahlem. The Gestapo ransacked her offices, probably on Vedder's orders, and sent one of her daughters to a concentration camp.

Furtwängler's turn was next. Vedder, acting with his boss Hans Hinkel and a nod from Goebbels, got the Gestapo to hound Berta Geissmar out of Germany. Without Geissmar, Furtwängler could barely tie his shoes and with the Wolffs gone there was no one to relieve him of the painful necessity to make decisions. He railed privately against the regime and, angered by a ban on Paul Hindemith's music, flailed against it in the press. But his resistance was futile. Goebbels, who had the conductor's measure, manipulated him like a puppet on a string and tarnished his name by using it as a symbol of Nazi legitimacy.

Vedder's public career was short-lived. He was sacked within a year from the Reichsmusikkammer for financial improprieties but, shielded by high-ranking SS friends, set up an independent agency. Among his protégés was a young Austrian conductor, Herbert von Karajan, whom Vedder launched in 1938 as a rival to Furtwängler and as the Nazis' first home-grown maestro (he would ultimately succeed Furtwängler at the Berlin Philharmonic in 1955[25]). By 1941 Vedder controlled all the leading conductors in Germany except Furtwängler – namely Karajan, Eugen Jochum, Clemens Krauss, Hans Swarowsky and the compromised Dutchmen, Willem Mengelberg and Paul van Kempen. He also ran the Berlin Festival and stacked it with his favourites. Although he only joined the party in 1940 he was commissioned as an SS officer by Himmler's adjutant, Ludolf von Alvensleben, commander of the notorious mass-murder squads in Poland. In July 1942 Vedder suffered a serious setback when he was 'definitely excluded from the Reichskultur-kammer at the personal directive of Reichsminister Dr Goebbels'[26] who had been swamped with complaints about his dealings. After 'massive SS intervention', Vedder was eventually reinstated. He continued to assist his protégé Karajan in various ways, not least by sending Frau Karajan two pairs of shoes for collection at the Dresdner Bank in Bucharest, where he had sent the conductor to work after Goebbels shut the German theatres in August 1944. Vedder received SS honours that summer from Heinrich Himmler, but time was running out for Nazi music business. He was last sighted before the collapse of Berlin, working at the SS offices for race and colonisation. After the war, he set up successfully as a concert agent in southern Germany, with Karajan as his principal artist.[27]

To stand above the fray, an agent in *nouveau-siècle* London and Paris needed to offer an added value or attraction. He needed guile, daring and a nose for novelty. The prince of innovators was Gabriel Astruc, a Parisian dandy with pearl tie-pins, a gold bracelet and a crimson carnation that bloomed daily in his buttonhole until he replaced it with the well-deserved Légion d'hon-neur.[28] Son of the rabbi of Brussels, Astruc combined a regard for ancestral traditions with an insatiable appetite for new sensations: he would date documents by the ancient lunar calendar, while whistling a theme from an impressionist score. A polemicist in literary journals, he joined the music publishing firm of Enoch's, married the boss's daughter and founded a Société Musicale with backing from a sephardic banker and the socialite Comtesse Greffulhe, the model for Marcel Proust's Princesse de Guermantes. He imported Richard Strauss and Emmy Destinn to give the sexiest of *Salomes* in 1907 (three years before Beecham conducted a bowdlerised version in London) and manipulated a scandalous stage career for the seductress Mata Hari. *Around the World in Eighty Days* was another of his spectacles. He brought the Cakewalk and Foxtrot to Paris, with indelible consequences for Debussy and Satie. He was an incurable xenophile,[29] indiscriminate in his enthusiasm for anything foreign and exotic.

A capable musician, Astruc did not trust his own ears. When Arthur Rubinstein applied to join his agency, he invited him to audition before a panel consisting of the composers Maurice Ravel and Paul Dukas, and Jacques Thibaud, the foremost French violinist. On hearing that Rubinstein wanted to play a Saint-Saëns concerto at his début Astruc exclaimed, 'I will arrange right away for a rendezvous for you with the master. I want him to come to the concert!'[30]

Astruc was formidably well-connected. He gave the pianist a monthly retainer of five hundred francs and took sixty per cent of his concert fee, blending enlightened management with outright greed. Both Rubinstein and the harpsichordist Wanda Landowska owed him their continental careers.

Astruc was not overly concerned with individual talent. He itched to do something different, to change the culture. In 1906 he was introduced by Comtesse Greffulhe to a Russian of parallel aspirations. Serge Diaghilev was the discoverer of a new school of painters in St Petersburg. While showing an Exhibition de l'Art Russe in Paris, he offered Astruc a season of Russian music – not just familiar symphonies of Tchaikovsky and the tinklings of Rachmaninov, but gritty arias of the 'Mighty Five' intoned by the peerless Feodor Chaliapin, along with novelties by Skryabin and Liapunov. Their five concerts in the latter fortnight of the May 1907 season were the talk of tout Paris, overturning previous scorn for Russian music. The applause for Chaliapin was so prolonged that the conductor, Nikisch, threw down his baton and refused to conduct an encore. Skryabin made fashion headlines by promenading hatless, fearing that covering his head would render him prematurely bald.

Diaghilev furnished his concerts with four Grand Dukes of the imperial court and Nikolai Rimsky-Korsakov, the living link in Russian music between Glinka and Glazunov, who was there to conduct his own Poème Symphonique. This was an unprecedented array of a nation's musicality and French composers were thrilled to discover in it an alternative to otiose Wagnerism. Richard Strauss sat in Diaghilev's box grumbling about 'this circus music' and muttering 'we are not children any more'. Rimsky-Korsakov retaliated at Salome, shouting at the singers to shut up. Paris pullulated with excitement.

The following year, Diaghilev and Astruc brought Boris Godunov to the Opéra with Chaliapin in the title role. Canny Albert Carré at the Opéra-Comique countered with Rimsky-Korsakov's Snow Maiden; the Opéra Ballet enticed Mathilda Kschessinskaya from St Petersburg to dance *Coppélia*. Paris was awash with Russian culture and Astruc, wanting to stay ahead, broke with Diaghilev. They were, in any case, unlikely allies. Astruc had an accountant's eye and an Old Testament regard for personal morality; Diaghilev spent other people's money and slept with male dancers. Their only common bond was an urge to innovate.

Hearing that Astruc was talking to the Metropolitan Opera about a first overseas tour Diaghilev, who could not get by without him, turned up in Paris with the boldest of his schemes – a Ballets Russes season that would present the best of new music, choreography and stage design from Russia and France alike. Astruc was enraptured. He agreed to book theatres and handle administration, publicity and ticket sales for two and a half per cent of box-office, half his normal commission – on the understanding that Diaghilev would bear the entire financial risk. In the event Astruc had to raise emergency cash, but his press campaign was so effective that extra performances were added to meet an overwhelming demand. It seemed as if the two impresarios had captured the very essence of the age.

Any prospects of profit, though, reckoned without Diaghilev, whose expenses were so exorbitant and budgetary control so derelict that, before the season was out, Astruc sent bailiffs to sequester clothes from his hotel room, dragged him before a bankruptcy tribunal and wrote an eleven-page letter to Tsar Nicholas II denouncing him for disgracing the Russian court by signing his worthless contracts as an '*Attaché à la Chancellerie Personelle de Sa Majesté l'Empereur de la Russie*'. None of this prevented the resumption of their partnership once Diaghilev had somehow settled his bills and come up with fresh ideas.

The advent of the Ballets Russes in 1909 was relatively sedate – introducing Pavlova in *Les Sylphides*, Nijinsky in a pastiche by Tcherepnin, and *Ivan the Terrible* by Rimsky-Korsakov, starring Chaliapin. But the next four summers were, literally, epoch-making. They changed the nature of ballet from demure dance to shattering drama and invented a post-Wagnerian *Gesamtkunstwerk* that harnessed composers, dancers, writers and painters to a single work of art. Nijinsky danced Debussy's *Faun* against a Léon Bakst backdrop; he partnered Karsavina in Ravel's *Daphnis et Chloé* with choreography by Fokine. Stravinsky, Rimsky's favourite pupil, wooed Parisian ears with *Firebird* and *Petrushka*.

Astruc was so bedazzled that he built a Théâtre des Champs-Elysées with a grandiose deco exterior and an opening season of Russian, French and German extravagances, including Debussy's futuristic *Jeux* and Fauré's romantic opera, *Pénélope*. The exteriors of the house were carved at great expense by famous sculptors and interior murals were painted by Vuillard and Sem. This folly might have survived on an overnight hit. It was blighted instead by Stravinsky's *Rite of Spring*, whose pounding rhythms and jerky movements provoked uproar from bewildered balletomanes. Leaning almost headlong out of his box on opening night, Astruc begged people to 'listen to the music and whistle afterwards'. In vain; blows were exchanged, police were called and the riot entered musical folklore. Astruc shut the theatre and declared bankruptcy. 'You are wrong to abandon *our* theatre,' said Debussy. 'It would be preferable, in my humble opinion, to continue the struggle and if you have to die, better to die a beautiful death.'[31] Marcel Proust sent 'profound sympathies' and wondered why Parisians who spent so much on snobbery could not support 'this most interesting and noble of enterprises'.[32]

For Diaghilev, who scorned balance sheets, Astruc's insolvency was a minor irritant. For Astruc, it was a mortal blow. Though he lived another twenty-five years, the jovial impresario lost his zest and faded from the scene, leaving Debussy lamenting his 'infinitely sad and thankless adventure'.[33] The Ballets Russes moved on to other backers, and its historians accord him scant mention. Yet without Astruc Diaghilev could not have conquered Paris, and without their combined assault the development of French music would have remained bogged down in its tedious trench between classicists and Wagnerists. Astruc's importations invigorated a generation of composers and ran a seditious streak through Parisian culture. Costumes of the Ballets Russes appeared in the windows of top couturiers and Russian delicacies infiltrated *haute cuisine*. Ragtime percolated from Astruc's visiting American bands into the scores of Les Six and the 'jazz age' of the 1920s. He had infected a notoriously self-obsessed society with the sounds of two worlds.

On opening nights for many years later he would wander down the crowded boulevards, buttonholing old acquaintances and besieging them with the nostalgia of an Ancient Mariner. 'Opposite the exit of the Châtelet theatre,' he recalled in his memoirs,

> the most elegant participants of the Grande Saison would gather at a restaurant on the rue Royale. In a corner reserved for the Ballets Russes, where Diaghilev and Nijinsky devour their chateaubriand steaks, Reynaldo Hahn and Jean Cocteau are telling pretty stories while, some distance away at a slightly isolated table, Marcel Proust is writing combative letters and savouring a *bavaroise au chocolat*.[34]

No wonder it was known as the *belle époque*.

*   *   *

The character and function of the European concert agent were thus well established before the First World War and have changed very little since. The typical agent was a musical amateur of the educated classes, wealthy or sufficiently well connected to start up in business or buy into an existing firm. He was personable and gregarious, able to converse intelligently about music but not expert enough to leave artists feeling threatened. He did not chew cigars or tout for custom. A trader in human failings, he lived off a fund of spiced gossip, knowing that musicians loved nothing better than hearing of each other's peccadilloes, while journalists could be fed sanitised versions of the same material. Shy of public exposure, his relations with the press were mildly paranoid. He needed its daily cuttings to plug his artists but feared its fickleness like a dose of plague. Bribe as he might, he could never guarantee a good review.

The public image of the concert agent was predominantly male, though within each company there existed a stratum of female agents, more discreet and severe than their partners. These were the nuns of the music business who, wedded to the muse, revered its divinities in mute adoration. Some reputedly sacrificed their virtue to the cause but their lips were impermeably sealed.

By the turn of the century, artists regarded some form of agency as essential – except in London where, until the Second World War, it was possible for an artist to get by without personal management. Henry Wood, conductor of the Proms, had no agent; his concerts were organised by the lessees of Queen's Hall and financed by a Harley Street laryngologist, Dr George Cathcart. Sir Edward Elgar, England's foremost composer, channelled conducting dates through his publisher, Novello. Many of his concerts were paid for by a rich admirer, Leo Schuster. Joseph Joachim's annual chamber music series was underwritten by another Elgar backer, the German-born banker Edward Speyer.

Careers were launched on a letter of introduction to a couple of noble homes. An Australian violinist, Leila Doubleday, arriving for the Coronation of George V in June 1911, had her début concert attended by two royal highnesses, seven dukes and the Australian prime minister, and accompanied (on Melba's recommendation) by Landon Ronald's New Symphony Orchestra.[35] Such concerts were never advertised; they sold by word of mouth within the same social set.

Night after night, artists went from their public concerts to play in the great houses. 'Musical parties reflected the social position of their givers,' recalled the piano accompanist Ivor Newton. 'If the Astors had Paderewski and Melba, the Rothschilds had Caruso and the Howard de Waldens Edvina,

Martinelli and Yvette Guilbert. Less eminent artists were heard in South Kensington and Bayswater. And so on, down the social scale.'[36] These appearances were munificently rewarded, one duchess allocating a thousand guineas per night to her entertainers. Kreisler, invited to dinner by a millionaire and asked to bring his instrument, replied sweetly, 'My violin does not dine.' Not without proper terms being agreed in advance.

Agents played no part in these transactions, lacking admission to good drawing-rooms. An exception was Lionel Powell, a Shropshire lad of landed stock whose family bred eminent churchmen. Powell, though, had no liking for the dog-collar. An amateur violinist, he took a stake in 1906 in the Schulz-Curtius agency and proceeded to diversify the firm away from its Wagner fixation. Powell took a room in Claridge's, drove a white Rolls-Royce and threw weekend house parties at his country mansion, Sutton Court. Fair-haired, slightly built and feverishly impetuous, he was broader in outlook than the Woosterish playboys of his era. Neither chauvinist nor imperialist, his interests were uncommonly international.

He assigned one room to each continent in his suite of offices. It was said in his obituaries that 'he went forty times to America and eight times around the world.'[37] During the war he bought out Schulz-Curtius at a knockdown price and removed his German name from the letterhead; London's first agent died soon after, allegedly of a broken heart. More an event promoter than an artist manager, Powell booked the Royal Albert Hall for Sunday Celebrity Concerts with Melba and Tetrazzini, Chaliapin and Kreisler. Divas were milked for the last drop of publicity. He sold five thousand seats a month in advance by exhibiting exotic photographs of Amelita Galli-Curci.

Other managers regarded records with foreboding, but Powell shepherded his artists into dog-and-horn studios as early as 1909 and assiduously nursed connections between his stars and the Gramophone Company, later EMI. His enthusiasm was not without self-interest; record producers commended new artists to his care and co-ordinated releases to tie in with his concerts. He might have made more by granting limited licences that required the label to renegotiate rights to each record every five years or so. But such foresight would have been half a century ahead of his time. In the gritty age of wind-up gramophones, no one attached long-term financial or historical value to records. They were musical snapshots, taken on the spur of the moment, sold as living souvenirs and discarded once the scratches became unbearable.

More hazardously, Powell was the first to import orchestras on a regular basis: the Berliners and Viennese with Wilhelm Furtwängler, New York with Toscanini. The cost was disproportionate to any likelihood of profit and Powell usually lost a packet. But he added colour to a smug season and enabled London's musicians to measure themselves against the finest in the world.

So bewitched was Powell by foreign talent that he came to believe that no young musician with an English name was worth the price of admission. Henry Wood once sat next to him on a bus in Oxford Street and was treated to a diatribe about the difficulties of importing foreign artists in wartime. 'Why don't you take up Albert Sammons?' suggested the conductor, mentioning a soloist of whom Kreisler thought highly.

'How can I push an *English* violinist?' snorted Powell.[38]

British talent, and there was much of it, needed a different outlet. Powell's alter ego, called Ibbs & Tillett, functioned as a clearing house for musicians of all grades. The agency was founded by a Spaniard, Narciso Vert, who presided over a supper table at the Café Royal on Piccadilly with the literati George Grossmith and George Moore. Vert managed Hans Richter and Anton Rubinstein and represented, according to one well-fed conductor, 'all that was noble in Victorian Concert Music management'.[39] Bernard Shaw chaffed him for sending his worst seats to music critics.

Vert's office was open daily from eleven to five for on-the-spot auditions. He welcomed 'applications from composers desirous of having their works published and introduced to the public'[40] and accumulated a mountain of dross. At his death in 1905, Vert & Simkins were circulating a mass of performers to the music clubs and societies in every town in the land. Percy Grainger, one of few bright sparks on the books, called the firm 'a fatal agent'.[41] Its only world star was Sergei Rachmaninov.

Vert left the firm to his nephews, Pedro and John Tillett, who raised capital by forming a partnership with R. Leigh Ibbs. As Ibbs & Tillett, they established an English code of honour that was adopted by the rest of the music business. 'Ibbs & Tillett never had a written contract with an artist. If a relationship didn't work, the artist was free to get up and go somewhere else,'[42] related the company archivist, Wilfred Stiff. 'Their word was as good as a contract,'[43] said the violinist Henri Temianka. Honesty evidently paid, for Ibbs wore an appearance of stability while the hot-headed Powell veered from one crisis to the next, helped down the slippery slope by his profligate conductor, Sir Thomas Beecham.

Powell and Beecham were kindred spirits: close in age, born rich and bent on forcing foreign culture on reluctant Brits. Beecham, heir to a brand of laxatives, burnished his fabled wit on the creative efforts of his fellow-countrymen. 'British music,' he drawled, 'is in a state of perpetual promise. It might almost be said to be one long promissory note.' Beset by creditors, Beecham knew more than most musicians about the value of promissory notes. What British music there was, however, he meant to get his hands on. Having crashed two opera companies, he went fishing for an orchestra in 1929 and, with Powell as rod-master, almost landed the London Symphony Orchestra. Traumatised by the Great Depression and the dawn of subsidised state broadcasting, the LSO were in a state of shock. After a quarter-century of proud autonomy, its best players were being tempted by a weekly wage at the BBC's new symphony orchestra. Morale and playing standards hit rock-bottom. Beecham, spinning a seductive line, offered to employ the LSO for his Covent Garden opera season; Powell, with extra bait, set up a two-thousand-pound record deal.

Both men were out to beat the BBC. Powell saw his audiences being eroded by wireless stay-at-homes and Beecham called broadcasting 'the world's greatest misfortune'. This did not prevent him, even as he forced the LSO to rewrite its constitution twice to his autocratic specifications, from pulling every string he knew to get the BBC to name him chief conductor of its orchestra. At fifty years old, he was the most accomplished conductor in the kingdom. But the prospect of capricious Beecham and his agent running the musical output of national radio did not appeal to BBC governors. They chose instead the self-effacing, entirely trustworthy Adrian Boult and let Beecham learn of his defeat from the newspapers. The LSO, getting wind of his duplicity, broke off their talks. Beecham was left high and dry.

In 1931, Powell suffered a series of box-office flops. The worst was a Paderewski tour which dropped four thousand pounds; at a dinner after the final concert the pianist, learning of the losses, wrote his agent a cheque for the full amount. In January 1932, while spinning a new Beecham line to the LSO, Powell died suddenly at the age of fifty-four. He had been a central figure in music for half his life, but no one seemed to know anything about him. Within days, the official receiver was called in. The agent who once boasted of paying out fees of a hundred and twenty thousand pounds a year had died penniless, owing money all over the world.

The only man who could pay it back was his former partner, a South African-born solicitor who fell out with him in 1929 and had recently made up. Harold Holt was blessed with a diamond fortune, a Jewish mother ensconced at Claridge's and two overweening maiden sisters, Miss Mattie and Miss Hilda. Tubby, rumpled and well-scrubbed, his smiling disposition concealed a firm resolve. Implored by Powell's staff to avert a scandal he sprang into action, picked up the tab for current bookings and effected an almost imperceptible transition. The only sign the public might have spotted was in the programme booklet for the Berlin Philharmonic concert on 7

February, which contained only one advertisement for a future Powell promotion. By the end of the month, Powell's name had vanished from the concert scene and the firm was reborn as Harold Holt Ltd.

Holt proceeded to sort out the orchestral situation with a single, brutal letter. In July 1932 he wrote to the LSO, calling off negotiations because 'in the opinion of his Board the LSO had lost most of its former prestige and no longer commanded the confidence of the public'.[44] Three months later he formed the London Philharmonic Orchestra for Beecham on exactly the same recording and opera basis. The LSO, miraculously, survived. It banned Beecham from its podium, along with his accomplice Malcolm Sargent, but acquired a grudging respect for Holt and by 1936 was dealing with him again. Directly after the war, with Beecham forming yet another orchestra, it was Holt who rescued the LSO from insolvency with three years' worth of bookings for Sunday afternoon concerts.

Tactful, imaginative and inherently good-natured, Holt could do business with anyone. Even the Nazis sent him orchestras, in the full knowledge that he was organising concerts in aid of 'innocent victims of persecution' in Germany. He promoted Marian Anderson and Paul Robeson when they could barely get a hearing in the United States and put on Cossack choirs from the Soviet Union alongside anti-communist émigrés. Beecham he kept quiet by forming a limited company to operate his concerts, with money from the conductor's long-suffering mistress, Lady Cunard. Holt was unawed by Beecham and cultivated friendships with his much-abused rivals, Henry Wood and John Barbirolli. He was also more open than Powell had been to native-born musicians, especially when war broke out and the ports were closed, though he could not quite conceal his opinion that they were little better than second-class. The young Benjamin Britten walked out to join Ibbs & Tillett after hearing Holt disparage his music. The English, said Holt dismissively, 'never had much confidence in home products'.[45]

His international roster featured Horowitz and Menuhin, Milstein and Schnabel, Beniamino Gigli and Jussi Björling. He rarely needed to go scouting, as rising stars were sent to him first. Auditioning for Holt at thirteen years old, the violinist Ida Haendel waited anxiously after playing her pieces. Dispensing with platitudes, Holt said, 'I think I shall call you my little sister, now that you are going to be my artist.'[46] No musician could resist so warm an embrace, and Haendel was Holt's for life. He exploited her cruelly with a salaried contract that required her to play whenever he ordered. Later, she found he was taking a fifteen-per-cent commission instead of the standard ten. Behind the charm lay an acute concern for personal financial gain.

Most nights Holt was to be found backstage at Queen's Hall and afterwards, like Vert in former days, at a corner table at the Café Royal, regaling his guests with good stories and fine wine. Night creatures of this species rarely married, though Holt had an eye for ladies of a class he could never take home to mother. Years of gourmandise and mild debauchery engraved a mark on his features; Diana Menuhin recalled 'dear old hung-over Harold Holt's red cabbage face' at her wedding to Yehudi in 1947.

John Tillett, too, grew into an elderly bachelor in a homburg hat, prowling the concert halls after dark. The master of Ibbs felt a fatherly concern for his artists and worried what would become of them when he was gone.

One day in 1943, when the fate of civilisation hung in the balance, he called in his young secretary, Emmie Bass, and asked her to marry him. 'It was not a love match,' says Wilfred Stiff, 'more a marriage of convenience to continue the business.'[47] Emmie, who had trained at the music publishers Chappells, carried her artists' list in her head. She upholstered her chairs and made her own curtains. Even when she became head of the firm, she took the bus in to work at Wigmore Street, arriving ahead of the switchboard girls. If a town clerk called from deepest Cumbria with plans for a gala, she would have an artist instantly to hand – someone like the gracefully ageing soprano Eva Turner, who tended to mingle with dignitaries after her recital and sweeten their connection with Ibbs & Tillett. Emmie liked artists who brought in extra work.

'One has the distinct impression that a firm like Ibbs & Tillett deliberately refrains from promoting its artists as an ungentlemanly pursuit, alien to the British concept of good sportsmanship. They are confident that concert societies all over the British Isles will keep coming back year after year,' wrote an American violinist.[48] Emmie always went in to work on Saturday mornings. That, she knew, was when music clubs got hit by last-minute cancellations and she could provide substitutes. One of the criticisms of Emmie was that she functioned not as an agent but as a clearing house, in which big names got good dates and the rest had to wait until they dropped out. 'When Pouishnoff dies, I'll be all right,' said a patient pianist. 'Until then, I've got to keep well in with Emmie and hope for a break.'[49]

Her shining star was Kathleen Ferrier, taken on by John Tillett in 1942 as a half-trained oratorio singer from Blackburn and groomed by Emmie to world fame. It was at Emmie's house in Elm Tree Road, near the Abbey Road studios, that Ferrier relaxed with her paints and canvas from the strain of spiralling success and sudden cancer.

Peacetime paid dividends for Emmie, with five orchestras playing in London and Ferrier's creamy contralto conquering all. The birth of Covent Garden as a state-funded, year-round opera house sent her off signing up continental singers; Dietrich Fischer-Dieskau was a prize catch. Emmie took to driving a ferocious Jaguar, dropping in at three concerts a night, to make sure her artists felt appreciated. 'My dear, I thought you were wonderful,' she would gush, not having heard a note they had played or sung.

Holt had his chance to run Covent Garden in 1944, but could not be bothered. He was dissipating in a cloud of cheap perfume and vintage port. He took on some Americans, notably the influential Isaac Stern, but when Rafael Kubelík arrived on his doorstep as a fugitive from the 1948 communist *putsch* in Prague, he told the Czech conductor – son of one of the firm's greatest violinists – to seek world representation with a Dutch agent, Johanna Beek. 'I don't think I could manage it,' sighed Holt. Kubelík went on, under other managements, to head the Chicago Symphony Orchestra, Covent Garden, Bavarian Radio and the Metropolitan Opera.

Ian Hunter, director of the Edinburgh Festival, visiting Holt to negotiate a Menuhin concert, remembers that 'all the staff were in their fifties and so were most of the artists. What I remember more than anything else was his enormous bonhomie. He had an inexhaustible fund of stories, that were musical and Jewish and very funny. There's nothing artists love more. But he had lost all ambition and his money was running out.'[50]

Fearing a repeat of the Powell disaster and a knock-on effect on the industry as a whole, Emmie Tillett bought shares in Harold Holt Limited together with the publishers Boosey & Hawkes. The sclerotic Harold Holt meanwhile was being dragged through the courts by a lady friend, charged with breach of promise, that most English of amorous indiscretions. 'Impresario sued by Singer,' screamed the evening papers. He lost the case and married another singer, but died not long afterwards in 1953, at the age of sixty-seven. One night Miss Mattie and Miss Hilda were seen leaving his house with two large bundles. They returned to Claridge's by limousine and told the concierge to place their packages in the hotel incinerator. Holt had written a memoir filled with scurrilous stories about all the musicians he had known, but his sisters would not allow it to sully the family escutcheon. After the *auto-da-fé*, they retired to South Africa.

The late Harold Holt had left a few thousand pounds, no property worth mentioning and a business on the brink of ruin. 'No one thought he was a brilliant agent,' said Ian Hunter. 'He wasn't hungry enough.' Hunter was picked by the shareholders for his youthful bustle. He was a festival man, adept at convincing local authorities in Bath, Brighton, the City of London, Hong Kong and elsewhere that they needed an annual musical jamboree. His own artists understandably took precedence in these festivals. Hunter introduced Isaac Stern's Israeli sparks – Daniel Barenboim, Itzhak Perlman, Pinchas

Zukerman – and the rising conductors Bernard Haitink and Claudio Abbado. By the late Fifties, the firm of Holt was on the mend and Emmie was delighted. 'We were never rivals,' says Hunter. 'She thought of me as an impresario – "you're no agent, Ian," she'd say. Eventually she offered me her shares in the business on easy terms. I won't tell you how much – but it was nothing. She was terribly anxious that Harold Holt's name should continue.'

Tradition, friendliness and probity were watchwords of the British music business in Emmie Tillett's time. New agencies proliferated in the post-war boom, but they followed rules of rectitude that emanated from Ibbs & Tillett. There was Sandor Gorlinsky, a continental refugee who looked after Maria Callas and Lorin Maazel. Victor Hochhauser was the exclusive importer of Soviet products. Joan Ingpen founded an eponymous firm that launched Joan Sutherland and Georg Solti. Her partner, Howard Hartog, advanced the cerebral qualities of Alfred Brendel and Pierre Boulez. They competed for artists, but preserved a high degree of mutual respect. The British Association of Concert Agents (BACA) had a code of practice that prohibited the poaching of an artist by one agent from another – not that anyone would indulge in something so squalid.

Emmie, in her later years, was pressured to modernise. 'Her kind of business was bound to have problems unless it changed philosophy and took on fewer artists,' said Wilfred Stiff. 'No one realised how near Emmie came to insolvency.' She took on the leading English vocalist Janet Baker, the prize-winning pianist John Ogdon and the supreme cellist Jacqueline du Pré in an era when telecommunications were faster and careers became international. But Emmie saw herself as a booking agent for Britain, concerned that she had enough talent to meet any regional contingency.

'Ibbs & Tillett should have been the greatest agency in the world,' said Jasper Parrott, one of her young lions. 'It wasn't too late to take up opportunities for reconstruction.'[5] Parrott, a Cambridge-educated polyglot, and his colleague Terry Harrison argued that the future lay with small agencies like Ingpen's, which built world careers for a handful of artists. Emmie was an unregenerate wholesaler. In October 1969, Harrison and Parrott walked out of Ibbs & Tillett, taking with them the pianist-conductors Vladimir Ashkenazy and André Previn. Emmie was bitter but unbowed. She struggled on for ten more years until, aged eighty-two, she yielded the firm to younger hands and enjoined them to preserve its hallowed name. 'Emmie was very correct, you know,' said her competitor Joan Ingpen. When the liquidators were called in, agents all over London muttered: 'Thank God Emmie never lived to see this.'

*   *   *

No one thought there could be another Wall Street crash like 1929 or a slump like the Thirties. Confidence was the buzzword in the Reagan–Thatcher years, when businesses were urged to expand at all costs, whether by loan-backed growth or take-over. Such was the shock of the Black Monday share collapse in October 1987 that it paralysed executive brains. Many businesses carried on borrowing, believing they could invest their way out of trouble. When interest rates roared into double figures, they were unable to meet debt repayments and resorted to selling out cheap, declaring bankruptcy or siphoning cash from unorthodox sources.

Holt was among the firms that over-extended in the Eighties. It co-funded an ambitious Japan Festival with Harrison–Parrott and lurched into the potentially lucrative area of orchestral touring, where the agent took a share not only of concert fees but of every air ticket, hotel room and meal supplied for up to one hundred travelling musicians. Touring was a high-risk, high-return game, where the agent placed a large sum up front and hoped to recoup a fortune. Holt were in the process of paying the Berlin Philharmonic sixty thousand pounds a night to play in Japan when recession took hold in the Far East and the gush of profit turned into a trickle. With cashflow drying up, Sir Ian Hunter – knighted for his services to music festivals – went hunting for a white knight investor.

Over at Ibbs & Tillett, managing director Richard Apley had Georgia on his mind. Ibbs had staged a remarkable recovery after Emmie's death by signing a new generation of stars from the Soviet Union – among them the prize-winning pianists Mikhail Pletnev and Vladimir Ovchinnikov and two towering bass-baritones, Dmitri Hvorostovsky and Paata Burchuladze. While scouting for more artists, Apley was persuaded by his Soviet contacts to invest in state ventures, mostly in Georgia and Armenia. None of the schemes had much to do with music. They included trading in tea, wine, fine arts and the Spartak Moscow soccer team.

Apley had joined Ibbs while managing an orchestra for the choral conductor Richard Hickox. He left the agency to retrain as a solicitor in August 1989, but his wife, Fiona Blyth, continued to work in the firm and he remained the majority shareholder. Four months later, Ibbs & Tillett called in the liquidators. With the Soviet empire disintegrating and the domestic market mired in recession, it could not pay its bills.

Creditors gathered at a suburban hotel in Hendon to learn that Ibbs & Tillett owed a total amount of £212,327 to, among others, a top advertising agency, a hotel chain and the Royal Opera House. Cries of 'incompetent', 'disgraceful' and 'bumbling' were hurled at the shamefaced directors. Some victims were still unaware of their loss. It transpired at the meeting that, in

THE COMPANY OF WOLFF'S

order to finance exotic ventures, Ibbs & Tillett had dipped into the cash accounts of top artists. Dietrich Fischer-Dieskau, for example, was owed twelve thousand pounds. Ovchinnikov and Hvorostovsky had seventeen thousand pounds and fifteen thousand pounds missing from their accounts. 'There was gross mishandling of funds,' said the liquidator, David Rubin.

'If this is true, I would be deeply shocked,' commented Joeske Van Walsum, BACA's president. 'It is a clear legal obligation of the agent to protect monies due to their clients.'[52] It proved, regrettably, all too true. Apley, facing threats of prosecution, reached an out-of-court settlement with creditors and retired from the scene. 'The expenditure on Soviet projects was considerable,' he said, 'but so was the potential. We had been regarded by the top US managements as *the* agency to ring about Soviet artists. You could hardly say we speculated wildly when you look at the string of artists we had uncovered . . . The Soviet venture was always an organic growth, never a matter of shooting in the dark.'

The liquidator agreed that Apley had been 'naive, possibly negligent, but not criminal or dishonest'.[53] 'Agents in classical music generally work for very little profit,' said Van Walsum, 'and I can easily see how a business can get into trouble if not properly controlled.'[54]

A fortnight after the creditors' meeting, two directors of Ibbs & Tillett set up again in business as Artists Management International with finance from Andrew Lloyd Webber's Really Useful Group and an undertaking to repay more than half of Ibbs's liabilities. They were granted a licence by the Department of Employment and sought readmission to BACA, pledging to abide by its 'strict code of ethics and professionalism'. Apley's wife, 'formerly of Ibbs & Tillett', went into partnership with a French agency, Transart. The trading name of Ibbs & Tillett was acquired by Lloyd Webber and quietly laid to rest.

BACA tightened its rules and expelled deputy chairman Terry Harrison and two others for refusing to set up separate accounts for their artists, but this amounted to locking the stable door after the horse had bolted. For the first time in a century of fair dealing, the British music business had been caught playing around with money that belonged to its artists. In the midst of the scandal, Howard Hartog was carried to his grave in a cortège that tolled the passing of the last romantic. Hopeless at paperwork and careless of figures, Hartog was more interested in the music his artists played than the money they earned. He was loved for this shambolic eccentricity and mourned as a man of integrity and ideals, an antediluvian relic of an agency world that was no more.

'Emmie Tillett was so respectable.' Sir Ian Hunter sighed at the terraced house in west London that now served as Holt's offices, far from the centre of town. 'To see her firm go broke, and in that way, was a terrible thing.' Harold Holt's name was the last symbol of former values, but the firm was in alien waters. In trying to rebuild its fortunes, Holt had gone swimming in a sea full of sharks and lost a large chunk of its torso. Its fate, as the century entered its closing decade, was suspended parlously between a crunch of converging jaws.

NOTES

1 Flesch, p. 115
2 His son, Emil, ran an agency in Munich from 1906 to 1913, numbering Richard Strauss among his artists and organising the world première of Mahler's 'Symphony of a Thousand'. Like his father, Emil Gutmann wound up in an asylum for nervous disorders.
3 Flesch, pp. 50–1
4 Lebrecht, *Mahler Remembered*, p. 109
5 document in possession of Rosé family
6 Hellsberg, p. 308
7 La Grange, vol. I, p. 612
8 Stargardt-Wolff, p. 56
9 Stresemann, p. 48
10 Walter, pp. 40–1
11 Schuh, p. 378
12 Flesch, p. 133
13 Hambourg, p. 161
14 Paderewski, pp. 175–7
15 Paderewski, p. 317
16 *Die Musik*, I, 10, p. 906
17 Ysaÿe, p. 86
18 Finck, p. 443
19 Knepler, p. 43
20 Gerhardt, p. 19
21 letters in Otto Klemperer archive, Zurich, and Pierpoint Morgan Library, New York
22 Walter, *Briefe*, p. 189
23 Geissmar, pp. 31–2
24 Geissmar, p. 33
25 see Lebrecht, *The Maestro Myth*, chapter 5
26 Rathkolb, p. 218
27 Vedder resumed at Bodensee until his death in 1952, when his son Walter re-established the agency in Munich. Karajan was still listed among its principal artists in 1959, alongside Elisabeth Schwarzkopf, Paul Hindemith and Benny Goodman. The firm moved in 1978 to Frankfurt-am-Main, where it continues to operate under new management since Walter Vedder's death in 1986.
28 Inghelbrecht, *Mouvement*, p. 170
29 Astruc, p. 240
30 Rubinstein, *Young Years*, p. 130
31 Nichols, p. 279
32 Astruc, p. 290
33 Inghelbrecht, *Mouvement*, p. 193
34 Astruc, p. 133
35 DOUBLE, vol. I. pp. 57ff

36 Newton, p. 213
37 *Musical Times*, February 1932
38 Pound, p. 132
39 Glover, p. 93
40 Andrew Green, 'Bach in Edwardian Times,' *Classical Music* Magazine, 22 February 1986, p. 19
41 Grainger, p. 327
42 Wilfred Stiff, interview with the author
43 Temianka, p. 220
44 Pearton, p. 94
45 Haendel, p. 201
46 Haendel, p. 79
47 Stiff, author's interview
48 Temianka, p. 220
49 Joel, p. 14
50 author's interview
51 *CM*, 19 October 1991, p. 48
52 author's interviews
53 interviews by Andrew Green
54 author's interview

CHAPTER V

O, COLUMBIA, THE
GEM OF THE OCEAN[1]

C odes of conduct counted for naught in old New York. A man might impress a soubrette by telling her he was a concert agent, but to polite society he was just another hustler. 'Some agents are honest, some are not,' warned the *Evening Post* critic Henry Theophilus Finck. 'Some managers agree for the sum of two or three thousand dollars to secure sufficient engagements to launch the beginner successfully; and if the girl happens to be good-looking but penniless, they have the effrontery to suggest dishonourable ways of securing the sum required.'[2] There could be no seamier testimony of the profession's low standing.

Concert agents abounded, and there was not much to choose between them. Leader of the pack was the high-spirited Henry A. Wolfsohn, who kept a parrot that he trained to sing Wagner – but only when suspended upside down. 'My experience has taught me that only about five per cent of those who struggle and aspire can have their ambitions gratified,'[3] he would tell newcomers as he pocketed their signing-on fee. Wolfsohn liked to see money up front. Five thousand dollars, he told the Texan pianist Olga Samaroff (she was plain Lucie Hickenlooper before he changed her stage name), would just about cover promotional expenses for one season. Five grand was a lot of money in the opening decade of the twentieth century. It was the amount Gustav Mahler asked for, and was refused, for conducting twenty concerts with the New York Philharmonic. Mahler, at least, turned up to conduct. Wolfsohn cashed the cheque, made no promises and, often as not, produced no dates. Taken to task, he would blame the artist for lacking sex appeal. His greatest coup was to entice Richard Strauss, chief conductor of the Court Opera in Berlin, to give the world première of his *Symphonia Domestica* in Carnegie Hall, followed by two performances in Wanamaker's department store. It is a tribute to Wolfsohn's powers of persuasion that he got Strauss to conduct during normal shopping hours. A tougher customer was Sergei Rachmaninov, who waited until the agent was dead and his widow was running the office, before finally agreeing terms for a US début.

Mrs Wolfsohn faced immediate competition from a new force in New York music, an Ivy League operator with a society wife who sat on all the best committees. As an artists' agent, Loudon Charlton earned a refined reputation for indolence. He was nevertheless appointed manager of the New York Philharmonic Orchestra at seven thousand dollars a year in 1910, Mahler's second season as conductor. Charlton reckoned that if he ran the orchestra, he could engage his own clients as soloists. Mahler soon put a stop to that, complaining of the manager's 'naive, brutal egotism'. Charlton retaliated by adding twenty concerts to the schedule for Mahler to conduct at no extra fee, scheming all the while to replace him with a more malleable maestro. When Mahler fell mortally ill in February 1911, Charlton quickly wrote to the *New York Times* denying responsibility for his collapse. 'Mr Mahler and the management are now, and have been throughout the season, working in perfect harmony,' he lied.[4] Mahler's tragic death three months later was attributed by the press to 'the killing demands of American artistic life'[5] and by his widow to the ladies of the Philharmonic committee. If blame had to be pinned on anyone, it should have been Loudon Charlton. Mahler, carrying a known heart ailment, was intentionally demoralised and, incidentally, exposed to fatal infection by the insidious manoeuvrings of the agent who managed his orchestra.

Charlton did not escape entirely unscathed. The music press, which turned a blind eye to most shenanigans, grew alarmed at the sight of a major orchestra being harnessed to its manager's commercial interests. 'The finale of this will be an ultimatum which Mr Charlton will one day put to himself, and that will be that it must be either the Philharmonic or his own bureau, and his own bureau will win,'[6] predicted the *Musical Courier*. Sure enough, after just two seasons Charlton quit the orchestra and went back to his bureau, where the business ethic was unclouded by artistic considerations.

The New York Philharmonic, in this and other precedents, was merely following a pattern set in Boston where the man who ran the leading orchestra had a bustling little business on the side. Charles A. Ellis was working for a mining concern in Minnesota in 1885 when his boss, Major Henry Lee Higginson, switched him to running his symphony orchestra. After three tentative seasons under Georg Henschel, a friend of Brahms, the BSO was beginning to find its bearings with an Austrian conductor, Wilhelm Gericke. Better players were brought in from Europe and Ellis kept them busy by extending the concert calendar into high summer with lazy evenings of light classics. His scheme proved popular, profitable and durable; it was the forerunner of the famous Boston Pops. Gericke cultivated a competent ensemble, which the young Arthur Nikisch then raised to international quality. Ellis all the while kept the administration running like clockwork. He was the first full-time manager of any orchestra in the United States, 'a quiet gentleman'[7] with a 'kind, patient'[8] manner who preferred to co-operate with sister-orchestras rather than compete. Towards the players, who were barred by Higginson from joining a union, he adopted a caring though strict paternalism.

He toured Europe each summer to audition soloists and was received respectfully wherever he went as an architect of American culture. His musicians were regularly invited to play at Bayreuth, and Boston was the first US community to earn overseas musical recognition. It would be stretching the truth, however, to depict Ellis as a selfless emissary. Once he had things running smoothly at the orchestra, and Symphony Hall was being built, Ellis set out to make a little something for himself.

His great asset was an air of unflappable calm that had an instantly tranquillising effect on volatile visitors. Nellie Melba, within twenty minutes of meeting him, sacked her agent and asked Ellis to organise her US career. He added to his list Kreisler and Paderewski, the two hottest concert virtuosi, together with two home-grown heroines, Geraldine Farrar and her friend Olga Samaroff. He kept his agency exclusive, representing only a handful of top stars and, unlike Wolfsohn, making no crude demands for 'promotional expenses'. He had no need for petty cash. He took twenty per cent of the five highest fees in the musical world.

At Melba's behest, he joined the socialite New York conductor Walter Damrosch in 1898 to form a travelling opera company in competition with the Met. Damrosch found him 'a delightful partner' whose 'equable temperament and fair-mindedness had made him many friends'.[9] There was unusually no rancour when the Damrosch-Ellis Opera Company folded after four years, but Ellis avoided opera ever after. In symphonic music, he had no need for allies or encumbrances. From a modest office in Boston, he controlled the entire economy. As agent to the most desirable stars, he named the top fees. As manager of the Boston Symphony Orchestra, he paid the highest market rate. Wearing both hats, he fixed the fee structures that governed the content and development of American concert life.

The way he called the shots can be judged from his handling of Kreisler. Hearing that the Viennese violinist was fed up with Wolfsohn's, Ellis offered him a concert tour with the Boston Symphony Orchestra at eight hundred dollars a night, two hundred higher than any other player. Kreisler was delighted and asked Ellis to become his agent. Having established a record fee for his new client, Ellis then challenged other orchestras to match his rate or miss out on the top fiddler. Whatever people made of Kreisler's playing, everyone now knew he was the highest-paid violinist in the world – and that had to mean he was the best. It was a simple trick that Ellis worked time and again.

In orchestral circles, Ellis's word was law. 'A letter from him was more potent than the most feverish personal efforts of road agents sent out by other managers,'[10] said Samaroff. Adella Prentiss Hughes, founder of the Cleveland Orchestra, on being told by Ellis's deputy, William H. Brennan, that 'Mr Ellis is most interested in a young American pianist and would like you to present her,' booked Samaroff on the spot without even asking her name – 'such was my faith in the integrity and knowledge of Charles Ellis.'[11] Above his desk hung the motto: 'The Lord helps those who help themselves.'

He was boss at Boston for more than thirty years, retiring with Higginson in the post-war doldrums of 1919. Months later, the orchestra went on strike. Ellis had always avoided industrial unrest by means of old-world civility and a grasp of employee psychology he had acquired down the mines. To censure this dedicated public servant for abusing his position with the BSO by running a private racket would be churlish. It would also misrepresent the nature of the American music business, which was founded on insider trading and flourishes to the present day on naked conflicts of interest. Ellis showed that the way to get ahead in music was to get your feet under the desk in a major institution and set up a parallel operation for your own profit. That lesson was not lost on a hungry young man from Ohio who set out to industrialise musical America and monopolise its music business. Arthur Judson called Ellis 'the greatest manager America ever produced'.[12] Not many people would ever dare to challenge Arthur Judson's authority in musical America.

'AJ', as intimates were encouraged to call him, was the archetypal giant among pygmies. He stood above six feet tall in his socks, knew more music than most virtuosi and was richer than many of the benefactors who founded his orchestras. He was an imposing presence — 'the son-of-a-bitch exuded power,' recalls Harold Schonberg, chief critic of the *New York Times*. 'He was a gorgeous man, maybe six foot four, wonderful carriage, extremely handsome, craggy face. He was a personage,' said a member of his personal staff. 'His face could reflect anger, sadness, joy and compassion in equally readable terms,' wrote another aide, Schuyler G. Chapin. 'He was not somebody I ever wanted to cross.'[13] Like Rupert Murdoch and Bill Gates, Judson was a circumspect man who seemed at first glance an ordinary kind of magnate rather than sole lord of a slice of the universe. Like Murdoch and Gates, he had the talent to live at the right time for his talents. He went into orchestral management in the decade that US orchestras doubled in number; he penetrated broadcasting a few moments before its dawn. He was, in common with Murdoch and Gates, a bold improviser, a master of the possible.

Judson ruled music in America for two-thirds of the twentieth century, from Verdun to Vietnam. At one time he headed three major symphony orchestras, along with a concert agency that managed a majority of the top conductors. Pressed about his 'knack of serving conflicting interests at the same time',[14] he would shrug wordlessly as if the issue was not worth his valued consideration.

His agency, the biggest on earth, had branches in every city; a subsidiary sent musicians to every small town in America. He co-owned a broadcast network. His profits were planted in buildings all around Carnegie Hall, a ring of Judson real estate that mutely affirmed his stranglehold on the musical citadel. No man ever wielded such hegemony in music. 'He ran a kind of protection racket,' said one of his conductors. 'If you wanted a career in America, you had to sign with Judson.'[15] 'Those who maintain that Judson enjoys playing God are not far from right,'[16] wrote a sympathetic observer. Even sworn admirers admitted a 'tinge of dictatorship'[17] in his governance.

Like most divinities and tyrants, his antecedents are shrouded in mystery — not so much shrouded, perhaps, as shredded. Judson rarely discussed his past. When his grandson sought to commission a posthumous biography, he found no papers of any personal interest either in his estate or in any of the organisations he once ruled. 'He never wanted to be written about,'[18] said a press aide. How he eliminated the evidence is unknown, but the effectiveness of his cover-up was questionable. Any misdeeds, short of murder, would have seemed inconsequential beside the monolithic scale of Judson's calculated abuse of musical power.

If there was a compelling reason for Judson to cover his tracks, it was because he was ashamed of having sprung from the wrong side of the tracks.

He was born in the 'musically ignorant small town' of Dayton, Ohio, on 17 February 1881 – we know this from a biographical note he sent to a music journal, *The Etude*, in January 1940. His parents were Irish immigrants who scraped together enough to send young Arthur to study the violin in New York with Max Bendix, retired concertmaster of Theodore Thomas's orchestra. In his own recollection, Judson went on and 'played the violin in small orchestras; and then conducted an orchestra of one hundred men in Ocean Grove, New Jersey'. He returned to the Midwest to be appointed, at nineteen years old, Dean of the Conservatory of Music of Denison University in Granville, Ohio. He lacked any academic qualification for this position; thirty years later, Granville awarded him an *honorary* doctorate in music.

Judson claimed to have made Denison into a modern music college; he also bragged of having played there in 1903 the first American performance of a violin sonata by Richard Strauss. Neither assertion has been validated. It is safe to assume, however, that he was a competent musician with a degree of scholarly ambition. While at Denison he published a pamphlet, *History of Music (An Investigation of Causes and Results)*. 'One day when I was professor of music [sic] at a midwestern university,' he told *The Etude*, 'I sat down and began to appraise my assets. I soon realised the truth, when I compared my talent with that of the great violinists I knew. There was no use to be pushed on by well-meaning relatives and friends [into a performing career]. I resolved to get into my present field.'[19] The reality was rather less reflective. Judson was twenty-six years old, married, a father, and going nowhere.

In 1907 he took his family to New York in the hope of making a living as a musician or as a musical ancillary of some kind. 'I wake up at night,' he confided to his partner many years later, 'and my mind goes back to the time my wife and son and I came to New York to make my way, and the trouble I had was nobody's business. I taught violin, conducted orchestras, and gave musical festivals throughout the country. Finally, I decided it was too much. I then went on the staff of *Musical America*.'[20]

This was one of three US journals devoted to the art in a golden age of music criticism. None paid their writers enough to feed a family and even doyen critics on the daily newspapers had to supplement their income by teaching college. Judson, as a newcomer to the critics circle, was sent around the orchestral circuit on a third-class rail ticket, covering concerts and orchestral news. To make ends meet, he also sold advertising for the magazine to the orchestras he visited. The temptation to temper his reviews according to the size of his commission must have been well-nigh irresistible. Although the conductors he interviewed and the managers he pitched to viewed him as a fairly subfusc species of musical fauna, the experience gave Judson an entry card to the twin power points of concert life.

Passing through his home region in 1910, he discovered something unusual at play in the city of Cincinnati. A young English church organist had been surprisingly appointed to conduct the orchestra in preference to Wolfsohn's nominee, the Berlin-born Bruno Walter. Cincinnati was predominantly a German community and its orchestra was co-founded by the wife and family of the serving US president, William Howard Taft. Any fears that its choice was eccentric were dispelled by some electrifying opening concerts. Arthur Judson described them in *Musical America* as the best he had ever heard outside New York. His interview with the young lion was headlined: 'Leopold Stokovski – Thinker, Philosopher and Musician.'

Judson did not leave town without forming a lifelong alliance with the Tafts, who relied upon him ever after for musical counsel. In Stokowski, however, he found an apparent soulmate. The conductor was a man of his own age and humble, half-Irish origin, beset by an identity crisis that prompted him to spell his surname temporarily with a 'v' and fake a Slavonic accent. He had been taking image lessons from his fiancée, Olga Samaroff, who had Russianised her own name for professional advantage and had moved heaven and earth to get Stokowski his first job. Her cousin, General Andrew Hickenlooper, ran Cincinnati's gas and electric company and was a future lieutenant-governor of Ohio; she also knew President and Mrs Taft. 'Mr Stokowski,' gushed Olga to anyone who would listen, 'is the greatest conductor in the world.' After three seasons, she broke his contract with Cincinnati and applied the same methods to secure him a more prestigious pulpit in Philadelphia.

The Quaker City, ninety miles from New York, took a perverse pride in its reputation for dullness. Stokowski blew in with a concert of Russian fireworks and Arthur Judson was there to report that 'the reception to Mr Stokowski was not that of an audience merely glad it had a competent conductor, but wildly enthusiastic because it had discovered a genius.'[21] While Olga blitzed the social front, paying seven hundred calls in her first winter, Stokowski galvanised a dormant ensemble in a dormitory town into America's dazzle-band. Stokowski was a sound freak who changed seating plans on the concert platform to achieve a unified yet transparent timbre. He encouraged string players to find their own bowings and play freely in an ever-flowing melodic line. Applying himself to technical details of sonic wizardry, Stokowski needed a Charles Ellis to sort out the organisational side of his orchestra, and someone in the Barnum mould to promote 'The Stokowski Sound' across the world.

Judson, who had been promoted on *Musical America* to advertisement manager and was finally earning a decent wage, heard that Philadelphia were looking for an administrator and raced over to catch Stokowski on vacation in Vermont. 'That's the man for me,' said the conductor, and in the autumn of 1915 Judson took office as manager of the Philadelphia Orchestra. It was locally rumoured, and never refuted, that to make doubly sure of getting the position and retaining it Judson seduced the wife of a member of the orchestra's governing board. Handsome and imposing, he magnetised many women in his life and, unlike Stokowski, preserved a proper discretion about his conquests. To public appearances Judson was a blameless family man. Stokowski, by contrast, wanted the world to know that he was irresistible to women and made a public fetish of his flirtations. 'He prefers any inconsequential flapper who comes along,' lamented the long-suffering Olga.[22] Sex would surface as a painful bone of contention between the maestro and the manager.

Judson's arrival could not have been better timed. Philadelphia was ready to erupt in March 1916 with the American première of Mahler's eighth symphony, known as the 'Symphony of a Thousand'. Stokowski, who heard the composer conduct the elephantine score in Munich six years earlier, amassed 1,068 instrumentalists and singers. Judson was in charge of logistics and publicity. Rave reviews pushed the Battle of Verdun off the front pages of Philadelphia newspapers. Tickets were scalped (or so it was reported) at one hundred dollars a seat. Judson sold out eight more performances before the army decamped on two private trains for New York, where critical accolades served notice that Philadelphia had reached the top of the orchestral tree. With Boston on the wane, New York leaderless since Mahler's death and Chicago unimpressive, the orchestral future belonged to Philadelphia, Stokowski and Judson.

Both men claimed credit for the transmogrification. Stokowski rebuilt the orchestra in his image, established its recording fame and ignited public involvement. When finances flagged in 1919, he led a 'Save the Orchestra' parade through the streets and raised a million dollars. Judson's achievement was less loudly sung. He went to the board and asked to see the budget. On being told there was none, he wrote the first financial forecast ever prepared for an American orchestra, providing the fiscal instrument that underpins the functioning of every professionally run business. Trustees looked at the Judson spreadsheet and knew exactly where the orchestra was heading. Investors drew confidence from his predictions. The chamber of commerce read his balance sheets and issued a pamphlet on *The Commercial Value of Music to Philadelphia*.

Judson resented Stokowski's relations with the business community, especially with the doting *Ladies Home Journal* publisher Edward Bok and his wife Mary. Stokowski, he told them, 'needed a cohesive public and a malleable audience'[23] which only his expert management could organise and keep docile. Left to his own devices the maestro would self-destruct, he warned – a prophecy that was uncannily fulfilled when they parted. 'They say Stokowski built that orchestra,' grumbled Judson in later years. 'He didn't – I did.'[24]

That assertion is too far-fetched to demand contradiction. Without Stokowski's pin-up looks, his ear for sound and his eye for sensation, Philadelphia would never have risen above the humdrum, no matter how efficacious its manager. Stokowski was the making of Philadelphia, so much so that a colourless successor could keep the orchestra on course for decades beyond.

But Judson's contribution was not inconsequential, even in an artistic sense. In addition to the financial framework, he brought a measure of musical judgement and a much-needed decisiveness to the enterprise. Until Judson turned up, Stokowski lacked the heart to sack ailing and incompetent players. Judson, untroubled by sentiment, dismissed thirty in a year. He was the steel behind Stokowski's smile, the muscle in his orchestral miracle. Together, they were unbeatable.

Yet, in a partnership that lasted twenty years in Philadelphia and was resumed thereafter, neither addressed the other familiarly as 'AJ' or 'Stoki'. They remained 'Mr Judson' and 'Mr Stokowski' to the end of their lives. A natural reserve, possessed by both men in unnatural abundance, turned cool and gradually adverse. Stokowski, who trusted no one, was the first to become suspicious when he saw Judson invading his domestic domain.

The manager, within months of taking office, founded Arthur Judson Concert Management. He delegated routine orchestral matters to Ruth O'Neill, a convent girl who became his Girl Friday, while he went out touting for talent. His first private client was Stokowski, followed by his wife Olga, who had pledged to give up work and devote her life to Stoki, was bored with playing hostess and wounded by his infidelities. Judson offered to rekindle her appeal as America's favourite pianist. Stokowski was furious. He told the manager he could no longer study symphonic scores at home because his wife was forever practising piano. At Judson's suggestion, he built her a sound-proofed studio. A wall went up between the unhappy couple.

Torn between professional renewal and hopes of saving her marriage, Olga suffered a breakdown. When she failed to meet Stokowski for dinner one night in February 1917, the conductor called Judson, who informed the police. Olga was found safe and well in New York's Roosevelt Hospital, where she had walked in, pleading amnesia. Judson told the press she was overwrought after playing too many concerts, sixty in half a season. She returned to the concert hall in triumph, only to suffer a memory lapse during a concerto conducted by Stokowski. If they could not trust each other as musicians, there was little left to keep them together. Just as they were about to part, Olga fell pregnant and gave birth to a daughter, Sonya. Twenty months later she sued for divorce and moved to New York. While organising her belongings in her new apartment, she tripped over a packing case and tore a ligament in her left arm, ending her career.

Olga never loved another man and Stokowski never found another wife who matched him in mind or musicality. He did not go so far as to accuse Judson of messing up his marriage, but Stokowski rarely let on what he really felt. On learning of Olga's death, alone in her West 55th Street apartment in 1948, he did not shed a tear or send a wreath. Behind the mask of impassivity, he was a passionate man who funnelled his emotions into music. He would have needed to be completely insensate not to have experienced a twinge of jealousy over Judson's role in offering Olga an escape from their marriage. A seed of sexual resentment infiltrated their relationship.

Stokowski, for all his glamour-boy appeal, had difficulties with girls. His marriages were rocky, his divorces painful and at least one of his limelit affairs – with the screen star Greta Garbo – was unconsummated. A long-serving record producer said he delighted in making 'drawing-room conquests' but did not pursue them to the bedroom. Troubled by fears of erotic inadequacy, he had only to look at Judson to see masculinity at its most masterful. When told of the manager's notorious affair with the board member's wife, Stokowski went all prim and puritanical. He called it 'unseemly'[25] and felt threatened in more ways than he could acknowledge. In the two areas of life where the conductor craved dominance, music and women, Judson had all the answers.

It speaks volumes for both men's dedication that they were able to transcend any personal differences that might impede professional progress. Indeed, the further they drifted apart the better they worked together. So much so, that in 1922 when Judson was named manager of the Philharmonic concerts in New York the newspapers automatically assumed that Stokowski would join him. This was the last thing Judson wanted as he struggled to run three orchestras in different cities at one and the same time. He had taken on Cincinnati and its dynamic conductor Fritz Reiner, and was helping New York to unravel an orchestral nightmare. The Philharmonic, smitten by a musicians' strike, was fighting an audience war with the City Symphony under the Dutchman Dirk Foch and with Walter Damrosch's New York Symphony Society. Judson settled the unions, crushed the City and absorbed the Symphony, leaving the Philharmonic-Symphony the only orchestra in Manhattan. Willem Mengelberg of Amsterdam was chief conductor, sharing his seasons with Wilhelm Furtwängler of Berlin and Arturo Toscanini of La Scala, until the Italian claimed the rostrum in 1929.

With New York uppermost in his mind, Judson needed Stokowski to stay put and keep his Philadelphia story running. The orchestra was making lots of recordings, thanks to Judson's guile and Stokowski's flair, but was missing out on better opportunities. It gave the first nationally broadcast concerts on three Sundays in October 1929, only for Judson to announce that the New York Philharmonic with Toscanini would broadcast forty-two Sunday concerts from Carnegie Hall the following season. Stokowski, whose starring role as conductor and commentator had reached Europe on shortwave, was rightfully aggrieved. Having begged Judson for years to take the Philadelphia on a European tour, he was outraged when the manager sent the New York Philharmonic to Europe with Toscanini in 1930 (the tour, as it happens, had been the bait by which Judson tempted Toscanini to take the New York job).

As a sop to Stokowski, Judson switched the maestros around for a fortnight in the spring of 1930 — an arrangement that caused a box-office rush in both cities, but left both conductors less than satisfied. Toscanini had to reverse Stokowski's careful seating plan before he could get the Philadelphians to play as he wanted, while Stokowski faced ripples of abuse from Toscanini lackeys in the Philharmonic. 'Give us an upbeat before the downbeat,' demanded the objectionable oboist, Bruno Labate. The word 'charlatan' reached Stokowski's ears and he expelled three players from rehearsals. Eleven years would pass before he conducted the New York Philharmonic again.

Judson was not bothered. All he saw was packed houses in two cities and praise from the boards of both orchestras. Reducing his commitments, he stepped down at Cincinnati and asked to leave Philadelphia but was detained by emotional appeals from the directors. Judson recognised that he could not personally run every big orchestra in America. If, on the other hand, he won the respect of their boards and the compliance of their conductors, he could control the entire industry.

He had a way with the men and women who founded and funded America's orchestras, speaking to them as one self-made success to another. 'Mr Judson always worked *with* the board,'[26] said a Stokowski ally in Philadelphia. 'Judson has never forgotten for a moment that he is a businessman, and he has never claimed to be a simon-pure idealist,'[27] noted a journalist. He talked dollars and common sense and the benefactors trusted him implicitly. They liked the way he always paid cash for his concert tickets, never accepting a free seat.

When dealing with maestros, Judson introduced himself as a 'disappointed conductor'.[28] But he had observed in Stokowski all he needed to know about the insecurities of an orchestral conductor and he made no obeisances before their pedestal. Blessed with a gift that could not be appreciated without a good orchestra, conductors were an easily unsettled, furiously jealous species and Judson stoked their anxieties. Recruiting new batons all the time, he gave each maestro the impression that there would always be someone to replace him if he did not obey Judson's law. The big three – Toscanini, Koussevitzky and the disaffected Stokowski – were beyond his command, but the rest succumbed tamely enough. Any guest conductor who showed promise at Philadelphia or New York was signed up on the spot by the orchestral manager's private company.

He was building the biggest concert agency ever seen, with the inimitable Jascha Heifetz at the head of his soloists' list and dozens of lesser lights who also needed to eat. When a Judson conductor took charge of an orchestra, he was expected to follow agency instructions. Massimo Freccia, Italian maestro at New Orleans, received a letter that read: 'Dear Freccia. So-and-so is a marvellous pianist, a Hungarian. You must engage him. Regards, Judson.' Freccia naively asked to hear the candidate play first. Judson's response was a frosty silence. He did not like having his authority questioned. His decisions, said a journalist, 'leave no room for appeal – there is no higher court of judgement.'[29]

It was Judson's boast that, in seventy years at the summit of musical affairs, he never interfered in artistic policy.[30] This was not so much a lie as a mark of his benign detachment. Sitting on both sides of the fence, as manager of an orchestra and most of its soloists, he felt serenely impartial. If a conductor wanted to perform loss-making repertoire, he would veto it. That was not artistic interference, just realism. If a board was determined to give more dates than it could afford, Judson withheld his soloists until sanity was restored. It was in no one's interest for an orchestra to overspend. He was the voice of reason and the enemy of adventure. The unfamiliar was outlawed, the outrageous suppressed. Mahler, whose eighth symphony had given Judson the springboard to his career, vanished from American concert halls. Mahler required a large orchestra and expensive promotion. Why play Mahler when the public were satisfied with Beethoven? Otto Klemperer blamed his banishment by Judson from major podia on having programmed the *Resurrection* Symphony in New York to a predictably half-empty house. Had it not been for Koussevitzky's patronage of native composers in Boston and Stokowski's eclecticism in Philadelphia, American music in the Judson era would have narrowed to a thin band of proven favourites. 'Judson didn't seem to have any musical tastes,' recalls a conductor's widow. 'He'd talk about artists and tell gossip but I can't remember that he ever expressed a preference for any music at all.'[31]

Stokowski worked tirelessly to force modern music past his manager's veto. Seeking to strangle his sources, Judson volunteered in 1926 to run the International Composers' Guild, which fed Stokowski dangerous scores. The Guild, led by Edgard Varèse, should have been warned. It folded within a year, to Judson's quiet satisfaction.

But its successor, the League of Composers, had wilier leadership and in 1930 spurred Stokowski to his greatest gamble – the US ballet première of Stravinsky's *Rite of Spring*, twinned with Schoenberg's abstruse *Die glückliche Hand*. 'You cannot possibly think that you could fill the Metropolitan Opera House with that programme,' said Judson to the League's chairman, Claire Reis. 'You will really have all my sympathy if you insist on carrying out this programme.'[32] He begged the Philadelphia board to oppose the plan, but Mrs Reis had independent financing and Stokowski was adamant. The audience fidgeted through Schoenberg and roared for Stravinsky, landing Stokowski on the cover of *Time* magazine, the first maestro to enter that ephemeral hall of fame. He proceeded with Alban Berg's *Wozzeck*, followed by a Prokofiev ballet and *Pierrot Lunaire*. Judson, struggling with a runaway horse, held sway with the board until, in 1934, Curtis Bok was elected chairman and gave Stokowski free rein. Reaping a quarter-million-dollar deficit from an opera season that Stokowski conceived but refused to conduct, Judson announced his resignation. Weeks later Stokowski quit as well, accusing the board of failing to appoint an acceptable manager. The truth is, both were bored by Philadelphia and preoccupied elsewhere.

Judson, masking his 'intense dislike'[33] for Stokowski, stayed on just long enough to secure the podium for his favoured nominee. He managed Fritz Reiner, who was much liked by Philadelphia critics and taught at the Curtis Institute, but had a volatile Hungarian temperament and an independent mind. Judson decided instead to replace Stokowski with a balding teetotaller of low charisma. Eugene Ormandy, born Jenö Blau in Budapest, had caught Judson's eye in New York while leading the band for Isadora Duncan at Carnegie Hall. 'I came to see a dancer and instead I heard a conductor,'[34] said the manager.

Judson kept Ormandy busy with dates until a music director dropped dead in Minneapolis in 1931. Reading the orchestra's antiquated contract, Judson saw it had not taken in the advent of records and radio. The musicians were paid a weekly salary and could be deployed at no extra fee in whatever musical activity their management saw fit. Judson called an RCA record producer, Charles O'Connell, and told him he could record the Minneapolis Orchestra with Ormandy for free. O'Connell hopped on a train and recorded two sessions a day for a fortnight, including Sundays. By the end of his second trip he had a hundred works in the can and Minneapolis was the most recorded orchestra on earth. The organisation earned royalties of $163,362.58 over the next ten years; the musicians got nothing. 'Mr Ormandy was not paid for his heroic efforts,' reports O'Connell, 'but the records won him nation-wide attention and were largely responsible . . . for bringing about his eventual appointment as conductor of the Philadelphia Orchestra. That, I suppose, was sufficient compensation.'[35]

Philadelphia needed a celebrity, and no one matched Ormandy's fame on vinyl. He was thirty-seven years old, married-plus-two and modest to a fault; hard-working, meticulous and completely unimaginative. Under his kapell-meister-like conductorship in the next half-century, Philadelphia recovered its treasured reputation for dullness.

Stokowski went off to Hollywood, where he consorted with Garbo and made *Fantasia* for Walt Disney but could not settle. He returned to conduct the New York Philharmonic for Judson and rejoined his agency. For a while it was almost like old times as Judson orchestrated publicity for Stokowski's third marriage – to the heiress Gloria Vanderbilt, a girl forty years his junior – and audiences were smitten by his aura. But Judson refused to make him music director, splitting the title with the impressive Greek, Dmitri Mitropoulos. Stokowski objected, and the symbiotic partnership of maestro and manager broke up again in 1950, this time for ever. Unwanted in America, Stokowski cast in his lot with Beecham's agent, a gentle Hungarian named Andrew Schulhof who despatched him to England to conduct the Royal Philharmonic Orchestra, and onward into Europe. Schulhof was summarily sacked after five years' devoted service for the insufferable offence of letting a photographer sneak into a Stokowski rehearsal at Stuttgart; the conductor hated to be seen growing old. His fate, between leaving Philadelphia and a final nonagenarian flourish, was fractious, unfulfilled and tragic – doubly so, in the sense that it commanded little sympathy.

Judson, by contrast, was a picture of contentment. From twin power points on either side of West 57th Street, he controlled America's lynchpin orchestra and most of its concert artists. Elegant in English tailoring and a near-British drawl, he had kicked over his humble traces and modest musicianship to become supreme sovereign of all music in the whole of the United States. His ascent had been almost imperceptible. It owed everything to an uncanny sense of timing.

Back in 1916, as Philadelphia awoke to Mahler's eighth symphony, an assistant manager of the Marconi Wireless Telegraph Company of America sent a memo to his boss. 'I have in mind a plan of development,' wrote David Sarnoff, 'which would make radio a household utility in the same sense as a piano or phonograph. *The idea is to bring music into the house by wireless.*'[36]

Arthur Judson, playing with his son's crystal receiver one day, 'foresaw the potential of radio *as a means of disseminating music*'.[37] A brief spasm before the birth of mass media, two of the architects of broadcasting saw its purpose purely as a means of satisfying public demand for music.

Sarnoff, a Russian-Jewish immigrant who liked to be called 'General', applied for radio patents and acquired manufacturing interests. As makeshift stations sprang up in farmyard barns (the first was KDKA Pittsburgh in November 1920), he offered to link them by telephone. By 1926, he had twenty-five stations carrying the first World Series baseball game to fifteen million listeners. His embryonic National Broadcasting Company (NBC) was the only organised force in a rabble of two-bit independents. A typical station was WCAU in Philadelphia, sold in 1922 by its founder-engineer to a sharp young lawyer, Isaac Levy. Ike had many other ventures on the go, so to run WCAU he roped in brother Leon, a sybaritic dentist who wooed and in 1927 wed the fragile heiress to the Congress Cigar Company, Blanche Paley. Her brother, William Paley, college-educated son of Russian Jews, took an immediate interest in his in-laws' cat's-whisker operation.

Sarnoff was now ready to agglomerate. He raised a million dollars, bought a year's worth of telephone lines from AT&T and canvassed independents to take his national service. They could join either the Red or the Blue network, one slightly cheaper than the other, but in reality they had no real choice. Custom-made programming from NBC would be cheaper and more popular than local efforts, and most of the independents took up the franchise – though not Philadelphia's WCAU.

Arthur Judson had been waiting for this moment. In September 1926 he formed the Judson Radio Corporation to supply music to the NBC network. The new broadcasters had no expertise in the worlds of music. Judson would act as their intermediary. His proposal went to Sarnoff. When no reply was received, Judson went to the General and asked what he meant to do about his scheme.

'Nothing,' snarled Sarnoff.

'Then we will organise our own chain,' said Judson coolly.

'You can't do it.' The NBC chief laughed. It had taken him ten years to build the world's first broadcast network. No jumped-up music agent was going to steal his airwaves. He had taken care of musical programming by granting a consultancy to the conductor Walter Damrosch, whose New York orchestra was in the process of being dismantled by Judson. Damrosch, a metronomic practitioner of reactionary outlook, invented the NBC Music Appreciation Hour, a weekly sermon delivered to millions of schoolchildren which made him, in Sarnoff's tribute, 'America's leading ambassador of music understanding'.[38] NBC had Damrosch. It did not need Judson's offer.

Rebuffed but not dejected, Judson went straight from Sarnoff's office to see Betty Fleischmann Holmes, a Cincinnati yeast heiress on the New York Philharmonic board. He told her that NBC would pollute the airwaves with indecent vaudeville and promised to build a rival network on the sweet and uplifting sounds of symphonic concerts. Mrs Holmes wrote him a six-thousand-dollar cheque and Judson set up United Independent Broadcasters, Inc. Back in Philadelphia, where his orchestra was cock of the walk, the Levys became one of his sixteen founder-affiliates. The Columbia record company, worried by Sarnoff's take-over of its Victor competitor and swoops on music copyrights, gave him a hundred and sixty-three thousand dollars to buy telephone time. On 18 September 1927, an orchestral manager called Arthur Judson produced the inaugural broadcast of the Columbia Phonograph Broadcasting System.

It was an unqualified disaster. Judson had acquired a new American opera, *The King's Henchman*, by composer Deems Taylor and the popular poet Edna St Vincent Millay, with singers from the Metropolitan Opera, the Ohio-born conductor Howard Barlow and a twenty-three-piece orchestra plucked from the New York Neighborhood Playhouse. Just as they went on air, lightning struck the telephone system and half the affiliates received no signal. In the few cities that picked up the broadcast, the opera overran by seventy-five minutes, taxing the patience of advertisers and listeners. Columbia Records pulled out within a month, leaving its totemic name on the masthead. Only a forty-thousand-dollar float from the Philharmonic's Mrs Fleischmann Holmes (she would eventually sell her investment for three million dollars) kept the improvisatory network on air. Judson pressed on with a weekly concert series, the first, on 9 October, starring his new mistress, soprano Sophie Braslau.

Yet not everyone was unhappy. William Paley in Philadelphia saw sales of his La Palina cigars skyrocket from four hundred thousand a day to one million when Columbia aired the La Palina Smoker comedy hour. Paley had a million dollars of tobacco cash to burn and, aged twenty-six, rode to New York to rescue CBS. In September 1928 he got himself elected president. By the end of that year, with receivers now in ten million homes, the Columbia Broadcasting System had forty-seven affiliates against NBC's sixty-nine; by 1935 they were level pegging and taking profits of almost three million dollars a year.

Against the populism of NBC's *Amos 'n' Andy* show and the paternalism of Damrosch's lectures, Columbia positioned itself as the 'Tiffany Network', a broadcaster dedicated to quality and culture, to the best journalism and the highest standards. It had Toscanini and the New York Philharmonic every Sunday afternoon, Bing Crosby in his national début, Ed Murrow, Orson Welles. It was a class act. General Sarnoff, eat your heart out.

Paley owned the biggest stake in the network. The next largest was Judson's, amounting by his death in January 1975 to one-third of a million CBS shares. Anyone who had bought one hundred CBS shares at ninety dollars each when they were publicly quoted in 1932 could have made $682,832.55 on their quoted value in early 1975,[39] some seventy-five times their original worth. Judson owned foundation stock in CBS, and a lot more than one hundred shares of it. With the spread of affiliates and the birth of television, he became 'immensely wealthy',[40] almost beyond computation. Strangely, no one wondered where the overtaxed manager of three major orchestras had found the time and the vision to erect a media empire.

Money did not change Judson's life, apart from the purchase of a Connecticut estate with a swimming pool and his move to an uptown apartment, 'decorated with great taste and no individuality'.[41] He ate at good restaurants and became an ardent bibliophile, rewarding friends with rare editions of English classics. But he never contemplated giving up orchestras and becoming a mogul. He was too much of a musician for that. What he saw in CBS were the benefits it could bring to his musical enterprises. As a CBS director, he could sell the network hundreds of hours of orchestras and artists. His conductor, Howard Barlow, became the network's music director and his composer-chum Deems Taylor was the Sunday concerts commentator. He got Paley to buy the Columbia Phonograph Company in 1938 so he could fix new recording contracts for his New York and Philadelphia orchestras. When the network needed to appease federal commissioners, Judson coined the motto 'Good music equals public service' and plugged in extra concerts. He was in the happy situation of selling his own artists to his own company, fixing the prices and taking a cut on both sides of the table. That is how he liked to do business.

*   *   *

It is a measure of Judson's genius – and no lesser noun will do – that in the midst of creating CBS he pulled off the biggest coup of his career. In 1928, sensing a twin threat from regional organisers and an affronted NBC, Judson bought the Wolfsohn Musical Bureau and proposed a merger to four other agencies. He warned that operators in Los Angeles and Chicago were side-stepping New York agents and snaring their artists. Sarnoff, meanwhile, was forming an NBC Artists Bureau to feed talent to his network. Agents could not fight these forces single-handed. They could either amalgamate, or capitulate.

NBC opened its bureau late in 1928. The following year brought the Wall Street Crash and a collapse of concert bookings. By the turn of 1930, Judson had sweet-talked his competitors into accepting his terms. The six biggest New York firms linked arms as the Columbia Concerts Corporation, managing 'one hundred and twenty-five artists and organisations', or two-thirds of the top musicians active in America. CBS provided finance and Paley was named president of the new agency. Judson was chairman of the board and the largest stockholder. To have merged two hostile managements would have been a diplomatic *tour de force*; to combine five was a near-miracle of tenacity, vision and vigorous persuasion, proof of the unstoppable drive of the Judson juggernaut.

Each agent was allowed to keep an independent division within Columbia. Judson looked after his artists and Wolfsohn's; his latest recruit was Vladimir Horowitz. Lawrence Evans and Jack Salter had the young Yehudi Menuhin and Lawrence Tibbett. Francis Coppicus and Freddie Schang of the Metropolitan Musical Bureau handled ballet and opera tours, including the Trapp Family Singers. The Haensel and Jones office dealt mainly with new European artists. Together, they outgunned NBC and dwarfed any regional competitors. Columbia, said Judson, was 'the largest booking bureau in the world'.[42]

And so it remained, despite federal intervention in 1942 accusing both networks of running an illegal cartel in artists. To avoid a monopolies investigation, CBS and NBC sold the agencies to their directors. Judson renamed his firm Columbia Artists Management. The NBC bureau recon-stituted itself as the National Concert Artists Corporation (NCAC), forming an alliance with the flamboyant Russian-Jewish promoter Sol Hurok, but never challenging Columbia's primacy. The difference was easily discernible. NCAC had old-fashioned, hard-talking musical salesmen. Columbia had Judson.

'Arthur Judson possesses something rarer than insight,' eulogised his old friend, Olga Samaroff. 'He has *foresight*. Sensing the tendency of the age, he first proceeded to create a managerial coalition that all but controls the entire country. Instead of fighting among themselves, most important American musical managers are engaged in apparently peaceful concerted action under his leadership. The chief outcome of this joining of forces is the community concert.'[43]

Community Concerts grew out of an 'organised audience' movement started in the Chicago area in 1921 by Dema Harshbarger, a polio-stricken concert agent and her partner, Harry P. Harrison. Instead of sending out performers and hoping to get paid by local managers from ticket sales, Harshbarger whipped small-town enthusiasts into forming Civic Music Associations that raised the full booking fee in advance. Her scheme eliminated financial risk, along with a strand of provincial middlemen. Judson took a look and, together with a leading agent Daniel Meyer and five others, transplanted the idea to fifteen towns in New England. He saw it as a blueprint for winding a chamber music circuit around the United States and, ultimately, for extending Columbia's influence into every corner of the country.

He took the idea to Paley, who liked the thought of CBS stars trailing their acts all around the boondocks so much that he set up Community Concerts as a nation-wide operation under CBS control. NBC lured Meyer away and bought up Harshbarger's Civic Concerts. Lines were drawn across the land. There were Civic towns – two hundred and thirty-seven of them in 1933 – and Community towns, one hundred and twenty-five at the same count. Civic towns heard NBC artists, Community received Columbia product. Exclusively, and collusively.

Depending on the amount of money it raised, a city chose the level of artist it could afford. Nelson Eddy, Mario Lanza, Jascha Heifetz and Paul Robeson were among the top attractions. Less affluent places might be offered Joseph Szigeti or Rudolf Serkin, excellent soloists who were planning a tour of the region and had vacant nights. Wisconsin got to hear the French composer Francis Poulenc with his chosen chansonnier Pierre Bernac, a privilege that was rarely, if ever, afforded to remoter regions of France. Even a wayside town like Paris, Texas, could raise the cash for a concert of some kind. 'This corporation,' declared the Columbia Artists Almanac of 1931, 'claims that it is able to supply all concert demands, however great or modest, of every club, school or college, organisation or individual entrepreneur . . . In the task of recovery the solace and inspiration of music will play its accustomed part, and the artists listed in this book, couriers of that lovely muse, are ready and eager to spread the message of cheer and joy to the four corners of this great land.' There was a religious zeal to Judson's message and there were plenty of musicians in the 1930s, unemployed or exiled, who were willing to play for next to nothing. The Roosevelt administration took its cue from Community and Civic when founding the Federal Music Project in 1935, aimed at putting laid-off musicians back to work around the country.

'Our purpose was to step into the breach and to save concert management during the Depression rather than any great hope for a profitable business,' reflected Paley in a glow of philanthropic retrospection. 'We did indeed sustain some losses for a while but ended up making a modest profit.'[44] The musical mapping of America went ahead through the Depression and reached a peak of nineteen hundred towns by 1940, when the Justice Department intervened. It violated the Freedom of Speech amendment, said the feds, for entire towns to be treated as sole fiefdoms of a network subsidiary. CBS and NBC, fearful of Congressional interference, severed their ties with Community and Civic, and the market was supposedly opened to competition. Nothing changed, in fact. The two 'organised audience movements' continued to be run by Columbia and NCAC, each offering an exclusive list of artists to their subscriber towns.

It worked like a charm. The Community rep hit town for a week – 'a missionary of culture,' Judson called him. He addressed a banquet of leading citizens, sang the glories of Heifetz and Horowitz, launched a Community membership drive and departed with enough cash to book some of Columbia's lesser-known performers. 'It's not that we told them they couldn't book other artists,' recalled Harry Beall, one of a force of sixty-five field representatives. 'It would just never occur to them. You were the hero from New York. You gave speeches and were treated like royalty.'[45]

There were few complaints from the townsfolk, who were not hugely deprived by conflictual exclusivities. Most towns could not afford Heifetz and could not name another violinist. They received, on the whole, reliable performers, a raising of their cultural self-esteem and a considerate, attentive service. There could be nothing detrimental in that – except, perhaps, for the artists.

To a musician, a Community tour of middle America looked, on paper, irresistible. It provided a block of work and sell-out houses. The fees were respectable, the expenses moderate and the hospitality heart-warming. 'A famous singer, once under our management, was engaged to sing in a rough Pennsylvania mining town,' Judson related. 'When she arrived in the early morning a cold rain swept the dreary railroad platform. The enthusiastic Mayor was there with the public and a brass band to greet the prima donna. The tired and worn prima donna, half awake, stepped upon the platform and said, ''Great guns, why does my manager send me to a God-forsaken town like this?'' '[46] It was a manager's misfortune, sighed Judson, to reap a harvest of ingratitude for his venturous idealism.

Yet Community artists on the long and lonely trail often took to wondering why they were never offered big time Columbia dates and why they always came home flat broke. There were two traps in the Community contract. The first was cash – or, rather, cashlessness. Although the fees seemed attractive, artists only ever received a fraction. 'Where does all the money go?' demanded the British contralto Kathleen Ferrier. A singer booked for a thousand-dollar date might budget a hundred for the accompanist and another couple of hundred for travel and hotels for two, coming away with two-thirds of the fee. In Community country, she would be lucky to net thirty per cent.

The difference lay in what Community called 'the differential'. Before an artist got paid, Columbia took a twenty-per-cent commission. On top of that, Community – which was part of Columbia – took a second cut, usually another twenty per cent. Thus, of a thousand-dollar fee, four hundred went back to Columbia, thirty per cent went in expenses and the artist was lucky to be left with three hundred dollars, before tax.

'Without the differential, Community and Civic could not operate,' excused an apologist. 'They would have no source of revenue – that is, unless they changed their whole policy and exacted a flat fee from each association. This they do not want to do, for they hold that the artists who benefit . . . should be the ones to shoulder the expense.'[47] The truth was that squeezing artists was a lot easier than raising the cost of Community membership, easier indeed than taking candy from a child. Yet it was not loss of earnings that ruined performers but the Community tag that stuck to their careers like well-chewed gum. Once Columbia started taking forty per cent from a Community artist it gave up getting him conventional dates. 'The straight engagement nets Columbia twenty per cent, the Community Concert approximately twice as much,' reported the experienced violinist Henri Temianka. 'Community Concerts wins. The soloist anxiously trying to build his career is the loser. Of course, he rarely finds out.'[48]

A musician who became popular on the Community circuit was withheld from agents who took Columbia's orchestral bookings. In time, local fans realised that he lacked star rating and the small-town dates dried up. Van Cliburn, who started out as a Community pianist, was 'in an acute state of depression'[49] by 1958, his fourth season, when only five towns wanted him back. Happily, he entered the Tchaikovsky Competition in Moscow, won the contest hands down and returned to a ticker-tape parade down Broadway and the biggest-selling concerto album in history – another Columbia triumph, it seemed, until Cliburn tore up his contract and joined Hurok. Less resolute prize-winners got lost on a Community tour of Louisiana or gave up in Oregon, their dreams destroyed.

A brilliant immigrant Russian pianist, unrecognised by Columbia after two years with Community, threatened to quit unless he got a New York début. 'If he won't carry on, there are a hundred others to take his place,' shrugged his Community booker. 'The concert chains control the touring business in a manner closely approaching monopoly,' wrote the composer-critic Virgil Thomson. '[They] have almost a life-and-death power over musical careers.'[50]

Judson, who described Community as 'a healthy and progressive'[51] system, had an intriguing justification for its operating system. Columbia, he explained in a 1945 *Current Biography* article, had advanced a large amount of money to launch Community Concerts. That, he said, 'was a loan not to the communities *but collectively to artist clients*'. What he meant by this was that every hundred-buck pianist who played at Plainsville, Iowa, owed a share in a 1930 debt to the unbelievably wealthy Arthur Judson – and Judson was not going to be bilked of his rightful due. Staggering in its effrontery, this statement does reveal an essential truth about its author. Judson, whatever his musical ideals, was out to make money out of musicians. In an age when entertainment became a bi-media monopoly and artists were more in need of an agent's protection than ever before, the most powerful agent in America came out, in word and deed, firmly on the side of the exploiters. That, needless to add, is not quite the image he wanted enshrined for posterity. In a ninetieth-year interview, Judson spoke of 'the financial investment he [*sic*] made in . . . spreading the cause of good music to thousands of cities and hamlets across the nation'.[52] The underside of the operation was nowhere to be seen.

While America writhed in the coils of the Depression, Judson waxed ever more omnipotent. Every Wednesday after lunch he left Columbia's head-quarters and jaywalked across 57th Street, sitting for the next three hours in a darkened Carnegie Hall to audition a parade of talent. 'During the course of a year I hear hundreds of applicants and possibly pick ten who seem worthy of the effort of being "built up" into "names",'[53] he said. A young conductor, invited to sit beside him, heard a Parisian violinist give a dazzling exposition of difficult virtuoso pieces.

'What do you think?' said Judson.

'Incredible,' said the conductor.

'I agree,' said the manager.

'Are you signing him?'

'No.' Judson shrugged. 'There's something missing.'

The disappointed aspirant was Ivry Gitlis, a master of the instrument who never became a star, because Judson sensed a possible flaw in his make-up.[54] Whether Judson could have made Gitlis famous is anyone's guess; the trouble is, he would not make the effort unless a performer seemed perfect. 'You cannot force a success,' he liked to say. 'I don't believe in throwing money around in attempting the impossible by force.'[55]

'He was passionately interested in new talent and never bored by auditions,' said one of Judson's aides. 'Anyone who wanted could just turn up on a Wednesday afternoon and play.'[56] The line of aspirants was never ending. This, they knew, was the doorway to Shangri-la. Little did they imagine that few would be chosen and, of those who were, most would wind up in a dusty Community chest. Those who made the beginnings of a career were encouraged by Judson aides to drench the boss in flattery. 'As for Mr Judson, he is one of the greatest and most honest men I have ever met,' gushed the short-lived pianist William Kapell in a letter to the ever-watchful Ruth O'Neill.[57]

Judson was less choosy about conductors, needing large numbers on his books to supply the ever-growing band of American orchestras, which in the course of his lifetime would amount to half the professional symphony orchestras on earth. European conductors were encouraged to believe that if they wanted to work in the United States they required a Judson contract. 'It was like a green card,' says Massimo Freccia, who decided to emigrate when Benito Mussolini took an unsettling personal interest in his concerts. 'On the advice of Vincenzo Bellezza, a conductor at the Met, I wrote to the Judson office and was sent a contract by mail. I promised to give them fifteen per cent of any concert fees I got in America. In exchange I got – nothing.'

Freccia arrived in New York in 1937 and conducted at Lewisohn Stadium on Toscanini's recommendation. A Cuban lady booked him for four seasons with the Havana Philharmonic, then found him a better band in New Orleans. On both contracts Columbia exacted an unearned commission. Judson claimed credit for his next promotion, to the Baltimore Symphony Orchestra, although Freccia insists he secured the position independently. 'Judson came down once to hear me conduct at New Orleans and perhaps one more time at Baltimore,' says Freccia. 'He was my manager for twenty-two years and I saw him only a couple of times.'[58]

He knew all too well that there was no escape. Conductors who switched to other agents vanished from the map and those who confronted Judson were consigned to oblivion. In 1932, after a season in Cincinnati, Eugene

Goossens decided to stop paying Judson his commission. Goossens was a gifted Englishman of Belgian stock who had set up an excellent orchestra in Rochester, New York, for the Kodak philanthropist, George Eastman. A dozen years into his American career, he reckoned he did not need Judson any more. Judson called in Ralph Colin, the attorney he shared with Paley. After a brief exchange of lawyers' letters, Goossens was obliged to pay up his agent's commission, plus costs. 'I took my lawyer's advice and decided to settle out of court,' he told his parents lamely. 'Nevertheless, I was and still am in the right.'[59] Whatever the rights and wrongs, Judson made sure he never got another job. Goossens, hoping to inherit Boston or New York, was stuck in Cincinnati until 1946, when he departed for Australia. He remained a Judson artist to the end of his life, and Judson did not lift a finger on his behalf – doubtless *pour encourager les autres*. No one ever denied AJ his rightful due.

Once a Judson conductor took over an orchestra, it became Columbia property for ever. On elevating Ormandy to Philadelphia, Judson handed his Minneapolis post to Mitropoulos. Moving Mitropoulos on to New York, he gave Minneapolis to the Hungarian Antal Doráti, whom Judson duly replaced at Dallas with the assistant New York conductor, Walter Hendl. Reiner in Cincinnati relinquished his podium to Goossens, before taking Pittsburgh from Judson's Otto Klemperer. Goossens's post in Rochester went to Columbia's José Iturbi. In a nation-wide game of musical chairs, Judson owned the players and manipulated the positions. His major gaps were Chicago, under the veteran Frederick Stock, and Boston, where Koussevitzky had an aesthetic distaste for Columbia. But Judson had ways of neutralising hostile forces. He took both sons of the Boston Symphony Orchestra manager, George E. Judd, to work for him at Columbia. Koussevitzky's beloved protégé Leonard Bernstein was taken on as a Columbia artist and assistant conductor in New York. Like a medieval warlord, Judson held hostage the sons of neighbouring chieftains to assure himself of their docility.

With most orchestral boards eating out of his hand, their managers were exceptionally deferential. Many owed Judson their jobs. When he had something to tell them, he called a national gathering. In 1942, facing the threat of a wartime entertainment tax, his informal reunion consolidated into the American Symphony Orchestral League (known by its coarse acronym, ASOL). Calling on his Cincinnati Symphony connections with Senator Robert Taft, Judson led ASOL's successful lobby of Congress against the tax. He was a keynote speaker at ASOL conferences for many years and won Columbia a uniquely privileged position with the increasingly influential symphonic association.

Judson had prudently avoided any practical investment in opera. The Met hired out its artists for concert recitals for the same commission as Conried once took, only it now used the income to balance the budgets rather than feather its manager's nest. In 1916 it devolved the concert careers of some singers to the Metropolitan Musical Bureau formed by Francis Coppicus and Frederick Schang, and when that firm was merged into Columbia Judson found himself with nightingales under his roof. He relied on a long-term mistress, the retired opera singer Sophie Braslau, to advise him on operatic lore and looked after such Met eminences as Jussi Björling, Lily Pons, Grace Moore and George London. Bill Judd, his young trainee, forged links with New York City Opera. Before long, Columbia won the dominant position in opera that it already held in concert life.

It was also going global. In February 1937 Columbia set up office in Vienna 'to promote a more active international exchange of artists and organisations between Europe and North America'.[60] The firm shut down a year later when the Nazis marched in, and Judson's man, André Mertens, moved to Manhattan. Once the war was over, however, wider ambitions were quickly rekindled. Judson was not content with being the biggest in America. He wanted to rule the world.

Even Arturo Toscanini, whose dictatorship of American music seemed absolute, needed to reach a private accommodation with its *de facto* controller. He and Judson shared an anti-modern, illiberal outlook, but distrusted one another. To safeguard their domains as conductor and manager of the New York Philharmonic, Judson erected a boundary wall and sent his assistant manager Bruno Zirato running missions along the top. Zirato's job was 'to make sure [Toscanini] would always have someone to whom he could express any dissatisfaction, and to report any problems to Judson'.[61] Zirato had been hired by Judson back in 1922 while mourning his former employer, Enrico Caruso, with whom his main responsibility had been to play endless games of cards on performance days to protect the great tenor's voice from wasteful conversation. A Neapolitan fixer with shady contacts, Zirato knew little about music and less about singing, an innocence underlined in an opportunistic little book he wrote on Caruso's vocal method. He was, however, a delightful man, tall, garrulous and 'a lovable rogue' with the ladies. With Zirato as buffer, Judson and Toscanini barely needed to acknowledge each other's existence. For taking care of Toscanini, Zirato was rewarded by Judson with a key job at Columbia, handling daily communications with his conductors. Zirato, in due course, controlled their access to Judson. That was his power, and he used it to the best of his sinisterly charming ability.

Toscanini raised Philharmonic standards to levels unheard since Mahler's day. His resignation in 1936, announced as his retirement, was widely lamented and left Judson with an unfillable vacancy. His board wanted to appoint the Berlin conductor Wilhelm Furtwängler, provoking protests from Jewish and anti-Fascist groups. Toscanini preferred Artur Rodzinski, a headstrong, combustible Pole whom Judson disliked. Judson proposed John Barbirolli, an unheralded Englishman of limited experience. The Cockney-sparrow grandson of a Scala violinist who played in the première of Verdi's *Otello*, Barbirolli was imbued by equal measures of tradition and romanticism. He was thirty-six years old and conducting in Glasgow when a telegram arrived from Judson telling him to drop everything. Judson, who had been in touch with Barbirolli since 1928, produced recommendations from Heifetz and Horowitz praising his concerto accompaniments. He wanted a trouble-free conductor and later confessed to 'misgivings'[62] about the callow appointment but he could not deny his original enthusiasm and personal sympathy for Barbirolli. 'I admired Judson for having the courage to take John,' says Lady Barbirolli. 'Where it went wrong is that he never supported John. Probably, he wanted someone unknown who would do as he was told. John had a mind of his own.'[63]

Toscanini learned of the appointment while summering in Italy and swore terrible vengeance against Barbirolli and Judson, 'offended by this lack of respect'.[64] Abandoning plans for a twenty-five-concert American tour with the New York Philharmonic, he agreed to receive an emissary from the mighty kingdom of David Sarnoff. The intermediary, a maestro worshipper named Samuel Chotzinoff, arrived with a proposal to create a new radio orchestra in New York for Toscanini to conduct, in flagrant opposition to Judson's Philharmonic. It did not take him long to decide. 'Very surprised [your] acceptance radio proposal,' cabled Zirato to Toscanini, acting as ever on Judson's instructions. 'Want to know if Maestro considered bad effects this contract would make *our* season.'

'Was surprised at your surprise,' replied Toscanini. 'I will ask nothing of Sarnoff, who will arrange things to suit his own interests just as the Philharmonic has done and will always do.'

'You are wrongly advised and falsely informed,' retorted Zirato.[65]

The situation was developing into a full-blooded vendetta when Judson, who abhorred confrontation, calmed things down. Much as he resented NBC's coup, he held enough cards to secure a peaceful co-existence. Rodzinski, whom Toscanini wanted as his 'drillmaster'[66], was a Judson conductor, guesting with the Philharmonic. If NBC needed any more conductors, it would have to get them from the same source. Chotzinoff, who built the orchestra, was married to the sister of Jascha Heifetz, Barbirolli's referee. Toscanini's own son-in-law, Vladimir Horowitz, had his career in Columbia care. Judson possessed enough ammunition to inflict serious discomfort on the Toscanini enterprise, and the Toscanini clique knew it. Chotzinoff, doubling as a music critic, offered an informal truce by writing in a review that fears of a slump in Philharmonic support when Maestro returned were proving groundless (Barbirolli's Philharmonic audiences were, in fact, larger than Toscanini's had been). Sarnoff, fearful of federal curbs, ordered NBC publicists to play down rivalries and signal the birth of a radio orchestra as a means of 'encouraging the support of local symphony orchestras everywhere'.[67] He willingly agreed not to play Sunday afternoons, when Philharmonic concerts were aired on CBS.

Judson 'never mentioned Toscanini,' remembers Lady Barbirolli, 'too close to the knuckle.' Toscanini, for his part, besmirched Barbirolli to his cronies but avoided public criticism of the Philharmonic or its manager. Years later, he apologised to the English conductor for having behaved 'like a pig'.

Barbirolli's five Philharmonic seasons were embittered by Toscanini's 'lies and innuendos'[68], compounded by libels circulated by a jealous Thomas Beecham to orchestras and music societies ('If Beecham felt it was worth writing to everybody,' said Judson to Barbirolli, 'he must have thought you are pretty good.'[69]) There was insubordination from Toscanini loyalists in the orchestra and the Philharmonic's financial constraints forced the Englishman to conduct twice as often as the Italian, leaving him doubly at the mercy of the New York critics. Judson, who kept Lawrence Gilman of the *Herald Tribune* and Olin Downes of the *Times* on his payroll as programme annotator and intermission commentator for Philharmonic concerts, dismissed Downes in mid-season. The *Times*'s chief critic then let it be known, amid a string of vile notices, that he 'would never accept Barbirolli'.[70] Judson, asked why he had unnecessarily offended the mighty scribe, said, 'Oh, I thought I'd get myself a better man.' Gilman died in 1939 and was replaced on the *Tribune* by the composer Virgil Thomson, a committed Beechamite with a vinegary turn of phrase. As the press turned poisonous, Judson comforted Barbirolli and shed tears at his occasional ovations. 'I think there was a softer side to him,' says Lady Barbirolli. 'He genuinely liked John, but in the end he would not stand by him.'

The end came in 1941, with the Barbirollis returning to bomb shelters in Britain and the Philharmonic entering its centenary season without a chief conductor. For the next two years the orchestra lacked artistic direction.

Koussevitzky was approached, but withdrew on the death of his beloved wife. Finally, against Judson's better judgement, the combustible Rodzinski was named musical director in 1943.

The previous twenty years had been the most turbulent in New York Philharmonic history. Yet whether the orchestra improved or declined, grew rich or poor, one man stood above criticism. Judson was deemed infallible by his directors and, when he erred against anyone else, he had the muscle to avoid being named. In the depths of the Depression, he took on the unions by suggesting a merger of the Philharmonic and Met orchestras. The musicians issued an appeal, imploring concert patrons to 'prevent any concert bureau or artists' manager (with their multiple interests at stake) from obtaining an almost complete control of these important institutions in the American musical world'. Judson's name was never mentioned. Violently as they loathed him, union bosses knew that Judson did not like to see his name in the newspapers and they dared not violate his taboo. He was too awesome to be crossed.

An authorised history of the Philharmonic, published in 1975, gives the board's-eye view of Judson as an immaculate administrator with a good business head. 'Since Judson's flair for making money out of music led him constantly to seek expanding audiences,' wrote the head of Columbia University's music department, Professor Howard Shanet, 'he could honestly combine profit-making with the democratic ideals of public service and reconcile his private business interests with his administration of the New York Philharmonic.'[71]

Honesty and democracy, the watchwords of George Washington, were thus officially attached to Arthur Judson. If the Defence Secretary of the United States had been running a private arms dealership from his Pentagon office, there might have been a twitch of public concern. If he additionally co-owned a warplane factory and a clothing concession for the Marines, his impartiality in Cabinet discussions on issues of war and peace could conceivably have been called into question. In the timid world of music, however, no one dared suggest that Judson might be swayed in the slightest by inadmissible personal interests. The music press was comprehensively muffled. *Musical America*, the trade bible where Judson had cut his professional teeth, was now secretly in partnership with him. 'It was an interlocking corporation with Columbia,' said one of its editors. 'There were certain artists of other agencies we were simply not allowed to review – Mischa Elman was one of them, I remember. If they weren't reviewed in those days in *Musical America*, they didn't get booked in middle America.'[72]

The grapevine was rife with rumours of Judson's corruption, but none was

117

ever printed or proven and the gossip served only to increase the perception of his power. 'I don't know of artists who paid kickbacks to AJ,' said one orchestral manager, 'but I do know of situations where young artists were told by him "we're going to have to make an investment in promotion. Pay $10,000." '[73]

'In his own terms, he is inviolably honest,' commented a music journalist, Cecil Smith. 'He is always being loyal to someone or some interest, no matter how much evidence there may seem to be to the contrary. He may be being loyal to an orchestra and its public, or simply to the art of music, when he refuses to settle one of his importunate conductors in a position for which he does not think the conductor is equipped. He may be showing loyalty to some better pianist when he refuses a booking to one of his pianists who would dearly love to have it. By sentimental standards, Judson is not always a friend to his clients. He will not go through hell and high water to get them everything they want. He will try to get what he thinks they ought to have, without violating his other allegiances.'[74] In his celestial sway over music and its tiresome mundanities, Judson began to assume the attributes of deity.

His sixtieth birthday in February 1941 marked the apex of his authority. For services to music – unspecified, but possibly connected with a grateful pianist, Robert Casadesus – he was awarded the Order of the Academie des Beaux Arts by the government of France. In America, he shunned recognition. His music empire had earned him what William Randolph Hearst and Howard Hughes craved but for all their wealth could not procure: the power to be unseen.

Any concert goer, asked to name the biggest music mogul, would have picked Sol Hurok, who billed his own name bigger than his stars. Hurok introduced America to Anna Pavlova and Leonide Massine; toured the boondocks with Feodor Chaliapin and Arthur Rubinstein; discovered Jan Peerce, Andrés Segovia and Isaac Stern. He presented Marian Anderson before a seventy-five-thousand-strong multitude at the Lincoln Memorial after the Daughters of the American Revolution barred the black contralto from Washington's Constitution Hall. Few were aware that Anderson had been with Judson until, dismayed by a lack of bookings and racist slurs, she fled to Europe. Hurok revived her career as 'the voice of a race'. He fostered the legend of a galaxy of stars who longed for nothing more in life than the privilege of appearing beneath the rubric 'S. Hurok Presents'

In the mêlee of social gatherings, Judson would tower above the company saying very little. 'The fact he didn't speak much made him appear stronger,' thought Lady Barbirolli. His magnitude and taciturnity magnetised the opposite sex. 'He was good-looking and a tremendous womaniser,' said an agent's wife. 'It's alleged that he had many affairs,' said an aide. 'He had the reputation of being something of a stallion,' the Barbirollis heard. Shortly before the war he took a second wife, Daphne – 'a meek little woman, American middle class,' recalled Freccia. 'I think he needed someone at home to tell him how wonderful he was,' felt Lady Barbirolli.[75]

It is comforting to imagine that Judson's compulsion for secrecy exposed a domestic yearning for reassurance, a human weakness in the music machine. At work, the only vulnerability ever seen was an occasional over-reaction to the unmanageable and the unpredictable. So efficiently had Judson regimented American music that the range of ideas he received was as homespun as any *Time* reader's and he was caught unprepared by the perfumed iconoclasms of composer-critic Virgil Thomson. Fresh home from the fleshpots of Paris, Thomson trained his cosmopolitan monocle on music in New York and disliked almost everything he saw and heard. He deplored the taste for Sibelius, lion of embattled Finland, described a Heifetz recital as 'silk-underwear music', belittled Barbirolli, sniped at Toscanini and quoted his artist-boyfriend's comment on the New York Philharmonic as 'not a part of New York's intellectual life'. His motives did not preclude vanity or self-interest. 'The general standard of music reviewing in New York had sunk so far that almost any change might bring improvement. Also, I thought perhaps my presence in a post so prominent might stimulate performance of my works,'[76] said Thomson. Conductors like Beecham and Ormandy who programmed his fluent prairie suites and Francophone symphonies were assured of favourable reviews. Others received tart, though rarely sanguinary, reproofs.

The article that incensed Judson came at the end of Thomson's second week as chief critic of the *Tribune*, when he dismissed the black soprano Dorothy Maynor as 'immature vocally and immature emotionally'. Columbia, unused to such cavalier treatment, called a board meeting and, so Thomson was told, threatened to withhold concert advertising from the *Tribune* until the presumptuous chief critic was sacked. The ultimatum, from Judson's office, carried the implication that Philharmonic ads might also be cancelled.

Word reached Ira Hirschmann, a pianist's husband who ran a Sunday chamber music series and worked weekdays as advertising manager of Bloomingdale's department store. He told the *Tribune*, 'Mr Thomson has not yet reviewed my concerts unfavourably, though he well may do so. But whatever happens I shall match, line for line, any advertising you lose on his account.'[77] Judson was thwarted, but Thomson did not forget him. In a book, *The State of Music*, published a year beforehand, the composer had pledged 'to reveal the manipulators of our musical distribution for the culturally retarded profit-makers that indeed they are'. Thomson had Judson in his sights but, as a hedonist and dilettante ('I was out to have fun,' he confided[78]), was prepared to bide his time.

His opportunity arose in February 1947 when Rodzinski's tenure at the Philharmonic, never tranquil, ended in furious recriminations. Rodzinski was not, by any lights, an easy man. His photograph could have illustrated an aspirin poster: tense, nervous headache. He had inherited martinet tendencies from Toscanini and was a preaching convert to Moral Rearmament, a self-important evangelical movement with authoritarian undertones. He kept a goat farm in Massachusetts and was convinced that his milk and cheese could cure America's chronic dyspepsia, as it had his own.

He had given orchestral managers in Los Angeles and Cleveland a rough ride and he blamed Judson, his agent since 1926, for failing to appoint him Toscanini's heir at the New York Philharmonic, an injustice re-echoed in his wife's memoirs:

> The power-loving manager had gnawed his lip and chewed his cigar through an eleven year Toscanini reign. With Maestro gone, Judson saw his chance to take control. Barbirolli would program according to the manager's tastes, invite the right soloists and conductors (all from the Columbia Artists stable) and generally behave himself. Judson knew that in Rodzinski he would have another strong-willed, musically-independent artist of the Toscanini and Stokowski stripe, a man who would take no orders . . . For a fact, Judson had not helped Artur to a single post, and any guest engagements he got were usually through his own efforts. Artur had never forgiven Judson for advising the Cleveland Orchestra's board against him. Nevertheless, he was under personal contract to the man and regularly paid Judson his percentage, a sum that seemed and felt more and more like payments to an extortionist . . . 'I will not suffer this quietly,' he said.[79]

Had they felt this way about each other in December 1942, Judson would never have given Rodzinski the New York job. The orchestra cried out for artistic leadership, but Reiner, Georg Szell and Pierre Monteux were all available, not to mention Stokowski. Clearly Judson and Rodzinski came to some kind of initial understanding.

It lasted exactly six weeks. In February 1943, Rodzinski demanded the dismissal of fourteen players, one seventh of the orchestra, including the concertmaster Michel Piastro. Rodzinski had first consulted Toscanini, who told him to do what he felt necessary. He then went to Judson, who urged him to seek divine guidance before making any rash decisions. Rodzinski returned next morning, saying he had prayed to God, who told him: 'Fire the bastards.'[80] Judson relieved him of the duty of telling the victims, but someone leaked the list to Olin Downes, who lambasted the orchestra's management in the *Times*. Eleanor Roosevelt appealed for clemency. Union boss Jimmy Petrillo ordered the remaining players not to sign new contracts. Rodzinski was threatened with impeachment.

Judson, fielding the flak, met quietly with Petrillo. He reinstated five men and raised minimum salaries in the orchestra from ninety to one hundred dollars a week[81] (he got even with Petrillo four years later with the Taft-Hartley Bill, a law drafted by Cincinnati Senator Robert Taft penalising union funds). The storm died and Rodzinski, surprisingly, won over the orchestra by treating them humanely. He would cut short rehearsals on a fine day to take his little son for a stroll and he initiated social activities for the players' wives. His programmes incorporated more gentle modernities and his attendances were generally high. Nevertheless, rumbles of volatility were never far below the surface.

.He would interrupt rehearsals with a proselytising MRA sermon. He was said to carry a loaded gun in his back pocket. He once grabbed Leonard Bernstein by the throat after catching him playing truant. Judson extricated the frightened assistant conductor and sent him away on tour. Rodzinski went around slandering Bernstein, saying he had given him the job because he was the only young American conductor out of uniform. He became ever more irritable as Bernstein's concerts and compositions gained front-page notices and national acclaim.

Thomson, knowing Rodzinski's antipathy to Judson, praised him to the skies. He was 'healing neuroses' in the orchestra, bringing 'a faint blush' to the string sounds, variegating the repertoire. 'Today,' wrote Thomson on 9 February 1947, 'the Philharmonic, for the first time in this writer's memory, is the equal of the Boston and Philadelphia orchestras and possibly their superior . . . Artur Rodzinski has done more for the orchestra in that respect than any other conductor in our century has done. Mahler and Toscanini were greater interpreters, not such great builders.'

Six days earlier, Rodzinski had appeared before the Philharmonic board to discuss a new contract. Such matters would normally have been settled between himself and Judson, or between his lawyer, Allen Dulles, and Ralph Colin – who, in addition to being the CBS and Columbia attorney, was also a director of the Philharmonic. But Rodzinski was unhappy and asked to address the board. He denounced first the contract, then Judson, calling him 'a dictator who made musical progress impossible'. As Judson paled and Colin muttered 'This can't be true', he added, 'As manager of many soloists and conductors, Judson engages as many of his own clients as appearances will allow. He uses the Philharmonic as a testing ground for unproved performers. He uses it to give them publicity. And, of course, he doesn't run from the profits he reaps.'[82]

The next day Rodzinski resigned, announcing his secretly negotiated transfer to the Chicago Symphony Orchestra. He also went public. 'The three pillars of a soundly run orchestra,' he declared, 'are the board, the manager and the musical director. As the New York Philharmonic is run, these three pillars are not of equal importance, as they must be. The board and musical director revolve around the manager as if they were satellites.' The invisible Judson was finally exposed, and the press had a field day. Rodzinski made the cover of *Time*, and *Newsweek* carried a major feature.

None delighted more at the manager's embarrassment than Virgil Thomson. 'Arthur Judson,' he wrote, naming the devil for the first time, 'is unsuited by the nature and magnitude of his business interests to manage with the necessary self-effacement a major intellectual [sic] institution doing business with his other interests.' The *Herald Tribune* devoted an editorial to the theme. Everyone sat back and waited for Judson to be sacked.

It never happened. The manager, unruffled, brought in the ultra-respected Bruno Walter to serve as musical adviser while he took his time appointing a successor with the full support of his board. Rodzinski, by contrast, fell out with the Chicago board inside nine months and went into tailspin. 'The man's a trouble-maker,' Judson told other orchestras. 'You'll regret getting mixed up with him.'[83] Rodzinski suffered a nervous breakdown and his devoted wife begged Judson to forgive him, for the sake of his sanity. Judson, ever the gentleman, received her graciously in his office. 'I have always had a warm spot for you, my dear, but I could never get along with your husband, and I don't intend to try now. I don't ever want to see him again,'[84] he said firmly. Rodzinski died in 1958, his reputation in tatters. Judson was not a vindictive man, but his empire was constructed on pledges and threats and from time to time, as he demonstrated with Goossens, he needed to enforce his writ. When Eugene Ormandy tried to settle the Thomson affair by asking Judson to find the critic work as an orchestral conductor, the manager was immovable. He informed Thomson, in no uncertain terms, 'that he had been angered by my denunciation, that he was now more than ever my enemy, and that he would remain so'.[85] As a conductor, Thomson never got past first base. Nor would anyone else who affronted the supreme authority.

Rodzinski went to his grave convinced that Judson was utterly corrupt, taking kickbacks from the players he had refused to fire and plunging his hands into the Philharmonic till. The fact that he was independently wealthy made no difference; rich men always like to make more money, he said.[86] Judson associates say he was a scrupulous orchestral manager, knowing that any false accounting or whiff of bribery would have been detected by the businessmen and women who packed his boards and paid his wages. He was also careful not to overload the Philharmonic with his own soloists. Barely a quarter of New York's guest artists were Judson clients; a further quarter belonged to his Columbia partners. Apologists say the key difference between Rodzinski and Judson was not that the manager wanted more of his own soloists but that the conductor wanted more stars than the budget could support. The same apologists added, rather stretching credulity, that the commission Judson drew in any season from soloists' fees was less than the personal cheque he paid to the Philharmonic to buy his own concert seats.[87]

Whatever the truth in Rodzinksi's charges and for all the mud Thomson could muster, Judson's position at the Philharmonic was unaffected. He installed another of his clients, Mitropoulos, as music director and permitted him more modernities than ever before. Audiences shrank from his challenging concerts, senior musicians hated playing dissonant scores and directors muttered that Judson, now in his seventies, was losing his grip. But the orchestral budget, Judson's invention and lifelong adjunct, was firmly balanced, though it topped a million dollars for the first time in 1947 and a million and a half five years later.

The orchestra was still playing every Sunday on CBS – joint proprietor: A. Judson – and its European tours in 1951 and 1955 were significant cultural victories in the developing Cold War. A British administrator who got the better of Judson in a minor tiff over Edinburgh Festival broadcast fees was surprised to find him accepting the setback with good grace, 'He came up to me and said, "well done!" There was nothing mean about him.'[88]

'More and more,' wrote a sympathiser, 'Judson seems less the czar people once thought him to be than a substantial, gentlemanly link with a past and – we now like to think – less naughty era of the concert business . . . Judson's continuing regard for the values of a generation ago, combined with his hesitation (I wish one might say his complete refusal) to go out after a quick but meaningless dollar, makes him seem old-fashioned . . . Already there is a tendency on the part of musicians to forget their one-time heat and see Judson as a solid citizen upholding values that are in danger of being crowded out.'[89] He had time for unhurried conversation, especially with conductors who entered his office and tried to avert their eyes from the magnificent desk of many drawers that stood in the corner, his famous 'contract desk'. 'As a young conductor, you dreamed of the moment when AJ took you by the arm and led you to the contract desk to start your career,' recalls one visitor.[90]

Sensing his relaxation, the Columbia partners who had endured his writ for twenty years staged a *putsch* against his presidency in 1950, shooting down his proposal to inaugurate a lecture division and replacing him as head of the company with Ward French, chief salesman for Community Concerts. Judson accepted the reversal with apparent equanimity, as he could well afford to. He was still the biggest stockholder in an agency that managed one hundred and fifty conductors and soloists and thirty-five ensembles, controlling more than half America's bookings of classical talent to a value of twenty-five million dollars a year. Judson personally retained the all-important conductors' list. His Community venture was at the height of its profitability. His CBS network was opening the silver casket of television. His New York orchestra was gaining international renown. And his own role had reverted to near-invisibility. At seventy-five years old, Arthur Judson could look out across his empire with undisguised satisfaction, for he and Columbia had achieved a superpower status that fulfilled the poet's fond vision:

> O, Columbia, the gem of the ocean
> The home of the brave and the free,
> The shrine of each patriot's devotion,
> *A world offers homage to thee.*

NOTES

1 attrib. Thomas à Becket
2 Finck, p. 443
3 Finck, p. 443
4 Roman, p. 467
5 Roman, p. 482
6 Roman, p. 393
7 Samaroff, p. 50
8 Howe, pp. 86–7
9 Damrosch, pp. 128–9
10 Samaroff, p. 51
11 Hughes, p. 102
12 Samaroff, p. 323; cf also Hart, p. 59
13 Chapin, p. 60
14 Smith, p. 38
15 Freccia, author's interview
16 Smith, p. 38
17 Samaroff, p. 321
18 Audrey Michaels, author's interview

19 Unless specified, all Judson quotes in this chapter are from *The Etude*, January 1940, pp. 6–7, 'The Making of a Name' by Arthur Judson.
20 Ruth O'Neil, quoted in Daniel, p. 154
21 *Musical America*, 26 October 1912
22 Daniel, p. 189
23 Kupferberg, p. 49
24 interview with William Malloch
25 Chasins, p. 126
26 Mary Louise Bok, in Daniel, p. 320
27 Smith, p. 34
28 Daniel, p. 315
29 Smith, p. 33
30 Hart, p. 71
31 Lady Barbirolli, author's interview
32 Reis, pp. 92–3
33 Daniel, p. 342
34 Kupferberg
35 O'Connell, p. 66
36 Lynes, p. 41
37 Hart, p. 79
38 Horowitz, p. 203
39 Metz, pp. 316–17
40 Schuyler Chapin, author's interview
41 Lady Barbirolli, author's interview
42 *The Etude*, loc. cit.
43 Samaroff, p. 321
44 Paley, p. 330
45 authors interview in *Classical Music*, 29 October 1994
46 *The Etude*, loc. cit.
47 Smith, p. 62
48 Temianka, p. 216
49 Temianka, p. 215
50 *Herald Tribune*, 21 January 1951
51 *The Etude*, loc. cit.
52 Hart, p. 83
53 *The Etude*, loc. cit.
54 interview with Antonio d'Almeida
55 *The Etude*, loc. cit.
56 Chapin, interview
57 Roger Gross Ltd sales catalogue, December 1995
58 author's interview
59 Rosen, p. 156
60 *Musical America*, 10 March 1937, p. 19
61 Sachs, p. 217
62 Hart, p. 89
63 author's interview
64 Sachs, p. 255
65 Sachs, p. 257
66 NBC, p. 11
67 Horowitz, p. 159
68 Kennedy, p. 133
69 Lady Barbirolli, author's interview
70 Kennedy, p. 130
71 Shanet, p. 249

72 Gene Bruck, author's interview
73 Philip Hart, author's interview
74 Smith, p. 39
75 author's interviews with Lady Barbirolli, Belle Schulhof, Schuyler G. Chapin, Massimo Freccia
76 Page, p. 147
77 Thomson, p. 325
78 author's interview, 1985
79 Rodzinski, pp. 151–2
80 Hart, p. 90
81 This was no small salary. A hundred a week was exactly what Elizabeth Taylor was earning at MGM that year for her appearances in *Lassie* films. An orchestral musician in the 1940s was a citizen of consequence. 'If you played in the Symphony,' recalled Isaac Stern, 'you were someone – a *pay-son.'*
82 Rodzinski, pp. 289–90
83 Rozdinski, pp. 318–19
84 Rodzinski, p. 321
85 Thomson, p. 391
86 information from Richard Rodzinski
87 Smith, p. 38
88 Sir Ian Hunter, author's interview
89 Smith, pp. 34, 40
90 Jonathan Sternberg, author's interview

CHAPTER VI

HEY DIDDLE DIDDLE, THE SILVER FOX AND THE FAMOUS FIDDLE

T he President of the United States played the piano. His daughter, Margaret, sang arias. While Harry S. Truman nuked Hiroshima and brokered the Cold War, his only child set her heart on a soprano career. Success did not come easily and she was 'starting to feel very discouraged' when an opportunistic conductor in Detroit, Carl Krueger, offered her a début, which was broadcast nation-wide. 'The entire Truman Administration was glued to the radio at 8:28 Eastern Standard Time on March 16, 1947,' recalled Margaret happily. Orchestral bookings followed in Pittsburgh, Cleveland, the Hollywood Bowl and, inevitably, in the capital, Washington, DC.

Music critics, gifted a chance to strafe the White House, dipped their nibs in acid. The President responded with a note to Paul Hume, critic of the *Washington Post*. 'Mr Hume,' wrote the head of the most powerful nation on earth, 'I have just read your review of Margaret's concert . . . Some day I hope to meet you. When that happens, you'll need a new nose, a lot of beefsteak for black eyes and perhaps a supporter below. Harry S. Truman.'

'I never claimed that I was one of the great singers of all time,' said Margaret Truman, 'but I did feel that I had achieved professional competence.' This was not a feeling widely shared within the profession and her career petered out before her father left office in 1952. It left, however, one lasting resonance.

In 1948 Margaret Truman got herself an agent, James A. Davidson, 'a topflight professional who handled only a small number of first-rate singers'[1] as well as the faltering affairs of the unsettled Fritz Reiner. When she complained about the trickle of bookings, Davidson sat Margaret down and told her the facts of life: that the concert circuit was controlled by Columbia and NCAC, which blocked other agents from getting their artists into affiliated towns and cities. 'You had better tell that to my daddy,' said Margaret. In no time at all, Davidson and his partner Kenneth Allen were in the Oval Room elucidating the iniquities of the music business to the President of the United States. 'Get me J. Edgar Hoover,' was his reaction.

The Federal Bureau of Investigation, busily rustling alleged communists out of Hollywood, dragged its heels for seven years on the music case. Finally, in October 1955, it gave the Department of Justice enough ammunition to file suit, in the Southern District Court of New York, against four defendants: Columbia Artists Management (CAMI), its subsidiary Community Concerts, NCAC and its offshoot, Civic Concerts.

The charge was that 'beginning in or about 1933 and continuing thereafter', the companies had 'combined and conspired in unreasonable restraint of interstate trade and commerce in the management and booking of artists and in the formation and maintenance of organised audience associations, and . . . monopolised said trade and commerce in violation of Sections 1 and 2 of the Sherman Act'.

It was hands up and surrender for the 'organised audience' game. Pleading *nolo contendere* – no contest – the guilty parties paid a token penalty of twenty-six thousand dollars, plea-bargained on their behalf by Judson's attorney, Ralph Colin. The real punishment lay in a slip of paper they were forced to sign, promising to release their stranglehold on regional concerts and open them up to artists from other managements.[2] By signing the so-called 'consent decree', the two big agencies confessed to having acted together as a cartel to control American music-making. 'Because of legal hazards it has always been difficult to document specific instances of close co-operation between the two giant booking agencies,' noted one orchestral manager, 'but from personal experience . . . I can testify that I was myself involved in such "gentlemen's agreements" and was well aware of their operation in other situations.'[3]

Having carved up the country between them for so long, the two colossi were unable to function in a free and open market. NCAC and Civic were hurriedly sold off to a baritone, Luben Vichey, and sold again to the Summy-Birchard Company, steadily falling to pieces; Sol Hurok alone escaped from the wreckage. Community Concerts survived, but was never the same force. By 1987 it posed such a minimal threat that rival agencies agreed to the lifting of the 'consent decree'. With fewer than five hundred customers and only seventeen field representatives, Community was begging managers to loan their stars to its wizened roster in the hope of rekindling local enthusiasms. The solo vocal recital, once a Community mainstay, had withered on the vine; big singers were no longer prepared to tour the boondocks, and no one wanted to hear also-rans. An attempt by the mezzo-soprano Marilyn Horne to revive the art-song evening proved quixotic. Community Concerts was a distribution network with a declining product line.

As for Columbia, the loss of Community income and the shame of judicial exposure rocked the empire to its foundations. Ward French, the Community salesman who removed Arthur Judson from the presidency in 1950, was himself sacked for trying to grant 'a decent degree of independence' to local promoters just ahead of the consent decree. His successor, Frederick C. Schang, decried the 'French Revolution' that aimed to sunder Columbia from Community Concerts – only for that wedge to be driven fatally home by the federal courts.

Columbia, said one manager, 'was a snakepit – all the directors were biting each other'. The founding partners were near retirement and anxious to protect their pensions, while younger bloods were jockeying for a position that had never been vacated. Aloof from the Lilliputian strife stood Arthur Judson. The principal stockholder rarely descended now to the general office from the sixteenth storey where, with the trusted Bruno Zirato, his Philadelphia aide Ruth O'Neill and his Boston princeling William ('Bill') Judd, he ran the Judson, O'Neill and Judd Division of CAMI as a walled-off private enclave. O'Neill was, additionally, treasurer of the entire corporation. No sum, however small, could be disbursed without her reluctant signature. 'Columbia was in chaos,' recalls a young assistant, Schuyler Chapin, 'but Judson held the power, because Judson controlled all the conductors.' He called the shots at most American orchestras and still managed the New York Philharmonic, though not for very much longer.

Nemesis arrived one springtime Sunday morning in April 1956, in the form of a *New York Times* headline: 'The Philharmonic – What's Wrong with It and Why'. The orchestra was going through a rough patch. Attendances had slipped from two hundred and fifty-two thousand in 1949–50 to two hundred and twenty-eight thousand latterly – due mainly, it seems in hindsight, to the rival attractions of domestic television. The *Times*'s new chief critic, Howard Taubman (Olin Downes having died in August 1955), went to every concert for nine months before delivering his verdict on the orchestra in a full-page piece, blasting conductor and management for the blight.

The playing had become imprecise and the tone coarse, wrote Taubman. The conductor, Dmitri Mitropoulos, was a poor trainer, 'overmatched by the requirements of the Philharmonic post'. His attempts to modernise the repertoire were compromised by a 'lack of delicacy' in classic and romantic works. The players felt mutinous against the conductor, and each other; there were 'divisions among the men on a basis of nationality and religion'.

The board lacked a 'vibrant up-to-date philosophy' and the manager had an external interest in looking after fifty conductors. All but one of the Philharmonic's guest conductors were represented by Columbia, as well as more than half the soloists. 'It should be emphasized,' wrote Taubman cautiously, 'that there is not the slightest evidence of wrongdoing. But disaffected people, with or without axes to grind, keep insisting that the Philharmonic is being used to magnify reputations of Columbia artists.' No-hopers from Columbia appeared as soloists with the Philharmonic, while hot stars like Lisa Della Casa and Victoria de los Angeles could not get a look-in. 'Would it not be better if there were an independent management in charge of the orchestra?' demanded the *Times*.[4]

The *Herald Tribune* followed up this attack with three successive Sunday diatribes by Paul Henry Lang, describing the Philharmonic as 'a deteriorating artistic institution' and blaming its decline on Judson. 'It is indefensible,' echoed Lang, 'for a person involved up to his neck in the exploitation of the concert industry to serve at the same time as the paid manager of what to all intents and purposes is a public trust.'[5] The charges were no different from the ones that Rodzinski and Thomson had trumpeted a decade earlier and which, said Judson associates, remained groundless as ever. 'When Zino Francescatti, who was a Judson artist, played concertos with the Philharmonic, I saw Judson send back his commission to the orchestra,' said Columbia salesman, Harry Beall. 'Judson never made money from the Philharmonic while he was its manager.'[6]

There was no denying, though, that the orchestra was in poor shape. Its NBC competitor had been disbanded on Toscanini's retirement in 1954 and complacency prevailed. Under pressure from two newspapers, the directors finally took decisive action. In an annual report, published in September 1956, president David M. Keiser thanked the press for 'valuable recommendations' which were under 'active consideration'. By the start of the new season in October, Judson had been retired as manager and Mitropoulos had been demoted from Musical Director and obliged to accept his one-time acolyte Leonard Bernstein as joint principal conductor, and successor-in-waiting.

An era was over, and Judson's enemies rejoiced. What they failed to perceive was that the same hand still pulled the orchestra's strings and would do so for some years to come. The new Philharmonic manager was Judson's deputy and Columbia employee, Bruno Zirato. He retired in 1959 to make way for Columbia's former press chief, George E. Judd jr, whose brother, Bill, was Judson's partner. On George Judd's death of cancer in 1961, the next manager was Carlos Moseley, an ex-pianist who owed his first job in the press department to Judson. The arch of influence continued to stretch across West 57th Street, from CAMI headquarters to Carnegie Hall.

Bernstein loathed Judson, but could not have got to the top without him. Denied Koussevitzky's mantle by upper-crust trustees of the Boston Symphony Orchestra, Bernstein's baton prospects sputtered through the McCarthy years, sustained periodically by a grudging word of encouragement from his manager. 'Judson told some friends of mine,' reported Bernstein in 1955, 'that it was time for the Philharmonic to get a Jew there as conductor so that it can get out of the doldrums it is in. The old bastard said that he doesn't like me much, but that I was the only guy around that fitted the bill.'[7] Stripped of its crude hyperbole, that statement has an authentic ring of Judsonian legerdemain.

Bernstein was put up for the New York job by the departing Philharmonic manager, and sworn in by Zirato, his puppet successor. It proved the most exciting appointment the Philharmonic ever made, tripling audience numbers and reaffirming the Americanness of the orchestra's repertoire and musicianship. His was a musical Camelot to match John F. Kennedy's at the White House. He was a Broadway hero and a household name, mobbed at Young People's Concerts, master of ceremonies at Kennedy funerals, handsomer and more lusted after than any American musical hero of his time, bar Frank Sinatra. He owed all this to the position that Judson won for him at the Philharmonic and on CBS Records and television. He must have known that Judson would call some day to collect the debt.

The only organised resistance to Columbia came from Sol Hurok – and the notion that Hurok was organised strains the tolerance of English usage as much as his much-quoted Goldwynisms. 'When people don't want to come,' Hurok would say in his deep Russian-Jewish accent, 'nutting vill stop them.'

He was a master of the bifocal aphorism. 'If we sell out, we'll lose less,' he said. 'Of all the great people in the world, I have the smallest ego.' He loved to see his name in lights and persuaded Hollywood to make a movie of his life, *Tonight We Sing*. He even got them to tone down his colourful accent, solemnly emphasising, 'This is the story of a successful man.'[8] Judson, from his patrician height, looked down on Hurok as a frumpish, greenhorn hustler. 'AJ considered himself more genteel than Hurok,' recalls CAMI staffer Mary-Ann Zeitlin, 'but Hurok had more flair.'[9]

Hurok lived on a diet of daily enthusiasms. 'I am a hero-worshipper,' he said. 'I belong to that fraternity who crowd the aisles, run down to the platform and stand agape, eyes turned upwards, until the last encore. I am one of that clamorous throng that rudely wedges its way into dressing-rooms after each performance. I am star-struck!'[10] 'I don't think he was capable of the truth,'[11] said the dancer, Agnes de Mille, who was married to Hurok's chief associate, Walter Prude. Scrambling free of the disintegrating NCAC he turned eastward for new blood, to the land of his birth some seventy years before. Dealing with Russia was a hazardous business in the mid-Fifties, risking arrest as a spy or blacklisting as a communist. Several Hurok artists, among them the choreographer Jerome Robbins, had been grilled by McCarthy's committee on Unamerican Activities. Paul Robeson had fled the country. Aaron Copland's music was deemed unfit for a presidential inauguration. Leonard Bernstein had his passport confiscated.

Behind the thought-war, however, there were stirrings of a post-Stalin thaw. President Eisenhower met the Soviet leadership in Geneva in July 1955 and reopened cultural exchanges. Three months later, under State Department auspices, Russian musicians began streaming to America for the first time since the Revolution. Emil Gilels caused a box-office stampede in Philadelphia and drew every pianist for miles around to his Carnegie Hall début. David Oistrakh introduced the recent violin concerto by Dmitri Shostakovich. The 'Red Cellist', Mstislav Rostropovich, heralded as heir-apparent to the crown of Pablo Casals, gave a recital tour. All three were managed by the Schang Division of Columbia, through the agency's formidable connections in Washington.

Hurok could not watch this influx and do nothing. He flew to Paris and contacted Soviet cultural officials and 'interpreters', one of whom, Edward Ivanyan, was about to be assigned as watchdog on Rostropovich's US tour. Hurok convinced Ivanyan, in eloquent Russian and at expensive restaurants, that Soviet interests in America would be better served by a man like himself, who understood the Russian soul. Ivanyan found the Columbia people 'stingy

. . . and not very pleasant to deal with' (or so he told Hurok's biographer)[12] and advocated a change of agency.

Hurok, in the meantime, sent his two favourite artists on a goodwill mission to the USSR. The violinist Isaac Stern and tenor Jan Peerce were Jewish-Americans of Russian extraction, able to communicate uninhibitedly with musicians, audiences and officialdom. 'We send them our Jewish violinists from Odessa, and they send us their Jewish violinists from Odessa,' quipped the ebullient Stern,[13] whose cheery tour paved the way for a Hurok visit to Moscow, his first in two decades.

Hurok came out with contracts to tour the Moiseyev folk-dance ensemble, followed by the Bolshoi Ballet, David Oistrakh and the populist Armenian composer, Aram Khachaturian. By 1958, he held an informal monopoly for presenting Soviet artists in the US, adding spice and vivacity to a humdrum, sophomoric culture of Hitchcock thrillers and John O'Hara novels.

The profits Hurok earned were considerable – close to a million dollars on the Moiseyev tour alone – and the prestige incalculable. He achieved the improbable feat of gaining the confidence of the Soviet authorities and of their often-unhappy artists. If musicians looked hungry, he fed them at his own expense; when KGB goons docked their *per diem* for the cost of free meals, he slipped the players discreet wads of cash. 'With Hurok you felt protected,' wrote Rostropovich's soprano wife, Galina Vishnevskaya. 'Wherever you appeared with him in New York – be it a restaurant, an elegant store, or a splendid hotel lobby – you would be noticed and indulged, not because you had come in with a rich and famous man, but because if you were with Hurok, you had to be important.'[14]

Bypassing the state music agency Gosconcert, Hurok dealt with the Minister of Culture, the fearsome Madame Furtseva. When Rudolf Nureyev fled West, Hurok obtained personal permission from Nikita Khrushchev to continue presenting the defector without prejudice to his Moscow connections. He covered his back by feeding tidbits about the Soviet leadership to an ill-informed US intelligence service.

Columbia could only gaze in frustration as Hurok snatched their trophy and raised himself from the commercially dead, disguising an often-precarious liquidity behind a dazzling front of showmanship. His list, never large, boasted 'The brightest stars of Music, Dance, Theatre, Film, Radio, TV and Records'. Apart from a handful of singers – Maria Callas, Janet Baker and Victoria de los Angeles – Hurok's artists overwhelmingly reflected his own ethnic make-up. In a brochure that featured Nathan Milstein, Gregor Piatigorsky and Henryk Szeryng, the defining personalities were Arthur Rubinstein among established stars and Isaac Stern at the head of the rising sons. Rubinstein and Stern represented the Hurok style at its most combative, and it was their artistic morality that engineered confrontation with Columbia, which aspired at best to moral neutrality. Arthur Judson's artists were told 'to avoid anything remotely associated with political sentiments that might offend the business power structure'.[15]

Battle lines were drawn in 1948 when Wilhelm Furtwängler, a Judson client, was approached to succeed Rodzinski at the Chicago Symphony Orchestra. Furtwängler was hesitant, anticipating trouble from his arch-enemy Toscanini and from victims of the Nazi regime with which he had been publicly, though uncomfortably, associated. He finally consented to an eight-week probationary season. News of his return provoked uproar. Heading the protests were Vladimir Horowitz, Toscanini's son-in-law, and Arthur Rubinstein, who had lost two sisters and most of his family in Nazi death camps. 'I will not collaborate, musically or otherwise, with anyone who collaborated with Hitler, Goering or Goebbels,' said Rubinstein in a telegram to the orchestra, issued to the newspapers. 'Had Furtwängler been firm in his democratic convictions, he would have left Germany. Many persons like Thomas Mann departed from that country in protest against the barbarism of the Nazis. Furtwängler chose to stay and chose to perform, believing he would be on the side of the victors . . . Now he wants to earn American dollars.'[16]

A score of soloists pledged to boycott Chicago if Furtwängler conducted there, among them Piatigorsky, Heifetz, Milstein and Stern. Yehudi Menuhin took the conductor's side and Milstein soon recanted his condemnation, saying he saw no difference between a German conductor and the Nazi rocket scientists recruited by the Americans in 1945. Rubinstein replied that the scientists and their knowledge were 'spoils of war' rightfully claimed by the victors; German musicians, on the other hand, could use their public position to inseminate Nazi ideas in the United States.[17]

As the enormity of Nazi crimes dawned upon America, reactions were understandably heated. The German pianist Walter Gieseking was arrested in New York by immigration officers days after his arrival and sent home without playing a note. The union boss, James C. Petrillo, pledged to block the issue of work permits for German fellow-travellers. A union activist added, 'Furtwängler will never come to Chicago. He wouldn't have an orchestra to lead.'[18] As tempers rose, neither the Chicago Orchestral Association nor Columbia Artists spoke out in defence of the absent conductor. A sheaf of testimonials from musicians he had saved from the Nazis was never shown to the press.

After a fortnight's furore, Furtwängler announced his withdrawal, claiming – in contravention of his normal pretence at political naivety – that he was the victim of a sophisticated conspiracy. He was determined to expose the plotters and, four years later, told the Vienna Philharmonic that he had 'just learned from a reliable source that Hurok was one of the chief figures in the fight against my engagement in Chicago'.[19] Hurok had told the impartial Bruno Walter that he would do 'everything in his power' to keep Furtwängler out of America.

The agent proved as good as his word, scrapping a 1952 Vienna Philharmonic visit when the orchestra stood by the contentious conductor. Furtwängler was convinced that Hurok was taking his instructions from Toscanini, 'who was determined to prevent [his] appearance in America at all costs',[20] but Hurok had nothing to gain from currying favour with the declining Maestro. A conscientious member of anti-fascist, democratic-left organisations, Hurok had raised pre-war appeals on behalf of Republican Spain. He had also lost family in the Holocaust. His campaign of retribution, however, was not self-impelled but artist-led – driven by Rubinstein, who swore he would not make music with child-murderers, and by Stern who throughout his illustrious solo career refused ever to set foot on German soil.

Furtwängler died in November 1954. A Berlin Philharmonic tour, organised by Columbia's André Mertens for the following spring, was taken over by Herbert von Karajan, an unrepentant, card-carrying ex-Nazi. There were demonstrations outside Carnegie Hall and denunciations from Petrillo and Jewish organisations. Two concerts sold out in advance; the third was hit by a boycott and heavily 'papered' with a non-paying audience.

Mertens, whose sympathies lay with ravaged Europe, brought the Berliners back in 1956 without further disruption. The connection he formed with Germany's super-orchestra and its unprincipled conductor would prove valuable to Columbia in the long term, giving the agency a European foothold and favoured status with Karajan's future powerhouse. It also served to define an inherent difference between Columbia and its main domestic competitor.

What Hurok's artists had raised in the Furtwängler affray was not so much the case of an individual morally ambivalent musician (a case so compelling that forty years later Ronald Harwood and Harold Pinter made a stage-play of it) as the question of whether music existed in a moral vacuum. Were musicians to stand silent while minority races were murdered in Europe and stigmatised in the American South? Could music ignore the Soviet invasion of Hungary and America's saturation-bombing of Vietnam?

The Columbia line was that music was a business like any other and had no cause to poke its nose into other people's politics. Hurok had some sympathy for this view and certainly never criticised Soviet human rights abuses while he was amassing Moscow gold. But Hurok was a hostage to his artists in the Furtwängler affair and was unable ever after to restrain their outrage. While Columbia sent musicians to perform in racially segregated Alabama halls, Hurok artists led civil rights marches. When Israel was surrounded by Arab armies, Hurok musicians flew in to play solidarity concerts in the desert. When the arms race ran out of control they drew up mass petitions. Right or left, they took the ethical high ground and defended it vehemently. Columbia, by contrast, took no stand on any public issue. In the eyes of young musicians Columbia was a WASP-led, conservative, faceless corporation, while Hurok's was multi-racial, artist-led and socially committed. Given the choice, young artists preferred Hurok's.

Isaac Stern was the firm's conscience. Born in the former Pale of Jewish Settlement in 1920 and brought up 'poor as a church mouse' in San Francisco, the stubby, pugnacious Stern made his concerto début at sixteen and was acclaimed at Carnegie Hall in 1943. Blessed with a commanding stage presence and a distinctive tone of unsentimental warmth, he was sharp enough to know he would never outplay Jascha Heifetz and hungry enough to need an alternative supremacy. 'The greatest influence of our time was Heifetz,' he admitted. 'Because I had such an awe for what he did, I let my awe remain untouched by jealousy and chose another way of saying something. I wish I played better. I know people [who] can play rings around me. But my whole being is made up of wanting to know not *how* you play, but *why* do you play.'[21]

If he could not be the greatest living fiddler, Stern would make himself the godfather to violonists. No sooner was his own career up and running than Stern searched out talented kids in shanty-towns, got them an instrument and saw them through the Juilliard School, where his friends Ivan Galamian ('he could take a chair and teach it how to play') and Dorothy DeLay applied the finishing touches. Early protégés came from the new state of Israel, where Itzhak Perlman and Pinchas Zukerman formed a so-called 'Stern Gang' or 'Kosher Nostra' that grew to include Gil Shaham, Shlomo Mintz and Yefim Bronfman. Later on, Stern plucked Yo-Yo Ma and Midori from urban tenements. 'Isaac has produced more fine players than anyone,' said DeLay. 'There have been so many over the years and not all became stars. Some are good orchestral musicians or teachers. But he'll do the same for anyone. I've known him call his dentist to fix the teeth of kids who were no great shakes musically.'[22] Stern said all he was doing was emulating those who had helped him as an immigrant child – 'it was in the air, a tradition that was instilled in me unconsciously' – but not every rags-to-riches star remembers to repay his social debts. There was a moral imperative about Stern, and he instilled it insistently in his children and protégés. His daughter was ordained as a rabbi. Successful beneficiaries were expected to help his latest fledgelings with coaching, advice and engagements.

Raised on folk memories of pogroms and persecution, Stern showed a heightened awareness of world events. 'I'm not a politician,' he told me, 'but whatever they do affects you and your children. So you have to be aware to some degree, to get over this terrible feeling of impotence about what is being done to you by others.' Hurok once told him that musicians were better at diplomacy than politicians. Stern sniffed the wind and ran ahead of the State Department in forging cultural links with the Soviet Union and China. He was among the first to propose state aid for America's arts – an idea that was anathema to Arthur Judson, who had reason to resent federal intervention in artistic affairs. Judson declared 'a repugnance of government subsidy'[23] but Stern sensed that the Kennedys were willing to incorporate cultural renewal in the New Frontier and played his heart out at a White House recital. A Congressional report warned meanwhile that the Soviets were winning the battle for hearts and minds by portraying Americans 'as gum-chewing, insensitive, materialistic barbarians' and themselves as 'a cradle of culture'. Congressman (later Senator) Jacob Javits, a friend of Hurok's, spoke of 'an enormous propaganda weapon which the Russians are using against us, with the most telling effect, all over the world'.[24] Hurok, summoned to testify on Capitol Hill, implored legislators to provide funding for America's arts.

In 1965, after four years of deliberation, Congress established a National Endowment for the Arts and Isaac Stern was co-opted on to its Council. There was no sudden rush of government funds – seven million dollars at first, rising to one hundred and sixty-seven million in three decades – but the decision marked a reversal of national indifference. It was a testament to the persuasive power of a committed musician and his business minder.

Although he played at the White House for every president since Kennedy it was on the New York stage that Stern scored his greatest political triumph. In 1955 Arthur Judson announced that the New York Philharmonic would abandon Carnegie Hall for modern, purpose-built premises at the Lincoln Center on 62nd Street. America's most august concert venue would then be demolished and replaced by an office block, or a parking lot. Musicians were appalled; Bernstein raged from the Philharmonic rostrum; but only Stern took action. 'You want to know how Carnegie Hall was saved?' he reminisced around his seventieth birthday. 'The real beginning was a Passover Seder I attended at the home of Rabbi Israel Goldstein. It was an ecumenical Seder with people of all faiths there, and I was seated beside Bob Wagner, who happened to be the Mayor of New York . . .'[25]

Wagner remembered going to concerts as a child and told Stern that if he could raise enough support, he would go with him to Governor Nelson Rockefeller and demand state legislation enabling the city to effect a compulsory purchase. Stern collected signatures from every musician of consequence, from Pablo Casals to Bruno Walter, and rounded up donors to pay for the hall's upkeep. The state law was enacted in June 1960, hours ahead of the growling bulldozers, and the city of New York became a musical landlord. It leased the hall to a non-profit Carnegie Hall Corporation, with Isaac Stern as its president. Thirty-five years later, he was still president. 'As they say in the song, "I Just Can't Say No",' he laughed. When a centennial refurbishment was required in 1986, Stern chased around the donor circuit and raised fifty million dollars to pay for it.

Whatever causes he took on, Stern's violin-playing never slackened. He embraced strenuous concertos by Berg and Bartók, Stravinsky and Shosta-kovich, gave the première of Leonard Bernstein's *Serenade* for violin and orchestra, and commissioned new works from Penderecki, Rochberg and Maxwell Davies. He recorded for CBS more than two hundred works by sixty-three composers. The trio he formed with Eugene Istomin and Leonard Rose brought chamber music to big halls. At his busiest, he played two hundred concerts a year.

But Stern was always more than a famous fiddler. He possessed a midas touch where money was concerned, buying up Stradivarius and Guarnerius violins as a young man for twenty to thirty thousand dollars each. Half a century later they were worth a hundred times more (and most of his collection was permanently out on loan to beginners). In his spare time he played the stock markets, achieving a comfortable upper-middle-class life-style – 'I'd love to have a private plane but I can't afford it,' he complained. He also earned handsomely from music, becoming America's highest-paid soloist, at forty-five thousand dollars a night. 'We give it all away.' Stern sighed; but his inflationary aspirations hastened the erosion of America's fragile musical economy, nursed so carefully through the course of its history by the almighty Arthur Judson.

It was Judson who felt the brunt of Stern's incursion. The rescue of Carnegie Hall made a mockery of the old man's future planning for the New York Philharmonic. The orchestra wound up in an acoustically disastrous hall facing nightly competition from Carnegie – which, with undisguised delight, turned up the heat by cutting seat prices. The Philharmonic lost close to a million dollars in its opening season at Lincoln Center.

Stern was 'the spiritual leader of Carnegie Hall – his speeches were like papal sermons,' said a fellow board member.[26] Lincoln Center lacked a figurehead of equal weight and lost out on public affection. In the clash of concert halls Columbia was the big loser. Its arch of influence no longer stretched across West 57th Street, from CAMI headquarters into the heart of America's music. Carnegie was in alien hands and the Philharmonic was adrift. Judson's omnipotence was broken, while the octogenarian Hurok was, with Stern's support, rompingly in the ascendant.

Stars of the new generation who would formerly have seen no escape from the Columbia clutch drank chicken soup around Stern's hospitable table. He befriended Lorin Maazel, Zubin Mehta and other luminaries of the podium. His empathy with Bernstein was so intense that he refused ever to discuss it in public. The 'Stern Gang' in its broadest constellation offered unaffiliated artists a gleaming alternative to Judson, haloed with ideals and untainted by sleaze. They could either accept admission to the Hurok fold or enjoy the benefits of mutual back-scratching with Stern and his circle. The myth of the indispensable manager was called into question, as successful young artists planned their careers collaboratively – 'I'll conduct your festival if you play a Brahms cycle at mine: my secretary will confirm the dates.' As the Sixties' climate turned libertarian, this independence option seemed so alluring that the giant Columbia was finally roused from its torpid self-absorption and forced to bring out the long knives.

It was around his eightieth birthday in February 1961 that Arthur Judson began thinking about a successor. Like all self-made rulers he was reluctant to let go and, like most of them, he refrained from grooming an heir who might unseat him prematurely. He had yielded the presidency of Columbia some years before but clutched the conductors' division possessively to his massive chest. Now, he finally let it be known around Columbia that, when the time came, Bill Judd would inherit his conductors and, with them, the power to manipulate concert life across America. Judd had a privileged upbringing and, unlike Judson, had never known hunger. 'He was a kind, dear and gentle person, a true Bostonian gentleman,' said his secretary.[27] He wore preppy shirts and had a half-hidden secret life, but his knowledge of orchestral affairs was encyclopaedic and his kid brother, George, was in charge of the New York Philharmonic.

Early in 1961, when the snows melted and spring blossoms came into bloom, the erect figure of Arthur Judson boarded a Pullman car at Penn Station and embarked on a coast-to-coast farewell tour of America's orchestras. To the assembled board of each ensemble, he introduced Bill

Judd as his heir. Conductors were informed by letter that Judson was bowing out and Judd was their new manager.

Then, something happened. Months later Judson went on a second Pullman tour with a different successor, a man no one in the orchestral community had heard of before. Exactly what transpired between the first tour and the second has never been revealed and thirty-five years later is still protected by vows of confidentiality. Asked about her husband's role in the crucial transition Elizabeth Weinhold, widow of Columbia partner Kurt Weinhold, said testily, 'That's an in-house affair and no business of anyone else.'[28] Other witnesses died with their lips sealed, or were bound to silence by the victorious heir. His name was Ronald Andrew Wilford.

Finding out what happened inside Columbia in the spring of 1961 is like reconstructing a lost concerto from scattered sketches without sight of the solo part. The central player in the drama will never reveal his role. But there are a few survivors who have nothing to lose from speaking out, and from their accounts there emerges a saga of intrigue and ambition that would do justice to a John Le Carré thriller. Bill Judd was a Smiley-type character, a dedicated department head of high intelligence who bore his domestic wounds with great dignity. In the summer of 1961 Judd lost his beloved brother, aged thirty-six, to cancer. He was distraught, but dared not take time off from CAMI, where his inheritance was under daily siege. One day he got a call from Jascha Heifetz ordering him to the West Coast. He could not resist a summons from that quarter and may have welcomed an escape from the plot-thickened atmosphere of 57th Street. Everyone in the office knew Judd had a fear of flying and, if he planned to spend the weekend in Santa Monica, would be gone for the better part of a working week. 'During those four days that Bill was on the road, Ronald Wilford moved in,' recalled Naomi Graffman, a secretary in the Schang Division. A Columbia manager, insisting on anonymity, takes up the story, 'There was a lot of turmoil. Wilford, who ran the very small theatrical division, chose this moment to call a crisis meeting. Judd was on the West Coast and could not get back in time. At the meeting, Wilford ousted Judd from the conductors' division. It was as simple as that.'[29]

The case that Wilford made to the meeting, and that Judd was not there to answer, was that the conductors' division lacked impetus and initiative. Judd was marking time rather than strategising growth. He was good with artists but could not see the larger picture. Since his brother's death, Judd had been hitting the bottle. He was potentially unstable. Someone – and no one is prepared to identify the speaker – someone at the meeting added that Judd was also a well-known homosexual.

This was not a word to be uttered lightly in 1961 when carnal relations between consenting males was an imprisonable offence and gay men lived in nightly fear of blackmail. It was especially not to be uttered at Columbia where, according to responsible reports, 'many of the managers were homosexual, and all were in the closet'. The furtiveness of their private lives added a conspiratorial strain to their managerial work, a further thread of intrigue in the CAMI web. The agency was, like British Intelligence, viewed as a gay enclave, profoundly insecure and susceptible to hostile penetration. As such, it mirrored the state of New York music in the early Sixties. A conductor's wife alleges, 'It seemed to us that being gay was a distinct advantage to anyone looking for career advancement. Whatever games [they] were playing to fool board members, the rank and file musicians knew. Bernstein, Mitropoulos and Schippers, fairly or otherwise, were so labelled and the impression was that they ran a "closed shop". The expanded circle, which included Copland and Barber, seemed to outsiders to be extremely powerful. Add to that, the collection of New York concert managers (excluding Ronald Wilford) were known to be gay.'[30]

Whatever social prejudices they suffered, gay men saw the artistic community as a haven where they could expect to find tolerance or benign disinterest. Whoever raised the homosexual issue at the anti-Judd *putsch* intended not only to attack the excluded Judd but to strike fear into every gay man in the music business. Abandon Judd, was the message, or we'll purge you all. It was imperative, declared one of Wilford's supporters, that Judson's division, the mightiest in CAMI, should not be entrusted to *'one of them'* – a phrase that has been quoted verbatim by three independent sources. No one around the table hated Bill Judd or despised him for his sexual preferences. They wanted only what was best for the company. And what was best in the fragile trade of artistic reputations was a conductors' chief who conformed to the normative expectations of American orchestras and audiences: clean-cut, discreet, clever, respectably married and emotionally stable. Ronald Wilford was the only man present who fitted the bill.

Throughout the discussion Judson kept his own counsel. There is even some question as to whether he was in attendance at the crucial meeting. He had been responsible for Columbia's recruitment of gay men. 'He hired talented men for a pittance because they had a hard time getting jobs,' confirmed Mary-Ann Zeitlin, a violinist's wife who worked for Judson. After Wilford's victory, she said, 'Judson suddenly claimed he never knew there were so many homosexuals at Columbia.'[31] He threw his weight behind the winner.

When Judd came home from the coast he found Wilford at his desk. He put up no resistance, bowed as he was by family tragedy and fearing, like all active homosexuals of his day and age, the implicit threat of exposure and abandonment. 'He just got drunker and drunker, and fatter and fatter,' said colleagues. 'I don't think he was psychologically equipped for all that responsibility,' said a Wilford supporter.[32] Judson, on his second farewell tour, explained that he had 'offered the conductors' division to Judd and was disappointed he hadn't grasped it with both hands'.[33] Wilford was more ambitious, a man after his own heart. If Bill Judd belonged to a Le Carré novel, Wilford seemed more at home in the world of Michael Dobbs's political thriller, *House of Cards*. Having won his first boardroom battle on an anti-gay ticket, Wilford would wind up one day shielding a top conductor from homosexual scandal.

His immediate conquest was satisfyingly complete. 'Judson adopted Wilford,' observed Belle Schulhof, wife of Stokowski's ex-manager. 'He loved him. He told other managers, "He is like my own son".'[34] That endorsement was priceless to Wilford as the two men travelled the orchestral circuit. It counted for less within Columbia where the founder, shorn of his conductors, was mercilessly treated as yesterday's man. 'He had this aura about him of a nineteenth-century empire builder, a Cecil Rhodes. He was a larger than life figure and he had done so much. He was the man who pioneered classical music in America,' said Mary-Ann Zeitlin. But his fellow-directors could not wait to get rid of him.

The impassive Judson countenance relaxed slightly as he ordered his martinis seventeen parts gin to one part vermouth and made time for office jokes and gossip. He came in one day as agents were flapping over Michael Rabin, the brilliant violin prodigy. 'Oh AJ,' fluttered Ruth O'Neill, 'what *shall* we get Michael as a birthday present?' Judson looked down from his six-foot-plus and drawled, 'A gun to shoot his mother.' His instinct was unerring as ever – Rabin would die of drug abuse at thirty-five – but his sense of propriety was faltering. Judson, in his prime, would not have permitted himself the luxury of rancour and there was some justification for CAMI directors to exclude him from sensitive deliberations.

Exactly what prompted his explosive departure no one knows. 'There were one or two things he wasn't included in and he hated, after having so much power, being treated as a figurehead,' said Mary-Ann Zeitlin, who left the building with him in summer 1963, two years after he yielded his conductors' list to Wilford. 'I think he just got mad at [Columbia president] Kurt Weinhold,' said Janice Roberts, who was married to Wilford.[35]

Whatever the trigger, Judson blew out with the faithful Ruth O'Neill at his heels, two octogenarians bent on vengeful rejuvenation. The faintly comic pair 'rented a small office a few buildings east of the CAMI headquarters on

57th Street, where they speedily set up what was in effect a government-in-exile', relates the pianist Gary Graffman. 'At first, this geriatric kingdom followed a benign course. Old friends and well-wishers were the only visitors, dropping in to pay homage to the deposed sovereigns. However, these sovereigns had other plans. One day Frederick Steinway, then affiliated with his family's piano company next door, stopped by to pay his respects, and found himself seduced . . . "Before I knew what was happening, they offered me a job." '[36]

Next to join was Harry Beall, an ex-Community salesman who worked at the Boston Symphony Orchestra. 'Ruth O'Neill called via a mutual friend in Boston and said Judson wanted to see me,' recalled Beall. '"Don't take off your coat," she said when I arrived. I'll never forget AJ's opening words. He said, "God is a damn fool to let me start a new company at the age of eighty-two. But I will pay the bills and you will do the work." '[37]

In November 1963, the month Kennedy was assassinated, they went into business as Judson, O'Neill, Beall and Steinway, known for short as JOBS. It was to be Judson's last stand. Throughout that winter Columbia shivered in fear of defections. Judson was so confident of corralling conductors that a press release boasted of Leonard Bernstein's recruitment. The New York Philharmonic maestro owed Judson his job, and the debt was due for repayment. But Judson could not get past Bernstein's secretary. Three months after the press statement the conductor sent a letter to his former manager, copied to the *New York Times*, ordering Judson not to use his name.

Bernstein no longer needed Judson, or Columbia, or all they stood for. He had formed his own company, Amberson Enterprises, to manage his compositions, his conducting and his television films. His personal income was bigger than most agencies' turnover and his secretary spent much of her time fending off engagements. Bernstein had put the past behind him. He never saw or spoke to Judson again.

With Ormandy, the let-down was considerably more painful. Judson had plucked the Philadelphia conductor raw from the banana boat and earned him a celebrity that, many believed, vastly exceeded his natural talents. Ormandy, it was said, would not cross the road without consulting Judson. 'In Judson he confides as in a father,' wrote his record producer, 'and this has been to their mutual profit; for AJ is lord of all conductors (except two or three) and wisely chose, years ago, to put golden opportunities in Eugene's way.'[38] It was rumoured in podium circles that Ormandy paid Judson thirty per cent, twice the normal commission. 'The only one of us he was interested in was Ormandy,' said the Baltimore conductor, Massimo Freccia.[39]

Judson waited weeks for Ormandy to call his new number. 'Each had an enormous ego, and neither would ask first,' remembered Beall. 'When Judson finally swallowed his pride and called Philadelphia, Ormandy said, "Thank you very much for all you have done, but I have decided to stay with Ronald Wilford." '[40] In a subsequent conversation, Ormandy protested, 'But *you* taught me to love Ronald so well that now I cannot leave him.'[41]

'The crucial artist was Ormandy,' said an orchestral manager. 'If Ormandy stayed with Wilford, then Judson was fixed – and Ormandy stayed with Wilford. There was a strong feeling among musicians that Ormandy had really double-crossed Judson.'[42]

Judson, incensed by the betrayal, blanked the Hungarian out of his life. 'Ormandy bombarded him with letters which Judson binned unopened,' said Beall. 'Finally the Philadelphia Orchestra manager called and begged us to make peace between them, because Ormandy was becoming impossible.' A tearful public reconciliation ended four years of silence, after which Ormandy told an interviewer, 'I owe him [Judson] everything.'[43] That same year, Ronald Wilford provided Ormandy with overwhelming cause for gratitude.

In 1968 Wilford brought to an end Philadelphia's thirty-year contract with CBS Records and set up a five-year, two-million-dollar deal with their opponents, RCA Victor. The budgets were unprecedented and the recordings, predictably enough, unremarkable. Ormandy conducted the same old repertoire in the same unexciting manner. The records sold in driblets and the outcome was the eradication of RCA as a classical entity. When the contract was completed in 1973, the label called off all further orchestral projects and became a backlist distributor. Deprived of competition, CBS slimmed down its own orchestral commitments. Philadelphia, which had put American orchestras on the world's turntables, now tolled the death-knell of American classical recording. The deal that had looked so dazzling for orchestra and Ormandy turned into their epitaph. The only man to come out smiling was Ronald Andrew Wilford.

Judson had one last shot. Having failed to woo back his maestros, he moved heaven and earth to persuade Wilford to join his new agency. 'It broke AJ's heart that Wilford did not go with him to JOBS,' said Mary-Ann Zeitlin. 'Wilford, when we asked him about it, said Judson had not put up enough money for him to leave Columbia.' This seemed a thin excuse, even at the time. Wilford knew that CAMI had the biggest assets and the best prospects for a man of his ambition. By the end of the decade he would be president.

Judson's new agency did not demand much of his formidable attention, attracting very few celebrities and a lot of European hopefuls. 'JOBS was a catastrophe,' said conductors' manager Belle Schulhof. Fritz Steinway soon quit and the agency reverted to its original name of Arthur Judson Concert Management, under which it had been incorporated more than fifty years before in Philadelphia. Judson would come to the office each morning and demand, 'Harry, what's CBS stock going for today?' And when Beall, having checked the business columns, told him the shares were worth twelve or fifteen dollars each, Judson would ask happily, 'Now, Harry, what's that times one third of a million?'[44]

On his ninetieth birthday, attorney Ralph Colin contributed an article to *Variety* extolling Judson's role in the birth of American mass media. Colin sent two copies to the *New York Times*. One was for Judson's obituaries file, the other for Paley's. Colin feared that Judson, shunning the limelight to the last, might be deprived of the credit he deserved for conceiving CBS.

His gesture was premature, for Judson was not yet ready to die. 'Still a veritable monument of a man,' noted Philip Hart in 1973, 'he continues to wield a great influence, less directly now than through the many managers, conductors and board members in whom he indoctrinated his principles . . . Judson exercised a great power in his time, not always wisely in the opinion of some in specific instances, but firmly and efficiently, bringing into the symphonic institution many elements of strong and sound management.'[45] He took a third wife in his nineties, a professional nurse who read aloud to him classics from his library of first editions that he had purchased and read while riding the railroads back and forth between the orchestras he managed in Philadelphia and New York.

Death caught up with Arthur Judson days before his ninety-fourth birthday, on 25 January 1975, and the eulogies were as sparse as he would have wished. There are no stone memorials to the great musical magnate, no daisy-chain of civic relics like Hilton's or Woolworth's. When Judson quit Columbia, he made them remove the nameplate from the Judson Recital Hall (it was renamed the Columbia Recital Hall). With his death, the last firm to bear his name faded into nothingness and no trace remained of his legendary domains.

Yet, for a man who ruled a whole world, the enduring memories are unexpectedly affectionate. 'He never screwed anyone unnecessarily,' reflected orchestral manager Philip Hart. 'I never saw him do an unkind thing to anyone,' said New York Commissioner of Cultural Affairs, Schuyler Chapin. 'Say what you like about AJ,' said his secretary Mary-Ann Zeitlin, 'but he certainly loved music.'[46]

*　　*　　*

No one knew much about Ronald Wilford and he did his best to keep it that way. Where Judson was publicity-shy, Wilford was obsessively secretive. He forbade his second wife to visit his home town and stymied her attempts to discover his real name. A pianist who had known him since college was dropped by Columbia when Wilford became president. He blurred his background so thoroughly that, looking in his bathroom mirror while shaving, Wilford may well have had cause to wonder who it was he saw there.

At Columbia, they first became aware of him as a downstairs tenant one floor below, a faintly vulpine young man running a shoestring agency and looking to make connections. He wore sedate suits and made bland conversation. There was nothing conspicuous about him, except a certain predatory inconspicuousness. He would come up at twilight hours and vanish as swiftly as he came. Someone dubbed him 'the Silver Fox', and the nickname stuck.

Neither in his years of struggle nor at the pomp of his power was there any similarity to Judson. 'When Arthur Judson walked into a room he always made an impact,' recalled aides.[47] When Wilford entered, no one noticed — and that is what he wanted. He avoided the press and averted his face at the pop of a camera. I have seen him standing for several minutes just outside a circle of musicians, enjoying the state of being unnoticed. In forty-five years as a manager, he grudged five press interviews.

His excessive need for anonymity was unrelated to his business, which was to all appearances respectable and legitimate. Nor did it stem from social unease, since Wilford could be convivial in the right surroundings. His diffidence was an exceptional trait, distinguished from normal timidity by a coiled aggressiveness, an angry reticence that seemed to be rooted less in the nature of his activities than in his character and origins, those mysterious origins that he fought so fervently to obscure.

The entry in *Who's Who in America* records his birth in Salt Lake City, Utah, on 4 November 1927, six weeks after Judson put CBS on the air. He disclosed nothing more than the Christian names of his parents, Andrew and Marcile, and of his third wife, Sara Roosevelt Wilford. One son of a previous marriage is noted, but not his daughter. His two colleges are listed, but not his failure to graduate. The rest of the entry consists of a chronicle of company positions and a club membership, the New York Athletic. There are no honours, no hobbies, no affiliations, no publications to his name — nothing to differentiate the number-one deal-maker of classical music from the second vice-president of an agrarian bank in Wisconsin. For business partners who might read *Who's Who*, he volunteered a life stripped of colour, character and conviction.

Wilford only ever once discussed his antecedents, in a 1971 interview with Stephen E. Rubin of the *New York Times* from atop the CAMI pinnacle. He talked then of a 'miserable' childhood and a desperate quest for self-definition. 'My father was Greek, my mother was Mormon,' he confessed. 'I had a hard time knowing who I was. Mormonism stresses the family; but when your father is Greek Orthodox, it's not a family any more. Automatically, you can't conform. This area is a problem for me.'[48] These revelations, never to be repeated, indicate that he was undergoing a period of fairly intense self-absorption. He was between wives and freshly installed in a position of power. Fascinated by psychoanalysis, he may, at this time, have been undergoing a period of therapy. 'The psychoanalytic field has always been very interesting to me and I have indulged myself in it. And I have found that it is extremely valuable to me in what I do,' he later admitted.[49]

The clash of cultures in his background was formative, the more so since both are autocratic. Mormonism is a messianic, American-born sect ruled by a shadowy board of elders. It collects population data around the world, apparently with the purpose of claiming the souls of the citizens it catalogues. Its founders retreated under threat of persecution to Utah, where the Church of Latter-Day Saints enjoys the status almost of a state religion. Greek Orthodoxy, by contrast, is a reactionary, colourful relic of Byzantium, in which a powerful priesthood was inextricably associated with national leadership. Concepts of manipulative authority underpin both faiths in the Wilford family.

As the second of seven children, he was subject to the will of an overbearing Greek father. Andrew Wilford was fourteen when he came to America around the outbreak of the First World War. Settling in Utah where there was a small Hellenic community, he changed his name and got a job. His children were never allowed to discover the original family name. 'All we knew was that it began with B and was very long,' said Janice Wilford, Ronald's second wife.[50] When Ronald and Janice went to Greece on vacation, Andrew forbade them to make contact with his relatives or search out the ancestral home. Andrew Wilford never met his daughter-in-law, though he conversed with her in a rich Greek accent on the telephone. She, in turn, was prevented by Ronald from visiting Salt Lake City. She never knew what he was hiding there, but she sensed that he had inherited from his father a pathological fixation with secrecy. Many immigrants came to America with a dark deed in their past; sometimes that deed cast its shadow on the next generation.

To portray himself in an all-American mould of self-made man, Ronald Wilford underlined the poverty of his upbringing and let it be known that his father was a janitor, or maintenance man. Those who knew the Wilfords, however, said they lived 'in a good middle-class house on a downtown thoroughfare in Salt Lake City'. The pianist Grant Johannessen, a native of the town, said, 'It doesn't seem to jell that he came from a poor family.'[51] Andrew Wilford was a building and maintenance contractor working on commission for Greek magnates who owned hotels and movie houses. 'Ronald told me that his father drove a Cadillac and was friendly with some of the richest Greeks, until he got into tax trouble,' said Janice.

There may have been vicissitudes in the family finances but the Wilfords could afford to send their son to college. His mother, an American-born Mormon of German and Swedish descent, wanted him to have professional qualifications and Ronald enrolled at Utah State University in the summer the war ended. He was too impatient, however, to sit out his course in business studies and collect a graduation certificate. He kept nagging his tutors for business opportunities.

In the summer of 1945 Salt Lake City staged a ticker-tape parade for its heroes home from the war. In the summer of 1946 the city turned out again to welcome Grant Johannessen home in triumph from a Carnegie Hall début and a big concerto success with the New York Philharmonic, conducted by Georg Szell. Johannessen, at twenty-five, was back to give concerts in his home state. 'A friend of mine, Gail Plummer, the former manager of the Utah Symphony Orchestra, was teaching a marketing class at college and told me about one of his kids,' recalled Johannessen. 'He said, "This boy doesn't know a thing about music, but he is dead keen to become an artists' manager." So Gail sent him off on tour with me through that summer vacation.'

Plummer had not exaggerated. Ronald Wilford had never been to a concert or played an instrument. On bus-rides from one small town to the next, the student pumped the pianist for information about music and the musical world. 'He was always very inquiring, anxious to find out my opinions of music and my colleagues. He never had much feeling for music himself. We went driving around colleges, playing one recital at ten in the morning, driving on, and playing again at eight that night. It was terrific training to play inches from the sprawled knees of big-boned football players. Ronald Wilford was a very good road man. What struck me above all was his industry. I thought to myself, here is somebody who will probably profit from being in this business.'[52]

Latter-day prophecy is not uncommon in Utah and the pianist, that summer, looked deep into the student's soul and saw the future. Ronald Wilford may have had no aptitude or sentiment for the art of music, but he was going to make a very great success at it. On their return to Salt Lake

City, Johannessen put Wilford in touch with his agent in New York, a former musicologist called David Rubin who was 'in a precarious position and needed help'. Wilford dropped out of college, got married and opened an office in Salt Lake City to sell Rubin's artists to orchestras and communities in the Pacific region. 'He was known in the trade as The Greek,'[53] said Philip Hart, who ran the orchestra in Portland, Oregon. The unfriendly appellation indicates that managers found Wilford gawky and perhaps untrustworthy. He had a lot still to learn.

In 1948, he moved to New York, leaving his wife and daughter. 'He had divorced his first wife when I knew him,' said David Rubin, who took him on as a full partner in Rubin & Wilford. New York was at its artistic zenith in the few short years between victory and McCarthyism and it must have seemed the easiest place in the world to find stars and develop their careers – another Bernstein, another Stern, another Cliburn. But the big agents were fairly efficient at sniffing out talent and Rubin & Wilford were, with one or two exceptions, left combing the leftovers. Neither man earned much of a living. 'It was a hand-to-mouth existence,' said Mary-Ann Zeitlin whose violinist husband, Zvi, was a Wilford client. 'The big stars went to Columbia and they were getting the lemmings. Ronald was doing all he could just to get a foothold.'[54]

'Ronald was very effective in sales and in running that kind of office, but he did not bring *any* artists to our partnership,' said Rubin.[55] His emphasis is significant. Wilford could sell a package of entertainments to a Pacific Coast manager, but he lacked the panache to attract the allegiance of a refined classical artist.

The firm broke up after five years on what Rubin insists were amicable terms. Wilford's friends were told that he, while out of town, heard that Rubin was bringing over the Nazi-tainted pianist, Walter Gieseking. Wilford refused, as a Greek-sympathising anti-fascist, to be party to that deal and broke the partnership on a matter of principle. If this account of events is true, the episode sits uneasily with Wilford's future alliance with the mightiest of musical Nazis, but there are so many twists and contradictions in his spiralling ascent that it may, perversely, be accurate.

Rubin went on to manage the brilliant Juilliard String Quartet, before taking a staff position at Steinway. Wilford found himself on his own in a strange city, virtually friendless and with no visible means of support. Johannessen, his ice-breaker, forsook him for Columbia. Things were looking bleak. 'I never worried about success,' he later maintained. 'I didn't have money. I remember cashing a cheque in a drugstore on 57th Street for five dollars on a Friday for the weekend, and on Tuesday it would bounce.'[56]

'He'd come hanging around my desk a great deal at Columbia,' recalled Mary-Ann Zeitlin. 'He would ask me out to lunch, but never had money to pay.' She introduced him to a secretary at the opposite desk, a girl called Janice Roberts, whom Wilford took out and in 1956 married. Janice knew he had an ex-wife, but ten years would pass before she discovered he had a child. The couple spent many evenings baby-sitting for the Zeitlins. Wilford had nothing better to do.

What changed his life was a tip-off – reputedly from a Vienna-based conductor, Jonathan Sternberg – about the French mime, Marcel Marceau, who was drawing vast crowds in Europe to see a performance art that had seemed defunct. Wilford went to watch Marceau in Quebec in 1955 and signed him up for a United States tour. Where he found the money is uncertain, but Janice had a small legacy and was a full partner in Ronald A. Wilford Associates.

Marceau's two-week run at the Phoenix Theater had to be moved to a bigger Broadway house and ultimately to the City Center for a six-month stay. Wilford had found himself a meal-ticket. He got Marceau on to comedian Red Skelton's top-rated CBS TV show, where his chalk-faced act was watched by millions. Marceau's next television spots were alongside Fred Astaire, Victor Borge, Dinah Shore. He was seen on screen by Arthur Judson, who had been pondering this new medium and wondering why he could not make money out of it. When radio went on air, Judson knew how to make it play music. With television the obvious option was opera, and NBC seemed briefly receptive after scoring massive ratings at Christmas 1951 with Gian-Carlo Menotti's *Amahl and the Night Visitors*. The network issued more commissions to Menotti, Bohuslav Martinů and Lukas Foss. It began showing mainstream operas in hour-long, *Reader's Digest*-like versions. With static cameras, boxy sound and condensed plots, NBC's *Carmen* and *Otello* bore scant resemblance to the live experience, but to millions who had never set foot in an opera house it was the real thing and NBC, for a while, showed eight operas a season.

At the crest of this chimera, Bill Judd and NBC's Samuel Chotzinoff hatched a scheme to send NBC's *Butterfly* and *Figaro* on tour around middle America. Audiences were receptive but the receipts were poor and NBC shut down its opera slot in midstream upon realising that *Amahl* was a sentimental one-off, belonging more to Broadway than to bel canto. Broadway was then at the summit of its musical success, with *My Fair Lady* and *West Side Story* drawing record crowds. Judson decided to get in on the act. He knew the fellow downstairs was trailing a French mime around local theatres. In 1958 he called Wilford up to form a theatrical division in CAMI, sending Broadway shows out on the ailing Community circuit.

Thrilled to get a foot in the Columbia door (Janice had to resign from her job as the price of his admission), Wilford knew that theatre was peripheral to the main agenda and if he wanted to get ahead he needed to get conductors. He had scored one coup in the podium by – as he told it – stealing four of Judson's top batons and selling them to an orchestra in Oregon. Judson, he said, 'didn't like me for that'.[57] Judson, in all probability, barely noticed his presumption.

What happened was that the Portland orchestra had got rid of a weak conductor and, in the upheaval, lost its manager and most of its 1953–4 season. Wilford, hearing of the trouble on his Pacific grapevine, volunteered to book a series of guest conductors. The season he produced was the best Portland ever heard – Igor Stravinsky, Otto Klemperer, Arthur Fiedler of the Boston Pops, Fabien Sawitsky (whose uncle was Serge Koussevitzky), Paul Strauss and – to ice the cake – Strauss's close friend Dmitri Mitropoulos, music director of the New York Philharmonic. Four world stars and two satellites was more than Portland could ever have afforded, but Wilford was unusually persuasive.

He solicited Mitropoulos as a fellow-Greek, only to be told that he would conduct for nothing if Portland auditioned his protégé, Strauss, as its next music director. So long as Mitropoulos took no fee, Judson could not object to his bit of moonlighting. 'The key to Wilford's operation was Mitropoulos,' said Philip Hart, who soon afterwards resumed managing the orchestra. 'His participation enabled Wilford to approach other big names.'[58] To sign Stravinsky, Fiedler and the sound-alike Sawitsky, Wilford went on bended knee to Bruno Zirato and begged their release from CAMI, which exacted its commission. There was nothing daring about his raid on Judson's conductors.

The one stroke of flair that Wilford showed was in tracking down Otto Klemperer, who was in trouble with Washington and had been dropped by Judson. 'My father was having a difficult time,' said his daughter, Lotte. 'The authorities had taken away his American passport [for having friends among the Hollywood suspects] and we were living in a shabby hotel in New York without any work. It was a wonderful thing for us when Ronald Wilford got in touch.'[59] The sharp young agent took the conductor's physically imposing and intellectually formidable daughter to lunch and waxed lyrical about a *Messiah* he had heard Klemperer conduct in Salt Lake City in December 1946. It had stuck in his mind and he wanted him to conduct the Portland orchestra.

The invitation stirred Klemperer from a bout of depression and reignited his career. 'I paid him more than anybody else, because he needed it more,' Wilford told the conductor's biographer.[60] 'I think I was kind of in love with

Lotte,' he confessed in a separate reminiscence.[61] On 2 November 1953 Klemperer conducted a Weber overture, Mozart's *Eine Kleine Nachtmusik*, Strauss's *Don Juan* and the seventh symphony by Beethoven in Portland, Oregon. 'It was a feeble orchestra and he made them play fantastically,' said Hart. 'People remember that concert in Portland to this day.' The fee paid Klemperer's passage to London, where he took up the reins at the Philharmonia. Wilford, raw as he was, had found out what it took to set a world conductor back on his feet. From that moment Wilford's foxy eye was fixed on the podium portfolio.

'Once Ronald Wilford got into Columbia, he was Machiavellian,' said Mary-Ann Zeitlin. 'I knew he existed but never saw him,' said Harry Beall. Wilford entered Columbia in 1958, took over the conductors' division in 1963 and achieved the presidency in 1970, his eye never wavering from that chalice. Silver-spooners like Schuyler Chapin glimpsed the gleaming edge of his ambition and got out within months of his arrival. The gay brigade withered beneath the heat of an assumed hostility; several died mysteriously in their thirties, victims of a pre-AIDS syndrome. Bill Judd finally quit in 1969 to form a small agency, just before Wilford won the presidency of Columbia. 'Bill never really liked corporate life: he just wanted to represent artists,' said his secretary sadly.

For Wilford, the key artist was Herbert von Karajan who commanded much of western Europe. Wilford's devotion to Karajan was almost filial. The two men shared a bond of Greek blood and common dreams of dominance. Wilford considered Karajan to be a unique historical force. 'I liked him very much,' Wilford confided. 'More than liked. Adored him.'[62] 'With Karajan he had a special understanding,' confirmed Janice Wilford. 'Ronald had an enormous admiration for him. He was the greatest of conductors. But the only things I ever heard out of Karajan's mouth were matters related to business.'

Wilford eased Karajan's entry to the Metropolitan Opera in 1967, assuaging general manager Rudolf Bing's antagonism to ex-Nazis. The Met became a staging post for Karajan's Salzburg *Ring* and a platform for his American ambitions, but Wilford's next move on his behalf was unfortunate. In 1969, Wilford offered Karajan to the Chicago Symphony Orchestra which was looking to replace the lacklustre Jean Martinon. The Chicago board was thrilled at the prospect of time-sharing a music director with the Berlin Philharmonic, but when Wilford broached the idea to Karajan he rejected it out of hand. 'He was not happy in America,' said Janice Wilford. The Chicago board showed less compassion. 'Wilford messed up,' said an orchestral manager. 'He was unable to deliver.'[63]

Chicago gave its podium to Georg Solti, a 'Stern Gang' sympathiser. Loss of credit with a Big Five orchestra was a blow to any artists' manager, let alone one who presumed to fill Judson's giant shoes. Wilford, if he was worried, never let it show. Where Judson cultivated the admiration of orchestral executives, Wilford was prepared to court their hostility, knowing that he held the best cards. 'I really don't care,' he shrugged. 'If I have an artist they want, they will have to book him.'[64]

If he could not be loved, Wilford was content to be feared. He increased the number of conductors on CAMI's list from a few dozen to more than a hundred, controlling the supply to orchestras of their most essential commodity. Contrary to some assessments, he did not prune his list of dormant or unsuccessful conductors. He preferred to keep it as large as possible to confound clients and competitors with the crafted illusion that Ronald Wilford held the reins of most of the available conductors. And he was forever out prowling for more. One independent manager tried (unsuccessfully) to place an advert in *Musical America*, appealing to the nation's orchestras: 'Why don't you take a conductor from me? Ronald Wilford does. Every year.'

He viewed his conductors in two categories – 'the ones I care about' and the ninety-odd others, exposing his favouritism by the repeated use of that phrase[65] and encouraging his chosen ones to feel 'really close to him'.[66] Conductor-clients who were not central to his plans were treated with an indifference verging on contempt. Antonio de Almeida, a French conductor of noble mien, had been launched by Judson and boosted by Sir Thomas Beecham before settling as music director in Stuttgart. Back home on a visit, he met the Philadelphia Orchestra chairman, Wanton C. Balis, at a social affair and was astonished to hear that the orchestra had been trying, at Beecham's instigation, to book him for three concerts in the following season. 'We kept asking, but Ronald Wilford said you weren't free and offered [Seiji] Ozawa instead,' said Balis. 'He actually showed me Wilford's letter,' said de Almeida, who headed for New York to confront his agent. Wilford laughed off the incident as a misunderstanding. He turned graver when de Almeida gave him the sack. 'That's fine,' said Wilford. 'But remember: I *never* take anyone back.'[67] Conductors who left him – and few ever dared – found it difficult to obtain an important podium in the United States.

Trusting his instincts, Wilford preferred to pick conductors himself and was dismissive when they approached him. Ursula Sternberg, wife of the man who alerted Wilford to Marceau, went to discuss her husband's prospects with him in 1967 on their return to the US. 'He was extremely negative, coldly destructive,' she said. 'He showed me a drawer that he said was full of conductors who would always remain there. I ran out crying into 57th Street.'[68]

José Serebrier, a Uruguayan working with Leopold Stokowski in the mid-1960s on his last ensemble, the American Symphony Orchestra, was advised to seek an appointment with Wilford. 'The first thing he said to me was, "You've got to get away from Stokowski. That man destroys orchestras." ' Serebrier, suppressing his outrage at the slur on his hero, produced the reviews he had received for recent New York concerts. 'I'm not concerned with that,' said Wilford. 'All my conductors get bad notices, but they get all the work.'[69]

Surveying the hopefuls at his office door, Wilford would laugh aloud at their discomfiture. 'Someone comes in and tells me, "I am the greatest conductor you will ever hear." I stood up and said, "Well, it's nice to know you. You don't need me." That man hasn't been heard from since. It's obvious nobody like that is going to make it,' he chortled to a BBC interviewer.[70]

The only trait he shared with Judson, apart from a demon drive, was the knack of fine timing. Wilford took over the division just as a new wave of talented young conductors was breaking on the scene, perhaps the last the world would ever see. It included the Italians Claudio Abbado and Riccardo Muti, the Americans André Previn, James Levine and Michael Tilson Thomas, the Germans Carlos Kleiber and Kurt Masur; Bernard Haitink in The Netherlands, Colin Davis in England, Seiji Ozawa in Japan and the United States. Maazel, Mehta and Barenboim clung to Stern's circle and eluded his net.

In later years, Wilford claimed credit for the emergence of this generation. 'Most of the artists I manage now, I worked with before they had a career,' he said. 'Abbado was assistant at the New York Philharmonic; he wasn't known. Muti was a young man in Florence when I met him. Ozawa was a little boy who wanted to get a visa to come to New York. Previn was a jazz pianist who had conducted one concert in his life, and I told him he should be a conductor. I did what I believed in. I did it before I came to Columbia; I had my own business.'[71] This was the image he wanted to foster – of a dedicated manager whose nose for talent made him the 'king-maker' of classical music. This was, of course, less than half the portrait of an immensely contradictory character.

He craved power and the status it bestowed but, having achieved it, shrank from recognition and denied the 'king-maker' tag. 'I don't play God,' was a frequent assertion. He drawled the adverbless argot of international executives but, when pressed for a self-definition, spoke of his 'calling'. He assessed artists with the impartial eye of a cattle auctioneer but, once smitten, could not resist their aura. 'That's my problem,' he reflected. 'When I hear somebody good, I want to be involved with them. I want to understand who they are and how it works and what it is. I want to feel it. I want to be involved with them.'

The fervent, furtive emotionality of Ronald Andrew Wilford was his secret weapon, an assault tactic so open and unaffected that – allied to the golden benefits he promised – it could scarcely be resisted. When Wilford approached a conductor, he offered not a glittering career but his body and soul. It was a remarkable process to observe for, at the moment of seduction, the seducer seemed acutely more vulnerable than his intended victim. From each and every artist, and there were more than six hundred on his list, Ronald Wilford longed for the grace of acceptance. 'As a child I was slighted a lot,' he volunteered in a psychoanalytical aside. 'This is my whole kind of emotional involvement.'[72]

Into the fulfilment of a passion so belatedly requited he threw himself unstintingly. 'The minute he came home from the office he got on the phone and carried on working. Then it was out to a concert and off to dinner afterwards. It never stopped,' said his wife. 'He wanted to do the best he possibly could for his artists. Their lives depended on him.'[73]

The first life he transformed was Ozawa's. 'I was working with Judson then, and Lenny Bernstein had sent him over,' Wilford recalled. 'He couldn't speak much English. I listened to this guy and I said, "I'll work with you for five years – sign a contract?" He said, "Yes." I then went [with him] to an acoustical test at Lincoln Center's Philharmonic Hall, which wasn't open yet. The New York Philharmonic . . . had three assistant conductors. It was the last day of the Philharmonic season; they had been engaged for two weeks to do these tests. Following that rehearsal they were all going on vacation for a month. The musicians were slouching, they were not paying any attention, they were giggling at the back. The second conductor finished and Seiji was the last. 'Suddenly I see this kid, Seiji, run up on the stage and the musicians are like somebody bolted them back in their chairs, posture perfect, edge of their seats, and they *played*.'[74]

He placed Ozawa at Chicago's Ravinia Festival in 1964, at the Toronto Symphony the next year, with the San Francisco orchestra in 1970 and, two years later, at the pinnacle of American music, the Boston Symphony Orchestra. Ozawa's exotic looks and Beatles fringe drew younger audiences, but musicians complained from the outset of his lack of engagement with them and the music. He was forever arriving or leaving for Japan or Europe, learning barely enough English to order a cab. He showed a mastery of impressionistic music but, in the view of many critics, never came to grips with core symphonic repertoire. His recordings were bland to the point where reviewers wondered aloud why labels like Philips and Deutsche Grammophon let him conduct Mahler and Prokofiev cycles. Yet Ozawa, notwithstanding opposition, stayed at Boston for twenty years and, with Wilford's backing, could expect to remain there until retirement. Like Ormandy at Philadelphia, he was protected by an all-powerful manager with an unshakeable faith. 'Seiji has it, Abbado has it, Muti has it, this kind of presence,' said Wilford. 'When they put their hand out, there's music. These people are geniuses. I don't know where they come from.'[75]

Muti he met through a record producer, Previn through Schuyler Chapin. He picked up Levine as a nineteen-year-old Juilliard kid, told him to 'get as much repertoire as you can under your belt . . . until you're around twenty-seven', checked up on him each summer at the Aspen Festival and in 1971, a year behind schedule, installed him as principal conductor of the Metropolitan Opera. Levine calls Wilford 'one of the most phenomenal human beings I know'.[76]

By the end of the Sixties, Wilford's new generation was making its mark on America, Karajan ruled unchallenged in Europe and the man from Salt Lake City was ready to seize command of Columbia. He had the blessing of the outgoing president, Kurt Weinhold, and the acquiescence of his board. All he needed was cash. Although he made a good living from Marceau and some of his maestros, Wilford was not yet a man of means, seemingly not rich enough to buy a controlling share in Columbia. Yet, as Weinhold's widow confirmed, 'by the time he became president he certainly had enough stock.'[77]

The market value of this most private of companies is difficult to assess. Apart from a block of office space in midtown Manhattan, its only asset was the reputation of its artists and managers, a stock that could plummet with a few poor performances. Yet even if the valuation set by the directors was nominal, Wilford would have had to raise a sizeable sum to gain a majority holding. Where he found that money may be linked to a parallel development in his domestic circumstances. After a dozen years of childless marriage, Ronald and Janice Wilford had adopted a son, Christopher. 'He made me feel human,' said Ronald.[78] In the summer of 1968, with students rioting all over Europe and the Russians poised to enter Prague, the Wilfords went on holiday to Italy. Their good friends Anthony and Sara di Bonaventura came along with their five children. Anthony was a formidable concert pianist with a taste for contemporary music (he would commission a concerto from György Ligeti) and a disregard for careerism. Sara Delano Roosevelt Whitney di Bonaventura, his wife, was born a Roosevelt and adopted by the plutocrat Jock Whitney, growing up amid two of America's greatest fortunes. She was keen to go off touring that summer and so was Wilford. Anthony was preoccupied with his music and Janice Wilford volunteered to look after the children. 'That, I suppose is when it all began,' she reflected years later.

Janice first became aware of the tension at a forty-second birthday party she gave for her husband in October 1969. Four months later, Anthony di Bonaventura stormed into his manager's office and declared, 'I don't like what's going on between you and my wife.' Janice remembered Ronald coming home that night in a fury. 'How could he talk to *me* like that?' demanded Wilford. The pianist went off to Australia for a Wilford-organised chamber music tour with the violinist Zvi Zeitlin. 'He came back to find that his wife was leaving him for his manager,' recalled Mary-Ann Zeitlin.

Sara would later assure Christopher Wilford that nothing untoward had passed between her and his father while they were married to other people. At all events, both marriages ended swiftly. 'We separated in 1970, and that was when Ronald became president of Columbia,' said Janice Wilford, who had no doubts about the source of his newfound fortune. 'His money came from Sara,' she said. 'Where else could it have come from?'[79]

And so Ronald Wilford sat at last at the head of Judson's table, surrounded by tame partners and satraps, cloaked in a fug of secretiveness that grew thicker with each passing year. Among the early business he attended to was the departure of Grant Johannessen from the Columbia list. 'I had been at Columbia for twenty years until Ron came into control,' said the Salt Lake City pianist who put Wilford on the road to success. 'He used to introduce me at parties as his very first artist, but now he had his own agenda. He sort of erased me from his mind. We had very little to say to one another, and I went of my own accord and without rancour. He probably wanted me out because I knew something about his past.'[80]

Janice Wilford left New York with their son, Christopher, and was shut out of the world of music. 'I miss taking care of the artists, some of whom were my friends,' she said, quarter of a century later. The Zeitlins, for whom Wilford once baby-sat, never saw him again. At the age of forty-two, Ronald Wilford reinvented himself as a man without a past, without a shadow.

One enigma bred another. Under Columbia rules, Wilford could not own more than a slim majority of the shares, purchased apparently from the retiring Weinhold and the Judson estate, but the size of his holding was unknown even to his partners. 'CAMI is a company owned by its employees,' he liked to say, but his authority was not open to challenge. People who left the firm were made to sell back their shares, at Wilford's valuation. 'There was no independent way to measure their worth,' complained one outgoing director.[81] When Chris Schang, a founder's son, objected to inflationary new shares that Wilford was issuing in the company, the president told him to back off — or sell his stock at a risibly low price.

At board meetings Wilford would sit silent or laconic, while division chiefs discussed proposals and policies. Votes were taken and measures agreed, but anything Wilford disliked he would simply veto at the point of implementation. CAMI was supposedly an amalgam of independent divisions, but Wilford oversaw their accounts, resolved any internal clashes and formed new operations at will. 'He doesn't make a habit of interfering in the work of colleagues, so we don't really see what the limits of his authority might be,' said division chief Doug Sheldon.[82] Wilford himself insisted that he never indulged in long-term planning. 'I walk backwards into the future,' he said, cautious as a fox with prey.

When I asked him in 1988 how the company had changed since Judson left, he was momentarily stumped for an answer. 'I guess we started the specialisation,' he finally suggested in his rambling style. 'I hired people who specifically specialised in opera. We have a conductors' division, a theatre division, a festival division, a television company. In Judson's day, you took a boat when you went to Europe. Now with the Concorde the whole business of building a career is entirely different. So one can make a trip to the Orient, the United States and Europe all in one season.'

As Columbia expanded, he averted the risk of a monopolies investigation by tempering domestic growth while retaining market leadership. 'We were always much bigger than Hurok,' he bragged. 'Hurok was basically a local manager who became an impresario. We were always in management, and not locally.'[83]

To expand the business he had to go abroad. He flew to Moscow to wrest artists away from Hurok and came away with a Kirov ballet tour, but the Russians preferred dealing with one of their own and deprecated CAMI's 'mass-production style, with all its corporate divisions'.[84] Hurok's agency fragmented after his death on 6 March 1974, its key performers eventually settling at ICM Artists, which was run by Isaac Stern's former secretary, Lee Lamont. For the last quarter of the century ICM became the leading alternative to CAMI. Stern, with his many public duties, avoided confrontation, but many among the fiddler's extended family made no secret of their gut-hostility to the Silver Fox and all he represented.

'I have never wasted a word of greeting on that man,'[85] said Zubin Mehta, who conducted the New York Philharmonic for fifteen years, keeping it firmly out of CAMI's clutches. Lorin Maazel walked up to him once and said, 'Wilford, one day I am going to buy up your business and throw you on to the street.'

Wilford claimed to be perplexed by the animosity he aroused, though his actions and body language were undeniably aggressive. He was widely credited with getting his former CAMI colleague, Schuyler Chapin, replaced as manager of the Metropolitan Opera, after telling the company's president, 'If you want to save the Met, get rid of Schuyler.' Wilford later told a reporter, 'I can't take credit for Schuyler leaving the Met – though I might like to.'[86] Chapin did not talk to him for ten years afterwards, but Wilford was at peace with himself. All he had done was protect one of the artists 'we care about' – in this case, the Met future of James Levine.

All Wilford ever did was for the benefit of his artists. 'I learned a long time ago what one's fiduciary responsibility is,' he told me. 'When you're married, you don't necessarily have to do everything for the benefit of your wife. But when you have a fiduciary agency responsibility, which is what I have with these musicians, I must do only that which is in their favour. And that's what I do.'[87] His metaphor may have been ill-chosen, given his personal history, but the meaning was unmistakable. Ronald Wilford was wholly committed to a handful of conductors in whom he had found emotional fulfilment – Karajan, Ozawa, Previn, Levine. Their welfare was his mission in life, and for their sake he would sacrifice anything. Anything except his power – that invasive, all-pervading musical autocracy whose very existence he so strenuously denied.

NOTES

1 Truman, pp. 365, 439, 441
2 In a similar case in 1963, the showbiz conglomerate MCA was ordered to stop acting as both an artists' agency and a producer of shows and films. MCA had represented both sides to each other, actors and producers, during the great Broadway strike.
3 Hart, pp. 52–78
4 NY Times, 29 April 1956
5 Shanet, p. 324
6 author's interview, January 1995
7 Toobin, p. 102
8 Robinson, p. 321
9 author's interview
10 Hurok, p. 11
11 Robinson, p. 4
12 Robinson, p. 348
13 Robinson, p. 337
14 Vishnevskaya, p. 208

15 Hart: *Reiner*, p. 58
16 *NY Times*, 6 January 1949, cited in Gillis, p. 103
17 *Chicago Daily Tribune*, 20 February 1949; quoted Shirakawa, p. 355
18 Gillis, p. 116
19 Gillis, pp. 130–1
20 Gillis, p. 129
21 Stern quotes, unless stated, are author's interview, November 1990
22 author's interview, 1990
23 Hart, p. 94
24 Lynes, pp. 423–4
25 'Stern at 70', by Herbert Kupferberg, *Classical*, July 1990
26 private communication
27 Marylynn Fixler, author's interview
28 author's interview
29 author's interviews
30 personal communications with the author
31 author's interview
32 Janice Roberts Wilford, author's interview
33 Harry Beall, author's interview
34 author's interview
35 author's interviews
36 Graffman, p. 115
37 author's interview
38 O'Connell, p. 61
39 author's interview
40 Beall, author's interview
41 information from Naomi Graffman
42 Hart, author's interview
43 Hart, p. 87
44 anecdote related by Marvin Schofer
45 Hart, pp. 92–3
46 Hart, Chapin, Zeitlin, author's interviews
47 Audrey Michaels, author's interview
48 Stephen E. Rubin, 'Ronald Wilford: Muscle Man Behind the Maestros', *NY Times*, 25 July 1971
49 Andrew Decker, 'Classical String Puller', *Manhattan Inc.* magazine, September 1989, pp. 144–62
50 author's interview
51 author's interview, February 1995
52 author's interview
53 author's interview
54 author's interview
55 author's interview
56 interview with Natalie Wheen, BBC Radio 3, 20 June 1991
57 Dekcer, loc. cit.
58 author's interview
59 author's interview
60 John Lucas, communication with the author
61 personal communication
62 author's interview
63 personal communication
64 author's interview
65 in, for example, interviews with Natalie Wheen and myself
66 Decker, loc. cit.
67 interview with Antonio de Almeida, December 1993
68 author's interview, January 1995

69 author's interview, November 1994
70 interview, June 1991
71 BBC interview, June 1991
72 both quotes – BBC interview, June 1991
73 author's interview
74 BBC, loc. cit.
75 BBC, loc. cit.
76 both quotes – Frederic Dannen, 'Twilight of the God?', *The New Yorker*, 3 October 1994
77 author's interview
78 *NY Times* interview, 1971
79 author's interview
80 author's interview
81 private communication
82 *Classical Music* magazine, 22 December 1990, p. 26
83 both quotes – author's interview
84 Robinson, p. 438
85 comment to the author
86 *New Yorker*, 3 October 1994
87 author's interview

CHAPTER VII

THE MONEYING
OF MUSIC

There were two economic miracles in post-war music. The first broke around 1960 when west European governments, having rebuilt their shattered cities, began pumping money into orchestras and opera houses. 'In Germany,' said Wolfgang Stresemann, son of a Weimar Chancellor and manager of the Berlin Philharmonic from 1959, 'there was a tradition that the state is custodian of the arts. Originally, this was the responsibility of the royal courts. When they were dissolved after the First War, the Weimar Republic (of which my father was one of the architects) inherited that duty. Support for the arts was sustained even during the years of inflation, making Berlin the most exciting city in the world.'[1] Under the Nazis, the state ruled the arts with punitive rigour. Once the Federal Republic of Germany found its economic footing, governments of its individual *Länder* resumed a tradition of benign patronage. By 1960, every opera seat in West Berlin received a twenty-Mark (five-dollar) subsidy from the city, while Hamburg subsidised its opera house richly enough to afford seasons of George Balanchine and the New York City Ballet.

Public funding for the arts in Britain, inaugurated in 1946, took its leap forward around the same time. In January 1959 the House of Commons held its first-ever debate on arts provision, passing a resolution 'That this House welcomes the increasing interest of the people of Great Britain in the arts; endorses the principle that artistic policy should be free from Government control or direction; proclaims the importance of maintaining the nation's cultural heritage . . . and while grateful for the increase in Government support for the arts . . . urges a substantial increase'. Covent Garden, recommissioned after the war on a grant of twenty-five thousand pounds received five hundred and fifty thousand pounds that year.

The Treasury's generosity seems scarcely credible in retrospect. All an opera house had to do was outline its plans and the state would underwrite the bulk. In 1962, the Royal Opera was told that its subsidy would be pegged to 87.5 per cent of its previous year's income. The more shows it put on, the more public money it would get. Running an opera house under that kind of formula was like letting a child loose in a sweetshop: a nifty manager or music director could grab as many bonbons as he could stomach. It was early in the 1960s, under Sir David Webster and Sir Georg Solti, that Covent Garden finally achieved world rank.

In France, meanwhile, culture minister André Malraux waved a blank cheque at anyone who could revitalise musical life. A proposal by Pierre Boulez to burn down the Opéra was declined with regret and millions of francs were poured into Rolf Liebermann's reformist regime. All over western Europe, the hand of government was open to art. It did not enter anyone's mind that a false market was being created in which bad orchestras received as much money as good ones, on the grounds that all orchestras were a good thing. Every small town in Germany had a state-funded orchestra, but no more than three of them attained international standard. Those were the days, seemingly so distant now, when huge industries – from steel-making to telephones – were owned or run by central government, with vast subsidies to protect manufacturing jobs. The dread alternative was mass unemployment, widely regarded as a leading cause of the last war. The arts, on the other hand, were seen as a symbol of national revival and a golden photo-opportunity. French ministers crowded into frame with Igor Stravinsky; Berlin's cultural senator, Heinz Tiburtius, walked arm-in-arm for the cameras with 'his' chief conductor, Herbert von Karajan. Giving money to the arts felt good and was a fairly cheap way of exercising power (few sensations are headier for an elected official than the exercise of power without responsibility). No minister was ever fired in the Sixties for spending too much tax-payers' money on the lively arts.

The renewal of public benefice in Europe coincided with a burst of corporate generosity in the United States. In 1962, the Ford Foundation announced a programme which, over a dozen years, would give seventeen hundred million dollars of automotive profits to performing and educational bodies. In the past, American rail, road and food barons had atoned for lives of avarice by building temples to music – Andrew Carnegie in New York, Henry Ford in Detroit, H. J. Heinz in Pittsburgh. The Fords and Rockefellers had also given six-figure cheques to opera houses. But this Foundation bequest was so munificently in a scale of its own that it rewrote the ground rules of US concert life.

There was a minor condition attached to this allocation. In order to claim a share of the $82.5 million that Ford set aside for orchestras, an ensemble had to raise exactly twice as much from other sources. Philadephia put in for two million dollars in 1966 and was told to raise four million in matching funds within four years. So irresistible was this incentive that the orchestra hit its target three years early and went on to raise a chest of ten million. Orchestras, seeing the glitter of Ford gold, built up large fund-raising departments. Executive time that might have been devoted to artistic planning and audience building was diverted to courting corporate and private donors. A euergetic[2] ethos, unmatched since the free bread and circuses of ancient Rome, was sweeping corporate America under the rule of two Democratic presidents, Kennedy and Johnson, who set the tone for cultural supportiveness by establishing a National Endowment for the Arts.

There were no obvious strings attached in the early stages, but as their involvement in the arts expanded some blue-chip firms saw it as a means of obtaining strategic advantage. Big brands had used the arts in the past to advertise their wares. There was a Lucky Strike orchestra that played on NBC and the Texaco oil company brought operas from the Met live into every American living-room. Whether these initiatives sold more cigarettes or gasolene was debatable, but around 1970 big players in both sectors saw the arts as a means of softening their brutal corporate image. Exxon (oil) and Philip Morris (tobacco) set the ball rolling with major art exhibitions that attracted unprecedented television coverage. Mobil (oil) and AT&T (communications) invested directly in screen time by sponsoring public television series of drama, music and visual arts. 'It takes art to make a company great,' was the Philip Morris slogan.[3]

It was no coincidence that tobacco's love for the arts began just as the surgeon-general of the United States stamped health warnings on cigarette packs, announcing that smoking caused cancer. Nor was oil altruism entirely unrelated to Congressional alarm at rising prices and environmental blight. 'We want to be associated with your leisure and pleasure,' said a music-sponsoring tobacco boss.[4] When cigarette advertising was banned on British television, brands like John Player and Embassy sneaked onto BBC screens as sponsors of concerts and sports. By forming a link with the arts, the tobacco industry could also appeal 'to a more discerning group – the opinion formers'.[5]

Britain, as it so often does, provided American business with a beachhead for invading Europe. The tobacco legions came first, with Peter Stuyvesant flicking small sums into the London Symphony Orchestra and Glyndebourne Festival in the early 1960s. Stuyvesant also offered a competitive scholarship for young singers. At the auditions, ciggy bosses sat puffing smoke rings while candidates choked on their notes. 'What's wrong with that?' said one executive. 'Geraint Evans [the Welsh baritone] smokes like a chimney – our brand, too.' 'Music sponsorship is a way of increasing awareness of our product,' said the man from John Player, the brand that brought Simon Rattle to national attention when, in 1974, he won its conductors' competition.

Compared with what was to come, the amounts involved were trivial. In 1960 the only music sponsor in Britain was the John Lewis department store, which had given twelve thousand pounds to Glyndebourne since the war. Ten years later, British business was giving half a million pounds each year to the arts. By 1990, sponsorship exceeded sixty-five million pounds,[6] the bulk of it spent on opera, concerts and ballet.

It became an industry in its own right, as consultancies sprang up to advise performers how to find sponsors, and vice versa. An Association for Business Sponsorship of the Arts was founded in London in the offices of Imperial Tobacco. Its director, Luke Rittner, went on to become secretary-general of the Arts Council under the premiership of Margaret Thatcher, who saw business contributions as a legitimate substitute for state funding. The arts climate changed, as it had done in America. Newspaper critics were ordered to name in their concert reviews the sponsors 'without whom this event might not have been achieved', and businessmen were flattered by artists and politicians into posing as a new Maecenas class, heirs to the ducal patrons of Haydn and Mozart. Royalty granted a seal of approval. 'The artist,' declared the cello-playing heir to the throne, 'should be the partner of the business man and woman in making communities better places to live and work.'[7] Amid a glow of giving, no awkward questions were asked.

The catalyst for unlocking corporate coffers on a massive scale was the inauguration, on 3 March 1982, of London's hundred-and-fifty-three-million-pound Barbican Centre, presented as 'a gift to the nation' by the Corporation of the City of London. The Barbican gave a home to the London Symphony Orchestra, the Guildhall School of Music and Drama and the

Royal Shakespeare Company, along with a substantial annual subsidy. With this token of credit from the Square Mile, the arts embarked on a Yukon-like rush for business funding, inhibited by few rules or restraints. One arts centre considered renaming itself after a Japanese computer. The Edinburgh film festival took the name of a whisky liqueur. Arts chiefs tumbled over one another in their keenness to accommodate sponsor wishes. Throw out the logo? No problem. Change the programme? What would you prefer to hear, sir? Sometimes a sponsor would have to remind the ensemble of the need for artistic integrity. 'Here's a promise,' said Digital's chief executive to English National Ballet at the start of a seven-year agreement. 'You don't sell computers, I won't dance.'

The risks, however, were widely ignored. The Philharmonia Orchestra in 1981 accepted six hundred thousand pounds from British American Tobacco in return for redesigning its concert programmes and Beethoven recordings in the maroon livery of Du Maurier cigarettes. For two seasons the musicians even wore dark-red bow-ties to match the packaging. Then, having achieved brand recognition sooner than expected, BAT discontinued its support. The Philharmonia, which had relied heavily on the backing, almost went bust. Cigarette cash, the players learned, could seriously damage your welfare.[8]

It became glaringly apparent that any ensemble which allowed its identity to be dominated by a sponsor was at risk the moment the sponsorship ended. This did not prevent one opera company from allowing singers to be smeared in sponsor's ice-cream and another from allegedly offering to stage *Carmen* in a named tobacco factory. In a 1994 poll of European arts groups, two-thirds said they would welcome tobacco money, knowingly promoting cancer and substance addiction through the sustainment of art. Times were tough as state cash withered. By the late 1980s sponsorship was saving British arts from Margaret Thatcher's many cuts, accounting for one-eighth of national music budgets.

The trend was also spreading across Europe. The Groupe Caisse des Dépots in France gave twenty-seven million francs in 1985 to revive musical life at the Théâtre des Champs-Elysées; France Télécom became a major supporter of regional opera. In 1986 the manager of Amsterdam's Concertgebouw orchestra, Hein van Royen, called a British colleague to ask naively, 'This sponsorship money – should we be interested?' The next year's fiscal crash left no one in any doubt as to the answer. The European Commission issued a policy paper[9] describing business support as 'essential' for arts growth and in 1991 formed a Comité Européen pour le Rapprochement de l'Economie et de la Culture (CEREC) to promote pan-EU sponsorships.

American firms stymied by EU trade barriers channelled their cash to eastern Europe, where a few well-spent bucks could buy a great chunk of national kudos. IBM got in on the act of Czech liberation, underwriting such emotional events as the return to Prague of the musical exilarchs, Rafael Kubelík and Rudolf Firkušný. These concerts, released on video, earned Big Blue untold friends in former communist territories.

With the Iron Curtain a shade of the past, sponsorship spread unchecked from Ballymena to the Black Sea. Promoted by governments, recipients, media and commerce, it fostered a universal illusion of euergetic benevolence. Not many sponsors were honest enough to admit that they were in it for what they could get – or, as the Digital chief executive confessed, 'We believe very clearly that the amount of money we've spent on the arts has more than repaid itself – we can measure the business we have got as a result of it.'[10] As the arts went on bended knee to business, few remembered a time when music paid its own way.

These twin bursts of largesse – state funding and Ford grants in the 1960s and the sponsorship boom of the 1980s – caught the music business unprepared. It was a conductor who grabbed the moment and milked the cow for all it was worth. In 1955, on being named chief conductor of the Berlin Philharmonic, Herbert von Karajan demanded as a matter of principle that he and his soloists should be paid more than anywhere else in Europe. His starting fee was two thousand Marks (one hundred and sixty pounds) a night, fifty per cent more than any musician earned in London, which then paid the top rates in Europe. He applied the same strictures in Vienna, where he became head of the state opera in September 1956. The state subsidy he negotiated amounted to four million dollars which, as one writer put it, 'makes him the richest, most envied opera director on earth'.[11]

'Money does not interest me,'[12] said Karajan on numerous occasions. His concern was control. As head of the highest-spending institutions, he would command the most public attention and professional respect. The best soloists and conductors would flock to his summons and the loyalty of his Berlin players would be bought with high salaries and record deals. And if at any time they murmured, he could always retreat to Salzburg and Vienna where another sovereign state would pay his ransom note.

That was Karajan's formula, and it worked brilliantly for thirty-five years. His personal enrichment was almost incidental to his empowerment. Once his Berlin fee hit ten thousand Marks in 1973 he stopped bothering to ask for a rise since the few thousand he could get for conducting concerts were insignificant beside the millions he made on the side. His 1962 LP of

Beethoven's fifth symphony sold 1.2 million copies in the next fifteen years, earning Karajan ten per cent of the shop price of every record. In total, he made close to nine hundred recordings. At least half of them were regularly on sale on four different labels, increasing his wealth every day of the year, and that of his estate for seven decades after his death. His estate was declared for probate in July 1989 at five hundred million Marks (£163 million), most of it sheltered in Liechtenstein and Switzerland, away from the grasp of tax-collectors. For a man who was not interested in money, Karajan made more of it than any classical musician in history – and much of what he made came, directly or otherwise, from the public purse.

Many of his recordings were taped during rehearsals of the state-salaried Berlin Philharmonic, or at the Salzburg Festival in time paid for by the Austrian government. If the record companies had paid Karajan and his orchestra the commercial rate for session time, outside of rehearsals and concerts, his work would have become unaffordable and his record output would have been halved. The West Berlin Senate covered the bills for many of his foreign tours with the orchestra, on the grounds that they served as important diplomatic missions for the isolated city. Karajan exploited their naivety, demanding extra fares for a fictitious entourage and exorbitant fees for screening his films on national television in the countries he visited. His greed was exposed by *Der Spiegel*, when a 1985 trip to Taiwan aborted after the conductor demanded three hundred thousand Deutschmarks per concert and a ten-film season on local television. The Taiwanese were outraged and the tax-payers of Berlin, who plunged nineteen million Marks into the Philharmonic that year, had strong reason to feel abused. Karajan, when confronted, showed no sign of remorse.

In Vienna he put his personal secretary, André von Mattoni, on the state payroll and tried to install his lawyer, Emil Jucker, as manager of the opera house. Mattoni, a former film actor, was accused in the local press of packing Karajan's casts with singers who paid him a commission. This was untrue: it was Jucker who worked that scam. The only claim against the immaculate Mattoni was that he engaged a new prompter from Italy, as no Austrian could be trusted by Karajan. Money, public money, leaked left and right to the conductor and his cronies. In his last full season Karajan increased his spending by more than twenty per cent and still went over budget. When officials attempted to stem the flood Karajan, citing 'reasons of health', quit in August 1964. Truth to tell, he was bored by Vienna and had virtually drained it dry.

He also resigned as director of the Salzburg Festival but that was merely a ruse: he retained invisible control of a board stacked with acolytes. He made

Salzburg spend nine million dollars building him a Festspielhaus for thirty days' use a year and when the good burghers complained, he borrowed the hall for his own private festivals at Easter and Whitsun. Two official investigations cleared Karajan of outright corruption at Salzburg, but very narrowly. Any tourist could see that only Karajan's record labels were able to book advertising space at festival time and only his favourite artists got on to the stage. Opera productions, paid for by every Austrian citizen, were filmed and marketed by Karajan's company, Telemondial. If film and recording equipment interfered with public enjoyment the audience knew better than to complain. 'Der Chef', as he liked to be called, did precisely as he pleased.

Administrators, dazzled by Karajan's performances and personality, covered up his use of public funds and abuse of public trust. Diehard fans were deaf to discordances and the press, both local and global, was heavily muzzled. In a 1983 interview with the *New York Times*, Karajan threatened to sue for libel and to boycott America if the paper quoted documents about his Nazi past.[13] Neither the documents nor the interview were published in his lifetime. The music press sang unblemished hymns to his greater glory. Deftly calibrating his own reputation, Karajan became a symbol of the power and the glory of classical music. His orchestra was magnificent and his festivals extraordinary – an ascendance that he founded on a patented form of public embezzlement.

Karajan, more than any other individual, undermined the probity of musical affairs and the delicate balance of musical economics. No longer was a performer's pay fixed by his or her drawing power at the box-office, but by what a power-mad conductor decided he or she ought to receive – with a dip into the public or corporate pocket. The process of organising a concert lost all contact with realities of cost and revenue and became dependent on extraneous funding.

Karajan rallied around him an élite corps of artists who shared his bounty, and raised the going rate for performers everywhere. A soloist who made twenty thousand dollars at Salzburg would not settle for less a month later in Paris. So opera fees, which had been stable for forty years, soared into the high Gs. Maria Callas stuck at a thousand-dollar top fee, and sang perhaps thirty times a year. Under Karajan, a favourite soprano like Katia Ricciarelli could make in one night what Callas earned in six months. A pet conductor who raked in a hundred thousand dollars from guest appearances at Salzburg and Berlin could no longer be tempted to buckle down to the hard work of building a municipal orchestra or opera ensemble. And players in the Vienna Philharmonic became accustomed to make more in a Salzburg month than musicians in British orchestras earned in the entire year.

By the time Karajan died, the trickle-down effect of his sweetheart deals meant that mediocrities were claiming ten thousand Marks for conducting a concert anywhere in Germany and orchestras were being choked to death by their demands. Karajan's game had been founded on the presumption that some public body somewhere could always be persuaded to pay for the necessity of having good music. Neither he nor anyone in his circle envisaged a time when public wealth would severely contract and concerts would be allowed to go begging.

The music business watched Karajan with envy and admiration, but could not get in on his act. The most agents could hope for was to sign his protégés and take a share of their golden fees. Karajan kept up a sentimental attachment with Rudolf Vedder's firm, but otherwise had no time for any manager — except Ronald Wilford. He wanted to impress America with recordings and tours and turned to Columbia for support. Karajan and CAMI became the 'K und K' of a secret Habsburg-like state that ruled invisibly over music.

In Wilford, he found an intelligent ally and blind admirer. 'Wilford had the antennae of a sycophant,' said a witness to their dialogue. 'He always seemed to know what the Maestro was about to say, and tried to say it first.' 'He made it quite clear that Karajan was his artist,' said another watcher.[14] Wilford wanted so much to be part of Karajan's world that in 1970, the moment he won the Columbia presidency, he proposed setting up CAMI-Europe in conjunction with Sandor Gorlinsky, London agent for Maria Callas, and Karajan's EMI producer, Peter Andry. Hitched to two megastars the agency would have conquered the continent but Gorlinsky, as his price for the waning Callas, demanded shares in CAMI which Wilford was either unwilling or unable to sell; the venture aborted.

This did not stop Wilford making persistent bids to establish CAMI on European soil. In the 1980s he merged with a Zurich agent, Rita Schütz, only to part in acrimony. His next link-up was in Munich with Karin Wylach, daughter of a veteran manager who looked after James Levine in Germany. Wylach was an agent after Wilford's own heart. In October 1989, as the Berlin Philharmonic met to elect a successor to Karajan, she caused ructions across musical Europe by demanding a quarter of a million Deutschmarks per night for a concert tour with Levine. Brussels, Amsterdam and Florence duly paid up, but London's Royal Festival Hall balked at having to pay twice as much as they normally did for the same orchestra with Karajan. 'There was no unreasonable increase,' insisted Wylach,[15] but the London concert was called off. Days later, the orchestra snubbed Levine in private caucus and elected Claudio Abbado as its new chief. 'If Mr Levine wants an agent to look after his interests that's fine,' said Klaus Häussler, the players' co-chairman. 'But that agent will not handle any dealings for the orchestra.'[16] Several years elapsed before Levine recovered in Berlin, but his link with Wylach remained and Wilford's regard for her increased (though, as one associate insisted, it 'involved no cash injection from CAMI'[17]). Wylach had toughed it out, and Wilford liked that. Being an agent meant never having to say you're sorry.

He continued to woo young British agents with a view to setting up a European office and once made an airy offer for the ailing firm of Harold Holt Ltd, only to back off when they asked to see the colour of his money. He finally hired Sir Colin Davis's secretary, Judy Salpeter, to run a modest London bureau. 'The trouble with Ronald is that the first thing he does is lecture you on how to manage artists,' said one of the agents he pursued. 'He has no understanding of Europe or knowledge of languages. He thinks Europe is just Berlin, Vienna, Salzburg, Dresden, Munich, Milan, Paris and London, wherever he has got someone working as music director.'[18]

Whatever his limitations, the sight of Wilford's footprint sowed panic among European agencies. They sought political cover and, in some countries, secured it. In Switzerland and Austria, laws were enacted requiring opera houses and orchestras to book artists only from a local agent, a form of protectionism that was highly conducive to corruption. Viennese firms took to bribing opera officials to tell them who was being cast in future productions; all it then took to earn a commission was a call to the foreign singers with an offer of essential representation. In Germany there was a custom by which singers paid just four or five per cent commission to their agent, the other five per cent coming to the agent from the engaging opera house. This was designed to give local firms an advantage over foreigners, but it sowed doubt in artists' minds as to whether the agent was acting on their behalf or the opera house's.

Wilford viewed these procedures with contempt and carried on growing. 'It isn't done to conquer Europe or become multinational, which is what a lot of people are accusing me of trying to do,' he said. 'Those are terms you use with commodities, not with our field of endeavour. I have my own convictions and I want the ability to put them into practice . . . When I have the desire to make an international career, I want the ability to do that. It is not to conquer or compete: it is to offer better service to the people we represent.' Unlike Judson, who could not care what artists did when they were out of America, Wilford meant to manage them world-wide.

So long as Karajan was alive he needed no other ally. The Berlin potentate provided glittering careers for CAMI conductors and singers. In the Salzburg summer of 1987 Levine conducted one-third of the opera nights, as well as orchestral concerts. The Karajan connection unlocked Deutsche Grammophon doors to CAMI artists and eased their passage in other high places. With Karajan dead, the going would get bumpier but Wilford could afford to bide his time, having spread the maestro's monetary principles around the world. 'It was Wilford who established the market value of artists,' said festival organiser Peter Diamand.[19]

The day Wilford became president of Columbia, American concert fees started going through the roof. Until 1971, the rewards for live performance in the United States had been relatively modest. In 1949 there was a misleading rustle of C-notes as Arthur Rubinstein, Jascha Heifetz and Gregor Piatigorsky were acclaimed as the Million Dollar Trio on signing an RCA recording deal. But this, on closer inspection, turned out to be a piece of *Life* magazine hype that bore scant relation to their concert income. Heifetz, the greatest living violinist, was getting three thousand dollars for a Carnegie Hall date at the time. Vladimir Horowitz, his co-equal at the piano, received the same top fee.

The next echelon of performers – Rubinstein, Menuhin, Schnabel, Milstein and three or four others, got five hundred dollars less. One rung below them, a score of soloists rated two thousand dollars at Carnegie Hall and a fraction of that on tour. When Horowitz or Heifetz played Carnegie Hall the house made a five-thousand-dollar profit. If the artist's agent booked the concert independently he could cut out the local promoter and double his soloist's take. Even so, the money made by top musicians was unspectacular. 'Three or four pianists and an equal number of violinists earn $100,000 or more in a good year,' wrote the well-informed critic Howard Taubman in 1943. 'A limited group averages $50,000. Then there is a precipitous decline, and a fine talented musician considers himself lucky to earn $10,000.'[20] Quarter of a century later, the same proportions held true. Heifetz, nearing retirement in 1968 but still as big a draw as ever, received ten to twenty per cent more than the next-best violinist. The size of his fee represented supremacy, not avarice, and his recitals were self-financing without any need for subsidy.

Ronald Wilford would change all that with a little help from Sol Hurok. Just as Karajan had done in Europe, Wilford overturned an applecart that had trundled along happily for half a century. Wilford's weapon was the baton. By amassing a majority of maestros he could dictate terms to the orchestral sector. The tenure of a music director, understood since Mahler's time as occupying half a year or more, was reduced by Wilford to twenty, then fourteen, weeks, enabling his conductors to hold parallel jobs on other continents. Wilford then imposed a rule that the music director of one

American orchestra could not conduct any other. This helped create guest openings for his many floating maestros and sustain a spirit of opportunism across the profession.

Judson, himself an orchestral manager, would never have tolerated conditions that imperilled a sector he had helped construct. If any of his conductors sought a wage that was uneconomic, Judson would refuse, in the collective interest, to submit to his demand. Wilford, however, was unhampered by split loyalties or sentiment. He set out to get the most for his men, whatever the impact on the industry at large. 'My client is the artist – not the Philharmonic, not the Metropolitan Opera, not anyone else,' he told the *New York Times* in 1971, 'and I am absolutely ruthless if it comes to telling an orchestra to go to hell if I feel something is unfair to an artist of mine. I really don't care, because if I have an artist they want, they will have to book him.'

His attitude hit orchestras like a tax bill from the Borgias. Cities that reckoned on paying conductors a thousand bucks a night and a music director seventy thousand for the season suddenly had to cough up twice as much, and double again a few years later. In Philadelphia, where the podium was held by Wilford clients, the maestro price quadrupled between 1970 and 1990 for half the amount of work. In Boston it merely trebled. Other maestros, seeing what Wilford men were getting, wanted parity or better. In Chicago, where Wilford was shut out by successive managements, the music director's salary in 1995 was fifteen times what it had been in 1960, rising four times faster than national wages. In Los Angeles the seven hundred thousand dollars that Esa-Pekka Salonen earned in 1995 carried one whole digit more than Zubin Mehta's payslip in the 1960s. In Pittsburgh, Lorin Maazel struck gold as the first million-dollar maestro in 1990. Whether or not a conductor belonged to Wilford, his near-monopoly of major names enabled him to bludgeon orchestras into submission and give conductors a standard of living they had never expected or, perhaps, earned.

Hurok, meanwhile, was upping the ante for instrumentalists. 'Hurok would push the fees up, but just a little under what the artist was really worth so that he didn't really gouge the local impresarios,'[21] said Isaac Stern protectively. But the name of the game was getting top dollar. When Heifetz quit, Stern became the top soloist in America and made sure to stay that way. In 1995, turning seventy, Stern had a non-negotiable concert fee of forty-five thousand dollars, an amount matched only by Itzhak Perlman. That year, for his fiftieth birthday, Perlman played one hundred concerts around the world. Allowing for some discounting, his concert income was well in excess of three million dollars, to which he added royalties from the lifetime sales of four million records. When Perlman or Stern played at Carnegie Hall sponsors were needed to cover their fees and the house saw no profit.

Perlman was a prodigious artist and a kindly, charming man on crutches: no one grudged his great fortune. Trouble was, what Perlman got, others coveted. Agents for Anne-Sophie Mutter, the Steffi Graf of German music, sought record fees on her home turf and, when her version of the *Four Seasons* with Herbert von Karajan sold into six figures, inflated them abroad. Pinchas Zukerman, Midori and Yo-Yo Ma did not lag behind. A clutch of pianists hit the high Gs – Daniel Barenboim, Evgeny Kissin, Ivo Pogorelich, Maurizio Pollini – along with a range of vocal soloists, like Jessye Norman, Kiri Te Kanawa and Kathleen Battle. Since these performers usually guaranteed a full hall, orchestras paid up and swallowed the losses. There were pockets of resistance, like the year London orchestras buried their historic hatchets to impose a collective ban on Miss Mutter until she dropped her fee to below a thousand pounds in 1993. But in the end, pressured by conductors, agents, sponsors and audience expectations, orchestras usually paid up.

If large fees had been restricted to two conductors and soloists per generation, as they were in the era of Toscanini, Horowitz and Heifetz, orchestras might have absorbed the impact. But Wilford set out to make unrealistic increments the norm. His success (and Hurok's) slipped a noose around orchestral necks. If they wanted to fill a hall they had to pay a star more than he or she could ever recoup at the box-office. The loss, however, could not be made up at lower-profile concerts since they rarely sold out. And if by chance they did, the next season that orchestra would wind up paying the lesser-known soloist an unaffordable rate.

This was the CAMI catch-22 that grasped US orchestras warmly by the throat, pushing several to disbandment. California lost a fine band in Oakland. Denver and New Orleans went briefly to the wall, before reassembling as player-managed teams. The trail-blazing Louisville Orchestra, a fount of new music in the 1950s, sacked some players in 1995 and slashed the salaries of those who remained to twenty-four thousand dollars a year, just over half what Perlman, Stern, Mutter or Jessye Norman were making in a night. Freelancers in nine New York orchestras came out on strike in January 1993 over concert pay of less than a hundred and twenty dollars that barely kept their fiddles in spare strings. The richer the stars became the poorer was the fate of ordinary musicians and the fare of regional concerts.

A California agent took a call from a regional orchestra, wanting to know, 'Who've you got that's good and cheap?' When the agent asked why, they said, 'We've had an anniversary season and blew our entire soloists' budget on a concert with Isaac Stern. Now we've got to fill the gaps.'[22]

The cumulative effect of the fee explosion came to light in a 1992 ASOL report which showed that orchestral expenditure had risen eightfold, from 87.5 million dollars in 1971 to almost seven hundred million in two decades. More than half of this haywire hike – triple the cost-of-living rise – was ascribed to 'artistic costs'. In five years, between 1986 and 1991, these costs rose by half to $335.8 million. Since players' wages were being squeezed, the ball-breaking item on the budgets of American orchestras was the fees of conductors and soloists: the preponderance of whom were engaged from CAMI, the stars from Ronald Wilford in person.

The only way an orchestra could afford Wilford's artists was to pursue alternative sources of income. So they stacked the sales side of their staff and pushed artistic values into second place. 'Today, when the administrative operation of a major orchestra resembles that of a huge international corporation,' wrote the pianist Gary Graffman, 'most of the marketing techniques employed – the selling of the symphony – have nothing to do with the original purpose of the symphony being sold: that of presenting the finest music played in the best and most skilful manner for an audience that wishes to listen. In the desperate search to find a way for the orchestra to be all things to all people, these artificial gimmicks, with their continual emphasis on "relevance" succeed only in lowering the standards for everyone.'[23]

The American orchestra in the Wilford era entered a desperate fight for its survival. 'Judson never screwed us,' said one orchestral manager. 'Wilford is a different matter.' The master of 57th Street, sitting in his darkened office behind drawn Japanese blinds, unseen and unknown to the music public, shrugged off complaints with practised disdain. If an orchestra wanted to engage his artists, they must be able to afford them. No pay, no play. 'I don't care,' said Wilford, 'what anyone else thinks.'

Scoff as he might at Sol Hurok's weakness for self-advertisement, Wilford was easily unsettled by the old trickster. When the octogenarian impresario recruited back from CAMI his sometime aide, Sheldon Gold, an infuriated Wilford reportedly cut off Gold's phone and held him 'virtual prisoner . . . in a closet-like office'[24] until his contract expired. This was not the act of a confident man, and Wilford conceded that he may have been overcompensating for his sense of backwoods insecurity. 'I guess part of the reason I have this ruthless reputation is that, when I came to New York, I cut out a lot of feelings,' he told the *Times* in 1971. This was the last public glimpse he yielded of his inner self but, even after the shutters slammed down, managers and artists found themselves warming to an underlying, humanising vulnerability. 'There is something lovable about him,'[25] said an aide he sacked. 'When he wants to charm,' noted Stephen Rubin in the *Times*, 'he has men and women mesmerized.'

Hurok's death in 1974 brought his empire to rest, after three years of turmoil and lawsuits, in the hands of Sheldon Gold and the giant Hollywood agency, International Creative Management. Any anxiety Wilford may have felt at the rise of a movie-backed competitor, stacked with Isaac Stern gangers and run by an ex-CAMI man with a grievance, was allayed by Gold's laid-back attitude. Gold was a caring manager, after the European manner, who stayed close to a select handful of artists and was mourned by them long after his early death in 1985. 'Shelly Gold was the last of the old-fashioned managers,' grieved Itzhak Perlman.[26] 'CAMI is the General Motors, with models from A to Z,' Gold liked to say. 'We are the crème de la crème, the Rolls-Royce of the music business.'[27]

His successor, Lee Lamont, was made of sterner stuff. She set up a London branch and had bruising encounters with European agents but fought clear of Wilford, each respecting the other's lines like felines on the prowl. Lamont at ICM had the top violinists, plus Yo-Yo Ma, Wynton Marsalis and the pick of the Juilliard graduates. Wilford at CAMI had the conductors and most of everything else.

Using music directors as his agents of influence, Wilford proceeded to harness their institutions to his ideas. Who needed to manage an orchestra, like Judson, when its strings could be pulled through a surrogate? The Metropolitan Opera joined Wilford's domains the day it installed James Levine in its podium in 1973. The Boston Symphony Orchestra began listening to Wilford when it appointed Seiji Ozawa in 1972. Philadelphia, San Francisco and Detroit hired music directors exclusively from his office: Muti and Sawallisch, Blomstedt and Tilson Thomas, Järvi. CAMI men shuttled in and out of key administrative posts at these companies. When the Met opened an electronic-media department it was headed by a CAMI director, Peter Gelb, who had previously worked for the Boston Symphony Orchestra and continued to serve as its artistic adviser. The vocal consultant at Chicago's Lyric Opera and Santa Fe Opera was another CAMI partner, Matthew Epstein. The public was unaware of this subtle penetration, but musicians felt the thrust. Word went out among singers that if they wanted a role at the Met or Chicago, it helped greatly to be signed with CAMI. As for conductors, they knew all too well that an American career lay primarily in Wilford's gift.

By allowing these impressions to flourish, CAMI doubled in size under

Ronald Wilford's rule to eight hundred artists. Inevitably, some felt neglected. 'Ronald told every manager at CAMI to be attuned to the psychology of each artist. But how do you psychoanalyse five hundred singers? How does anyone get individual attention in a division of 150 artists?' asked a departing agent.[28]

Singer defections were commonplace. Wilford, in the space of five years, lost Kiri Te Kanawa, Cecilia Bartoli, Montserrat Caballé, Galina Gorchakova, Barbara Hendricks, Katia Ricciarelli and Dawn Upshaw, seven of the world's top sopranos. He appeared unconcerned. 'We have some who are terribly loyal, those who have succeeded in making a career,' he shrugged. 'Others don't succeed [sic], so there is turnover there. The turnover doesn't interest me. It's the ones whose careers we have been active with for years and years. Those are the ones we care about.'[29] The ones that mattered to Ronald Wilford were conductors, most of all his two favourites, Ozawa and Levine. Ozawa held the fort at Boston and earned CAMI a foothold in Japan, a connection of inestimable value to Wilford's global strategy. Levine was his key to the Met, and much, much else.

From the outset, Wilford's faith in Levine was boundless. 'I couldn't care if [New York Times critic] Harold Schonberg, Rudolf Bing, Sol Hurok, [Met chief] Goran Gentele and 25 people in Gregorian chant said James Levine is a failure. I wouldn't believe it,' declared Wilford in 1971.[30] His support was vindicated once Levine was entrenched at the Met, his unstinting application steering the company through patches of financial and managerial uncertainty to a plane of supreme confidence. Rehearsing in polo shirt and sneakers, a bright-coloured terry-towel splashed over his left shoulder to catch the drenching sweat from his two-hundred-pound frame, Levine made the orchestra the match of any in America and the chorus a formidable force. The Met was the only house in the world where the biggest stars turned out every season – not for the fees, which were capped at thirteen thousand dollars, but for the pleasure of working with a congenial music director and a strong all-round cast. Levine was an assiduous vocal coach and sensitive piano accompanist, often partnering his stars in lieder recitals.

Many of them were his personal discoveries. Kathleen Battle, Jessye Norman, Dawn Upshaw, June Anderson and a host of American singers made their names at the Met and their international careers through CAMI. With flowers from Levine's nursery, Wilford was able to supply Bayreuth with the Wagnerian voices it could no longer find in Germany and Deutsche Grammophon with its last Ring cycle of the twentieth century. Levine's success took him to Bayreuth, Salzburg and almost to Berlin as Karajan's heir, Wilford lighting his way and planting new flagpoles for his own podium empire.

There were purists (there always are) who carped at the overparting of young singers and the overuse of superannuated stars. Such gripes were generally wide of the mark. Under Levine, the Met reached a period of peak prosperity both in the calibre of its artists and the state of its organisation. No opera house in the world offered governmentally unsubsidised seats at such affordable prices. None was seen and heard so widely via satellite broadcasts, as well as on disc and video. It was, of all the world's opera houses, unbeatably the most international in quality and outreach.

Yet there were flaws, the most visible of which lay at the nexus of the music director's link to his agent. Unlike almost every other CAMI conductor, Levine spent most of his year in one podium. This was less out of choice than necessity: he could not find reliable conductors to lead revivals at the house. Apart from an infrequent visit by Ozawa or the maverick Kleiber, the Met was conducted by makeweights. The cause of Levine's difficulty was Wilford. He would not let maestros waste six weeks rehearsing a Met opera at a weekly rate of ten thousand dollars when they could be earning twenty thousand a night giving concerts in Pittsburgh, Cleveland, Dallas, Chicago and twenty other cities. 'It is not to the advantage of other conductors to go to the Met,' he told me. 'I want them to go here, here and here. And no, just because I manage you [Levine], it doesn't mean I help you for your opera house, that's your problem.'

When Levine came to complain, Wilford administered a powerful unguent. 'Ronald said something interesting to me a few years ago,' Levine confided to the New Yorker. 'He said, "Do you have any idea how many people think of you as the sun coming up each day?" '[31] His ego polished to full beam, the music director leaned back and let the praise wash over him. Many marvelled at Levine's energy and enthusiasm; few were aware of the pit stops that refuelled them.

Wilford's support saw him through untold crises. Had Levine looked closer, he might have felt that some of them were of his manager's making. He was accused, for example, of turning the Met into a mausoleum of well-worn hits by Mozart, Verdi, Wagner and Puccini. Levine replied that the Met had three thousand eight hundred seats to fill. Nevertheless, his caution seemed excessive. It took Levine eighteen years to commission an American opera, John Corigliano's Ghosts of Versailles. It was 1992 before the Met risked Janáček's Katya Kabanova, a 1921 masterpiece that was acclaimed across Europe. Unlike most conductors, Levine never dabbled in modernism – let alone the avant-garde – even for curiosity's sake. He had been guided from age nineteen by Ronald ('We advise on everything') Wilford. If the Met was ultra-conservative, it bore the stamp of its music director's mentor. One-third of its Levine-era playbills were Puccini nights. 'Ronald has strong views on repertoire, and he makes sure his conductors know them,' said a CAMI defector. 'He treated some of his artists in a completely dictatorial manner,' said Peter Diamand. 'He decided whether they accepted an invitation or not. He'd say, "I won't let Seiji conduct a third-rate orchestra like yours." Which wouldn't stop him a few weeks later from saying, "Can't you take such-and-such a conductor? It would be such a glory for him to conduct the wonderful Orchestre de Paris." '[32]

'I'm on their side in finding out what it is that makes them function best. That's my job,' said Wilford. So, on his advice, Levine conducted grandiose romanticisms when his particular gift was for classical clarity. Ozawa recorded Mahler and Prokofiev cycles with bland impersonality, when his flair was best evidenced in French impressionisms. Their records failed to set critics alight and left no mark on the sales charts, except in Japan. Yet this is what Wilford, who never studied music and did not attend a concert before he became a manager, advised them to record. His conductors aimed for the familiar, the failsafe, the overplayed.

Evidence of his involvement was witnessed at the début of Daniele Gatti, a rising Milanese whom Wilford introduced as 'the next Riccardo Muti'. Gatti had been invited to the Met for Donizetti's *Lucia di Lammermoor*, only for Wilford to recommend *Madama Butterfly* as 'more of a conductor's opera'. Young and uncertain, Gatti switched operas and made a relatively subdued début. *Lucia*, with June Anderson in the title role, would have given both soprano and himself a greater triumph. Anderson quit CAMI over the deflection; Wilford was typically unmoved. He was doing what he liked best, calling the shots at the Met and moulding his new maestro.

His influence, along with Levine's security, was finally challenged when their soprano of choice, Kathleen Battle, was sacked in February 1994 for what the Met management described as 'unprofessional actions . . . profoundly detrimental to artistic collaboration'. Battle, at forty-six, had become a backstage byword for diva-like excesses. She refused to share transport with other singers, dismissed the stretch limo that was taking her to the Clinton inauguration because it was not long enough, pushed Trevor Pinnock off the podium to direct a Handel rehearsal and pulled out of a Vienna Philharmonic date at three hours' notice, provoking the first cancelled concert in the orchestra's history. A 'wonderful friend' and fellow-Ohian of Levine's, she could do no wrong in his eyes, nor in the ears of a hundred thousand fans who bought their Mozart recital on CD. The seventh child of a black steelworker, she was the stuff of American dreams and an icon to the unempowered. To fellow-musicians, she was the epitome of uncollegiality.

At Lincoln Center she refused to sing until her dressing-room was provided with a bigger cake of soap. At San Francisco Opera orchestral players wore a T-shirt with the motto 'I Survived the Battle'.

Her credit began to run out at the Met when, rehearsing *Der Rosenkavalier*, she lashed out at a young guest conductor, Christian Thielemann, and called for general manager Joseph Volpe. When he refused to attend, she went home. On hearing from Wilford's office that Volpe backed the conductor, she walked out on the production. Volpe, an ex-carpenter at the Met whom Pavarotti affectionately dubbed '*grande capo*', was the wrong man to offend. She toured blamelessly with the Met in Japan but Volpe had marked her card.

Back home for Donizetti's *La Fille du Régiment*, she kept changing rehearsal times and persisted in coming late. She threw one Friday tantrum too many at a veteran mezzo, Rosalind Elias, who had been friendly with Volpe in his scene-building days. The house trembled all weekend, anticipating a show-down. Wilford, sensing trouble, called a meeting with Volpe first thing Monday morning but appears to have succeeded only in stiffening his resolve. Hours later, the Met issued Battle's marching orders in unusually harsh wording. Battle replied, denying misconduct. Wilford said, 'It is my position that she was wrongfully terminated and should be paid for the engagements. Kathy Battle is a perfectionist and she always fights for that perfection.'[33]

The case was called to arbitration by the American Guild of Musical Artists, of which Battle was a paid-up member, and the lawyers got to work. Whatever the outcome of any settlement, Battle was out of the Met with a badly bruised career, notwithstanding her agent's best efforts. She could still get concert dates wherever she liked, but her return to the American stage was dependent on Volpe's mercy, and the *capo* was not known as a compassionate man. Battle's few defenders blamed her advisers who, they said, should have warned her years before of the likely consequences of her conduct.

Levine, who was away at his father's deathbed when the row broke, returned to find his own future at stake and some of his authority eroded. A new artistic manager, Sarah Billinghurst, had been appointed by Volpe. Levine's foes were murmurous, among them some board members who barely suppressed their outrage at extra-mural activities that, according to *Time* magazine, involved 'liaisons with people of every age and hue'. The Met needed Levine for the time being and renewed his contract to 1999, but the rule of 'What Jimmy wants, Jimmy gets' no longer applied. Volpe let it be known that he was vetoing some of Levine's artistic proposals.

The real loser, however, was Ronald Wilford, whose armlock on the Met was broken with suprising ease in the Battle fracas. Volpe had called his bluff and the agent, needing to protect Levine and his many singers at the Met, folded like a house of cards. His name was in the papers again, and that hurt. The damage was widely seen. A myth of Columbia invincibility stretching over decades had been dented. Some said the music business would never be the same again.

The Nineties had not been kind to Ronald Wilford. Karajan's death in July 1989 left him without an idol. Levine's failure to win Berlin was an added blow, although the chosen Abbado was also a Wilford client. André Previn, a long-time favourite, was wearily out of the running for top jobs. Klaus Tennstedt, his German hope, had taken early retirement. Giuseppe Sinopoli, his Italian investment, was not winning hearts and minds. Riccardo Muti and Bernard Haitink were distancing themselves from his advice. Worse, the younger generation of Simon Rattle, Esa-Pekka Salonen and Riccardo Chailly were shunning CAMI as a doddering monolith, casting their lot with boutique-like personal agents who attended to their every need.

One young contender who came Wilford's way was Daniele Gatti, chief conductor at thirty-one of Rome's Santa Cecilia Orchestra. Gatti was called to New York by the American Symphony Orchestra and, at the end of a rehearsal that left the players gasping, found Ronald Wilford waiting in his green room. 'We'll work together,' said the agent. 'Fine,' said Gatti, 'but at my tempo.' Wilford, accustomed to snaring conductors with promises of Boston and Philadelphia, had to bear with Gatti as he worked his way through small-town orchestras, before taking on the Big Five. In 1995 Gatti accepted a post with the Royal Philharmonic Orchestra in London, an unsettled band in poor repair. It was not a move Wilford would have advised but good conductors were scarcer than ever and the master-agent was prepared to bide his time.

He thought he had signed the exciting St Petersburg conductor, Valery Gergiev, in November 1989, but the deal he struck with the Gosconcert state agency collapsed with the Soviet Union. Gergiev came forth with a mind of his own, leading the Maryinsky Theatre by example and urging his singers to give it their first loyalty. On tours abroad, conductor and stars chipped back a tithe of their dollars to the theatre's coffers. This was not the kind of dedication Wilford applauded in a conductor. When the tireless Gergiev took a part-time job in Holland as music director of the Rotterdam Philharmonic, he did so without the benefit of agents. Wilford, none the less, kept him on the CAMI list and was often to be seen at Gergiev performances, waiting his moment.

Back home, Wilford was feeling competitors' breath on his nape. The sports king, Mark McCormack, had invaded classical music with his International Management Group and ICM was staying the course longer than Wilford had reckoned. In 1995, Lee Lamont stepped down as ICM president, to be succeeded by the avuncular David Foster, a CAMI partner previously seen as Wilford's heir apparent. Wilford calmly allowed Foster to walk out, together with his deputy, Caroline Woodfield. Both found their phones still working and their doors unlocked.

A spate of further departures, some less peaceable, aroused press speculation about CAMI's stability. There were whispers of overdue mortgages and fraying credit lines. The *New York Times* assigned two reporters to investigate CAMI over several months. They came up with no evidence of liquidity problems or managerial decay. 'This company is owed two to three million dollars in commissions,' Wilford told employees. 'Any company in our business that is owed that much can't be in a great deal of trouble.'

Yet stretch-marks were clearly appearing on the Columbia epidermis. Wilford suddenly put a stop on staff buying any more stock. When Foster and others departed they had to sell back their shares in Columbia, at Wilford's valuation, and presumably to him. There was, remarked the *Times* pointedly, 'no outside monitoring of [CAMI] finances'.[34] Except for a tax inspector and an accountant or two, no one but Wilford knew the precise disposition of a company that was allegedly 'wholly owned by its employees'. Wilford told fellow-directors what he felt they needed to know, and nothing more. The secrets of Columbia were held by its chief shareholder and he, for some reason, was getting jittery. The *Times* inquiry made him uneasy, and his discomfort at my investigations was reported back to me by several sources. Never a trustful man, he no longer knew whom he could trust. He shut down the publicity department.

A sign of his edginess was a decision in 1990 to sue one of his artists. The pianist André Watts had defected to IMG and told promoters to pay commissions to his new agency. CAMI, represented by Ralph Colin's old law firm, claimed breach of contract and was awarded judgement of three hundred and thirty-seven thousand dollars, plus interest and costs against the pianist. Watts would have to play a lot of concertos to repay his debt to Ronald Wilford. Since anger alone would not have provoked the secretive Wilford to risk a fully reported fight in open court, it must be assumed that he feared Watts's defection was the first trickle from a cracked dam and launched the action demonstratively, *pour encourager les autres*.

Inside CAMI headquarters Wilford's tetchiness was manifest. A young associate, questioning the heavy workload he was lining up for a vulnerable opera singer, was dismissed on the spot. 'Your contract will not be renewed,' said Wilford. A soprano, daring to question his career advice, was told, 'This lunch is now over' — and so was her CAMI contract. Foster, who had been the friendly face of CAMI, found two of his limelight projects whisked away by the boss and realised there was no future for him in the firm.

The roughening brusqueness, though, was mitigated by streaks of sentimentality. I have seen Ronald Wilford gently escort Sir Rudolf Bing, befuddled by Alzheimer's Disease and barely knowing the time of day, into his personal limousine to be taken to a performance at the Metropolitan Opera that he once ruled. Wilford allowed Nelly Walters, a CAMI partner in her nineties, to keep her office and personal staff and ensured that everyone in the office treated her with courtesy and deference. A Mediterranean respect for white hairs became increasingly pronounced in his demeanour as he passed the conventional retirement age.

Nearing seventy, the Silver Fox had no son or daughter in the business and, avowedly, no long-term strategy. 'We go project by project,' he once said, using each advance to plant another stave in the CAMI fence that ringed the world of music. To accelerate this process, he now encouraged his associates to infiltrate arts organisations. In 1991 Matthew Epstein, a director of CAMI and adviser to two US opera houses, was named general director of Welsh National Opera. Epstein, in his early forties, was an astute judge of vocal quality and a trusted friend of many singers. He was often seen on the town with Kathleen Battle on his arm and freely lent his apartment to the Welsh baritone Bryn Terfel when he came to New York to make the outstanding Met début of the Nineties. Epstein remained, however, an active artists' agent and his appointment to run a state opera house raised questions of conflictuality not previously encountered in Britain. It was soothingly reported that Epstein had given the Welsh board certain formal assurances about his position.

He need hardly have bothered for, within eighteen months, Epstein was gone. An Arts Council funding squeeze elicited a swift letter of resignation. While other opera directors stood and fought for their companies Epstein, an agent by trade, saw the cash had run out and there was no point in staying. Stung by seeing himself described as an operatic butterfly, he retorted, 'Perhaps a bee might be more apt. Indeed I do move about with some speed looking for artistic situations of excellence and real promise (as WNO has provided) but when honey begins to evaporate, I am left starved, and go on . . .'[35] His metaphor was the more revealing for being mixed. Real bees do not consume honey. They make it for others to enjoy. True to CAMI creed, Epstein did not readily give up a position of influence. Two years after his resignation, the busy agent was back in Cardiff as a judge of the Singer of the World competition, earmarking future clients for his expanding division.

Wilford counted Epstein's band of singers as a proof of his own foresight. He was still hungry for growth and assigned strained resources towards a television foray, the strengthening of the music theatre department and the formation of an ambitiously named division of Twenty-First Century Culture under Alexander Castonguay, a section that promoted supposed futurisms like cabaret singer Ute Lemper, minimalist Michael Nyman, movie composer Michael Kamen and rock dissident Stewart Copeland. These cults were peripheral, however, to CAMI's main concerns, whereas opera and television were quintessential. CAMI made waves in television for only twelve years, but that tactical venture would prove crucial to Wilford's endgame.

In the summer of 1981 Wilford, ever on the look-out for agency talent, offered a job in his office to an assistant manager of the Boston Symphony Orchestra. The young man came warmly recommended and extremely well connected. Seiji Ozawa was so impressed by his many qualities that he had lent his house at Stockbridge, Massachusetts, for the aide's wedding to Donna Grey, a public relations executive. Wilford, noted a Boston staffer, 'was jealous of anyone in orchestral management who got too close to his conductors, especially Ozawa. But this person was an exception.'[36]

The assistant manager, who was just twenty-seven years of age, was called Peter Gelb. His father, Arthur, was a managing editor of the *New York Times*, with special responsibility for cultural coverage. His mother, Barbara, was a writer. Given that *Times* reviews and features carried more musical clout than any other US newspaper's, the Gelbs were useful folk for Wilford to cultivate.

Arthur Gelb would be eased into early retirement in 1990, after allegations that he used the arts pages to advance the careers of his wife and son. 'Over more than a decade,' reported *Variety*, 'the *Times*' former editors A. M. Rosenthal and Arthur Gelb have been accused of practising a form of cultural tyranny, of imposing their tastes and priorities on the community at large . . . Gelb was most frequently criticised for lavishing coverage on any event involving Eugene O'Neill. Gelb and his wife, Barbara, co-wrote a biography of O'Neill; Barbara Gelb also wrote a one-act play based on the life of Carlotta Monterey O'Neill. Joseph Papp (its producer) . . . dictated coverage – even the reporter he wanted to do the story – and Arthur would set it up.

'Clients of Arthur Gelb's son, Peter, an agent who represented many classical musicians, were said by staffers at the time to be given what one described as "ridiculous overcoverage".'[37] Independent publicists were startled to find that the Boston Symphony Orchestra was getting more feature columns in the *Times* than the New York Philharmonic. 'Before Peter Gelb worked for the Boston Symphony Orchestra, this paper never covered out-of-town orchestras unless they came to New York,' recalled a music staffer. 'When Peter was in Boston, we were running features on Ozawa, BSO tours and anything that went on there.'[38] Small wonder Ozawa was impressed. The paper even ran a hatchet-job on the senior Boston critic, Richard Dyer, who was frequently hostile to Ozawa.

The *New York Times* would prefer to draw a line under its Arthur Gelb era when 'an electric, almost showbiz snap and tension [was brought] to the newsroom, much of it the result of the restless Gelb's unending flow of ideas'.[39] The quality of these ideas was contested by the paper's critics who, in 1978, threatened mass resignation, protesting 'that critics should feel free to express their own point of view rather than try to express the opinions of their editor'.[40] Their challenge was faced down by executive editor Rosenthal and for twelve more years the lanky, bespectacled, conspiratorial Gelb ruled as the closest equivalent America ever had to a cultural commissar. The *Times* set the tone for what the nation should see and hear and Gelb set the agenda for the *Times*. One consequence of his sovereignty was the impressive rise of his son, Peter.

Gelb junior's first job was a stint in Sol Hurok's office in 1971, when he was seventeen. He went on to Yale but dropped out after a semester – 'he was not cut out for academia,' said a contemporary – and went to work for the New York public relations firm of Gurtman and Murtha, advisers to comedian Victor Borge. His first client was the Harlem Boys' Choir which 'by some coincidence acquired a great deal of publicity in the *Times*'.[41] In 1974, reading that Vladimir Horowitz was planning one of his famous comebacks, Gelb offered to organise his publicity. 'Of course, it did not escape Horowitz's calculating mind that Gelb was the son of Arthur Gelb . . . and one of Arthur Gelb's domains was the [*Times*'s] cultural coverage,' wrote Horowitz's biographer and the newspaper's fastidious chief music critic, Harold Schonberg.

Gelb senior issued a self-distancing memo to the effect that 'Peter was on his own' and any Horowitz item 'would be run at the discretion of the music editor', who 'leaned over backward not to print Horowitz stories'.[42] This did not keep Horowitz off the front news page of the *Times* after a Peter Gelb press stunt at the Met in 1978. The coverage was admired by Tom Morris, manager of the Boston Symphony Orchestra, who offered Peter Gelb the position of publicity director. Boston had to take on an extra assistant to prepare press releases 'because Peter was very insecure about writing', but the PR man proved himself an able organiser on Boston tours to Japan and China in 1978–9. 'Peter is one of the most brilliant publicists I have ever worked with and very successful in making tour deals,' confirmed Morris.[43]

Gelb's enthusiasm for famous musicians could lead him easily astray, as on the day he let a *Life* photographer invade a Rostropovich recital at Tanglewood. The audience was unsettled by clickety flashes and Gelb was punched in the mouth on the Tanglewood lawn by an outraged artistic administrator. He had a lot to learn about music and seemed more focused on celebrities than on what they performed. He became Ozawa's tennis partner. He was exactly the kind of man Ronald Wilford was looking for.

Wilford, never one to court rejection, made sure that his offer to Gelb in 1981 was irresistible. Knowing the young man's greater ambitions lay not in music but in the movies (his father, Arthur, claimed credit for 'discovering' Woody Allen and Barbra Streisand), Wilford asked him to set up a division at CAMI making films about famous musicians and selling them to public television. His motives were uncomplicated and his need immediate. Herbert von Karajan was devoting his declining years to filming himself conducting the core symphonic repertoire and Wilford, as ever, wanted in on the potential new market for music videos. Gelb consented without much hesitation and, by way of a dowry, brought Vladimir Horowitz back to CAMI. The pellucid pianist, in a rare interview, told the *New York Times* (who else?) on 13 August 1981 that he was changing agents because he needed somebody like Gelb to look after his special needs. Over the next few months Gelb coaxed him into giving his first London concert in almost thirty years, followed by a coast-to-coast US tour and a début trip to Japan. Back in his upper-Eastside studio, Horowitz spiralled into precipitate decline. Ronald Wilford, throwing him an eightieth birthday party in October 1983, worried whether he had contracted Alzheimer's Disease. Between themselves, Horowitz and his wife, Wanda, referred to Wilford as 'the barracuda'.[44]

Gelb stayed close to them, however, and when Horowitz showed signs of revival in April 1985, made a film of his late-afternoon musings at the piano. 'I never play anything exactly the same twice,' said the last relic of the great Russian school. American record labels, accustomed to his eccentricities, showed no interest in the sound-track, so Gelb sold it to a producer called Günther Breest at Deutsche Grammophon in Germany. The deal would prove fateful, not so much for Horowitz, who had five years to live and fewer records to make, but principally for Gelb and Breest.

The Horowitz film was Gelb's first international television coup. Although classical music was banned on ratings-led American networks, it had a popular following and powerful credits in Europe. Filming music was where many movie directors cut their milk-teeth – Franco Zeffirelli, John Schlesinger, Ken Russell – and Gelb was intelligently following their route.

It was a good time to be selling documentaries. European networks were becoming budget-conscious and starting to accept input from apparently independent producers. 'When I first started in this field,' Gelb told a television conference in 1992, 'there was a great deal of enthusiasm amongst the major players in Europe to back programmes that had a lot of international appeal and glamour having to do with classical music.'[45] As a CAMI agent, Gelb could deliver celebrity performers and some finance without being cross-examined too closely about his editorial agendas, or who got final cut of his star portraits. Most of the funding came, Karajan-fashion, from the public purse as state-supported channels purchased the CAMI programmes. This was a neat way of making music films and it won Gelb six Emmy awards. It also gained him access to decision makers in television who could put CAMI clients in the public eye. Gelb willingly used his contacts on Wilford's behalf.

In July 1988, he called the head of music at Austrian Television (ORF), urging him to relay James Levine's performance of Haydn's *Creation* from the Salzburg Festival for the second year in succession. 'At first, Peter Gelb was all honey,' said the executive. 'Then, when I remained adamant in my refusal, he said, "OK, but you will get no more Karajan recordings on ORF."'[46] An intervention by the festival director, Franz Willnauer, nullified the Karajan threat (if ever it held substance), but the incident reveals how thoroughly Gelb had learned his craft from Wilford, brandishing big names to promote smaller CAMI fry and dictating to a state organ what music it should play. *L'état*, as Karajan might have put it, *c'est moi*.

In the course of a dozen years, the fifty-odd movies that Gelb produced amounted, in the main, to glossy profiles of CAMI artists – Ozawa, Jessye Norman, Rostropovich, Abbado, Kathleen Battle and a stream of relays from Levine's Metropolitan Opera, where Gelb was executive producer in charge of television programming until Joseph Volpe turfed him out (reportedly threatening to throw him bodily across Lincoln Center). In addition, Gelb organised and filmed all-star concerts in St Petersburg and Prague and an historic relay of Horowitz's return to Moscow in 1986. Using reputable directors and top sound teams, his films looked like bona-fide music programming, until the relentlessly flattering camera angles and soundbites led viewers to suspect otherwise.

'Peter's films were not always as bad as they seemed,' said Richard Dyer of the *Boston Globe*, a long-standing Gelb-watcher. Dyer sensed a glimmer of idealism in the Prague film when, into an all-star line-up, assembled for the centenary of Dvořák's *New World* Symphony, Gelb slipped on the august keyboard artist Rudolf Firkušný to play a Dvořák Ballade. 'Firkušný had never been on world television, and those three minutes of his were out of this world,' said Dyer. 'Peter didn't have to put him on. The mass audience had never heard of him. But Firkušný was in the film, and Peter deserves credit for that.'[47]

There was documentary merit, too, in the Horowitz and Karajan films where the subjects were too old or weary to care much what the world saw of them. As a genre, however, Gelb's films trod a dubious line between art and self-advertisement, and Dyer was among the first to attack their impropriety. 'You can't go putting on public television profiles of artists made by their agent,' he said. Similar complaints were voiced in Europe. By the time of Karajan's death, Gelb was being cold-shouldered by many broadcasters (with one notable exception, Britain's Channel 4).

'I would probably be out of business, if the record companies hadn't stepped in to fill the gap,'[48] Gelb confessed in 1992. That salvation, though, was short-term. The record industry was hoping to stimulate demand for videodiscs of musicians in action but the recession was fierce and the public uninterested, except in Japan. CAMI Video was becoming a drain on the agency. 'Do we make money on that? No,' said Ronald Wilford. 'Do we break even? Yes.'

At this point, Gelb pulled off a deal that saved his career and CAMI's future. Through Seiji Ozawa, he had got to know the heads of Japan's Sony Corporation, Akio Morita and Norio Ohga. Both men were ardent music lovers and Ozawa fans – to the extent that they were preparing to build a $9.7-million concert hall bearing his name at Tanglewood, Ohga donating two million dollars from his own pocket. 'It has long been my wish to be able to perpetuate Seiji Ozawa's name in connection with the Boston Symphony Orchestra,' said the Sony president.

Sony brows were furrowed in 1993 by public resistance to their laserdisc and minidisc players. The only reason for people to buy the machines would be the quality of the programmes available to play on them. Sony owned Columbia Records and Columbia Pictures that pumped out dozens of new releases each month, but head office felt insecure and in need of fresh ideas, especially in the high-spending consumer area of classical music.

On 14 July 1993, Sony announced that it had bought CAMI Video and appointed Peter Gelb president of Sony Classical USA and deputy to Günther

Breest, his erstwhile Horowitz partner, now Sony Classical chief in Hamburg. 'Peter Gelb, with his special talent in classical music production and repertoire and music-based film-making, is ideally qualified to become an invaluable resource for Sony,' said Michael P. Schulhof, president of Sony Music Entertainment. The price Sony paid CAMI for Gelb's operation was around six million dollars, plus a seven-figure signing-on fee to Gelb. For a venture that was struggling to break even and had fifty movies no one wanted to see, six million was some price. Ronald Wilford could barely conceal his glee. 'We're not doing this for the money,' he said. 'The sale simply represents what everyone should be doing. Peter is a brilliant talent, and it is time for him to move on.'[49] Some time later, Wilford modified that statement. 'He didn't leave,' said the CAMI chief. 'I sold him.'[50]

The brilliance of Gelb's talent, echoed by a Sony press release, was said to have 'involved the creation of musical productions with virtually all major orchestras and opera companies throughout the world'. He had devised projects in Japan and was producing a new version of Walt Disney's *Fantasia*. The former publicist, it seemed, had invented his own myth. He was certainly conscious enough of its importance to employ the publicity director of the Boston Symphony Orchestra, Kim Smedvig, to handle his personal PR, alongside Ozawa's. Detractors said Gelb placed image above substance, even delaying Horowitz's funeral by a day to match the date reported in the *New York Times*. At a New Year's concert in Vienna, he had the cards on the artists' bouquets changed from Sony to Peter Gelb. 'He is totally without any presence or personality, that is why he is so ego-conscious,' said a Sony producer. Detractors, though, became fewer and less willing to be named as Gelb's power increased.

At thirty-nine, he had his own record and movie label and unlimited backing from Tokyo. As for Ronald Wilford, he had lost a son ('I adore Peter, but I cannot hold Peter back') and gained a dominion. In the small print of Peter Gelb's Sony contract was the appointment of Ronald Wilford to the board of Sony Classical USA. This gave Wilford what every agent coveted: access to the easiest means of plugging his artists. Things were looking up again at the fortress on 57th Street and a smile was seen playing on Ronald Wilford's pursed lips.

The curve of Peter Gelb's amazing career stayed in the ascendant. Within twenty months the curly-topped ex-publicist took over as global head of Sony Classical, replacing the outsmarted Breest. 'Günther resigned because Ohga was not prepared to back him against Peter Gelb,' said a Sony producer.[51] Gelb announced an 'aggressively eclectic' policy for the ailing label, pruning the existing artists' list and dismissing the Hamburg production team. In their place he appointed CAMI colleague Matthew Epstein as vocal consultant and Laura Mitgang, a video producer, as head of artists and repertoire. The direction was recklessly populist. Bobby McFerrin, a conductor in dreadlocks who yodelled his way through symphony concerts, was plastered on all Manhattan buses and bus shelters. Michael Kamen, composer for the *Lethal Weapon* movies and a new CAMI client, was the kind of artist Gelb looked to promote. Although Gelb relinquished his shares in CAMI, the ties between Columbia Artists and Sony Classical were now indivisible. Ronald Wilford went around calling Peter Gelb 'one of the most brilliant men I know'.

While the music business was engrossed in these movements, the market for music was mutating in alarming ways. Star-studded certainties of the record industry were gathering dust, concert audiences were waning, and funding was hard to come by. European governments were cutting public spending, the NEA was under threat of extinction by 1997 and the panacea of business sponsorship was starting to look chimerical. Early in 1996 Covent Garden found itself two million pounds in the red because corporate funding was down by one-third that season.

'Changing priorities in the private sector have affected giving patterns to orchestras and will probably continue to do so,' warned a gloomy 1992 report from the American Symphony Orchestral League. Orchestras were losing ground to medical and environmental causes. Personal donations predominated in US arts support, but music was missing out on fast-growing business sponsorship, which tripled its volume in the Nineties. Only six per cent of US business sponsorship went to the arts in 1994; the bulk went to sports (sixty-seven per cent), rock concerts (ten per cent) and insatiable causes like AIDS research and geriatric hospitals. Windsurfing, with twenty-five million dollars' worth of sponsorship, outstripped the entire US orchestral sector, which raised just $7.5 million in business grants. British banks, pitching for student accounts, switched backing from classical concerts which needed subsidy to rock gigs which did not.

Music was losing out on every front. A new generation of social lions were less keen on concert going than their parents had been. In the 1960s, recalled Joseph Silverstein, ex-concertmaster of the Boston Symphony Orchestra, 'people like Henry B. Cabot would come to every Friday night concert at the Boston Symphony, and when we played Mozart his handkerchief was out. Today, there are board chairpersons in orchestras across the country who don't even come to concerts. We have people on the boards simply because they are CEOs of organisations that give money to the orchestras.'[52]

The few who gave demanded more for their money. In exchange for covering five per cent of a concert's costs, a sponsor expected to have his name plastered over the hoardings and programme, and even mentioned in newspaper reviews. 'Sponsorship is where it gets way out of hand.' Ronald Wilford sighed. 'When commercialisation means you have to drape the stage with the logo of the sponsor, it leaves me [cold].'[53] Yet the sponsor was in a position to dictate terms and forward-looking agencies set up sponsorship departments to obtain direct funding for individual artists. Conductors went into job auditions waving sponsorship packages rather than batons.

Orchestral and operatic seasons were planned in accordance with the preferences, real or imagined, of those who held the purse strings and sat in the best seats. As the centre stalls filled with the cream of corporate society, the atmosphere thickened and younger listeners were deterred, by price and ambience, from sharing the experience of great music performed by living masters. Concert going became a preserve of the moneyed and the middle-aged.

The state machine that was supposed to support music in Europe squandered limited resources on an ever-spreading arts bureaucracy. In 1992 the Arts Council of Great Britain employed one hundred and seventy-five staff to disburse one hundred and ninety-four million pounds, of which eight million pounds went on Council salaries and administration – enough to fund an opera house. The Council was a relatively efficient, low-paid body, which is more than can be said of the Department of National Heritage, which employed almost four hundred civil servants to oversee arts and leisure in the UK. Net costs of running this superfluous agency trebled from nine million pounds in 1989–90 to twenty-eight million five years later – at a time when arts funding was frozen and government was cutting spending on everything but itself. The department's expenses did not include the salaries of a Secretary of State, a junior minister, their personal staff, five departmental cars, chauffeurs, international travel and all the usual perks.[54] A ministry designed to give the arts a seat at the Cabinet table was leeching off their dwindling cash flow.

The British figured fairly low on the profligacy scale. Cultural bureaucrats of the European Union were to be found daily in the finest restaurants in Brussels, disbursing funds to politically motivated causes. Ministers in Rome fiddled while the Opera was raided by fraud detectives, as its director, Gianpaolo Cresci was charged with mishandling public funds and fined sixteen million lire (one hundred thousand dollars) by Lazio region high court for running up debts of forty-five billion lire. A veteran festival director raged against 'the hypocrisy of state funding' that nurtured delusions of grandeur in the givers and dependency status in the recipients.

And music meanwhile was running out of time and money, its orchestras collapsing, its opera houses reduced to showing musicals. London's state-funded Coliseum proposed staging *My Fair Lady*. Aachen, a German city with a thousand years of musical culture, relied on Lionel Bart's *Oliver* and a rock musical *Gaudi* to balance its operatic books. Its much-praised intendant, Elmar Ottenthal, headed a new breed of management experts who replaced conductors and stage directors at the head of arts institutions, which they ran like district hospitals. Knowing there was no possibility of profit in classical music, they concentrated their efforts on minimising losses.

Feeling the squeeze on artist engagements, the music business upped its fees, determined to get the most out of the system while it lasted. A sampling of artistic budgets in major companies across Europe and America shows that fees rose by thirty to fifty per cent in the five years after Karajan's death, testimony to the blend of greed and desperation that now prevailed.

How much the major agents took out of taxpayers' pockets cannot be assessed with total accuracy. But if Covent Garden is taken as a working example, agents would be paid a nightly dividend on six to eight performers – the leading singers, the conductor and usually the stage director. With a top fee of ten thousand pounds and a median of two thousand to five thousand pounds, it can reasonably be reckoned that agents take about as much per night as the leading baritone. Multiply that by one hundred performances a season and the agents' share of the Royal Opera budget comes to three hundred and fifty thousand pounds – enough to fund four new productions, or double the company's outreach activities.

In the micro-economics of modern music, the agents' take constituted a chunk of working capital that opera houses and orchestras could invest more profitably in new work. Yet no company has dared outlaw agents for fear of losing their stars, and most preferred their artists to be professionally represented as a means of reducing the risk of contractual misunderstandings and uncontrollable tantrums.

One British agency, the fourth or fifth largest, took eight hundred thousand pounds in commissions in the year to April 1991, returning one hundred and seventy-five thousand pounds in profit to its directors after salaries and expenses. The company, founded by a former flautist, Joeske Van Walsum, on capital of one thousand pounds, could not fail to make money while taking twenty per cent of the world earnings of high performers like Esa-Pekka Salonen, Mitsuko Uchida and Yuri Bashmet. 'Agents are meant to be leeches on society, but we are not leeches if we are doing a good job for everyone,' said Van Walsum.[55] Agents of his order of minitude preserved old-fashioned virtues of individual care and artistic development. 'I'm against the idea of big agencies,' declared Van Walsum. 'What I would like to see is a greater number of strong managers, not huge empires. We have a role as an honest broker and we would like to have a reputation as presenters of enterprising, risk-taking projects.'[56]

Brave words but, as the recession squeezed, agencies big and small put pressure on artists and public promoters to increase their share of the cake. Artists relied on them more than ever to get work and company managers turned to them to keep their artists in order. The tithes paid to agents crept up in Europe, nearing US levels of twenty per cent. The music business, like it or not, leeched off the ailing body of musical performance.

Agents, however, were acutely aware of the decline and went out seeking higher returns than they could possibly get from a night at the opera. Ogling the millions made by the Three Tenors concerts, they invested their energies in attractions that could fill an arena and move a CD mountain. Ronald Wilford overcame a fastidious distaste for mass spectacle when, stuck with a star who was banned from opera houses, he set about rescuing Kathleen Battle's career with a Three Sopranos extravaganza planned for Naples, Florida. His A-team of Jessye Norman and Kiri Te Kanawa dropped out after initial enthusiasm, and Wilford spent much of the next year making up alternative casts for a substitutes night in Rio. The lowest-rated soprano at this comic event would bank a million dollars, but it was an undignified venture for a man who prided himself on discretion and discrimination. Still, times were tough and Columbia Artists was not impervious to the winds of change.

Values were wavering, too, at its historic rival, Hurok–ICM. Isaac Stern, moral godfather and campaigner, hit seventy in 1995 and shocked the fiddle world by walking out on Vera, his wife of forty years. Stern's gang had been built on tribal loyalties. The collapse of its family home removed a pillar of certitude from a besieged profession where it was now every man for himself. Classical music, buffeted by modernity, lacked epic heroes and moral leaders. At a time when people pursued virtual reality in computer games, music offered no escape from everyday stresses and strains. Coming under the hammer of change in all its heartlands, the art had never been in greater need of guidance and leadership. Yet, when music cried out for help, the music business turned its back on the traditional concert hall and opera house, and went all out to make money.

NOTES

1 interview with the author
2 for definitions of euergetism, see Paul Veyne (transl. Brian Pearce), *Bread and Circuses* (Penguin Books, London) 1990
3 CEREC press release, 27 April 1994
4 Len Owen of Benson & Hedges, interview with the author, 1981
5 Shaw, p. 19
6 'Business in The Arts' supplement, *The Times*, 9 December 1993
7 ABSA annual report 1991, p. 9
8 author's interviews with Jack Prosser (Peter Stuyvesant Foundation), Don Whiting (John Player), Michael Reynolds (BAT), 1981
9 'A fresh boost for culture', Brussels, 1987
10 *The Times*, loc. cit.
11 Joseph Wechsberg, in H. Rosenthal, *Opera Annual No. 8* (John Calder, London) 1962, p. 13
12 Lang, p. 27
13 letter from Fred K. Prieberg to the Executive Editor of the *NY Times*, copy in the author's possession
14 personal communications
15 author's interview
16 author's interview
17 Doug Sheldon, in *CM*, 22 December 1990, p. 27
18 personal communication
19 author's interview
20 Taubman, p. 33
21 Robinson, p. 290
22 related by Jacques Leiser
23 director's message to Curtis Institute students, 1994
24 *NYT*, May 1995
25 author's interview
26 author's interview
27 recalled by Schofer
28 author's interview
29 author's interview
30 *NY Times* interview
31 issue of 3 October 1994
32 author's interview
33 *New Yorker*, 3 October 1994
34 Ralph Blumenthal, 'Gray Eminence of Classical Music's Stars', *NY Times*, 24 May 1995
35 letter to the *Sunday Times*, 13 March 1994
36 personal communication
37 'Culture Shock at *New York Times*', *Variety*, 30 May 1990, p. 1
38 interview with the author
39 Gay Talese, *The Kingdom and the Power* (Bantam Books, NY) 1970, p. 429
40 *Variety*, loc. cit.
41 Boston colleague of Gelb's, interview with the author
42 Schonberg, *Horowitz*, pp. 229–30
43 author's interview
44 Schonberg, pp. 258–61
45 comments in 'The Deal', IMZ conference, Toronto, 1 October 1992
46 related by H. Tanzmayr
47 author's interview
48 comments in 'The Deal', IMZ conference, Toronto, 1 October 1992

49 'Sony Purchases a Little Help In a Classical Video Venture', *NY Times*, 14 July 1993
50 *NY Times*, May 1995
51 Michael Haas, author's interview
52 *Symphony* magazine, May–June 1995, pp. 22–3
53 BBC interview
54 see Norman Lebrecht in the *Daily Telegraph*, 22 January 1996
55 *Financial Times*, 6 December 1992, *Weekend FT*, p. vii
56 interview with the author, 1991

III

MAESTROS . . .

CHAPTER VIII

THE MANAGER
AS MAESTRO

A s the twentieth century slithered to a close, it became ineluctably
apparent that the age of the music director was at an end. Inter-
continental travel, maestro greed and the universal weakening of one-to-one
human relationships had reduced the chief conductor's presence at major
orchestras to less than four months a year. Like the non-executive chairman
of a multinational utility, the music director was rarely to be found at his post
or in charge of the business. His leadership was adventitious and his
infrequent interventions disruptive rather than inspiring. He received a
massive emolument for sticking his celebrated name on the company
letterhead, signalling its credit-worthiness to investors. Many employees,
however, wondered what he was there for.

The top conductors had turned into time travellers. Daniel Barenboim
divided his working year between 'heading' the Chicago Symphony Orchestra and the Berlin State Opera, allocating July to Bayreuth and any weeks left
over to Israel, France and England. Lorin Maazel spent fourteen weeks in
Munich and as much again in Pittsburgh. His Pittsburgh successor, Mariss
Jansons, held paid positions at the Oslo, London and St Petersburg
Philharmonic Orchestras and limited his US directorship to a new low of

ten weeks a year. Jansons, a shyly intense performer, was a slow energy burner who preserved at fifty enough combustion to ignite any ensemble he attended. He took the trouble to learn the players' names and always had fresh insights to impart about the symphonies he interpreted. Some of his contemporaries, by comparison, barely bothered to scan the music or look up at the musicians they led. They came like visitors from outer space, untouched by earthly needs and oblivious to the requirements of building an orchestra.

Nature abhors no vacuum like a power vacuum. When conductors began podium-hopping, the charismatic rule of the music director gave way to the slide-rule of the executive director. While Beecham bestrode the London Philharmonic and Furtwängler held the baton in Berlin, few apart from the players knew the name of the man who fixed their rehearsal schedules and mailed their payslips. But once Karajan signed a contract with the Berlin Philharmonic that limited his attendance to just twelve concerts a year – an obligation that he once threatened to fulfil in a fortnight[1] – an ulterior authority was needed in the office to plan events and maintain player morale while the master was away. The incumbent Intendant (or artistic administrator) when Karajan was appointed was an ex-Goebbels radio boss and sometime composer called Gerhart von Westermann. He was nearing retirement and felt unhappy without an all-seeing führer at his shoulder. In 1958 this self-effacing functionary stepped down, tendering his position to a social luminary, latterly restored to West Berlin with his American wife and credentials.

Wolfgang Stresemann, son of a Weimar hero, had worked as a music critic and conducted small-town orchestras during his exile in the United States. Back in Berlin in 1956 as Intendant of the US-zone radio orchestra, RIAS, he continued to conduct some of its public concerts. Stresemann was a competent musician and organiser, but his strongest claims to the Philharmonic vacancy were an emotive surname, a clean political record and a close friendship with the trail-blazing new Mayor, Willy Brandt. The force of Stresemann's personality and connections would, it was hoped by the players who approved his appointment, compensate for the chief conductor's wilful absenteeism. Karajan was initially suspicious of the new Intendant, but Stresemann's old-world diplomatic skills and unflappable professionalism provided the basis for a partnership that was outwardly unruffled and inordinately triumphant.

'It [works] like this,' Stresemann explained in 1978. 'I ask Herr von Karajan to give me his dates, if possible in the spring for the season after next, which he does. Sometimes he changes them and then you have to see how you can work it in. I should add that he doesn't change things out of spite . . . Guest conductors are then invited for the numerous dates that Herr von Karajan has not claimed for himself.'[2]

Stresemann invited the same eminent guest conductors year after year, men who complemented Karajan in their diversities but were too well-mannered to outblaze him. Karl Böhm, Eugen Jochum, Carl Schuricht and Sir John Barbirolli were regular seniorities; Zubin Mehta, Lorin Maazel and Claudio Abbado were the rising stars. The Intendant quietly accommodated Karajan favourites like Seiji Ozawa, and reluctantly downplayed his anathemas, Bernstein and Barenboim. By finessing his human resources and reasserting a tradition that transcended maestro-magic, Stresemann fortified a Philharmonic ethos that stood separate from Karajan's golden halo and would withstand his ultimate scorched-earth assaults.

In just under twenty years, Stresemann imprinted on the orchestra something of his urbane cosmopolitanism and public-service heritage. A great German institution began admitting foreign players and personnel. Where his predecessor employed just three assistants in the office, Stresemann recruited a staff of fifty to cope with the torrent of recordings and tours that stemmed from Karajan and star guests. By 1995 the administration had grown to eighty-one, almost equalling the number of players in the orchestra – proof positive of the shift in authority from podium to planners' desk. In a centennial monograph, written as he prepared to depart, Stresemann assigned the orchestra's chief strength not to its baton lineage but to its democratic system of 'self-administration'.[3]

His relations with Karajan were mutually wary. Photographs of them together show the tall, aristocratic Stresemann inclining his head concurringly or quizzically towards the diminutive, ramrod-like conductor. A closer rapport developed on tour, where Karajan relaxed in the luxury of a well-run operation. He asked Stresemann to head the jury of his triennial conductors' competition and, on his retirement from the orchestra in 1978, issued an unusually warm valediction. Contacts cooled, though, after Stresemann published a personal history of the orchestra[4] in which the difficulties of working with a distant, autocratic conductor were unconcealed. Karajan did not acknowledge receiving a dedicated copy of the book[5] and when Stresemann was summoned back in 1984, at eighty years old, to resolve an ugly quarrel between orchestra and conductor, he achieved no more than a temporary respite. Karajan was too old and pain-ridden to show much of his former flexibility. Nor was he concerned for social niceties. When Stresemann at his second farewell concert paid public tribute to the conductor – 'I'm happy and pleased that you, dear Herr von Karajan, are with us here on this occasion, since you weren't able to be here last time' – Karajan left the stage without a word of reply. The barbed remark about his absences had struck home: Karajan would never admit that Stresemann might have shared the credit for building *his* orchestra, *his* hall, *his* posterity.

Other conductors, visiting Berlin, were more impressed by the management. Having a Stresemann in the office, they realised, would set them free to fly the world. The pairing of butterfly conductor and assiduous manager was taken up by US orchestras, starting at Boston where Seiji Ozawa's lengthy and often distracted tenure was kept smoothly on the rails by a contiguous line of executive directors, Tod Perry, Tom Morris and Kenneth Haas.

The longer conductors were away, the more decisions managers had to take – until their ascendance was unchallenged. If a music director now clashed with his executive director, it was the conductor who had to give way – or go – no matter how proficient or popular he was. It happened first at the Concertgebouworkest in Amsterdam, where Bernard Haitink was ousted after twenty-five years by an Intendant, Hein van Royen, who wanted his own way. It happened in Hamburg where the headstrong John Eliot Gardiner received short shrift from the radio orchestra's manager. It happened spectacularly to André Previn in Los Angeles and miserably to Vladimir Ashkenazy in London, where barely a season would go by without one music director or other being given his marching orders by an increasingly assertive corps of managers. It was out of this surging cauldron of London's squabblesome orchestras that the Supermanager found his *métier* and his philosophy, a credo that proclaimed the death of the traditional symphony orchestra.

In the season that Wolfgang Stresemann took charge of the Berlin Philharmonic, a German-Jewish exile in South Africa found himself standing at the crossroads of two budding careers. He could either become chief conductor in Capetown, or drop the baton for ever and take a job as general secretary to the London Symphony Orchestra. To Ernest Fleischmann, thirty-four years old, it was a straight choice between being number one in a self-satisfied, self-isolating society or playing an important but frustratingly invisible role on the world stage. Fleischmann, who had been conducting since he was eighteen, was intelligent enough to know that he was a notch or two below top class in the maestro league. 'I was not totally immodest about having a talent for conducting,' he said, 'but I was very worried whether I would measure up to what is needed of a great conductor. I did not know whether I had the self-discipline to master this most difficult of all performance arts.'[6]

Managing an orchestra, on the other hand, was a challenge to his restless ingenuity, the augury-watcher's adaptability of a former refugee. Fleischmann had demonstrated his organisational flair by putting together a six-week international festival in 1956 for the seventieth anniversary of the city of Johannesburg. He commissioned a festive overture from William Walton and imported the London Symphony Orchestras to play five concerts. When Josef Krips fell out with the players and cried off at the last minute, Fleischmann called in a conductor whose reputation for perfectionism was so unyielding that orchestras no longer dared employ him. Nursed by Fleischmann through a nerve-racked night-before, Jascha Horenstein gave a performance of Mahler's *Resurrection* Symphony that resounded the world over and revived his career. The LSO were impressed by Fleischmann's verve and caring and when their Secretary, John Cruft, opted for a quieter life with the British Council, they called Fleischmann and offered him a job no careerist would ever have considered.

Even in the semi-anarchy of self-governing orchestras, the London Symphony Orchestra was a byword for mayhem, an organism whose interior heaved with would-be conductors. It had Neville Marriner leading the second violins; Barry Tuckwell was principal horn and Howard Snell was second trumpet; Gervase de Peyer played clarinet; Erich Gruenberg was concertmaster. Pursuing solo careers, they were ill-disposed to take orders. No conductor or manager could tame them for long; Krips, in frustration, punched John Cruft in the teeth while attempting to assert his authority.

Their vibrancy and disorder, though, were enchanting to Fleischmann, living as he did in a conformist ex-colony with a propensity for enforcing homogeneity. Like many liberal Jews, especially ones who had endured the Hitler trauma, Fleischmann loathed apartheid and risked his skin helping police fugitives escape over the Rhodesian frontier, disguised as black-tie concert goers. He moved his family to London in November 1959 and vowed never to go back.

Into a managerial circle dominated by ex-players, Fleischmann landed like a gazelle on adrenalin, oblivious to lurking dangers. All the London orchestras were in some kind of trouble and the LSO, at the end of the Fifties, looked by far the most vulnerable. Its chairman, Harry Dugdale, had retreated back into the cellos, fed up with trying to whip seventy-odd colleagues into concord. There was no chief conductor and essential functions like concert manager and librarian were being carried out by players in their spare time. State funding was minimal, corporate support unknown and London's oldest orchestra survived from one concert to the next in nightly contention with three independent competitors and the BBC.

'When I came to the LSO, it was a far, far better orchestra than it was being given credit for,' reflected Fleischmann. 'What I did, maybe out of naivety, was persuade them to stick their necks out and promote a lot more concerts with good conductors. I wanted to make people realise how good the orchestra was. You can't just do that by playing well.' He began by upgrading the printed programmes and professionalising the office. Image-consciousness was still alien to British culture and Fleischmann was perceived as a pushy self-publicist, but the younger look he gave the LSO would suit it admirably when the Sixties started to swing.

Reshaping a concert season that had been strung together like odd-sized beads on a string, he booked quality time with top-class conductors, some already involved with the LSO, others newly contracted. 'If I produce for 1961 Monteux, Solti and Stokowski, will you take us?' he asked the head of the Vienna Festwochen. That weighty line-up earned the LSO its first visit to the birthplace of symphonic music. In Vienna, at the Imperial Hotel, as Kennedy and Khrushchev were carving up the globe in another room, Fleischmann beseeched the eighty-six-year-old Pierre Monteux to become principal conductor. Monteux, who had premièred Stravinsky's great ballets half a century before, was universally revered as a repository of performing traditions and a kindly, spiritual leader. 'If I accept,' he told Fleischmann, 'I want a twenty-five-year contract – with,' he twinkled, 'an option for renewal.' Like all great men, Monteux never spoke wholly in jest. After a lifetime in music, he wanted to pass on his experience while time remained. The LSO, under his baton, 'played as if every concert were likely to be the last . . . the players held Monteux in professional admiration and personal affection – and it showed in their playing.'[7]

Self-belief returned, and with it a measure of serenity. Record companies awoke to the excitements of LSO concerts and recorded them the morning after. Clifford Curzon's spine-tingling account of the first Brahms piano concerto with Georg Szell, Martha Argerich playing Chopin with Abbado, Aaron Copland conducting his own works, Monteux repeating *The Rite of Spring* on its fiftieth anniversary with Igor Stravinsky growling audibly in the stalls – concerts and recordings such as these were self-assertively epochal. A sense of moment descended upon the LSO and conductors clamoured to be part of it – 'virtually everybody except Karajan, Klemperer and Giulini came to conduct us,' bragged Fleischmann. His connections with conductors were highly charged. With Monteux he played a dewy-eyed grandson; with Solti and Bernstein a clever facilitator; and with his contemporaries – Abbado, Zubin Mehta, Seiji Ozawa and Colin Davis – a brotherly ally. No orchestral manager had the range of conductor relationships that Fleischmann developed; nor, perhaps, the depth. As a former conductor, he knew better than anyone how to play on their vanities and vulnerabilities.

When Monteux died in July 1964, months before an intended ninetieth birthday concert, the LSO mourned him with a Berlioz *Grande Messe des Morts* conducted by Colin Davis, the most persuasive British interpreter since Beecham. Fleischmann recommended Davis for the principal conductorship and took him on an Asian tour that should have achieved endorsement by the players. Davis, however, was desperately involved in trying to spring his future wife, Shamsi, from Iranian captivity and by the time the orchestra reached India he was almost too distraught to conduct. Summoned to choose their next chief conductor, only two players could see past the personal crisis to vote for Davis (one of them, recalled Fleischmann, was Neville Marriner who was in the process of forming his own chamber orchestra, the Academy of St Martin in the Fields). Thirty years would elapse before Davis returned, cerebral and calm, as music director of the LSO.

In February 1965, the orchestra elected István Kertesz, a mercurial Hungarian, 'against considerable opposition from Ernest'.[8] The administrator accepted defeat with good grace and worked equably with Kertesz, which cannot have been easy since both had tinderbox tempers. The orchestra was on a roll, and touring the world. Visiting Israel in 1964, the strictly-raised Fleischmann was so taken with its relaxed social and sexual mores that he nearly accepted a job with the Israel Philharmonic. It was the first of many glamorous propositions that would start coming his way.

Credit for the orchestra's success clung to the General Secretary rather than to its conductors. Fleischmann did nothing to shun the limelight and his self-advancement stung some board members, who argued that the artistic turning point had begun with Stokowski's concerts in 1956 and the parallel arrival of Tuckwell, now the orchestra's chairman. They resented Fleischmann's bustling independence, his willingness to make commitments without clearance from the board. Marriner dubbed him 'Flick-knife Fleischmann' and many suffered the sharp edge of his tongue and the shortness of his temper. But Fleischmann could turn on the charm to disarm critics and his diplomatic skills were crucial in securing the LSO pole position on a dangerously crowded race-track.

Shortly after taking office, Fleischmann initiated contacts with his opposite number at the London Philharmonic Orchestra, a retired trumpeter called Eric Bravington whom Bernard Haitink considered 'one of the best managers I have ever worked with'.[9] In an unusual show of unity, Fleischmann and Bravington went together to the Arts Council to initiate discussions of the long-term future of London orchestras. Their timing was immaculate. In

March 1961 Sir Thomas Beecham died, leaving the Royal Philharmonic rudderless. Three years later, the Philharmonia was disbanded by its founder, Walter Legge. The Arts Council put up emergency funds to keep the bands playing while a committee of inquiry, headed by Lord Goodman, pondered a strategy. Its Solomonian verdict, that London needed 'rather more than three but less than four orchestras', left no one with enough funding to feel secure. But while two of the orchestras struggled for survival, the LSO and LPO now stood perceptibly above the fray, their futures apparently above question.

Fleischmann moved fast to cement that advantage. Hearing that the Corporation of the City of London were talking to the Philharmonia about occupying a new concert hall in the Barbican, he called Tuckwell to the office on a Friday afternoon and by Monday morning produced a winning bid for the residency. 'Fleischmann's attitude was: go for what you want first. Get it. Then sort out the details,' said Wilfred Stiff, a manager who later revised his Barbican estimates. 'Ernest hadn't thought of things like having to renew carpets, or run an air-conditioning system.'[10] Fleischmann was untroubled by the costings of such trivia. He was a man of vision, a man of achievement. For the first time since its foundation in 1904, the LSO would have a home to call its own.

He was starting to plan the orchestra's triumphant entry into the promised hall when, one Monday morning, a thunderbolt struck that he cannot, to this day, recount without an air of bewilderment and a catch in his throat. On 30 March 1967 Tuckwell typed and sent a letter resigning from the orchestra as both chairman and player. 'The real reason for my resignation,' he wrote, 'is that I cannot for another day associate myself with the General Secretary.'

The Australian-born hornist had a flourishing solo career and a connection with royalty through his sister, Patricia, who was about to marry the Queen's cousin, the Earl of Harewood. An articulate, gregarious man, Tuckwell had worked with Fleischmann for three years in apparent harmony. His letter, however, exposed a savage resentment at what he saw as the administrator's theft of authority from the players who rightfully owned the orchestra. 'I do not think the Board of Directors is any longer in a position to control the affairs of the Company; that is, not while Mr Ernest Fleischmann is the General Secretary,' charged Tuckwell. 'And while I must admire his almost unequalled flair for presentation and advertising, I find it too undignified and embarrassing trying to justify his inability to accept or apportion blame, which results in frequent rows and recriminations, his constant evasiveness, and the impossibility of getting a plain and accurate explanation from him. In short, I do not wish it to be thought that his methods are my methods.'[11]

'I was shocked,' said Fleischmann in a choked voice, quarter of a century later. 'I really had no idea that Tuckwell and his friends were plotting. He and his wife were at our house three nights before the fatal letter, until about three in the morning.'

Tuckwell would always deny plotting against Fleischmann or coveting his job. 'There was a problem with Ernest – he's that sort of person,' he said in 1991. 'There was a general disagreement with the way he conducted his job. He will always be a controversial person, a man of almost unlimited ideas.'[12]

The LSO board, meeting in emergency session, fired Fleischmann and begged Tuckwell to return – which he did, though only for a year. Fleischmann would one day make his peace with Tuckwell and invite him to play concertos with his next orchestra, but the act of reconciliation did not diminish the devastation he felt at having been sacked by the LSO. The orchestra had been his home, the conductors his family, the Barbican his future. Losing all three at once was a trauma that awoke in his consciousness the memory of being spat upon as a nine-year-old Jewish boy in the streets of Nazi Frankfurt-am-Main.

It did not take him long to land a new job, as European director for CBS Records, or to enjoy a smirk of *schadenfreude* as the LSO faced an inevitable backlash. A Philips recording chief, learning of his dismissal, wrote to the orchestra, 'I must tell you in all honesty that our artists and the company as a whole are so shocked by this turn of events that there may be no need for further correspondence.' A year later, once Tuckwell and Kertesz had both quit, the LSO board wrote to Fleischmann asking him to return. The orchestra had suffered an eighteen-thousand-pound loss, Philips and Decca had stopped their recordings and morale was sinking. Fleischmann weighed the offer momentarily, then demanded that a formal appeal should be made to him signed by every member of the orchestra. He knew that unanimity was unattainable in any musical grouping larger than a string quartet. He was also starting to sense that the days of the old-fashioned symphony orchestra might be numbered.

The news that Fleischmann was being headhunted by an American orchestra drew unflattering comment in the British press. IS THIS MAN WORTH £20,000 A YEAR? wondered one headline writer. Little did anyone imagine that the ousted general secretary of the LSO would end up with a half-million-dollar salary and something approaching Hollywood stardom. In June 1969, Ernest Fleischmann left London for good (or so he thought) to become executive director of the Los Angeles Philharmonic Orchestra and general director of its summer home, the celebrated but derelict Hollywood Bowl. An article he had written in *High Fidelity* magazine attacking the provincialism of US orchestras and the weakness of their managers had brought him to board attention. A 'supermanager', said Fleischmann, was needed to run a modern orchestra. Los Angeles challenged him to prove it.

In a country where the orchestral superhighway ran down the East Coast from Boston to Philadelphia and stopped dead at Chicago, Los Angeles barely figured on the musical map. Its orchestra, formed in 1919, boasted Klemperer and Eduard van Beinum among past maestros, but classical concerts did not count for much in Dream City. 'This is a movie town,' sighed Fleischmann years later. 'Don't believe *anything* you read here about the movies.'

Surviving in traditionless California where the state did not grant a single tax dollar to musical performance or education, the LAPO ranked fifteenth in the money league of US orchestras and lower still in glamour; Walter Matthau was its only showbiz subscriber. Attendances were running at fifty-six per cent and players were taking home eight thousand dollars a year. Strikes flared; two managers came and went in quick succession. Zubin Mehta, music director since 1962, begged Fleischmann to join him. 'I assured him we would not sit on separate pedestals and communicate only through memos, as most conductors and managers do,' said Mehta. Fleischmann flew out, first-class, and was duly impressed.

'It was extraordinary,' he said. 'These were committed players. The rapport they had developed with Zubin was absolutely thrilling. It was clear they were on their way to becoming one of the world's major orchestras.'[13] He took the job and infecting the players with his zeal and conviction, talked them into breaking the national union agreement that forced record companies to pay the entire orchestra, even if only half were playing in a Haydn symphony. He also wanted to make it easier to dismiss weak players. In return, he promised higher salaries and more work. The musicians voted seventy-seven to one for Fleischmann's new deal and saw their recording sessions triple. 'For the first time, a player doesn't have to worry about moonlighting to make a decent wage,' said trumpeter Irving Busch. 'And we thank Ernest for that.'[14]

He engaged architect Frank Gehry to design a nine-million-dollar renovation of the Hollywood Bowl. Having sold the plan to the civic authorities, he began selling the LAPO's eleven-week Bowl season at all prices, from private boxes with sumptuous catering to one-dollar snuggle-seats for students. He set up free concerts for underprivileged groups and school visits to ethnic communities. At the upper end of the social stratum, he organised visits by Covent Garden and the Teatro Communale of Florence, and was a driving force behind the formation of a Los Angeles opera season. The cultural desert of southern California was beginning to bloom.

Mehta, whom Fleischmann loved 'like a brother', was away most of the year in Israel and Europe, and happy to be relieved of organisational responsibilities. When he departed in 1978 for the New York Philharmonic, his successor was the patrician Carlo Maria Giulini, a serene Italian who was concerned primarily with refining tonal quality.

Fleischmann shamelessly manipulated maestros. 'There are only four or five superstar conductors,' he mused while choosing a music director. 'Fortunately I know them all on a first-name basis, and all I can do is talk to the ones we're interested in – and make bloody well sure each man feels he is the only one we want.'[15] A double-edged quip began circulating the world's green rooms. There are three great orchestras in the United States, conductors joked. Chicago is famed for its brass, Philadelphia for its strings, and Los Angeles . . . for its management.

Transitions of power from one class to another are rarely achieved without ruffled feelings, and Fleischmann was never reluctant to confront those he dispossessed. 'Every day, the most incredibly rude – but well deserved – letters go out to greedy agents and lousy sopranos,' said Mehta. 'That man will never play again in this town,' was one of Fleischmann's stock reactions to a maestro who had given what he considered to be less than his best. He reduced his own employees not merely to floods of tears but to fits of primal screaming. Working for Fleischmann, said a former marketing director, 'meant being humiliated on an almost daily basis . . . He's fabulous if you're in trouble, but he always has to have the upper hand'.[16] He is, said another ex-staffer, 'the most totally egocentric, completely unprincipled and yet incredibly brilliant monomaniac in music'.[17]

Whether Los Angeles would ever be large enough to contain his ego was an open question. Bigger fish soon came beckoning. In his file at the LAPO I found a 1972 letter from Pierre Boulez lamenting Fleischmann's refusal to join him at the New York Philharmonic. Metha, six years later, tried to take him to New York, but Fleischmann, though tempted, was still unready to leave the golden lures of the sunshine state. The LSO beseeched him to return in 1973, as artistic director of the Barbican; 'they could never have delivered,' snorted Fleischmann derisively. The Metropolitan Opera came sniffing in 1983 and both the San Francisco Opera and Boston Symphony sounded him out. In November 1985, at the second time of asking, he finally resigned from the LAPO to become head of the Paris Opéra, charged with preparing its move into the magnificent Bastille. A week later he changed his mind because of an 'immense outpouring of appreciation for my work here, and affection for me personally, not only from the board of directors, the musicians and my staff, but also from many members of the public . . .'[18] It was a prudent, not to say prescient, decision. Every subsequent head of the Paris Opéra was devoured in the kitchen of French politics, where presidents and couturiers meddled incessantly in cultural affairs. 'One has to be aware that if you take a job in France politics will play a very large part,' reflected Fleischmann. 'I had the backing of Pierre Boulez. It was at his urging that they asked me. Then I got cold feet.'

In Los Angeles, at least, he was boss of all he beheld – as André Previn discovered to his cost. When Giulini retired in 1985 to tend his ailing wife, Fleischmann had the idea of appointing a young conductor whom he could mould to his own specifications. The man he had in mind was Simon Rattle, barely thirty and promising great things as music director in Birmingham. He also had an eye on Esa-Pekka Salonen, a Finn of twenty-seven who had made a sensational London début in Mahler's third symphony in 1983. But the board refused for once to let Fleischmann have his way, as wealthy directors clamoured for a Name to keep Los Angeles in the limelight. The Name Fleischmann came up with was Previn, a Hollywood sound-track composer who had made it into the international podium thanks largely to the dates he was given at the LSO when Fleischmann was its general secretary. Previn went on to lead the LSO for eleven heady years, an era of glitz and razzle that sagged into fretful tedium when the relationship outlived its avowedly superficial attractions. Previn moved on to Pittsburgh and to London's Royal Philharmonic Orchestra. At fifty-five, he was well liked by the record industry and was looking for a comfortable, career-crowning appointment. Los Angeles, for this former studio slave, was a dream fulfilled and he headed West in high hopes with his new English wife, Heather.

'Ernest should never have hired him,' said an LAPO board member, 'but there were no other Big Names available. He envisaged it as a homecoming, forgetting where Previn really came from.'[19] Like Fleischmann, the conductor was German-born, raised in exile and hardened in the London incinerator. He thought he was being welcomed home to tinseltown as the man in charge of music. It did not take him long to realise that someone else had feet planted beneath his desk. 'I wasn't allowed to have an opinion,' Previn told the Los Angeles Times when the conflict burst open. 'Ernest is physically, mentally and psychologically incapable of uttering these words: I will have to check with the music director.'[20]

After an overhyped start, Previn's concerts failed to catch fire and sell enough seats. When his contract came up for renewal in 1988, Fleischmann went into neutral gear and Previn got worried. The sparks began to fly when he found that Fleischmann had, without his consent, offered Esa-Pekka Salonen a Japanese tour with the LAPO and the position of principal guest conductor, alongside the well-liked Rattle. Previn stormed in to see board president Michael Connell and succeeded in overturning Salonen's appointment, though not in securing his own contract renewal. Finally, in March 1989 the sympathetic Connell took him aside and said, 'Fetch your wife, go out and have a good dinner. When you come home, there will be good news.'

'What about Ernest?' asked Previn.

'Ernest has nothing to do with this,' said Connell. 'We're tired of feeling that he is the Philharmonic. From now on . . .'

When it came to the crunch, however, Fleischmann rallied his friends on the board and outgunned the president. Previn, hearing that his contract was still in abeyance, resigned and went public. Fleischmann, sleek as a panther, named Salonen as his next music director. 'The whole thing was planned beautifully from day one,' said Previn. 'Esa-Pekka Salonen has never been a music director in his life. He will do as he is told.'

'Preposterous, totally untrue,' said Fleischmann, though he could not deny that events had worked out exactly as he had wished. He had a young conductor and, with Salonen, could drive the orchestra into contemporary, challenging works. He hired the young stage *provocateur* Peter Sellars to create community events and attract a new public. The Los Angeles Philharmonic was ahead of the game and Ernest Fleischmann was still in command, reaping the highest managerial salary in the concert world. Even Michael Connell sang his praises. 'I don't think that there is anyone better than Ernest Fleischmann at figuring out, within the bounds of what is truly classical music, what sells and still meets the artistic goals,'[21] said the LAPO president.

But there was a hefty price to be paid for his single-mindedness. Previn's attacks, coming as they did from a fellow-refugee and self-made musician, hurt Fleischmann more than he cared to admit. The conductor's departure left stains on the carpet and the board, no longer the manager's puppet, rushed in to punish him with budget cuts the moment his balance sheets were hit by recession. 'It was pure vendetta,' said one observer. Fleischmann, gritting his teeth, had to cancel his education and outreach programmes and lay off staff. The LAPO's twenty-four-million-dollar endowment was the lowest of seventeen top US orchestras. It was not big enough to indulge Fleischmann's social conscience.

The personal toll was even higher. His marriage to a professional architect had not survived years of late hours and occupational preoccupations; his children had grown up and away. Although he enjoyed fine food and attractive companions when he could spare the time, he was starting to take on an isolated, rumpled look. 'If Ernest doesn't work sixteen hours a day,' said one associate, 'he's not happy.'

'I'm kind of sorry for him in my own weird way,' said Previn in a barb that struck home. 'He is driven by that extraordinary need for solitary power. The man hasn't got anything except the orchestra . . . Everything he does has some connection – tenuous or blatant – with the orchestra.' Previn was right, up to a point. He saw his antagonist immersed in running the Los Angeles Philharmonic and concluded that this was his whole life. But Fleischmann had not been brought out of Hitler's Germany, South African apartheid and London's musical fratricide only to devote his life to a Pacific Coast orchestra. What occupied his waking thoughts was not so much the Los Angeles Philharmonic as the state of orchestral music as a whole at the end of the second millennium – a state for which he felt an acutely personal responsibility. On 16 May 1987, invited to give the commencement address at the Cleveland Institute of Music, Ernest Fleischmann delivered himself of a manifesto on the musical future. He called it: 'The Symphony Orchestra is Dead. Long Live the Community of Musicians.'

Speakers at college ceremonies are expected to reminisce fondly about their student years, crack two jokes, compliment the teaching staff and send everyone off in an optimistic glow. If that is what the Cleveland Institute was looking for, they had booked the wrong speaker. Fleischmann, from his opening sentence, was positively inflammatory. 'It's high time we began to set fire to the symphony orchestra,' he declared. For musicians, he said, the orchestra was a factory floor where they spent soul-wasting shifts. For audiences it represented a dull habit, and a dying one. For managers like himself it was difficult to breathe fresh life into a defunct form. If we want to save the symphony orchestra, he urged, 'we must accept that the orchestra as we know it is dead.'

To gasps of incredulity, Fleischmann continued reading his text:

It's dead because symphony concerts have become dull and predictable, musicians and audiences are suffering from repetitive routines and formula-type programming, there is an acute shortage of conductors who not only know their scores inside-out but are inspiring leaders, and there is just as great a shortage of administrators who possess artistic vision and imagination, as well as fiscal responsibility and negotiating skills.

It's the rite of winter that's killing us. Every year we end up with the same sort of sacrificial dance as we try to ring the changes and vary the ingredients in what is essentially a rather limited, fairly standard nine-teenth and early-twentieth-century orchestral repertoire stew . . . Is it then so very surprising that our audiences seem to get older every year and our musicians more bored and frustrated, particularly as the conducting of that standard repertoire tends often *not* to throw any new light on yet another *Eroica*, Tchaikovsky Fifth or *Unfinished*?

His solution: to demolish the symphony orchestra and replace it with a free community of musicians who could form into smaller or larger ensembles according to public demand and artistic need. Those who were not playing concerts could be teaching kids in ghetto schools, rehearsing with prisoner groups or working at the coalface of creation with local composers. Some might play period instruments or form string quartets; others could get involved in jazz, folk and ethnic music. Some would develop conducting skills; a few might even like to help out in the office and groom themselves for a career in management. A dozen nights a year, they might all get together with a capable conductor and give a well-rehearsed, thoroughly professional symphony concert.

To achieve this ideal, all that was needed was a spate of local mergers – the Philadelphia Orchestra with a local chamber ensemble, the New York Philharmonic with the Orchestra of St Luke's. Putting together two orchestras would provide a pool of '140 to 150 highly skilled musicians, *under one expert administration*'. In dismantling the formal symphony orchestra, the only function that Fleischmann considered indispensable was a professional administration. As in all revolutionary societies, from commune to kibbutz, power would pass to the bureaucracy. The idyll that Fleischmann envisaged was to be run by Fleischmann-clones. 'I see myself as a facilitator and a catalyst who can help the musicians realise their potential,' he later clarified.

In a concluding exhortation – part Pierre Boulez, part *Animal Farm* – Fleischmann rekindled the incendiary metaphor. 'I want you to become arsonists,' he told the students, 'to join me and lots of musicians, administrators and trustees in setting the symphony orchestra ablaze. If the music we love so deeply is to survive, we must accept that the orchestra is burnt out, but from its ashes something infinitely richer, more varied, more satisfying can arise if we all work together to create it.'

The lecture was widely circulated and superficially reported. '*Das Sinfonie-Orchester ist tot*,' shouted the normally subdued *Die Welt*. The music business, for its part, treated the furore as 'Ernest chasing publicity again' and waited for the wave to subside. Only one commentator, the *New Criterion* publisher Samuel Lipman, himself a professional pianist, examined the ideas in detail

213

and rejected them as authoritarian. 'The centrepiece of Mr Fleischmann's new order is not the concentration of musicians; it is the concentration of administration,' wrote Lipman. 'There can be little doubt that a few powerful administrators would indeed stand to benefit from the enactment of Mr Fleischmann's proposal . . . only strong administrative control in the hands of one individual, would have any hope of making sense out of such a chaotic situation.'[22]

The symphony orchestra, said Lipman, was still alive and bravely 'accomplishing the vital function of preserving and extending civilisation'. It was admittedly in a weakened condition, but euthanasia was no remedy. The sickness lay not in the orchestra but with celebrity maestros – he cited Zubin Mehta by name – who were imposed upon the players and inhibited their artistic potential by restricting them to routine repertoire and interpretations.

Fleischmann's retort to reasoned criticism exculpated his favourite conductors and struck a characteristically emotive note: 'I find myself caring and worrying more than ever about the art and the artists from whom I and millions of others have derived so much profound joy, so much life-enhancing music. My working contacts with countless musicians over some four decades have convinced me that most of them are unable to realise their full potential as artists within the rigid structure of the conventional symphony orchestra . . . That is why I have put forward certain ideas and proposals . . . [which] have evoked a spirited and constructive response from a number of concerned musicians.'

Lipman replied, 'The sad fact is that each passing year sees a decline in the vitality of American orchestras. This decline has been superintended by the masterful administrators of whom Mr Fleischmann is a representative. It is time that *their* failure be recognised for what it is.'[23]

His was a wilderness voice, however, as Fleischmann's manifesto was reinforced by world recession. Within a year of his lecture, funding authorities in America, Britain, Holland and Germany began talking about merging orchestras to cut costs and create a deployable pool of multi-tasked musicians. Major halls started reducing their concert dates, because audiences were shrinking and the symphony was provenly 'dead'. The Arts Council of England made its annual grants to orchestras conditional on the players undertaking educational work, like it or not.

Ernest Fleischmann, now executive vice-president of the Los Angeles Philharmonic Orchestra, found himself garlanded as a visionary of the orchestral future and offered prestigious consultancies. The LAPO became the first US orchestra to win a residency at the Salzburg Festival. In place of the Big Five US orchestras, some numbered Los Angeles among the Big Six and credited Fleischmann with its ascension. 'I still feel we need supermanagers,' he declared to an ASOL assembly. 'I have done what I thought needed to be done,' he told me. 'It was not to create a power base but to do the job as I perceived it had to be done. I suppose if there was something that was driving me it was the awareness that you are dealing with artists and an art-form, and that creates a specific set of responsibilities. Music is not a business. The money has to be found to pay for it, but the art must come first.' Only a principled supermanager, he argued, could ensure that the interests of art remained uppermost in an epoch of greed and expediency.

One Friday afternoon every three months or so, four men and a woman alight from separate cabs at a city hotel and vanish hurriedly into the lobby. The men are managers of Big Five orchestras in Boston, Philadelphia, Chicago and Cleveland. The woman is Deborah Borda, executive director of the New York Philharmonic. The first female to head a major orchestra, Borda was unresistingly admitted to the inner clique of senior managers. This embattled group faced daily pressure on several fronts – from musicians and their union, from conductors and their agents, and from rich patrons who funded the orchestras but were quick to criticise aspects of their operation.

Unable to relieve their feelings with anyone of equal rank within their own organisation, they turned quarterly to one another in an anonymous hotel in a different city. 'We don't share confidential artistic plans and financial information,' one of them told me, 'but we let our hair down and let rip about our boards, conductors, soloists, the unions, anything we want to get off our chests. And we come back to the office on the Monday morning feeling a bit better.' Star performers might be forgiven for getting anxious on reading about these meetings. An over-coffee tale of misconduct in Chicago could easily cost the miscreant his US career. If a maestro got locked out by the Big Five managers, no power on earth could retrieve his American prospects.

The managers are not as a rule vindictive, but they are bound by a common instinct of mutual self-protection and they formed a defence union against the wilder elements of the concert platform, and other perils of their lonely profession. Arthur Judson apart, the office of orchestral manager in America formerly involved getting musicians on stage at night and paying them the next morning. In the Wilford era, however, absentee music directors and ever-rising costs called for a tougher breed of executive with wider artistic powers. 'To help keep the orchestra's often leaderless musicians busy and at the same time to meet ballooning expenses, the manager evolved from a kind of backstage uncle – whether kindly or crusty – into a chief executive with a greatly enlarged staff to handle the day-to-day details of his [sic] work. Most of the new generation came up through the American Symphony Orchestra League's management training programme and the ranks of minor-league orchestras,' noted the New York Times in a 1987 class report on the new managers.[24]

'At its highest level,' sniped Samuel Lipman, 'the world of musical administration today is a tight little place; if anyone should doubt this fact of institutional life, he need only be aware that recently the Boston Symphony Orchestra and the Cleveland Orchestra have dealt with their need for bold new policies and fresh administrative blood by the simple expedient of exchanging top administrators – Thomas Morris leaving Boston for Cleveland, and Kenneth Haas leaving Cleveland for Boston.'

Amid this incestuousness, Deborah Borda preserved something of her chastity. Sexual discrimination had forced her to fight twice as hard for advancement, and when she got to the top she owed no favours, having risen by way of positions that no male manager wanted. After eight years as artistic administrator of the San Francisco Symphony Orchestra, where she broke through to the walled-off East German music director, Kurt Masur, she took charge in 1986 of the chamber ensemble in St Paul's, Minnesota, a modest group eternally eclipsed by the state symphony orchestra. What Borda did was to give the SPCO a plural identity by splitting the conductorship between an American composer, John Adams, an early-music expert, Christopher Hogwood, and a rising youngster, Hugh Wolff. Stylistic diversity kept the players on the edge of their seats and the audience in a state of excited uncertainty.

In two years Borda was off – to the Detroit Symphony Orchestra 'which was already such a complete disaster that I knew I could only go up'.[25] In an automotive capital with mounting unemployment, the orchestra was under attack for racial prejudice and on strike over enforced pay cuts. The all-white ensemble, embittered by poor conditions, refused to give black musicians the kind of gentler audition procedure that had broken race barriers in other bands. Borda, smoothing the path for minority musicians, terminated the aloof music directorship of CAMI-backed Günther Herbig and got the town buzzing with a renovation of its historic but dowdy concert hall. By effecting an institutional merger between orchestra and hall, she was able to diversify their offerings, introducing free educational concerts and African-American programmes. Neeme Järvi, the eclectic Estonian, was booked from CAMI as music director.

In eighteen months Borda was back in Minnesota managing the state symphony orchestra but still, to her frustration, being ignored by the Big Five. 'They said they couldn't have a woman there,' she noted of one vacancy. Inside a year, however, she was approached by the New York Philharmonic, an orchestra with the biggest purse and lowest buzz. In the view of some of his toughest critics, sixteen years of Zubin Mehta's play-safe programming satisfied blue-rinse subscribers, but it stultified the repertoire and taught the players that ordinary was good enough for a city that had only one symphony orchestra. A hundred-million-dollar endowment enabled the Philharmonic to lose $2.4 million in 1991 without flinching. This was an orchestra that had forgotten what it meant to live and play as if life depended on it. Long removed from the hub of New York intellectual life, the Philharmonic had lost its recording role and was seeing its social centrality eroded by computer-age counter-attractions. Still, there were plenty of players, staff and members of the board who saw no crisis with a hundred million bucks in the bank.

'When the board of directors was interviewing me . . . and it became really serious,' recalled Borda, 'I asked them, are you sure you want me, Deborah Borda, because I do want to change things. I'm known for doing that and if I come to the Philharmonic it will not be to maintain the *status quo*.'[26] She was forty-three when she accepted the position, working alongside her former San Francisco associate, Kurt Masur, as music director. 'I had worked very hard to position him in New York,' she confided.

Even those familiar with Borda's power-suited pushiness were amazed at her blitz on Philharmonic performance. Her new executive team, many of them women, sharpened the orchestra's salesmanship of seats and sponsorship packages. In Borda's first season, the house was full again and the deficit was halved to $1.2 million. Tackling the confrontational atmosphere between musicians and management, she promised players the highest orchestral wages in America in return for flexible working practices and conciliation procedures. A co-operative committee was set up to resolve grievances. Its first meeting heard complaints against Masur, who agreed under Borda's persuasion to moderate his rehearsal tongue-lashings. Borda herself was sweet-talked out of overloading a touring schedule.

The new union contract, achieved in two years of tough talking, gave her the freedom to redesign programming and reconnect the Philharmonic to a public that had forgotten its existence. Into the routine of subscription concerts, she introduced Rush-Hour Concerts at 6.45 p.m., advising commuters that if they delayed their homeward journey they could catch an hour of great music, miss the log-jams and still get home at around the same time. For those who wanted to stay on there were post-concert cocktails with the players and conductor. Masur, a forbidding figure in the past, mingled happily with his listeners. Uptake at Rush-Hour Concerts reached ninety-nine per cent, one-third of whom were converted by Borda's sales team into regular Philharmonic subscribers.

Masur endowed the orchestra with a richer tone and a deeper seriousness. It was playing better, said James Oestreich in the *New York Times*, 'than it had in years, perhaps decades'. The chief critic, Edward Rothstein, felt 'something resembling civic pride'.[27] A 1993 Europe tour drew bouquets of accolades. 'Perfection,' said *The Times* in London. 'Wonderful,' extolled *Die Presse* of Vienna. In Warsaw, the cheering lasted almost half an hour. In Masur's home town, Leipzig, where standing ovations are rare, the Gewandhaus audience stood for twenty-two minutes to acclaim the local hero with his American orchestra. In its hundred and fiftieth anniversary season, the New York Philharmonic was being restored to its rightful pinnacle.

Masur and Borda credited each other with the success, seeming almost over-careful of each other's sensitivities. 'When Masur's around, Deborah walks on eggshells,' said a Philharmonic supporter. But behind the scenes neither was afraid to let rip – or to give ground in a lost argument. Masur spent just fifteen weeks of the year in New York and bore weighty responsibilities in Leipzig. He had to trust Borda to look after guest programming, especially in the realm of American music where he had little expertise. Never one to shrink from enhanced authority, Borda pushed women composers and conductors into prominent concerts and named a Cuban-born New Yorker, Tania Leon, to advise Masur on musical Americana. She once threatened, only half jestingly, to obtain a court order against a Carnegie Hall concert by the all-male Vienna Philharmonic on the grounds that the US Constitution enshrined equality of opportunity. Deborah Borda was unremittingly feminist.

The daughter of a four-times-married politician mother, Borda played the viola well enough in her teens to win places at London's Royal College of Music and the New England Conservatory of Music. But playing in orchestras left her larger ambitions unslaked and she made her way into orchestral management with Boston's Handel and Haydn Society.

'I found I couldn't leave music,' she said. 'It occurred to me that there was another way I could use other skills that I have. I love music more than anything. Other people go to church. I go to concerts. I'm such a wise guy sometimes, but I mean this very seriously. It's my religion, it's my spiritual basis.'[28]

An excess of spiritual fervour is not necessarily a safe attribute of sound management. Borda, however, tempered her zeal with an engaging tendency to self-parody and a raucous, ready laugh. New Yorker born and bred, she cut through the precious phraseology of musical discourse like a motor-bike cop in a mile-long snarl-up. Her tolerance for bullshit was zero. Unlike many male counterparts, she refused to abase herself before venerated maestros. The press called her 'tough' and 'feisty', adjectives that she found offensive. 'I'm articulate, decisive,' she said. 'I'm willing to take risks and I've been pretty successful. Say that about a man and people will say, "Oh, he's a really good manager . . ." Say that about a woman, and she's "tough" '.[29] The private Deborah Borda lived serenely with a long-term companion and two much-loved cats.

The speed of her ascent led to charges of 'reckless careerism'[30] and doubts were aired about her staying power. 'I sometimes wonder what I'll be doing at fifty,' she would muse,[31] but the vigour of her Philharmonic input could not be gainsaid. Her job, she said, was 'to look two or three blocks ahead'[32] and by the end of her fourth season she was widely, if resentfully, regarded as the tone-setter in American orchestral management. Simmering player resentment was defused in July 1995, minutes before a strike deadline, by Borda springing the best salary offer in any orchestra in the world – a minimum of $81,120 a year, plus health and pension deals, for a twenty-hour week that allowed musicians to pursue a full external career. Only the New York Philharmonic could afford it. In Borda's view, her orchestra and a small handful of other big-city establishments would survive whatever the new millennium might hold. As for the rest of the musical world, it was up to them to find their own solutions. Called upon to rebut a morbid ASOL prognosis of symphonic futures, she likened the situation to an automobile driving towards a precipice. 'So, as the car heads towards the cliff,' she orated, 'we need to remind ourselves that *we basically have control* of a vehicle which has many choices for action.'[33] It was up to managers to grab the wheel and change direction, as she was doing in New York. Her pugnacious positivism starkly counterpointed Ernest Fleischmann's reductionist merger-ism which, in Borda's vicinity, was shrugged off as menopausal male talk. 'I'm confident there will be orchestras,' said Deborah Borda, 'but maybe not as we've known them. Maybe better.'[34]

It was London that came closest to validating Fleischmann's death sentence. In the 1980s the London Symphony Orchestra came several times to within days of disbandment. Internal strife, indifferent management and a calami-tously mishandled entry to the Barbican resulted in debts of three hundred and seventy thousand pounds and a clamour of creditors. In June 1982

Lloyd's Bank had a debenture drawn up over the orchestra's assets and the board promised to pay off its debts within two years. In October 1983 the chairman, Anthony Camden, took a month off playing the oboe to raise emergency funds in the City, while every player was asked to chip in forty-three pounds a month to keep the company afloat. Then the Arts Council, without warning, slashed a hundred thousand pounds off the LSO's annual grant. An interest-free loan from the Musicians Union narrowly saved the day.

A second-row cellist, Clive Gillinson, walked into the management office and found 'there were no financial controls: the business wasn't being run as a business.'[35] Having once run a Hampstead antique shop with his wife, Penny, Gillinson was one of the few members of the company who could make sense of a balance sheet. In November 1984 he was asked to stand in as managing director; four months later the Arts Council issued a final ultimatum, warning that it would cut off all funding if the LSO debts were not paid up within three years. Gillinson, under pressure from desperate colleagues, signed a five-year management contract. Before that term was up he had turned the LSO around, sold his cello and established himself as Britain's most successful symphonic manager – but the threat to orchestras had not gone away.

Among Gillinson's earliest embarrassments was an attempt to persuade music director Claudio Abbado to abandon his ambitious 'Mahler, Vienna and the Twentieth Century' series, the most expensive venture the LSO had ever undertaken. Abbado refused point-blank. 'Claudio gave me the best possible lesson of my life,' said Gillinson later. 'He said, "You don't compromise on the artistic side." ' To pay for Mahler, the players scrimped, cut corners, screwed non-premier rehearsals to a bare minimum and played a lot of junk dates they would prefer to forget. But Abbado's brainchild was a turning point, endowing the Barbican with artistic credibility and, in Gillinson's estimation, 'giving the musicians back the beginnings of their self-respect'.

There was a long haul ahead, but by 1987 the LSO was in the black and by 1989 it was breathing easier on a corporate endowment and a pledge of permanent funding from the City fathers. Cannily, Gillinson wielded this patronage to squeeze matching sums out of a discomfited Arts Council that had nearly written off the LSO.

Setting art once more above prudence, he contracted the expensive cellist Mstislav Rostropovich to play a sixtieth birthday retrospective series with the LSO. Out of that engagement grew symphonic cycles of Shostakovich and Prokofiev, the first ever heard in London and the envy of continental capitals. Leonard Bernstein returned to relive his favourite works with the LSO, which in 1988 elected his protégé, Michael Tilson Thomas, as Abbado's successor. Colin Davis came back with an epochal Sibelius cycle and in 1995 assumed the music directorship on Tilson Thomas's departure. But Davis explicitly stated that he was responsible only for his own programming, as *primus inter pares* in a cabinet of conductors that included Boulez, Ozawa, Previn, Rostropovich, Solti and Tilson Thomas. The director of these musicians, if not actual music director, was Clive Gillinson. 'What's important to me,' he said modestly, 'is what the great artists want. Essentially, I go looking to fulfil their musical vision.'

A colonial boy, born in Bangalore and raised on a farm in Kenya, Gillinson studied mathematics at university, before switching to the Royal Academy of Music. On graduation, he found a warm welcome in the LSO cellos. When called to the rescue, he felt he was fighting not only for his job but for the livelihoods of his closest friends and the survival of an institution that mattered to all of them far more than any football club does to its easily transferred players. The LSO, to Gillinson, was family, history and religion in one.

As soon as funds were available, he set about improving the players' quality of life. Installing co-principals on most instruments, he gave top players time off for personal development and created openings for them to work with composers, school groups and, for the socially conscientious, mental patients and prisoners. 'It's terribly important to enable players to reclaim their personality from the orchestral experience,' he believed. 'You take up music to express your individuality, then you join an orchestra and have to repress it.'

As a manager Gillinson was, first and foremost, the players' advocate and his position depended on their support. But he knew that better conditions would attract superior musicians and the LSO was able to recruit into its ranks some outstanding young soloists, despairing of freelance uncertainty on the chamber circuit. Despite the Barbican's muffled acoustic, the LSO most nights outshone its three historic rivals. Bernard Haitink, who was attached by long ties of loyalty to the London Philharmonic, gazed across at the LSO with open admiration. 'Eric Bravington and Clive Gillinson are the only examples of people I have met who came out of an orchestra and knew how to pull them together,' he said. 'The LSO is therefore doing well, because they have continuity, good programme ideas, and you have a feeling that they are well managed. I miss that with the other London orchestras. You must have a consistent policy. When the LPO came to me – I am their president, whatever that means – I said, "don't concentrate so much on a new music director. You must have artistic direction." '[36]

From the security of his Barbican fortress, buttressed by seven-figure grants from the Arts Council and the City, Gillinson watched the disaster that he had so narrowly averted at the LSO loom over the remainder of England's orchestras. By 1993 only two of them — the LSO and Simon Rattle's Birmingham orchestra — were confident of continued funding. That year Gillinson was elected chairman of the Association of British Orchestras and the Arts Council, in one of its most capricious acts, announced the withdrawal of funding from two London orchestras. The selection was to be made by a star chamber headed by Lord Justice Hoffmann, before whom the three threatened bands would beg for their lives. Gillinson, whose LSO was exempted from the cull, was attacked by brother-managers for lacking solidarity. To victims of this inquisition it looked as if the LSO was lined up on Torquemada's side. 'Where were they, you might ask, when we were going under?' retorted LSO partisans.

When the dust settled and the Arts Council plan collapsed, the LSO found itself paradoxically weakened by the unexpected survival of all four orchestras. Competition between them turned hostile and Gillinson was tarnished in the fray. For three years in a row he could not afford to raise wages at the LSO. There were rustlings in the ranks and unhappiness at the Barbican, but LSO players had only to look at the London Philharmonic to convince themselves that Clive Gillinson still knew best.

The LPO, which had been primed to win the Hoffmann contest, came out of the débâcle in deep trouble. Resident at the Royal Festival Hall, it was racked by internal squabbles that precipitated the departure of two managements and a music director, Franz Welser-Möst, in as many years. Together with the Philharmonia and the Royal Philharmonic it took a tide-over loan from the Musicians Union and in 1995 was forced to relinquish its exclusive RFH residency. Leaderless and despondent, the orchestra found a new patron in the former Thatcherite cabinet minister Lord Young, who took a political overview and proposed a cost-saving administrative merger with the RPO. It took a few weeks before anyone realised who was behind this dazzling initiative. But when talks between the two orchestras broke up and the plan was proclaimed unworkable, its invisible architect was none the less retained on a consultancy basis. Ernest Fleischmann was back in town, six days a month, striving to put the London Philharmonic back on its feet and settle some old scores. 'Crisis management,' said Esa-Pekka Salonen, 'is something Ernest very much enjoys.'[37]

The flick-knife was seventy years old but, said friends, he was keen for challenge and uneasy in LA. He had given the Dream City a better orchestra

Outbreaks of Lisztomania, orchestrated by an
unseen manager. (Above)

Anton Rubinstein at the piano. He pocketed Steinway's gold but
refused to return for an encore.(Below left)

Jenny Lind, stony-faced and even tougher on the inside, the
patron saint of an embryonic music business.(Below right)

Queen Louise Wolff (front table right) dominating a music business lunch with (r. to l.) Frederic Steinway, Mrs Carl Flesch, Emil Bohnke, Melanie Kurth, Erich Kleiber, Mrs Georg Bernhard, Mrs Fritz Kreisler.(Above)

Giulio Gatti-Casazza, unflappably elegant, restored financial probity to opera in America.(Above)

Sol Hurok, the magnificent, in his own favourite portrait.(Left)

Phineas T. Barnum, first bringer
of music to mainline America.(Top)

Hermann Wolff, patriarch and oligarch
of the European music
business, with its capital in Berlin.(Left)

Enrico Caruso endorsed French wines
for hard cash, but kept his
operatic fees to affordable levels.(Top left)

CAMI headquarters on West 57th Street,
two doors up from Steinways and directly
opposite Carnegie Hall.(Below)

Harold Holt in full
flight, ashtray over-
flowing and reaching
for the stars. *(Photo:*
Sir Ian Hunter)
(Above)

The future Salzburg
founders gather at the
1911
premiere of *Der*
Rosenkavalier.
Standing (l. to r.)
Max Reinhardt,
Hugo von
Hoffmanstahl,
Alfred Roller; seated
(l. to r.)
Dresden Intendant
Count Nikolaus
von Seebach, Richard
Strauss,
conductor Ernst von
Schuch.
(Right)

Walter Legge shares a score with Herbert von Karajan in 1955, a pivotal year in their relationship. Legge's uneasy expression suggests that power is rapidly slipping from the record industry's puppet master to its new dictator. *(Photo: Roger Hauert)*(Above) Isaac Stern, convenor of world violinists and centrepiece of an agency counterculture. (Top Left)

Arthur Judson in his pomp was lord of America's music and its mass media. But his handwriting on this 1940 dedication to Evelyn Barbirolli is the shaky scrawl of a semi-educated clerk, or a powerless wallflower. *(Photo: Lady Barbirolli)*(Top right)

The tobacco industry comes puffing up music as health authorities start attacking the weed.(Right)

An ailing Herbert von Karajan and Sony chief Norio Ohga cut the ribbon of a compact disc factory at Anif, near Salzburg, in 1985. (Left)

Three tenors sing in a public bath on a night that spelled doom for the classical music industry. (l. to r.) Placido Domingo, conductor Zubin Mehta, Jose Carreras, Luciano Pavarotti. (Photo: *Decca/ Vivianne Purdom*) (Below)

CREDIT DECCA / VIVIANNE PURDOM

DECCA

Chairman Norio Ohga, conductor of Sony's disaster- ridden music invasion. *(Photo: Sony)*(Above)

Deborah Borda, power-suiting the New York Philharmonic. *(Photo: Lisa Kohler/NYPO)*(Bottom right)

Camera-shy Ronald Wilford (left), caught socialising with Eckard Heintz, 1993 President of ISPA *(Photo: ISPA)* (Below)

The sunny side of Ernest Fleischmann, orchestral manager in a maestroless world. *(Photo: LAPO)* (Right)

The fast-rising Peter Gelb, heir to Sony's music empire and CAMI's favourite son. *(Photo: Sony)* (Bottom right)

Mark H. McCormack, smilingly expressionless and relentlessly expectant. *(Photo: IMG)* (Below)

All pictures, unless otherwise noted, are courtesy of the Lebrecht Collection.

than it deserved, but orchestras in Fleischmann's view were a figment of their manager's imagination and could degenerate on his departure. He wanted to leave behind something permanent in the shape of a magnificent concert hall and persuaded Walt Disney's family to build it. The architect was his favourite Frank Gehry and the interior was modelled on the Philharmonie of Berlin, music capital of Fleischmann's *Heimatland*.

Balconies were to be abolished in the interest of audience democracy; raked tiers would ensure excellent sightlines at all price levels. The site was to be open day and night, for universal enjoyment. 'It was Walt Disney's ideal that art be available to everyone,' puffed Fleischmann. 'We don't want a temple of culture, rather a welcoming kind of place.'[38] The opening was scheduled for September 1997, when Fleischmann would be seventy-three and still in harness. But few great edifices ever open on time and, as the date kept slipping, the costs ran one hundred million dollars over Fleischmann's projected budget. The county, which was meant to run the hall, called a public inquiry and a pall of negative headlines settled over the scheme. Not a man to quit when he was behind, Fleischmann showed more than his average signs of irritation. He began to reflect longingly on the golden overseas opportunities he had passed up. 'If I were conducting, I might start a new career now,' he quipped in 1991, 'but anyone looking at my age in my job would not consider me a good investment.'

The lure of London, though, was irresistible – a chance to erase lingering bloodstains, a chance to prove that his doomsday theory might work, not just for one orchestra but for an entire orchestral culture. Commuting first-class between LA and the London Philharmonic at a time in life when most men are tending gardens and grandchildren, Ernest Fleischmann could shut his eyes and imagine he was a grand maestro, sought after by orchestras the world over.

As orchestral managers assumed the maestro mantle, willingly or otherwise, their counterparts in opera houses and newfangled 'arts centres' entertained a wilder delusion. It is not clear which salaried officer first called himself an impresario, but it was probably Rudolf Bing, bowler-hatted boss of the Edinburgh Festival and Metropolitan Opera House.

Bing, whose headiest moment was the firing of Maria Callas in 1958, was (in his publisher's words) 'without doubt one of the greatest musical impresarios of the twentieth century. Berlin, Glyndebourne, Edinburgh and above all the Metropolitan Opera owe an enormous debt to his great creative genius'.[39] From this description you might picture an entrepreneur like Domenico Barbaia of Naples or Gabriel Astruc of Paris who risked the bread on their children's plates to bring a new Rossini opera or Stravinsky ballet before a fickle public; an impresario like Sol Hurok who shipped a nation's culture at his own cost, or Mark McCormack who staged operas wholly without public subsidy. But Bing was never more than a hired hand, spending his board members' money on predictable entertainments and milking the applause for himself and his presumptuous profession.

'I am not prepared to enter into a public argument with Madame Callas,' declared Bing when announcing her dismissal, 'because I fully realise how much more skill and experience she has than I do in such matters.' This was a double-lie, issued to the press directly after Bing sent the telegram that terminated the diva's US career at the age of thirty-six. He seized the advantage in manipulating public opinion. As for any reluctance to mud-wrestle, the second sentence in his press release deliberately set out to destroy Callas by asserting that 'her artistic qualifications are the subject of violent debate between her friends and her enemies' – this of the supreme dramatic singer of the modern era. Her fondest fans would not have denied that Callas was a difficult, devious colleague, but Bing's argument with her was not about dates or money. It was, as one Callas biographer correctly perceived, a 'trial of strength' in which an increasingly vain and confident class of managers, serving an increasingly wealthy, sensation-seeking audience, manifested its newfound muscle by penalising a vulnerable artist.

The sacking of Callas, wrote the German cultural commentator Jürgen Kesting, constituted 'the overshadowing of a capricious, moody and yet magnetic and brilliant performer by a colourful, expensive and luxurious business . . . with the all-powerful manager/impresario/conductor in the economic background and with a self-regarding public in the centre'.[40] It marked a turning point in artistic relations, for while it did not change the high-handed way some artists behave, nor the demands made on them by major institutions, it introduced the company-manager as a power-player, flexing his biceps in a vacant ring. By styling themselves impresarios, company-managers sought to conceal the artificiality of their position, assuming the glamour of entrepreneurship without the risk of personal outlay. An International Society of Performing Arts, ISPA by acronym, provided a woolly definition for their rising occupation and a world network for its machinations.

These managers were the masters of opera in the latter half of the twentieth century, the Machiavellis of casting, the dispensers of patronage. Their emergence was less sudden than in the orchestral sphere, since music directors in opera had long shared certain artistic functions with a trusted, if invisible, administrator. The model relationship in opera had been Arturo

Toscanini's with Giulio Gatti-Casazza at La Scala and the Met. Where the neo-impresarios differed from Gatti-Casazza and his self-effacing heir, Edward Johnson, was in their desire for control and celebrity. Bing was an acid-tongued aphorist who liked getting quoted and loved to be thought of as 'Mr Met'. In Europe, the name to conjure with was Rolf Liebermanns, a dormant composer who fomented a frenzy of new operas and styles as director of the Hamburg State Opera (1959–73) and Paris Opéra (1973–80). Acclaimed by company publicity as a 'creative influence', Liebermann was more fêted and flamboyant than any of the conductors he employed.

Not all the neo-impresarios were glory seekers. Carlo Fontana, sacked as Sovrintendente at La Scala in 1993 during one of Milan's political ructions, 'felt bitter about being hauled out from my detached and discreet position behind the scenes'.[41] A quiet facilitator, cherished by Luciano Pavarotti and Sir Georg Solti, who threatened to boycott La Scala unless he was reinstated, Fontana none the less shared the inflated self-image of his caste. His job, as he saw it, was not just to book good singers and conductors, keep the orchestra and chorus in line and ensure the productions were of a high standard and the house was full. It was, rather, to develop a 'cultural strategy' that would turn his theatre into a 'symbol of cohesion' and intellectual stimulus: 'To do for culture, and with culture, what politicians and politically motivated persons have so far failed to do.'[42] Beside such high-flown aims, Riccardo Muti's task as music director seemed a mere technicality.

Sentiments such as Fontana's were symptoms of a musculature that had outswelled its shirt. Few modern conductors had an ego to match the untrammelled ambitions of their tenured 'impresarios'. In the 1980s, the Vienna State Opera lost two of the world's finest music directors, Lorin Maazel and Claudio Abbado, to a *putsch* by cultural and political bureaucrats. The house that Mahler ruled wound up without a conductor to call its own, directed by Ion Holender, a former artists' agent. The modern era's most impressive opera house, the Australian Opera in Sydney, had an accomplished artistic director, Moffat Oxenbould, but no music director. Command of San Francisco Opera passed from a conductor, Kurt Herbert Adler, to a record producer, Terence McEwen, to a stage director, Lotfi Mansouri. The new Nederlandse Opera was personified from opening night by its general director, Pierre Audi, rather than by any conductor.

The marginalisation of maestros achieved its apotheosis at multi-disciplinary arts festivals and multi-purpose 'arts centres', that fashionably combined the functions of concert hall, movie house, theatre and art gallery. In Amsterdam, the managing director of the operating company of the Concertgebouw hall had more say in concert planning than the music director of its resident orchestra. When Martijn Sanders, a University of Michigan MBA, devised a Mahler cycle for 1995 he allocated Riccardo Chailly and the Royal Concertgebouworkest just two concerts in his series. The rest were shared out between international orchestras and conductors, with Chailly's predecessor, Bernard Haitink, getting twice as many symphonies as he did to conduct. There was a power point being made here, but neither Chailly nor his orchestra was in a position to resist. Ironically, the historic event that Sanders sought to commemorate was the world's first Mahler cycle in 1920, played entirely by the Concertgebouworkest under its chief conductor, Willem Mengelberg. No house manager would ever have told Willem Mengelberg which symphonies he was permitted to conduct. The gulf between 1920 and 1995 was a measure of the loss of maestro potency and the rise of 'impresario' managers.

London's South Bank Centre was designed to operate without a music director under Nicholas Snowman, who started out in 1985 as an imposer of Boulezian programming, but shed his convictions under pressure of dwindling audiences. The South Bank's central attraction was the Royal Festival Hall, but no conductor was allowed to draw up its concert planning. Where the dapper Snowman manifested *dirigiste* tendencies, Judith Aron at Carnegie Hall was more like a traffic cop, neutrally allocating lanes to incoming vehicles, but occasionally dressing up in full regalia to direct a Bernstein or Solti parade.

Some of these quasi-impresarios slaved around the clock, others were habitually out to lunch. Some abused their position for sexual or financial gain, others were monastically virtuous. As a group, they were neither more nor less effective than hospital administrators and foreign ambassadors. They did a job that needed doing and were generally well paid for it. What raised them above the parapet of public attention was, pure and simple, the privilege of being involved in art. Where hospital chiefs and diplomats got noticed only when epidemics or war loomed, neo-impresarios could steal a headline any time they liked with a bold stroke of concert planning or opera production. Even in an information-saturated society, art was still a magnet of controversy, and controversy was the fast lane to fame. The impact of art, however, was perceptibly diminished when the promoter was a salaried Snowman or Sanders, rather than a flaring, daring Beecham or Diaghilev.

As administrators stole more and more maestro clothes, the impetus of concert giving suffered a subtle mutation. Where music directors were primarily concerned with putting on well-rehearsed, widely advertised performances of relevant works, house managers had a higher objective. They had to ensure that budgets balanced and the paymasters were content.

This entailed grotesque investments in the imprecise art of marketing, alongside daily acts of obeisance to politicians and sponsors. Their programming was directed not by musical imperatives, but by what was politically correct and business approved. The American composer Gunther Schuller lashed out futilely at modern managers for allowing 'corporate mentality' to dominate their concert planning. A pall of expediency settled on the concert hall.

Ernest Fleischmann, in the end, found no bold solution for the London Philharmonic's problems. He jacked in his mission after installing a brother-administrator, Serge Dorny of the Flanders Festival, in the newly created position of Artistic Director. 'Ernest feels that, with the appointment of Serge, the orchestra is now in the best possible hands,' said its chairman hopefully.[43] A week later in Los Angeles, as his Disney dream hall drifted ever further into the fuggy future, Fleischmann finally gave up the struggle and announced his retirement, effective June 1997. 'It will be very difficult to find anyone who could begin to fill Ernest's shoes,' said the LAPO president.[44] Where orchestras once aspired to attract the best conductor, their survival now hinged on head-hunting an imaginative administrator.

Few cities now had a music director with the vision or persistence to regenerate their musical life. Few conductors were, in any case, capable of seeing beyond their professional routines and personal ambitions. Their lives were split between several cities and their menu restricted to personal specialities. By the end of the century there would be no maestro under the age of fifty who had mastered the central concert repertoire, from Bach to Shostakovich.

The last stand of the waning music director was staged in a deserted city in the middle of 1994. Paris in the second week of August is no place to pick a shoot-out if you want to get on screen. Populace and press have fled to the Riviera and only tourists come gawking at the temples of art. Mid-August, though, is when opera staff reassemble to rehearse the season's curtain-raiser. Fresh from festival success in Florence, music director Myung-Whun Chung drove up to the Opéra Bastille, eager to get to grips with Verdi's *Simon Boccanegra*. Chung, a Korean in his forty-second year, was the artistic conscience of a storm-tossed company. In the five years since he took the job, breaking a conductors' boycott over Daniel Barenboim's dismissal, Chung had kept a cool head amid the labour unrest and political caprice that were the hallmark of Parisian opera, celebrated in István Szabó's 1990 movie, *Meeting Venus*. Rallying his musicians with a mixture of naive idealism and commercial acumen, Chung raised the orchestra and chorus to a standard that

Deutsche Grammophon recognised with a prestigious recording deal. His personal achievement was rewarded with a lavish new contract worth two-and-a-half million francs a year (£330,000) and signed with a flourish by the outgoing Bastille director, the socialist fashion millionaire Pierre Bergé. Despite a change of government, Chung had good reason to feel secure in his position.

Arriving at the artists' entrance, however, Chung found his path blocked by an official who gave him a letter from the newly appointed director-general of the Opéra Nationale de Paris, Hugues Gall. It announced his immediate dismissal and barred him from entering the premises. Chung was stunned. 'I have been treated, forgive the expression, like shit,' he told me some days later, his natural fastidiousness dispelled by shock and anger. 'They are saying that I have chosen to leave because I refused to renegotiate my contract. That's an outright lie. I was always prepared to do whatever I could to help the Opéra, even to renegotiate, but they have ignored my artistic rights.'

'I have been absolutely fair to M. Chung for six months,' was the explanation of Hugues Gall, Rolf Liebermann's former right-hand man who had been summoned by Gaullists to bring the Bastille to heel and stem its spiralling deficit of seventy million francs (£8 million). Gall had been running the Geneva Opera on a tight budget and was famed for standing up to labour unions and artists' agents. 'I aim to put order in this house,' he said. 'I need to freeze salaries and make redundancies. M. Chung would have been the highest-paid music director on earth. Why should artists get the same fee at La Scala, Vienna, Berlin, a little less in London – and double when they come to Paris? I am not a French cow and I am not going to be milked. I can live without power, but someone has to be head.'[45]

These two versions of the events at the Bastille entrance did not so much conflict with as deflect off one another, as if the principals were discussing separate issues in different languages. No one reading of the contention could fail to be reminded of the Barenboim imbroglio of 1989, when a strong-headed music director with a clear if unaccommodating artistic outlook was ousted by a political appointee who accused him of greed and intransigence. Barenboim's offer to halve his fees had been similarly rebutted. French public opinion in both instances was deftly turned against the uncomprehending foreigners. Both disputes would be resolved predictably with a discreet million-dollar pay-off to the evicted conductors.

But there the affinities ended. Barenboim's dismissal made world headlines and drew protests from conductors of every confession, from Karajan down. Chung's sacking five years later was staged in the dead of August and settled before the summer was over. No maestro raised a voice in anger and, though the orchestra offered to stage a sympathy strike, Chung politely declined their gesture. 'I don't want anything that would be at the expense of the house,' he said. 'It would only give them grounds to accuse me of playing power games.' His principled solitude had an affecting dignity and a wounded charm. Unlike Barenboim, who had lined up a parallel music directorship in Chicago, Chung had nowhere else to go. He was totally dedicated to the Bastille and its musicians, wasting weeks in ministry offices, negotiating pension rights and parking places for second violinists and superannuated altos. He was a music director in the full sense of the title, and anyone listening to his DG recordings would agree that he was worthy of his hire.

'I can't accept comparison with Daniel Barenboim,' Chung complained. 'Barenboim never conducted at the Bastille. I have worked here for five years and even *they* admit the results were not bad. We were all looking forward to someone thoroughly professional like M. Gall coming in and taking control. But he has shown that he hasn't the tiniest grain of respect for anyone in this house. He has told me as much. To ask a musician to accept his conditions is like making me go into an artistic dungeon as a prisoner for three years. They want me to accept whatever he dictates. How could I hold my head up in front of the musicians?'

Gall did not dispute the charge. 'Every artistic decision has financial consequences,' said the administrator. 'Under M. Chung's contract, he had rights of veto. I cannot live with a nice chap next door who has a grenade in his pocket. Only one person can take the responsibility, and that's me.'

Over the next few days their confrontation degenerated into near-farce as Chung, contract in his hand, went to court and secured a judicial order requiring the Bastille administration to let him conduct. Fifty orchestral musicians in the public gallery cheered the decision. But when the music director returned to the Bastille he was once again refused entry.

In any Anglo-Saxon jurisdiction this would have constituted a flagrant contempt of court and resulted in Gall's probable imprisonment. In France it marked the opening of private negotiations between the government-backed administrator and an appeal court judge. The outcome was a concession by Gall, allowing Chung to enter the building but stipulating that he no longer worked there. Gall refused to reinstate him, despite Chung's offer to conduct without pay for the next six years. Faced with the impossibility of making music in Paris, Chung told his lawyers to negotiate a financial settlement.

The key difference between his case and Barenboim's lay in the calibre and intentions of their opponent. Bergé, as music critic Alain Lompech noted in *Le Monde*, 'was an independent spark with no other qualification than that he was a friend of President Mitterand'.[46] Gall, on the other hand, was a highly regarded opera professional whom insiders considered the best candidate for an impossible job. Anglophile in dress and tastes, he masked a reputed toughness behind a courteous manner. His attitude to conductors, however, was unyielding. In Geneva, Gall produced low-budget seasons with up-and-coming Anglo-American singers, clever directors and no resident conductor. In the media eye, company chiefs like Gall were credited with artistic innovation and looked upon music directors as a dispensable expense.

'With the kind of man I am and the kind of experience I have,' said Hugues Gall, '*I don't see the need for a music director.*' These were dire words from an influential oracle. They spelled doom for musical authority and demotion for the musical component in opera. Yet they were, in many ways, in tune with an epoch when armies could not fire a missile without permission from defence ministry accountants and hospital managers, not doctors, took critical decisions of life and death.

Gall was probably aware that his declaration was a tad too harsh and modified it with a suggestion that he might 'find somebody who will be music adviser, or regular conductor'. His choice fell upon James Conlon, a quiet American who was Generalmusikdirektor of the city of Cologne under an efficient German administration. 'My career is not going to end if I get fired,' said Conlon, who described himself as 'completely fatalistic'[47] about the Bastille.

Chung's dismissal cost the company its record contract and the trust of young conductors. Gall attracted Sir Georg Solti and Seiji Ozawa to his opening season, but failed to achieve a quarter of the staff redundancies he required. Wildcat strikes blacked out one in twelve performances in 1994–5, costing the company a million francs a night. Barely had Chung departed than his unhappy orchestra and chorus went on strike, demanding parity with players at Radio France. People going to the Opéra could never be sure that the show would not be cancelled at the last moment.

Gall's position elicited a chorus of sympathy from the ruling classes of world opera. 'What Hugues is doing is not greatly different from what Liebermann did,' said Sir John Tooley, former general director of Covent Garden.[48] Yet, whether or not he succeeded in whipping the Bastille into order, it was clear that Gall had struck a mighty blow for managership. He would go down in history as the opera boss who abolished the position of music director and reduced the conductor to a cipher on his schedule. After the second sacking of the Bastille, the newly empowered manager was well on the way to becoming the maestro of the musical future.

NOTES

1 see Stresemann, . . . *und Abends*, pp. 147–8
2 Lang, p. 125
3 Stresemann, *Berlin*, pp. 114–15
4 . . . *und Abends in die Philharmonie*, 1981
5 Stresemann, to the author
6 all Fleischmann comments in this chapter are from the author's interviews, unless indicated
7 Pearton, p. 162
8 personal communication from LSO board member
9 author's interview
10 Stiff, author's interview
11 copy in the author's possession
12 author's interview
13 both quotes: 'The Importance of Being Fleischmann', by Thomas Thompson, *New York Times Magazine*, 11 April 1976
14 *NYT Magazine*, loc. cit.
15 *NYT Magazine*, loc. cit.
16 'The Philharmonic's Once and Future King', by John Henkin, *LA Times Calendar*, 10 July 1988
17 *NYT Magazine*, loc. cit.
18 Fleischmann to Lang, 6 December 1985
19 interview with the author; identity withheld
20 all Previn quotes from: 'The Tyrant of the Philharmonic', by Martin Bernheimer, *LA Times Magazine*, 8 October 1989
21 *LA Times Magazine*, 8 October 1989
22 *New Criterion*, September 1987, pp. 1–7
23 *New Criterion*, December 1987, pp. 38–41
24 'Orchestra Managers: Bridging Worlds of Business and Art', by Andrew L. Pincus, 2 February 1987
25 interview in *Classical Music* magazine, 10 April 1993
26 *Classical Music*, loc. cit.
27 *NYT*, 23 May 1993, 16 July 1993
28 *Classical Music* magazine, 10 April 1993, pp. 17–19
29 *CM*, loc. cit.
30 *NY Times*, 15 February 1994
31 conversation with the author, June 1993
32 *NYT*, loc. cit.
33 ASOL–92, p. B–2
34 ASOL–92, p. B–6
35 all Gillinson quotes, unless stated, from conversations with the author, 1985–95
36 author's interview
37 author's interview
38 *NYT*, 1 June 1988
39 jacket blurb to Hamish Hamilton edition of Bing memoirs
40 Kesting, pp. 209, 211
41 *La Stampa*, 13 April 1993
42 *La Stampa*, loc. cit.
43 Bob St John Wright, press statement dated 19 January 1996
44 Robert S. Attiyeh, press statement dated 26 January 1996
45 all quotes by Chung and Gall are from author's interviews, August–September 1994
46 *Le Monde*, 6 September 1994
47 *International Arts Manager*, September 1995, pp. 18–19
48 comment to the author

CHAPTER IX

THE FESTIVAL RACKET

F ew summer resort are remote and ethereal as the Dolomite mountain village of Dobbiaco. Four hours from the nearest airport, Dobbiaco is a haven for walking wounded from the metropolitan fray, a place to 'wander in the mountains [and] seek peace for my lonely heart',[1] as Gustav Mahler discovered. The air is pure, the water sparkling, the slopes beckon to be climbed or skiied. In Mahler's time, Dobbiaco (under the Teutonic name of Toblach) was a refuelling station on the Vienna–Venice–Munich railway. Today, it is well off the main line and no larger on the map.

Mahler stumbled off a train in the late summer of 1907, mourning the death of his daughter, the collapse of his health and the loss of his Vienna hegemony. Calmed by the serenity, he rented rooms for the last three summers of his life at the neighbouring hamlet of Alt-Schluderbach where, gazing across the meadows and rambling beside the lakes, he composed an ode of self-consolation, *Das Lied von der Erde*, followed by the ninth and tenth symphonies. The forester's hut where he composed those scores survives as a rickety shrine, owned by a leading hotelier.

When Mahler reconquered the world's concert halls in the 1980s, Dobbiaco commissioned a statue for the village square, renamed the main street in his honour and inaugurated an annual Mahler festival. A week of concerts in the school hall and a symposium of international scholars lured

Mahler-seekers from all over central Europe. The festival, costing around a hundred thousand pounds, is as other-worldly as the village itself. There is not a Mahler record to be bought nor a biography to be read throughout Dobbiaco. There are no Mahler T-shirts or key-rings, no chocolatier with a tourist line in Mahler-balls, no sponsorship by Fiat or Firelli. 'We are only a little village,' explained one of the organisers, firmly intending to keep it that way.

For music critics, Dobbiaco is a time-warped anachronism on a turbo-charged festival chase that starts in Florence at the Maggio Musicale, moves on to Glyndebourne and cracks open the midsummer aspirin bottles at Bayreuth and Salzburg, Edinburgh and Lucerne. Like the Grand Prix circuit, no venue contributes much more than a backdrop to the caravan of stars and groupies that flutters from one festival to the next, barely pausing to change costume and currency. Bayreuth's Isolde becomes Salzburg's recitalist; Edinburgh's American orchestra moves on to Lucerne; if Figaro catches flu at Glyndebourne, a *doppelgänger* is whistled up from Bregenz. What began as a local expression of the artistic spirit has turned into a network of permanent institutions, buttressed by state subsidy and gridlocked in a global game-plan.

The train ride from Dobbiaco to Salzburg — no more than three changes on a good day — administers a culture shock of coronary severity. Where the Dolomite village flies a lone festival banner outside its tourist office, every shop window in the Austrian mountain town beams with artists' portraits and even the cab doors are decorated with record insignia. Deutsche Grammophon, the 'yellow label', distributes yellow showerproofs to rain-drenched callers at its festival office. Salzburg is so vital to the record trade that some labels spend half their promotions budget at the festival and one has been known to splash three-quarters of a million Deutschmarks on window space alone; a hundred thousand CD sales would not recoup that outlay. Salzburg is where the record business goes for broke. No one in the music world attends Salzburg for fun. The music is serious and the deals are deadly.

Innocent visitors enter a citadel of monstrous prices and merciless self-interest. Concerts are timed according to the preferences of leading restaurateurs and there is no such thing as a sell-out. Tickets (and tables) are always obtainable, at a price, whether from your hotel major-domo or at the stage door from cupiditous personal assistants of celebrated singers.

Players in the Vienna Philharmonic earn more in a Salzburg month than their whole year's salaries, according to an Auditor General's report. Conductors who challenge the players' tradition of sending half-paid deputies to rehearsal are taken aside and advised that festival is a time of rest and relaxation. If the music is not up to his expectations, maestro can always call expensive extra rehearsals. Those who upset these arrangements – like the Italian Riccardo Chailly in 1987 – are not invited back.

Mozart, who was kicked out in his teens and denied a statue until he was fifty years dead, is Salzburg's number one money-spinner. He is merchandised on sweet-wrappers, ties, scarves, umbrellas and dolls, many manufactured in the Far East for a Japanese-dominated tourist trade. Even the Mozart birthplace is an ersatz reconstruction. Salzburg is not fussed by the provenance of profits.

Pilgrims who visit Mecca, Lourdes or Amritsar expect to be scalped by locals as the price of faith. Salzburg offers no spiritual compensations. Its Mozart worship is fake and its biggest hit is *The Sound of Music*, a Hollywood musical that sanitises recent history. There is little truth in festive Salzburg, and scarcely any beauty. Yet Salzburg, the fount of modern festivals, was conceived as an artists' idyll, a refuge from materialism. Its surrender to mammon dealt a mortal blow to musical idealism.

When the theatre director Max Reinhardt dreamed up a festival in Salzburg before the First World War, he talked in utopian terms. His *Festspiel* concept was rooted in the medieval German *Fest*, which brought together rich and poor, landowner and serf, to witness passion plays under the aegis of a unifying Church. It aspired to purify the souls of its beholders and reconsecrate performers to a divine purpose. Reinhardt's historical whimsy sat uneasily with his drive to modernise the German stage. He introduced a liberal style of interpretative direction at Berlin's Deutsches Theater, along with imaginative lighting and mass open-air productions. He took over two more companies, gave birth to expressionist theatre and supported new writers; he rarely backed a loser. Barely thirty when the century dawned, Reinhardt was the Kenneth Branagh of his age. By fifty he was the Peter Hall, rich enough to buy himself a seventeenth-century castle, the Schloss Leopoldskorn, there to gaze over Salzburg and envisage a stage where there were no stars but a community of artists, dedicated to art alone. Whatever his progressive inclinations, Reinhardt privately yearned for Baroque values. He sank ever deeper into such reveries as Austro-Germany crumbled to defeat in the First World War.

Reinhardt had become attached to Salzburg as a young actor and had schemed back in 1903 with the playwright Hermann Bahr to use it as a springboard for a Sarah Bernhardt–Eleanor Duse company. If he could only detach great artists from great cities, he believed, he might help them achieve that ever-elusive perfection. Nothing came of the idea, though Bahr pulled political levers in Vienna and preached the dream to his protégés, the writers Hugo von Hofmannsthal and Stefan Zweig. Salzburg itself showed little enthusiasm for this, or in a 1906 opera festival for Mozart's hundred and fiftieth birthday, conducted by Gustav Mahler and Richard Strauss.

Twelve years on, however, Austria was another country and Salzburg a different town. The empire had gone, the populace was starving and the former Alpine bishopric awoke to find itself the second city of a new republic. It needed a civic emblem and in July 1918 sent an emissary to Reinhardt asking if he was still thinking of a festival. Reinhardt replied with a rambling essay about lost virginity and the need to bring together 'countless men who would be redeemed from this horrible time through Art'.[2]

He called for a theatre with no barriers between actors and audience and a programme of the highest seriousness. Salzburg was bemused and uncertain. To his colleagues Reinhardt talked in more practical terms of the need to find summer employment for indigent actors and musicians. He found support from a polemicist who, with profounder sensitivity for local patriotism, suddenly pushed Mozart to the fore. Hugo von Hofmannsthal began, as the war ended, to campaign for a festival of music and drama. 'We want to take Salzburg and raise Mozart and the town of his birth to a truly Austrian symbol of artistic creation,' he declared.[3] A dazzling poet in his youth Hofmannstahl, when his muse dried up, turned to writing librettos for Richard Strauss. He appalled polite society with *Elektra* and appeased it with *Der Rosenkavalier*. With Reinhardt he recreated the medieval *Everyman* in 1911 as an open-air spectacle in Berlin. Both teamed up with Strauss on *Ariadne auf Naxos* and discovered a common yearning for antediluvianisms.

Hofmannsthal viewed the Salzburg festival as 'a moral mission', a necessary corrective to modernity. To achieve it, he would use whatever means necessary – including incendiary devices of German racialism. He propounded a unity of 'all the forms of theatrical expression which spring from the south German soil'[4] and preached a blood brotherhood between Wagner's shrine in Bayreuth and Mozart's at Salzburg. Bayreuth was Europe's only music festival but its dedication was to Wagner alone and its administration was (and is) an internecine family affair. Salzburg, in Hofmannsthal's vision, would be a shrine for the totality of German music and drama. He co-opted Richard Strauss, the most successful living German composer, together with Franz Schalk, his co-director at the Vienna Opera and Alfred Roller, Mahler's stage designer, who proposed the origination of a distinctive Salzburg style of Mozart performance.

This Mozartian identity was just beginning to germinate when Reinhardt jumped the gun. On 22 August 1920, almost without warning, he directed Hofmannsthal's adaptation of *Everyman* in the open square outside the Salzburg cathedral. The seats were snapped up by Bavarians and Viennese and, after a run of five performances, a sixth had to be put on solely for Salzburgers. 'Priests said the play was stronger than any sermon,'[5] said the director and *Everyman* became a festive perennial. 'Through the great door of the cathedral came the voice of the Lord calling for the testing of *Jedermann*,' reported an English visitor. 'Trumpets sounded from the high towers. In the silences of the afternoon, as Everyman listened and heard his name echoed, now near, now far – "*Jedermann! Je-der-mann!*" – all sorts of common everyday sounds took on significance, the flapping of the wings of the pigeons, the chiming of the clock. The cortège of *Jedermann* entered the square in poignant perspective, slowly approaching, Sorrow and Repentance trailing behind . . . I have never seen acting of such pity, eloquence, power and sweetness.'[6] Reinhardt's ideal was achieved at a stroke. Only Karl Kraus, the Viennese iconoclast, questioned the outrageous seat prices and the potential for blasphemy on the cathedral steps.

The first concert was conducted the following summer by Bernhard Paumgartner, director of the Mozarteum academy. Strauss, who scorned Paumgartner's Salzburgian provinciality, threatened to resign from the festival board, thought better of it and in 1922 transferred four Mozart productions from Vienna with sensational casts and the superb Vienna Philharmonic. Salzburg hummed with music lovers. In late August, the Socialist Party demanded the expulsion of all tourists and the restoration of pre-festival food prices.

Opera goers were threatened with cudgels by jobless locals. Under intense pressure, the deputy provincial governor issued a proclamation ordering tourists to leave by 3 September, by which time the festival was profitably over. Resentments simmered among those parts of the populace that derived no direct benefit from the festival, but the Salzburgers who counted – the politicians, hoteliers, shopkeepers, bishops – were quick to take their cut. As early as 1922, journalists spotted town notables selling their complimentary tickets to hotel porters. As the festival grew famous, Salzburg became a compulsory pleasure spot for sybaritic steelmakers and currency speculators, purring all day around the lovely Salzkammergut countryside in their Daimlers, pausing for lucullan feasts at country inns and returning in time to enjoy the best music and drama to be experienced anywhere in Europe.

The artists who came to Salzburg, inspired by Reinhardt's vision, gave of their best with scant thought of reward. Reinhardt waived his fee, as did the conductor Arturo Toscanini. Hofmannsthal took only half his royalty and many singers appeared for expenses alone, happy to work in congenial surroundings and the company of their peers. Paumgartner conducted free concerts of Mozart serenades beneath the stars. Toscanini was never so relaxed as in Salzburg, sporting an informal beret, waving to fans from his open Cadillac and neglecting to throw a tantrum at every musical misdemeanour. Franz Schalk was found most afternoons at the chessboard in the Café Bazar, tearing himself away five minutes before his baton was due to rise on *Fidelio*. Alexander Moissi, the original *Jedermann*, presided in the same coffee house over a table-length of admirers.

Reinhardt would end a première night with a sumptuous banquet at his fantasy castle. Stefan Zweig, Europe's top-selling biographer, threw rival parties at his villa on the Kapuzinerberg. They never ate at one another's table — not out of any personal animus, but in order to avoid offending Hofmannsthal, who was insanely jealous of Zweig's massive royalties.

Zweig's house guests included, at one time or another, the Nobel laureates Romain Rolland and Thomas Mann; the modern composers Maurice Ravel and Béla Bartók; and the visionaries H. G. Wells and James Joyce. Carl Zuckmayer, Germany's most bankable dramatist, held court at nearby Henndorf: 'There were sixteen guests in the house,' he wrote, 'and it remains a mystery to me where we found room for all of them . . . There was Chaliapin, the great Russian singer with his wife, several friends and his lovely daughters . . . There was a Dutch scholar who had recently set up a precious music archive in Vienna. There was a theatre director, a Catholic prelate from Germany, a few writers, some actors and artists with their wives or girl friends.'[7] A visitor did not need to be rich to share the festive spirit. 'We would go to Morzg, a few miles across the meadows,' recalled the English critic, Neville Cardus. 'We sat under lilac trees at tables which were covered with cloths in red-and-black check, and members of the Wiener Philharmoniker were there, witty, ironical and, of a sudden, as noisy as children. Mairecker, the first violin . . . insists on my having an omelette, despite that I have lunched on *Forelle* (trout) and *Kartoffeln* (potatoes). The omelette is brought to the table by a *Mädchen* who carries the tray on high. Apparently the omelette is made of snow and air and music. Mairecker stands up, all attention like a soldier, salutes the omelette and plays the first of the gorgeous melodies of the *Kaiserwaltzer*.'[8]

Rows over deficits and artistic preferences, whipped up by the Viennese press, could not blight the festival's benign sense of purpose. A festival hall was built in 1927, frugally upholstered yet equipped for all but the biggest operas. A Bavarian bank underwrote the festival that year and Thomas Cook inaugurated package tours, involving an eight-hour train ride from Zurich.

The first Americans arrived, among them the movie mogul Louis B. Mayer who sat through egalitarian *Everyman*, his brow beaded in nervous perspiration. 'You cannot put that on in America,' he warned Reinhardt. 'There are too many rich people there.'[9]

Hofmannsthal's death in July 1929, struck down as he dressed to attend his son's funeral, devastated the colony of artists that grew around the directorate. But 1930 brought the longest festival yet, with six operas, four plays and sixty thousand tickets sold, twice as many as Salzburg had citizens. Two British prime ministers and the President of France attended and the festival showed a substantial profit. In less than a decade Salzburg had redefined the festival for modern times. It was to be high-minded, yet light-hearted; desirable for the rich, yet accessible to the impecunious; attracting the finest artists, but paying them pin-money. It occupied the slowest month of the year but offered a prospect of perfection. Above all, it signalled a reborn belief in art as an eternal remedy for human woes. Like most innovations of the inter-war years, it was quickly copied – and corrupted.

Among the early visitors to Salzburg was an English landowner, John Christie, who dropped by after the rigours of Bayreuth. A bald, one-eyed Old Etonian and ex-Eton schoolmaster of primordial persuasions – England was the centre of the universe, Wagner the acme of all music – Christie built an organ room in his Sussex mansion and summoned musical friends and young professionals to share his recitals. In 1931, at the robust age of forty-eight, he fell in love while singing duets with a five-guinea soprano twenty years his junior, Audrey Mildmay. They honeymooned in Salzburg and, on their return, Christie built an opera house on to his Glyndebourne mansion.

He talked of producing a *Ring* in summer and *Parsifal* at Easter, but the stage was small, the house sat three hundred and Audrey was a Susanna, not a Brünnhilde. Glyndebourne was made for Mozart. In 1934, the conductor Fritz Busch and producer Carl Ebert, partners in a 1932 Salzburg *Entführung*, opened Glyndebourne with *The Marriage of Figaro* and *Così fan tutte*. Critics hailed an 'English Salzburg' and EMI rushed down with recording vans to capture the freshest performances ever heard in the British Isles, sung in Italian by a flawless ensemble. 'In the production of Mozart operas,' wrote the learned J. A. Westrup in the *Daily Telegraph*, 'Glyndebourne has set a standard which Salzburg . . . cannot quite equal.'

Christie had not bothered to announce the festival until a month beforehand. He expected patrons to turn up in formal dress. Interval dinners were served at half a guinea or five shillings (about the same as first- or second-class rail returns to London), as well as Afternoon Tea.

Opera goers could also picnic on the lawns. A chauffeurs' room was provided, 'where servants may obtain refreshments at reasonable prices'.[10] Seats at two pounds were pricey but not prohibitive and the audience was an English allsorts of idle rich and opera nuts. 'The poor could go to Glyndebourne if they had sufficient enthusiasm to save up for the experience,' noted one music critic, 'but it was too easy by comparison for the rich to go merely because it was the thing to do.'[11] 'Though it may cost a poor man more than he can usually afford,' sermonised art historian Herbert Read, 'nevertheless, art is too important, and the sacrifices we must be prepared to make for it too imperative, for any feelings of social differences to matter, or even to arise. It would be a tragedy if Glyndebourne became merely a social occasion – it would destroy its aim and dispirit the enterprise.'[12]

The opening season cost Christie less than ten thousand pounds, a pittance for a man who owned a hundred thousand acres, his own construction firm, the biggest car-dealership in Sussex and a long stretch of the North Devon coast. He did not begrudge the cost and was unstinting in his devotion to the assiduous Audrey – 'a good pro,' according to fellow-singers, who 'won her place in the company fair and square'.[13] He expanded the house to hold six hundred, then eight hundred, its intimacy preserved by the Christies who lived next door and greeted their artists as friends and their customers as guests. Christie's eccentricities added to the homeliness of the place. He refused to wear underpants or trouser-belts, regardless of involuntary exposure. When the Queen Mother came, he unscrewed his glass eye and rolled it in her hand. The King's nephew he snubbed because he forgot to wear a black tie. Seeing a young schoolmaster wheeling a baby in its pram while his wife watched the second act of *Figaro* from the single seat they could afford, Christie gave the sleeping baby to a gardener's wife to mind and sat the grateful father in his private box. If he liked a young singer, he would pay his or her tuition fees.

Christie was an English anachronism, with history on his side. Glyndebourne, opened in the first year of the Thousand Year Reich, became a haven for talented refugees whose ambition was not merely to subsist but to transplant the art that Hitler was destroying. Ebert and Busch enlisted the Darmstadt administrator Rudolf Bing, the vocal coach Jani Strasser and, for one season, the brilliant Berlin designer Caspar Neher. The singers were a hypertense admixture of exiles and German or Italian loyalists, but the bucolic surroundings subdued political passions and the lack of anything else to do kept the casts rehearsing way past midnight. 'Even work is more attractive than the night life of Lewes,' Busch remarked.[14]

The company was lodged mostly in cottages on the estate and a fleet of cars from Christie's garage was on hand to ferry them around. They had nothing on their minds for weeks except music, and the music they produced, often as not, approached the perfection that Reinhardt had envisaged from the heights of his Salzburg *Schloss*.

Salzburg, meanwhile, shuddered amid economic depression. The upsurge of German racialism found an ugly echo among local malcontents and its first victim was Moissi, his *Jedermann* career destroyed by a scandal involving the chief surgeon at the Salzburg hospital, one Ernest von Karajan. Moissi had asked Dr Karajan, a keen festival goer and sometime second clarinet in the Mozarteum orchestra, for permission to watch a baby being born in order to describe it in a novel. Karajan obtained the consent of an expectant mother, in return for a small amount of money, but the woman subsequently retracted and ran to the right-wing press claiming she had been abused. Moissi was subjected to ferocious attacks from Nazis who identified him (mistakenly) as a Jew. He was stink-bombed while playing Everyman at a Vienna theatre, harried by women's groups and ostracised by old friends. The Archbishop of Salzburg demanded his removal from the festival and Moissi was sacked in April 1932, the first founder to depart in sorrow, though by no means the last.

Zweig was next. When the Nazis seized power in Germany they burned his books at the top of the pyre and erased his name from the opera he wrote with Richard Strauss. His Salzburg villa was raided by local police. Zweig, a nervous man, sold up and emigrated to England, then to Brazil, where he committed suicide. Reinhardt, another Nazi target, went to work in Hollywood and came home only at festival time. 'The nicest part of these festive summers,' he told Zuckmayer, 'is that each one may be the last . . . you can feel the taste of transitoriness on your tongue.'[15]

To the unsettled world, however, Salzburg smiled through the 1930s as a rare island of tolerance that attracted an ever-wider mixture of artists and audiences. Arturo Toscanini decamped from Nazified Bayreuth, challenging its claim to Wagner with an exemplary *Meistersinger*. Salzburg groaned at the expense of his annual productions, but exulted at the influx of maestro-worshippers. Toscanini's rampant personality cult gave rise to slurs that the festival was becoming a 'Hollywood of music',[16] but his perfection-ism dispelled summer laziness and any monopolism was mitigated by the parallel presence of Bruno Walter, Clemens Krauss, Bernhard Paumgartner and Wilhelm Furtwängler. The Toscanini era, in any event, lasted only four seasons. In February 1938, hearing that the Austrian chancellor had gone to see Hitler at Berchtesgaden, the Italian anti-fascist cabled from New York: 'Because of the changed situation must cancel my participation.'[17] A month later, German troops were heiled in Salzburg with outstretched arms, a burning of books (the only literary *auto-da-fé* in Austria) and a referendum in which 99.71 per cent of the citizens acclaimed the union with Germany.

The idyll was over. Joseph Goebbels cleansed the festival of Jews, confiscated Reinhardt's castle and held court at Moissi's table in the Café Bazar. A box was built for the Führer in the festival hall and Hitler twice made the twenty-minute drive from his mountain lair to hear Mozart operas in August 1939, as he prepared the invasion of Poland. The festival became a stop on the 'Strength Through Joy' circuit of Nazi party entertainments. Furtwängler, Krauss and Karl Böhm conducted submissively.

In the final summer of peace, Toscanini joined Walter, Busch, Sergei Rachmaninov and Pablo Casals at a new event in the Swiss lakeside resort of Lucerne. Glyndebourne went on tour to Belgium and gave a six-week home season. On the final night Chistie came out to address the audience with 'serious news'. He had just been informed that, for the first time in a generation, Harrow had beaten Eton at the annual cricket match. The world, he said, would never be the same again.

During the war, Christie volunteered Glyndebourne as an evacuation centre for children of the London blitz. Salzburg continued as a temple of Aryan art until it was shut down on Goebbels's orders in August 1944, after the generals' attempt on Hitler's life. The eighty-year-old Richard Strauss, who came for the première of his last opera, *Die Liebe der Danae*, was allowed to see a general rehearsal and left in tears, never to return.

The Americans, liberating Salzburg in May 1945, put on a three-week festival that summer. The town was strewn with bomb debris and clogged by refugees. Food was short and fraternisation with the occupying force was forbidden. A conductor was smuggled in from the British zone on the back of a truck. Performers were perfunctorily checked for political cleanliness. Böhm was barred as an avid Nazi, but the *Entführung* bill was topped by Maria Cebotari, until lately the Führer's favourite soprano. The purpose of the festival was propagandist, a show of restored normality.

The engine of Salzburg's regeneration was Bernhard Paumgartner who, accused at the Mozarteum of Jewish ancestry and sexual relations with students, had spent the war on a government research grant in Florence. Back in Salzburg, the innocent Paumgartner – in alliance with a Dachau survivor, Egon Hilbert, who was chief administrator of Austrian theatres – took charge of the 1946 programme.

Paumgartner planned to rebuild the festival around his protégé, a Salzburg conductor who blazed to fame in Hitler's Berlin and was now under Allied embargo. Heribert von Karajan, son of the surgeon, had been spotted by the Mozarteum director as a boy and admitted as a piano student. With his father absent day and night at the hospital, Paumgartner took him on mountain hikes, played tennis and football with him and taught him to ride a motor bike. In January 1917, when Heribert (he would drop the weakening middle vowel of his baptismal name) was eight, he played Mozart's Rondo in D major, K485, at a public recital. Some time afterwards Paumgartner told him, 'My dear Herbert, you will never be a pianist. You will become a conductor.'[18] Paumgartner had detected in his football a certain physical fluidity and leadership quality. In a seventieth birthday greeting to his mentor, Karajan recalled 'the crucial conversation when you explained that, with my particular way of listening to music, I could only find true satisfaction in conducting . . . I must thank [you] for that crucial stimulus in my life.'[19]

The festival filled his teenage summers as he watched Paumgartner produce incidental music for Max Reinhardt's inaugural *Jedermann* ('he was not a good conductor,' said Karajan[20]). Graduating from the Mozarteum in 1927, he was sent to study technology in Vienna, rooming with his elder brother, Wolfgang. He dropped out of the Technische Hochschule and spent his time at the music academy, where he made no friends, chased no girls and left no impression on his teachers. Short, silent and single-minded, he returned home within eighteen months and booked himself a concert with the Mozarteum orchestra. His father played clarinet that night and took pains to organise a professionally useful audience.

The opera house at Ulm in Germany was one conductor short and pressure was brought to bear upon its intendant to make a three-hundred-mile journey to hear Salzburg's débutant. Impressed, he offered Karajan a chance to conduct *Figaro* and subsequently a conductor's job at eighty Marks (then forty dollars) a month. Over the next four years Karajan learned the basic repertory at Ulm, around thirty operas each season. He cycled to Bayreuth to hear Toscanini and assisted at Salzburg most summers. Paumgartner fixed him a festival début in 1933, conducting incidental music for Max Reinhardt's production of Goethe's *Faust*.

By this time, the twenty-five-year-old conductor had taken a fateful decision. On 8 April 1933, the day German newspapers published a decree dismissing all Jews from public office, he joined the Nazi party. He enrolled first in Salzburg and again three weeks later in Ulm, as if to make sure his application did not go astray. It did him no immediate good. Instead of getting promoted, he was released by the Ulm manager, who told him he stood no chance of getting noticed there. He moved to Berlin and signed with a concert agent, Rudolf Vedder, an SS-officer and associate of Heinrich Himmler's. The months that followed are unaccounted for in his biography. Early in 1935, hearing that the opera intendant of Aachen was in town looking for a chief conductor, he secured an interview. 'I told the man, don't give me a contract until after you have watched me conduct a rehearsal. If you like that, give me the first production in your season. If I do it well, then you take me.'[21]

Such preternatural confidence qualified him for high office in a state that lionised leaders. Within months he took over both the opera and the town's orchestral concerts, ousting an inept Nazi, Peter Raabe. At twenty-seven he was the youngest general music director in the Reich, heading a town with a thousand years of culture and a seventy-man orchestra. His performance of a Hitlerite hymn, with a uniformed phalanx of seven hundred and fifty male choristers, was the centrepiece of the party's 1935 National Community Celebration in Aachen. He was alleged, though never proved, to be an agent of the Sicherheitsdienst[22] (SD). Blond-haired, blue-eyed, clean-cut and loyal, he was dubbed 'Das Wunder Karajan' by Goebbels's publicists after a luminous Tristan und Isolde at the Berlin State Opera in October 1938. On Hitler's fiftieth birthday he was named kapellmeister of the Berlin Opera. Heads of state were taken to hear him conduct. When the Wehrmacht swept into France, Karajan led his orchestra into occupied Paris. He was a willing figurehead of wickedness, a standard-bearer of supremacism.

Goebbels used his ascent to unsettle the politically wayward Wilhelm Furtwängler at the Berlin Philharmonic, who called on Hitler's support to crush his rival. In April 1941, while in Rome with the Berlin State Opera, Karajan was sacked by Aachen for absenteeism; that same month Allied bombers laid waste to his Berlin opera house. For the remainder of the Reich he was kept occupied with guest concerts. He upset party officials in 1942 by divorcing his first wife, an Aachen soubrette, and marrying an industrial heiress, Anita Gütermann, who had a Jewish grandparent. While this did not outlaw her under the Nuremberg Laws, she was an injudicious choice of partner for a supposedly invertebrate Nazi.

He conducted in Paris six weeks before D-Day and remained in Berlin almost until the end. Six weeks before the city fell he was given leave to make a recording in Milan, taking his wife with him. He went into hiding beside Lake Como, emerging in September 1945 to conduct for the British Army in Trieste. He was rewarded with a lift home to Salzburg, where he was promptly arrested.

'We were transported in lorries, like beasts,'[23] he complained, never once sparing a word of compassion for the millions who rode the Nazi death convoys. Interrogated by US officers, he was exculpated by an ex-tenor called Otto von Pasetti who ruled that 'by taking responsibility for his racially persecuted [sic] wife and shouldering the related consequences [Karajan had] compensated for his membership of the NSDAP.'[24] Clutching this clean sheet, he took a call from the Vienna Philharmonic in January 1946, conducted a stunning concert and was banned by the four-power Commission. A full-scale inquiry in Vienna resulted, after much delay, in a verdict that barred him from the podium until December 1947.

Throughout his investigation Karajan travelled eighteen times between Vienna and Salzburg, setting up the 1946 summer festival. 'Each trip took 24 hours. I would wait on the Russian-manned frontier to be treated like a beast in order to consult how to make Salzburg work,' he moaned.[25] Egon Hilbert, on behalf of the new Austrian government, warned that Karajan could not conduct 'in a leading capacity'.[26] But Paumgartner went for Karajan or bust, allotting him unprecedented prominence with ten opera performances and two concerts. The aged festival president, Baron Heinrich Puthon, backed him up with a threat to cancel the festival if Karajan was not allowed to conduct. The Americans dithered, awaiting a verdict from Vienna, as Karajan began rehearsing *The Marriage of Figaro* and *Der Rosenkavalier*. When they finally ruled him out, he hid in the prompter's box and gave cues to the visible conductors, Hans Swarowsky and Felix Prohaska. 'It didn't matter,' he said. 'I had done everything.'

The Americans credited him in private memoranda with the success of the 1946 festival, recommending that 'his talents are urgently needed to rehabilitate Austria's musical life.'[27] He could not have imagined that, despite Paumgartner's best efforts, it would take him a decade to win control. Blocking his ascent in 1947 was the gaunt and rehabilitated figure of Wilhelm Furtwängler, who swore he would boycott Salzburg if 'that man K' played a prominent role. Apart from two operas in 1948 and one the next year, Karajan was barred from his home podium so long as Furtwängler lived. He did not apparently miss it much; indeed, during the Nazi epoch he had not bothered to conduct there at all.[28] What Karajan wanted from Salzburg was not applause, but obeisance. And he was prepared to wait for the mountain to approach his Muhammad. In the meantime, his career shot off with EMI and the Philharmonia Orchestra in London. The Musikfreunde society, which runs Vienna concerts, named him artistic director for life. Before his Allied ban expired the Lucerne festival invited him to conduct. He returned every summer for the rest of his life. Lucerne's founder-president, Dr Strebi, became the first of his Swiss attorneys and financial advisers.

Salzburg no longer had the summer to itself. Lucerne, with Karajan, was pitching for rich patrons; the Catalan cellist Pablo Casals put together an anti-fascist festival in a French Pyrenean village, Prades. In the United States, Serge Koussevitzky turned his country estate at Tanglewood into a gathering place for young musicians; Adolf Busch, brother of Glyndebourne's conductor, was among the founders of the Marlboro chamber music festival in Vermont. Each of these venues won the allegiance of a nucleus of outstanding musicians and their community of followers, diverting them from Salzburg and threatening its centrality.

Glyndebourne, too, was under pressure. Christie could no longer fund the festival from his own pocket, having yielded more than half his income to socialist rates of taxation. There was not much point in applying for funding from Britain's Labour government, particularly when the artistic purse strings were held by the economist, Lord Keynes, who had bickered with Christie since their schooldays at Eton. As a stopgap, Glyndebourne became a base for Benjamin Britten and his English Opera Group, which split away from Sadler's Wells after the triumph of *Peter Grimes*. Acclaim for *Grimes* in a dozen capitals made Britten the country's most successful composer for two centuries. He gave Glyndebourne its first world première with *The Rape of Lucretia*, starring Kathleen Ferrier, followed in 1947 by *Albert Herring*, a comedy of rural manners. In between, there was a disastrous national tour and the composer huffed off to found a festival of his own in the Suffolk fishing village of Aldeburgh. A garland of Britten commissions opened the new Holland Festival; *Lucretia* was staged at Salzburg. The field was becoming crowded and all the flowers looked the same.

Bing, however, was not despondent. A lean-faced refugee with the hand-kissing courtesies of a Habsburg courtier and the bowler hat of a Whitehall civil servant, he concealed behind a façade of servility a ruthless instinct for self-advancement. His other qualities were an analytical brain, beguiling salesmanship and a complete absence of sentiment.

Idle at Glyndebourne for much of the war, Bing perceived that Britain's bravery could be turned to cultural advantage. Great artists would want to honour the land that stood alone against Hitler and their governments would pay for the propaganda value of an artistic success. An international festival in a British city would also provide Glyndebourne with a second outlet, offsetting its production costs. Audrey Christie proposed Edinburgh and

Bing, seeing parallels with Salzburg, sold the idea to the Lord Provost. 'My mind kept returning to the castle on the cliff in Edinburgh,' wrote Bing, 'not really like the castle in Salzburg but equally memorable.'[29] Glyndebourne supplied managerial know-how and two operas for the inaugural Edinburgh Festival of 1947. The French government, mindful of Stuart alliances, sent an orchestra and theatre company. The Old Vic and Sadler's Wells Ballet rode up from London, the Hallé and Liverpool orchestras from Lancashire. Edinburgh had not magnetised such attention since the murderous days of Mary Queen of Scots. Calvinist killjoys muttered darkly of 'long-tailed squanderbugs' and predicted 'a complete fiasco'[30] but the festival sold a hundred and eighty thousand tickets in three weeks, made a forest of headlines and cost the city council no more than twenty thousand pounds. In a culture of ration books and fuel shortages, the festival burst upon a weary public like a waterfall in the Sahara.

One concert in particular resounded around the globe, defining the festival's identity and setting its future standards. The Vienna Philharmonic Orchestra, reunited by Bing with its exiled conductor Bruno Walter, gave a heart-rending performance of Gustav Mahler's *Das Lied von der Erde* with Ferrier and Peter Pears as soloists. The response was so intense they gave an extra concert, of joyous waltzes. It was as if the golden years of Salzburg were magically reincarnated on the windy heights of Lothian.

For eight years Glyndebourne gave Edinburgh its administration and its operas, and brought through a procession of the world's great orchestras. Music was the main course, but the table groaned with supplementary gourmandise.

A festival of art cinema brought visits from Roberto Rossellini and John Huston. Renoirs, Rembrandts and Gauguins were assembled at the Royal Scottish Academy. A seminal retrospective on the balletmaster Serge Diaghilev was shown on the twenty-fifth anniversary of his death. And away from the international menu, a fringe of snoot-cocking revues opened a window on undiscovered talent. Something would be showing at all hours of the day and night. No festival, before or since, achieved Edinburgh's clock-round activity. By the end of its first decade the Edinburgh International Festival was drawing some one hundred thousand visitors, one-third of them from abroad.[31]

Salzburg could not equal Edinburgh's variety or match the festivals that were flowering all over western Europe. An impecunious Austrian government passed a festival law in 1950, setting up an official directorate and enshrining a pledge of state subsidy. Furtwängler was to be the guarantor of artistic integrity, and the composer Gottfried von Einem would inject elements of modernity. Married to a Bismarck and ensconced in a Salzburg *Schloss*, von Einem had done time in an SS prison and was a fine figurehead for a reformed festival. Salzburg, however, was unregenerate. It hated von Einem's new music (albeit by traditionalists such as Carl Orff, Frank Martin and himself) and bemoaned the cost. When the composer was caught asking the communist Bertolt Brecht to write a replacement parable for the *Jedermann* perennial, the reactionaries slashed his authority. By the time Furtwängler died in November 1954, Salzburg had a power vacuum that only one man could fill.

'I shall be a dictator,' announced Herbert von Karajan, assuming office as artistic director of the Salzburg Festival in March 1956. That same month he took over as artistic head of the Vienna State Opera, having succeeded Furtwängler at the Berlin Philharmonic. He was in charge of German repertoire at La Scala and was still making records with the Philharmonia. Salzburg seemed like an optional extra to his bulging portfolio and local opponents, like von Einem, were convinced that his attentions would be far too heavily engaged elsewhere for him to alter the nature of the festival. They could not have been more mistaken. Karajan saw Salzburg not as a feather in his cap but as the cornerstone of his empire. Everything he achieved and became would proceed from this seat of power. To reach his goal, he would need to distort the festival beyond recognition.

His priority, like Hitler's in 1933, was to master and emasculate the machinery of government. He ignored the artistic advisory board and stacked the statutory directorate with his cronies, acolytes like his future biographer Ernst von Haeussermann, whose duties included providing visiting politicians with pliant female company. Having failed to secure von Einem's dismissal, Karajan tormented the composer until he resigned in confusion. Why, von Einem asked him, did he need to control so many institutions? Karajan, smiling, replied that he loved '*Das Spiel der Mächtigen*', the game of the mighty, playing for the love of power and its unlimited rewards.[32]

When Baron Puthon resigned the festival presidency in 1959 on the eve of his ninetieth birthday, Karajan replaced him with the trusted Paumgartner. He then gave up his own title as artistic director, knowing that he could run Salzburg from behind the scenes without the accountability attached to a formal position. 'He liked to avoid unpleasantness and preferred that other people should bear the responsibility,' said a long-suffering associate.[33] After Paumgartner, others served as his puppet-presidents. From the moment Karajan came home in 1956, until his death in July 1989, nothing twitched in Salzburg without his say-so.

He bragged of shattering 'all the windows in the old town' with the explosives that blasted a hole into the mountainside for his massive new festival hall. The edifice was built in Karajan's image and to his detailed specifications. He wanted a stage big enough to accommodate a *Ring*; if Mozart got lost in its vastness, too bad. The mark of his productions was monumentalism. His preferred choreography was static, his lighting gloomy. All eyes were drawn to the conductor, the immortal leader. The dimensions and dynamics of Karajan's hall were insidiously authoritarian, recalling the Berlin ministries of Albert Speer and the railway stations of Benito Mussolini. It is a building that evokes awe rather than festivity. Abandon joy, all ye who enter.

The new Festspielhaus was the symbol of Salzburg reborn, its confidence restored, its purpose subtly altered. 'Times have changed,' wrote one Austrian apologist in time-honoured Goebbels terminology. 'We must accept this for better or worse, *as well as the iron, sometimes brutal, laws of management.*'[34] Karajan was an irresistible force of history, a superman of the scientific future. The cars he drove were the sleekest, the yacht he raced the fastest. Police held up traffic around the Festspielhaus when his Mercedes approached. The chief of customs stood to attention on the tarmac at Salzburg airport as Karajan skilfully landed his private jet. A piste was cleared when he went skiing; paparazzi spotted a miniature Beethoven score protruding from his ski-jacket pocket. He was the embodiment of scientific progress and artistic redemption. His price was unqualified power and Salzburg felt it was a price well worth paying.

The grandeur of his performances, the efficiency of the orchestral playing and ensemble singing, encouraged audiences to imagine that they were purchasing perfection: the ultimate, insurmountable rendition of a masterpiece of western art. Karajan encouraged this delusion, styling himself 'the greatest conductor of our time'[35] and producing close to one thousand recordings and videos. His relentless self-dissemination was disguised as a desire for 'the democratisation of music', a way of bringing truth and beauty to millions in the comfort of their living-rooms. His true intention was, so far as can be surmised, the very opposite. In the control rooms of the record industry and throughout his dominions, Karajan compressed the range of music that was performed and the manner in which it was played. He outlawed authentic period performance and experimental modernism, sanctioning a restricted index of certified masterpieces, performed in a predictable mid-romantic fashion. In the art of interpretation he customised a sang-froid smoothness that left Bach and Bruckner, Haydn and Hindemith, sounding much the same. There were *frissons* of excitement, but no coils of emotion. Like Alfred Hitchcock, he was a master of tension and incapable of passion. Karajan knowingly pursued uniformity in music and uniform is, by definition, a token of totalitarian authority.

In order to restore Salzburg's appeal he offered leading singers twice what they would get elsewhere and awarded himself a princely two thousand dollars a night, five times higher than the top London fee. No artist would ever attend Salzburg again for love of music. Karajan created a dependency culture for mercenary musicians: the more he paid them, the more they needed his patronage. He brought in the Berlin Philharmonic in 1957 to keep the Viennese in line and paid them both over the odds to secure their unwavering allegiance.

The Karajan culture outlawed fraternisation. Artists and orchestral players no longer drank with friends and fans in downtown cafés and open meadows. They raced off from rehearsals in sports cars, like the supreme leader himself, to private quarters or a rich man's table. An artist who came to Salzburg was protected from the prying public.

The public, too, underwent strategic reconstruction. Karajan, in a 1956 memorandum, talked of 'eliminating' (a good Goebbels word) occasional tourists and rebuilding the festival on a *Stammpublikum*, a permanent group of wealthy supporters who would return year after year to subscribe to its ritual. When the directorate refused to scrap single tickets, or make them unaffordable, he withdrew the idea, only to resurrect it at an Easter Festival that he founded in 1967; a Whitsun Festival followed. These private enterprises came to dictate both the repertory and demography of the publicly funded summer festivals. Their success was overwhelming. A survey in 1981 showed that fifty-five per cent of summer festival goers had attended regularly for the previous six years.[36] Karajan had carved himself a captive public out of Germany's economic miracle, corpulent new plutocrats of the Ruhrland boom who thought nothing of paying a thousand Deutschmarks for a brace of seats and as much again for dinner afterwards. While synthetic reproductions of his performances were peddled to the masses, the live original was reserved for an élite who could afford Salzburg prices.

Being in Salzburg was a mark of social distinction. Music critics revelled in its expense-account luxury and uttered paeons of praise. If it happened in Salzburg, it had to be excellent – just look how much it cost. In *Der Rosenkavalier*, Karajan used a rose of pure silver. The glass that got smashed at the end of the champagne aria in *Don Giovanni* was crystal, even in rehearsals.

The extent of Karajan's power has been exposed elsewhere[37] and, like most forms of human governance, was based on a collusive chimera of mutual self-deception. People wanted to believe in something perfect and Karajan gave them what they wanted. Unlike political rulers he was not overly concerned with the workings of power, relinquished most of his positions and did not bother to designate a successor. Nor was he obsessed by wealth, though he owned four homes and amassed an estate worth five hundred million Deutschmarks. These were merely the means to his intended end: to control the way music was performed and perceived, now and for all eternity, to stamp his mark on an ephemeral art in an unsurpassable pile of indelible compact discs and laserdiscs. 'I shall be available for coming generations to regard me as a kind of ultimate witness to our age,' he prophesied.[38] When Karajan, a twice-divorced atheist, conducted Mozart Masses before the Pope, he did so not in homage to divine authority but as a gift from one spiritual potentate to another.

Recordings were the key to his revelation and Salzburg the hub of his industry. His publicly funded rehearsals doubled as private recording sessions, Austrian taxpayers' cash streaming directly into his tax-proofed accounts in Switzerland and Liechtenstein. State cash flowed sweetly into his private festivals. No one demurred. He had foes in the socialist government but he was 'Austria's greatest musician' and in Salzburg he was a law unto himself. When he needed extras for an opera, he ordered a platoon of conscripts from the local army commander. His closest friend was the chief hotelier, and the hotel barons adored him. 'Karajan was a magnet,' said Johannes, Count Walderdorff, owner of the *Goldner Hirsch*.[39]

He encouraged the music business to regard his festivals as a stock exchange of recording options. The classical record industry moved office in August to Salzburg's grand hotels, trailed by a caravan of concert agents and television brokers. The companies Karajan shunned – chiefly CBS and RCA – were mysteriously unable to book advertising space in central Salzburg. When Leonard Bernstein made a rare appearance in 1971, CBS pointedly plastered his portrait along the road where '*Der Chef*' motored each morning from his Anif home to the festival hall.

Favouritism and corruption were endemic. A federal investigation in 1983 revealed that festival staff were receiving eighteen months' salary for twelve months' work and artists were paid more than anywhere in the world. Nothing changed. A second inquiry five years later unearthed a million-dollar overspend on lighting. The report blamed the directors for abdicating financial and artistic control to the unaccountable Karajan. 'He was the grey eminence in the background, not taking any responsibility but making all the decisions,' said the investigator, Dr Hans Landesmann.[40] Before publishing his report, Landesmann showed it to the conductor. 'It was a very amicable and objective atmosphere,' he recalled, 'until he read my recommendations black on white. Then he got very, very annoyed.' Karajan got his lawyers to attack Landesmann as 'a dilettante blowing soap bubbles'. But his strength was ebbing in his eightieth year and his opponent was unexpectedly resilient. Landesmann had fled Vienna as a child, to be hidden from the Nazis by Hungarian priests. A prosperous businessman, he had fostered a modernist counter-culture at the Vienna Konzerthaus, working with Claudio Abbado and Pierre Boulez to combat the dead-wood programmes of Karajan's Musikfreunde allies. He formed a European Community Youth Orchestra for Abbado and followed it up with a diplomatic coup, assembling players from both sides of the Iron Curtain into the Gustav Mahler Youth Orchestra. Landesmann was everything that Karajan feared – Jewish, progressive, intelligent and formidably well connected in politics and music alike. He was also financially secure. He stood urbanely at the gates, while the dying tyrant raged within.

He urged the government 'to restore the special Salzburg aspect and return to the roots of the founders, Reinhardt and Hofmannsthal'. A team of three professionals should preside, eliminating the possibility of another dictatorship. His plan was quickly accepted, but before it could be implemented Karajan died of a heart attack on the eve of the 1989 festival in the arms of his newest corporate partner. His Anif grave was covered by music industry wreaths. He had inherited a shining ideal and perverted it for personal gain. The refuge that Reinhardt had built for art in its greatest purity had been transformed by Karajan into a musical market-place. Reinhardt had preached to all creeds and classes, Karajan only to the rich. Reinhardt believed people would flock to Salzburg to see something unique. Karajan offered the assurance of predictable uniformity. By the time of his death, the Salzburg festival was exceptional only for its opulence.

It was nothing short of miraculous that Glyndebourne managed as long as it did with no outside assistance, other than eight years of Edinburgh revenues. The year Karajan took over Salzburg saw a split with Edinburgh and sent John Christie looking for alternative subventions. Grumbling in *The Times* about state support for Covent Garden ('while we produce the best opera in the world on no grant'), he was alarmed by a published letter the following day questioning the fifty pages of advertising that filled Glyndebourne's programme book. Since arts donations could not be set against tax, Christie had been persuading business friends to rifle their advertising budgets on his behalf.

A page in the Glyndebourne programme might not sell many shoes at the John Lewis or Marks & Spencer department stores, but it could be set down as a legitimate business expense and Glyndebourne could charge what it liked for the space. The festival had, in fact, been rescued in 1950 by the John Lewis chairman – 'a gesture which was the cornerstone of the whole present-day financial structure of Glyndebourne',[41] according to the official historian.

To relieve his two children of the financial burden, Christie formed a trust for the opera company and, in 1959, handed control to his twenty-four-year-old son, George. With stubborn pride, the younger Christie and his wife, Mary, devoted their lives to the festival, strengthening the original network of business friends. In 1992, Sir George Christie took pickaxe in hand and began knocking down the opera house, confident in the knowledge that he had raised thirty-three million pounds from 'friends' to build a new auditorium of eleven hundred and fifty seats, more than half the size of Covent Garden. He was said to be 'drained by continuous corporate entertainment, sitting through the same half-dozen productions night after night for three months'.[42] In fact, he took pride in his ability to attract money. 'We now find ourselves looking into the next century with, I believe, the first purpose-built opera house to be constructed in this country since the original opera house was built here by my father,' he declared. 'We have been through the worst recession since the 1930s. To be so close to target [funding] in such conditions says "oceans" for the loyalty and extraordinary generosity of the companies and individuals who have responded.'[43]

Not all donors wanted to advertise their generosity. While cutting workforces in Margaret Thatcher's recessions, they did not want to be seen supporting a privileged event with company cash. To square their shareholders, chairmen said they had to contribute at Glyndebourne to bolster City confidence. It was a business expense.

'George's prowess with sponsors has led the way in Britain,' wrote his former productions director, Sir Peter Hall, with a serpentine sting to his praise:

> It is George who has revitalised Glyndebourne's sponsorship from business – and it is huge. The finances of the opera house are also enormously helped by the comparatively low fees paid to the artists. It is a tradition that you work at Glyndebourne because you want to, not to earn money – leading singers getting a tenth of their normal fee. They go there because the working conditions are superb and it is a good place for a young artist to develop or for a mature artist to learn a new role. But they pay for it. Glyndebourne has always been subsidised by its casts.[44]

There was truth in Hall's allegation. The top singing fee at Glyndebourne in 1992 was twelve hundred pounds a night; a good soprano could earn six times as much at Covent Garden. But, though artists called it 'Glynditz', after the escape-proof German prison at Colditz, many preferred lunch on the lawn and a cuddle in the shrubbery to the high rewards and heartless slog of opera in the city. Whatever its parsimony, Glyndebourne had a knack for tracking new talent, introducing Luciano Pavarotti, Elisabeth Söderström, Teresa Berganza, Maria Ewing and Elena Prokina to the British stage and retaining such conductors as Bernard Haitink and Simon Rattle.

Under the younger Christies, the season lengthened from May to August and new operas were commissioned from leading British composers, Nicholas Maw, Oliver Knussen, Nigel Osborne and Harrison Birtwistle. A touring company was formed. Tickets to the festival were less than half the subsidised top seats at Covent Garden, but there was a waiting list for membership. Christie, sensitive to criticism, denied that Glyndebourne had become a corporate club. 'It's a private opera company,' he told reporters at the reopening of the house. 'Nothing wrong with that. [But] it has never allowed the corporate element to have a presence exceeding thirty-five per cent of capacity.'[45]

Nevertheless, the atmospheric alteration was undeniable. Gone was the madcap come-ye-all catholicity of John Christie and the eclectic admixture of his guests. In the 1990s you might still encounter a breviary-clasping young prelate on the lawns, stunned to the fundaments of his Anglican faith by a harrowing *Jenůfa*. But you were doubly likely to meet a sales director blankly unmoved by Janáček's tragedy, or staggering legless on a surfeit of Dom Perignon. Sprawled across the lawns with their Harrods hampers and hired waiters, City brokers supplanted the gentler manners of the country set in their dowdy gowns. Busy bosses landed by helicopter, Silver Clouds preponderated on the parking lots and, while portable phones were politely discouraged, the place was geared towards power-dining. There is nothing eccentric or unserious about the new Glyndebourne. If the battle of Waterloo was won on the playing fields of Eton, as John Christie believed, then the corporate take-over wars of the late twentieth century are plotted every summer between the acts of a Mozart opera in the walled gardens of Glyndebourne.

Edinburgh retained the quintessence of its character, thanks to a native frugality and the fizz of the fringe. Scots prudence kept public subsidy to around five million pounds (less than one-fifth of Salzburg's), and foreign ensembles continued to appear at their own government's expense. It took forty-seven years for the city to furnish an opera house. The festival survived on inspiration and improvisation, introducing works that London, for decades, dared not stage – Paul Hindemith's *Mathis der Maler* and Bernd Alois Zimmerman's apocalyptic *Die Soldaten* – and uncovering major talents. Unfortunately it could not afford to invite them back. In terms of star performance, low fees pushed Edinburgh down the glamour league. It could not offer Salzburg emoluments and Bayreuth recording contracts, or match the spectacular opera stagings on the lake-top platform at Bregenz. Peter Diamand, Edinburgh director from 1965 to 1978, remembered the visiting Karajan's astonishment at his budgets. 'We talked about the finances of the Festival,' Diamand recalled. 'He said, "I can't understand how you can have a Festival like this with such little money. It's a fraction of what Salzburg gets." Then he asked, "Will I get a fee for my broadcasts?" When I assured him he would, he said, "It's not necessary. Keep it for the festival." '[46]

The salvation of Edinburgh was its anarchic Fringe, which sold half a million tickets each festival and swelled the number of Edinburgh visitors to three quarters of a million. Day and elongated night, in church halls and leaking marquees, the Fringe flourished a bewilderment of entertainments – anything from foul-mouthed comics to a student string quartet. In a good year it added spice and surprise to the official cake. In a mediocre festival the Fringe consoled tourists that their trip had not been wholly in vain. Yet the Fringe, for all its youthful babel, could not protect the Festival against competition. Festivals were no longer a scattering of seasonal diversions but a year-round leisure industry, worth forty million pounds in ticket sales in Britain alone.[47]

Every Scandinavian town with a sense of civic pride started up a white-nights festival. Cathedral towns in Poland came up with esoteric themes. In the agrarian German state of Schleswig-Holstein, the pianist grandson of a Baltic prime minister drew in entertainments from all around the northern seaboard. With his own prime-time television show and a taste for political hot potatoes – German xenophobia, protectionism, expansionism – Justus Frantz envisaged the modern festival as a gypsy caravan of options and causes, grounded in no single site or idea. His focus was Israel one year, Japan the next. In two months he ran one hundred and fifty events in forty venues, some of them no more salubrious than a converted barn, earning Schleswig-Holstein seventy-five million pounds in visitor revenue and a niche on the cultural landscape. While Reinhardt reached out to a spiritual élite, the Frantz formula was predicated upon mass tourism. By the time he was ousted in 1994 for a two-million-pound overspend, Frantz had established Schleswig-Holstein as a fixture in the arts calendar.

Even stuffy Lucerne felt the pressure to modernise, allowing the conductor Matthias Bamert to experiment with street musicians and new scores. A network of festivals encircled the Pacific, from Sapporo to Perth. The Boston conductor Seiji Ozawa founded a Saito Kinen festival at Matsumoto, in the foothills of the Japanese Alps, with funding from his media supporters and the highlights distributed world-wide on video. America's music festivals at Tanglewood and Ravinia were integrated into the organisational empires of the Boston and Chicago Symphony Orchestras. Where Salzburg and Edinburgh once commanded cultured attention without much challenge in a sultry August, fickle critics and epicures now went haring after hard-nosed attractions in ever more exotic locations. Gone was the liberation of art from material concerns. Gone was the freedom to take artistic risks without damage to career or country. Festival time was not a flight from the treadmill, but a trade fair for the music business and its corporate associates.

It is a quarter to eight on a rain-soaked Salzburg morning and Hans Landesmann, breakfasting on a ham roll and coffee in Karajan's former office, is ringing around desperately for a tenor. A well-known singer has turned up without having learnt his cantata, breezily announcing that his purpose in coming to the festival is to launch a new recording. For Landesmann, the singer is a roseate symptom of a corrosive malaise. His role is reassigned, after two dozen calls, but his attitude represents all that is rotten in the state of Salzburg. Five years after Karajan's death, the festival remains a temple of egotism. No one performs there for the sake of art or spirituality, only for personal gain. No one attends for the shock of inspiration, but for the assurance of familiarity.

Landesmann, as concerts and finance director, has struggled to cleanse the Augean stables and revert to Reinhardt rules. With his Belgian director of opera, Gérard Mortier, he has reinstated musicians and modernisms banished by Karajan. Landesmann has brought in Claudio Abbado, Pierre Boulez and György Ligeti; Mortier is *au fait* with new-wave deconstructionists, opera directors like Peter Sellars who reset *Don Giovanni* in a New York tenement. 'Gérard and I are very much outsiders,' says Landesmann, 'but the politicians felt there was a great need for change and were anxious to bring in people who are in a position to make changes.'[48]

The auguries were favourable – even from hoteliers who suffered from the stagnation of Karajan's last period. But the obstacles were immense and cracks quickly appeared in the festival leadership. Mortier, who shoots from the lip, called a press conference to denounce Abbado for not agreeing to conduct *Elektra*. Landesmann, Abbado's ally, avoided being seen with Mortier in public for several days. 'In private, Hans and I understand each other very well,' declared the opera chief. Landesmann had nothing to add.

Although they shared the same objectives, they kept hitting land-mines left by Karajan in his mortal retreat. The old intriguer bequeathed his Easter Festival to his widow Eliette, his secretary Beate Burchhard, and his Swiss lawyer Werner Kupper. These legatees signed a co-operation treaty with the summer festival but promptly locked horns over who got first crack at a 1995 *Elektra*. While the directorates bickered, Abbado plumped for the Easter *Elektra*; Mortier swiftly announced a summer *Elektra* under Lorin Maazel. Two *Elektras* in three months would have made Salzburg a laughing stock and he shamefacedly withdrew, substituting an ill-conceived *Rosenkavalier*.

It was the latest of many climb-downs. Mortier unleashed a colourful attack on overpaid stars who abused Salzburg's hospitality. With two tenors and a soprano threatening a boycott, he issued a contrite clarification. 'We don't want the festival to be dictated by record companies,' he declared, especially ones that had used 'mafia tactics' to exploit their links with Karajan. Objections by Deutsche Grammophon and legal moves by the Karajan estate produced a hasty apology. Mortier told Salzburg shopkeepers they should do more for the festival, 'instead of always milking it'. Another retraction. He attacked the mayor of Salzburg, who controlled one-fifth of the festival's funding, and withdrew his remarks before the print was dry on the morning papers. 'Say what you like about Karajan,' snorted a veteran observer, 'but he never apologised.' 'Mortier suffers from an irresistible need to talk,' said a sympathiser. 'He smashes his own windows by talking too much.'

The only fight Mortier won was with the Vienna Philharmonic, which he successfully confronted over its habit of sending deputies to Salzburg. The Philharmonic threatened counter-attractions in Vienna but, without Karajan, were powerless and increasingly dispossessed. In the mid-1990s Mortier flew in the Philharmonia from London to cover modern repertoire that the Viennese played indifferently.

Landesmann meanwhile was striving to reduce Salzburg's dependence on Karajan's heavy German industrialists. A triumvirate of neutral sponsors, Nestlé, ABB and Allianz – two Swiss groups, one Bavarian – formed the first corporate involvement in Salzburg, injecting one million pounds a year. It amounted to just three per cent of the festival budget but added a welcome counter-presence to the steel barons and the music industry.

Landesmann also led the way in encouraging an expansion of the fringe-like *Szene*. He threw open Salzburg to back-packers and turned for the first time to its eastern neighbours. The president of Hungary, Arpad Göncz, opened the 1993 festival with a lyrical evocation of all that Salzburg meant to sentimental central Europeans – 'the music of the angels filtering through the wall, the glowing that vanishes slowly into darkness . . .'[49]

Yet, for all their good intentions and connections, Landesmann and Mortier were impeded wherever they turned by structures that Karajan had embedded in the mountainside. They were unable to evict the record industry or slash artist fees without decimating the festival's appeal and its revenue. They needed the rich to return year after year if there was to be any chance of achieving Reinhardt's idea that top-priced seats should subsidise the rest. As it was, the front rows stopped selling once Karajan died. The old guard of maestro-worshippers who snored through the Karajan's Mozart fled at the sight of Monteverdi, departing in a convoy of Mercs for the Schubert festival at Hohenems and the floating Verdis at Bregenz. Landesmann and Mortier hoped to replace them with Eurocrat glitterati and million-salaried chiefs of privatised utilities, but the gaps yawned large in the centre of the auditorium and the top restaurants and hotels complained of vacancies.

Nor was there much sign of social renewal. Salzburg had, for the lifetime of anyone under forty, symbolised all that was élitist, conscienceless and impervious in modern Europe. To expect people to believe overnight in its change of heart was unrealistic. Around town, the name-signs were defaced by two angry lines scrawled through the initial: $alzburg. Dissident posters went up on walls in poorer areas declaring 'culture-free zones' – because culture had become so synonymous with privilege that its popular appeal was permanently damaged. The festival, detached from the lives of ordinary people, appeared to many Salzburgers as a perversion of common decency, a lavish pasture for the world's oppressors.

At nine o'clock one bird-sung morning of the seventy-fourth consecutive festival, I spotted a bedraggled queue of men, women and children slouched outside a locked door, guarded by armed police, close to the gates of the old town. The door belonged to the German consulate and the half-starved supplicants were just off the night train from the killing fields of Bosnia, half a day's ride away.

Reinhardt intended his festival to be a haven from the horrors of war. Now the war in Europe returned to mock his escapist dreams, deriding art as irrelevant to the causes of conflict. Salzburg could not palliate the strife of Sarajevo. On the contrary, it bore a share of the responsibility. On the steps of the Mozarteum. I ran into the NATO secretary-general deep in discussions with a well-known armaments manufacturer; Mozart, so far as I could overhear, was not on their agenda. The deals that kept the guns roaring in Bosnia were sealed between symphonies at Salzburg.

The 'virginity' that Reinhardt idealised was unprotectable in the terrors and turmoil of crumbling supra-national states. The borderlands were dangerously near and the more Salzburg ignored them, the more artificial the festival seemed. The intrusion of politics, finance, commerce and communications conspired to destroy the elusive dream.

Few music festivals could offer a relief from modern woes, or preserve their innocence against external pressures. Edinburgh, outside its festival, was the crack–cocaine capital of the United Kingdom. Lucerne's fish was struck off one summer's menu, after suffering fall-out from the Chernobyl nuclear disaster. When I last passed the schoolhouse in Dobbiaco, they were building a wooden platform outside. It was designed to hold an orchestra of one hundred musicians and several television gantries for a global transmission of Mahler's ninth symphony. The idyll was over. A troubled composer would never again come to Dobbiaco to seek peace for the torments of his lonely heart.

NOTES

1 *Das Lied von der Erde*, final stanza
2 Gallup, p. 9
3 Szeps, p. 214
4 Sayler, p. 200
5 Sayler, p. 191
6 Cardus, pp. 277–8
7 Zuckmayer, p. 22
8 Cardus, pp. 274–5
9 Zuckmayer, p. 40
10 GLY–36, p. 12
11 Blom, p. 249
12 GLY–36, p. 5
13 Franklin, p. 52
14 Bing, p. 55
15 Zuckmayer, p. 44
16 Gallup, p. 98
17 Gallup, p. 101
18 Haeusserman, p. 24
19 Bachmann, pp. 52–3
20 Vaughan, p. 99
21 Vaughan, p. 107
22 the Nazi 'security service'
23 Vaughan, p. 133
24 Bachmann, p. 150
25 Vaughan, p. 138
26 Bachmann, p. 154
27 Vaughan, pp. 141–3
28 see Jaklitsch
29 Bing, p. 84
30 ED–56, p. 29
31 ED–56, p. 14

32 Gallup, p. 160
33 Stresemann, p. 261
34 Gallup, p. 166
35 DG record advertisements, 1964
36 Gallup, p. 184
37 see Norman Lebrecht, *The Maestro Myth* (Simon & Schuster, London) 1991
38 VF, p. 118
39 *Salzburg Spectakel 1993*, p. 44
40 author's interviews, 1989–94
41 GLY–63, p. 78
42 *Observer*, 6 February 1994, p. 19
43 GLY–92, pp. 2–3
44 Peter Hall, *Making an Exhibition of Myself* (Sinclair-Stevenson, London) 1993
45 *CM*, 19 February 1994, p. 6
46 author's interview
47 source: PSI–ARTS
48 author's interview
49 opening address, 24 July 1993

CHAPTER X

IF YOU WISH
UPON A STAR

O nce upon a time, there was a promising young pianist. He was a very good pianist with a brilliant technique that won him first prize in an international competition and the admiration of all who knew the intricacies of keyboard lore. For reasons that will become apparent, his identity had better be withheld.

Unusually for a struggling musician on the competition circuit, our hero had a fatherly agent who shielded him from the razzmatazz, resisted the quick-silver offers and signed him with a record company that produced long-term career plans. His début recordings were warmly received in *Gramophone* and *Diapaison* and everyone was quietly satisfied.

One day, a new marketing director was appointed and, surveying his products, decided that the pianist was under-performing. Not that he was playing too little or too softly, but that he was selling less than, all factors taken into account, might exponentially be expected from an artist of his potential. What was needed was a campaign, a personality refit that would position him as a totem for thirty-something ABs and upwardly mobile C1s and turn him into the musical equivalent of, say, fish fingers. The pianist was taken down the King's Road, Chelsea, kitted out in snazzy shirts and ties, groomed to the cutting edge of his receding hairline and plastered across full-page spreads in men's magazines and family newspapers. He gave thoughtful interviews on issues of the day and the problems of sustaining intimate relationships. For a whole month his name and his music hummed across the media.

And then – silence. The release on which the promotion hinged failed to breach the top ten or, indeed, to sell any faster than its unpromoted predecessors. Stacks of unsold discs piled up in the shops. Overnight, the ads were stopped, the interviews dried up. The marketing director homed in on an under-age violinist and the pianist's name was never mentioned again at board level.

He bore the disappointment bravely, carried on playing as cogently as ever, made two records a year, travelled hectically and switched agents and labels in the hope of preferment. But his moment had passed and younger artists were popping up every other month. He had not lived up to his moment and he would not get another until he reached eighty, when the image-makers might feel he was ripe for presentation as a living immortal.

Less secure performers, stunned by this all-too-familiar rush of fame and fall, sought solace in drink, drugs and street-corner shysters who promised unattainable second comings. The road to classical celebrity is littered with fallen aspirants, many twitching in frustration as inferior musicians clamber over their prone forms to reap the glittering prizes. Success, in music as in business, is a matter of timing, of being the right person in the right place at the right time. More cruelly than commerce, though, classical music only ever gives you one shot.

Kiri Te Kanawa seized hers when, engaged to sing at the Prince of Wales's wedding in 1981, she radiated an appeal that outshone the ceremony and outlasted the marriage itself. It was, she said, 'the chance of a lifetime' and she turned out in canary colours and a cheeky pillbox hat that could not fail to captivate the cameras. Prince Charles, signing the Register at the opposite side of St Paul's Cathedral, was distracted by a 'marvellous . . . disembodied'[1] sound and became her greatest fan. The wedding, watched on television by half the world's inhabitants, made Kiri a prime-time star. Most singers who sang at royal occasions were forgotten names before the archbishop had finished pronouncing his blessing.

The violinist Anne-Sophie Mutter, at thirteen years old, made the most of Herbert von Karajan's fickle patronage to conquer German hearts with the security of her technique and maturity of her poise. She was hailed as the lioness of German music – efficient, invincible and as materially enviable as a new Mercedes, all pain concealed behind the façade of success. A young cellist adopted by Karajan around the same time was left mutely admiring Mutter's slipstream.

No winner of the prestigious Chopin Competition ever made as big a splash as Ivo Pogorelich did when he was omitted from the final round in 1980, provoking a walk-out by Martha Argerich, the 1965 gold-medallist. The ensuing outcry, allied to his devil-may-care attitude, turned the young Serb into a hot ticket at a thirty-thousand-dollar fee, rising to any price he cared to name. 'America needs me, as much as I need America,' he greeted the *New York Times*. 'When I first met Karajan,' he bragged, 'I was shocked at how little there was in him of a musician. I said to him, "Maestro, before we get going with the orchestra, I need to tell you a few things . . ."'[2] He recorded the Tchaikovsky B-flat minor concerto with Abbado at distorted tempi and declared his interpretation to be the standard setter for the next millennium. He rode the wave of critical outrage like a surfer heading towards the ever-stretching golden sands. One hostile review was sent to Paris for forensic psychoanalysis. The doctor's opinion – that the critic was homoerotically obsessed with the pianist – was mailed to every newspaper editor and concert manager in London. 'My true cosmopolitan heart pushes me, as it has indeed done on so many occasions in the past, to overcome my natural shyness and outgrow my personal ego, in driving me towards the matters of the general public's interest,' explained Pogorelich, obtusely.[3] The offending critic was sent a portrait of the pianist, with a recommendation to utilise it for the purpose of self-abuse.

Make what you might of Maestro Igo Pogorelich (as he signed his letter), but no one would ever accuse him of failing to make the most of his moment. It was this talent as much as any other that won him a massive Deutsche Grammophon contract and a passport to posterity. Was he a better pianist than the unnamed performer at the head of this chapter, a superior technician or more thoughtful interpreter? Would he ever join Horowitz among the untouchables? The answer is probably negative on both counts; what Pogorelich possessed, in addition to keyboard mastery and a sly charisma, was a hunger for success that made him specially prized by the masters of the classical market-place.

Unlike the pop machine, with its efficient turn-out of exchangeable stars, serious music has no monster-maker. The pop sector operates a scattergun strategy, swamping stores and the airwaves with a monthly plethora of new acts and moving fast to support whichever of them sells best. The cost of fifty failed launches is easily recouped in the receipts of one big hit. In classics, recording costs are so high and the margins are so slim that no label can afford more than a handful of monthly releases – hence the inordinate faith and fees that attach to famous names whom the public might be expected to recognise.

Yet what makes a star in classical music remains an enigma. The one in a lifetime who outshines all peers — Heifetz, Horowitz, Caruso, Callas — is divinely fingered. The rest are essentially self-made, risen to great heights by seizing their moment. The corridors of record companies are thronged with image men and superagents who claim to have 'made' Pavarotti, or Jessye Norman, or Nigel Kennedy, and promise to do it again. But the truth is that none of these wizards has ever made lightning strike twice. The birth of a star is a mystery that defies marketing theory and the wondrously comic best efforts of an increasingly desperate industry.

THE FATTENING OF BIG LUCY

Luciano Pavarotti, in his pomp, would wonder from time to time how he ever got to be so big. He was the most celebrated tenor since Caruso and the richest in history. When his wife, Adua, was reported to be contemplating divorce in 1995, Pavarotti's fortune was conservatively estimated at one hundred and fifty million dollars, plus twenty million in future bookings. His possessions included a millionaire's villa at his birthplace Modena, a Central Park apartment in Manhattan, the obligatory tax haven in Monte Carlo, a property firm and finance company, an agricultural co-operative and an internationally recognised racing stud. He was the only classical musician whose countenance beamed forth indiscriminately from society magazines and gutter tabloids.

His father was, all his life, a humble baker and Luciano's early struggles gave no hint of the phenomenon he would become. He was turned down for roles in his home theatre and was twenty-five before the regional capital, Reggio Emilia, gave him a break in *La Bohème* in April 1961. He married Adua on the security of that engagement and made a Covent Garden début in the same opera two years later. This was followed by twelve appearances in Mozart's *Idomeneo* at Glyndebourne where he learned to work hard, and with a settled cast. His technique, however, was insecure and his future uncertain. The voice reached top C without apparent effort, but many felt it lacked physical ballast and could burn out young. He took to selling insurance on the side as a possible alternative occupation, manifesting an apparent *joie de vivre* that would, in time, become his most winning mannerism. What was it, then — or who, rather — that leap-frogged this cavalier youngster over every opera singer of his time, and several times beyond?

Pavarotti, a man wholly without false vanity, put his fame down to his prodigious size. At well over twenty stone, he was unmissable wherever he went. 'Because of my size, people see me once and they don't forget me,' he opined.[4] Until he was twenty he played left wing on a local soccer team. 'I was built for sport. When I gave up sport, I put on weight,' he reflected.[5] Obesity was something he joked about, while being ultra-careful about camera placings. 'I am happy *in spite of* my weight,'[6] he lamented. But many fans believed, perhaps superstitiously, that bigness was an integral part of the man and his art. It was the source of his irresistible televisual bonhomie, the bottoming of his bell-like top notes. His personal representative, Herbert Breslin, said, 'When Luciano sings, people are not conscious of his size. They are conscious of his voice and the joyfulness of singing that he communicates. A skinny Pavarotti with twenty-five per cent of his voice wouldn't mean anything.'[7]

As his fame spread, pictures and measurements of his rise and fall in girth were relished by the popular press and dissected by the broadsheets. An American writer described him as 'only slightly smaller than Vermont'. Closer to the knuckle, Milan's *Corriere della Sera* punched his 'bulging gut' and complained that he had turned into 'a kind of grotesque Carnival king to the masses'.[8] Wounding as these comments must have been to Pavarotti, they were meat and drink to the machine that manufactured his magnificent image. Although he reacted angrily to suggestions that he wielded clout in casting the operas he sang in, 'Big Lucy' never sued anyone who wrote that he was fat. He knew, better than anyone, the value of recognisability.

Many would claim credit for his fame. The key players, however, were few, random, mutually wary. Joan Sutherland was the near-altruistic first. She liked the callow Italian because he was taller than she was; not many tenors were. So she persuaded Greater Miami and Fort Lauderdale opera companies to book him for her four nights of Donizetti's *Lucia di Lammermoor* in February 1965, his US début. Afterwards, she took him home for a six-week Australian tour. Like a grateful puppy, Pavarotti bounded around the local heroine in *Lucia*, *Sonnambula*, *Traviata* and *L'Elisir d'Amore*.

He sang, by all accounts, wondrously, but his projection was under-developed. It was Sutherland who, standing in front of him and placing his hands on her stomach as she sang, taught him to use his diaphragm. 'Every time I'd turn around, there he'd be with his hands on my wife's tummy trying to figure out how she supported her voice, how she breathed,' said the conductor Richard Bonynge.[9] It was Down Under that Pavarotti learned to swell his voice, seemingly from below the knees. He began to frisk around the stage as his confidence rose. Back together at Covent Garden in June 1966, Sutherland and Pavarotti had 'a lot of fun' in Donizetti's *Daughter of the*

Regiment and, though critics sniffed at the 'sentimental, slapstick' piece, it eventually earned his passage to America.

He sang with Karajan at La Scala and achieved a stage understanding with his fellow-Modenese, Mirella Freni, but at thirty-two he was wholly unrecorded. His tapes had gone round the major labels but tenors were plentiful in the late Sixties and producers did not want to risk offending their house-stars with a presumptuous newcomer. 'There were twenty excellent tenors when I began – Corelli, Gedda, Raimondi, Bergonzi, di Stefano, del Monaco – so I tried to choose things they were not doing,' he recalled. Bonynge pointed him towards Bellini and Donizetti bel canto operas that were his wife's great forte.

The couple then did him their third great favour by pressing him on to Decca, over the objections of its European chief, Maurice Rosengarten, who 'worried himself sick about what [Mario] del Monaco would say'. Rosengarten, said the Decca producer John Culshaw, 'did not want Pavarotti, and he did not seem to care which of our competitors grabbed him'.[10] He finally sanctioned a 45-rpm record with one aria on each side, a pop single which the classical division did not know how to project. The man with the biggest headache was Terry McEwen, head of Decca-London's US operation and Sutherland's close friend and admirer.

McEwen, a corpulent Canadian, knew he had a big tenor on his hands because Joan and his own ears told him so. But the single he was sent from London was unsellable and Pavarotti was making no headway in America. His Miami début went unnoticed and his San Francisco *Bohème* with Freni in November 1968 fared little better. His advent to the Metropolitan Opera the following year was stymied by a heavy flu that caused him to break down after a single *Bohème*. He flew home to Modena, cancelling thirty outstanding engagements and getting himself branded in US opera circles as untrustworthy. McEwen was mortified. He had fought for Decca to sign Pavarotti as Sutherland's duettist and needed him to make good. So, like many another businessman in distress, McEwen got himself a publicist. When Pavarotti returned to the Met with Sutherland in *Daughter of the Regiment* in February 1972, the press was primed to await a sensation. Pavarotti tossed off nine top Cs in the general rehearsal and the orchestra stood in ovation. McEwen's publicist, the quick-thinking Herbert Breslin, rechristened him 'King of the High Cs' and from then, there was no turning back. The senior opera critic, Irving Kolodin, spoke of his 'infallible sense of line'. Harold Schonberg in the *Times* called him 'the thinking man's tenor'.[11]

He proved himself to be a natural television personality, stealing Johnny Carson's *Tonight* show with naïf charm and sly wit; he got asked back on more than a dozen occasions. His 1977 television *Bohème* with Renata Scotto drew twenty-five thousand viewer letters. He made the covers of *Time* and *Newsweek*.

This, for Breslin, was just the beginning. A former schoolteacher, born in 1924, Pavarotti's publicist came out of the US army at the end of the Second World War with a passion for opera and a study grant at the Sorbonne. After a Detroit spell in motor industry advertising and corporate speedwriting, Breslin applied for a lower-paid job in his native New York with the Ann Colbert concert agency. The first artist he was given to look after was Sutherland, for whom Breslin learned to snarl at slavering reporters. 'The idea was to deaden her publicity because she got too much,' said Miss Colbert. His next project was Elisabeth Schwarzkopf. 'I thought it would be a good idea for a nice Jewish boy like Breslin to look after her, because she had this difficult Nazi reputation,' said her agent. 'Was he successful? Oh, yes.'[12] On Schwarzkopf's behalf, Breslin sweet-talked the same pressmen he had formerly snubbed. Banned from the Met by Rudolf Bing, Schwarzkopf did a round of concerts and recitals, appeared on television and made a Handel recording in Detroit. Breslin's vital role in her American rehabilitation is unexplored by Schwarzkopf biographers.

Having spent the Sixties with Colbert, Breslin set up an independent office with Sutherland as his first client. 'She paid him to the end of her career to keep the press away,' said an associate[13]. He met the Spanish pianist Alicia de Larrocha. 'He thought she was a wonderful artist who was not making it, and he could help,' said a *Times* journalist[14]. Breslin prevailed on feature writers to give Larrocha a higher profile, but transferred her management to Ronald Wilford at CAMI. He did not feel he could cope with fee negotiations and record contracts. Nevertheless, he continued to exert 'artistic control' over the pianist's burgeoning career. Met favourites Richard Tucker, Marilyn Horne and Leontyne Price were among those who applied for Breslin's special assistance.

To the dowager world of musical PR, Breslin added a braggard muscularity. His competitors were efficient women in their middle years – Dorle Soria of Angel Records; Margaret Carson, who looked after Bernstein; Audrey Michaels, who handled Arthur Judson's special artists; Sheila Porter, sister of the *New Yorker* critic. These were the ladies who lunched the editors and tickled the critics with a rustle of press releases. Breslin used the telephone where they used the fish-knife and splattered a prose style that was overripe to the point of self-embarrassment. He once called Sutherland 'the supreme soprano of the century', qualifying his hype immediately with the rider: 'She *may* be the greatest soprano of the century, but we have no way of judging. We *do* know she is the only person in the world who can sing *Esclarmonde.*' Away from the hype he poured forth for public consumption, Breslin had the telephone manner of a recently maimed longshoreman. He never conversed when he could yell, never schmoozed when he had the chance to abuse. To those on the receiving end of his gratuitous rudeness, Breslin made a name for himself as 'the most cordially loathed man in the music business'.[15]

Public relations brings, at best, a vicarious satisfaction to its practitioners and Breslin sought a creative role. His involvement with Sutherland was limited by Bonynge and his other singers were shadowed by agents. In Pavarotti, however, Breslin found an artist who was young, impressionable and entirely unmanaged − except for Adua who took care of his European diary while raising their three daughters in Modena. Shortly into their collaboration, Breslin ceased to be Pavarotti's publicist and became his full-time manager. 'Some people say that I had a big effect on Luciano,' said Breslin modestly, 'that I changed him like a Svengali masterminding his whole career. I suppose I've had some effect on him.'[16]

Sutherland confirmed that Breslin had 'given him much good advice'. Bonynge said, 'I know there are those who say we helped Luciano get started. He didn't need any help from us or anyone else.'[17] Genius, it is said, will always out − but it does help to have a Sutherland opening the doors for you and a Breslin blazing the trail with a fanfare of media attention. So effective was his manager's campaign that one reporter renamed him P. T. Breslin, after the inimitable Barnum.

Breslin's first initiative was to take Pavarotti out of opera for a month and send him on a recital tour with piano accompaniment. The vocal circuit was ailing, as CAMI's Community Concerts knew to its cost, but some towns were still booking and Breslin reckoned that recitals would enable Pavarotti to project his personality, free of the distracting impedimenta of operatic production. On 1 February 1973 Breslin booked Pavarotti into William Jewell College, a small Baptist school in the town of Liberty, Missouri, where a local benefactor had left enough funds to attract top-fee artists. Before setting out, he told the tenor, 'Don't go there to see if the public likes you. Go and see if you like the public.' Pavarotti, alone on stage, sang as he pleased and pleased as he sang. No critic was admitted, either at Liberty or at the follow-ups in Dallas and Denver, but word of mouth spread quickly to the east. On 18 February 1973, on the strength of one small ad in the *New York Times*, Pavarotti sold out Carnegie Hall. Some months later he announced recitals in Chicago. To a journalist's warning that vocal evenings did not sell well, Pavarotti replied, 'My plan is to sing here in a concert with the house full. That is my plan. Okay?'[18]

By 1980 he was filling seven-thousand-seat halls and earning more than all his kind. 'Luciano feels he has something to offer and he is anxious to offer it to as many people and in as many different places as possible,' said Breslin.[19]

'It was clear to Herbert Breslin at once that in terms of publicity Luciano's personality was almost as big an asset as his voice,' commented Adua Pavarotti,[20] who settled on a cautious coexistence with his manager. Adua had ambitions of her own; in 1986 she set up State Door Opera Management in the grounds of the Modena mansion, offering her services as an agent in response, she said, 'to all the requests I had for help from young singers'.[21] A sensible demarcation was established, with Adua looking after her husband's Italian affairs and Breslin managing him in the rest of the world, subject to her co-ordination of the all-important diary. La Signora Pavarotti was not without influence.

The solo recital was hailed as Breslin's master recipe for making a star, but Pavarotti was not the only one to whom he suggested it. The Spanish tenor, Placido Domingo, was also on Breslin's books as a publicity client. 'Herbert went to Luciano and Placido,' said Merle Hubbard who joined Breslin in 1972, 'and said to them, "You are the two greatest tenors in the world today. If you want to go beyond that, the way to do it is recitals." Placido was nervous about this and declined. Luciano was game for anything.'[22] Domingo, said Breslin, 'is a first-rate tenor, but he didn't want to do concerts or some other projects I suggested to broaden his audience.'[23] In particular, Domingo refused to place his management in Breslin's hands. Domingo quit Breslin some time later with a burning sense of resentment. Any ill will that subsequently arose between the two tenors stemmed from the years when they paid the same publicist and competed for his favours.

Breslin went on to place Pavarotti in an American Express poster campaign that appeared on bus-shelters the world over. He got him to ride a black charger on his forty-fifth birthday in New York's 1980 Columbus Day Parade, to sing at the Academy Awards ceremony and to double-bill with Frank Sinatra at Radio City Music Hall. His audacious and expertly timed publicity yielded an avalanche effect. After appearing on public television 'Live from Lincoln Center' with Zubin Mehta, Pavarotti received no fewer than one hundred thousand letters. Singing *Rigoletto* in Central Park, he drew an audience estimated at two hundred thousand. Decca's records sold like fresh pasta. At one point, Pavarotti had eight discs in the *Billboard* top forty.

As his tenor grew fatter, Breslin devised ingenious forms of camouflage that turned grossness into grandeur – a multi-coloured shawl, a Borsalino hat, the tablecloth-sized white handkerchief that served Pavarotti as a security blanket in solo recitals. He also made errors of judgement – and they were well camouflaged, too. A 1981 movie, *Yes, Giorgio*, in which Pavarotti at his most obese played a bumptious food-throwing gump, can occasionally be caught on very late-night television.

As Pavarotti rose in fame and flamboyance, many others flocked to Breslin for a dose of the magic elixir. Christopher Hogwood, the period performance specialist, sought his assistance and was dubbed, somewhat risibly, 'the Karajan of Early Music'. Sir Georg Solti, music director of the Chicago Symphony Orchestra but eternally image-anxious, was pictured in a red hat. Some singers who joined Breslin – Susan Dunn, Kallen Esperian, Nucia Focile – landed big-house roles opposite Pavarotti. The tenor denied that he or his manager had any say in choosing his operatic partners. This did not stop aspiring opera stars from imagining that a proximity to Pavarotti's manager might enhance their chances of selection.

With a staff of seven, Breslin's office handled some two dozen artists. None, however, attained the celestial success of the magnificent man from Modena. There were two ways of interpreting this. Either artists were too stupid to swallow Breslin's proven potion, or he was unable to pull off the same coup twice. Whatever the case, Breslin's agency got a reputation for having a high artist turnover in the industry. 'One day Herbert will be touting an artist to the heavens,' said a journalist. 'The next, they'll be poison because they have left him.'

Domingo's defection was an irritant that the Spaniard was not allowed to forget. Wherever he turned up to sing he found simultaneous feature coverage of his great contemporary. He almost walked out of an opera on finding a Pavarotti advertisement in the programme booklet. Rumours of ugly rivalry were fed to the media. No one admitted fuelling the feud, but Domingo pointed his finger at the Pavarotti camp. 'I don't care what they do as long as it's fair,' he told me in 1991. 'They are trying to sell a product and it would be stupid on their part to describe it as second-best . . . Whatever they say about him, that's fine. But don't touch me.'[24]

Comparison between the two tenors was misleading, for they were antipodal in most aspects of character and attraction. Domingo was the *Otello* of a lifetime, while the cheery, chubby Pavarotti had trouble representing tragedy. The Italian was a born Nemorino where, with Domingo, a faint sullenness marred his comic roles. Pavarotti exuded a peasant love of life and its pleasures; Domingo exhibited a refined and calculating intelligence. The Italian had a mass following among aesthetes and opera queens; Domingo was more the housewives' choice.

On most artistic counts, Domingo held the upper hand. He sang a hundred roles, from Rossini to Massenet and, later, Wagner. Pavarotti mastered thirty, mostly in his own tongue. Domingo was athletic, trim and young-looking, allowing him to play an annual Salzburg soccer fixture and to act most parts with dramatic verisimilitude. Pavarotti, as his weight increased, became a static stage presence with a limited expressive range. Domingo was a capable conductor, had a grasp of stage direction and planned a retirement career as head of an American opera house. Pavarotti was a singer, plain and simple. His voice and serenity, however, were in a class of their own. Beautifully as Domingo sang and credibly as he acted he could not produce those orotund upper tones that seemed to start at the soles of Pavarotti's calf-leather shoes and rise volcanically through his mountainous form to an awesome eruption.

That Pavarotti loyalists should have felt the need to smear Domingo was proof itself of the Spaniard's potency. Unable to malign him vocally, the Pavarotti camp attacked the weak spot in every artist's make-up – his age. A whispering campaign alleged that Domingo had been born before his admitted birth date, 1941, and was probably older than Pavarotti and closer to the final curtain. A fake date of 1934 crept into at least one standard music dictionary. Domingo, distressed by the aspersions, produced an authenticated copy of his birth certificate from the registry office in Madrid, but failed to quell the rumour-mongering. 'It gets to the point where you don't know whether some words have been said by Luciano or by newspaper people,' he griped. 'I trust Luciano. I cannot say I trust everything that is behind him.'

That was unsurprising, given the cultivated belligerence of the Pavarotti machine. 'I want it clearly understood,' Breslin told a British magazine writer, 'that if [Luciano] does not get on the cover I will return to London and personally castrate you.'[25] 'Why the fuck do you wanna know?' was his response to my inquiry about Pavarotti recording dates. At Larrocha's Decca producer he yelled, 'You don't fuck around with Alicia.' 'I have never had anyone talk to me like he does,' said the producer. Breslin, said a Decca boss, 'is very badly behaved. He is the pits.'[26]

'Once Luciano got big, Herbert got abusive,' said his associate, Merle Hubbard. 'I used to say to him, "Herbert, don't burn all the bridges. We still need them for our other artists." But if someone was of no use to Luciano, he'd just hang up on them. No one else on our list really mattered to him.' A pianist who went to seek his advice was told, 'There is one thing you have to remember: our minimum fee is fifteen thousand dollars a year. This is the most important thing for you to bear in mind.' Fees for Breslin representation ranged from two hundred and fifty dollars to fifteen hundred dollars a month. Breslin took eighty per cent of the commissions earned by his associates. On

Pavarotti he made twenty per cent on most engagements and recordings, creaming upwards of two million dollars a year.

He made no excuse for rudeness and needed none. With Pavarotti on his list, he was made for life. His Rottweiler snarl liberated the tenor to beam upon all comers, knowing that his manager would savage anyone who demeaned him. Pavarotti was, by nature, faithful to those who rendered him service and, it seemed, genuinely fond of Breslin. He addressed him as 'Herbert, my friend' and stroked his bald head in family snapshots. 'Luciano can be very loyal,' said producers at Decca, where he was exclusive for a quarter of a century. Philanderous proclivities notwithstanding, he was tenderly devoted to his wife and daughters.

When Glyndebourne needed big names for a fundraising concert, Pavarotti responded in a trice, mindful of a debt of honour that he owed for the tradecraft he had learned in Sussex thirty years earlier (once the event had been published with his name in big letters, Glyndebourne received notice of his withdrawal). He was sentimentalist and patriarchal and few ever left his circle in prolonged disfavour. He perhaps needed a Breslin to protect him from his own generosity. 'If it wasn't for Herbert, I would find myself doing nothing but benefits . . .' he told his biographer. 'Herbert's way of telling people No is not my way, but Herbert has his style of operating.'[27]

There could be no question that Breslin had raised Pavarotti to a plateau of success unattained by any singer of his time, but a plateau is where Pavarotti stood at the peak of his vocal powers, in the early 1980s. He had the highest fees attainable, was singing in the biggest halls and was attaining saturation press coverage. He could name his own productions and conditions and was 'writing' a ghosted autobiography. There was nowhere else for him to go within classical convention. For Breslin to justify his Barnum soubriquet, he would have needed to invent a new framework for his tenor. But the opera buff was constrained by his own cultural aspirations and, when someone dared to suggest the unconventional, Breslin threw the impertinent man bodily out of his office and on to West 57th Street – or so the legend goes.

There are two versions of Pavarotti's encounter with Tibor Rudas. They are identical in every respect – except in their account of Breslin's reaction. A boy soprano at the Hungarian State Opera, Rudas lost his income when his voice broke and formed a dance and acrobatics act with his twin brother. On tour in Australia in 1948 when the communists took power, Rudas stayed abroad. He married, set up a dance school and sent graduate troupes touring around Asia. Entering America, he organised floorshows at casinos in Las Vegas and Atlantic City. The takings were good but the taste was low and

Rudas was nagged by an artistic conscience. He booked the New York Philharmonic with Zubin Mehta for Las Vegas. The conductor told him about a wonder-tenor who could fill any house on earth. In Pavarotti's account, Rudas went to see Breslin to book the tenor for his resorts. He was evicted bodily, time after time, until he uttered the words 'one hundred thousand dollars' – whereupon Breslin sat him down to talk turkey. 'In 1981,' said Pavarotti, 'you must remember that $100,000 was an enormous amount of money for a classical artist to earn for just one appearance.'[28]

In the narrative that Rudas gave his friends, he pursued Pavarotti to Italy and convinced him to get his unwilling agent to negotiate. Rudas then marched into Breslin's office and refused to leave until they agreed a date; one concert was all Breslin would allow. The discrepancy between the two stories is small, but it indicates Breslin's gut-resistance to everything Rudas wanted and stood for. Rudas was a courteous man in rimless glasses, dark suits and grey ties. He may have dealt with mysterious figures in his casino world but he wore the air of a retired physician and he communicated in an accent as warming as goulash. Breslin, who swore like a stevedore and looked uncomfortable in collar and tie, was outclassed – and knew it. 'When Tibor came along, we were into helicopters, bodyguards, the whole Andre Agassi mould. That's not where Herbert Breslin is,' said a member of his staff.

Pavarotti summoned Rudas and Breslin to meet him at La Scala before he went on stage to sing *Aida*. He refused to sing in a gambling den, he said, but by the third act had accepted a Rudas compromise – that he should sing not in, but *near* the casino in a specially designed tent. The venue was Atlantic City, and Rudas hoped for a crowd of nine thousand. His hotel partner, Resorts International, were sceptical and pulled out, leaving the Hungarian bearing the risk.

Ahead of the Rudas event, Breslin exposed Pavarotti to ever-larger crowds and spaces. After singing in a Miami convention centre where the sound system was first plagued by feedback and then switched off altogether, he was ready to pull out. In desperation he called Ray Minshull, head of the Decca Recording Company in London. Minshull summoned James Lock, one of his best sound engineers, from a Solti session in Chicago and sent him on the next flight to join Pavarotti in Montreal. The tenor was in the middle of a press conference when he saw Lock walking into the Four Seasons Hotel. Breaking off in mid-sentence, he sighed, 'I am *so* happy to see you, my friend.' Without Lock, the arena concerts, the Three Tenors, the transmogrification of Pavarotti from opera star to superstar, could never have come about.

'My involvement was trivial,' Lock shrugged with British understatement. 'I had to get the equipment sorted out from scratch and vet local crews to work with. I wanted to let people listen to Luciano the way I'd want to listen to him myself – to hear the voice, and to hear classical sound.'[29] Lock designed a sound system that gave Pavarotti the confidence to sing at his best in the Atlantic City tent on 19 October 1983. 'He was very happy that it came across so well,' said the engineer. 'Luciano loved the atmosphere and the applause,' said Rudas. He also loved the loot.

After three more Rudas events at ever-higher fees, Pavarotti gave the Hungarian control of his extra-mural activities. Rudas asked for a dozen nights a year and Breslin was obliged to give way. 'Herbert always goes to the events to support Luciano, but there's not very much for him to do there,' commented Lock. 'Rudas organises these things very well.'

The British engineer, on the other hand, was indispensable to the enterprise. Pavarotti insisted on his presence at all outdoor events and Rudas paid Decca handsomely for his services. Lock, though he did not complain, received no share of the receipts. 'And here we are more than two hundred concerts later,' he reflected in 1995. 'I must say I have got a bit fed up with it and trained a young colleague to replace me. I much prefer making records in the studio.' Crucial as his contribution was, it is surprising that Lock was not rewarded commensurately – or even given a mention in Pavarotti's memoirs. His input did not, however, elude Domingo, who sought and received Pavarotti's permission to hire Lock's team for his own outdoor events.

As Pavarotti waxed larger in the public eye, Domingo spent the late 1980s trying to trounce him on grass. Where the Italian drew two hundred thousand into Central Park, Domingo attracted eight hundred and fifty thousand for the Statue of Liberty centennial concert, half a million into a Tel Aviv park and three hundred and fifty thousand on to the Madrid University campus. Yet Pavarotti still outshone him monumentally in publicity and profitability.

In 1986, hearing that Pavarotti had filled a London stadium, Domingo ordered his UK agent, Margherita Stafford, to book Wembley Arena for a pre-Christmas concert. Bad press dogged the event from the outset. Domingo, hearing that only half the tickets had sold on the eve of the concert, called it off and went on the prime-time Wogan show to complain that tickets prices were too high. The cancellation cost him public support, a loyal agent and lengthy litigation with the promoters, ultimately settled out of court.

The difference between Pavarotti and Domingo could not have been more amply illustrated. The Italian was a popular commodity, the Spaniard an acquired taste. Pavarotti was constitutionally at ease, Domingo was in a perpetual fret.

Above all, Pavarotti had behind him the high-octane Rudas organisation, closely watched by Breslin, who was himself closely watched by Adua. Domingo had only a male secretary, his wife Marta, and an international assortment of *ad hoc* agents. He could not hope to compete with Pavarotti except in the opera house, where the Italian was becoming an infrequent visitor. For much of the Decade of Greed, Pavarotti avoided Covent Garden because he felt its general director, Sir John Tooley, was too chummy with Domingo. One last-minute cancellation was cabled from a South Sea island where the supposedly unwell tenor was 'resting' with a buxom companion. Between 1981, when Rudas entered the picture, and 1989, when he was finally banned from the house, Pavarotti fulfilled only fifteen of his forty-one scheduled appearances at Chicago's Lyric Opera. Often his relinquishing of opera was attributable to a parallel appearance at Rudas's or Breslin's behest in a supermarket car-park or an international tennis court. His star shone so bright that it was in danger of soaring out of the operatic firmament altogether.

Domingo, when he sang for the masses, made no bones about his motives. 'In some of these performances we can make real money,' he said, 'because in opera we don't.' Pavarotti preferred to pretend that his was a missionary campaign, designed to recapture a popular following for grand opera. Rudas, too, waxed lyrical about luring time-killing gamblers away from the one-armed bandits and back to high art. Yet each time he staged a Pavarotti event he removed a premier attraction from the opera stage and, by paying him ten times his highest opera-house fee, weakened the economic foundations of the opera industry. Fellow-singers saw what Pavarotti was earning and wanted some for themselves, whether through Rudas or other promoters. 'I don't take anything out of my opera performances – so why should I be criticised?' protested Domingo. The Spaniard, however, was isolated at the summits of artistic principle and appetite that drove him in his fifties to commission new operas and drive himself deeper into the thicket of Wagner's *Ring*.

By 1990, Pavarotti and Domingo were further apart in style and aspiration than ever before. It took a third tenor to bring them together in a common purpose. José Carreras, a chirpy Catalan with a knack for breaking hearts backstage and front, fell ill with leukaemia and miraculously recovered. To give thanks for his restoration, he asked his good friends Placido and Luciano to join him in a concert for children's cancer charities. Carreras was no threat vocally to either of the big men and they volunteered their services readily, as did the conductor Zubin Mehta.

Then the music business took over. A computer salesman turned music agent, Mario Dradi by name, fixed up a link with the soccer world cup finals, which all three tenors were mad keen to watch. James Lock set up Decca's digital console and television networks came charging in with transmission offers. For reasons still uncertain, whether because they doubted its viability or were badly advised, the tenors decided to take a flat fee for their recording and broadcast rights – a sum not hugely in excess of what Pavarotti got paid per night in a Rudas marquee. When three hundred million people watched the telecast and Decca sold twelve million discs, the singers rued their lost royalties.

The concert remains compellingly watchable on video. More than just a variety show, it brought together three epic timbres and techniques and allowed three effulgent personalities to strike sparks off one another. The outbreak of peace between two great artists was itself cause for thanksgiving. That night, said Domingo, three tenors 'were really one: we worked for each other, were breathing with each other'.

'Whatever tension there had been in the past was long since forgotten and we had very good relations,' declared Pavarotti, 'I thought it was time for the press to forget.'[30]

That winter, Pavarotti asked Domingo if he could watch him rehearse *Otello* and took away a tape of his performance. Five years later, he was working himself up towards playing Otello for the first time on the opera stage. Competitiveness persisted, but it had been turned to mutual advantage.

Once the Three Tenors concert was over, Rudas stepped in to make sure neither he nor Pavarotti got ripped off again. For a repeat performance at the Los Angeles World Cup he held the media to ransom and earned the three tenors and their conductor more money than they could sensibly spend in two lifetimes. Sales of the discs and videos slipped to eight million, but there was plenty of life left in the Rudas formula. Pavarotti took to singing for him so often in the open air that the voice was under stress. A 1991 concert in London's Hyde Park attended in pouring rain by the Prince and Princess of Wales left Decca's engineers frankly dismayed. The leading Italian newspaper, *Corriere della Sera*, accused Pavarotti of 'descending to the level of Madonna'. He was booed at La Scala in December 1992 when a top note cracked on opening night in Verdi's *Don Carlos*. He admitted that the audience were right to have barracked him: he had gone into the performance under-prepared.

A 1994 Verdi *Requiem* at Wembley Arena, with people paying up to ninety-five pounds ($150) to hear him, contained 'woefully out of tune meanderings'.[31] Critics commented that anyone paying for a concert ticket had a right to expect 'that the basics are in place'.[32] Before the *Requiem*, instead of resting, the star attended the inauguration of a Channel tunnel train named 'Pavarotti'. He travelled on to the Philippines, where his tickets were priced at twenty-five thousand pesos (six hundred pounds), or the equivalent of five months' average wages – so much for claims that his concerts expanded the popular audience for classical music.

A 1996 Three Tenors roadshow was announced by Rudas on Pavarotti's sixtieth birthday, with concerts planned in London, New York, Tokyo, Munich and Melbourne and tickets priced between thirty-five pounds (fifty dollars) and three hundred and fifty pounds (five hundred dollars). 'It would be hypocrisy if we said we are not looking for success for our sponsors and ourselves,' said Domingo on behalf of tenors united.[33] Rudas, this time round, had a German co-promoter, Mathias Hofmann, and the involvement of a rock-label patriarch, the celebrated Ahmed Ertegun of Atlantic Records.

Singing Verdi's *Ballo in Maschera* at Covent Garden, Pavarotti took time off to launch a new perfume – then cancelled performances because of fatigue. BBC plans to televise a concert from his horse show in Modena were hastily scrapped when it was discovered that Pavarotti was not actually singing, but miming to a pre-recorded tape. 'I don't think there is a more difficult or *honest* profession [than mine],' he told television viewers.[34] Home in Modena, apologists said, he was professionally less rigorous. In September 1995 he gave a benefit concert in Modena for child victims of the Bosnia war. He improvised duets for Decca with the pop singers Meatloaf and Simon Le Bon and was pictured embracing the Princess of Wales. The world of Luciano Pavarotti was far removed from the haughty, disciplined formalities of fine, high art.

Herbert Breslin was still in attendance, 'watching over Tibor Rudas like an axeman over a turkey'[35] and Adua Pavarotti was never far away, alternately threatening divorce and accepting contrition for an affair with his travelling companion, Nicoletta Mantovani.

Adua's Stage Door Management employed more staff than Breslin's agency and supplied entire casts to certain Italian opera houses. Her conductors included the talented Daniele Gatti, and Carlo Rizzi of Welsh National Opera. 'Luciano's dream – and mine, too,' she declared, 'would be to find, perhaps through . . . Stage Door, a young tenor who has all the essential qualities required to build a big career.'[36] It was Adua's stated ambition to produce a second Pavarotti. Some hope.

Breslin no longer harboured such fantasies. At the age of seventy he formed a profound attachment to a young man whom he announced as his heir to the agency. Three of his oldest associates walked out, taking their artists in tow. The spate of defections left the Breslin agency looking battered, tattered and more than a little bewildered. From his second home in France Breslin was able to refurbish his list with assorted Gallic musicians.

As Luciano Pavarotti surveyed his hospitable table in Modena he might well have asked himself which of his partners – Adua, Breslin or Rudas – had exercised the greatest influence on his spectacular career. Breslin had been crucial on the first lap, but Rudas overtook him on the straight. Adua, meanwhile, had tended his domestic affairs and prepared to share the fruits of a happy retirement. Others had played their part – Bonynge, Sutherland, James Lock, Terry McEwen, his secretary and occasional impresario Judy Kovacs – but no individual was responsible for more than a fraction of the Pavarotti phenomenon, and none of those who grew rich on his percentages was able to justify their fortune by repeating the feat and producing another money-maker out of the hat. This did not stop a myth taking wing in the world of music, a notion that Pavarotti was somehow man-made. If only the music-biz could latch on to the forces that made him, classical music would be rolling in money.

THE UNDOING OF NIGEL

The dog and horn had fallen on hard times and was heading for the scrapheap. EMI, one of the foundation stones of the record industry, announced it was discarding Francis Barraud's picture 'His Master's Voice' in the interests of homogeneity and modernity. The logo could not be used in the United States, where it belonged to RCA, and was out of tune with the dynamic corporatism that Thorn-EMI wished to represent. Heritage had a low market value in the thrusting ethos of late-Thatcherdom. Like most record labels, EMI was pitching for now, pursuing laser-age imagery and teenage idols. In cheeky Nigel Kennedy it possessed a cross-generation communicator who appealed to rock fans without deterring classical purists. In his manager, John Stanley, EMI believed it had the means to generate an infinite succession of Kennedys. Forget the dog and horn, the future belonged to EMI.

Kennedy's recording of Vivaldi's *Four Seasons* had rewritten the label's marketing score. This was one of the most recorded works of pre-classical music with eighty-odd versions stacking the racks, from Karajan's expensively upholstered Berlin sound to a skeletal rendering by sixteen Swedes on period instruments. Kennedy's disc was musically unremarkable, except in its aggressively forward placement of the solo violin and some spotlighting of other parts of his anonymous backing group. What set the disc apart and sent it storming the pop charts was the strategic forethought that attended its release in September 1989. Kennedy, who had recorded concertos before without making waves beyond the classical press, was determined this time to make it count. He had the *Four Seasons* segmented into twelve tracks instead of four, and got EMI to plug them to DJs as three-minute chill-out snippets for interspersion between heavy metal and polysyllabic rap. He was aiming unapologetically for a mass listenership. 'The Vivaldi concept was totally structured in my mind beforehand,' said Kennedy.[37]

When the disc hit the airwaves, it was backed with a national tour of television chatshows, shop signings, interviews in soccer-match intervals, women's magazines and children's media. The blitz continued in micro-planned detail for six months. The disc sold a million copies inside a year and two and a half million before it slowed. 'Only he and Pavarotti have done that sort of figure,' marvelled EMI bosses.[38] Nigel Kennedy was penetrating homes that had never owned a classical disc. He was reaching out to spaced-out souls of his lost generation – and also captivating their mothers, who could not resist a tug of sympathy for this waif-like, stubble-cheeked urchin with his butchered hair and touchingly tender tone.

The son of a Royal Philharmonic cellist who walked out before Nigel was born and migrated to Australia, the budding musician was sent to the Yehudi Menuhin school at the age of seven, when his mother remarried. 'There was a faint threat,' he recalled, describing his audition, 'that you were going to be taken away from home and put into some horrible institution like *One Flew Over the Cuckoo's Nest* if you played too well. Unfortunately, I played that little bit too well and got took into the fucking madhouse.' Menuhin, who paid for his tuition, sent him to New York for finishing off at the Juilliard School for Music and Drama. 'It was a shocking place that tried to make people into little professionals before they knew what music was about,' said Kennedy. Assigned by his mentor to the Harold Holt agency, he was sent out on the concert circuit with a precious Guadagnini loaned to him by a sympathetic violin dealer. After the *Four Seasons*, he was able to afford a much costlier Guarnerius.

He won *Gramophone* magazine's Record of the Year award in 1985 with the Elgar concerto, but made no secret of his disaffection with the classical milieu. He was pushing thirty when he got the award and was being talked of as a boy wonder. How old would he have to be before the classical world took him at face value?

Behind the frustration, a keen intelligence was at work. He left Holts, declaring the ways of the music business to be antiquated, complacent and isolated from the real world. 'I don't think there is such a thing as classical management,' he said. 'There are plenty of classical musicians with amazing power – a violinist like Gidon Kremer or the pianist Martha Argerich – who have got what's needed to put music over at the highest level and with great communication, but don't get the public they deserve. In classical music, the managers sit by the phone and wait for everything to come to them.' Too fidgety to hang around, Kennedy wanted a manager who made things happen.

His public demeanour was changing with the times. The middle-class boy from Brighton took on a demotic accent and talked in a hip dialect with an almost calculated disregard for formal syntax. 'Monster' and 'damage' were favourite words. He dressed like nothing on earth, mostly in gear picked up in street markets and worn with an impudent grin at the snootiest of concerts. He had originally extemporised the attire and trademarked it when people applauded. 'I'd come over from New York and done a bitta brain damage there,' he recounted. 'It was Sat'dy afternoon and I had a gig at the Royal Festival Hall. I was baht to hang up my cloves so they wouldn't be crumpled but when I opened the case they weren't there. I went down Camden Market looking for tails and they didn't have any. So I just bought a lotta black stuff off the stalls and went and played in it. Afterwards, everyone came up and said, "Hey Nige, that's great what you're doing for classical music." '

At EMI they thought so, too, but the suits were terrified where it might lead. They loved his populism and feared its consequences. Nigel liked to swig champagne from the bottle; his father, they reminded themselves, died of alcoholism. Fresh off a flight from Amsterdam, he would extol the substances he had encountered in exotic cafés. EMI did not want to see him boozed up or getting busted. Nigel needed a minder, they felt, a man he could trust and they could rely on to keep him in order.

In 1987, the British EMI chief Rupert Perry introduced him to John Stanley, former manager of the Bay City Rollers pop group. A well-groomed guy with greying hair, thirteen years Kennedy's senior, Stanley viewed himself as a creative facilitator. 'I take responsibility for drawing somebody's dream through their life,' he intoned persuasively. 'Agents don't do that.'[39] Stanley saw what Kennedy wanted to do with the Four Seasons and said he could help. The violinist was entranced by his practicality, his sensitivity and his undisguised prosperity. Stanley drove a blue Rolls-Royce. 'Somehow, with all the success he enjoyed, I thought he'd be pretty flash – you know, the kind of moneyed medallion man. It wasn't the case at all and he seemed quite normal . . . He was actually standing back and looking at my career overall and pulling together in his mind what the real potential was for me,' said Kennedy in a reminiscence he dictated to Stanley.[40] The manager kept him waiting several weeks for an answer. 'I spent a long time making up my mind before taking on Nigel Kennedy,' said Stanley. 'I knew nothing about classics, but he was interested in getting into popular music and that's where my credentials were.' He was finally won over by a concert in which Kennedy mixed classics with jazz, winding up with a violin solo rendition of the theme to BBC television's *Match of the Day* football programme. 'Very soon after that,' said Kennedy, 'John started the mission.'[41]

Five years later, when the partnership was over and Kennedy had become a near-recluse, opinions were divided as to precisely what John Stanley had contributed to the making of Nigel Kennedy. The *Four Seasons* had been recorded and segmented before his arrival. The promotional ideas were in place. What Stanley added, it seemed, was a sense of military discipline and purpose. He installed a command centre at EMI and governed Kennedy's activities day by day, even hour by hour. No approach to the violinist, no matter how trivial or music-intrinsic, was allowed to bypass his controller.

'John was brilliant at timing, especially in the first six months of *Four Seasons*,' reflected Barry McCann, EMI's marketing director and a personal friend of Kennedy's. Stanley engendered a thrill and tension around Kennedy that spilled into showbiz and earned his client the kind of exposure reserved for film stars and national heroes. He was picked for *This Is Your Life*, a peak-time television institution, and *Club X*, a teenie show. Nor was the fame locally confined. Less than one-fifth of Kennedy's record sales were British. He was big in Scandinavia, huge in Australia, growing fast in America. 'A superstar, "the Nige", had been born,' wrote K. Robert Schwarz in a *New York Times* profile.

Stanley retuned his presentations with laser-lights and an all-girl string ensemble. *Kennedy — A Monster Bash* was staged in December 1990 at London's Dominion Theatre. George Martin, the Beatles' producer, was supposed to be making the video. Not everyone approved. John Drummond, the BBC's controller of music, attacked Nigel Kennedy as 'the Liberace of the Nineties'. *The Strad*, bible of the violin trade, found his new persona veering 'from the distasteful to the disgusting'.[42] Classical critics deplored distended mannerisms in his concerto playing. Musicians hired for the Monster Bash were still waiting two years later to be paid. People who paid good money for an open-air concert were charged extra for deck-chairs.

Kennedy was distressed by the backlash and tried to mend his bridges with the classical world. He elected to record the Brahms and Beethoven concertos, having formed a keen rapport in these works with Klaus Tennstedt, EMI's top German conductor. Tennstedt was a willowy individual whose reaction to sudden celebrity after a lifetime in the provinces was to suffer a succession of physical breakdowns. Kennedy responded warmly to his wispy vulnerability. Tennstedt, for his part, was drawn by Kennedy's boyish respect, his prodigious technique and his formidable sales record. Barely able to understand each other's utterances, they shared a non-verbal irony for the absurdities of record-making. In each concerto, Kennedy interpolated his own cadenza – a four-minute mixture of classical pyrotechnics with echoes of his new hero, Jimmy Hendrix. He bought the rock-martyr's sweat-soaked bandanna at auction and wrapped it round his brow as a talisman whenever he played.

Neither the Brahms nor the Beethoven shifted anything like the haystacks of *Four Seasons* discs, but sales still topped six figures and that, for classics, was massive. Kennedy's ability to communicate with any kind of audience was beyond contradiction. In Kiel, Tennstedt's home town, he marched out in June 1992 to face a half-empty hall of Holsteiners in their Sunday-best – wearing a black silk shirt, velvet trousers and calf-length bovver boots. There were giggles as he greeted the penguin-suited Konzertmeister with a High Fives greeting and 'Wotcher, monster'. But once the Beethoven concerto was under way he was into total communication. Never immobile, he nestled up to the conductor one moment and nuzzled the violas the next. His delight in the orchestral interplay was surmounted only by a constant awareness of his audience. He played that frigid Baltic house as conscientiously as a gigolo on his last lira, wheedling, stroking, flattering, touching, appealing with his little-boy-lost look. At the close, the applause was eruptive and the encores endless. That Kiel concert is lodged firmly in my memory, because it was one of the last Nigel Kennedy would ever perform in public.

John Stanley had been fixing him a multitude of deals – a ghosted autobiography, a feature video, a world tour. 'Stanley pushed like mad to have the video made,' reported McCann, but Kennedy was growing weary and suspicious. 'Once we started working on other things after *Four Seasons*,' said Kennedy, 'I didn't have enough time or information put in front of me to make valid artistic decisions on these things, with the result that I wasn't happy with the standard. I was losing control.'

His girlfriend, Brixie, walked out and took their pet dog to California, his classical friends were cutting him loose, he was tired of playing the same pieces over and over again, and his loneliness was palpable. That summer, he called an end to his concert career and retired, at the age of thirty-six, to a remote house in the Malvern Hills. If EMI wanted any more records, he said, they could build him a studio at home. As for John Stanley, he wanted no more of his bag of tricks; during that summer their connection was dissolved. 'Nigel's enthusiasm for what he called Dead Composers was always mixed,' explained Stanley. 'When he decided to stop performing after recording the Beethoven concerto, there was no point in us staying together. There was never any dissent. It was abrupt, not acrimonious. All his relationships were ending at the time. The machine had been running too fast and he stopped it the only way he knew how.'

Stanley denied overtaxing Kennedy, but he admitted that their rupture followed an Australian tour where in five days the violinist gave fifty-six interviews, set up by his manager. He slipped out of Kennedy's life as smoothly as he had entered, leaving a joint-venture memoir that the violinist refused to promote in paperback. Kennedy transferred his dormant diary to a rock agency and set about preparing a reinstrumentation of Hendrix hits for future release by EMI.

'This Hendrix thing has taken me over,' he said. 'Everything else is off until this is sorted out. When I have ideas I want to try out, I'll just pop up at the last minute in small places with two or three hundred people to try out the Hendrix and get the structure in my head. One of the things I liked about the classical world is that you don't make a record until you know you can play it well enough.'

EMI had a Berg concerto and two French string quartets already recorded, but Kennedy refused to sanction their release until his new preoccupation was out. Later, he put the Hendrix project on ice and prepared an album of his own compositions. He had a new girlfriend and a small circle of friends, but his detachment from the current of musical activity was total. He would turn forty in December 1996 and, while not quite forgotten, was unlikely ever to recover his mass following. The fans, like himself, had entered middle age and their mothers were past caring for waifs.

To say that he was sorely missed by the record business was a desperate understatement. The British music industry had lost its biggest classical draw and there was no one to replace him. Menuhin, no less, led the appeals for his return. 'I am thrilled that he is going back to chamber music and I think he is shedding his rather juvenile and iconoclastic attitude to old culture,' said his childhood patron. 'My prayer is that his spontaneity will take an absolutely impeccable idealistic form.'[43] What Menuhin did not know or could not face was the innocent idealism that lay at the core of Kennedy's rejection of everything to do with the classical music machine. Whatever the future might hold, Kennedy was adamant that he would not return to that environment. 'I can't ever go back to the classical music world,' he assured me in 1994. 'You don't make a decision like that, just to go back on it.'

*   *   *

And where did Kennedy's withdrawal leave John Stanley? Why, at the peak of his classical popularity, with managers and musicians lining up to buy a draught of his priceless advice. Stanley was, everyone knew, the man who had 'made' Nigel Kennedy, and if Kennedy somehow got unmade that was down to the artist's temperament rather than the manager's sagacity. So Ronald Wilford at CAMI sought Stanley's view of the black soprano, Jessye Norman. Mark McCormack of IMG sent him to Barcelona to devise a film of José Carreras's life. 'I took him back to the hospital where he had almost died and made him sing the piece of music that ran through his head in those months,' related Stanley, who could not remember a year later what the music was. Sir Georg Solti, still fretting about his image, came to him for a year's worth of consultation. Stanley said he made himself useful in sorting out Solti's position at Salzburg, though he had no previous experience of the festival.

'John had not run out of ideas,' said EMI's McCann, and the company continued to approach him. Stanley claimed they ignored his advice to record more Baroque music after *Four Seasons* and misapplied his Kennedy techniques to other, less suitable soloists. 'That's hindsight.' McCann shrugged. In 1994, two years after Kennedy's disappearance, John Stanley went on tour as the author of a blockbuster book on *Classical Music: The Great Composers and their Masterworks*, with an introduction by Sir Georg Solti who professed himself 'extremely sympathetic to John Stanley's intention'. A review of the contents revealed that Stanley had written only a brief foreword, afterword and seven pages of text. The rest had been word-processed by an unnamed team of writers.

Stanley, to his credit, never claimed to be an expert on classical music and his background showed him to be a jack of many trades. After attending art school in Oxford, he took a news camera and went chasing floods and accidents across the West Country. Contact with BBC newsrooms and a convivial manner led him into the corridors of light entertainment.

By the early 1970s he was representing 'three-quarters of the DJs on Radio 1'. He was involved in setting up Capital Radio, London's first commercial pop station, and then went to California to market the BBC's *Dr Who* series. According to press reports, he was called in to advise Governor Ronald Reagan on international affairs. 'I was English and involved in broadcasting: it was logical of him to ask me,' said Stanley. 'It's not my fault that some papers called me his manager.' His best deal was selling the Bay City Rollers' hit 'Saturday Night' to an eponymous American chatshow. His experiences sounded colourful enough when strung together, but separately contained none of the strategy for which he became so admired in the classical world.

Stanley did not go on to puppeteer the BBC's disc-jockeys, run a record label, or get a post in the Reagan Administration. Yet classical bosses and artists were taken in by his aura, and Reed International paid him a small fortune to assemble a supposedly authoritative guide to classical music.

As he polished off that assignment, Stanley thought he had stumbled upon a solution for the joint salvation of classical music and the established Church. Many in the Nineties, he felt, were looking for a spiritual dimension to their pressured lives. 'It would take so little imagination to use music as a catalyst to draw people back towards faith,' he preached winningly. On this occasion, the music business was unmoved and the Church untempted. John Stanley went home to Norfolk to write a book about classic cars. He continued, said his book-jacket blurb, 'to develop multimedia projects for the promotion of classical music'.

INTIMATIONS OF SEX AND INCENSE

Desperate times breed desperate measures. In the depths of recession, classical music encountered a personality problem. The problem was lack of personality. The titans — Herbert von Karajan, Leonard Bernstein, Vladimir Horowitz — were dying. Joan Sutherland, the last of the divas, announced her retirement. Pavarotti could not go on for ever. Kennedy was gone, perhaps for good. The stars whose names were universally recognised could be counted on the fingers of one hand. Beyond them stretched a faceless anonymity. The top performers had terrific technique, but it was impossible to tell them apart. This is what agents meant when they moaned about 'presenter decline'. Shut your eyes and you could not be sure if a Stradivarius was being played by one Juilliard wunderkind or another. Midori, Anne Akiko Meyers, Sarah Chang, had no gripping individuality to convey in music and all sounded much the same.

The recognisability of singers was, if anything, feebler. This was supposed to be a golden age of American singers, but it would take a consultant laryngologist to distinguish between Carol Vaness and Cheryl Studer, Dawn Upshaw and June Anderson, Deborah Voigt and Susan Dunn. And these were supposed to be the shining stars of the lyric stage. Raised by superteachers and agents to be ultra-profesional and free of obvious fault, young performers shed whatever colour and fire they once possessed and settled into dread conformity. Many were, beyond doubt, better technicians than the divas of yesteryear, but who would not give all the faked orgasms of the modern model-vocalists for one half-shriek from Callas? Opera houses prized their efficiency, but music lovers crept away in mounting numbers to the comfort of their ancient recordings. This was a dire omen that called for emergency measures.

As patriotism is to the scoundrel, so are sex and God to the music business – the last refuge. Classical music was a late developer in sexual activity. It had regularly produced female stars of physical beauty and tonal sensuality – Maria Jeritza, Guilhermina Suggia, Emmy Destinn, Maria Cebotari – but felt no need to advertise their god-given attributes. What these women could do to a buttoned-up audience was well known to all who heard them and would not have borne description in those pre-liberated times. It would also have misrepresented the totality of their impact. Any depiction of Maria Callas as 'sexy' diminishes the complexity of her magnetism, a phenomenon fiercer and more durable than mere tumescence – as her huge gay following would proudly attest.

Other female sensations of the post-war era were equally unsuited to sex-treatment. Kathleen Ferrier possessed a granitic, aloof beauty. Joan Sutherland was an imperious, somewhat forbidding diva. Jacqueline du Pré, although she arched her body and flung back her blonde mane lasciviously while playing the cello, preserved an angelic aura that defied crude imagery. An avid child of London's Swinging Sixties, du Pré was tragically struck down by multiple sclerosis in 1971. Long after her death in 1987, her records remained among EMI's top-sellers without a penny having to be spent on promoting her glamorous physical attributes.

The first signs of sexual awakening in classical music cropped up in opera, where once-radical stage directors ripped the clothes off their sopranos and sent them cavorting naked as never intended. While this imposed an ultimatum on many singers to slim down or lose work, it did not turn the strippers into vocal stars. Maria Ewing, when she flung off the last of Salome's veils and exposed her pubic regions to the Covent Garden public, failed to achieve a higher fee or more recordings. Leslie Garrett, who bared her butt at English National Opera, was not snapped up by Salzburg. In the cultivation of a musical career there were still, it seemed, more cogent considerations than carnality.

It was the record industry which, ever responsive to media need, plunged headlong into the honeytrap. In the mid-Eighties, stirred by Hollywood's spiral into flesh and gore movies, newspapers and television demanded an ever-higher quotient of juvenile pulchritude. There was no point giving space to a sublime pianist if she was fifty and frumpish; what editors wanted were budding stars who looked like sex-goddesses – and never mind how or what they played. Whether by chance or design, the ailing edifice of RCA obliged this appetite with a Canadian cellist called Ofra Harnoy.

RCA had virtually given up recording anyone except the flautist James Galway by this time, as it awaited take-over. It was never much of a nursery for new talent and had no career plan for débutants. What pushed Miss Harnoy on to the label was, principally, a pair of pouting lips and a body to die for. Born in 1965 in the Israeli truck-stop town of Hadera, she fast outgrew her native land and the musical confines of Canada. At seventeen, Harnoy became the youngest winner of the Concert Artists' Guild award in New York. Several cello authorities vouchsafed her gifts and serious reviewers were cautiously enthusiastic. This was not enough to get her to the top. Every record label had its resident cellist – Yo-Yo Ma at CBS, Rostropovich at EMI and DG, Lynn Harrell at Decca, Julian Lloyd Webber at Philips – and there was neither the repertoire nor the demand for them to sustain more than one cellist at a go.

But RCA had an idea. Pout those lips and bare those shoulders, they hinted, and there is no telling what might happen. Media interest perked up at the sight of Ofra in a flowing green frock and her discs started shifting in respectable numbers. Phase two of RCA's campaign was to dress her in something slinkier and plaster the cellist on roadside billboards in major conurbations. Irish brickies in London would turn up at dawn to find Ofra reclining languorously on the hoardings around their site. Euro-capital railway stations were dominated by her sultry figure. For two or three years, Ofra Harnoy became a half-familiar name and an RCA asset. But her concert career failed to prosper and a flirtation with Hollywood produced little more than screen tests. A whiff of sexiness had raised her name, but could take her no further. When RCA was bought out by the Germans, Harnoy's visibility diminished.

Still, the sex-lesson was not wasted. At every record label and many concert agencies, décolletages were deepened and limbs bared. Nadja Solerno-Sonnenberg, media-friendly 'bad girl' of the Juilliard Academy, was pictured in a derelict house in a skirt that barely covered her shapely thighs. To relaunch Anne-Sophie Mutter in America, publicist Sheila Porter put the German violinist in a strapless gown that, said Time magazine, accentuated 'the alluring curve of her shoulders and the luxurious corona of her billowing tresses'. Given that Miss Mutter had previously been perceived as Brünn-hilde's baby sister, this was no mean achievement for the publicist. 'I know what I'm doing with Anne-Sophie,' said the experienced Miss Porter, shrugging off New York Times gripes about the 'extra-musical thrust' of her violinist's projection.[44] Miss Mutter, however, was planning ahead to marriage, motherhood and a sedater approach to celebrity. Sex, in her case, was a transient diversion from serious industry and would not be attempted again.

There was some discomfort about the crassness of such methods, but classical music was merely responding to a world in which sex sold everything. When a bare bottom advertised mountain boots and bodily fluids could symbolise motor oil, why not use the same visual language to identify musical products? If simulated intercourse sold overpriced ice-cream, let the authentic sensuality of young performers attract a new audience to classics.

Before long, every hopeful with half an inch of overspill was being encouraged to show her all – or almost – by an industry that was seriously short of stars. Many of the soloists – female and male – who were hyped as sex-objects vanished after one or two recordings. As in pop music, marketing inventions were good for a quick hit, but no power on earth could preserve an overhyped product. More worried than ever, the music-biz dug deep into the conservatories and came up with a class of kid violinists the like of which had not been seen since the turn of the century. Midori, Sarah Chang, Helen Huang and heaven knows how many Asian youngsters were taken out of school and put on the concert circuit as they reached puberty. It did not take a Freudian analyst to detect something suspect in a line of teenies being paraded before a concert audience – and particularly a record-buying public – that was overwhelmingly male and middle-aged. The emphasis was unwaveringly focused on youthful precocity, but the undertext whiffed of unuttered temptations.

This procession reached its pallid nadir in the case of Vanessa-Mae Nicholson, a sixteen-year-old Singapore-born girl who had appeared with various orchestras and recorded concertos on a private label without exciting great expectations. Her press pack was filled with thrilling quotes from the *Victoria Regional News* (Canada), and the *Northamptonshire Chronicle and Echo*. In 1993 Vanessa-Mae shed her surname, teamed up with pop promoter Mel Bush and signed a contract with the classical division of EMI. Her début single was a rocked-up version of Johann Sebastian Bach's Toccata and Fugue in D Minor. It reached number eleven in the UK pop charts. When her Guadagnini violin was stolen from her Kensington home a fortnight before the record launch, Vanessa-Mae made the nightly news and tugged the nation's heart-strings (the instrument was later recovered). In this personable teenager, EMI had a potential revenue generator to pay for less profitable recordings.

Her next recording was to be Mendelssohn and Bruch. Having lost Nigel Kennedy to early retirement, EMI Classics was in acute need of an outreach artist. However, to project its young violinist EMI and Mel Bush employed imagery that broke all bounds of classical convention. Two pictures of

Vanessa-Mae were circulated for press use. The first showed her standing in a shallow, calm sea, holding a white violin and dressed in a flimsy wet shirt over a white see-through bodyform. Her pelvic hair was plainly visible. The second shot showed her on a ski-slope, dressed in a short halter and high-cut hotpants, bare legs akimbo. In a photo-session for the *Sun* newspaper, the girl wore slinky lingerie and gave a practised come-on look to the camera. What might have passed muster in a movie actress was truly shocking when coming from a supposedly classical musician with aspirations to spirituality and a record label with cultural pedigree.

Hardened arts editors blanched. 'The packaging of classical music now-adays relies as much on flashing knickers as on flashing artistic credentials. But the marketing campaign for young violin star Vanessa-Mae borders on kiddie-porn,'[45] commented the London *Evening Standard*. 'Keyed up by jungle rhythms blasting from a radio, she plants her knee-high boots four provocative feet apart and thrusts her hips at the camera, dangling an electric violin from her crotch,' reported *The Times* of one photo-session.[46] 'A lot of people have said the pictures are raunchy and sexy. But I'm only sixteen and I don't think that much about sex . . . If people find me sexy, it's not my fault,' said Vanessa-Mae. This was 'a young girl having a bit of fun in the water with her violin . . . the top just happened to get wet,' said her agent.[47] What she was doing in the sea with her fiddle was not that readily explained away.

The classical press elected, for once, to ignore urgent stimuli from the record industry and refused to display glossy features. EMI, for its part, wondered what the fuss was about. 'Get real,' said Roger Lewis, head of EMI Classics in the UK. 'What are being projected here are images you would associate with any new pop artist. For classical, she will be projected in a completely different way.'[48] Lewi sounded agitated, and with good reason. Vanessa-Mae, he confirmed, was 'one of our key strategic projects'.

In an attempt to assert her outreach credentials, she visited schools for a television show and played a Bruch concerto on a nation-wide tour, 'bringing live classical music to young people all around the UK,' she said.[49] Audiences were modest and the critics unimpressed. American sales of her début album were sluggish. EMI's press releases were still likening her to Menuhin, Heifetz and Kreisler, when the order came from corporate heights to retarget Vanessa-Mae as a pop star for whatever recording future she had left.

This was a morbid outcome for denizens of the dog and horn who, in the Vanessa-Mae venture, surrendered their virtue and gained little in return. The label that made the names of Caruso and Karajan, Menuhin and Perlman, was looking tacky and threadbare, ripe for corporate restructuring. Sex had failed to fertilise a cash-cow. In the subtle realms of classic recognition sex was too crude a marketing tool. What turned people on in serious music was not necessarily an erogenous prod – and, if it was, the audience was divided into straight, gay and all shades between. Sex, naughty or nice, was not going to make new classical stars. The gloom of that defeat was beginning to settle upon EMI when salvation was promised by a superior power.

The anticipated pre-Christmas rush of 1992 turned to a trickle, as millions were thrown out of work in the third winter of recession. Record stores were dismal mausoleums, the seasonal fare of Kathleen Battle carols and King's College chorales gathering dust on the top-priced shelf. People who came to browse were after a different kind of consolation. They kept asking for a record whose name few could remember. 'Have you got that symphony where the girl is singing but you don't catch what she says?' whispered customers, and assistants soon got to know what they meant.

The third symphony by Henryk Mikolai Górecki contained a devout finale, sung in Polish and containing inscriptions to the Virgin Mary found on the wall of a Gestapo dungeon. The music was exceedingly quiet and slow, in everything except popular ascent. Released in the United States by Warner in June 1992, it hit sixth spot in the classical charts after a few plays on public radio. At Christmas, it was one of *Time* magazine's three classical discs of the year.

Released in Britain in the summer, it topped the classical charts for months and reached number six in the pop album sales, one place behind Paul McCartney, selling six thousand copies a day. By the middle of 1993 world sales were nudging half a million. Three years on, with five rival recordings on the market, the three-quarter million mark was in sight. The unstoppable rise of Henryk Mikolai Górecki defied every tenet of record industry faith. No living symphonist had sold in tens of thousands since Dmitri Shostakovich in the Second World War, and none had neared a million. No composer from the contemporary music ghetto had ever penetrated the pop charts. No classical work had achieved high sales without a title and a performer that the public could memorise. What this humble Pole from Katowice was doing was turning the world's most sophisticated merchandising machine on its head and teaching it the virtue of simple things.

'I never asked that anyone should play my music,' said Górecki. 'Why do they buy it? Maybe they are looking for something . . .'[50] A Roman Catholic of sixty years old and prolonged physical infirmity, Górecki had spent his whole life in an industrial town under a cloud of noxious pollutants and official disapproval. He started out as an avant-gardist and, while admired by the Boulez circle, was banned by Stalinists at home. That oppression turned vicious when, in 1976, he abandoned atonality for the innocent affirmation of spirituality expressed by his third symphony. The tranquil work alienated western modernists and contributed to his dismissal as rector of the Katowice conservatory. A dozen years passed before communism tottered and Górecki found a British publisher who admired his unshakeable convictions. Through suffering and success, the composer insisted that his symphony was not a religious credo. 'In my understanding,' said Górecki, 'it is a love song.'

For the recording industry, however, it was nothing less than a revelation. In the recessed winter of 1992–3, the classical music business found God in a record store. Warner signed Górecki to a long-term contract and two western publishers went to war over his unassigned scores. Warner, which made its initial recording on a buy-out basis, paid no royalties to soprano Dawn Upshaw, conductor David Zinman or the London Sinfonietta. They were coining a fortune from Górecki and looking for more like him. In the next few years there were modest successes on various labels for composers writing in a similarly calming vein. The Greek-Orthodox Englishman John Taverner struck a chord with *The Protecting Veil* for cello and orchestra. The Georgian Giya Kancheli made waves with his sixth symphony, the Estonian Arvo Pärt with his choruses. Two long-cloistered Russians, Galina Ustvolskaya and Alemdar Karamanov, awoke the world with spiritual sounds. The late Frenchman Olivier Messiaen was promoted as a Catholic. The Scotsman James Macmillan scored a potent blend of minimalism, Catholicism and nationalism.

Had classical music gone religious? Is the Pope a Catholic? God had returned as the rock and salvation of the record industry – or so it seemed until you examined the sales figures, which showed that no other composer had achieved one-tenth of Górecki's astounding impact. Nor did any of Górecki's subsequent releases take off in any comparable manner, for he was the shyest and least promotable of modern heroes. It took an effort of will and a promise of future privacy to persuade him to attend one press conference in Brussels and make a single television documentary. His symphony, he said, was 'a miracle' and the record business was beginning to write it off as a one-off, when lightning struck for the second time.

During 1993, bean-counters at the Spanish branch of EMI noticed a startling demand for one of their older recordings. It consisted of monkish chants recorded a quarter of a century before and bought as a job-lot from a defunct Catholic label. Reissued as *Canto Gregoriano*, it was getting played on middle-of-road radio stations to help gridlocked motorists simmer down their road rage. Suddenly it became a best-seller. Months later, it was issued world-wide. In the next two years it sold five million records and produced EMI's best market figures for a decade. Apparently, God's songs achieved unprogrammed popularity at acid-house parties where DJs played them at dawn to send ravers obediently to their homes.

The monks, like Górecki, were untouched by success. They continued to rise at 5.30 each morning, to sing their prayers and till their fields at Santo Domingo de Silos. Unlike Górecki's musicians, they earned a three per cent royalty and were therefore able to install central heating at their eleventh-century monastery. There was some disquiet at increasing levels of tourism but in general the monks presented a picture of happiness, an ancient community living in harmony with the modern world. They even travelled occasionally to promote spin-off discs in plush hotels and restaurants. For the record industry, and EMI in particular, this was confirmation that God was on their side in the struggle against starlessness.

But like most revelations, there was to be no happy ending. In October 1995 the monks announced that they wanted nothing more to do with the organised record industry. 'EMI was interested only in making money, not in respecting our culture,' said their choirmaster, Father Jose Luis Angulo. Any future releases, he intimated, would be channelled through Jade, an obscure religious label. Its producer, Alejandro Masso, told Spanish journalists, 'The monks didn't even want to talk to EMI any more. They feel the Gregorian chant is being degraded with people using their holy music for dancing, getting stoned and porn.'

EMI rejected the assertion, but conceded that it was powerless to protect sanctity after it appeared on record. 'We're a record company: it's our job to market and sell as many [copies] as possible. We've never given any licence to a porn company but, frankly, once the records are sold they are out of our control,' said EMI Spain's business director, Pablo Arrabal.[51] And with that admission, the hopes for a musical-religious revival petered out. For even if the public was seeking God through the wonders of classical music, the record industry – which interfaced with all the impurities of movies, television and media, and was itself demonstrably sex-obsessed – was an unsuitable instrument for the cleansing of souls. It was high time, said the monks, for the Church to reclaim its musical glories and restore them to the faithful in dedicated places of worship.

That clanged like a giant nail in the coffin of classical recording. Starless, sexless and now declared godless, it was condemned to wander like a thrice-wounded nomad, scanning the musical horizons for the next mirage.

NOTES

1 Fingleton, p. 179
2 Umbach, pp. 67–9
3 letter to the author, and others, dated 15 May 1987
4 Pavarotti/*World*, p. 263
5 interview with Hunter Davies, *Mail on Sunday*, *You* magazine, nd
6 op. cit., p. 50
7 *Daily Telegraph*, 3 March 1992
8 *Daily Telegraph*, 13 August 1991, p. 10
9 Pavarotti/*Story*, p. 100
10 Culshaw, pp. 345–6
11 Mayer, p. 93
12 author's interviews
13 Merle Hubbard, author's interview
14 Peter G. Davis, comments to the author
15 Michael Walsh, 'Snakeoil and the Fat Man', *New York* magazine, 13 November 1995
16 Pavarotti/*Story*, p. 162
17 op. cit., p. 102
18 Mayer, p. 131
19 Pavarotti/*Story*, p. 165
20 Adua Pavarotti, pp. 131–2
21 interview with Robert Turnbull, *Sunday Telegraph*, nd
22 all Hubbard quotes: author's interview
23 Pavarotti/*Story*, pp. 167–8
24 All Domingo quotes: author's interview, Salzburg 1991
25 *Sunday Times Magazine*, 22 October 1989, p. 26
26 author's interview
27 Pavarotti/*World*, p. 52
28 Pavarotti/*World*, p. 53
29 author's interview
30 Pavarotti/*World*, p. 63
31 *Daily Telegraph*, 12 March 1994
32 loc. cit.
33 *Guardian*, 12 October 1995, p. 9
34 interview with Melvyn Bragg, *South Bank Show*, LWT productions, transmitted 8 October 1995
35 Merle Hubbard, author's interview
36 Adua Pavarotti, p. 156
37 all Kennedy quotes from author's interviews, 1991–3
38 Roger Lewis, author's interview
39 all Stanley quotes: author's interview, 1994
40 Nigel Kennedy, *Always Playing* (Weidenfeld & Nicolson, London) 1991, p. 34
41 Kennedy, op. cit. p. 35
42 the words of *Strad's* North America editor, Dennis Rooney
43 author's interview
44 Barbara Jepson, 'The Strapless Violinist', *Vanity Fair*, February 1990, p. 196
45 *Standard*, 15 December 1994, p. 42
46 Joanna Pitman, 'Bow belle', *Times Magazine*, 25 February 1995, p. 9
47 *The Times*, loc. cit.
48 author's interview
49 interview with *Classic FM* magazine, February 1995
50 Górecki comments from conversations with the author, 1993–4
51 *Sunday Times*, 15 May 1995, p. 22

IV

. . . AND THE CORPORATE
MURDER OF CLA$$ICAL MUSIC

GOING OFF THE RECORD

A t one in the morning, when London sleeps, I look out of my loft window and see the lights still blazing at Abbey Road. No one makes music at that time of night and the suits that run the record business are all safely abed, but somewhere in the bowels of the famous studios sits a lone producer tinkering, in his own unpaid time, with an almost-perfect symphonic recording, striving into the small hours for the eternally unattainable.

Record producers are the unsung heroes of classical music. Poorly paid, overworked and lacking the clout of pop artist handlers, the classical producer is lucky to get his or her name spelled correctly – or at all – on the record sleeve. Yet, more than any conductor, soloist or orchestra, the producer is responsible for what we hear on the record, and many regard that responsibility as sacred. I have known producers to throw up their jobs rather than condone a false note or work with an inferior artist. I have heard them tell celebrated conductors to go home and learn their score. When Claudio Abbado sought to delay the release of *Boris Godunov* over a bad bassoon note, it was the producer who told him bluntly and in front of the entire Berlin Philharmonic Orchestra that the label had spent a million dollars on his pet project and if any flaws had got through they were nobody's fault but his own. The outraged conductor rushed to head office demanding the producer's head; he was told that the man would be rewarded and promoted for doing his job properly.

Conflicts of this kind are less common than one might expect. Intelligent artists – Abbado wept publicly on the death of Rainer Brock, his Deutsche Grammophon recording partner – generally respect their producers' expertise and trust them on the final cut. Bernard Haitink, at a Philips party for his sixtieth birthday, credited his veteran producer, Völker Straus, for any success he had enjoyed on record.

As salaried staff in a star-led industry, producers are kept out of the public limelight. But theirs is the hand that guides the stars and theirs the personality that stamps classical labels with a mark of authority. In conductor-producer teams, it is often difficult to determine which is the more creative influence – Georg Solti, or John Culshaw in the Decca *Ring* cycle? Leonard Bernstein, or John McClure in a host of CBS recordings? Culshaw was responsible for inventing the much-praised Decca Sound, an amalgam of technical ingenuity, *esprit de corps* and shrewd publicity. Brock turned DG into the pianistic label *par excellence*. EMI was moulded by a line of producers who made hard-working British orchestras sound like heavenly ensembles. Whoever is nominally head of a record label, it is the producers who pick the talent, the venue and the technical team, deciding the acoustic and human character of each and every recording. A good producer can make or break a label – and there has never been an excess of good producers.

The father of the guild was Fred Gaisberg, a Washington schoolboy who squeezed into Emile Berliner's bedroom one day in 1891 to watch the great inventor cut the first gramophone record. Gaisberg was earning pocket money playing piano accompaniments to singers as they recorded cumbersome cylinders for the Columbia Phonograph Company, which held the licence to Thomas Edison's patent. Recognising the superiority of Berliner's flat disc, Gaisberg did not hesitate when the cranky immigrant offered him a job as piano player and talent scout. Eight years later, aged twenty-six, Gaisberg was sent to Europe as Chief Recorder. He shared a ship berth with Berliner's nephew, who was setting up a pressing plant at the family's Hanover base – the future Deutsche Grammophon Gesellschaft, or DGG.[1]

Berliner's London firm, incorporated as the Gramophone Company, had acquired as its trademark Francis Barraud's kitsch painting of a dog and horn, promoting itself as 'His Master's Voice'. Gaisberg took a small room in the Maiden Lane offices and set up his gear. By Christmas 1900 the Gramophone Company had a catalogue of five thousand records, a tribute to Gaisberg's work ethic and the eclecticism of foreign reps, who inclined their horns to Hindi singers and Hebrew cantors. In the scratchy dawn of recording, anything sold. A Red Label (or Seal) was attached to premium artistry and Gaisberg went searching for star quality.

In March 1902, he checked in at Spatz's hotel in Milan, where Verdi had died the year before. Signor Spatz was the father-in-law of Umberto Giordano, composer of *Andrea Chénier* and *Fedora*, and his premises were popular with singers. Gaisberg, with his brother Will and a local gramophone agent, went off to see Alberto Franchetti's *Germania*, an overblown piece of nationalism that had just opened at La Scala to huge acclaim. Unable to get tickets, they invaded an aristocrat's box, were thrown out and narrowly avoided fighting a duel. The following night, sitting through the full opera, Gaisberg was overwhelmed by its tenor, a Neapolitan of twenty-nine in only his second season on stage. He sent an emissary to ask what fee the man would require for recording ten songs. The answer was one hundred pounds sterling. 'In those days, these were really staggering terms,' wrote Gaisberg, 'but I transmitted them to London with a strong recommendation . . . A cabled reply came back quickly: *Fee exorbitant, forbid you to record*.' Gaisberg crumpled the telegram and summoned Enrico Caruso to his hotel. On the sunny afternoon of 18 March 1902 Caruso, 'debonair and fresh, sauntered into our studio and in exactly two hours sang ten arias to the piano accompaniment of Maestro Cottone.'[2] He was paid one hundred pounds and over the next twenty years earned a million more from records. His ten songs are still selling strongly on compact disc.

The records, released for his Covent Garden and Metropolitan Opera débuts, proved unerringly close to reality. Caruso's voice possessed a singularity of richness that pierced the crackle of primitive players. He was the first star of the gramophone and, in many ways, the greatest — generous in voice and heart, scattering his wealth among dozens of dependents and struggling to learn new roles even as he lay dying. He was a unique performer, universally adored, the first to break down the walls of the opera house and embrace a world audience. His recordings, said Gaisberg, 'made the gramophone'. Without him, it might have gone the way of the barrel-organ and pianola.

After Caruso, every other singer wanted to get on record. Francesco Tamagno, Verdi's Otello, was the hit of 1903; Nellie Melba signed the next year, on tough terms. She demanded a mauve label all to herself and the selling price of a guinea per record, one shilling more than anyone else. She refused to visit Gaisberg's studio; the equipment had to be carried round to her drawing-room in Great Cumberland Place. In 1906 Adelina Patti was wheedled out of rural retirement to trill into Gaisberg's horn at her castle in Wales. She was sixty-three years old and enchanted by the sound of her own voice. On hearing the records she exclaimed: '*Maintenant je sais pourquois je suis Patti!*' (Now I know *why* I am Patti!)

Gaisberg journeyed to St Petersburg to record the stars of the Maryinsky Theatre, headed by the mighty bass, Feodor Chaliapin. He turned Luisa Tetrazzini into a household name and ghosted a book in her name. He was the making of the Irish tenor John McCormack, the mentor of Beniamino Gigli. He recorded Paderewski and Kreisler, Mascagni and Prokofiev, Artur Schnabel and Arthur Nikisch. Remarkably, he does not rate a mention in any of their memoirs, existing, it seems, as no more than a shadow on the retina of their artistic vision.

Artists of their era saw recording as a way to earn money, big money. Mischa Elman in 1913 netted thirty-five thousand dollars in record royalties; Fritz Kreisler, ten years later, was getting an annual cheque for a hundred and seventy-five thousand dollars. Most of the money came from single discs consisting of a short encore that artists regarded as trivial. Few bothered to rehearse for their recording sessions and Gaisberg counted no more in their estimation than a box-office clerk at Queen's Hall.

He never ventured an artistic opinion. It took all his courage to beg Patti to stay close to the horn. 'She did not like this and was most indignant, but later when she heard the lovely records she showed her joy just like a child and forgave me my impertinence.' Patti, he felt, 'was the only real diva I have ever met – the only singer who had no flaws for which to apologise'.[3] His brother Will (who died of influenza in the 1918 epidemic) 'regarded artists as children and would mother them all',[4] but Fred revered them and rarely overcame his inhibitions. Once, when Schnabel was having technical difficulties (as he often did) in a Beethoven sonata, Gaisberg broke the tension by strolling over to the piano and doing a soft-shoe vaudeville shuffle that plunged everyone into giggles. After a short tea-break, the sonata was successfully completed.

A myopic bachelor with a toothbrush moustache, Fred Gaisberg was one of those men who live for their work. His methods were simple, his motives pure and his sense of history uncannily prescient. He recorded Bruno Walter conducting Mahler's ninth symphony in Vienna and Pablo Casals playing Dvořák's cello concerto in Prague, moments before the Nazis destroyed the essence of *Mitteleuropa*. When war broke out and he went into reluctant retirement, Gaisberg had given half a century to the record industry and seen its output exceed a quarter of a million titles. His contribution was historically and numerically the most significant of any man's on either side of the Atlantic – but he was never appointed to the board. He was a modest cog in a media machine that, after the Wall Street crash, saw the senior labels, Red Seal and

Columbia, subsidiarised by the RCA and CBS megaliths and their British outposts merged into Electrical and Musical Industries (EMI). Gaisberg saw his industry overshadowed by broadcasting, his techniques outmoded by technology and his pioneership usurped by his own office-boy.

'I was the first of what are called "producers" of records,' bragged Walter Legge, probably the most disagreeable personage ever to intrude upon musical performance. A Wagner buff and lover of all things German, Legge never mastered an instrument but professed an insuppressable urge to make his mark on music. He found his slot in the record world. 'Before I established myself and my ideas,' said Legge, 'the attitude of recording managers of all companies was "we are in the studio to record as well as we can wax what the artists habitually do in the opera house or on the concert platform." My predecessor Fred Gaisberg told me, "We are out to make sound photographs of as many sides as we can get during each session." My ideas were different. *It was my aim to make records that would set the standards by which public performances and the artists of the future would be judged.*'[5]

The task that Legge set himself was to make records seem 'superior' to live performance: 'I decided that recording must be a collaboration between artists and what are now called producers. I wanted better results than are normally possible in public performance: I was determined to put on to disc the best that artists could do under the best possible conditions.'[6]

The son of a Shepherds Bush tailor, Legge landed a job in 1926 with the Gramophone Company as a product demonstrator to provincial audiences. The job ended within weeks when the twenty-year-old salesman was heard disparaging some of the discs he played. Unfazed by dismissal, Legge reapplied in 1929 to become Gaisberg's factotum and sleeve-note writer. 'Without any guile or malice in his make-up, Gaisberg readily allowed Walter to turn up at recordings of special interest,' recalled Legge's sister.[7] The senior producer soon had reason to regret his generosity when Legge went over his head in 1930 with an irresistible proposal to the company's top management. Why not eliminate the financial risk from making records, said Legge, by getting customers to pay for them in advance? It would, for example, take thirty shillings from five hundred subscribers to fund a première recording of the sepulchral songs of Hugo Wolf. To general surprise, Legge hit this target in two months – thanks to a mysterious rush of one hundred and eleven subscriptions from Japan and a flagrant puff in the *Sunday Times* by the critic Ernest Newman, who was Wolf's sole English biographer.

Legge's Wolf Society series, sung by the luminous Elena Gerhardt, was issued in April 1932. He then formed a Beethoven Sonata Society with Artur Schnabel as pianist and a Mozart Opera Society, which captured the early Glyndebourne casts. The Society gimmick was a goldmine. Bach's organ music was recorded in France by Albert Schweitzer and his cello suites by Pablo Casals; Sir Thomas Beecham recorded Society issues of Delius and Sibelius; the complete Haydn quartets were produced in Belgium; Kreisler and Franz Rupp played the Beethoven violin-and-piano sonatas. The première recording of Mahler's *Das Lied von der Erde* was conducted by Bruno Walter on advance subscription without costing EMI a penny. Three volumes of Schnabel's Beethoven netted eighty thousand pounds. Legge, in his mid-twenties, became the company's blue-eyed boy.

A tubby little chainsmoker, prematurely aged in a permanently rumpled suit, he was the least congenial of colleagues. In the corridors, he was 'forever fumbling with the secretaries'; a junior associate once found him 'giving dictation with his flies wide open'. He liked to pose as a Don Juan; by most accounts he preyed on vulnerable girls in his ambit, EMI clerical staff and Covent Garden soubrettes who could be sacked or promoted on his say so. Memos from Legge were like misguided missiles. 'You seem to be hopping, bumbling and fumbling mad,' he swiped at a junior.[8] He particularly loathed the Columbia sister-label within EMI and its ever-courteous chief producer, David Bicknell. Where Gaisberg and Bicknell cultivated a team spirit, Legge refused to help carry sound equipment and erected a class barrier between producer and sound engineers. He held orchestral musicians in contempt and boasted he would replace any player if he found one who was five per cent better.

A musician who met him on the street told Gaisberg's secretary that Legge had not seemed as vile as everyone said he was. 'He never is,' she replied tartly, '*not the first time.*' From the lash of his tongue he exempted two species – the artists who made his name and the critics who sustained it. Ernest Newman, the senior English Wagnerian and *Sunday Times* columnist, was best man at Legge's wedding to the German soprano Elisabeth Schwarzkopf (his first marriage, to the Glyndebourne mezzo Nancy Evans, ended in divorce). Legge formed a mutual admiration pact with Newman in print, though in private Newman did not conceal his distaste. Legge's, he once said, 'is the tragedy of a brilliant brain in a twisted mind'.[9] Neville Cardus, the most widely read British critic, 'let it be known that Legge was one of his pet aversions'.[10] His know-all mien, caustic wit and naked Machiavellianism put Legge beyond the pale of normal intercourse – though not beyond Sir Thomas Beecham, supreme intriguer in English music, who employed him as assistant artistic director in his pre-war Covent Garden seasons. Legge blatantly imitated Beecham's lordly manner. The conductor described him as 'a mass of egregious fatuity'.[11] Beecham's dazzling wit and luminous art allowed him to get away with blue murder. Legge's wit was malicious and his art invisible.

When Beecham fled his country in its hour of need, Legge stepped into his shoes as music provider for the masses, forming a concerts network for ENSA, the armed forces' entertainment organisation. Its reception was so intense, and the performers so grateful to Legge for giving them wartime work, that he was uniquely positioned on VE-Day to meet a hugely increased demand for cultural consolations. Together with his ENSA colleague Joan Ingpen, a pianist working in marine insurance, and the cellist James Whitehead, Legge rounded up the best players they had met in the war into a new orchestra, the Philharmonia. Beecham, returned from his American haven, conducted its all-Mozart launch, but was soon sent packing by Legge. This was to be Legge's orchestra, and there was room for only one maestro. Whomever he engaged to conduct the Philharmonia, Legge would stand beside him in rehearsal and tell the orchestra what *he* wanted. The Birmingham conductor, George Weldon, got so fed up with this, recalled Ingpen, that he challenged Legge to conduct a recording himself. For weeks he practised in private, but when it came to facing the orchestra he threw down the baton in embarrassment. Legge was constitutionally incapable of producing a musical gesture.

Although he remained a full-time employee and ran his orchestra on EMI's time, the company 'appeared to ignore'[12] the Philharmonia. Legge kept it going with work from the busy British film industry, but by 1947 he was putting on public concerts that his employers dared not miss. Richard Strauss, octogenarian and impecunious, came to conduct the Philharmonia at Ingpen's invitation; Furtwängler responded to a summons from Legge. The rest of the season was led by Issay Dobrowen, Alceo Galliera and Paul Kletzki, and much of it was recorded by Legge for EMI.

Once Herbert von Karajan was released from post-Nazi limbo, Legge used him as his mainstay conductor. There was a polish to the playing and a crispness to the sound in his Philharmonia recordings that was a credit to both men and outshone anything on the market. Toscanini, jealous of the glistening sound, sailed over to conduct the Philharmonia. Legge ventured into America, setting up Angel Records with Dario and Dorle Soria. He retrieved Otto Klemperer from the doldrums of exile to perform late-romantic masterpieces. Guido Cantelli and Carlo Maria Giulini added glamour and style to the London concert scene. The Philharmonia was cock of the cockney walk and Legge the pride of his profession. He 'made himself exceptionally unpopular at times,' wrote John Culshaw, 'yet over and over again he made records which were the envy of us all'.[13]

But the dark side of Legge left an even larger residue. Culshaw privately called him 'Decca's best friend – we picked up all the artists he fell out with'. 'He was a kind of megalomaniac,' said Joan Ingpen, who was evicted from the Philharmonia by Legge's paranoia. Ingpen was a strong-minded woman who, alongside the Philharmonia, set up and ran a concert agency representing, among others, the much sought-after Miss Schwarzkopf. Legge became anxious that Ingpen's husband, the Viennese agent Alfred Dietz, was passing on too much information about his wife and his other discovery, Herbert von Karajan. 'Once Karajan came on the scene, Walter wanted everything,' said Ingpen. 'He engineered an almighty row and got rid of me from the Philharmonia.'

The cause was trivial, a trumped-up accusation that Ingpen was withholding work from Schwarzkopf. After a blazing confrontation, Ingpen was made to sell Legge her forty per cent shareholding in the Philharmonia in exchange for his forty per cent share in her agency and a lump sum. EMI seemed unaware that Legge was the orchestra's sole owner, or that he had previously been hiring artists from an agency that he co-owned. Having got rid of Ingpen, Legge used his EMI clout to punish her. 'When we had the final bust-up,' Ingpen reported, 'he told my artists they wouldn't get their EMI contracts renewed if they stayed with me. He warned them that things tended to happen to people who crossed him.'[14] Luckily for Ingpen, she discovered Joan Sutherland and took her straight to Decca.

Within the record world Legge was roundly detested. For a whole Bayreuth month he sat shoulder to shoulder with Culshaw's Decca team without once assaying a 'Good Morning'. This was not absent-mindedness or bad manners; Legge simply relished other people's unease. At EMI he was forever scheming to sabotage other producers' projects. At the dawn of stereo, EMI found themselves unable to produce a major choral recording because Legge had sequestered all its stereo equipment for a solo recital by his precious wife.

His power lay with Karajan, Schwarzkopf – who called him 'my Svengali' – and Maria Callas who was quoted in EMI publicity releases praising Legge's musical judgement. Yet he was unfulfilled. The job he longed for was to be 'in control of opera' at Covent Garden, where he could imprint his ideas on live performances of the greatest living artists. After running a campaign of withering whispers against the Royal Opera House, he was co-opted in 1958 as a non-executive director on the assumption that he could do less harm from within. That illusion was soon dispelled as Legge sought to usurp authority. 'Having been on the Board for five months,' he blustered, 'no official of the theatre has told me what operas we are doing next season, what casts have been engaged or what casts it is proposed to engage. It seems to me quite ridiculous to have me on the Board if I am not to be consulted on these things, in which I have an acknowledged expertise.'[15] It should be noted that he had never cast a live opera in his life.

Legge, wrote a co-director's wife, 'was an extremely dangerous man. Widely experienced and with impeccable taste in music, he possessed a certain coarse charm and wit, but was nevertheless arrogant, unreliable and with a contempt for other people easily aroused.'[16] He attended few meetings, preferring to pepper the chairman, Lord Drogheda, with aggressive memoranda. Some directors, like the philosopher Sir Isaiah Berlin, found his nihilism mentally stimulating; others saw him as a flatulent nuisance. When his tirades were exhausted he resigned gracelessly, claiming that Covent Garden had only appointed him to get their hands on his wife. Schwarzkopf, in fact, quit the house shortly after he joined, dismayed at press attacks on her coquettish Marschallin in *Der Rosenkavalier*, a role she had been moulded in by Legge.

In June 1963, resentful and bored, Legge wrote EMI a letter of resignation. To his evident surprise it was accepted with relief. He had never realised how much a man of his vitality and venom could be detested in a dusty British boardroom. Nine months later, while working out his notice, he sacked the Philharmonia. 'It is impossible for me to express my regret that this is necessary,' he wrote to the musicians, 'I feel as if I am cutting out my own heart from my living body; but better that than that the name Philharmonia, which has been representative of a new and higher standard of performance than Britain has ever had, should deteriorate.' The inference from this phoney martyrdom was that if *he* was not in charge, the Philharmonia would damage its reputation. The orchestra was his company; he had every right to liquidate it.

The first the players heard of their dismissal was on the BBC's eight o'clock morning news. 'It came as a complete shock,' recalled the clarinettist Basil Tschaikov. 'The orchestra would have ceased to exist in a fortnight if Klemperer had not thrown his lot in with us.'[17] The august conductor, apprised of the crisis while recording *Messiah*, urged the players to resist. A co-operative was formed, backers were found and the band played on. Legge did everything in his power to stop them. He wound up the company and in 1968 sold his shares to EMI for fifty-three thousand pounds (equivalent to half a million in 1996 values). The name 'Philharmonia' was sold on to a Chinese conductor, Ling Tung, for use on his neighbourhood orchestra in downtown Philadelphia. The London musicians, unable to use their own name, were forced to play as the 'New Philharmonia'. 'I ran the Philharmonia as a benevolent dictatorship,' lied Legge,[18] whose tyranny was as manifest as his altruism was fake. Unknown to the players, he received a five-per-cent royalty on every Philharmonia recording. As the orchestra's sole owner, he knew the figures to be accurate, having previously approved them at EMI.

One cause of his resignation, never revealed before, is that EMI awoke to Legge's double-dealings. The chairman, Sir Joseph Lockwood, took legal advice and was told that Legge was doing nothing criminal in hiring his own orchestra to EMI, but the time he spent on the Philharmonia might be considered a breach of his employment contract. Faced with an ultimatum to give up his job or his royalties, Legge took the money and left. His income from US sales of Philharmonia recordings alone amounted to seventy-five thousand pounds a year. When Lockwood later held a full inquiry, he found that every financial document signed by Legge relating to the Philharmonia had vanished from the files.

In her loyal memoir, Schwarzkopf maintains that Legge was shabbily treated. 'When one realizes that his salary in 1953 was only four thousand pounds per annum, it is quite astonishing that Walter didn't pack up, take along some of the artists he had brought to EMI . . . and move on.'[19] As it happens, Legge was well paid; a staff producer, in 1953, could afford to run a car on one-eighth of his salary. As for his employment prospects, Legge found himself in enforced idleness, friendless and unwanted. Karajan, for whom his usefulness had expired, gave orders to his secretaries not to let him past the door and simultaneously stopped engaging Schwarzkopf for his productions. Schwarzkopf, tenderly solicitous, took her husband on tour as her constant companion. In later years, she privately opined that her live recordings were a truer reflection of her art than the studio work – suggesting that all those hours of ultra-refinement with Legge could not match the stimulus of a real audience. When their retirement was being planned, Legge favoured Californian sunshine but Schwarzkopf overruled him and they settled in Switzerland. Legge was left irritably cultivating his Swiss garden until his death in 1979, at the age of seventy-two. 'He was an arch-shit,' said the festival director Sir Ian Hunter, 'but charming company at dinner.'[20]

The eulogies were fulsome. He had 'probably done more than anyone else alive to raise standards of musical performance', said the influential critic Andrew Porter. 'The world owes him a debt for having sought out, sifted, promulgated and preserved for posterity the best in mid-twentieth century musical culture.'[21] Tributes of this kind established Legge's posthumous stature. They are, in essence, spurious. Legge's contribution to mid-century culture was minimal. His favourite British composer was William Walton; he loathed most contemporary music and chose performers as reactionary as himself. His concept of perfection was anti-art. Getting it right on record was what mattered to Legge. He sought to supplant the unpredictability of concerts with a synthetic correctness stitched together on the editing table. Each recording was meant to be the 'definitive' performance for its time, a totalitarian notion that appealed most to Karajan. Klemperer, however, dissented. 'Listening to a recording,' he growled, 'is like going to bed with a *photograph* of Marilyn Monroe.' Real art, as real artists know, is a matter of chance and compromise, of error and inspiration.

'To Otto Klemperer the making of records was an economic necessity,' said his daughter, Lotte, 'and in the making of them he was always uncomfortably aware of the lie that any so-called final statement embodies. Such thoughts, considerations, were not in Legge, as [Schwarzkopf's] book makes all too clear. Perhaps the difference is best explained by Legge's statement about himself: "I'm a midwife to music." By Klemperer's lights, an artist – conductor, instrumentalist, singer – could be midwife to music (though it's most unlikely he would have used this simile) – but a record producer would be at best a midwife to *the business of music*.'[22]

No record producer would ever hold such power again – Karajan saw to that. Taking command of Berlin, Vienna and Salzburg in 1955, the *übermaestro* inherited institutional contracts with Deutsche Grammophon and set about turning the German label into a world leader. Risen from Third Reich ruins and owned by the Siemens industrial group, DG was enjoying the early fruits of the German economic miracle when Karajan dictated a global agenda. Starting with his 1962 Berlin Beethoven cycle in stereophonic sound, he positioned himself and the yellow label in the public ear as models of acoustic excellence and artistic authority.

A techno-freak who believed that science and industry would reveal the ultimate solutions of artistic creation, he subjected the symphonic and operatic repertoire to continuous sonic upgrading. Four times he repeated the Beethoven symphonies on DG, each time in an enhanced format: digital LP, videotape, CD, laserdisc. By the time of his death, in July 1989, Karajan accounted for one-third of DG's sales and the label held twenty per cent of the world market, overtaking all competitors.

Alongside his DG commitments, Karajan recorded concurrently with

Decca and RCA, or EMI, attracted by their overseas markets and, in Decca's case, by its distinctively spatial acoustic that made stereo seem so much more vivid. Legge's illusory perfectionism and Decca's realism were the base ingredients of the 'Karajan sound' – not that admiration ever stopped him from sabotaging other labels. He tried to stop Decca recording the *Ring* by block-booking the Vienna Philharmonic for his own projects. He left EMI heavily in the red on his recordings. When DG chiefs wearied of his tyranny he wooed the Japanese. Throughout a thirty-five-year hegemony, he ruled the record industry divisively and brooked no interference. Instead of letting producers run sound tests before rolling their tapes he began recording as soon as he entered the podium and ordered changes after hearing the first take. 'If he had agreed to rehearse for as little as ten minutes at the start of a session, he might have saved himself and a lot of other people from wasted energy,'[23] wrote Decca's John Culshaw. For Karajan, it was just another way of exercising muscle. He demanded absolute obedience from record personnel and, as his empire grew, prostrate obeisance. Setting one company off against another, he controlled the introduction of new technology and ensured that he was always the first to use it. Swamping the stores with almost nine hundred recordings, continuously reissued, he monopolised the market and homogenised music.

At almost precisely the same moment in the United States, a new force leaped on to the deck. In 1956 Leonard Bernstein became the first native-born conductor to head a major American orchestra. Brash, handsome and a star of the *Omnibus* cultural show on CBS television, Bernstein was wanted by both big US labels. He had cut some early records for RCA, but inclined temperamentally towards the classier Columbia, the so-called 'Tiffany network' which had a long-standing Judson contract with the New York Philharmonic.

For twenty years Columbia Records had lagged behind RCA Victor which, backed by NBC Radio, built an orchestra for Arturo Toscanini and convinced America of his invincibility. So long as Maestro conducted, all other musicians were minims. RCA also had exclusivity with the Boston Symphony Orchestra and a solid partnership with Philadelphia and Eugene Ormandy. In 1944 Columbia poached Philadelphia and Ormandy from RCA to create a core orchestral catalogue of more than three hundred recordings over the next quarter-century. In addition, the label paid Judson for New York Philharmonic recordings with Dmitri Mitropoulos and Bruno Walter. Taken together, it was a credible and modestly profitable enterprise, but no match for the Toscanini machine. All that was about to change.

In the summer that Bernstein raised his baton in New York, a new president took office at Columbia Records. Goddard Lieberson was the staff producer behind the long-playing record invented by a CBS scientist, Peter Goldmark, nephew of the romantic Viennese composer. Lieberson argued a demoralised top brass into spending a quarter of a million dollars on developing a vinyl LP which rotated thirty-three times a minute and could embrace a whole symphony. Its launch in 1949 rattled RCA, which responded with a forty-five-rpm, four-minute disc. After a brief but entertaining 'battle of the speeds', defeat was conceded when Toscanini heard that Bruno Walter was recording symphonies that did not have to be turned over in mid-theme. RCA went scuttling to the underdog label for a licence to manufacture LPs and Lieberson was wreathed in glory.

A former composer, Lieberson believed in the music of the future. 'In 1940, though still in a subordinate position at Columbia Records, he managed to record Le Sacre du Printemps and Pierrot Lunaire conducted by their respective composers, an event that changed the highest level of musical awareness in America,' wrote Robert Craft.[24] 'He understood music fairly well and loved to be taken for a musical intellectual,' said the violinist Nathan Milstein. 'But scratch the surface and you'd find a businessman. His genius at keeping a balance between music and commerce took him to the top of Columbia Records.'[25] Once there, he signed Stravinsky to record his entire musical output, retrieved Charles Ives from oblivion, lured the iconoclastic pianists Vladimir Horowitz and Glenn Gould to the label, protected the slow-selling Duke Ellington and was first backstage with a contract to record any Broadway hit. His original-cast album of My Fair Lady sold five million records in 1957 and helped pay for comprehensive Schoenberg and Webern editions.

He told Schuyler Chapin, his Masterworks executive, 'This company makes a lot of money out of music – it's your job to pay back the debt.' Lieberson made the popular pay for the unpopular. He was a liberal thinker whose far-sightedness far outshone the restrictive, reactionary notions of Walter Legge. 'He was the best boss you could ever imagine,' said Chapin, who went on to become general manager of the Metropolitan Opera and Culture Commissioner for the City of New York. Chapin once slunk into Lieberson's office, resignation letter in hand, after spending sixty-five thousand dollars on live recordings by Sviatoslav Richter that the pianist refused to have released. Lieberson heard him out, his head buried in a sheaf of papers. When Chapin had finished and was waiting to be fired, all Lieberson said was, 'Well, you'll never make that mistake again.' For a boss like that, said Chapin, 'You would have jumped off the Empire State Building without a parachute.'[26]

English-born and expensively dressed, Lieberson owned a box at the Met and married George Balanchine's ex-wife, the dancer Vera Zorina. Unlike other record producers, he was a fully accredited member of the social élite. He signed his letters 'God' and knew everyone who was culturally anyone, from Somerset Maugham to Jacqueline Kennedy. Leopold Stokowski pronounced his name 'God-ahr', like the French film-maker.

As president of Columbia Records, he offered Leonard Bernstein a twenty-year contract 'to record anything he pleased at any time he desired to do so'.[27] The conductor took him at his word and set about recording the entire concert repertoire from Bach to Bartók. Over Chapin's protests, he recorded Liszt's monumental, unmemorable *Faust* symphony – 'a sales disaster'.[28] No one at the company could stop him doing as he pleased once Lieberson had given him the green light. His Sibelius series covered an over-recorded composer who was going out of fashion, his Beethoven was gratingly immature. On the credit side, he announced that Mahler's time had come at last and recorded an historic cycle of symphonies. His Shostakovich performances were compelling and he put more American composers on the map than any other conductor.

During the course of one year he made a new recording every week, earning an advance of three to five thousand dollars on each, up to quarter of a million dollars that would take decades to earn back. Other top conductors, like his teacher Fritz Reiner at the Chicago Symphony Orchestra, did not gross more than twenty thousand a year from recordings. Bernstein's contract with the Philharmonic gave him thirty per cent of its CBS royalties, reduced to twenty per cent when a soloist was engaged.[29] This may help explain why Bernstein played the solo part in so many concertos when a better pianist might have boosted sales.

The volume looked impressive, reaching four hundred thousand albums a year by 1969. But when accountants came to look at dollars and common sense, they found that the only individual Bernstein discs to make money were his Christmas specials – Tchaikovsky war-horses and sentimental lollipops. Given the same promotion, these records could have been made at a tenth of the cost with a hick conductor and Pomeranian orchestra and sold in equal numbers.

When he burst into opera, the costs ran amok. *Der Rosenkavalier* and *Falstaff*, produced in Vienna, spent one hundred thousand dollars each. His plan to record *Carmen* at the Met in 1973 at twice the price caused Lieberson's successors at CBS to demur. Bernstein took his project to Deutsche Grammophon and spent the rest of his career running up bills at the yellow label. The backlog he built up in New York was so vast that CBS were still issuing new Bernstein releases more than twenty years after his departure. His discs were heavily outsold by Ormandy's, which in 1995 still netted Philadelphia two hundred and fifty thousand dollars a year.

Lieberson, by letting Lenny loose, had precipitated economic madness across the entire American industry, and the consequences were not slow to follow. RCA, in 1968, matching its competitor dollar for dollar, gave the veteran Eugene Ormandy carte blanche to re-record his lifetime repertoire in stereo with the Philadelphia Orchestra. Before it let Ormandy go, CBS rush-recorded all the popular repertoire, leaving little for him to do on RCA. After spending two million dollars and five years making records young Americans would never want to buy, RCA pulled out of Philadelphia in 1973 and stopped orchestral recordings altogether. CBS, lacking the incentive of domestic rivalry, wound down its contracts with the Cleveland Orchestra and New York Philharmonic. By 1980, no American orchestra had a major-label US record contract.

The recognition had dawned that classics, as CBS executive Clive Davis put it, were 'at best, a break-even operation . . . Over a ten-year period, most classical recordings failed to recoup their cost.'[30] Popular music, on the other hand, was making big profits on relatively low investment and no union hassle. First came Elvis Presley on RCA, then the Beatles on EMI, the Rolling Stones on Decca and the Sixties folk heroes on CBS – Joan Baez, Bob Dylan, Simon and Garfunkel. The 'tiny business'[31] that Lieberson headed in 1955 was worth two hundred million dollars a year in US sales. That figure doubled in the next two years and quintupled by the time Lieberson retired. 'The classics accounted for only a tiny slice of this billion-dollar pie,' writes the industry historian Roland Gelatt. 'In share of market they dropped from around twenty-five per cent of total [US] sales in the 1950s to five per cent in the 1970s.' Whatever Lieberson's intentions, the music he loved best lost four-fifths of its commercial position during his presidency. Rock, as Gelatt notes, 'had created mass market expectations which the classics could not sustain'.[32] 'I remember going to a CBS sales conference, and when the classical presentation was announced it was booed,' recalled one producer. 'The sales force didn't want to know if a record could not sell like pop.'[33]

'Contemporary rock was changing with blinding speed,' wrote the ambitious Clive Davis. 'Much of the new music was also becoming a sophisticated new art form . . . My responsibility as a record executive was to involve myself deeply in this phenomenon.'[34] Davis took over Lieberson's job in 1966, signed Bruce Springsteen, Janis Joplin, Santana, Blood, Sweat and Tears and was sacked in a corporate *putsch* in 1973, accused of using fifty thousand dollars of Columbia money to decorate his apartment and twenty thousand to pay for his son's barmitzvah party. Lieberson was hauled out of retirement to find the company under federal investigation for mob connections and drug abuse. With his monogrammed handkerchiefs and gently puffed pipe, he looked quaintly antediluvian among the flowershirts and foulmouths who populated the executive floor of the Black Rock of 52nd Street. The CBS record division had swelled to half the size of the broadcast network and was showering cash like confetti – 'a little too much Louis Quatorze going on,'[35] he murmured.

'His return was like a Greek tragedy,' says Chapin. 'He was the last musician to run a record label. The industry had been taken over by bean-counters and lawyers.'[36] In Lieberson's day, a record contract was typed on a single sheet of paper and Columbia Records employed one staff attorney. Now, contracts ran to fifty pages and the Black Rock was sucking in the annual output of top law schools. Communications between artists and labels turned adversarial in the mid-Sixties when an accounts checker called Allen Klein went through the RCA books and won Bobby Darin a hundred thousand dollars in underpaid royalties. To counter the likes of Klein, who went on to make a bigger splash with the Stones and the Beatles, labels recruited legal-minded Rottweilers like Davis and his protégé, Walter Yetnikoff.

This was no environment for Lieberson who, sick with cancer, resigned in favour of the colourful Yetnikoff and died soon after. 'I was very angry about him dying on me,' said Yetnikoff. 'Because I thought Goddard had beaten the system. He had left CBS when he wanted to leave, not when *they* wanted him to leave . . . He was, I think, quite a happy man, certainly one of the most gracious, funny guys on the face of the earth. And he was doing what he wanted to do. He had financial security. He beat the system. And then the motherfucker *died* on me! It sounds facetious, but I was really pissed.'[37]

Yetnikoff ran Columbia uninhibitedly for fifteen years, forcing Billy Joel's lawyer to crawl on his knees for a contract and literally ripping the shirt off the man's back before giving him the document. At one convention, he motivated the sales force with a 'FUCK WARNER' sign above the rostrum. He womanised, boozed, called his enemies 'Nazis' and completely changed the tone of the recording world. Amid this violently altered ecology, classical music stood no chance.

Its last hope was to catch on as a visual medium, building an audience on television, but those dreams faded when Bernstein vanished from CBS screens as the network chased mass viewership. State television in Europe still carried concerts and opera as off-peak cultural heritage, but classical music had to be dressed up with gimmickry and nudity in order to achieve any kind of rating. The head of Britain's largest independent television company announced that he would never allow classical music to be screened before midnight. By the closing quarter of the twentieth century, classical recordings were in full retreat.

The dawn before compact disc was unnervingly dark. EMI, the British flagship, was sold off to the Thorn electronics concern. Decca, founded by Edward Lewis in 1929, was absorbed on his death in 1980 by the PolyGram group, a world-leading alliance of Philips and Deutsche Grammophon in which the Dutch manufacturer held seventy-five per cent of the shares. The big music decisions were increasingly made by lightbulb and weapons manufacturers. It seemed only a matter of time before classical music was 'rationalised', possibly to extinction.

Into this tenebrous prospect rose the compact disc, brightening record countenances with a laser beam. Gloom turned to boom as world retail sales of all recordings doubled in five years after 1985, from twelve to twenty-four billion dollars. A tenth of this revenue was classical, as serious music reclaimed a double-figure market share for the first time in a generation. Ecstatic label chiefs ordered an increase in studio activity. They grew even more excited when the hidden benefits were revealed. By adding an unforeseen clarity to ancient recordings, compact disc made the great performances of yesteryear sound more glorious than ever before. Demand soared for Furtwängler and Toscanini, Heifetz and Kreisler, Caruso and Callas. To reissue them cost nothing more than a quick pressing and a royalty cheque. Classics were back in the black, and business quickly cottoned on to their reborn profitability.

Richard Branson, the airheads-to-airline entrepreneur, equipped his Virgin label with a classical wing. Steven Ross, head of Time-Warner, went on a classical rampage, buying Teldec in Germany, followed by Erato in France, Elektra Nonesuch in New York, Finlandia in Helsinki. Sony, the Japanese hardware company, took over Columbia Records. RCA Victor, the other apple-pie US label, was acquired for above its perceived market value by the German book conglomerate, Bertelsmann. When Branson got bored, EMI eagerly bought him out for five hundred and sixty million pounds.

In the rock sector, the Japanese media group Matsushita bought out David Geffen, an independent producer, for half a billion dollars. Thorn spent one hundred and fifty million dollars on Chrysalis and two hundred and eighty-five million dollars for SBK. PolyGram, not to be outdone, paid over a billion dollars for A&M, Island and Motown. When the music finally stopped, four groups — Time-Warner, Sony-CBS, PolyGram and Thorn-EMI — were heading the industry with Matsushita-MCA and Bertelsmann-RCA some way behind. Together they commanded eighty-five per cent of sales worth twenty-six billion dollars a year. Of this total, classical turnover exceeded two billion, with the four majors holding three-quarters of the world market.

What triggered the take-over fever was not so much the teen appeal of Midori and Michael Jackson as the backlists of a century of recording which, on compact disc, were endlessly recyclable. After CD, there would be DAT, DCC, mini-disc and more besides. With better protection for copyrights and intellectual property, whoever owned the recorded past could control the multimedia future.

The classical controls at the reorganised majors were seized in the main by ex-Karajan aides. Günther Breest, his DG producer, became head of Sony Classical; Peter Andry, his EMI partner, became vice-president at Warner. Elsewhere, Culshaw trainees polished the Decca Sound and infiltrated Philips and DG. Across the classical labels there prevailed an air of collegiality that stopped just short of collusion. Producers might fight over a star but they were of much the same mind when it came to consumer prices. Thus, by mysterious coincidence, new releases cost exactly the same, give or take a penny or two, on all good labels around the world. Odder still, reissues appeared at a uniform mid-price, while cut-outs and commercial failures were comparably priced at bargain level. There were accusations of price-rigging, especially when CD prices hit fifteen pounds in western Europe, but official inquiries regularly exonerated the industry. Its senior labels were simply behaving like elderly members of a Pall Mall club, following time-honoured rules for which no one could remember the reason.

These cosy assumptions were, however, about to be exploded. In 1988, the year compact disc became a mass medium, a new line of digital classics appeared in British shops initially at a penny under four pounds. The packaging was crude and the artists unheard of, but the performances were acceptable and sometimes accomplished. The name on the spine was Naxos and the discs were made in Hong Kong. Over the next six years, Naxos breached the industry's price codes in all major territories and repertoire, trimming profits to a trickle.

The man who cracked the price cartel was a Frankfurt language teacher, Klaus Heymann, who had worked with the local US garrison in the Sixties and wound up in Hong Kong when his unit was posted to Vietnam. Wearying of the daily body count, he took to selling German cameras and hi-fis to GIs on furlough. When two of his suppliers, Bose and Revox, offered to stage concerts in support of their products, he booked the artists and imported records to sell in the foyer. By 1978, on his own reckoning, Heymann was the biggest record distributor in non-communist Asia. From there to making records was but a short step. Heymann's wife, Takao Nishizaki, a professional violinist, discovered a score by two Shanghai composers that detailed in glycerine sonorities the tragic fate of a maltreated working girl. The *Butterfly Lovers' Concerto* sold a quarter of a million copies in Hong Kong and was banned in Taiwan. 'For the Chinese,' said Heymann, 'it's like the Mendelssohn and Beethoven and Tchaikovsky rolled into one.'[38] Mrs Heymann soon filled football stadia with her soulful performances.

When compact disc arrived, Heymann was asked by a local businessman to provide a pack of the world's greatest classical music to be sold door-to-door in South Korea. Unable to organise sessions at short notice, he purchased thirty digital tapes, recorded in Bratislava, from a Slovak exile in Paris. Then his Korean partner went broke. 'So there I was, stuck with thirty classical masters. I couldn't sell them at full price because these were unknown east European orchestras, although the performances were not too bad. I had to put them out on a budget label. That's how Naxos Records was born.'

The discs went on sale in Hong Kong at six US dollars, 'the cheapest CDs in the world'. Woolworths sold mountains of his discs in Britain and Heymann booked more sessions in Bratislava and Ljubljana. 'The orchestras were completely flexible,' he relates. 'If they had to cancel a concert to make a recording they would happily do so.' If ten minutes were left at the end of a session, they would record an extra overture. He paid the players hard currency, one hundred and eighty Deutschmarks (seventy pounds) each per record, or half as much again as their monthly salary. 'For musicians in Bratislava it meant the difference between a life of hardship and a life of comfort,' he maintained.[39]

The conductors he used were often westerners – an American, Stephen Gunzenhauser, whom he discovered in Lisbon, and Barry Wordsworth, conductor of London's Royal Ballet. While major labels fought over the winners of international piano competitions, Heymann picked up the players in fifth and sixth place. He paid conductors and soloists a flat fee of one thousand dollars without further royalties. Underemployed radio producers and technicians provided studio supervision. Heymann himself claimed no specialist musical knowledge. A matter-of-fact businessman, his years in the East had barely touched a solid German mien, suspicious of flowery distractions. 'Actually, I don't like to meet artists,' he told the *Daily Telegraph*. 'Many musicians have a certain charisma that lets them push you into doing things that don't make artistic or business sense. Also, you shouldn't like your artists, otherwise how can you be objective?'[40]

He attacked the catalogue systematically, recording the complete symphonies of Beethoven, Brahms, Dvořák, Mozart, Tchaikovsky, Schubert and Sibelius. Followed by the concertos, the chamber music, the string quartets, the solo sonatas. Integrality was no proof of artistic integrity, as ill-conceived

Beethoven and Mahler interpretations would prove. The Dvořák cycle, on the other hand, was probably the best of its era and the Beethoven piano sonatas, played by Stefan Vladar, got the pianist poached by Sony. Popular operas, all from eastern Europe, contained some superb singing.

Any music that was off the mainstream he released at full price on Marco Polo, his 'label of discovery'. Much of it was tedious note-spinning but occasional revelations like Havergal Brian's monumental *Gothic* Symphony and the piano sonatas of Nikolai Myaskovsky won Heymann appreciable credibility among music buffs. Unwittingly, he was applying the Lieberson law of making profitable releases pay for uneconomic esoterica.

Not that Marco Polo was run altruistically. Heymann knew that if he covered enough composers some of them would pay off and his adventurousness would attract better artists. Antonio de Almeida, ex-conductor of the Paris Opéra who had appeared on both Philips and EMI, found him willing to produce the unfashionable Italian symphonist Gian Francesco Malipiero. Sir Edward Downes, principal conductor at Covent Garden, gave him Myaskovsky on Marco Polo and Elgar on Naxos. Raphael Wallfisch, one of the outstanding cellists of his generation, recorded obscure English sonatas for Marco Polo, followed by Vivaldi concertos for Naxos. 'I do not prepare or play any differently when I record for Naxos than when I record for anyone else,'[41] he declared.

As economic conditions worsened and major labels cut their output, Heymann attracted a superior class of ensemble. The BBC and Bournemouth orchestras recorded for Naxos for less than he paid in Bratislava. Pinchas Steinberg led Austrian Radio ensembles in Wagner operas. Naxos was becoming artistically competitive and commercially dangerous. Heymann was recording symphonies for one-fifth of major label expenditure. He broke even at two thousand five hundred sales and often sold six times that figure in four years. In 1990, before penetrating America and Japan, he sold three million records. By the end of 1994 he was up to ten million, with fifty per cent annual growth. He employed a staff of seven, spent pennies on promotion and cleared at least a dollar's profit on every disc sold. He was making three hundred new records a year and in Scandinavia was selling more than the rest of the classical record industry combined. In the United Kingdom he was third, just behind Decca and EMI but rising fast. One in every six classics bought around the world was a Naxos.

'The big companies stupidly created a star system, paying artists huge advances,' he said. 'Then they found they were having to delete good recordings to make room for releases by the people they had just signed up . . . Utterly stupid.'[42]

Their initial response was to ignore him. Record customers, they reckoned, were a conservative lot who would stick to the names and brands they knew. Why would they buy musicians called Krchek and Zsapka when they could have Muti and Rattle? But compact disc had a myth and logic all of its own. If digital sound was perfect, then all sound was equal and the only difference between two records of the same music was a matter of interpretation. Was any performer's input worth twice the price? Many purchasers, especially classical newcomers, felt not. Even hard-core collectors were tempted by the novelty and inexpensiveness of Naxos discs.

'I thought maybe we'd get to about fifty titles and then the majors would come at us with competition, and that would be the end,' reflected Heymann. 'But it didn't happen – though I think the majors wish they had taken notice in those days when we were so vulnerable.'[43]

Five years too late, the industry struck back with big-name reissues – Karajans and Kleibers for the price of an unknown Slovene. Heymann did not flinch. He had the distribution network, the repertoire and the resources to meet the onslaught. 'There's no question that he is causing us great pain,' confided one label chief. 'As long as he's around we shall have to keep discounting our product so heavily that we are making no money on it.'

PolyGram's chief executive Alain Lévy admitted in his end-of-1993 accounts that budget competition was hurting his classical side. At the first glimmer of a rumour that Heymann was thinking of selling up, label bosses went flying to Hong Kong with sweetheart deals in their briefcases. Heymann was not interested – not even at two hundred million dollars, which seemed an inordinate price to offer for his pick'n'mix catalogue. Nevertheless, the industry clung to a belief that as Peking rule and his sixtieth birthday approached in 1997, Heymann would retire to Australia and they could close him down. 'He'll record the whole repertoire and then sell out,' said one label boss. They refused to believe that he was into classics for anything other than money. 'The offers were very flattering.' Heymann laughed. 'But they still don't understand what I'm doing. My plans go beyond the year 2000 and I expect to offer a Naxos alternative to practically every classical work.'

Heymann, having made his point, was now embarked on a crusade. 'The major labels have become intoxicated by the taste of rock sales that they got from the Three Tenors,' he said. 'They have not only abandoned the classical business, they no longer understand it. You can make money in this business, but you've got to control your costs and have good repertoire ideas. I could live off my Johann Strauss edition – why didn't the major labels think of that first?'

Amid the exuberance of his challenge, the desire for recognition was unconcealable. Heymann, one sensed, wanted to join the club. He was aware of the Darwinian law of business which states that those who live by undercutting will themselves some day be cut under. Flying round the world, he found classic CDs in French supermarkets for ten francs, cheaper than the nastiest plonk and poisonous to the ear. 'Ridiculous price,' he snorted. Austrians were recycling village-hall *Messiahs* and puerile *Pastorals*. He took legal action in Germany to stop a producer of fake digital recordings. In the United States you could buy junk classics for three bucks. One of Heymann's own conductors, Alexander Rahbari, set up in competition with money from Iranian investors, founding a Discovery label. A British distributor, Tring, commissioned the Royal Philharmonic Orchestra to make one hundred and fifty discs – to be sold in supermarkets and service stations for one pound less than Naxos products.

'We are trying to get away from mass-merchandising,' said Heymann, who now found himself in the front line, defending sound quality, refined artistry and high production values, the tricolor of the traditional record industry. 'People look at us in a completely different light from other bargain labels,' he averred. 'Critics are aware that we are also doing Marco Polo, that we are not just in business to make a quick buck. I invest every penny I make in new productions.'

He hired a retiring producer from Decca to exert quality control over his output. Naxos would now carry only those recordings that bore a professional seal of approval (at worst, the rest could be shunted off on bottom-price catch-all labels).

A three-tier industry was taking shape – business class for star labels, cabin class for Naxos/Marco Polo, and both praying fervently that people would pay a little extra for quality rather than risk discomfort on the charter flights being scheduled by the undercutters. 'There will always be new artists, and the public will always want to buy recordings by top artists who are performing today,' declared BMG's chief confidently at an industry conference. There will also, he added in an undertone, be fewer new recordings made than ever before.[44] By the end of 1995, a world leader like EMI was making just four classical recordings a month.

The elevator door has a serpentine design and a Jugendstil blue-green colouring. The apartment is tall and airy, gracious as a ballroom and timeless as time past, a desired residence for dreamers and nostalgists. Bay windows bathe the rooms in winter sunlight, opening out on to an overhead U-bahn that every three or four minutes rattles commuters around Hamburg. Authentic to all appearances and elegant to a fault, this is the perfect home for a classical recording chief: reminiscent of bygone splendours, yet punctuated by forceful reminders of modern communications.

Roger Wright, artist and repertoire director of Deutsche Grammophon the largest classical label, sits in front of a wall cabinet of compact discs and agonises over production cuts. 'These things won't wear out.' He points despondently at the jewel-cased discs. 'So how will we ever persuade people to buy another Beethoven cycle when the one they have got will last forever?'

His anguish, in a television interview,[45] revealed a wormlike infestation that gnawed at the core of recording as it entered its second century. In 1983 Wright's company invested one hundred million Deutschmarks in new technology. Switching from analogue to digital production, it urged music lovers to replace their fault-ridden vinyl recordings with immaculate compact discs. Impervious to cigarette ash and undamaged no matter how often you played them, CDs were the first records that did not have to be handled with surgical gloves and rock-steady hands.

Their immaculateness was unnatural, out of this world. Instead of capturing and reproducing physical signals with all their ambient imperfections, the new system laserised sound into binary digits – up to four million each second – and replayed it faithfully, without hiss, crackle or surface noise. It was everything that records had ever claimed to be.

Like a flight of swallows, compact discs took off across the wealthier hemisphere in a silvery cloud, a harbinger of the dawning information revolution. The uptake exceeded all expectations. In the fragile instant before the arrival of facsimile machines and home computers, before the implosion of global recession, compact disc represented the shape of happiness to come. It was the gleaming chalice of a sacrament that promised salvation through invention – '*Vorsprung durch Technik*', in the jargon of German automakers – the defining gadget of an ephemeral yuppie generation. Along with AIDS, it would go down in history as the lasting emblem of the Eighties.

For classical recording, however, the rejuvenative elixir quickly wore off. In 1992 classical sales crashed by a quarter. By 1994 they were down to no more than five per cent of the world market, which was still growing at a rate of sixteen per cent each year.[46] Freak statistics made the classical figures look worse than they really were, but the underlying slump was undeniable. Not since the rise of radio in the late 1920s – when US record sales dropped from a hundred and four million to six million in just five years[47] – had the classical record industry felt so depressed. Then, as now, western economies were sluggish. But while previous recoveries were achieved by improving sound and extending choice, CD left little room for enhancement and the range of music on sale had never been greater. Minor embellishments, such as Sony's

20-bit methodology and DG's four-dimensional 4D gimmick, might still be asseverated. But, for the vast majority of record buyers, compact disc was the *ultima vera*. Now, having bought a symphony, they need never buy it again.

'For the first time in history we now have perfect recorded sound,' said the cellist Julian Lloyd Webber, 'and, with this achievement, one of the prime historical reasons for re-recording a piece of music disappears.'[48] The commercial impetus, though, was unchanged – to keep musicians in work and the record business in profit. The situation had the poignancy of comic opera. Having boasted for a century of her purity and high fidelity, the heroine is rudely spurned when her immaculate status is validated.

These reflections dappled darkly around Roger Wright's living-room as he surveyed Deutsche Grammophon's tactical options. A pensive Englishman with the physique of a rugby fly-half and an impressive track record at the BBC and the Cleveland Orchestra, Wright was engaged to energise a company that lost its headlights when Herbert von Karajan and Leonard Bernstein died in 1989–90. DG, with its bright yellow shield and elegant packaging, was the classical leader, but its Hamburg head office was dumbstruck by the downturn. Wright himself was so worried that he sometimes walked into a record store and purchased new releases on rival labels – just to show the dealer that someone was still buying.

At DG, for the first time in memory, no one was taping a Beethoven cycle with a major orchestra. 'There would have to be a compelling reason to record it again when we have digital Karajan, Bernstein and Abbado,' said Wright. Beethoven was a powerful brand name and if Beethoven was unrecordable the business was in trouble.

The economics were beginning to look absurd. It could cost a hundred thousand dollars to record a Mahler symphony in Berlin, half a million to cast a Strauss opera in Vienna. Most records sold two or three thousand copies on first release. It would take a lifetime to earn back the outlay on a Berlin production.

Any rational analyst would have told the industry to quit recording and repackage the back catalogue. Wright's role was to find an excuse for continuing to make records and his task was constrained by the dignity of his office. DG dared not stalk the catwalks of musical fashion without risking its hard-won authority. 'The scrabbling around for pieces with quick-fix appeal is an embarrassment to us all,' he sniffed, disdaining the half-million sales of Henryk Mikolai Górecki's meditative third symphony, which hit number six in the pop charts. 'The trouble with chart hits is that no one will want to hear them next year,' was the DG line. 'We are concerned with building an enduring list of great music.'

Yet the reality was that major labels had become overwhelmingly dependent on freak hits – Nigel Kennedy one year, Spanish monks the next – and on compilation discs designed to be played while driving a car, making love or weeding the garden. These peripheral products accounted for the vast majority of classical sales. The traditional symphonic recording, like the traditional hardback novel, was being left on the shelf and was in danger of disappearing.

The star system that had sustained the classical record business since Caruso's day was now contributing to its demolition. Singers who used to be satisfied with a one-off cheque and a mess of post-session potage were demanding an unpayable ransom. The first Three Tenors concert in 1990 cost Decca half a million dollars in fees to Luciano Pavarotti, Placido Domingo and José Carreras, not bad for a warm evening's work. It sold millions of discs and videos, and left Domingo seething. 'Decca obeyed the letter of the contract,' he told journalists, 'but as the concert sold so well they should have paid us more.'[49] Four years later, with the Los Angeles finals drawing near, the tenors changed the rules.

Acting through Pavarotti's outdoors-events impresario, Tibor Rudas, they staged a telephone auction for *Three Tenors II*. Six million pounds from EMI did not reach the reserve price, Sony dropped out at eight and Decca's ten million was vetoed by the grumpy Domingo. Warner stepped in with a winning offer of eleven million pounds. The three tenors and their conductor would get a million each in advance and would earn four times as much by the end of the year in royalties and broadcast fees. 'Thanks to the expansive international resources and expertise of the Warner Music Group, this remarkable reunion will reach a truly global audience,' crowed Rudas.[50] It would need to if anyone but the singers were to make any money on it.

'It is always better second time around,'[51] claimed Domingo – but better for whom? Certainly not for the record industry, which saw its stars pushed out of sight by a line of zeros, and least of all for opera houses that saw their prime attractions lured away by jamborees in open spaces.

Three Tenors II did roughly as well as could be expected, despite an appalling critical reception. Warners topped the charts and did not lose their corporate shirts, but the truly worrying statistic showed up in the industry's annual figures where *Three Tenors II* outsold the next biggest 'classical' record by a margin of nine discs to one. The new reality was that stars and their producers were no longer playing on the same side. The producers wanted to make the best operas and recitals achievable in modern times. The singers wanted to make the most money in history. The concept of a developing creative partnership was doomed, as stars flitted from one label to the next according to the sums they were offered.

Lifelong attachments like Sir Georg Solti's to Decca-London and Bob Dylan's to Sony-CBS were viewed as eccentric anachronisms. 'Star artists are our major asset, and exclusivity is essential,' protested Decca's outgoing president Roland Kommerell,[52] but in the new climate both sides in future would be looking after number one.

The nightmare of Three Tenor millions was bound to prove calamitous for classical recording. In the past, when a label struck lucky with a freak hit, the profits were reinvested imaginatively. Decca ploughed its Three Tenors pot into *Entartete Musik*, reviving valuable music that the Nazis had banned. EMI sank money from Nigel Kennedy's *Four Seasons* into young British artists. DG recycled Karajan cash into adventurous modernisms. Warner had spent its Górecki gold on a clutch of living composers.

These windfalls, though, were being ruled out by star greed. The record industry would no longer be able to take risks and extend the culture. Nor could it pay for the long-term development of new artists, an act of faith that could take years to redeem; EMI disclosed in 1994 that it had taken fifteen years to break even on Simon Rattle. Without its commitment, an important conductor could have been mired in obscurity. 'It's tragic: all we talk about nowadays is bottom line,' said a major-label A&R chief. 'We used to help artists plan careers, let them make mistakes and learn from them. Now we have to make projects pay, or drop the artist.' Classical record companies needed one big hit a year to fund artist development. If limelight releases were rendered unprofitable by star demands, there would be no money to create stars of the future and the industry would fall back on its century-rich backlist, a museum of recorded music. The danger was known to industry chiefs and they were powerless to avert it. In these fretful circumstances, the bond between star and producer – an amalgam of admiration, daring and a common sense of purpose that emanated from Gaisberg's original encounter with Enrico Caruso – was frayed beyond repair. Stymied on the one side by an indestructible disc, and on the other by insatiable avarice, the classical record was reaching the end of its playline.

NOTES

1 for further background, see POLY–100
2 Gaisberg, pp. 48–51
3 Gaisberg, pp. 86–7
4 Gaisberg, p. 45
5 Schwarzkopf, p. 10

6 op. cit., pp. 144–5
7 Marie Tobin, *Walter Legge: The Early Years*, ICRC, ix. 95, p. 12
8 Peter Andry, reminiscence in *Classical Music*, 3 June 1989
9 recalled by Joan Ingpen
10 Brookes, pp. 206–7
11 Jefferson, p. 77
12 Schwarzkopf, p. 91
13 Culshaw, *Record*, p. 180
14 author's interview
15 Schwarzkopf, p. 659
16 Donaldson, p. 115
17 author's interview, May 1994
18 Schwarzkopf, p. 106
19 Schwarzkopf, p. 68
20 Sir Ian Hunter, interview with the author
21 Schwarzkopf, p. 5
22 memo to Peter Heyworth, 26 July 82, copied to the author
23 Culshaw, *Record*, p. 218
24 Robert Craft, *Small Craft Advisories* (London, Thames & Hudson, 1989) p. 185
25 Milstein, p. 260
26 Chapin, author's interview
27 Chapin, p. 213
28 Chapin, *Bernstein*, p. 37
29 Burton, p. 253
30 Davis, pp. 231–2
31 Gelatt, p. 302
32 Gelatt, pp. 352–3
33 Paul Myers, comments to the author
34 Davis, p. 231
35 Dannen, p. 113
36 author's interview
37 Dannen, p. 115
38 all quotes, unless stated, from interview with the author
39 Brian Hunt interview, nd
40 Brian Hunt interview, nd
41 *CM*, 14 May 1994, p. 23
42 *Guardian* interview, 10 April 1993, p. 31
43 Brian Hunt interview, nd
44 Günter Hensler, BACA–94
45 *Late show*, BBC2, February 1994
46 source: International Federation of Phonographic Industries (IFPI). In 1994 the US accounted for one in every three classical records sold, spending $11.8 billion; the European Union spent $10.6 billion and Japan $5.9 billion.
47 Gelatt, p. 255
48 address to Association of British Orchestras, January 1992
49 *Classical Music*, 8 January 1994, p. 21
50 press release, 8 April 1994
51 *The Times*, 22 December 1993, p. 3
52 *BBC Music Magazine*, August 1994, p. 11

CHAPTER XII

THE PROPERTY
OF AN INTELLECTUAL

The French Revolution brought a promise of freedom and equality to suffering humanity with its Declaration of the Rights of Man and of the Citizen. The Declaration was promulgated in August 1789, six weeks after the storming of the Bastille, and among its subsidiary rights, legislated on 19 July 1793 as the Great Terror dawned, was the first formal recognition of an individual's entitlement to *propriété intellectuelle*, the fruits of his or her creative mind.[1]

Eighteen months prior to these excitements, in imperial Vienna, Wolfgang Amadeus Mozart was laid in a pauper's grave while his music sold like chestnuts on street corners. Had he lived a little longer, and in Paris, the poor composer might have seen some reward from the sale of each score. He might also have been stripped of his fortune by Pierre-Augustin Beaumarchais, founder of the Société des auteurs et compositeurs dramatiques and a doughty creative rights campaigner, who could now claim damages for Mozart's unauthorised operatic use of his original play, *The Marriage of Figaro*. Thus, like the Revolution itself, intellectual ownership was a mixed blessing for those it was meant to benefit. What the law gave with one hand, it could take away with the other.

Between the state and the artist, a third force seized the moment. The law was meant to benefit the owner of an original work but this, in law, was rarely the artist but a publisher who took possession of all rights in exchange for eking a royalty to the creator. The moment a piece of music went into print it ceased to belong to the composer for so long as it remained in circulation. Its publisher received the entire income and, if honest, passed a fraction to the composer. The result of revolutionary liberation was that publishers exploited the newfound rights and grew mighty, while artists remained downtrodden and poor.

The French attempted to redress this imbalance when, after their third political revolution in half a century, a second form of musical rights was enacted. One night in 1849, a dance composer of no particular consequence refused to pay his bill in a Paris bistro where the band were strumming his tunes. If they could play his music without paying for it, he argued, he would eat for free. The case went to court and judgement was given in his favour. In May 1850 France established a state agency, SACEM, to collect fees for copyright owners wherever music was played in public.

The beneficiaries were, once again, the publishers. This time, though, the boon was so great that it totally altered their priorities. Instead of printing scores and putting them on sale in much the same way as book publishers did, music publishers now turned the thrust of their operation to promotion and performance seeking. By getting their music played, they made money less from the sale or hire of a score than from its priceless performance rights. In the course of time, printing became secondary to music publishers: promotion was the art that kept them in the black. Success in publishing was judged by how much playtime, on stage and later on air, a company managed to get for its copyrights. Every minute was worth a mint.

The dawning of performing rights improved the status of composers only to the extent that the hit writer became a hot property, cherished by publishers and promoted to the ends of the earth. This concern was understandably restricted to proven composers and confined to countries that recognised performing rights. Britain did not protect such rights until 1912 and Germany, the heartland of serious music, was pressured into legislation around that time by a campaign led by Richard Strauss.

Music publishing in Germany traced its roots all the way back to Gutenberg, but German composers found it difficult to obtain fair treatment from an unsentimental industry. Schubert was underpaid and abused by Anton Diabelli, a dilettante composer who advised him to write fewer songs. Richard Wagner had his early works dismissed by the Mainz firm of B. Schotts Söhne and when he got *The Flying Dutchman* accepted in Leipzig by Breitkopf und

Härtel, it was 'on the condition that I abstained from asking any payment for it'.[2] Breitkopf, which made its fortune on posthumous volumes of Mozart and Haydn, claimed to have lost money on the Dutchman and its successors, *Lohengrin* and *Tannhäuser*. When Wagner proposed a four-night operatic saga on *The Ring of the Nibelung*, the directors collapsed in mirth.

Wagner went back to Schotts, which accepted the *Ring*, followed by *Meistersinger* and *Parsifal*, and reaped the rewards for seventy years and more. In this glow of Rhine gold, Schotts forgot their initial failure to support Wagner. On the seventy-fifth anniversary of the *Ring* première, a doyen of the Strecker family, which owned Schotts from 1859 onwards, wrote a fond monograph titled '*Richard Wagner als Verlagsgefährte*'[3] – Wagner as a publishing colleague. The composer would have relished this imputation of an equal partnership with a firm whose 'vain promises'[4] left him seething with fury. 'What he finds most disagreeable in his contacts with such people,' his wife reported, 'is their silence when he has explained to them how things stand.'[5] Wagner could tell publishers what he wanted but he was at their mercy when it came to printing and securing performances for his works.

The power of publishers enshrined by the French Revolution brought a flowering of music colophons all over Europe – Peters of Leipzig set up in 1814, Ricordi of Milan in 1808, Heugel of Paris in 1812, Novellos of London in 1811. Breitkopf und Härtel was incorporated in 1795; Schotts began in 1770. With the law on their side and new technology at their disposal, these firms dominated the Romantic era. Breitkopf made its pile on safely dead immortals and the piano works of Franz Liszt. Schotts soared on the spirit of Beethoven's ninth symphony. Peters did well on Chopin and Schumann, Heugel on Offenbach and Novello on Handel reprints. By 1843 Schotts had offices in Paris, London and Brussels and its competitors were not far behind in feeding a spreading public appetite for serious music. Behind the lustre of their complete editions, the publishers were respected as pillars of entrepreneurial propriety.

The supreme success story of the nineteenth century was Casa Ricordi which, almost alone, godfathered the golden century of Italian opera. Ricordi were the publishers of Rossini, Verdi, Puccini and several verismo composers, as well as some works by Bellini and Donizetti. They did not merely print full operas and peddle piano reductions for parlour playing. Ricordi exerted rigorous control of their operas from the point of commissioning to the moment of staging, never selling scores to producers but only ever hiring them out to ensure that an untampered version was presented to the public. They demanded approval of conductors and casts, especially at La Scala where their word was tantamount to law. They produced lavish artwork and exquisite set designs. When the score called for an unusual instrument – like the Japanese bells in *Madama Butterfly* – Ricordi manufactured the sound-machine to the composer's specifications. They were the first modern-minded music publisher, obtaining international copyright protection for their composers. Giovanni Ricordi, the founder, personally brokered an agreement between the Austrian empire and the Kingdom of Sardinia for mutual copyright recognition.

The son of a glassmaker, born in 1785, Giovanni Ricordi played first violin in a Milan theatre and earned spare cash as a music copyist. In 1807 he took himself to Leipzig and spent a year with Breitkopf und Härtel which had developed an improved font and copper plates for music printing. Back in Milan, Ricordi became the official copyist to several theatres, including La Scala, with a royal patent entitling him to print all their new operas. He opened a shop opposite La Scala and in 1825 bought the theatre's archives.

Pitted against wily *impresarii* in Naples, Florence and elsewhere, Ricordi did not always get the best bel canto works. But in 1838 he paid Giuseppe Verdi two thousand lire for his next opera, *Oberto*. The one after that was *Nabucco*, liberation opera of reborn Italy. It made Verdi a national hero and Ricordi a power in the land.

They remained allied for sixty years, never exclusively or in writing but with something resembling a blood bond between Verdi and four generations of Ricordis – Giovanni, his son Tito, his grandson Giulio, and his great-grandson Tito the second. Others sought to invade this relationship, and one succeeded for a while. Francesco Lucca, an engraver with Ricordi's, acquired a printing patent in 1825 and opened shop directly opposite his ex-employer. Lucca procured three operas from Verdi – *Attila*, *I masnadieri* and *Il corsaro* – by offering to relieve the overtaxed composer of the need to negotiate with theatres, a commitment quickly adopted by Ricordi and all other opera publishers. Only *Attila* made Lucca any money but he was a permanent thorn in Ricordi's side. His challenge reached its climax when, with Italian opera losing its lustre in 1871, he introduced the intoxicating sounds of Wagner to southern audiences. Verdi was incensed and Ricordi rightly alarmed. Although Lucca died childless soon after this coup, his semi-literate widow Giovannina promoted the alien cause with immense vigour just as Verdi entered a fifteen-year quietus. What saved the house of Ricordi was Verdi's reawakening and their own virility. *Otello*, in 1887, swung public favour back towards Italian opera. Months later, the widow Lucca sold her company to the fertile Ricordis, bringing Verdi and Wagner together under a single Italian roof. No other publisher would ever rival Ricordi's near-monopoly of music copyrights in his own culture.

Verdi himself had helped Ricordi enforce his rights by taking up French residency in 1854 to enjoy the benefits of Napoleonic law; he even thought of getting a British passport after the House of Lords limited protection of dramatic works to Crown citizens. He got his lawyer to draw up a copyright treaty between Britain and his home state of Parma and, as a member of the first Italian parliament, pushed through copyright laws useful to Ricordi.

His relations with the firm declined after *Aida* and almost ruptured in May 1875 in a row over unpaid royalties, only to be repaired in the autumnal glow of *Otello*. Tito Ricordi lacked his father's brio but his son, Giulio, a salon music composer under his German pseudonym, J. Burgmein, brought the firm its next great asset.

If Verdi was the glory of Ricordi's, Puccini was the goldmine. Giulio, who called him 'the Crown Prince', sacked the promising Alfredo Catalani from his catalogue to shield the slow-burning Puccini and stole for him the *Tosca* libretto from the laborious Alberto Franchetti. Puccini developed an operatic style that matched overripe melody to swampish passions. His lurid operas conquered the world's stages and earned Ricordi untold influence, resulting in a Metropolitan Opera commission for *The Girl of the Golden West* in December 1910. On Giulio's death in 1912 Puccini ran out of themes and fell out with Tito II who preferred the preposterous Riccardo Zandonai to his company's star. Puccini took his next operas elsewhere, without much success, until Tito was ousted in 1919 and the alliance could be renewed. Its climactic triumph was *Turandot*, which Puccini left almost finished on his deathbed in 1924 and Franco Alfano completed two years later for Toscanini to conduct an indelible première at La Scala.

But that was the end of the line. There were no more sons to run Ricordi's and, try as family-appointed executives might to renew Italian opera through the likes of Montemezzi, Casella, Respighi, Pizzetti, Malipiero and Nino Rota, the well had run dry with *Turandot* and the world lost interest in a stagnant art. Ricordi put its shares on sale to the public in 1952 and attempted a post-modernist revival with Luigi Nono, Franco Donatoni and Giuseppe Sinopoli, none of whom set the box-office on fire. The firm could still afford to back loss makers as royalties poured in from Verdi and Puccini, but copyrights were running out and the big bucks would stop at the end of 1994, seventy years after Puccini's death.

In August 1994 it was announced that three-quarters of the house of Ricordi had been bought by the Munich-based Bertelsmann Music Group. For Italians it was as if Fiat and its football club, Juventus, had fallen to BMW. 'In Milan, they can hear the tramp of German boots,' reported the *Frankfurter Allgemeine Zeitung*. 'Musical pearl in German hands,' shrieked the business newspaper, *Handelsblatt*. Bertelsmann's vice-president, Arnold Bahlmann, said that Italian creativity, under German proprietorship, would 'be taken more seriously around the world'[6] – a pledge that sounded unnervingly familiar to older Italians, casting their culture as the plaything of rampant German forces. Political objections, however, were overcome with assurances that La Scala's archives would remain on site and Verdi's autograph scores would be properly conserved. 'Those who are scandalised now said nothing when, to restore our Verdi manuscripts, I had to knock on the door of the University of Chicago [because] in Italy we received no help at all,' complained the Ricordi president, Guido Rignano.[7]

The take-over, in a country rocked by corruption scandals, was quickly pushed off the news pages. In the music world it was seen as sad but inevitable – part of a global trend in which giant media firms were increasing their software loads on the slipway to the information highway. Intellectual property was in high demand and the European Union, under French influence, had given it added value by harmonising copyright protection across fifteen countries to a minimum of seventy years after an artist's death. The beneficiaries, once again, were not creators but publishers whose share prices soared as media corporations strove to control a monopoly of available software.

Bertelsmann already owned the RCA Victor empire built by 'General' David Sarnoff and had bought licences to former Soviet archives. 'BMG is excited about the strategic opportunities which the acquisition of Ricordi will generate,' said vice-president Bahlmann, predicting a rosy future for its retail outlets and San Remo-style pop division. But the real Ricordi was no longer and serious Italian composers would have to look abroad for support and encouragement. 'The sad fact is,' said a London music publisher, 'that a medium-sized firm like Ricordi simply cannot survive in the modern corporate world. Its take-over is a sign of the times. By the end of the century there won't be any independent music publishers left – only three or four global giants.'[8]

The fate that befell Ricordi engulfed most other family firms in the twentieth century's three great revolutions – Soviet, Nazi and information. The Russians were the first to go. The rebirth of Russian music had been sparked by Peter Jürgenson, an Austrian in his twenties who opened a Moscow publishing house in 1861. While helping Nikolai Rubinstein found a music conservatory he met Rubinstein's pupil Pyotr Ilyich Tchaikovsky, four years his junior, took a liking to his opus one, *Russian Scherzo*, and printed much of his lifetime work. Tchaikovsky, despite crippling self-doubt and a mixed press for his symphonies, wrote songs that were sung in every civilised parlour. He made Jürgenson a mint. On the profits from Tchaikovsky's jingles the publisher, with his brother Josef and son Boris, branched out into the works of Russia's 'Mighty Handful' – Balakirev, Borodin, Mussorgsky, Rimsky-Korsakov and Cui.

Given the cultural rivalry between Moscow and St Petersburg, it was not long before the Jürgensons faced competition in the Baltic capital. In 1869 a viola player called Vasily Bessel opened a music shop on the Nevsky Prospekt and, renewing a student friendship with Tchaikovsky, published an 1872 opera, *The Oprichnik*, that had been turned down in Moscow. Tchaikovsky's first loyalty was to Jürgenson – 'I had no idea I could hurt you by going to Bessel,' he said – but the St Petersburg entrepreneur secured enough of his scores to make a tidy sum and secure less promising works by the handful. Never had Russian music been so well supported, or widely available.

The next surge came in 1885 when Mitrofan Petrovich Belayev, son of a St Petersburg lumber magnate, lavished his inheritance on Russian composers. To obtain good print and copyright protection, neither of which pertained in Russia, he founded M. P. Belayev Editions in Leipzig and began producing exquisite scores by Glazunov, Rimsky-Korsakov, Borodin, Liadov and Cui. 'Then came other young composers and the business grew literally every hour,' related Rimsky-Korsakov. 'In accordance with Mitrofan Petrovich's fundamental rule, no composition was acquired without fundamental payment therefor, as is frequently done by other publishing houses.'[9]

Belayev helped young composers, regardless of prior affiliations. Unable to separate Sergei Rachmaninov from his Moscow publisher Carl Gutheil, he programmed his orchestral works at the Russian Symphony Concerts he funded each year in St Petersburg, adding weight to a bantam reputation. He was equally fair to competitors, giving Jürgenson a contract to distribute his scores in Russia. Belayev's sole concern was the advancement and dissimulation of music by Russians of whatever creed or style.

On his death in January 1904 Belayev bequeathed the bulk of his estate to music and enjoined his executors Rimsky-Korsakov, Glazunov and Liadov, to promote his favourite protégé, the oddball Alexander Skryabin. The lofty Korsakov, whose kindest words for Skryabin were 'warped, posing and self-opinionated'[10] would have been hard pressed to comply, but help was at hand from a third benevolence.

Serge Koussevitzky was a double-bass player who became a conductor and music patron when he married a tea heiress, Nathalie Ushkov. Casting around for unfamiliar scores, he incorporated his own Editions Russes de

Musique in Paris in 1909, with a Russischer Musikverlag in Berlin. With Skryabin as his artistic adviser, he issued rowdy scores by unknown composers, mostly of the Diaghilev circle, who offended the refined editors at Jürgenson, Bessel and Belayev. Skryabin died in 1915 before Koussevitzky could fulfil his personal dreams but the other composers augured well. 'If you are in touch with [Koussevitzky's] Editions Russes de Musique, and if you are as kindly disposed towards me as before, please mention my name,' begged Sergei Prokofiev of Igor Stravinsky in 1915. 'I have a whole pile of manuscripts, including the second [piano] concerto, but [Boris] Jürgenson is jewing and bargaining, and I find him downright repulsive.'[11] During the First World War Koussevitzky annexed to his Edition the catalogue of Carl Gutheil who, as an Austrian citizen, had to leave the country. Rachmaninov, Medtner and Grechaninov were joined to Skryabin, Stravinsky and Prokofiev and the future of music was sounding increasingly Russian as the Germans squandered their symphonic hegemony in bombast and discordance.

All these Russian hopes and enterprises were demolished by the 1917 Revolution. Jürgenson's company was nationalised and his son Boris ended up working as a clerk in a building he once owned. Bessel's sons fled to Paris, as did Belayev's Edition, stripped of its funds. Koussevitzky's was the only list to keep growing. The conductor moved from Paris in 1924 to become music director of the Boston Symphony Orchestra, where he continued to espouse, discover and publish new composers of many nations.

For Russian composers, however, the Revolution brought hunger and despair. Their copyright situation, confusing enough beforehand, turned catastrophic. To protect rights in a country that was not party to copyright conventions, Russian publishers used to register scores in Paris one day before they were released in Moscow. This established ownership and enabled them to sell rights abroad. The Communists, proclaiming all property as theft, printed state editions of successful scores which they sold all over the world without paying a kopek to the original publisher or composer. Rachmaninov was robbed of income from his universally popular C-sharp minor étude. Stravinsky had to reorchestrate *Firebird* to create a new copyright. Prokofiev, visiting Moscow in 1927, tried to clarify his position with the dispossessed Boris Jürgenson:

> We kept our voices down, since we did not know who was in the next room . . . After his publishing firm in Russia had been nationalised, he gave foreign rights to a friend, a German publisher, Forberg. By this arrangement, Forberg reprints and sells abroad a number of works, including mine . . . In return he transfers money to Jürgenson from time

to time, but not very much and not on any regular basis. Of course, there is no question of accounts since it is all being done semi-legally. The aim of our conversation was to try to transfer the rights . . . so that the royalties from the sale of my works could be divided between me and Jürgenson.[12]

The firms that found refuge in Paris did not last very long. Bessel faded away on the rue de Moscou. Belayev in 1923 yielded representation of their composers to an Englishman, Ralph Hawkes, and Koussevitzky made a similar arrangement for the Gutheil and Editions Russes de Musique catalogues. He eventually sold them outright to Hawkes in 1945, in a settlement that earned Stravinsky an annual retainer of twenty-five thousand dollars in return for all future works. The glories of Russian music came to rest in British hands, which were held wide open to receive the fallen fruits of Europe's next storm.

In January 1933, once Hitler seized power, German publishers shed their Jewish composers and editors. 'A welcome cleaning up has been undertaken,'[13] wrote Willy Strecker of Schotts to Igor Stravinsky, whose violin concerto he had commissioned (on behalf of an American-Jewish soloist, Samuel Dushkin). Strecker asked the composer, living in France, to provide a 'declaration' of his Aryan and Christian antecedents for the publisher to use in refuting Nazi smears that Stravinsky was a 'Jewish Bolshevik'. The Nazis duly lifted their ban on Stravinsky. Strecker was unable, however, to alter their prejudice against the 'pure-blooded' Paul Hindemith and made no effort to protect his Jewish composer, Erich Wolfgang Korngold.

Hindemith, Korngold and hundreds of others joined a mass exodus, mostly to America, of atonalists, arch-modernists and composers of liberal or socialist inclinations. Kurt Weill, Hanns Eisler, Arnold Schoenberg, Ernst Krenek – leading lights of German music – were expunged by their German publishers and the industry itself was purged of Jewish proprietors. The Hinrichsen family, which had owned Peters Edition for sixty years, was ordered in 1939 to hand it over to a Nazi nominee, Johannes Petschull. One Hinrichsen survivor set up anew in London, another in New York; two directors were murdered in concentration camps.

The Berlin family firm of Adolf Fürstner, whose friendship with Richard Strauss stretched back to the turn of the century, endured identical expropriation. On reaching London, Otto Fürstner transferred all foreign rights in Strauss's operas into the grateful hands of Ralph Hawkes.

The custodians of German music, meanwhile, pandered shamelessly to the prevailing excrescence. Breitkopf und Härtel published an album of 'fighting songs' for the Hitler Youth. Ludwig Strecker, Willy's brother and co-director, edited a songbook for SA storm-troopers. Hitler sent diamond wedding greetings in 1942 to their parents, recalling that the elder Strecker had received in his youth fresh scores from the arch-racist Richard Wagner. Schotts provided the Reich with its only concert hit, the tramping rhythms and pagan choruses of Carl Orff's *Carmina Burana*, and became powerfully pre-eminent among German music publishers.[14]

When Nazism overwhelmed Austria in 1938, Ralph Hawkes took a train to Vienna to recruit editors from Universal Edition, which had been singled out by Goebbels as a nest of Jewishness and modernism. Hawkes appointed Ernst Roth, UE's head of publications, to a top position in Boosey & Hawkes – he eventually became company chairman – and Roth brought along Béla Bartók as his dowry. Erwin Stein, artistic adviser at UE, settled in London to nurse Boosey's brilliant young Benjamin Britten towards his first opera. Hans Heinsheimer, UE's head of opera, was instructed by Hawkes to set up an office in New York, to look after the fugitive Bartók and develop a new line of American composers, led by Aaron Copland. UE's part-owner, Alfred Kalmus, a musical enthusiast who began his career copying parts of Mahler's eighth symphony for its première, gathered his outlawed composers under Boosey's umbrella for the duration of hostilities and arranged concerts of their music in blitz-time London.

By the time Hitler was defeated, the vernacular of music publishing had shifted from German to English. The living greats – Schoenberg, Stravinsky, Bartók, Hindemith, Weill – were in the United States, their presence giving a moral and practical impetus to American music publishers. G. Schirmer Inc., founded in 1848 and headed by Gustave Schirmer III, produced the late works of Arnold Schoenberg alongside snappy new scores by Samuel Barber and Leonard Bernstein. Schirmer's had built its business on pocket scores of popular symphonies and its fortune on The Lord's Prayer, set to music by Albert Hay Malotte and jingling nightly as a close-down anthem on hundreds of radio stations. This deeply conservative firm now found itself among the leaders in new music, busily assisted by Hans Heinsheimer, who joined after being sacked by Hawkes for writing a humorous book about the music business.[15]

By 1950, on Hawkes's death, Schirmer and Boosey controlled the world's top composers. Schotts were still repairing bomb damage; Peters and Breitkopf were moving from communist Leipzig into the American zone, at Frankfurt and Wiesbaden; Universal in Vienna were locked in litigation with Boosey's over composers they had latterly dispossessed. Their common recovery, however, was gathering speed faster even than the national *Wirtschaftswunder*. 'In 1945 German music seemed a thing of the past. In

1951 it is one of the most vibrant voices in the concert of western Europe,' wrote the Munich critic, Karl Heinz Ruppel.[16]

The rebirth of German music publishing was founded on a faith in a united Europe. In musical terms, this meant endorsing the Darmstadt School doctrine of French and German composers who turned their backs on the past and restarted from scratch with a punitive regime of atonal and electronic music that lacked any national character.

The chief protagonists, Karlheinz Stockhausen and Pierre Boulez, hitched their careers to Universal. Schotts and Peters, more circumspectly, cultivated Bernd Alois Zimmermann and the Hamburg-based Hungarian exile György Ligeti. A wave of ascetic post-modernism cleansed German publishers of the taint of Nazism and restored them to continental command. 'French publishers made all the wrong decisions after the war, milking their old copyrights and becoming pretty much defunct,' explained a knowledgeable British editor.[17] Messiaen was the only famous composer whose works were mostly published in France. The rest followed Boulez across the Rhine where German publishers enjoyed access to the biggest pool of state-funded orchestras, opera houses and radio stations and every post-modernist knew that only German publishers could provide a regular calendar of performances.

'Pierre Boulez is a German agent,' griped the Schirmer composer Virgil Thomson, whose colourful suites were rarely heard in Europe. 'The Germans control music publishing today – not that they dare to speak up for Germany. What the Germans publish is music for the New Europe, and the business end of the New Europe is very largely an understanding between France and Germany.'[18]

Recovering international status, Schotts resumed operations in London. Petschull, the Peters boss, reached a settlement with the Hinrichsens which left him in control of the German head office, while they ran New York and London branches which recruited such avant-gardists as John Cage, Morton Feldman and Brian Ferneyhough. A musical Maginot line was thus drawn between Anglo-American-owned firms on one side, clinging to a traditional definition of 'good' music and 'great' composers, and Franco-Germans on the other, espousing 'new' music and paying for it with revenues of the old.

The division was mutually acceptable and the atmosphere within the industry was congenial to the point of connivance. Boosey and Schirmer's headed the traditionalist camp, which included such firms as Novello's, Oxford University Press and the Danish house of Hansen. Schotts and UE spearheaded the European vanguard, embracing occasional allies like Sikorski of Hamburg and Salabert of France. 'It is safe to prognosticate that fifty years from today the picture of music-making will not be greatly changed,' intoned Novello's official history in 1961, its hundred and fiftieth anniversary of doughty independence. No one could have foretold that Novello's would change hands three times in the next three decades, or that the array of autonomous music publishers would end up being covered by an unstoppable tide of corporate grey.

The idea that Universal Edition might look attractive to a serious investor was enough to curdle coffee-drinkers in a Ringstrasse café in fits of helpless giggles. Universal Edition existed as a licence to lose money. Started in 1901 with the aim of outselling Peters's distinctive green editions of standard ex-copyright classics, UE ran off fifteen hundred titles in six years and ran up a monumental debt of nine hundred thousand crowns ($180,000). Insolvency seemed certain until the dilettante directors turned to Emil Hertzka, a Budapest-born textile magnate with the flowing beard of a biblical prophet and a striking resemblance to Johannes Brahms. Hertzka's appearance was misleading, since he had no discernible knowledge of music. This advantage, it was said, rendered him immune to expert advice. 'Although I worked for quite a few years next door to him I never discovered whether he could even read music, nor did I ever hear him talk about it with enthusiasm or even sympathy,' recalled his fastidious assistant Ernst Roth,[19] doctor of jurisprudence and author of a treatise on aesthetic philosophy.

Musical ignorance, allied to fervent teetotalism, endowed Hertzka with a naive instinct for good composers. He took one look at Universal and decided there was no future in gems of the past. The only new publications in the list were symphonic poems by Strauss and Reger, picked up in a take-over of the Munich firm, Joseph Aibl. There was also a four-handed version of the second symphony by Gustav Mahler. Hertzka knew just enough about music to know that Mahler was all-powerful director of the Vienna Court Opera. He submitted an offer for Mahler's forthcoming symphony, the eighth, and in June 1909 signed Universal's first contract with a living composer. Four months later, he brought the unruly Arnold Schoenberg into the fold with his dangerous atonalities and his devoted acolytes, Alban Berg and Anton von Webern. Musical modernism was in a state of parturition and Universal Edition was the emergency midwife. Schoenberg declared tonality to be at an end; UE enabled musical Europe to sample his theories.

Hertzka bought a shop beneath the opera house arches to propagate his wares and bought up a dance publisher to pay for all the tunelessness. On Schoenberg's recommendation, he signed up his brother-in-law Alexander Zemlinsky and the Italian symphonist Alfredo Casella. Ferruccio Busoni came of his own accord. Karol Szymanowski joined in 1912, Frederick Delius some months later. There was no prospect of quick profit in any of them. Schoenberg was forever being advised by well-wishers (and others) to find some sounder means of eking out a living. His pupil Berg was put to work making a piano reduction for one of Hertzka's few early winners, a sexually decadent opera by Franz Schreker, *Der Ferne Klang*, that swept the boards of German theatres. Echoes of its sultry heat can be heard in Berg's two operatic masterpieces, *Wozzeck* and *Lulu*.

The First World War brought Béla Bartók and Leoš Janáček into UE from the outer reaches of the Austrian empire. Next came Zoltán Kodály, Darius Milhaud and Nikolai Myaskovsky.

In the fragile era that followed, Universal was internationalist and innovative, at the front line of cultural warfare and the front seat of musical scandals. It co-founded an International Society for Contemporary Music whose summer festivals were a shop window for UE novelties. As Schoenberg abandoned atonality for twelve-note music, Hertzka took on the dodecatonal pioneer Hauer and the microtonalist Hába. He recruited the Communist Eisler and the White Russian Medtner. He did not seem to care who or what he published, so long as it was provocatively new. Where the money came from was anyone's guess. On the rare occasions that one of his composers struck gold, Hertzka seemed mystified and not entirely pleased.

He had written off Ernst Krenek after one operatic disaster and refused to attend the Leipzig première in February 1927 of his jazzy *Jonny spielt auf*. By the close of that season, *Jonny* was playing in fifty houses and earning Nazi attacks on its heterodox raciality. Hertzka gave no sign of satisfaction then, or the following summer at the première of Weill's *Threepenny Opera*, a work that captured the frenetic amorality of inter-war Berlin and established Brecht and Weill as its oracle. 'As we watched the transformation of Kurt Weill,' reported Hans Heinsheimer, Universal's director of opera, 'we, too, were transformed.

> A lot of people who had avoided us through all of our professional lives like a boring plague, tried to find out how we spelled our names and were surprised to discover we had a telephone. Backstage . . . a man who looked like the personification of His Master's Voice and turned out to be just that had clawed his way towards Hertzka and had offered him money if he would let him record a show album of *Dreigroschenoper*. He did not *ask* for money to record one of our publications – he *offered* it. It was a shattering experience . . . a delicious disgrace.[20]

Hit or miss, Hertzka betrayed no emotion and formed no bond with his composers. Relations with Schoenberg were brittle and with Weill uneasy. He addressed all composers as 'Master' but did not reveal his opinion of any of them. 'He was not a kindly or genial man,' wrote Ernst Roth.

> It was said that Hertzka, for all his costly and unremunerative patronage of new ideals, never lost sight of his own personal interests . . . And still he did what no other music publisher at that time dared to do, and considerable sums of money were spent not only on engraving, printing, paper, binding and publicity, but also on supporting financially the struggling prophets of the new art. All this was done without charm, grace or warmheartedness, without any evident generosity – and yet it was still a unique undertaking.[21]

In 1927 Hertzka acquired the Vienna Philharmonic edition of popular pocket scores and appeared to be preparing himself for a shift in the political winds that would demonise modernism and restore the cult of romantic heroism. He was spared the trauma of seeing his Masters outlawed and exiled, collapsing in May 1932 with a fatal heart attack. His successors sought to reduce UE's offensiveness to Hitler by playing down Jewish composers and upgrading reactionary Germanists – to no avail. Alban Berg, who was racially acceptable, had extracts from his *Lulu*-in-progress banned in Berlin, a setback that delayed his work on the final act and resulted in the opera remaining unfinished at his death in 1935. When Hitler marched into Vienna in March 1938, Universal Edition was turned over to a pair of Nazi brothers, Robert and Ernst Geutebrück, who were charged with 'sanitising' its composers, staff and stock. On the completion of their mission in 1941, all shares passed into the hands of the acquisitive Johannes Petschull at C. F. Peters.

Among the few loyalists to keep their jobs was Alfred Schlee, UE's last salesman in Nazi Germany. Schlee paid lip service to the new rulers, but made it his business to steal one full set of every score Universal had ever published and bury them in church vaults and private houses. He 'risked his life many times for music,'[22] said Pierre Boulez and in June 1951, when UE was reconstituted, Schlee became joint head of the firm and part-owner, 'his reward for looking after the catalogue during the war,' said an insider.

Alfred Kalmus, Hertzka's long-bearded nephew and heir, remained in London to tend his Kalmus Edition, which discovered Harrison Birtwistle, the most important British composer after Britten. 'Dr Kalmus disliked going to Germany and Austria,' said members of his staff, but he worked amicably with Schlee and installed his son-in-law, Stefan Harpner, as co-director in Vienna.

It was Schlee who resuscitated UE by walking up to Stockhausen at the 1952 Donaueschingen festival and announcing 'I am your publisher.' Stockhausen's *Kontrapunkte* struck Schlee as a 'creative explosion' and UE became home for contemporary bleaknesses that were adored by a tiny intelligentsia and abominated by the general music public. The publication of these scores was subsidised by the sudden popularity of Mahler's symphonies and Janáček's operas. Hertzka's seeds were taking root in the second half of this century, enabling Universal to continue publishing new music without care or concern for profitability.

Back in 1942 Schlee had promised a Jewish fugitive in Italy that his music would be published when conditions permitted. Rolf Liebermann enjoyed some post-war success as a composer but gave it up to become a visionary opera administrator, running the Hamburg and Paris houses from 1959 to 1980.

Liebermann was sympathetic to new composers and intractable scores, forming around him a core of like-minded institutional managers. His *coup de grâce* was the long-awaited première of the complete *Lulu*, withheld until the death of Berg's widow who found within it proof of his extra-marital infidelities. The birth of *Lulu* on 24 February 1979 was a Universal affair. The opera, completed by UE composer Friedrich Cerha, was conducted by UE composer Boulez and staged at the Paris Opéra by UE composer Liebermann.

This was the last of Universal's glory nights. With Liebermann in retirement, the avant-garde in retreat and Mahler running out of copyright, the firm was reduced to marginal returns from intellectually chic but publicly unsaleable composers. UE was not financially unsettled and the list of concerts racked up by Luciano Berio and the Estonian Arvo Pärt were the envy of many small companies. But neither Berio nor Pärt was exclusive, Boulez had fallen silent and Stockhausen had repossessed his rights. During the 1980s with Kalmus dead, Schlee retired and Harpner removed, Universal Edition lost its links with the past and became just another colophon on the New European conformity. Alfred Schlee was preparing to receive ninetieth birthday tributes at Vienna's Musikvereinsaal in 1991 when UE received a shuddering jolt. A stranger turned up at a board meeting, saying he had bought thirty per cent of stock and expected to see a return on his investment.

The American was an unknown commodity. His name was Robert Wise and in the previous five years he had become the owner of some major publishing houses, among them Schirmer and Chester's. But Wise was not a member of the close-knit classical circle. His company, Music Sales Limited, founded in London in 1970, published pop songs for teenagers in piano and guitar transcriptions. He had no scholarly pedigree and made no effort to hide his scorn for the unbusinesslike ways of contemporary music publishers. 'I think they are more interested in their peers than they are in their composers,' he told the BBC. 'I'm not interested in being part of a club, and neither are our people. We are devoted to the composer and we are devoted to running our company efficiently.'[23]

His arrival stunned the UE boardroom. They knew where his shares came from – Kalmus's daughter, Susie Harpner, had sold up after her husband was ousted by Schlee's successor, Johann Juranek – and they knew they would have to dig deep to stop Wise gaining control. The gulf between them was colossal. The Viennese talked of art and ideals, Wise also asked to see the profit and loss account of every department. 'Their potential isn't being realised,' he said. 'They are contracting instead of expanding . . . I don't think it's the way to go, and the board clearly knows that: I'm on the board. I'm trying very hard to have them expand their activities and to generate some energy and life into the company. They have enormous potential, great rights, great opportunities in a market that's not overcrowded, especially in Germany and Austria, and they're not using it. I think we can wake them up.'

UE was awoken, but not as he had hoped. Reeling with shock, Vienna retracted its forces on to home territory and ordered the closure of the London office. An outcry from Harrison Birtwistle brought a stay of execution, but the retreat was unstoppable. By early 1995 all of UE's British composers had either fled or been set free and the firm was reorganised in a defensive trench. Birtwistle and the rising Scot, James MacMillan, went to Boosey & Hawkes, Simon Holt moved to Chester. Many of the remaining composers were unable to find a major publisher. In a world where the bottom line ruled, artists whose operas had been acclaimed at Glyndebourne and London were left high and dry in mid-career.

For Universal, retrenchment had the desired immediate effect. Wise, meeting majority resistance, sold his shares back to the board after little more than a year. Schotts, which already held a stake in UE, merged some of its operations and took a growing interest in its affairs. A veil of secrecy was clamped over these arrangements. 'The shareholders of UE do not wish to reveal their identities,' I was informed,[24] which seemed quaintly discreet for the custodian of so large a slice of our common European heritage. Not that it mattered much any more: UE was no longer a major player in the shaping of the musical future.

Wise came out of the transaction with a profit on his sale of shares and a much higher profile. He deplored UE's retreat – 'the worst thing they could have done,' he told them – and regretted the composer fall-out. He underlined his own commitment to living composers and would take libel action against any inference to the contrary. 'We turn the emphasis towards promotion of the composers,' he told the BBC. 'The more promotion, the more performance. The more performance, the more income. Very easy.' Wise believed he had a formula to make modern music pay dividends.

With or without UE, he was now the undisputed third force in music publishing. Back in 1975 it was reckoned that 'six main large firms operate in the field of serious music publishing.'[25] By 1995, due mainly to take-overs by Robert Wise, there were three left: himself, Boosey & Hawkes and Schotts with its German allies. In a shrinking pool, Wise was the expanding force and he had no reason to respect communal conventions. He did not share the background of his fellow-publishers and bore no debt to their traditions.

Born in New York into a family of music wholesalers, he was bored by the prospect of selling out-of-copyright scores to retail shops. Graduating from Cornell in 1959, he did well in the property market and wound up in London as the Sixties swung to an end. He liked the music of the Beatles and Rolling Stones and found it hard to obtain a playable score. Pop fans were considered musically illiterate and publishers could not be bothered with a minority who wanted to play the songs for themselves. 'Publishing in the old sense of printing sheet music has all but disappeared from the composition market,' noted a 1975 industry survey.[26] Wise saw a niche and founded Music Sales Limited. In due course he became the world's second largest distributor of pop sheets.

He had barely begun this venture when the venerable house of Novello came up for sale in 1969. Novello had Edward Elgar among its copyrights and an ailing trade in choral parts for great oratorios. It also owned a scatter of valuable properties in and around London. It looked like a perfect bet to Wise and he swooped on thirty per cent of the shares. He was beaten to the rest, however, by Granada Television whose vice-chairman, Denis Forman, was an opera buff. The Novello publishing house and its organ, *Musical Times*, was absorbed into the Granada group and hobbled on until 1986 when the network stripped down for a franchise battle and put its non-core activities up for sale. Wise put in a late bid but was beaten by a company called Filmtrax, which duly transferred its purchase to Classix Investments Ltd, an arm of the Ensign Trust that ran the Merchant Navy pension fund. Classix viewed the field of music publishing as a sensible investment and rationalised its properties. It seemed that Robert Wise was not fated to play a significant role in classical music publishing.

He had begun to develop a taste for it, though. In 1979, he picked up his first copyrights with the purchase of Campbell Connelly, a publisher of popular Forties songs, and found that by hiring a team of salesmen to plug the songs to performers and disc-jockeys he could prolong their shelf-life beyond the expected ephemerality. The same techniques, he reckoned, could be applied to classical backlists if only he got the chance.

In 1985 Wise bought the New York family business from his brother and partners and held the Music Sales Corporation in readiness for the eventuality of a publishing purchase. He did not have long to wait. Robert Maxwell, the rogue publisher, had just gobbled up Macmillan Inc. at the start of his US career and had no use for its musical subsidiary, G. Schirmer Inc. The four-generation family firm, sold to Macmillan in 1969 and still the major imprint in America, was put up for sale to the highest bidder. On his home turf Robert Wise faced no competition. Overnight he became the biggest classical music publisher on the American continent.

His acquisition triggered uncertainty among Schirmer composers, some of whom, led by Leonard Bernstein and Elliott Carter, scuttled off to Boosey & Hawkes. Their defection was irksome and did not increase Wise's esteem for his British competitor as he set about restoring Schirmer with the vigour of a revivalist. The firm was in poor shape, losing one and a half million dollars in its last Macmillan year. Over the next eight years Wise increased its income eightfold, by his own account. With Schirmer as his American base, he began building a European portfolio from London – Union Musical Ediciones, the largest music publisher in Spain; Edition Wilhelm Hansen, the most famous firm in Scandinavia, with its London subsidiary, Chester Music Group. Finally, in 1993, he claimed the prize that had twice eluded him, buying Novello from the seamen's friends for two and a half million pounds.

In a run of acquisitions, Wise gathered beneath a single roof the valuable copyrights in Sibelius and Nielsen (Hansen); Granados and Rodrigo (UME); Elgar and Holst (Novello); Barber and Menotti (Schirmer); Poulenc and Lutoslawski (Chester); as well as some Stravinsky scores. To these he added populist living composers like Philip Glass and Michael Nyman. He remained alert to opportunity and the music industry fluttered with rumours of his movements. His involvement in UE was one of several flirtations with small firms that failed to achieve consummation. From the moment that Robert Wise came on the scene, music publishing seemed up for grabs. Some firms, like the university presses, were protected by charter. Others huddled closer to big brothers. 'As a single classical music house, you can't plug in to a world network,' said Wise. 'Unless you can do that, you can't do the composer justice. A company like Faber or Peters cannot do what we can do.'[27] The writing was all too clearly on the wall.

His two major competitors moved firmly to secure their position. Schotts, still run by the Streckers, had UE in tow and other German imprints in thrall. On state-subsidised German territory they were unbeatable. Wise had no office in Germany; he channelled his classical business through the Hamburg house of Sikorski.

Boosey & Hawkes, as a publicly quoted company based in London, appeared more vulnerable and at one time its shares, mostly owned by Carl Fischer Inc., an American music wholesaler, were being eyed by take-over specialists. Any fears for its security were dispelled when share values sextupled on the strength of a Polish symphony and a Walt Disney lawsuit. *A Symphony of Sorrowful Songs* by Henryk Mikolai Górecki sold three-quarters of a million records world-wide in 1993, by far the biggest hit by a living serious composer since Rachmaninov was alive.

Around the same time, the use of a few Stravinsky bars in the video release of *Fantasia* landed the Disney Corporation with a two-hundred-million-dollar claim that the composer would surely have appreciated: he was paid only five thousand dollars for letting the music be played in the movie. It was musical quirks like these that indicated the unquantifiable value of intellectual property in the dawning information era and made music publishing a lucrative proposition. Boosey might find another Górecki at any moment, and it would earn from Stravinsky until the year 2042. Wise, not to be outdone, snapped up previous works by Górecki in a contract with his privatised Polish publisher and secured a handful of unassigned Stravinsky scores from the composer's heirs. Although classics accounted for less than five per cent of performing rights revenue, and companies like Music Sales were minnows beside the pop giants Warner and Chappells, competition for contemporary composers had never been keener and yields never higher.

Music Sales Limited, which did not include revenues from Schirmer and Wise's other US holdings, yielded profits after tax of £1.3 million in the calendar year 1993. The chairman and highest-paid director was paid £367,399. The previous year, he took a salary of £1,098,510.[28] These were happy days at Boosey, too, where pre-tax profits topped five million pounds and the highest-paid director, Richard Holland, received just under a hundred and fifty thousand pounds.[29] The accounts of Music Sales Corporation and Schotts Verlag were not published.

At the opposite end of the scale, and this comparison may appear unfair, it was reliably reported[30] that no more than two or three composers in any publisher's list were able to make a living from composing alone. In one comprehensive earnings survey, serious composers on average obtained less than one tenth of their income from musical composition.[31] The bulk came from teaching, copying, performing and non-musical activities. Beethoven may have died poor, but at least he died composing. Today's composers devoted less and less time to their calling. Many were unable to find a publisher, at a time when publishing profits had never been higher. Yet today's publishers earned more and more from the performance of music. Without composers what did the publishers amount to? It would be unwise to attempt an answer to that conundrum. All music publishers, no matter how small or benevolent, are uncommonly sensitive about their image.

Early in 1995 the last head of Universal's London office, Bill Colleran, gathered around him the rejected composers of modern publishing to form a new imprint at the University of York. Colleran was perhaps the final relic of UE idealism, devoted to his Masters and unconcerned with bottom lines. On paper, the team he assembled was formidable. It was headed by David Blake, a pupil of Hanns Eisler's who had written two political operas, *Toussaint* and *The Plumber's Gift*, for English National Opera. Blake lost his Novello contract after its acquisition by Music Sales. 'I was the first to get the chop, five days after the take-over,' he said. 'If you're not bringing in regular royalties, you've had it.'[32]

Vic Hoyland and David Sawer were left homeless when Universal withdrew from London. Anthony Gilbert and George Nicholson were released by Schott. Trevor Wishart was Britain's leading electronic composer. Anne Boyd was once published by Faber.

These were just a few of the fall-out victims in Britain. There were just as many deserving voices in other countries whom Colleran hoped to help by persuading performing, broadcasting and recording companies to reconsider their proven merits. For in an era of toughened copyright laws and ever-expanding media channels, there was more despair among composers and fewer outlets for their cries than at any time since the French Revolution. European harmonisation, which extended authors' copyright to seventy posthumous years and brought windfalls to the heirs of James Joyce and Thomas Mann, bypassed the composing profession whose rights were held primarily by publishers. Music publishers were in for a bonanza from contracts dating back to 1901 – mostly 'at the expense of the composer's estates', said a leading copyright consultant.[33] The individual composer ranked among the great dispossessed of modernity.

The roots of their powerlessness lay in the terms of a contract that had scarcely changed since Napoleonic times. Where authors would license a book to their publishers only for so long as it remained in print, and latterly for a shorter limit of ten or twenty years, composers who signed with a music publisher were required to sign away their rights in a score for all eternity. 'If you sign a contract with a major publisher, you surrender your birthright,' complained one American composer.[34] A few top earners, following Leonard Bernstein's lead, were able to form their own imprints and short-lease the scores to major publishers for world-wide distribution. But those who failed to achieve media stardom were forced to accept the publisher's terms, and think themselves lucky. For most composers the chances of performance and publication were now smaller than they had been when Mozart was alive. At the dawn of the twentieth century there existed two dozen music publishers of international consequence. By the mid-point there were half a dozen. At the end, there were just three major groupings. In score, as in every other aspect of the art, classical music was being corporatised to extinction.

NOTES

1 The British Copyright Acts of 1709 and 1775 applied only to printed books, giving their authors limited protection against pirate editions for up to twenty-one years.
2 *My Life*, p. 302
3 Mainz, 1951
4 *My Life*, p. 833
5 Cosima Wagner's Diaries (Collins, London) 1978, vol. II, entry for 17 July 1881, p. 690
6 loc. cit.
7 *Billboard* magazine, 12 August 1994, p. 38
8 identity protected, at informant's request
9 Rimsky, p. 275
10 Rimsky, p. 379
11 Stravinsky, *Selected Correspondence*, vol. I, pp. 67–8n
12 Prokofiev, pp. 52–3
13 Stravinsky, *Correspondence*, vol. III, p. 218
14 see Levi, pp. 159–65
15 *Menagerie in F. Sharp*
16 *Music in Germany* (F. Bruckmann, Munich) 1952, p. 77
17 author's interview
18 author's interview
19 Roth, p. 58
20 Heinsheimer, *Aida*, pp. 122–3
21 Roth, p. 58
22 Boulez, interviewed in *Lulu's Ziehvater*, Schlee's ninetieth birthday feature on ORF/ZDF.
23 interview on Radio 3, *Music Weekly*, 27 October 1991
24 official communication by fax, dated 12 January 1995
25 Peacock, p. 159
26 Peacock, p. 155
27 comments to the author, June 1993
28 source: Companies House. Music Sales Limited accounts for the year ended 31 December 1993
29 annual reports, 1993–4
30 BBC Radio 3, *Music Weekly*, 27 October 1991
31 Peacock, p. 23
32 author's interview
33 *Guardian*, 18 December 1995, p. 3, quoting Robert Montgomery, former head of the Mechanical Protection Society
34 conversation with the author

CHAPTER XIII

MASTERS OF
THE UNIVERSE

W hen Mark Hume McCormack was six years old, his godfather, the poet-historian Carl Sandburg, wrote a poem in his honour called 'Young Mark Expects'. It was a dotty pair of verses that barely deserved publication but, Sandburg being Lincoln's biographer and a national icon, it soon appeared in *Good Housekeeping* magazine. The title said it all: Young Mark had been pestering the old man for something and Sandburg, with a poet's insight, saw in the boy's eyes that what young Mark expects, young Mark usually gets.

Mark McCormack is proud of his poem. When he mentions it nowadays, however, the title gets transfigured in his normally infallible memory. He recalls the title as 'Young Mark Waits in Expectation',[1] subverting boyish nagging into something subtly more insistent. As an adult he would wait for no one.

McCormack's determination was formed in the year of the poem, 1936, by a near-fatal road accident. His skull smashed by a speeding car, he saw his parents at his hospital bedside thinking he would die – and, scared as he was, willed himself to survive. Barred from playing rough sports, he was taken out on a golf course where, keen to win, he threw a tantrum at the avuncular

Sandburg who played for pleasure. At fifteen, he was High School champion of Chicago and heading for college honours. Then he met Arnold Palmer and knew he could not win. Palmer was the best golfer he had ever seen, or dreamed of. McCormack played on, but the passion went out of his game. There was no purpose in playing a sport he could not win. Mark McCormack only ever wanted to be Number One.

Exactly why, no one can explain. Possibly something to do with being the almost-snatched only child of middle-American parents growing up in an era of limitless aspirations. His mother 'was a very precise, organised person . . . she laid out the next morning's breakfast before she went to bed, was always very punctual, with a routine that never changed'.[2] McCormack planned his life on parallel lines, segmenting the quarter-hours of each day into capsular tasks on pads of yellow lined paper and crossing off each deed as soon as it was done. Obsessively retentive, he keeps a daily record of the hours he sleeps, what he eats and drinks, how much exercise he takes; he can tell you to the minute what he will be doing on any day of the week six months hence. He inscribed his first book to his mother for inculcating in him 'an awareness that money was indeed worth being concerned about'. His father, a publisher of farming journals descended from the Scottish free-market philosopher, David Hume, was credited for teaching him 'the importance of being highly sensitive to people's feelings'.[3] The combination would prove deadly effective. McCormack has two mottos. 'Never underestimate the import- ance of money' is his public watchword. 'Observe aggressively' is his inner command.

He took a law degree at Yale, did army service in Georgia, married, had four children and played pro-am golf. The pros kept showing him their contracts. In 1960, aged thirty, he became Arnold Palmer's agent. Thirty years later, Palmer was still golf's top-earner, with a twelve-million-dollar annual income.[4] Motor cars and sweat-shirts bore his name; Arnold Palmer tea-houses flourished in Japan. McCormack had put a price on success and sold it for more than anyone imagined it might be worth.

As Palmer became golf's first millionaire, fellow-players thronged to McCormack's new agency, the International Management Group. First off the tee were Gary Player and Jack Nicklaus, Palmer's only real rivals. With the three champions in his pouch, McCormack could begin dictating terms to the well-meaning amateurs and retired professionals who ran the gentlemanly game. McCormack demanded more for his players, more contests, more prize money, more fame.

As tennis shed its amateur status, he snapped up the Wimbledon champions Rod Laver and Margaret Court, followed by the best of the rest. Barging into Wimbledon's marketing office, he brushed aside old colonels and ex-colonials to raise the championship's profits from a paltry thirty-six thousand pounds in 1968 to fourteen million pounds in 1993 – a surplus of one million pounds for every day of play. The following year he doubled the money, to £27.9 million. 'Imaginative selling of the championships by Mark McCormack, who is the All England's Club's international television consultant, has led to the spectacular rise in profits,' noted *The Times*.

To achieve these gains, McCormack altered the art of spectatorship. He had dirt walkways neatly paved and roped off privileged areas for sponsoring companies and their guests, liberally entertained in hospitality tents. True fans queued hopelessly in the rain, while financiers quaffed champagne and tennis chiefs flapped impotently. 'What happens is that sport allows him to find their money . . . and then finds he is gradually taking control,' said Phillipe Chatrier, president of the International Tennis Federation.[5]

Television was McCormack's stroke of luck. An increase in channels and transmission hours in the late 1960s sparked a surge in live programming. What could be easier on the eye, on new-fangled colour screens, than the fairways of a famous golf course and the flicker of white skirts on Wimbledon lawns? With McCormack at the media controls, the rolling greens began rolling in greenbacks.

His method was brutally direct. Taking over television sales at the Royal and Ancient golf club at St Andrews in 1977, McCormack told America's ABC network that the price for relaying the British Open had risen from one hundred thousand dollars to a million. Heavily reliant on sports ratings, ABC paid up without a whimper and paid again when McCormack doubled the whack. A lesser operator would have rested on his laurels, knowing the tele-ransom could be raised at will. But it was not in McCormack's nature to be content. He studied the television equation and saw a magic circle of mutual interests. The more TV paid for sports, the more his players would be seen on screen. The more they were seen, the more valuable they became to product sponsors who sewed logos on their nipples, rumps and forearms. The more insignias they wore, the more manufacturers would support the message with game-break advertisements, and the more profitable sport became to television. McCormack could then squeeze TV moguls for ever higher relay fees on behalf of the game's organisers. The more television paid to St Andrews, the more prize and appearance money there was for the players, and the more commission for IMG. Everyone was happy. Everyone was making money. Everyone hailed Mark McCormack as a genius who put jam on the sportsman's bread and butter and sport in the world's living-rooms.

To players who signed with his agency he promised total care and attention in exchange for a twenty-per-cent share. 'You will never have to open another brown envelope,' he pledged. Everything in a sporting life, from coaching to taxes to alimony payments would be taken care of by the nanny-state he created. IMG clients knew they could ring their minder at any hour of the day and night; the highest earners could disturb McCormack himself. 'IMG's personal representation activities begin with a responsive one-on-one relationship between client and manager,' purred the company brochure. 'All of its services are personalized to meet the exact needs of each individual client.' Proof of the formula was the fact that very few IMG sportsmen ever left McCormack's shelter.

To keep his players busy and television beaming all year round, he filled blank weeks in the sporting calendar with new tournaments – the Toyota World Matchplay at Wentworth in Surrey, the ATP tennis championships in Frankfurt, the Johnnie Walker golf championships in Jamaica, the International Nice Triathlon in France and the World Equestrian Games in Stockholm. In such events McCormack booked the venue, supplied the players, recruited the sponsors, fixed the television deal and made up the rules where necessary.

The mark of McCormack was soon felt wherever humans competed in athletic endeavour. He recruited more American football and basketball players than any other agency, the racing drivers Jackie Stewart and Ayrton Senna and the Romanian gymnast Nadia Comaneci. The Olympic Games, that summit of selfless endeavour, had long been in his sights. He emerged from the 1968 Winter Olympics with its star skiier, Jean-Claude Killy, winning himself a sizeable footprint on French television. Killy, when he retired, set up in business with McCormack co-promoting the 1992 Albertville Games.

IMG had been retained as a consultant by the Olympic organising committees of Calgary, Seoul and Lillehammer, but was held at arm's length by the International Olympic Committee, chaired since 1980 by the Spanish ex-Francoist, Juan-Antonio Samaranch. McCormack's bids to run Olympic sponsorship auctions were repeatedly rejected in favour of lesser-known associates of the secretive IOC. At Barcelona in 1992, IMG was pointedly shut out of the Olympic arena area and had to set up its hospitality tent some distance away. Yet the Olympics had been transformed, their amateurism destroyed, by the economic formula McCormack had invented between sports, commerce and media. In 1960, when IMG was founded, US rights for screening the Rome Olympics were sold for less than four hundred thousand dollars. By 1976 the price was twenty-five million. At Barcelona in

1992, NBC paid over four hundred million dollars[6] for the right to show the Games, a thousandfold increase in a single generation.

To capitalise on his media advantage, McCormack formed his own television company, Trans World International (TWI), to film tournaments and syndicate blameless documentaries about his clients. The dawn of satellite broadcasting earned him a deal to sell five thousand hours of programming every year to Rupert Murdoch. The sky was now literally the limit, and TWI proclaimed itself 'the world's largest independent source of televised sports'. McCormack himself took the lip-microphone from time to time to appear on the BBC as a pithy golf commentator in tournaments he organised, marketed and dominated.

To keep new talent flowing, he funded tennis schools in Florida, Spain, Italy and Belgium and planned more in Germany and Asia. Andre Agassi, Monica Seles and Jim Courier graduated from his academies and became clients of his agency. He liked to be described as 'The Most Powerful Man in Sports'. He also answered proudly to the nickname 'Mark the Shark'. There was nothing reticent about his aims or the methods by which he achieved them. In golf and tennis, he became Number One without ever having to strike a ball.

Between the day Carl Sandburg penned his poem and the night half a century later that he broke into song, Mark Hume McCormack showed no interest in the arts. His world was sports and sponsorship. He worked all hours of the clock and read company reports for relaxation. He had enough college French to decipher a restaurant menu but had no flair for the niceties of language and took no pride in a polished phrase. 'There are no literary prizes for the Great Memo,'[7] he wrote. His best-selling business manuals were composed of brief homilies that turned incidents from his own life into the anyone-can-make-it formula of a *Good Housekeeping* recipe. Everything he did was end-oriented. In bed, said his second wife, the doubles player Betsy Nagelson, 'Mark does not sleep. He accomplishes rest.' 'Getting to sleep is no problem,' confirmed McCormack, 'I decide to sleep in order to get my scheduled hours for that day on the yellow sheet.'[8]

Music never moved him much. He mooned to Frank Sinatra in his teens and admired the smooth ascent of Paul McCartney: 'I kinda grew up with the Beatles. As my career was starting so did theirs, as my career developed so did theirs. Their music was a part of my life. So I still get chills up and down my spine when I hear some of their stuff.' He was never tempted, however, to manage pop stars. 'Their longevity isn't much. Their reliability – with exceptions like McCartney – isn't very high. And competition in the field is more severe and sophisticated than in classical music. I don't want to tangle with people in that business.'

His interest in classical music was kindled by meeting the soprano Kiri Te Kanawa on a Surrey golf course. He, the tanned sportsman and tough businessman, would not wish to be mistaken for some lily-livered aesthete and he confessed total ignorance of her art. Te Kanawa offered to teach him the basics, taking him to a concert and, in a much-repeated anecdote, advising that 'the first thing you have to know is, it's intermission, not half-time'. McCormack was bored by the programme but intrigued by the possibilities. 'I decided that there was a tremendous parallel between sports and classical music,' he told me in the first of two extended interviews. 'Sports personalities and classical artists perform their profession without considera-tion of language. Both face identical tax and other financial considerations as they travel from country to country. We were eminently qualified on an internationally co-ordinated basis through forty-six offices around the world to deal with those problems.

'Also, we were very well connected world-wide with the corporations that sponsor sports. Many of the people that buy sports are responsible for buying cultural sponsorships and we sensed in them an interest in getting into that part of the arena.' In other words, there was money to be made from classical music, with little extra effort or expense, by doing exactly the same as he did in sports. Treading gingerly at first, he offered financial and tax advice to a couple of classical artists and set up concerts for Te Kanawa in conventional venues in Australia. By 1983 he was ready to take the next step and instructed John Webber, his senior international vice-president, to investigate the classical field. Webber had joined IMG fresh out of law school in 1972 and made its European office grow from six staff to a houseful. His personal clients included Nick Faldo and the jazz singer Shirley Bassey, and he was frequently used by McCormack as a trouble-shooter in areas the big man barely understood.

The first priority was to acquire artists and expertise. A showbiz contact pointed them towards the Hamlen-Landau agency in New York, a two-person team founded in 1978 with a reputation for personal care and an eye for young talent; its dozen-or-so clients included the violinist Joshua Bell and the soprano Arleen Auger. McCormack liked what he saw and bought the firm, renaming it IMG Artists but allowing Charles Hamlen and Edna Landau to proceed at their own pace. 'Edna and I were always given absolute independence to develop things the way we thought best,'[9] said Hamlen.

Their first coup, two years later, was to sign the supreme violinist, Itzhak Perlman. Like most protégés of power-fiddler Isaac Stern, Perlman worked with the ICM agency division run by Lee Lamont, Stern's former secretary, a circle that represented as much a collective world view as any managerial allegiance. Perlman's walk-out was a blow to the Sternists and a major coup for IMG, the more so when his concert fee hit forty-five thousand dollars and he began making television commercials for Fuji-Xerox films and the Paine-Webber bank. He also appeared on daytime cookery shows. 'Artists don't get a lot of those things,' said McCormack, 'because traditionally the representation of classical artists hasn't included that sort of thing. They're intrigued generally because they see sports personalities getting it all the time. They perceive us as the dominant company in sports and think, "my god, if I go with them, I might be drinking Diet Sunkist or get an American Express ad." And we are fairly good at that.'

Perlman's version of events was somewhat more downbeat. 'I didn't go to IMG,' he told me. 'What happened was, I started with Hurok and got together in his office with Sheldon Gold. Then Sheldon Gold became ICM. Then Sheldon Gold died. I never recovered, really. He was, for me, the last of the old-fashioned managers.

'After a while, I felt ICM was getting too big and I was looking for a small management and a friend of mine was with Hamlen and Landau. It was about the time that IMG acquired them. So I didn't go to IMG. I went to Hamlen and Landau, and then it became IMG. My going to IMG had to do with the kind of people there are at IMG Artists. It's the person I deal with that's important. I never did much by way of [product] endorsements. When I did American Express, it was way before I went to IMG.'[10]

If McCormack expected a rush of artists to follow Perlman, he was soon disabused. Even Kiri Te Kanawa, who shared his Wimbledon box, kept the better part of her stage career with other agencies and joined IMG only for one-off promotions. This did not stop McCormack from proclaiming their joint triumphs. 'We had Kiri do a concert in the [Australian] outback,' he bragged. 'We had her singing in vineyards in Victoria, we had concerts in Tokyo. We got sponsors for these things, we got public acceptance. We made Kiri more money than she'd ever made before, and made money for ourselves as well.' Dame Kiri protested to the press that she had been misrepresented. It was 'completely inappropriate', she wrote, to discuss her art in such pecuniary terms.

Impatient with classical reticence McCormack plunged into arena opera, a mass entertainment designed for yuppies who lacked the social confidence to venture into a conventional opera house. IMG booked the Earl's Court exhibition centre in west London and co-produced *Carmen* in 1987, with a cast of five hundred and Maria Ewing in the title role. It cost £4.5 million and was seen by one hundred thousand people in London, and a quarter of a million by the end of a tour to Australia and Japan. Placido Domingo came one night and liked it so much he asked IMG to offer him arena concerts. José Carreras, recovering from leukaemia, made his stage comeback in the Tokyo *Carmen*. Two of the top three living tenors were thus lightly hooked on IMG's brand of classics.

In *Aida*, imported from the Arena di Verona, IMG went one further and transferred its entertainment tents from Wimbledon. 'Techniques that we pioneered in promoting sports events and making them more enjoyable for the customer were unknown in classical music,' said McCormack. The delight among champagne-quaffing corporate guests was audible for miles around.

Then came *Tosca*. Timed for Wimbledon week in 1991, just as a world recession broke, it swallowed most of the two and a half million pounds McCormack was persuaded to put up. 'I should never have let them talk me into doing an opera I had never heard of,' he complained bitterly. The perfect timing that had graced his sporting life seemed to have deserted him in music. Artists were not rushing to his agency and the economy was sick.

At sixty, he could ill afford to waste much time. If music had been a minor sport, he might have quit after *Tosca*. But his pride was hurt by public failure and the bottom line still looked encouraging. In 1990, 'classical arts' amounted to four per cent of IMG's seven-hundred-million-dollar turnover, overtaking motor racing and equestrian sports in company ranking. By the time McCormack completed his next moves, music would be his fourth-largest earner, behind golf, tennis and team sports.

Like many another magnate unable to expand as quickly as he wanted, McCormack took a trip down take-over lane. Hamlen and Landau had given him a start but he needed a European bridgehead and, sitting up and begging to be bought was the biggest classical agency in Britain. Harold Holt Limited looked after such luminaries as Bernard Haitink, Simon Rattle, Sir Neville Marriner and Daniel Barenboim. Holt had lately bought the John Coast opera agency, representing Carreras and Luciano Pavarotti. It was conspicuously cash-starved and some of its active partners were on the wrong side of seventy. Holt was ripe for the plucking.

When McCormack showed interest the directors appointed Sir Claus Moser, former Covent Garden chairman and chief government statistician, to head its negotiating team. With the pomp of a galleon setting out to sea, the stately British firm voted unanimously to accept IMG's initial offer. McCormack, however, had a different way of doing business. He kept the deal on hold for eighteen months while Webber went through the books.

Then, in December 1990, he told Moser the figures did not add up and made a substantially – some say, insultingly – smaller offer for the firm. 'We did a whole financial review at Holt and things were not quite the same as we had believed,'[11] said Webber.

No sooner was his new offer rejected than Holt's youngest director, Stephen Wright, quit the agency to join IMG, taking with him twenty-five artists and the entire orchestral touring department. 'We got what we wanted,' gloated McCormack, 'the most profitable part of Holt's business – orchestral touring – and their most talented person in Stephen. It was like trying to buy the British Ryder Cup team and *only* getting [Nick] Faldo and [Ian] Woosnam.'

Wright had told Webber he would not go unless his former partners were generously compensated with a six-figure settlement paid over three years, giving Holt the cash injection it so keenly desired. Nevertheless, a wave of fear and loathing swept the normally placid waters of British music. Jasper Parrott, an independent agent, called Wright's defection 'a major moral lapse' and others shunned him as a leper. When the dust settled, it became clear that Holt had been left with seniorities, while McCormack had claimed the rising generation of conductors in Mariss Jansons, John Eliot Gardiner and Franz Welser-Möst. He had first call on Carreras. The golden flautist, James Galway, dumped his career-long adviser, Michael Emmerson, to join IMG. Riccardo Chailly, music director of Holland's Concertgebouw orchestra, signed up. Yuri Temirkanov and the St Petersburg Philharmonic topped the touring attractions. 'The McCormacks of this world,' reflected David Sigall, president of the British Association of Concert Agents (BACA), 'have realised that there is big money to be made in classical music. The traditional agent is limited by his resources. McCormack has enormous wealth.' The tremors were palpable. 'We're seeing a huge change,' fretted ICM's Lee Lamont, 'everything's being shaken up.'

McCormack was not going to be satisfied with fifty artists and a fleet of touring orchestras. Six months after the Holt raid he told me, 'We're looking for any intelligent way to cohesively develop a genuine world-wide management, event and touring classical company which is *the dominant force in the world*.'

He dismissed the all-powerful CAMI as 'an *American* outfit – have they got offices on five continents?' and mocked the small horizons of managers like Moser and Parrott. 'We saw that there wasn't anybody doing this very well in the [music] world, so we figured the competition was non-existent,' said McCormack, the leitmotiv bubbling combatively to his lips. 'We intend to be

Number One in music,' he said. 'We are looking for any strategy that will enable us to secure the Number One position.'

One morning in December 1992 a London agent, Tom Graham, requested a meeting with his chairman, Jasper Parrott. American born and a sometime CAMI trainee, Graham had linked up with Parrott and Terry Harrison in 1974 to provide their new agency with a vocal division. 'We were all the same age and decided we had the same outlook and somewhat aggressive approach,' he recalled.[12] Their agency claimed to be the largest autonomous classical management in Europe.

At the precise moment that Graham walked into Parrott's office, his close friend Diana Mulgan went in to see Robert Rattray, her co-director at Lies Askonas Limited. Their firm bore the name of its founder, a Vienna-born fencing mistress who served on General Eisenhower's staff during the Normandy landings and dedicated herself professionally from 1952 to the development of musical talent. Miss Askonas introduced Birgit Nilsson, Teresa Berganza and Nicolai Gedda to British audiences, and exemplified a traditional ethic of personal representation. She had bustled into recent retirement, confident that her hand-reared heirs would preserve the courtesies and conduct of her company.

It was a few days before Christmas and the music business was winding down. Wasting no time on seasonal pleasantries, Graham told his horrified chairman that he was leaving, with sixty top singers, to join IMG. Mulgan announced simultaneously that she was heading in the same direction with forty vocalists. Between them, the pair managed some of the sweetest voices in Europe, including Anne Sofie von Otter, Barbara Bonney and Thomas Hampson. Parrott that day lost two-thirds of his artists, Askonas about half. 'What we went through was completely out of the blue,' said Parrott some months later. 'Tom Graham told me he had been made an offer he could not refuse. A six-figure sterling offer. IMG is extremely good at singling out people and finding out their price.'

'We are giving talented people an opportunity to come with us of their own free will,' rebutted McCormack bluntly. 'No one's forcing any artists to go with them. If I lose a tennis manager, I don't necessarily lose his players.'

For the second time in two years, the music business was stunned by the arrogance and ease of McCormack's penetration. In a milieu that centred on money, there was no defence against bigger money – and McCormack with his sports fortune could outbuy anyone in music. He was also well aware that musicians were bound more closely to a personal manager than sportsmen were. Unlike golfers who fly in convoys from one contest to the next, soloists and conductors spend their working lives in single-occupancy hotel rooms, depending on a personal agent to keep them in tune with events. The agent, rather than the agency, is their lifeline. When an agent moves his artists follow like lambs. On being told that his personal manager had switched from Holt to IMG Sir Neville Marriner went along without a second thought. 'I have a personal relationship with Stephen Wright and I would not dream of mistrusting his judgement,' he reacted. 'I suppose IMG does represent a different style of management, but I don't see that I need to get drawn into that.'[13]

Thus, in two master-swoops, McCormack assembled the second-largest music agency in the world, based in a converted warehouse beside a roundabout on the motorway to Heathrow airport. The drab location, remote from any place of musical performance, underlined the change of style and priorities that McCormack brought to the music business. Unlike other agents, he did not woo and pursue solo players: he bought them wholesale. 'We're not hiring Mr X to get Singer Y as a client,' said McCormack. 'We're hiring Mr X, who's gonna get five hundred Miss Ys during the next thirty years.' For McCormack, the personal manager was the real talent, not the individual artist.

There was a redoubling of outrage in the agency world. Parrott demanded Tom Graham's removal as BACA chairman, but lost the vote. 'If Tom Graham and Diana Mulgan had been happy and fulfilled in their former positions, they would never have come here – and nor would their artists,' said IMG, and Mulgan let slip that she had been lunched by Parrott two months beforehand with a view to joining *his* agency. Poaching was an open game.

'I have no ill will towards IMG,' said Parrott months later, 'because that is the kind of business they are. In a way, it has made people like us think incredibly hard about what it is we can offer. It's a re-invigorating process. I have absolutely no doubt that the rest of the music business will adjust. It will defend itself better with tougher agent contracts and it will attack IMG's methods and approach. Smaller firms may merge. There will be more IMG raids, but as that process develops artists will peel off because they find that sort of thing intensely disagreeable. I am absolutely certain that there will be substantial defections of artists.'

McCormack, when I next saw him, looked like a bear who had collared the honey. 'We're right along the way to accomplishing what we want,' he said. 'We're getting close.'

He was planning Wimbledon-week concerts at the Royal Palace of Hampton Court; he was taking over marketing for the Arena di Verona, staging a festival at Aix-en-Provence in France and marketing the Sydney Opera House's twenty-fifth anniversary. He told a French journalist he might be interested in the troubled Bastille Opéra in Paris.

He was still on the prowl, ready and cash-rich to seize the day. His turnover was approaching the formidable figure of one billion dollars. Perched in a stiff armchair in his London mews house, in a lounge decorated with all the singularity of a Hilton bedroom, his ice-blue eyes registered their habitual impassivity. Not just the static expression but his flat, adverbless speech, his featureless casual clothes and his entire physical demeanour are designed to give nothing away. His control is uncanny and to some people frightening, though a rough warmth can percolate the mask of businesslike charm. He is neither an automaton nor as dispassionate as he likes to seem. 'I have a strong emotional streak in me,' he once confessed, 'which not much touches.'[14]

Music least of all. Was he ever moved by it? 'No, I'm not. I went to Solti's last performance [as music director] with the Chicago Symphony, *Otello* at Carnegie Hall. Everybody was in tears. It was moving just to watch the audience, not so much as to watch Pavarotti and Kiri and Solti. To listen to the fifteen-minute ovation and see everybody crying and yelling and screaming. That moved me because I knew that, my god, if they were doing that, this has to be an awfully momentous occasion.'

Most people who became concert agents did so because they were ravished by the sound, infatuated by its performers, or raised in a family firm devoted to the welfare of artists. Even Ronald Wilford has shed tears at a concert. Many agents are good amateur musicians, some might almost have made it as professionals. McCormack, on his own admission, 'could not tell a good violinist from a bad one'. One of his senior executives caused gasps at a BACA meeting by flatly refusing to recognise the concept of artistic integrity. All that counted was the bottom line.

Tom Graham took up this refrain on joining IMG. 'The take at an opera house can be quarter of a million [pounds] a night,' he told a television interviewer. 'It shows there's a lot of money in classical music.'[15]

'McCormack and many of his senior staff disdain classical music,' charged Parrott. 'They say it is not attuned to the mass market. There is a Masters of the Universe tone to some of their public statements.'

McCormack was stung by these charges into unaccustomed vehemence. 'What have we done that has been bad for this industry?' he railed. 'Is opera at Earl's Court bad? Is Carreras singing in Bath bad? Is giving a Nobel Prize ceremony concert bad? Talk to Itzhak Perlman, talk to Kiri Te Kanawa about some of the things we've done. I think they have been knocked off their feet by the imagination we have brought to their field of endeavour.

'You seem to feel that there is something wrong with the ambition to be Number One. To me, it means trying do the best possible job for our clients, the best promotion, the best financial management, to present classical music in ways it has never been done before, I am quite proud of all that. It isn't that we are just a bunch of renegades looking at f . . .' – he searched for the softest term – 'f . . . f . . . finance rather than artistic achievement. That doesn't work. You've got to present artistic achievement to the benefit of everybody, the public, the artists and ourselves. We saw an opportunity to do that, and we've done it and will do more. And I feel quite good about what we've done.'

If Mark McCormack has been so good for classical music, why does the mention of his name make concert managers blanch? Sheer financial muscle is one reason. McCormack could put up sixteen million dollars for a 1997 festival in Greece, the kind of cheque no classical body could sign without forming a consortium. Even without his sporting wealth, the combination of mass entertainments and personal management produced a classical business that, by the end of 1995, was conservatively worth one hundred million dollars in annual turnover. If just two per cent of that was profit, IMG would outearn every other music agency bar one. If the profit was much below that, its continuance would be in jeopardy.

The impetus for its activity was avowedly pecuniary. Where other agents responded to creative initiatives from their artists, IMG would envisage a business opportunity and go for it. This gave some of their promotions – such as London's Great Orchestras of the World Series – a functional identity that lacked the public perception of being driven by artistic need.

McCormack saw no reason to contradict this assumption. The deeper he plunged into music, the more proudly he wore his indifference to its integrity. He was surprised to find Kiri Te Kanawa upset after a Nobel concert because she had missed a note in a Mozart aria. 'How many people in that hall knew you missed?' asked McCormack.

'Well, Solti knew because he looked at me,' she sniffed, 'and I knew, but very few others.'

'So why get upset?' said McCormack. 'In an objective thing like golf, you finish a round with 65 and everybody sees it. When you play a tennis match and you have lost, everyone sees that. But in singing, how the heck do they know? More often than not, Kiri, you're the only one who knows, on a scale of 100, whether you have sung a 95 or an 82 or a 71.' He walked away believing he had consoled her, little realising that no true artist would ever mark her performance like a round of putting.

For McCormack, everything boiled down to the final score. Agents at IMG Artists were given quarterly quotas to fulfil. Any who did not produce profits were left feeling vulnerable. He paid them well and fostered a family atmosphere but he did not tolerate complacency. 'Every executive, no matter how senior, is made to understand that he is expendable,' said a former employee. 'They are not encouraged to form close relationships with artists, because the artists could be handled by someone else when they are absent or dismissed.' Very few personnel, however, found these restraints oppressive enough to return to their former agencies on a lower salary.

Nor were the artists noticeably unsettled. In five years of European operations only two conductors, Chailly and Semyon Bychkov, left IMG. Stephen Wright ensured that the ratio of agents to artists was higher at IMG than anywhere else, salving their fragile psyches with an unrivalled level of personal attention. In this respect, at least, the McCormack method worked beneficially for musicians.

Yet doubts persisted, particularly in the area of commitment. In golf, no one doubted McCormack's devotion. His attachment to some tennis players ran so deep that there were matches he could not bear to watch. In music, however, he had no emotional investment. He was in it for profit, and pride.

'Nobody gets rich in this business,' warned Ronald Wilford after McCormack's initial incursion. 'Those who are rich and want to fool around in this business eventually get out of it because you can't buy these people. It's a calling. You either love it or you don't. The people who just come for money leave because there is not that much money in it.'[16]

'There is an element of ego-trip in McCormack's involvement in music,' said Victor Hochhauser, his *Aida* co-investor, 'this is not a continuous operation.' Even John Webber was unwilling to make a long-term prediction. 'I am running a train,' said McCormack's confidant. 'I try to run it one station ahead of the rest. What'll happen if it stops, I can't say.' McCormack alone had the answer, and McCormack's way of stating a commitment was to strike fear in the rest of the field. There was nothing temporary about his music business, he said. 'We're in it long-term, and we mean to enhance the area in which we operate.' It was no longer enough for Mark McCormack to be Number One. He now needed to change the world.

The games of golf and tennis in the age of Mark McCormack had been comprehensively transformed. Top players had become preposterously rich, tournaments were dominated by television and sponsorships and seats became unaffordable to ordinary fans. Would the same happen to music under McCormack's management? What would become of the second-string players and unsponsored events? And would the challenge for musicians be dulled by unwarranted performances before uninvolved spectatorships, as was clearly happening in championship tennis? Was McCormack as good as he made out for the players he took under his protectorship? Look around the tennis courts, and the human casualties cry out for your sympathy.

His greatest boast is that players are safe in his hands. Once they sign an IMG contract 'everything is taken care of'. They need never open another brown envelope, book another flight, engage another coach. Trouble with the press? The PR department will fix it. Mental stress? IMG finds a counsellor. Heartbreak? IMG lawyers sort out the divorce settlement. But what happens when the players are ill advised or too young to understand the consequences of decisions taken by IMG and pushy parents?

McCormack backed Nick Bolletieri to train tennis talent from toddlers upwards beneath the burning Florida sun and consign them to IMG before they were out of short pants. The promise of wealth and fame turned kids who were good at games into paparazzi victims, their childhood destroyed, their relationships maimed. Andrea Jaeger rose to third in the world at sixteen and crashed out the next year, a victim of 'emotional trauma'. Tracy Austin entered Wimbledon at fourteen and vanished soon after, her body stressed beyond endurance. Jennifer Capriati was the tournament's youngest semi-finalist at fifteen. Two years later, another drop-out, she was arrested for petty theft and drug abuse and sent to a rehab clinic. 'What their stories sadly demonstrate,' wrote a British commentator, 'is the tawdry cruelty behind the glamour of international tennis. Children are signed up by agents before they reach their teens; their education and emotional development are crippled by demanding training routines . . . Strip away the glamour and it's just child labour.'[17] Capriati's father had threatened to sue tennis chiefs for illegal restraint of trade unless they let her play at twelve years old. 'There are fathers like Stefano Capriati all around,' wrote Rob Hughes in *The Times*, 'and there are agents like Jennifer's minders in Mark McCormack's IMG, scouting her successors at ever younger ages.'[18]

McCormack dismissed the charge of child exploitation and backed the tennis authorities when they raised the age of tournament consent to fourteen. 'The problem with young tennis players is parental,' he shrugged. 'It has nothing to do with the tennis establishment or agents. The kids associated with burn-out are often from families that are not very well off. The talented child offers financial security. Where we come in is to maximise the income and deal with other parts of the child's development.'[19] IMG, he maintained, was merely the instrument for realising other people's dreams.

The issue of damaged wunderkinder was no less acute in music, where prodigies overhyped by their agents vanished before puberty or descended into a drugged abyss. The ghost of Michael Rabin, a former prodigy found dead at thirty-five, still stalked Carnegie Hall as agents pushed forward with teenie successors. 'Everyone puts pressure on,' said Itzhak Perlman. 'It's also true in tennis where you can have young people shine at a very early age – in music you have the same danger of burn-out.' McCormack resented this suggestion, whether applied to music or sport. 'We're not stupid,' he said. 'It's simply not in our interest to exploit anyone to the detriment of his long-term career.'[20] The IMG Artists list generally steered clear of child prodigies. Its sole exception was Leila Josefowicz, a sixteen-year-old violinist whom McCormack read about in *People* magazine and added to his possessions.

It was not only children who suffered on the accelerated circuits of world sport. Bjorn Borg, the five-times Wimbledon champion who gave IMG Europe its pre-eminence, crashed out of the game at twenty-four and almost out of life in a reported suicide attempt. His life, after tennis, was a misery of aborted come-backs and broken relationships.

'Borg was exceptional,' said McCormack. 'I am particularly fond of him. He was a great influence on the game and we did some great work on planning his career and his income . . . Today he has launched into fashion wear and other such things and in so doing is associating with people who are not as capable as he.'[21]

When the German champion Boris Becker attacked the 'obscene amounts' of money that perverted tennis and its players, McCormack said, 'There's a bit of the poet in Boris and that part of him is rearing its head.' Becker had by this time earned forty million dollars from tennis; McCormack said he could have made him more. Yet Becker was not alone in worrying about the corrosive power of player wealth. Andre Agassi, McCormack's favourite player, said, 'It's all take, take, take.' 'The game has become a business, it's all money,' said the veteran Fred Perry. 'If you are wondering exactly when a wonderful game became such a lousy sport, the answer is the first time a corporate executive gave a fourteen-year-old a stretch limo to play with,' commented *Sports Illustrated*.[22] Becker returned to the theme. 'Quite often you show up at a tournament simply because you don't want to pay the fine . . . I have played matches when I didn't care whether I won or not: I was tired, I didn't want to be there, I wanted to go home. You take more interest in the flight time than who your opponent is . . . The problem is simple. There are too many tournaments.'[23] He did not name McCormack, but everyone knew who was responsible for the proliferation of meaningless tournaments. And when it came to music, critics started complaining of distracted artists who played at concerts that should never have been given. By allowing money – not art or glory – to set the performing agenda, McCormack had unleashed an uncontainable monster of avarice.

Nor were the personal lives of his players protected as well as he pretended. Look no further than the tragedy of Martina Navratilova, queen of the centre court. When Martina set up home with Judy Nelson, a Texan mother of two, IMG's PR department painted a touching portrait of two close friends with an absorbing common interest: Martina. Seven years later the champ walked out and Mrs Nelson was vilified by the same department as a 'malicious, money-hungry bitch', seeking millions in galimony – a tactic, she said, 'dictated very early on by Martina's management'.[24] Her lawsuit against Martina should never have come to trial. Instead it played out in an American district court and ran live on the CNN network. Millions watched Martina weep in the witness box while being questioned about gifts of love and deeds of property. She finally settled out of court, ceding Mrs Nelson a house in Aspen and a large lump sum.

While such upheavals can occur in the best-ordered lives, it seemed that Miss Navratilova's will to win, bolstered by IMG support, dragged her into an avoidable mess. In a TWI tele-documentary made in the summer of her retirement,[25] Martina was up-front about her lesbianism and attacked the media for intrusiveness. She made no mention of her management and its role in her life but, in the course of her domestic trials, she coined an aphorism as memorable as any of McCormack's business tips. 'You wanna know what committed is?' said Martina. 'Think of a plate of ham and eggs. The hen is involved. The pig is committed.'[26] She might well have been defining the relationship between agent and player.

When the eggs hit the pan, McCormack becomes invisible. His public persona is Mr Clean, realms apart from grubby ten-per-centers. He is a management guru, not an agent. His babelike complexion and churchgoing probity radiate an efficient innocence. He looks blank when you ask if there is any ethical conflict in his line of work. 'It would worry me,' says McCormack, 'if someone could point at something that was morally wrong, ethically wrong, wrong for our clients. But I don't think we've done any of that.'[27] His paragon is Arnold Palmer who, in retrieving his ball from the woods, places it ten yards further back than necessary so that no one might harbour any suspicion that he was getting an advantage. That, for McCormack, is sanctity.

His first, and only, line of response to criticism is that he acts in the players' interests and has done nothing to harm any area in which he operates. He cites as his model the Australian tycoon Kerry Packer, who persuaded underpaid cricketers to abandon Test matches and play night games on his Channel 9 in coloured pyjamas. Packer made cricketers rich but wrecked the culture of cricket, a game that is meant to run five days without necessarily yielding a result. Such tranquillity was valueless to a quick-return mogul. Packer replaced it with a one-day travesty of the game – replete with big hits and instant replays but stripped of grace and grandeur. It drew large crowds and was eventually forced upon the legitimate authorities, to the game's detriment. If McCormack meant to copy Packer, the future of music was in mortal peril.

In one of our conversations McCormack described the music circuit as incurably inefficient – 'just as cricket was before Kerry Packer moved in,' he said. IMG would shake it up with star recitals and massive sponsorship. There would be new talents and festivals every year. They would apply methods he had invented so devastatingly in sports. And the rest of the musical infrastructure would either have to sing in harmony, or simply disappear.

If music was to survive McCormack, it needed to find a chink in his armour – and that was no easy matter. For a third of the century McCormack had enjoyed unimpeded progress. Only once did officialdom intervene when, in 1983, a House of Commons committee led by a former sports minister, Dennis Howell, voiced concern over IMG's influence at national events like Wimbledon and the British Open. Political antennae had twitched when, during the 1973 professional boycott of Wimbledon, McCormack represented not only the championships themselves but also the leaders of *both* player factions, John Newcombe for the strikers and Roger Taylor for the participants. This kind of situation, said Howell, was 'pregnant with conflicts of interest and cannot carry public confidence'. This was strong language from a serious source, but it could not dislodge McCormack. Tennis, golf and the BBC needed him so badly that they would risk political anger rather than lose IMG. At the interface of sports and media, he had become indispensable and he worked all hours that God gave to remain so.

He rose each morning at 4.30, dictating to a waiting secretary while pencilling ticks and crosses on his yellow-lined pad of daily tasks. Toughing it out to the last cent in the deals he struck, he was not personally a greedy man, and the pay he drew from IMG was reportedly not excessive. But his zeal in pursuing goals was boundless and resisters wore the bruises of his mighty ambitions. What underlings found attractive was his willingness to listen to new proposals and to make long-term investments, happy to wait five or seven years before he saw a return. This gave him another unfair edge in music. No classical management could afford to take a breath that deep. Nor did they have his global reach. If a concert agent wanted to negotiate an orchestral tour to Japan, he would have to fly there several times and stay at outrageously expensive Tokyo hotels. IMG Artists set up tours through local staff in a Tokyo suburb, keeping the overheads down and prices affordable.

To musicians and their agents IMG looked universally impregnable. Yet there had been failures in various areas, none so large as to imperil the whole, but together suggesting a possible vulnerability. In tennis, McCormack missed out on Becker and Graf. By the time he got to the net they had been sewn up by European minders. He was known to be weak on Germans. Bernhard Langer was meant to be his Teuton hero and McCormack built a German Masters tournament around him, but the golfer lost his touch. He collared Michael Schumacher before he won a Grand Prix in his first season, but motor racing was a minority interest that could not produce the ratings of tennis or golf. As a mark of his intent McCormack removed Wimbledon – Steffi's and Boris's favourite lawn – from German public television and sold it to a cable channel. When Graf next raised the trophy, Mark zapped the channel tuner. Nevertheless, Germany – a state of central importance in classical music – was hard going for IMG.

Spain was another overflight. In the decade after Franco's death, the golfer Severiano Ballesteros emerged as the most marketable, popular, wholesome Spaniard anywhere outside the royal palace. His halo shone so brightly that when Europe lost the 1993 Ryder Cup to the Americans, usually omnivorous sports editors devoted their pages to commiseration for poor, downcast Sevvi. Ballesteros did not need to win; all he had to do was turn up and smile. McCormack, asked to name his greatest mistake, conceded, 'I would really have liked to have been the first guy to get to Ballesteros . . .'[28] The Spaniard possessed a certain insouciance that McCormack envied. He seemed not to care about earning top whack. He belonged to a milieu where money, though abundant, was not the main object. Until he had fathomed European style and made himself indispensable to its masters, McCormack knew that his world dominance would be incomplete – whether in sport or in any other sector. Classical music was a means of earning social class and European honours.

Back home, his supremacy was unchallenged. An agency called Pro-Serv of Arlington, Virginia, scooped up basketball players in the 1980s and made a grab for Stefan Edberg, Jimmy Connors and Ivan Lendl. McCormack got Lendl back and waited for the Virginians to overstretch. 'We had competitors once called Pro-Serv,' he said with a grin in 1992. 'They fell apart and most of their executives are now applying for jobs with us. There was another competitor I simply hated. We set out to destroy his business but then I realised just how incompetent he was, so it served our purpose actually to keep him going.'[29]

Few players left IMG with his blessing. 'Sebastian Coe is rather deceitful,' he snarled, after the golden boy of British athletics took off. 'He had no sense of loyalty and, as far as I'm concerned, no sense of honour.'[30] McCormack has been called vindictive, but maintained it did not bother him. 'If you took a hundred of those stories about our being ruthless or shark-like,' he said, 'ninety of them would centre on attitudes we have taken on behalf of our clients. I think being ruthless, in the context in which it is applied to me, is really sort of a compliment.'[31]

No one could touch him at his own games of golf and tennis, but a weakness could be glimpsed once he strayed on to alien territory. When Ronald Reagan left the White House, McCormack bid to handle the sale of his memoirs and his post-presidency career. Reagan, the old movie pro, consigned his affairs to the Hollywood agency, ICM, and barely gave McCormack a civil answer. Prior to this adventure, McCormack's only political catch was the disgraced vice-president Spiro Agnew, who was retained by IMG as a consultant for unspecified projects.

Undaunted by rejection, McCormack went haring after 'a bigger prize than Reagan ever would be'.[32] In June 1991, months after she was ousted as British prime minister, *Marketing Week* magazine ran a cover story titled, 'Can McCormack Make Margaret Thatcher Rich?' Inside, readers were told that 'The world's greatest sports manager and the world's most formidable woman are in negotiations for a partnership that could mean more wealth and prestige for both.' The article, flagged as an 'Investigation', was unsigned; most of its sources were 'IMG insiders'. (It neglected to mention that McCormack was linked to the magazine as a columnist.)

'Margaret Thatcher is in trouble,' purred the intro. 'She has the product but she lacks the management or the marketing . . . So step forward Mark McCormack as the obvious man for the job.' Contact had been made with Thatcher's son, Mark, and the deal was a foregone conclusion. McCormack, continued the article, 'has much in common with Margaret Thatcher. He is the most powerful manager in sport bar none and she has the same power in terms of her influence in UK politics.' As a token of his 'high regard', he was prepared to cut his commission from twenty-five to ten per cent and to give her a two-million-pound advance on a three-year management contract. He could make her ten million pounds a year, two hundred thousand pounds during Wimbledon fortnight alone from cocktail circuit appearances. IMG sources said McCormack had invested a lot of time in the project. A 'McCormack insider' supplied a guide to current social rank: 'In the first division there are Princess Di, Margaret Thatcher and Princess Caroline of Monaco. In the second division are the Queen, Prince Charles, Fergie and Madonna. The opportunity to acquire a first-division client – one of only three in the world – would crown Mark's career. He needs her as badly as she needs him.'

News of the deal was on the streets before McCormack was admitted to the Lady's presence. She apparently took an instant dislike to him and ended the meeting within minutes. Her memoirs, like Reagan's, went to ICM (and onward, for £3.5m to her erstwhile ally Rupert Murdoch). McCormack, who 'needed her as badly as she needed him', talked of 'being involved in a lot of other things for her, under Mark's supervision'.[33] None of them publicly materialised.

What went wrong? It seems that McCormack, rushing in like a moon-struck adolescent, misread the signals. He proposed to install IMG professionals at her side in place of her circle of sycophants. Thatcher saw attacks on her courtiers as a slur on her character judgement and went into a huff. McCormack suggested she had never been very good at looking after her personal interests; she replied that she had, after all, run a country for eleven years and won the Falklands War. He offered to strategise her return to active politics; she swatted him down. A fly on the wall risked having its ears withered by Thatcher's scorn in return for the rare sight of watching the Shark crushed to sardine paste.

Theirs was a perfect mismatch, heaven-made, and – though strangely unreported – it exposed McCormack's vanity and potential vulnerability. It spoke volumes for his self-assurance that McCormack, a sports agent, saw himself as counsellor to presidents and premiers – personal manager to the Pope himself. He believed he had the magic to enhance whatever he touched, no matter how little he understood of the subject and its sensitivities. Classical music would demonstrate that the Prophet Mark's homespun formulas – never underestimate the value of money – would work like an elixir in every situation. The trouble with such panaceas is that the cure has to be widely perceived, or the medicine loses its appeal. Unless music could be seen to have improved materially under McCormack's management, he would have to get out quickly to protect his formula's infallibility.

By now, however, he had grown so large that music would be decimated if ever he withdrew. There was no shortage of disaster scenarios at the end of the millennium, but one of the scariest was the precipitate closure of IMG Artists, with dozens of musicians and years of tours and festivals hurled into limbo. Classical music, like Wimbledon, had come to need Mark McCormack more than McCormack needed music or lawn-tennis.

Having made Wimbledon wealthy beyond its wildest dreams, he watched British tennis become a world loser. When McCormack came to SW19, locals like Roger Taylor and Virginia Wade were winning the singles and regular fans were sitting around the centre court. In 1995, the top native-born players were ranked 213 and 219 respectively and the best seats were reserved for the fat cats. McCormack had turned Wimbledon into a world event, well detached from its grass roots. Even the strawberries had lost their taste.

A similar process is conceivable in classical music. By whetting artists' appetite for high fees and the public's for artificially unsubsidised opera, McCormack created conditions that local players and promoters could not match. If he persisted, he would unsettle the musical economy and progress towards a dominance that, as in tennis, approached a global monopoly. If he withdrew, the audience he cultivated would wither away in a murmur of disappointment at lesser attractions and concert life would contract still further. Either way, music in the McCormack era was trapped between a rock and a hard place.

For individual soloists and conductors, the choice became agonising. The old establishment of the music business offered them familiar engagements and limited imagination. They saw Kiri Te Kanawa advertising a Rolex in their morning paper and José Carreras appearing in a soft-focus television documentary, the fruits of their IMG connection. They saw Itzhak Perlman and Evgeny Kissin earning unprecedented fees. They saw cosseting and comfort.

For the celebrated and successful, a life in music had never looked more rewarding. The fees were fabulous, the flights first-class and the fringe benefits felicitous. Life at the top was unfailingly sweet.

But for the majority of classical performers the outlook was bleaker than ever before. If they did not scramble aboard the IMG bandwagon, or if they were rudely pushed off, the alternatives looked slim and stale. The older agencies were in varying degrees of crisis and the boutiques were struggling on slim margins. Many excellent performers could not find an agent, because conscientious agents could not afford to invest in building anything less than a prospectively starry career, and the non-conscientious were not worth having. As temptations increased on both sides of the equation, the bond of mutual need between agents and artists was frayed by fear and mistrust. Agents narrowed their sights and thousands of musicians were left floundering in a complex, shrinking and unforgiving world.

NOTES

1 all McCormack quotes are, unless indicated, taken from two interviews with the author in June 1991 and May 1993
2 interview for *The Times Saturday Review*, 18 July 1992, p. 46
3 *MHM*, frontispiece
4 By 1992 he had been overtaken by the basketball player Michael Jordan at fifty million dollars p.a., negotiated by the Virginia-based Pro-Serv.
5 cf. Sylvain Cypel, 'Le Champion du Sport Business', *Fortune-France*, September 1989, pp 43–47
6 Four hundred and two million dollars, plus twenty million dollars' worth of video hardware. *FT*, 7 August 1992
7 *MHM*, p. 233
8 'A Life in the Day', *Sunday Times Magazine*, 1991
9 *Classical Music* magazine, 27 June 1992, p. 13
10 author's interview, April 1995
11 This and all subsequent agent quotes taken, unless indicated, from author's interviews in 1991–3
12 *Opera Now* profile, nd
13 author's interview, December 1990
14 *Sunday Times*, loc. cit.
15 *Omnibus*, transmitted 24 April 1995
16 BBC Radio 3 interview, 20 June 1991
17 Madeleine Bunting, 'Court Napping', *Guardian*, 24 May 1994, p. 24
18 'An American Princess who has moved out of the Court Spotlight', *The Times*, 22 January 1994, p. 34
19 interview with Michael Parkinson (an IMG client), *Daily Telegraph*, 2 July 1994, p. 20
20 *Daily Mail*, 9 May 1992, p. 73
21 *Figaro* magazine, 28 April 1990
22 all quotes: *Sunday Times*, 22 May 1994, p. 5
23 *Daily Telegraph Magazine*, 4 June 1994, p. 17
24 interview, *Observer Magazine*, 27 June 1993, p. 24
25 first aired BBC1, 28 July 1994
26 *Observer Magazine*, loc. cit.
27 *Independent on Sunday*, 18 July 1993, p. 11
28 interview, *Leisureweek*, 22 June 1990, p. 7
29 *Daily Mail*, 9 May 1992, p. 73
30 *Figaro* magazine, 28 April 1990
31 *Sports Illustrated*, 21 May 1990
32 McCormack aide quoted in *Management Week*, June 1991, p. 50; all following quotes from same article
33 author's interview, June 1991

CHAPTER XIV

INSIDE THE
GLASS TRIANGLE

T he headquarters are not, as one might expect, in the bustling centre of a world capital but out in the amorphous sprawl of Tokyo's charmless suburbs. Nor is head office an imposing edifice, like the company's black-marble palace on New York's Fifth Avenue or the Philip Johnson-designed former AT&T building on Madison Avenue that it picked up for a few billion yen during the decline of western real estate in 1991. Here the facelessness seems almost intentional. The command centre of the world's most design-conscious industrial concern is an eight-storey triangular block in the Goten Yama Hills district, a building that could easily be mistaken for the branch office of a medium-sized accountants' firm. The name 'SONY' is posted high above the eyeline of passers-by and the glass frontage is neutral enough to be missed by local cab drivers.

Inside, what strikes you is the silence. Past rows of bowing receptionists and mutely flickering television screens, you are escorted into a noiseless elevator, transported upwards and guided through corridors where the only sound is the intimate clack and whisper of secretaries' legs as they scurry between office suites. The heating is turned up oppressively high and the lighting is artificially neon. Any window light is screened by blinds. There are no directional signs or wall decorations. Authorised visitors to the upper levels of Sony, rigorously pre-screened, are made to feel like trespassers.

Into this hushed nerve-centre one gloomy day in November 1994 rolled an exquisitely tailored silver-haired man in an invalid's chair. Akio Morita, chairman and co-founder of Sony, was attending his first board meeting in a year and the entire staff were lined up in their fawn-coloured Issy Miyake uniforms to make obeisances. Morita, seventy-four, had been partly paralysed by a stroke that left his speech slurred and his gestures slowed. He exuded, despite these handicaps, an impressive authority.

Morita was one of the economic rainmakers of modern Japan, renowned alongside car-king Shoichiro Honda and electronics colossus Konnosuke Matsushita as a generator of post-war revival. A supersalesman of domestic products, Morita was red-carpeted in American boardrooms and his sayings were solemnly taught at Harvard. While Honda and Matsushita carried greater national weight, they rarely travelled. Morita was Japan's foremost spokesman in foreign parts, where he was known as 'Mr Sony'. His appearance at Sony's November 1994 board meeting was an indicator of its extreme seriousness.

Sony, his occidentally-named brainchild, was being overwhelmed by losses from its US entertainments division. Seven years earlier, Morita and his chief executive officer, Norio Ohga, had raided the Black Rock of modern media and, for two billion dollars, bought the entire copyrights and heritage of Columbia Records, canners of music since Edison's day. This was a glittering prize that looked even shinier when Ohga recouped half the outlay by floating twenty-seven per cent of Columbia's Japanese subsidiary on the Tokyo stock exchange. High on this flutter, Morita and Ohga pressed ahead in Hollywood with a $3.4 billion take-over of Columbia Pictures, gaining unlimited access to three thousand films, twenty-three thousand television episodes and some of the biggest names in cinema history.

Although some analysts warned that Sony were paying over the odds, the strategy had been coolly calculated inside the glass triangle. In the 1980s Sony had watched helplessly while its Betamax video recorder was routed by the cheaper, inferior VHS format whose makers, led by Matsushita, had provided a large menu of home movies. Betamax was Morita's baby and Sony's first defeat. Ohga swore the company would never again get caught without pictures and sound to go with its next-generation products. 'If we didn't have this software,' he told me in 1992, 'we could not launch new formats'.[1]

Sony's double-swoop on American culture stunned its competitors. Matsushita, playing me-too, rushed in with $6.1 billion in 1990 to buy

MCA Records and Universal Pictures. Toshiba, not to be outdone, took a billion-dollar, 12.5-per-cent stake in Time-Warner. 'We had a strong philosophy,' scoffed Ohga, 'I don't know if *they* did.' Whatever the relative intentions, trillions of yen from hardware investors changed the landscape of the music and entertainment industries. Against a torrent of press hostility, Hollywood and the hit parade were overrun by aliens. Japanese men in identi-suits owned King Kong and Bob Dylan, *Jurassic Park* and Frank Sinatra, Wet Wet Wet and Beethoven's Greatest Hits. Newspapers wailed of a 'fire sale' of apple-pie heritage and red-blooded Americans went to bed praying for the invaders to commit hara-kiri. No patriot, however, could possibly have envisaged the epic scale of Sony's catastrophes.

It began with the pair of *Batman* producers who were head-hunted for a two-hundred-million-dollar ransom to run Columbia Pictures. It then turned out that Peter Guber and Jon Peters, Barbra Streisand's former hairdresser, were still under contract to Warner Brothers and Sony had to pay an extra half-billion dollars in compensation. Peters began as he meant to continue, spending a hundred and fifteen million dollars on redecorating the studios and five thousand dollars a week on flowers for executive offices. He sent 'empty Falcon jets to London at thirty thousand dollars a pop to pick up his girlfriend,' who, together with his ex-wife, was apparently put 'on the Columbia payroll for quarter of a million dollars or more apiece'.[2] Peters annoyed Ohga by turning up sockless to meetings; he had the friendly habit of yanking employees out of their chair by the necktie. It cost Sony some thirty million dollars to ease him out. Frank Price, a studio chief who tried to impose restraint, lasted eighteen months and left with fifteen million. When Guber finally left in September 1994, he was reportedly *two hundred million dollars* the richer and had a promise from Sony to invest two hundred million dollars more in his own production house.

Laughable as these sums were to movie goers, they violently offended against the Sony work ethic which kept executives at their desks far into the night and required them to leave a note of their whereabouts each time they went to the lavatory. The conjunction of anally retentive Tokyo management methods and prodigal waste in tinseltown set the glossy magazines guffawing with *schadenfreude*. Sony lost a lot more than money in Hollywood. It lost face. Matsushita and Toshiba may have had their studio troubles, but neither was subjected to the scorn and derision that Sony reaped. Matsushita, twice Sony's size, made few executive changes and allowed incumbents in place to get on with their jobs. No one ever saw a hand from Osaka pulling strings at Universal, or cared much if they did. But Morita had spent his life courting western coverage and was now buried beneath an avalanche of gloating headlines. Back home, industrialists closed ranks to deny him the honours he coveted and undoubtedly deserved.

In November 1994 Sony directors gathered at Goten Yama to cut their losses, announcing a write-off of $3.2 billion dollars on entertainment operations. The loss was so huge it almost equalled the entire purchase price of Columbia Pictures. The detail was no less devastating. Of twenty-six Sony pictures released in 1994, seventeen lost money. Stephen Spielberg's *Hook*, billed in a Sony financial forecast as 'the entertainment picture of the decade', [3] sank almost without trace. It cost sixty-eight million dollars to make and was the mega-director's least memorable film. Arnold Schwarzenegger's eighty-million-dollar *Last Action Hero* was a monster-flop. Kenneth Branagh's *Frankenstein* was a box-office nightmare. *Radio Flyer*, budgeted at fourteen million dollars, cost forty million and recouped just over four. The best bean-counters in Japan were powerless to control an outflow that produced the first operating losses at Sony in almost half a century of self-generated, seemingly bottomless innovation.

It was a sombre set of Sony directors who assembled that November day at suburban headquarters. They ordained a series of crisis measures: spending cuts across the board, a search for investors to share production risks, tighter Tokyo controls. Morita, wretchedly impaired and shouldering responsibility, offered to resign from the main board. Four months later he relinquished his position as Sony chairman to the faithful Norio Ohga, his shadow for forty years.

The tallest man in Sony, with a strikingly deep voice, Ohga had kept a firm hold on head office while Morita posed with princes and presidents. He was respected as a tough negotiator and decisive leader, with a fiery temper and a fearsome eye for fine print. But Ohga was now sixty-four and had suffered three heart attacks. He was also known to be haunted by long-suppressed dreams. Nightly at 2 a.m., he would rise from his bed, stumble to his study and practise conducting a classical symphony. 'When I was young I told everybody that at sixty I would retire from Sony and start conducting,' he confided. 'Now, when I find a good successor, I will give up my title and become a full-time conductor.' For Ohga's sixtieth birthday the company bought him a celebratory concert with the Tokyo Philharmonic. It served only to whet his ambition. He wanted to conduct in Berlin and New York. Three hours a night, Ohga worked on his scores. He was loyal to Sony, but there were higher goals in life – and he wanted out.

Like most successful men, Ohga found it easy to dissemble. Music was his passion, but if it crossed his office desk he treated it with the same rigour as any other commodity. Ohga once pledged to make Sony the world leader in classical music. Now, *in extremis*, he slashed classical budgets and sacked top producers. Sony could not afford to fritter executive energies on the micro-economics of a minority culture when its mass entertainments were going down the tube. Its classical record label would have to make a profit, or else. In the maw of a multinational, classical music would have to pay the price for its parent industry's errors.

Japan's discovery of western art music began in the Meiji Period and attained its first milestone when Kosaku Yamada returned from studies with Max Bruch in Berlin to found the Tokyo Philharmonic Orchestra in 1915. Yamada was the first Japanese to conduct in Carnegie Hall in 1918 and the first to have an opera produced in his native land. Two younger composers, Tomojiro Ikenouchi and Kishio Hirao, completed their studies in Paris and brought home a timbre of French impressionisms that shimmered to local ears like traditional orientalisms. In the ensuing *Kulturkampf* between pastel French and German pomp, a decisive influence was wielded by the conductor Count Hidemaro Konoye who studied in both countries and favoured the Teutonic style. Konoye in 1924 founded the Japan Symphonic Association and the New Symphony Orchestra of Tokyo; in May 1930 he conducted the world's first recording of Mahler's fourth symphony.

Konoye's preference was typical of his class and his time. Japan was drawing closer to Germany, but could not tell good Germans from bad. Yamada, when the Nazis came to power, offered asylum to his Berlin teacher, Klaus Pringsheim, only for the refugee to be baited as a 'foreign enemy' under Japan's belated racial laws. Konoye conducted his affairs without fear of official interference since his brother was the prime minister, Prince Fumimaro Konoye, an enlightened politician who strove to build bridges between Tokyo and Washington. The prince's resignation in October 1941 put General Tojo in power and Pearl Harbor in the gunsights.

When atom bombs fell on Hiroshima and Nagasaki, bringing down the old order, Japan embraced the baseball, bobby-sox and chewing-gum culture of its American occupiers. But classical music kept its hold on the upper classes. To a young man planning his future in a ruined land it offered prospects of social advancement and material comfort. 'After the war,' reflected Norio Ohga, 'Japan was a really poor country. If I studied engineering I thought I could not find a job. But [to be] an artist was a wonderful life, I thought.'

The son of a wealthy family in Numazu City, Ohga enrolled in 1948 to study music at the national university of fine arts in Tokyo. He was blessed with a fine baritone voice and a restless practical curiosity. Family friends in Numazu asked him to look into a firm that was seeking to raise capital on a newfangled tape recorder. 'Ohga was interested in mechanical things,' notes an internal Sony history, 'and knew a great deal about foreign-made tape recorders.' He gave the manufacturers a grilling and suggested improvements to eliminate wow and flutter. 'The tape was the key to the future of our business,' wrote Akio Morita,[4] the company's co-founder.

Ten years older than Ohga and heir to a saké distillery, Morita on the day war ended found himself working in a naval unit that was developing a heat-seeking missile. The radio announced: 'We have lost the war, but this is temporary . . . Japan's mistake was a lack of material strength and the necessary scientific knowledge and equipment. This mistake we must amend.' Morita's generation would spend their lives amending. Emperor Hirohito, in his first address to the nation, urged his people 'to keep pace with the progress of the world'. 'It was brought home to me,' wrote Morita, 'that Japan would need all the talent it could save for the future . . . I felt somehow I had a role to play in that future.'[5]

With a naval friend, Masaru Ibuka, he set up a manufacturing company, Tokyo Tsushin Kogyo, in a shack in the Goten Yama hills. Ibuka had been making radar devices and using music students to check their oscillations with tuning-forks. He was married to a daughter of Tamon Maeda, a pre-war aide of Prince Konoye newly installed as education minister, and – until Maeda was purged by war-crime investigators – had access to top-level information and contacts.

While delivering equipment to the state radio, Ibuka caught sight of an American tape recorder and reckoned he could do better. Ohga's inquisitive visit came just as Ibuka's prototype was ready. They called the student 'the tough customer' and used him as a sounding board:

'My goodness,' thought the impressed Ibuka, 'his knowledge of tape recorders will put a professional to shame.' He fell for this meddlesome and magnanimous young fellow. From then on, Ohga would frequent [the company], serving as a self-appointed unpaid supervisor.[6]

In a ruined economy where the best hope for a small manufacturer was to make institutional sales, Ibuka's reps struck lucky on campus, where Ohga persuaded his college president to buy the machine.

Ohga then spoke to many people, insisting 'Tape recorders are a must for music schools. Musicians must train themselves with a tape recorder just as ballerinas study dancing by looking in a mirror.'[6]

Ibuka returned the favour by lending his machines to record Ohga singing the solo part in a university performance of Brahms's *German Requiem*. Out of these courtesies was born an eternal triumvirate, each partner taking a distinctive role. Ibuka was the visionary inventor, Morita the sales philosopher and Ohga the nit-picking perfector. Together they built from scratch one of the world's top companies and most recognisable commercial marques.

Ohga, however, was unprepared for a life of industry. In 1953, leaving university, he packed his knapsack, took his fiancée-accompanist Midori Matsubara and headed for Berlin, to become an opera and lieder singer. Ibuka and Morita insisted on paying him a salary for the duration of his studies. In exchange, he sent them back envelopes stuffed with newspaper cuttings on German electronic developments.

For three years he was immersed in music, singing Mozart roles in student productions and giving what he believes to have been the German première of Gian-Carlo Menotti's duologue opera, *The Telephone*. Ibuka, in 1955, sent him a pocket transistor radio bearing the trade-mark 'Sony', a logo that Morita reckoned would adhere better in western minds than 'Tokyo Tsushin Kogyo'. Ohga was not particularly impressed, unaware that the product and its makers would take sophomore America by storm. The tinny tranny was, to children of the Cuban missile crisis, what the portable Walkman became to teenies of the Reagan era. Both were Sony appliances, adapting and miniaturising for modestly priced personal consumption the latest advances of US military and space technology.

Morita visited Ohga in Berlin and together they went to hear the Philharmonic under its new chief conductor, Herbert von Karajan. Morita had met Karajan in Austria in 1953 on his first sales trip to Europe. 'They were already old friends,' said Ohga. The music student, more deferential towards a famous conductor, had been introduced to Karajan socially by the Japanese widow of the Austrian supermarket magnate, Julius Meinl, a lady who had shared her bomb shelter with the maestro in the last years of the Third Reich. Karajan, beguiled by the men from Sony, shared their burning interest in technological innovation. The axis they formed in the mid-Fifties would last literally to his dying moment.

A photograph of Ohga in 1956 shows him sitting, open-mouthed and alert, just behind the back row of violinists in a Philharmonic rehearsal. He is leaning forward, absorbing as much as he can of the music. He graduated from the Kunst Universität the following year, married his accompanist, Midori, and returned home to start a concert career. Sony was reluctant to lose him and Morita tempted him with a return trip to Europe and America, ostensibly to help recruit a new sales force.

The wily Morita waited until they were trapped together for four days on a transatlantic passage from Southampton to New York, before turning the conversation to Sony's future. 'Ohga, a strapping, barrel-chested fellow with a resonant voice, criticised Sony in beautiful tones, and I was most interested in what he had to say,' wrote Morita. Sony, said the young singer, had too many engineers and not enough doers and thinkers. 'All right,' said Morita, 'you join us and you will be one of the management team.'[7] Back in Tokyo, Morita's wife Yoshiko went to work on Midori Ohga, her former high-school classmate. Between them they wheedled Ohga into joining Sony, on the understanding that he would be allowed to continue his concert career.

His corporate climb was nothing short of spectacular. Within eighteen months Ohga was general manager of the tape division. The following year he founded a design centre that defined the striking differentness of Sony products from shoddy-looking Japanese goods. In 1964, aged thirty-four, Ohga was given a seat on the board. His concert giving began to suffer. A decision was forced on him one day when he would have had to skip a board meeting to make a rehearsal for the *German Requiem*; he cut the rehearsal and told his agent he was giving up the concert circuit. 'In my mind, I had trouble deciding which came first,' he reflected. 'I had many managers and workers under me and I could not leave them. My division was very profitable and successful.'

He was sent to Holland in 1963 on a mission to persuade Philips to lease their cassette recorder patent, marketed as a business accessory, for conversion into a music carrier. The talks were admittedly 'tough', as the Dutch resisted raids on their invention, but Ohga sweet-talked them into agreeing a single universal format for musicassettes. The Japanese then cornered the market by quickly producing a credible, affordable player, leaving the Dutch ruing their slow-wittedness.

No sooner were cassettes on sale than Karajan had himself photographed in the music press playing them in his sports car. 'When I became head of the tape recorder division,' said Ohga, 'we were in touch more and more.'

In 1967, sensing a growing Japanese demand for western rock music and indigenous clones, Ohga struck a deal with CBS Records to form a CBS-Sony subsidiary. 'Ohga said he wanted to make this the biggest record company in Japan, and ten years later he did it,' said the admiring Morita.[8] Nothing seemed beyond Ohga's formidable capacity. He founded and simultaneously headed five Sony divisions. In 1972, aged forty-two, he became corporate managing director; four years later he was deputy president; in 1982 he succeeded Morita as president and chief operating officer of the Sony Corporation. Not bad for a musician, a profession that Ohga never fully renounced.

During office hours, he insisted, 'I am a businessman. I make budgets, run divisions, project profits and sales. When I come back home, I make a big switch to being a musician.' Both he and his wife had recordings issued on CBS/Sony. Unlike Morita, he refused to wear the company jacket and dressed in sober-blue suits.

Inside Sony he was revered rather than liked. Product launches frequently had to be called off because Ohga rejected the look of a Play button or the placement of Sony's logo. His design ideas set standards for the entire industry. At Ohga's word, hi-fi went black and video players got a letterbox-flap. No detail was too small for his personal attention. Seeing a loose connection on my microphone, the Sony president called for a screwdriver and wordlessly repaired it. If it was a Sony, it had to function immaculately.

Outside the company Ohga was content to be anonymous, deferring to Morita's celebrity in the US and Ibuka's stature in Japan. Morita was intent on 'global localisation' – making Sony the first Japanese company that was truly universal; Ibuka was semi-retired. Morita even went to live for two years in the United States. From the late 1960s on, Ohga was shaping the company more decisively than either of its co-founders. It was Ohga who made the move into record production, strategised the 'synergy' between hardware and software and forced the pace of digital research and development. And every step of that progression he co-ordinated with the mastermind of classical music, Herbert von Karajan.

When Karajan brought his orchestra to Japan, Morita's was the only private home he visited and Mr and Mrs Ohga were the only other guests. 'Mr Morita's house has a marvellous pool. We went swimming together and afterwards to the jacuzzi. I saw many sides of the man,' said Ohga. They talked of music and aircraft, having both acquired pilot licences. 'He spoke very correct English,' said Ohga.

He was very charming but shy. Always when he bought a new jet he asked my suggestion. I gave him my idea for cockpit design. Once here in Japan I missed his first concert. The next day his secretary, Jucker, called me: 'Mr Ohga why didn't you come last night?' I replied that I had no ticket. Jucker said, 'Maestro will be waiting for you tonight. Please come to his room in the intermission.'

As soon as I entered he started, 'Why didn't you come?' and began asking me about jets. I said, 'Herbert, this one is not good for you.' He said, 'Unfortunately I have ordered it already, but can you advise me about the cockpit? I have to go in now, come back after the concert.' I returned to my seat and he started to conduct the Eroica Symphony.

The next time I saw him he had sold the first aircraft and bought the one I had recommended.

It was one of the basic assumptions of their friendship that Ohga kept Karajan briefed about audio breakthroughs and equipped his village home in Anif with state-of-the-art machinery. 'For Herbert von Karajan, art and technology were never opposing concepts,' observed his record producer.[9] They were twin articles of his faith, allies in his attempts to achieve and preserve the 'perfect' performance of a piece of music. As he entered his seventies, Karajan learned from Ohga and Morita about experiments in recording and reproducing sound with laser beams, eliminating ambient impurities of hiss and crackle. Dazzled by the digital future and fearing that it might render his life's work obsolescent, the conductor begged for machines that would enable him to re-record the whole of western music while he still had the strength. In some embarrassment, the Sony men had to admit that they were still some years away from digital production, the major advances in this area having been made by Philips. Flexing every tentacle of his influence, Karajan dragged Philips – part-owners of his DG record label – to meet Sony at a negotiating table where Ohga, for the second time, talked them into agreeing a common format and accelerating the production of a new gadget, the gleaming compact disc.

It was Karajan who presented the wonder-discs in April 1980 at a Salzburg press conference with Morita, famously declaring: 'All else is gaslight.' Flanked by Ohga in 1987, he cut the ribbon at the first CD pressing plant in Europe, built by Sony in his home village, Anif, with lavish state subsidy. Advised by Sony that visual images could in future be digitally stored, Karajan had himself filmed for posterity while conducting what he called his 'final word' on the core classical and romantic repertoire. 'He expressly intended the video productions that he began in 1982 to be released on laserdisc, a new medium which at that time was nowhere near ready for mass release,' said his record producer.[10]

Compact Disc and the Sony Walkman – Morita's inspiration for making music mobile – were Sony's salvation during the difficult Eighties in which Betamax was trounced out of sight by VHS videos with a bigger range of movies. Sony was simultaneously hit by a Walt Disney and Universal lawsuit, alleging that their 'time-shift' concept incited users to violate producers' copyright by taping films off air. It took eight years, a fortune in legal fees and a US Supreme Court ruling before Sony were vindicated, but by then Betamax had expired of aggravated software deprivation and Sony had switched to producing VHS machines. Morita's other vision, the implementation of a high-definition television screen whose 1125 lines would outshine the conventional 525- and 625-line sets, was stalled in its tracks by governments and broadcasters who balked at the idea of forcing all the world's viewers to buy new sets.

On the audio front, Sony's move to replace hiss-ridden cassettes with Digital Audio Tape (DAT) was thwarted by the refusal of record labels to lease music to a carrier from which pirates could make perfect copies. DAT died an unnatural death in 1991. Its Mini-Disc successor faced a mutually damaging head-on confrontation with a Digital Compact Cassette (DCC) developed by Philips and endorsed by Matsushita, Sharp and Sanyo. Ohga scorned a system that did not give youngsters the instant track access they expected on CD, and suffered in silence as both formats were indiscriminately dismissed as 'dodos'[11] by critics and retailers. What Sony needed was its own software archive to avoid producer blackmail and delay. When he swooped to conquer CBS Records and Columbia Pictures, Ohga had his eye on young customers who wanted the hottest music on the latest technology. 'The people who supported us when we established this company are now getting old,' he acknowledged. 'If we have a big hit we will get supporters for the company in the next generation.'

Before sealing the Columbia deal, Ohga sought the blessing of a near-octogenarian who was the intended lynchpin of the only part of the music business that really mattered to the Sony president. In conversations at Anif, Ohga secured a commitment from Herbert von Karajan that he would switch his recording work from Deutsche Grammophon to Sony, walking hand-in-hand into the future with his Japanese partners. Tragically for both parties, fate struck before the vision could be realised.

In July 1989 Ohga flew into Salzburg to visit Karajan with Michael P. Schulhof, chief executive of the Sony Corporation of America and the highest-ranked, most trusted westerner in the whole of Japanese industry. 'I received a message that he wanted me to come to him straight from the airport,' Ohga related.

I took along Mickey Schulhof, who is a physicist and a doctor, and also a good pilot – the ideal combination. When I arrived the butler told me to go up to his bedroom. He was sitting on the bed and said 'since – yesterday – I have had – pain'. I asked him what the problem was, he didn't know. The doctor had visited and said there was nothing wrong with his heart, but he should stay at home for a day and give up the *Ballo in Maschera* rehearsal. He assured him there was nothing to worry about. He asked me about the aircraft we had flown in on; the first half of our conversation was always about flying, which he loved.

Then he asked me, 'Norio, shall we have lunch together?' He called the butler and gave instructions in Italian, which I didn't understand. Another doctor came to give him an electrocardiograph test. He told him, 'I have my most important friend here today and even the king of China cannot disturb our discussion.' He sent the doctor away and we were chatting and laughing on many subjects. Just after one o'clock he suddenly stopped talking and said, 'I wish to have some water.' Mickey Schulhof gave him a bottle of mineral water. He took a sip, his face slumped to one side and he started to snort. Mickey Schulhof said, 'My goodness, a heart attack.' I said, 'Herbert, Herbert . . .' We called his wife – she was washing her hair – but he had already passed away.'

No wreath on Karajan's village grave was larger than Sony's. Two days after his death, Ohga was struck down by a serious heart attack. Exactly two years later, in August 1991, he cancelled an appointment with me in Salzburg at the last minute to undergo open-heart surgery. When I saw him in Tokyo the following spring he seemed fully restored, but the first mention of Karajan's name brought forth a stutter of anecdotage and a slurred hesitancy to his otherwise fluent English diction. Karajan had meant more to him than he cared to reveal. He had moulded Ohga's Bach-to-Bruckner preferences as a music student and served as his benchmark for excellence in orchestral performance. He was, to the ex-singer and corporate president, the supreme authority in matters musical. He had been an idol, a friend and a role model. After Karajan's death, Norio Ohga's thoughts turned increasingly to podium aspirations.

The classical record industry in the immediate post-Karajan period was like Lilliput the day Gulliver went home – a lot of little people running about the beach wondering what happens next. Nowhere was the bewilderment greater than at Sony Classical, a label made in the maestro's image. Eight months previously Ohga had hired Günther Breest, Karajan's producer at Deutsche Grammophon, to head the new label and transfer its head office from the CBS centre in New York combatively to DG's doorstep at Hamburg. In Ohga's perspective music, if it was any good, had to emanate from Germany. 'The appointment of Mr Breest, together with the transfer of the classical music headquarters, will enable us to capitalise on the tremendous opportunities that now exist to expand our artist roster and enhance our repertoire with the finest possible performances,' said Ohga in an unusually aggressive press statement.

Breest picked an office block in the most exclusive suburb of the priciest city in Germany and proclaimed a 'resurgence of interest' in classical records – only for the roof to cave in with Karajan's death and the onset of world recession. Sony's half-decade in Hamburg would turn into a comic miniature of its Hollywood hell.

The first thing Breest did was to have his ceilings edged in gold leaf and decorated with goddesses, to impress the many artists who would throng his palatial office. A chubby, ebullient man who had spent eighteen blameless years with Deutsche Grammophon, ending up as Artists and Repertoire chief, he embodied many of the finest qualities of the professional record producer. He was musical, meticulous, intelligent, resourceful and deferential. His role as Karajan's coat-hanger – the great man liked to humiliate producers by tossing a garment at them when he entered a room – had not given him much scope for imagination or leadership. Still, on half a million Sony dollars a year anyone could learn to lead. Breest was, expressedly, Karajan's nominee to head Sony Classical.

With Ohga's support, Breest moved confidently to outbid his former employers with ten million dollars for the forty-three symphonic films Karajan made in his dying years. 'The Karajan legacy will *never* become outdated,' declared Breest in Anif. 'I believe that for a long time to come, perhaps even for ever, Karajan will be the only artist to film musical performances in this way – that is, with sole responsibility for all [sic] aspects of production.'[12] As Karajan's producer, Breest's humility was touchingly apt. As Sony's man among the muses, he promoted the Karajan movies as the spearhead of the company's surge of new products – laserdisc, High Definition Television (HDTV) and other wonders yet unseen.

Unfortunately, the public remained impassive. Except in Japan, where new technology was a patriotic selling-point, the golden Lasers gathered dust. DG, whether in acumen or spite, rushed out Karajan's Seventies operas in household VHS format, mopping up whatever appetite there was for seeing the late maestro in action. Desperate to create a buzz, Breest persuaded the Munich maverick, Sergiu Celibidache – renowned for his refusal to make records – to have his concerts filmed in HDTV and released on laserdisc. To no avail: laserdisc was a loser from day one.

In the absence of Karajan, both as a draw on his own merit and as a magnet to other maestros, Breest needed big-name conductors and had the wherewithal to buy them. In pursuit of Claudio Abbado he gave a top A&R job to Olimpia Gineri, Abbado's former secretary at the Vienna State Opera – unaware that relations between the maestro and his minder were not invariably cordial. Gineri was the first in a long line of executive comings and goings, a procession that could not match Hollywood for expense but was no less entertaining to musical insiders. After Gineri went, Sony Classical lacked a cogent artistic policy because Breest promised her position to two different men and was unable to satisfy both.

One way or another, he managed in December 1991 to announce 'a joint interpretive [sic] venture' with Abbado and Karajan's former orchestra. The deal was that Abbado and the Berliners would have complete artistic control of their own mini-label under the Sony aegis. It was the first time a maestro and European orchestra had ever been told 'record what you like' and several players bought themselves new sports cars in anticipation of the proceeds. 'Sony's contribution to this project is enormous,' declared the business managers of the Berlin Philharmonic, Bernd Gellermann and Hansjörg Schellenberger. 'The very core of the Berlin Philharmonic's repertoire has been reserved for the new label,' they added. It was hard to believe that three months earlier, in a back room at the Philharmonie, I watched Abbado renew his long-term, first-choice record contract with Deutsche Grammophon. What Sony was getting from Abbado in Berlin was Second Hand Rose repertoire that DG did not want.

'Neither the conductor nor the orchestra was hired by the company with a view to recording a market-oriented repertoire,' said the signatories. Much innocent mirth was occasioned by the list of planned recordings: a series of Mozart symphonies, followed by Beethoven, Schumann, Dvořák and Richard Strauss. Not market-oriented in any shape or form.

The Berlin agreement was personally brokered by Ohga, who used the signing ceremony at the Japanese German Centre in Berlin to announce his intention to make Sony 'the most important classical label by the end of the century'. Breest was given *carte blanche* to recruit stars. Dollar cheques fluttered out like tickertape and, for a few heady months, a handful of artists were offered more money than they had ever seen in their lives. The sensible ones refused politely, knowing it could only end in tears.

One Salzburg summer Breest ushered me into his festival office with a lordly wave at the conductor portraits on his wall: Abbado, Giulini, Muti. 'Look,' he exulted, 'we have got the greatest living Italian conductors on Sony Classical.' Absolutely true, except none of them recorded primarily for Sony. 'My abilities to convince artists have not changed since I moved over from DG,' insisted Breest. Zubin Mehta, Lorin Maazel and, at Ohga's stipulation, Seiji Ozawa were recruited on a non-exclusive basis. He outbid the world for the reclusive Carlos Kleiber's New Year's concert in Vienna, but DG held on to the video rights. While Breest splurged, the yellow label sneaked off with two of his company's neglected stars, Pierre Boulez and Michael Tilson Thomas.

To counter the Sony strike, the market leaders donned combat gear. Professor Andreas Holschneider, musicologist president of Deutsche Grammophon, warned in a Hamburg newspaper of a 'yellow peril' that was jeopardising German dominance in music.[13] To raise a war-chest against 'the deep pockets of our opponents', PolyGram offered twenty per cent of its stock for sale on the New York, Amsterdam and Tokyo exchanges. 'After Karajan,' said Holschneider, 'the time has come to force the pace with new operas and twentieth-century repertoire.'[14]

Breest's policy was to record the symphonies that Ohga knew and loved. 'Everyone, from Günther down, was looking over his shoulder to see what Ohga thought,' said a Sony producer.[15] 'If I have a personal motivation,' Breest told me, 'it is that I do not want to disappoint Mr Ohga. He is a great visionary, with a sensitivity for business.' That sensitivity made itself felt when, after four years of untold losses, Sony Classical had moved not one percentage point closer to the goal of world leadership. Its market share was a fraction of DG's twenty-two per cent in Europe and it was slipping alarmingly in the United States. In Britain, the fifth-largest market, Sony sold fewer records than such cottage independent labels as Chandos and Hyperion.

Breest responded to Tokyo disquiet by shovelling out backlist recordings at bargain prices and cutting back on his principal loss makers. However, a decision to terminate Maazel's contract was overturned by Ohga, who had put up a million Deutschmarks in sponsorship to pay Maazel's fees as music director of the Bavarian Radio Orchestra. Breest refused point-blank when Abbado demanded to record Mussorgsky's massive opera *Boris Godunov*, only to give way under Tokyo pressure. After all, he was contractually obligated to let the Berliners call the tune on their mini-label. The budget for *Boris* was twice that of the most expensive opera ever previously recorded, Solti's half-million-dollar *Frau Ohne Schatten* for Decca. Despite every restraint in production, the opera still overran by a quarter of a million dollars – minuscule sums by Hollywood comparison but enough to make a dozen symphonic recordings. *Boris* sold fifteen thousand copies in its first year. At that rate, it would take half a century to break even. 'I am supporting this,' said Ohga. 'Otherwise no one would want to invest much money in classical recording.'

Breest and his chief producer, Michael Haas, resolved to resist runaway costs in the next Abbado extravaganza, Schumann's *Scenes from Goethe's Faust*. But Ohga, hearing the fellow-baritone voice of Welshman Bryn Terfel, insisted on his inclusion – whatever the price. Terfel sang magnificently and critics were ecstatic, but the discs – appropriately gold-tinted – stuck in the shops. Meanwhile, Terfel's solo recitals on DG were selling faster than new issues could be pressed. Even when Sony made a commendable recording, their rivals ran rings around the leaden neo-Hamburgers.

Breest, reading his reddening ledgers, made one smart move in buying up a post-Soviet job-lot of 'St Petersburg Classics' and releasing them at rock-bottom prices. In their fifth year of operation, Sony Classical staff were congratulated on breaking even for the first time. If Tokyo would only agree to write off the start-up costs – as it was about to do at Columbia Pictures – the label could look forward to a reasonable, reconstructed future. But time was running out as Breest came under siege on two fronts. The Japanese, everlastingly patient at their tea ceremonies, expected rapid returns from foreign ventures. And Americans at the New York offices of Columbia Records were vociferous in their resentment of the removal of classics to German soil. American record executives, many of whom were Jewish, referred to Breest's team as 'the Nazi gang'. They condemned their programming as boring and were outraged at German indifference to Columbia's American treasures that extended from Copland to Philip Glass, Horowitz to Isaac Stern.

The look of Sony Classical products, especially its early-music Vivarte label, was derided by American staff as 'German provincial' and heavily undersold. 'I feel that my time is over when there are not enough lovers of culture [in Sony] to understand what we have done,'[16] complained Vivarte chief Wolf Erichson, an ungimmicky producer with more than three hundred titles to his credit.

Once Peter Gelb entered the picture, the Germans knew they had lost the war. Gelb, as head of Sony Classical USA, heated up the strife between Hamburg and New York. He took over Breest's job inside two years, sacked the top producers and flew out the remaining Hamburg executives to Tanglewood to assure them of his best intentions. 'I would like to take this opportunity to reaffirm Sony Classical's dedication to its dual goals of artistic excellence and commercial success, and its commitment to our employees in Hamburg and New York,' said Gelb in his presidential greeting.[17] Weeks later, he put the Hamburg building up for sale, sacked most of the staff and transferred European HQ to London. 'With London and New York as our dual headquarters, we are now ideally positioned to accomplish our strategic goals,' Gelb announced.[18]

No one, it should be noted, left the Hamburg palace inadequately compensated. German law rigorously protects contracts of employment and Sony did not want to leave a legacy of litigation. It would be presumptuous to guess the total pay-offs involved in shutting down Hamburg, but Breest had three years of his half-million-dollar contract to run and his two senior producers received six-figure cheques. The redundancy bill was the least of Sony's write-offs. From start to finish – taking in all the hirings and firings, artist signings and sackings, productions and cancellations – Sony blew no less than eighty million dollars and probably more than one hundred million in its vain bid to conquer the classical summit. And the result? After five years, the label was back where it started – in New York, under an isolationist American management, without a hit to its name and with an artists' roster flimsier than any of its competitors.

The retrenchment of Sony Classical left Norio Ohga in a state of evident discomfort. He was the only man in the Sony boardroom with hands-on experience of classical music, and his hands had been on each and every one of the hapless classical initiatives. If Betamax had been Morita's blunder, Beethoven was Norio Ohga's. A new executive generation who knew not Karajan were coming on board, and they held Ohga responsible for the embarrassment. Fortunately, the disgrace was a relatively discreet affair. The music business clammed up and the music press was typically malleable.

Ohga, nevertheless, felt a need to reassert his classical authority and upped the frequency and visibility of his conducting appearances. There were two concerts in Tokyo, followed by Mendelssohn's *Scottish* Symphony in August 1992 at the Schleswig-Holstein music festival in northern Germany. The orchestra came from Warsaw and the reviews were muted. In pursuit of greater appreciation, Ohga asked for a date with the New York Philharmonic Orchestra. As president of Sony Corporation, he did not send an audition tape and wait patiently. He sent Mickey Schulhof, president of the Sony Corporation of America, with a million-dollar donation. Few orchestras would have refused, but the New York Philharmonic was conscious of being the richest and oldest band in America and went all huffy at the suggestion that it could be bought for the night. It also had as its treasurer the Time-Warner chairman, Gerald M. Levin, a media rival who might not mind seeing Sony's man humbled. Unwilling to take No for an answer, Ohga sent Schulhof back with a better offer, only to be rebuffed again. Music director Kurt Masur would not allow his orchestra to be conducted by a part-timer, was the reason given.

He got a more positive response from the Metropolitan Opera, which happily hired out its orchestra for an Avery Fisher Hall concert. On the night of 12 May 1993, Norio Ohga made his New York début conducting

Schubert, Beethoven and Johann Strauss. Tickets were mostly by invitation and critics were not encouraged to attend. This was an audience of many stars. Barbra Streisand was sandwiched between Tony Bennett and Billy Joel, Sony artists all. 'Do they tell you where to applaud?' squealed Dolly Parton. The hand that waved the baton was the one that signed their contracts.

Ohga appeared 'dignified and graceful' on the podium. 'His gestures showed sympathy and understanding for the orchestra playing going on around him, but they had minimal influence on it,' wrote Bernard Holland in the *New York Times*. 'One small example: by the time the famous chimes in Strauss's *Fledermaus* Overture had been cued, the percussionist had already played them.'[19] This was conducting for a different class of connoisseur.

Ohga's next stop was the Boston Symphony Orchestra, to which he had given two million dollars of his own money for building a concert hall in Tanglewood. Two million was a very generous personal gift. According to an authoritative survey, heads of major Japanese corporations earned between twenty-five and thirty million yen a year ($187,000 to $224,000), about one-hundredth the salary of the Chrysler chief Lee Iaccoca.[20] Ohga had either inherited a family fortune or been elevated to part-ownership of Sony. A new joke did the rounds of musical New York: 'Q. If you're president of a billion-dollar record company, where do you conduct a symphony concert? A. Anywhere you like.'

The following year, Ohga joined the board of Carnegie Hall, America's most prestigious concert venue. Ohga's involvement in US musical life was welcomed by music administrators but viewed with suspicion by some musicians, especially in the Boston Symphony Orchestra. 'We have been telling our board for years that Ozawa has been here far too long,' said a veteran BSO violinist. 'But they say there's too much Japanese money behind him for us to let him go. Ohga built him a hall. Nippon Electric pay for his overseas tours . . .'[21]

Ohga reacted to serious criticism and entrenched opposition with the same cultured impassivity. 'I know he speaks English,' said the Paramount chief, Martin Davis, who was trying to negotiate a merger with Sony. 'There's nothing more irritating than talking to a man who knows exactly what you're saying but just gives you this look.'[22]

Where Morita avidly sought the West's approval, Ohga shunned its barbs and hugs with a mien that was casually described as 'inscrutable' but was more likely a stiffened reflex of his upper-class upbringing. Four decades of familiarity with western manners had not prepared him for the racial prejudice that greeted Sony's cultural acquisitions and the gloating that attended its calamities. Confronted with the fall-out, Ohga followed recommended business-school practice and stonewalled: 'I know how to run a record company – I recommended the purchase to my board – I knew what we were buying,' he said.

The hesitancy and subdued tone of his delivery betrayed, perhaps, a deeper disappointment. All his life, Ohga had wanted to make a name for himself in music. Now, with finance at his fingertips and fine orchestras at his command, he was powerless to run a label the way he liked and forced to accept Peter Gelb's definition of a classical masterpiece: getting Yo-Yo Ma, the finest living cellist, to record a film-composer's gratuitous score on the Vietnam War. Nor was his own acceptance by fine orchestras achievable except by means of his cheque-book. These were chastening discoveries for Norio Ohga, fracturing the glass triangle of his Pythagorean self-image as technician, musician and manager.

Ohga had pledged that classical music would prosper in Sony hands, but pressures of technology and management forced him to retrench. He had promised that new Sony technology would make classics sound and look lovelier than ever, but record buyers resisted his gadgetry. He had reassured the West that pop music would, under Japanese management, retain its creative vigour and cultural autonomy. It did not take many months for that undertaking to be violently unsettled, breaching Ohga's well-intentioned aloofness and jeopardising the principles and practices on which the record industry had stood since Thomas Alva Edison's day.

The man Ohga trusted to look after the mass-market side of his record business was the inside man of the Sony take-over. Walter Yetnikoff was, apart from Karajan, Norio Ohga's oldest friend in the West. In 1967, as assistant general attorney at Columbia Records, he was Ohga's co-signatory on the agreement that founded CBS-Sony Records in Japan. They had remained on warm terms ever since. 'It's an unusual relationship between an easterner and an American,' said the lawyer. 'We talk about how people should develop their character, and what life's all about.'[23] This was an unusually sedate statement from Yetnikoff, whose normal mode of self-description ran more along these lines: 'I'm very spiritual. I commune with my higher power. I connect spiritually with my inner self . . . then I go out and I try to fuck people.'[24]

He refrained, by all accounts, from uttering obscenities in Ohga's reserved presence or trying to screw him in business. On the contrary, Ohga was Yetnikoff's insurance policy against the day when Columbia Records might go cold, or feel small, on him. That day dawned in November 1987 when

Yetnikoff, at loggerheads with his CBS bosses, heard that they were putting the record division on the market. He called Schulhof and told him to pass on the asking price to Ohga. Within twenty minutes, Ohga called back to say he was buying. Yetnikoff's reward was a cheque for ten million dollars, plus equity in the new business and Ohga's mandate to lead Sony's hunt for a movie studio and a management team to run it.

With Yetnikoff in command, Ohga could sleep easy about his record business. Exuberant, bearded and invariably open-shirted, Yetnikoff was the man rock stars rushed to with their confidences.

Michael Jackson cried on his shoulder. Bruce Springsteen was his buddy. The Rolling Stones, James Taylor and Cyndi Lauper were his signings. He had assembled an enviable rock list at CBS Records, but he also lost a number of top-selling artists. Joan Baez, back from Israel where CBS had booked her to sing on occupied Arab land, called Yetnikoff to complain. 'There's no such thing as occupied territory,' shrieked the label boss, 'those fucking Arabs want to throw me into the sea.'

'Which one, Walter?' said Baez, 'the Hudson River?'

That phone call ended the folk-singer's big-label career.[25]

Yetnikoff threw Paul Simon out of his office, then issued writs against him for failing to fulfil his last contract album before signing up with Warner. The singer, in a 1978 counter-suit, alleged that Yetnikoff had sworn to 'destroy Simon's professional career' in retaliation for his defection. The case, pre-echoing one of Sony's future nightmares, was settled out of court, with Simon paying CBS Records $1.5 million for the unmade album. The fight, Simon later said, cost him five years of creative infertility. Few who faced up to Yetnikoff escaped his biblical taste for bloody vengeance.

In Frederic Dannen's exposé of record-label corruption, *The Hit Men*, Yetnikoff was described as violent, drunken and abusive. He walked into a CBS board meeting covered in blood after smashing up a motor scooter. He was alleged to have connections with 'the Network', a blackmail ring that funnelled record company millions into radio stations on a No Pay, No Play threat. Dannen's book was a much-discussed best-seller in 1990, to Sony's evident distaste. With Ohga as his boss, it was widely reported that Yetnikoff was running amok in settling scores and chasing Hollywood dreams. Ohga was pictured in *Rolling Stone* with an arm around his shoulders. Not good for the Sony image.

Yetnikoff checked into a Minnesota drug and alcohol rehabilitation clinic in July 1989, the month Karajan died. He emerged to find himself unexpectedly excluded from the running of Sony Pictures. Worse, he was being blamed for the vast costs of hiring his friends Peter Guber and Jon Peters. Yetnikoff went raging again and artists took cover. The heat of his rhetoric could blister the nape of a New York cab driver. Jackson and Springsteen were reported to be on the point of leaving Sony. Ohga broke his Salzburg festival going to hit New York in mid-August 1990 and read Yetnikoff the riot act. But the warning came too late to save the flamboyant label chief.

The *Wall Street Journal* had it on good authority later that month that Yetnikoff was being promoted to Ohga's personal adviser and removed from the daily running of the label. By the end of the year Yetnikoff was gone from Sony, clutching the customary eight-digit golden handshake. Ohga's reaction to his departure – in circumstances that linked the pristine name of Sony with drugs, payola and profanities – was curiously roseate. 'Walter Yetnikoff is a wonderful man,' he said, his voice swelling with emotion, 'I love him. I can't criticise him. But unfortunately now we have lost him.' Under no pressure of questioning would Ohga admit errors of human judgement. Yetnikoff was 'a wonderful partner'. Jon Peters was 'a wonderful creator and an astute businessman'. Corporate discretion cloaked their pay-offs. Mickey Schulhof was credited with tamping down the turbulence left in their wake and forging new links between the music and movie divisions.

Yetnikoff's removal was, however, a painful blow to Ohga and it left the label with more problems than it solved. Tommy Mottola, the new record boss, described by a Yetnikoff ex-girlfriend as 'Walter's personal valet', was not a commanding presence or a remarkable talent-spotter – though he was married to Mariah Carey who would sing Sony's biggest hit of 1995, the 1.5-million-selling 'Daydream'. Mottola was never taken into Tokyo's confidence as Yetnikoff had been, and his appearance in Dannen's book embracing a 'Network' suspect did nothing to dispel the taint of decadence that was settling around Sony.

The one coup of comfort was that Michael Jackson, with Yetnikoff gone, was prepared in face-to-face negotiations with Ohga to agree a sixty-five-million-dollar contract for his next six albums. The amount was an industry record, as was Jackson's royalty rate of forty-two per cent of the selling price of each disc. 'His last recording was so successful for the company,' said a satisfied Ohga, who admitted listening to a Jackson record but would not pass artistic comment. 'If it makes money, that's good,' was all he would say. 'Michael Jackson is wonderful person,' added Ohga. 'He has a remarkable nose for what his fans want.' The scale of Sony's commitment seemed extravagant, but safe. Jackson was a high-energy, low-protein performer whose appeal transcended all known barriers of gender, age and race.

With a skin that was neither black nor white, a sexuality that was as explicit as it was indeterminate and conduct that was neither childlike nor fully adult, Jackson outsold all other pop stars in the Eighties. His 1982 *Thriller* album entered the *Guinness Book of Records* as the top-selling disc of all time, with forty-three million sales. His movie, *Moonwalker*, was a universal hit. His 1987–9 world tour grossed more than a hundred and twenty million dollars. With an entourage of two hundred people and a thousand tons of equipment, Jackson's was not so much an act as an industry, with a turnover larger than the GNP of many developing nations. He was also an extremely isolated and eccentric individual. Heavyweight newspapers referred to him as 'an alien from Mars';[26] the popular press dubbed him 'Wacko Jacko'. Even Sony bosses were heard wondering, 'Is Michael Jackson really as strange as he seems?'[27] 'Michael Jackson is not someone who finds it easy to form adult personal relationships,' reported the *Independent* newspaper in 1991. 'His constant companion on his last tour, for instance, was a ten-year-old blond boy.'[28]

Nemesis, in retrospect, was never too far off. The falsetto runt of the Jackson Five, a happy-family soul group from Gary, Indiana, there was always something disturbing about Jackson's gyrations. In the 1991 video of his 'Black or White' single, he was seen smashing up a car and apparently masturbating on its roof. Jackson later said, 'It upsets me to think that "Black or White" could influence any child or adult to destructive behaviour, either sexual or violent.' He had, said Sean O'Hagan in the London *Times*, 'the broadest fan base any artist could ever hope for.' He was also 'an object of fascination to a huge pre-pubescent audience who wait with bated breath for his videos'.[29]

This was the bait that hooked his Japanese backers. 'Our company needs fans among the young,' Ohga told me in 1992. 'If we have a big hit, we will get supporters for the company in the next generation.' Jackson was an integral element of Sony's renovation strategy – until his show was derailed in mid-1993 by allegations that the thirty-five-year-old singer had sexually molested small boys who slept over at his 2,700-acre walled-off Californian ranch. Jackson denied the charges. 'I am totally innocent of any wrong-doing,' he said, after police had submitted his body to an inch-by-inch examination to verify identifying marks on his penis and buttocks. 'It was the most humiliating ordeal of my life – one that no person should ever have to suffer,' said the beleaguered singer.

His next world tour was called off in mid-flight when the singer collapsed with 'exhaustion' and Pepsi-Cola withdrew its multimillion sponsorship. Sony, however, was hitched to Jackson for the long-term. 'We continue to stay in contact with Michael Jackson and his management with regard to his recording career,' said a spokesman. 'For Sony Music to comment further would not be appropriate, except to stand by the right that even a superstar is innocent until proven guilty.'

In the end, Jackson gave way to unendurable pressure and paid several million dollars to his principal accuser, thirteen-year-old Jordie Chandler. Claims from other boys continued to pursue him. He entered an iconic marriage with Lisa-Marie Presley, daughter of an earlier idol, and tried to resume his act. But while his televised interviews were compulsory viewing, his next album, *History*, was a maudlin self-justification that failed financially to justify Sony's thirty-million-dollar promotion with world sales of nine million albums. To compound his woes, Jackson immediately had to apologise for an anti-Semitic lyric and his wife unwittingly complicated his come-back by saying, 'He can't help it if children follow him everywhere – even to the bathroom.' The following summer Jackson and Presley went on separate holidays, he with puerile companions and she with her ex-husband. Just before Christmas 1995, as the singer lay stressed-out in a New York hospital, Presley told him she was suing for divorce over 'irreconcilable differences'.[30]

It was hard to resist a twinge of sympathy for Sony, who had signed Jackson in good faith and were as shocked as anyone by the allegations against him, predictable though they were. Sony took more than its fair share of flak and found itself stuck for the next five albums with an artist who was never going to recover his main attraction, that unisex wholesomeness that embraced viewers and listeners of all generations. Michael Jackson was damaged goods and Sony were damaged by association. Analysts were quick to remark that, had the record label been run from Manhattan rather than the Goten Yama hills, its leaders might have spotted the danger sooner and responded to it more constructively. There was a tendency to portray Sony as a company out of tune with music-biz realities and out of step with the needs of singers and listeners. These mutterings, non-specific and xenophobic on the whole, acquired pertinency and penetration with Sony's next courtroom drama.

In October 1993, in the midst of the Michael Jackson scandal, Sony was hauled into the High Court in London by a singer who wanted out. Georgios Kyriacos Panayiotou, better known as George Michael, was a former Wham! group member who went solo with the 1987 hit 'I Want Your Sex' and won a Grammy award for a fifteen-million-selling album called *Faith*. George Michael was hirsute, hetero and highly intelligent. He had an eight-album, fifteen-year contract with the London branch of CBS Records which he renegotiated in 1988 after the Sony take-over. His claim now was that this contract amounted to restraint of trade under British law and unfair exploitation under the European convention. It prevented him from making music with any other label if, as was now the case, he was unable to achieve artistic satisfaction with Sony. The company, he said, were refusing to release his records, authorise new productions – or set him free from what felt like enslavement.

His grievance stemmed from a 1990 follow-up album, *Listen Without Prejudice*, which sold less than half as well as *Faith*. This, the singer claimed, was because Sony had failed to promote it properly in America after he refused to appear on video as a sex-object. This was contrary to his new self-image, which was pitched at a more mature audience. 'I gained the very strong impression that the album had been killed to teach me a lesson,' he would tell the court. When Sony rejected his next album, Michael went to law.

The dispute, common enough in recording circles, would usually have been settled by common sense. Michael, anxious to avoid a costly and unpredictable prosecution, flew to New York in October 1992 to plead his case with Norio Ohga. He told him that Sony did not understand his creative process and they would be better off apart. Ohga listened impassively and promised him an answer the following day. The answer was No. A fortnight later, Michael's lawyers filed suit in London and the tone turned nasty. 'My years at CBS Records were creative as well as productive,' said Michael in a pre-trial statement, 'but I have seen the great American music company that I proudly signed to as a teenager become a small part of the production line for a giant electronics corporation . . . This arranged marriage to Sony simply doesn't work. We do not speak the same language.' The implication was that a foreign manufacturing company like Sony was unfit to run a creative enterprise.

Sony responded combatively, saying, 'Our contract with George Michael is valid and legally binding. There is a serious moral as well as legal commitment attached to any contract, and we will not only honour it but vigorously defend it.' The rest of musicdom quaked in its boots and blamed Sony for airing greyish linen. If Michael won, it would signal the end of long-term artist-label ties. 'It would make it much more difficult for record companies to invest heavily in new artists,' said a record-biz lawyer.[31]

Ownership was only one of the issues Michael challenged. Sony, he said, had made ninety-six million pounds out of his work in five years, while his cut was just seventeen million. For every compact disc Sony got £2.45 and the singer just 37 pence. Under their agreement, Sony had 'almost no obligation' to propagate his records, while Michael was required to give all his music exclusively to Sony. If he lost the case, said Michael, he would never make another record rather than have his work handled by Sony.

He lost, and appealed. With legal costs running over three million pounds neither side wanted the case to drag on, especially with the press gloating over every witness-box indiscretion. Michael was a hero to the public gallery, a gallant knight fighting the corporate dragon. In the end, both parties were got off the hook by David Geffen, a music-biz multibillionaire with a new Dreamworks label who, together with EMI's Virgin subsidiary, persuaded Sony to accept a forty-million-dollar 'release fee' for Michael, plus a four-per-cent cut of his future recordings. Michael was free and Geffen pledged to rebuild his image in America. Sony, for its part, had saved its face but lost mountains of credit in the record industry and beyond.

The model Japanese company had heard itself described in court as unsympathetic to artists and intent on enforcing harsh terms. Although the industry's long-term contracts had been ruled legal, it was clear they could damage the health and wealth of tenured artists. In future, singers and their agents would proceed more cautiously and not sign away more than two records at a time. This, wailed industry chiefs, could prove disastrous, since an artist's first releases often lost money and did not pay back until the fifth or sixth album. Label-hopping by artists, said Sony's UK chairman, Paul Russell, would cause the industry to self-destruct. A rash of new claims erupted. A singer formerly known as Prince walked around in 1994 with the word 'slave' etched on his cheek after Warner refused to release an album in a conflict over who owned the master-tapes, singer or label. Every time an issue of this kind came to a head, Sony was blamed for opening the floodgates.

By 1995, Sony had been pushed into third place in the US record market by Warner and PolyGram. Its share had slipped in three years from 17.2 to 13.6 per cent and there was no sign of new artists who might herald a recovery. Its movies were picking up with *Bad Boys* and *The Net* grossing over fifty million dollars apiece, but an embarrassment like *First Knight* recouped less than two-thirds of its sixty-million-dollar cost. In April 1995, Ohga was named chairman of Sony, yielding his executive presidency to Nobuyuki Idei, a fifty-three-year-old insider with pronounced hardware priorities.

Eight months later, Mickey Schulhof resigned from Sony under pressure from Idei. Newspaper reports focused on Schulhof's lavish life-style and Sony's string of expensive disasters. Schulhof had been denied the instant access to Idei that he had enjoyed for twenty years with the Sony leadership and his departure marked another personal blow for Ohga, who supported him to the last. Ohga was placed temporarily in charge of the entertainment division, but its future was open to question and his own position was seriously exposed. In the midst of the upheavals, Ohga permitted himself one small extravagance – an invitation to the Berlin Philharmonic Orchestra and Claudio Abbado to visit Japan in 1996 for the jubilee of the company's foundation. Ohga would have known by now that music would not bring Sony salvation. The company needed new home appliances and the introduction of HDTV for any hope of upturn. Music and movies were almost irrelevant to these technical and political missions, and their potential for causing fresh embarrassment was far from exhausted. Then, just as the troublesome arts were settling into sullen coexistence Matsushita, for the first time in its existence, gave Sony the glint of an idea.

The senior Japanese giant, owner of the Panasonic, Technics and JVC brands, had enjoyed a relatively easy time in Hollywood. Universal Pictures made *Jurassic Park* and a lot of money, MCA was looking to expand its music holdings, and its extensive television, theme-park and publishing interests were doing well. There were tensions between Tokyo and the old-Hollywood management of Lew Wasserman and Sidney Sheinberg, but that was only to be expected. There had been, at least, no Sony-like disasters. But in the middle of 1995 Matsushita startled the corporate world by pulling out. Edgar Bronfman, of the Seagram whisky family, offered $5.7 billion and the Japanese jumped at it. The price was less than they had paid – $6.1 billion plus a billion's worth of debt – but the relief was audible. 'The core business of Matsushita is electronics, which is undergoing a major change as the multimedia age approaches with the advance of digital technologies on a world scale,' said Yoichi Morishita, the company president. Reading the subtext, what he meant was that Japanese manufacturers should never have got into music and movies in the first place. How long, commentators asked, before Sony saw the light and went back to what it did best?

And what then, musicians worried, would become of its record label? Suddenly the corporate map of music that had been redrawn at the end of the Eighties was up for grabs again. Thorn in July 1995 announced the demerger of its EMI holdings and opened the door to bidders. Its classical division was comprehensively restructured to make it look more attractive.

Time-Warner had a top-level shake-out as the company geared up for market action. Two 'creative executives' were ousted and a potentially offensive gangsta rap subsidiary was sold off. Months later, Warner announced an enormous merger with Turner Broadcasting, creating a visual-media hybrid that pushed its music holdings down the priority table. Corporate question marks hovered over more than half the major groups in classical recording. Only Philips-controlled PolyGram, parent of Deutsche Grammophon, Philips and Decca, was entirely safe – thanks to Jan Timmer, the Philips boss, who started out as a bass-baritone singer and CD-producer.[32] But Timmer, too, was shortly due to retire.

Even at PolyGram, music producers were being nudged to consider whether the projects they had in mind might be useful to the parent company's movie, advertising and hardware interests. Music, especially its classical component, was being relentlessly subordinated to sister interests. Classical labels could be bought, sold or reformated overnight. Almost without anyone having noticed, the autonomy of the record industry had been destroyed. For the first time since Edison invented the means, record labels were no longer stimulated by musical need but by tactical positioning in trade wars and take-over strategies. The power to mould the world's musical tastes had become the plaything of dawn raiders, asset strippers, and hardware tycoons for whom music existed on the outer margins of their vision. In an ever-spinning roundabout of giant corporations, the needle slipped inexorably into the record industry's last groove.

NOTES

1 all Ohga comments, author's interview, February 1992
2 *Vanity Fair*, September 1991, p. 36
3 company report 1991, p. 23
4 Morita, p. 57
5 Morita, p. 4
6 both quotes from fortieth anniversary history, pp. 62–3
7 Morita, p. 159
8 *NY Times*, 18 February 1990
9 Günther Breest, speech at Sony Anif, 13 August 1991
10 Breest, loc. cit.
11 Robert Sandall, *Sunday Times Culture Section*, 18 April 1993, p. 18
12 Speech at Anif, 13 August 1991
13 *Hamburger Abendblatt*, February 1990, pp. 10–11
14 author's interview
15 comments to the author
16 *Early Music Today*, April/May 1995, p. 25
17 letter to Sony Classical staff, dated 7 March 1995
18 press release, 16 August 1995
19 *NY Times*, 14 May 1993
20 *Intersect* magazine, April 1992, p. 13
21 comments to the author, identity withheld
22 *Vanity Fair*, February 1994, p. 114
23 Dannen, p. 308
24 *Vanity Fair*, February 1990, p. 135
25 author's interview with Joan Baez, October 1995

26 *Observer*, 26 June 1988
27 *The Times Saturday Review*, 30 November 1991, p. 8
28 *Independent* profile, 23 November 1991
29 *The Times Saturday Review*, loc. cit.
30 *Daily Telegraph*, *The Times*, 19 January 1996
31 *Wall Street Journal*, 27 March 1995
32 for Timmer's career, see Gruithuijsen/Junge

CHAPTER XV

THE COCA-COLISATION
OF CLASSICAL MUSIC

And with each passing year of the millennium's final decade, more and more cultural assets were acquired by the mighty unaccountable. The relic of Columbia's glory, its CBS television network, was merged with the Westinghouse manufacturing concern. Some of the proudest names in English publishing – Secker & Warburg, Methuen, Heinemann, Hamlyn, Octopus, Sinclair-Stevenson, Mitchell Beazley and a dozen more – were agglomerated by the Anglo-Dutch Reed–Elsevier combine, stripped down to profitability and then put up for sale as a single lot. William Gates III, owner and inventor of Microsoft Systems that ran ninety per cent of all desk-top computers, bought the Bettmann image bank with the aim of incorporating in one database treasures of the world's great museums, creating 'a world-wide resource of visual information' – a veritable fortress of institutional copyrights. Rupert Murdoch, owner of many newspapers and innumerable satellite channels, swooped on popular culture by seizing premier rights to screen English soccer and both forms of rugby football, union and league. Pastimes and clubs that had kept a quirky independence from time immemorial were sent tumbling like ninepins in the bowling rush for information-age ascendance.

What chance did classical music stand in this onslaught? Internal optimists argued it was too small to interest corporate imperialists and would be allowed to play on regardless, but then optimism can seldom be trusted in a revolutionary age. Classical music, as this book has shown, got swept up in the early hours of the fire-sale of western culture. It may have been minuscule but it was a prestigious asset and without it no cultural conglomerate could call itself comprehensive. Sucked into the corporate maw, classical music was ruthlessly subsidiarised and subjected to the remote control of know-nothing bean-counters, its agenda dictated from without. The totalitarian reality of restricted cultural ownership by a handful of shifting global entities was taking on Orwellian dimensions — and the smaller the art form the more defenceless it appeared.

As this book went to print, key pieces on the classical chessboard were under renewed attack. Thorn-EMI was reported to be readying its music sector for sale and Walt Disney, newly merged with ABC television, was mentioned as a suitor. Warner threw its music division into the melting pot after merging with Turner television; Murdoch stalked the Warner perimeter, contemplating assault. In the classical pond, Ronald Wilford's CAMI nuzzled up to Sony while Mark McCormack's IMG explored an alliance with Isaac Stern's ICM associates. None of these moves might ever come to anything, but the wave of corporate rumours demonstrated how helpless music had become in the hands of global giants. A slip of paper signed in Sixth Avenue or Seattle could reallocate, or 'rationalise' to near-extinction, a quarter of the world's classical activity. The fate of organised musical life hung at the tip of an executive pen.

For this state of impotence, music had only itself to blame. An art that once paid its own way had, through ambition and greed, fallen upon the charity of politicians and businessmen. This dependency culture, created by the avarice of millionaire conductors, singers and their agents, reached a point where it was no longer sustainable by public and corporate funds. In the final years of the twentieth century, orchestras and opera houses that upheld the traditions of Bach and Beethoven were facing a daily threat of foreclosure.

As costs spiralled, audiences waned and the electorate was unmoved by the withering of arts institutions. Italy debated, without much heat, whether it should continue to fund thirteen opera houses, or close most of them down. There was no outcry in London when Arts Council officials sought to halve the city's orchestras. In fact, the only show of public spirit came when Covent Garden was awarded a seventy-eight-and-a-half-million-pound lottery windfall and the Murdoch press screamed foul. Yet this was a time when opera was supposedly at the peak of its appeal, with attendances soaring and every misdemeanour, vocal or marital, of three famed tenors reported in the mass media.

The reality was less demotic. Only the affluent could afford to witness the highest level of performance inside opera houses that were kept alive by state and corporate funds. The options open to everyone else were to hear amplified tenors in open spaces, or stay home and spin discs, imagining that by activating an electric current they were somehow participating in the musical process. Music, in the form disseminated by Japanese manufacturers, could be played in the bathroom or taken for a jog. The real thing, meanwhile, was stultifying in privileged or half-empty houses.

It would not take much to put music back on its feet. A billion dollars from Mr Gates, whose personal wealth was estimated at fifteen billion, would underpin every professional orchestra and opera house in the world for half a century hence. If even one of Mr Murdoch's many channels were turned over to concert relays, part of the public appetite for live action might retune away from rugby and mud-wrestling. Mr Gates flared a flicker of hope by promising some day to give away his entire fortune. Mr Murdoch put a forced smile on musical faces each time he attended the Metropolitan Opera. But to imagine that either man, or any of their ilk, would in a flush of public-spiritedness assist an art that was in such obvious trouble was to misrepresent the nature of modern philanthropy. Rich men like to back winners, whether on the race-track or on stage. Sport and rock music had the stench of success and were swamped with unneeded corporate support. Classical music, beset by self-doubt and a wobbly bottom line, was wanly unattractive to white knights. It needed more than the kindness of strangers to arrest millennial decay. To rekindle a sense of purpose, classical music needed to reassess its strengths and rebuild from basics – just as any other industry would do in difficulty.

But the music business was frightened of reconstruction. As the money ran out, maestros and their agents concentrated on making whatever money there was in a flurry of round-the-world orchestral tours and unnecessary promotions of gargantuan choral works.

When the music stopped, the big fish would be well provided for. Concert agents, facing an ever-darkening future, signed as many artists as they could get in the hope of cornering a market, or formed 'boutique'-style managements that tended two or three overpaid celebrities and turned their backs on the rest. Between these two approaches, old-fashioned methods of career building as developed by Hermann Wolff, Arthur Judson and Harold Holt fell into disuse. 'You don't go to the office any longer, excited about who might come in that day to audition,' said one agency vice-president. 'You spend all your time worrying about the few stars that make the money.'

New talent was now a non-priority, unless it was so young as to be almost jail-bait. Child wonders of Asian extraction were fiercely exploited, while profound interpreters were unable to get a paying date. If a young artist had not won a competition or made a name by the age of thirty, few agents would let him or her past the door. 'Much as I am attracted by what you have to offer, I cannot spare the time you would need to build an international career,' wrote one busy agent to an underused, mature conductor[1] – a well-polished brush-off line that amounted to a confession of collective guilt. The music business no longer looked after the orchestral trainers and painstaking rehearsers who kept the central repertoire in good repair, and their disappearance was sorely felt. Until 1970, you could expect to hear a Brahms symphony splendidly performed in any major metropolis regularly and as of right. By 1990, good Brahms was a rarity and great Brahms a distant memory. Globe-trotting star conductors had no time for intricate preparation, and their agents had no time for non-stars. For want of care and attention, great music was being depreciated and morale among musicians plummeted to mortal depths. Making a name and a living in music had not been this tough since Handel's day.

All possible outlets were somehow inhibited by corporate or political restraints. Recording was becoming a backlist business, with new releases down to a monthly handful. Eighty racked-up CDs of Beethoven's fifth symphony meant there was no incentive to record such masterpieces ever again and no opportunity for living interpreters to measure themselves against the granitic dead. Faced with limited repertoire and falling prices, big labels gave up on any artist who did not quickly make good. 'It used to be our philosophy to let artists make mistakes and learn from them,' said one major-label A&R chief. 'But now every project has to look profitable on paper and, if it fails, the artist could get dropped.'[2] There would be no more Kathleen Ferriers, Joan Sutherlands or Jacqueline du Prés, because their nursery playground had been sold to developers and turned into a parking lot.

For composers, too, horizons were contracting – and this despite the ephemeral success of minimalism and its Górecki-bred offshoot, 'holy minimalism'. Music publishing was ruled by three large groups that made most of their dough from exploiting lengthening terms of company copyrights. Movie sound-tracks might turn up an occasional winner like Michael Nyman, but the developmental wings of music publishing had been clipped by corporate ownership and a vanishing sense of cultural responsibility. There were no Emil Hertzkas around to shelter penniless dreamers who might become tomorrow's Kurt Weills. And without a publisher, struggling composers were starved of opportunities for commissions and performance*.

As for instrumentalists, the advice to musical Mrs Worthingtons was: 'Don't put your daughter on the concert platform.' 'Whatever area of music you choose,' warned a graduate career guide, 'there is no standard training programme and no fixed career path. You may have to acquire qualifications to demonstrate that you have the necessary expertise; but they will not automatically bring you work.

'Indeed, experience and "being known" are better guarantees of employment, and these can only be gained by working. Catch 22!'[3] Many highly trained musicians dropped out of music within months of graduation, and the conservatories themselves were under pressure to cut admissions and stop swelling the unemployment statistics.

If college leavers managed to find a job, the pay in all but the most lavishly funded orchestras was insufficient to feed a family. The despair felt by players in breadline bands was communicated, wittingly or otherwise, to those they were expected to entertain and uplift. People who had paid to sublimate their own problems in a Haydn symphony were met by a frowning reminder of earthly woes. There were many reasons for the audience collapse that befell classical music, but a loss of transcendence was not the least of them. Impoverished and frightened musicians were not the best advocates to restore popular confidence in classical music.

As earnings and employment receded, musicians played safe and took fewer imaginative leaps. Geared to the intrusion of microphones and cameras, they feared making any slip that could cost the chance of a broadcast or recording. Audiences, missing the thrill of highwire inspiration without knowing what they were missing, grew bored. A sense of virtual reality pervaded concert halls and opera houses, a drab illusion that was intensified by giant screens showing the pianist's hands at play, and other gimmicks of the media era. Might as well stay at home and watch telly, said once-loyal concert goers.

'Where has all the excitement gone?' wailed listeners and musicians alike. Gone in a haze of conformity, a process of palliation that one agent defined as 'the Coca-Colisation of concerts' – giving the public what it thinks it wants.

It was no longer possible to tell one top American orchestra from another, because they all aspired to the same inoffensive lustre. Fiddle-cubs who started out with a spark of invention emerged from college with a certificate of sameness, or their spirits crushed. 'The most important thing they teach is

---

* In March 1996, as this book went to print, Boosey & Hawkes added to its acquisitions the Berlin House of Bote and Bock, where Herman Wolff entered the music business.

how to socialise with sponsors and smile at conductors,' said one Juilliard misfit. In the hands of public officials, business donors and corporate owners, classical music was being dulled into extinction. The responsible authorities could not permit the risk of spontaneous artistry. Their job was to run a business, not rescue an art in its dying agonies.

Inside the belly of the corporate whale, classical music nestled contagiously with its new bedfellows. The masturbatory antics of Michael Jacksonish pop music, the moral decay of *Fatal Attraction* movies and the monotony of over-organised sport all left their mark on the classical slowcoach of the infotainment highway. When George Michael sneezed, classical recording seized up with pneumonia. Michael Jackson's arrest on child-sex charges precipitated emergency surgery at Sony Classical. Pitch brawls at the rugby world cup marred Kiri Te Kanawa's singing of the tournament anthem. Chasing redemption in connective media, classical music compromised its uniqueness and risked its integrity in a morass of amorality and violence. Weakened by internal conditions, it was exposed by conglomerate proximity to random, non-specific cross-infections.

While movies and pop music were less inclined to fraternise, Mark McCormack had rightly identified an affinity between classical music and championship sports. The top performers in both fields travelled more than was good for them and earned more than they knew how to spend; the tax nightmare that haunted Steffi Graf might just as easily have befallen Anne-Sophie Mutter had her affairs not been kept in meticulous good order by her lawyer husband.

Mutter was one of twenty artists who in 1995 earned well over a million dollars from classical music (see Coroner's Report p. 422). A million was the base rate for half the players in major league US baseball and peanuts for the top pugilist, Mike Tyson. But in most other spectator sports the champions were earning roughly the same as classical high-flyers. In 1993, motor-racing champion Nigel Mansell made eleven million dollars, the top golfer, Nick Faldo, ten million, the soccer striker, Gary Lineker, three million and the snooker champion, Stephen Hendry, just over two million.[4] This stacked up against fifteen million for Pavarotti, ten for Domingo, five for Perlman and two-and-a-half for Miss Mutter.

Mansell's total worth was assessed at seventy million dollars, earned by risking his life daily in the fast lane. Steffi Graf made about a million less, and she was the richest sportswoman in Europe. Neither, however, came close to the hundred million amassed by Luciano Pavarotti, an amount his wife, Adua, expected to share when she toyed with divorce in 1995. Classical music, apparently so enfeebled that it was on a life-support system of state funding, was creating greater wealth than all the commercial breaks of competitive sports. If a performer could make more singing arias at the Melbourne Tennis Club than hitting balls, priorities were plainly going askew. And if music was going broke, how did its maestros get to be so rich?

To unstring this expensive racket, we need to contrast the fortunes of classical music and organised sport down the twentieth century. Back in 1900, music and opera were mass pursuits that crossed class barriers and played in every small town. Sport was the idle pursuit of rich amateurs and the Saturday-afternoon fantasy of factory workers crowded onto unsafe football stands. Tennis, golf and horse-racing were the sport of kings; boxing and soccer were working-class affairs. Participants played for glory, not for gold.

Between the world wars, sports acquired an organisational framework, while music entered a communicative crisis in which many composers pretended to ignore their audience. These trends, together with the piping of radio into private homes, diminished popular involvement in classics and increased the following for sport. In terms of social importance, though, a rough parity prevailed. Hitler and Stalin used sport and music interchangeably as instruments of state propaganda. The 1936 Berlin Olympics were a showcase for Aryan physical supremacism; the Berlin Philharmonic under Wilhelm Furtwängler was paraded as a token of German spiritual sublimity. Soviet athletes and violinists were trained from infancy to win gold medals that would attest the unarguable superiority of Marxist-Leninist ideology. Measured in radio hours, there were more concert relays around the world than football broadcasts; newspapers employed as many music critics as they did sports writers.

Classical music was not eclipsed in the mass media until television entered the picture and Mark McCormack began selling live sports coverage – a critical moment in social history. Before McCormack moved in, the 1960 Rome Olympics took just under one million US dollars in global television revenue; for the Sydney Olympics in the year 2000 transmission rights were sold for one and a quarter *billion* dollars. Organised sport was suddenly awash in cash. The Charter that restored the Olympic Games in 1896 promulgated health-giving, run-for-fun ideals; a century later, the Olympics were a billion-dollar payday for which athletes wrecked their bodies on steroids. 'Most athletes set out as idealists, performing as well as they can for personal satisfaction,' wrote an Olympic reporter in 1992. 'It is not their fault that they became indoctrinated in a different code. The fault lies with those who have corrupted them by example.'[5] The rulebook of running, jumping and swimming had been rewritten by financial interests and the socio-political relevance of sporting life was transformed accordingly.

Television cleared its schedules to accommodate an ever-swelling calendar of sporting engagements. Newspapers heaped on extra pages with retrospective analysis of missed shots and strained tendons. Third-world nations measured their progress in sporting trophies. The dialectic of western political debate was recast in sporting metaphors as hapless ministers 'scored an own-goal' or 'fouled' each other in the struggle to forge a 'world-beating economy'. In the early 1960s John F. Kennedy noted, with mild surprise, that more Americans attended symphony concerts than watched baseball. A generation on there was no longer any room for comparison. Ball games had taken over week-night television and concert halls were half empty. In the match of the century, sport had overwhelmed classical music to win the leisure contest.

In drastic efforts to regain public favour, classical music courted state and corporate patronage. The visible influence of these ruling classes gave concert and opera houses an 'élitist' aura that stunted the audience base by deterring youngsters and radicals. Sniffing new money, agents upped their artists' fees, putting pressure on ticket prices and narrowing the attendance base still further. Classical music was moneying itself into a corner.

Its top names, meanwhile, were tempted by the novel rewards of mass entertainment. In the gold-rush that ensued after the 1990 Three Tenors concert, it was every soloist for himself and the taxman take the hindmost. Collegiality, commitment and any sense of proportion perished in the stampede. Placido Domingo thought nothing of cancelling a long-contracted date at Covent Garden in Puccini's *Fanciulla del West* in order to join the lucrative Three Tenors reunion in Los Angeles. José Carreras was under police investigation in Rome for demanding and receiving illicit fee boosters of a hundred thousand dollars a concert. Luciano Pavarotti made no apologies for charging twenty-five thousand pesos, the equivalent of five months' wages, to audiences in the poverty-stricken Philippines.

Jessye Norman had the backstage of London's Barbican Hall cleared for her personal convenience, closing the musicians' bar and banishing chorus singers to remote changing rooms. Star blackmail was invariably met by house managements. No one sued the tenors for breach of contract; the Met reportedly allowed some stars to use electronic vocal enhancement; the Barbican gave its chief conductor's room to Norman; and when Kathleen Battle was finally banned at the Met there were claims that she had been victimised for behaving no worse than anyone else. Money had made monsters of gentle musicians and music was corroded by their conduct. Comparisons with world sport were, once again, inescapable.

'Glory nights lost under weight of footballing greed,' lamented a *Times* headline[6] as Diego Maradona pocketed $1.75 million for playing an exhibition match in Korea. Cricket, a once-civilised game, became a battleground as batsmen donned medieval armour to face projectiles hurled with malicious intent at 120 mph. In US football and baseball, three out of four players were alleged to use performance-enhancing drugs. In Rugby Union a commentator choked, as his son's face was crushed by an opponent's boot, and a French player, Jean-François Tordo, needed to have his ear sewn back on after emerging from a South African scrum. Television advertising for a series between England and New Zealand featured a kiwi fruit being crushed to pulp in a British fist. George Orwell once defined sport as a surrogate for war. Bosnia apart, sport in the Nineties was bloodier and more personal than most forms of armed combat and was shown in gory slow motion most nights on prime-time television.

The ultimate bedlam of sporting madness occurred ahead of the 1994 Winter Olympics at Lillehammer when an American ice-skater, Tonia Harding, conspired with her former husband to attack and disable her main rival, Nancy Kerrigan. Despite facing trial, Harding was selected to skate in the Games. Neither she nor Kerrigan stood an icely hope of winning, but organisers reckoned that their contest would rivet a global television audience and delight advertisers. Ratings redoubled when Harding's ex sold unclad videos of their wedding night to a cable channel. The main talking points of the Lillehammer Olympics were boobs and greenbacks. Kerrigan took home a bronze medal and a Disney contract; Harding was offered a mud-wrestling deal in Japan after plea-bargaining a non-custodial sentence. Does anyone know who won the ice-skating at Lillehammer?

The shots in most sports were called by their media owners. Italy's biggest television baron, Silvio Berlusconi, proprietor of AC Milan soccer club, declared in 1993 that it would be 'unfair' for top clubs to be defeated in cup-ties by minnows. 'It is *economic nonsense*,' he complained, 'that a team such as AC Milan could be eliminated through bad luck. It is not modern thinking.'[7] French bosses went about winning in the old-fashioned Mediterranean way. FC Marseilles, owned by the socialist magnate Bernard Tapie, bribed its way to a European Cup triumph until someone squealed and Tapie, like Berlusconi in Italy, was charged with corruption. In Britain, Rupert Murdoch was able to switch soccer away from terrestrial broadcasters to his satellite channel through the inside help of Tottenham Hotspur chairman Alan Sugar, a leading manufacturer of satellite dishes.

The influx of money and media, it was said, made sports more pleasurable and accessible. Facilities at many grounds were certainly improved, but the benefits were intended for a corporate and membership élite, while working-class supporters faced restricted entry and were treated, in many instances, like animals. Dickensian disparities flourished at Wimbledon tennis championships. At the start of a second scorching week in 1993, free hats were finally supplied to ballboys and girls after six of them collapsed with sunstroke. The players, meanwhile, were being paid millions by manufacturers to wear branded headgear. Some games were delayed after the court coverers went down with food poisoning. The All-England Club, which made fourteen million pounds (twenty million dollars) from the tournament, had refused to provide food for casual staff and the coverers, who earned £22.75 ($34) for a fourteen-hour day, ate what they could find and afford – which happened to be a street-vendor's sausage rolls coated in green mould.[8]

It was not difficult to trace parallels in classical music, where a solo violinist facing a new orchestra would joyfully greet a former Juilliard classmate among the second fiddles. The gulf between them was, however, unbridgeable. Where the soloist was making half a million dollars a year, the orchestral player was lucky to take home a tenth of that amount. Could anyone imagine that soloist and ensemble player were making music 'together' when one was worrying about tax shelters and the other whether he could afford a new set of strings? Avarice had eroded any sense of community in classical music.

The competitive route that was the main gateway to a solo career had ravaged the comradeship that used to prevail when one young musician bumped into another. Competitions added a suspicious, combative edge to their discourse. Each aspirant looked at another wondering, will this person steal my only chance of success?

To keep up a supply of gladiators, conservatories geared students to compete, rather than to perform. The pleasure was taken out of playing, as teenagers were taught to impress a jury with flashy effects instead of giving rein to heartfelt expression. Contests were won with athletic bravura, not artistic invention. And if the winners went out emotionally repressed on to the professional circuit, what were audiences meant to feel? Or perhaps audience reaction mattered less to careerists and career makers than the response of a handful of power-players and corporate owners who controlled the outlets where music was played.

These authorities behaved, if not corruptly or violently, then with a snooty disdain for the broad constituency of music lovers. Little was done to lure back a mass audience. The overriding priority for arts centre managers was to please the plutocrats and politicians, and placate the stars. Upon such parlous policies was the future of music thinly predicated. Looking chic to a social élite and acting smarmy to financial providers was the way to run a concert hall.

The sporting parable preached by Mark McCormack spread a gospel of greed and envy among top performers. The mating of classical music with Hollywood movies, as plotted by Peter Gelb at Sony, was ephemeral to the movie business and unequal to the urgent need of restoring public faith in live performance. Luring Meat Loaf to record duets with Luciano Pavarotti would not send heavy metal fans streaming to La Scala. No matter what the moguls maintained, there were no benefits to be gained from being gobbled up by Bill Gates, Norio Ohga or Rupert Murdoch. In the morass of multimedia, classical music was the first art to fall, pushed to the periphery of public attention and redesigned for the privileged classes. In the daily lives of most people classical music now existed only as radio background, almost unnoticed.

The mass media were themselves in a state of flux. Television, at the zenith of its global outreach, was startled to discover that key people were turning off. Research by the Henley Centre in England showed that viewing hours were rising only among a 'cultural underclass' of the unwaged and low-paid. The occupied and educated AB sectors filled their leisure hours with more purposeful activities. Two out of five respondents complained that television was 'dull and predictable' and most felt it was 'getting worse'[9] – this in the world's most pampered small-screen society, where the BBC spent fourteen million pounds on adapting *Pride and Prejudice* and twenty million pounds on sustaining orchestras, out of a sense of civic duty and parliamentary requirement.

That the cultured classes were switching off was no great disaster, since most programming was pitched at achieving a high rating among a mass audience. But the alienation of middle-class audiences would necessarily result in an accelerated erosion of television's fickle commitment to high culture and its replacement by the instant gratification of daytime prurience and nightly nudity.

An excess of channels had bred a remote-control habit in which viewers zapped from one programme to another, taking in very little in content or advertisements. Broadcasters and advertisers, alarmed at low boredom thresholds, responded with sex-line chatshows and greed-struck games. Hands up anyone in the audience who slept with his sister and wants to win a Caribbean holiday. Adult genitalia and their demotic nomenclatures, inadmissible before 1980, became base ingredients of trash TV. Violence, supposedly banned until the infants were abed, was sneak-previewed in kiddie-hour trailers. Hustled and undercut by cable and satellite operators, network television went shamelessly tabloid.

Despite weekly Nielsen ratings and frequent academic surveys like the Henley Centre's, much confusion abounded as to what people really watched, and with what degree of attention. Competitive sport, a key attraction for thirty years, was losing its grip. In Germany, ratings for the ATP tennis championships fell by a quarter in 1994. The US Open shed one-eighth of its viewers. Australians, inexplicably, went off golf.[10] Sport, like much else on television, was blighted by ennui. Networks blamed low action levels and called for shorter game-breaks. What they could not admit was that modern players lacked zeal because television earnings had enriched them to the point of inertia. Media money was turning tennis into a game of automatons. 'I wouldn't buy a ticket to watch it,' said former world champion Ivan Lendl.[11]

In a match between the Croatian Goran Ivanisevic and the Swede Stefan Edberg, only four games out of twenty-three lasted more than a minute; when Ivanisevic played Boris Becker, all they could manage was three sixty-second bouts in two hours. Between smash and volley, the players towelled off, drank formula beverages, ate bananas and looked bored. The Central Statistical Office of Sweden, which stop-watched the matches, concluded: 'The problem of today's tennis entertainment is tied to the excitement factor associated with winning serves and returns. Consider, for example, the best scene performances in opera and the extended songs [arias]. They are longer in duration [3–4 minutes] than the corresponding excitement in today's tennis rallies.'[12]

This comparison was flattering, but misleading. If sport was so sluggish that some disciplines – wrestling and billiards, for example – were getting driven off mainstream TV, the music that was relayed on European television was gripped by *rigor mortis*. Television arts bosses shared the same clubs and predilections as the people who ran opera houses and concert halls. Indeed, they often *were* the same people. Both London opera houses and the Barbican arts centre were headed simultaneously by ex-television types. So were the Alte Oper in Frankfurt, Rome Opera, the Israel Festival and a host of ensembles and institutions around the world. But if anyone imagined that ex-media heads in live music houses could call in old favours to get classical music on to the small screen, they were sadly misinformed. Arts departments in network television were the mendicants of mass media, squeezed on budget and consigned to the wee hours. Arts houses went to television with cap in hand and a desperate look. They were beggars importuning the already beggared, hoping only for the cold comfort of shared misery.

On American television opera might get a minority PBS airing, but only if it was wholly paid for by a sponsor and relayed 'Live from the Met'. In Europe state broadcasters felt some obligation to the national culture, but the justification for producing music programmes was a presumed worthiness, rather than any journalistic or populist imperative. Knowing the viewership would be tiny and the broadcast slot late-night, there was an understandable reluctance to allocate stretched resources to anything involving orchestras, which had to be paid by the hour and paid again if the show was repeated. Cheapness, covert forms of subsidy and a pitch for political brownie-points seemed to be the major criteria for commissioning music films.

The result was a torpid predictability that failed to retain classical adherents, let alone attract new audiences. Televised concerts amounted all too often to overworn works played by overtired stars on spuriously manufactured occasions. Itzhak Perlman playing the Beethoven concerto for the thousandth time in his career, José Carreras singing Mario Lanza on the heart-throb's seventy-fifth birthday. Agency and record label manipulators lurked behind such events, facilitating their transmission in furtive ways, as public broadcasters gave way on editorial autonomy.

The *South Bank Show*, the only arts documentary series on British independent television, aired a roseate fifty-minute profile of mezzo-soprano Cecilia Bartoli that was produced and delivered by her record company, Decca. The BBC entered into a co-production deal with IMG to present McCormack crooner Shirley Bassey. Peter Gelb's Sony films went out on commercial Channel 4. Claudio Abbado's agents at CAMI produced the Berlin Philharmonic New Year's Eve concert in alliance with a consortium of public broadcasters. Warner's Erato division filmed its own artists on behalf of French television. These were, perhaps, lapses of editorial discretion. The normal practice was for a network to commission music projects from small-house producers, and not to inquire too stringently whether the programme was being made with record-company or agency backing. Generally, it was.

The only alternative to outright puffery of artists by their own agents was for networks to shake hands on musical co-productions. The French and German governments, enamoured of this route, went so far as to set up a joint ARTE channel for performing arts programming. An Internationale Musik Zentrum (IMZ) in Vienna co-ordinated multilateral music broadcasting. The difficulty, though, was that broadcasters could seldom agree across borders as to how a programme should be made. And, when they did, the product came out designed by committee and looked as lively as a

December afternoon in Düsseldorf. Film making gave way to deal making.

Given these constraints, it was unsurprising that music programming on network television was lightweight, apologetic or dubious. There was no obvious reduction in music transmissions but the 'mission to inform' that once inspired central broadcasters had been replaced by a brief to fill a certain number of music hours at the lowest achievable cost. The BBC, toying with a music documentary series, replaced it with a music quiz.

Television was, in any event, an alien environment for the aural intensity of classical music, which had once so dominated the radio waves. In the 1990s it receded into the small hours, with any aim of reaching a mass audience hopelessly forsaken. The vision of Arthur Judson, who founded a US network with the primary aim of propagating classical music, seemed quaint and quixotic in an era where the average adult attention span did not exceed two minutes. Television would contrive enough lurid trivia to fill its empty hours, while the sound of music faded into the ether.

So what future remained for the cornerstones of classical music? A tiny élite was assured of survival. The New York Philharmonic Orchestra, with an endowment of a hundred million dollars raised over a century and a half, had enough in the kitty to keep it alive for at least another lifetime. The same could be said for five more American orchestras, and for the Metropolitan Opera.

In Europe, the Philharmonic Orchestras of Vienna and Berlin, the Concertgebouw in Amsterdam and La Scala, Milan, were assured of the sustained elixir of public funding. So were the state opera houses in Munich, Vienna and Berlin. Ensembles of their history and pedigree were emblems of national continuity that could not be sacrificed without the risk of painful political backlash.

The cherished name of most of such institutions was enough to keep them bustling commercially with tourist packages and recording deals. When Sony slashed its massive commitment to the Berlin Philharmonic in 1995, the orchestra's impressive fee of a hundred and eighty thousand Deutschmarks (eighty-two thousand pounds) for a four-session CD was briefly in jeopardy. Chief conductor Claudio Abbado was sent out to scout for work with labels he had never met before. Vacant dates loomed for the first time in living memory. Just as players thought of remortgaging their second homes, in rode Warner to the rescue with two hundred and ten thousand Deutschmarks (ninety-five thousand pounds) per disc for a complete cycle of Bruckner symphonies with Staatsoper chief Daniel Barenboim. Abbado was abashed, his heir-in-waiting triumphant. It was business as usual at the glorious Philharmonie.

Joy in Berlin, however, was matched by disbelief everywhere else. The economics of the Warner deal looked wildly unreal to sister-orchestras who were having to waive their players' fees in order to get any recording work at all. While shunning or squeezing non-star orchestras, the record industry could not afford to dispense with deluxe brand-names that, like Rolls-Royce and Rolex, promised high quality or, at the very least, snob value. EMI in 1995 spent well over half a million Deutschmarks spent recording Beethoven's triple concerto in Berlin with Barenboim, Perlman, Yo-Yo Ma and the Philharmonic, by far the costliest concerto ever produced. The only way left to record classics in an overcrowded market, explained one EMI boss, was to make the biggest noise with the biggest names. There was no point in recording Beethoven with a London orchestra and iridescent young soloists (eat your heart out, Walter Legge).[13] Yet two of the three concerts from which the EMI recording was edited were conspicuously unfull. Berlin, it seemed, was sated to boredom point with classical stars. Decca, meanwhile, were letting Sir Georg Solti set a new opera-budget record with an all-star *Meistersinger* cast and the unmatchable might of the Chicago Symphony Orchestra.

Lesser orchestras were left scavenging for dates and improvising a short-term future. Managers of the five top US orchestras confided that they did not expect many lower-ranked ensembles to see out the century as full-time professional outfits. There was neither the economic demand nor the public will to sustain a symphony orchestra in cities of less than five million inhabitants. All over Europe, radio and municipal orchestras were going to the wall and the record industry was nearing the end of its tether. 'I haven't a clue what there will be left for me to do in five years' time,' a major-label A&R chief candidly confessed.

Music publishers, festival organisers, promoters of pop-classics, piano makers and all the cottage industries that once flourished on a thriving art now prepared for its feeble quiescence. None had any visible strategy that looked beyond the century's end. Wailing about 'the crisis', musical apparatchiks and entrepreneurs wrung their hands and protected their tenuous jobs.

If classical music was to have any future worth strategising, it would need to stop dreaming of past glories and focus on humbler origins. Orchestras had, after all, started life in a Leipzig coffee house. Baroque opera was played with chamber accompaniment. Composers wrote for whatever forces they, or their patron, could afford. Music was made within recognised bounds of economic feasibility. The grand orchestral concert was an occasional luxury, confined to large cities in high season. Travelling virtuosos like Franz Liszt and Fritz Kreisler toured adaptations of key tunes from new symphonies and operas that were not assured of an immediate wider hearing. Far into the twentieth century, new scores were published in scaled-down versions. In post-1918 Vienna, Arnold Schoenberg formed a Society for Private Musical Performance at which Mahler symphonies were reduced to sextets. Better to hear modern music in miniature, said Schoenberg, than mangled by unrehearsed orchestras obedient to a higher economic imperative.

In the following age of low wages and a rising tide of state responsibility for art, complexity became temporarily achievable. In pre-Hitler Berlin, Erich Kleiber accorded a reported one hundred and thirty-seven rehearsals to the première of Berg's *Wozzeck*, while Otto Klemperer staged a Schoenberg–Stravinsky double-bill at the proletarian Kroll Opera. Kleiber recreated *Wozzeck* for British audiences in 1951 – after which, for a dozen heady years, personal austerity combined with government generosity to bring Janáček's operas to a general audience and Schoenberg's *Moses und Aron* to Covent Garden. The BBC brought Mahler back to life with Europe's first post-war symphonic cycle and hired Pierre Boulez as chief conductor when France took fright at his incendiary modernism. Radical German directors took up Walter Felsenstein's time-intensive approach to operatic production, igniting a wave of cost-unconscious avant-gardism. The acme of extravagance was Bernd Alois Zimmermann's opera *Die Soldaten* (*The Soldiers*), requiring a cast of twenty-six, including six high tenors, and an orchestra of more than a hundred.

Premièred in Cologne in 1965 and hailed as a latterday *Wozzeck*, the opera received a spate of German productions, one of which needed three hundred and seventy-seven vocal rehearsals and thirty-three orchestral sessions. *Die Soldaten* was scheduled for several international houses, including Covent Garden, but never quite got there. Times were changing and public money was getting tight. 'It's a Sixties opera,' lamented Esa-Pekka Salonen who longed to conduct it. 'Works like that can't be done in the Nineties.'[14]

Die Soldaten joined a mournful mound of modern unrepeatables, topped by Karlheinz Stockhausen's seven-day *Licht* cycle and Harrison Birtwistle's half-electronic *Mask of Orpheus*. Alongside these casualties, grandiose romanticisms like Halévy's *La Juive*, Meyerbeer's *L'Africaine* and Fauré's *Pénélope* that had been planned by leading opera houses were now declared unperformable.

Advances in art required a low-cost, high-subsidy environment. The first condition was ruled out by fee inflation, the second by official loss of patience with unpleasant noises and empty houses. Subsidy, whether state or corporate, had to be justified in head counts. If audiences shunned innovation, sponsorship would be withheld. For modernism to revive in a hostile climate, new ideas and works needed semi-private cultivation in something like Schoenberg's society. Perversely enough, an exclusive circle of new music devotees might well become a compelling attraction. If the world première of the next Birtwistle work were a members-only event, the media and music lovers would batter the doors down to get in.

The solutions for new music were, however, peripheral to the main concern of rescuing established orchestras. With shortening attention spans, changing behaviour patterns and soaring ticket prices, the concert-going habit was being eroded and the subsidy for concerts undermined. For orchestras to survive, they needed to adapt fast. Ernest Fleischmann's idea of a flexible ensemble that could be dismembered into string quartets and wind chorales was one option. Deborah Borda's adjustment of concert times for commuters' convenience was another. All such schemes involved a redefinition of orchestral activity and the introduction of mechanisms that made a monolithic institution readily responsive to popular requirements. In effect, it meant the end of take-it-or-leave-it subscription concerts and their replacement by travelling players reaching out into the community. It called for greater ingenuity than any manager had yet shown. The reward was a chance to avert disaster, and await a better day.

The best success story of musical regeneration in modern times took place in Australia where, on 8 December 1945, an exiled Viennese viola player called Richard Goldner put on a chamber concert with money he earned from inventing a clothes fastener. Whipping sixteen fellow-refugees into weekly rehearsals for three months, the zip-maker stunned an unsophisticated audience in a half-blacked-out conservatory hall with a performance that was 'the best-rehearsed of any given in Sydney in the memory of the oldest critic'. Touring his group around the continent for the next six years, Goldner formed a national grass-roots organisation that he called 'Musica Viva'. From 1955, Musica Viva began importing well-known ensembles from Europe and America to appear alongside home-grown performers. Co-ordinating programmes with the national broadcaster, ABC, and with the country's orchestras, it fostered a diverse menu of music-making across the continent. With federal subvention, it took music to quarter of a million schoolchildren a year, commissioned new works from top composers and staged an international chamber music competition in Melbourne.

By 1995, Musica Viva was putting on two thousand performances a year to a total audience of three hundred thousand. It was 'the largest entrepreneur of chamber music in the world', yet its programmes were locally deter-mined, representing the tastes and inclinations of listeners across six thousand miles. When the chamber music competition polled an audience prize, farmers in deepest Queensland phoned in from their tractors to pass intelligent judgement on winners and losers. Quite apart from its educative achievement, Musica Viva helped ordinary Australians decide what they wanted to hear. While CAMI's Community Concerts in the United States was becoming unstrung by its profit motive and in Britain a network of music societies was undone by slack organisation, Musica Viva was planning for the next millennium, hand in hand with its audiences and in harmony with broadcasters and orchestras. Tastes might change and the box-office might dip, but Musica Viva was continually reinforced from its roots.

If Musica Viva were unique, it could be ignored as an antipodean freak. But the mission that gripped the impassioned zip-maker can be found glimmering in other quiet corners of the musical globe. In the Green Mountains of Vermont, participants in the Marlboro Music summer festival are warned in advance that 'no one should attend with the intention of performing'. The idea of Marlboro, founded by the exiled German pianist, Rudolf Serkin, in 1951 in a location made famous by cigarette advertising, is that young musicians should play chamber music with senior soloists in an unforced transmission of experience and tradition. Whether any music gets performed for a paying public is a secondary concern; but a performing schedule generally emerges and the purity of some concerts that have survived on record is simply dazzling. To hear Pablo Casals conduct the festival orchestra in Schubert's B-flat major symphony is to sense the Marlboro mission.

More than fifteen hundred musicians have summered in Marlboro over almost half a century and several famous quartets – the Cleveland, the Guarneri, the Vermeer – were actually formed there. When summer ends, the young musicians return to the rat race but something lingers in their style and character. Listen to the artistry of Yo-Yo Ma and Murray Perahia and you can tell that they have passed through Marlboro country, where time and motion stand still for a season and music is made without artificial additives. That Marlboro Music survives is a miracle of enlightened benefaction and devoted administration, but survive it does and in the very heart of musical America. What classical music needs in its temporal crisis is more Marlboros that nurture the spirit, and fewer Salzburgs and Tanglewoods that reduce it to dollars and cents.

Isolated though it is, Marlboro radiates a moral counter-culture around the world. Casals and his associate Alexander Schneider transplanted some of its ethic to small European festivals. The Hungarian violinist Sándor Végh has set up similar havens at the Cornish tip of England and around his Italian home at Cervo.

That summer festivals can flourish without commercialism is attested annually through the Baltic summer when every settlement in Scandinavia seems to organise musical events at no vast expense. A highway town called Mikkeli, two hundred kilometres north of the Finnish capital Helsinki, attracts the costly likes of Vladimir Ashkenazy and Valery Gergiev to lead its orchestral concerts. How? Because every artist under the microscopic pressure of media attention needs somewhere to find a summer refuge and is generally more than happy to repay the residents' neighbourliness with a joyous, gratis performance. Mikkeli, with its lakes and forests and endless light, is an idyll of seclusion where music is bartered summerly for simple friendship.

Even at the core of the music industry there are archipelagos of idealism. Klaus Heymann's Naxos onslaught showed how easy it was to break the star system with obscure performers adequately recorded at low cost. Others, less ambitious than the Hong Kong entrepreneur, confounded the system by placing musical integrity above artist demands. In March 1980, a former record-store assistant and small-label manager took a twelve-thousand-pound bank loan to record obscure classical music on his own label, Hyperion. To make ends meet, Ted Perry drove minicabs at night. Within a year he was heading for break-even. Moved by the songs of a twelfth-century nun whose music he heard on BBC Radio 3, Perry commissioned the first Hildegard von Bingen album from Christopher Page and the Gothic Voices. Titled *A Feather on the Breath of God*, it sold quarter of a million copies and, as Perry liked to say, 'paid for all my mistakes'[15] over the next fifteen years.

There were no frills or glamour to his operation. Occupying a warehouse in Eltham, south-east London, he sited the production office in the middle of the packing floor, where discs were stacked and shipped around the world. In a rush, the boss helped to pack. Most evenings, Perry was to be found sampling talent at the Wigmore Hall and other chamber venues. That was where he discovered Tatyana Nikolayeva, a lost titan of Russian pianism for whom Shostakovich had written his preludes and fugues. Her three-CD recording sold twenty thousand sets in two years. Another Russian pianist, Nikolai Demidenko, was his first exclusive artist and the mainspring of a Hyperion venture into virtuoso romantic concertos. 'My biggest advantage,' said Perry, 'is speed and flexibility. I don't have to go through an international planning committee . . . When an idea comes my way I can make up my mind that minute.'[16]

He commissioned Leslie Howard to perform the solo piano works of Liszt in forty volumes, recorded more of Purcell's music than anyone knew existed and retrieved the symphonies of a living British composer, Robert Simpson, from total neglect. His boldest stroke was to allow the piano accompanist Graham Johnson to plan a thorough thirty-two-disc survey of the six-hundred-odd songs of Franz Schubert for the composer's 1997 bicentenary. Much respected by the singers he partnered, Johnson recruited for his project such luminosities as Dietrich Fischer-Dieskau, Janet Baker, Elly Ameling, Thomas Hampson, Anthony Rolfe Johnson and John Mark Ainsley. They received no star fees or treatment on Hyperion; they were simply there to make music.

With ten employees, some of whom sang or played on his recordings, Perry produced eighty discs a year and built up a catalogue of six hundred. By the end of 1994, he was selling nine hundred thousand discs a year and in some territories overtaking Sony and BMG. At two or three per cent, Hyperion could not challenge the market leaders, but many customers bought no other brand and specialist stores often sold more Hyperion than big-label records. When the multinationals descended on Eltham with cheque-books at the ready, Perry sent them packing. 'What would I do with my life if I sold out?' he shrugged.

Hyperion was typical of a breed of independents that mushroomed in the 1980s to address major-label dereliction. Etcetera in Holland covered twentieth-century vocal repertoire. Opus 111 in France shed light on baroque oratorios. Chandos in England perfected a natural sound and an understanding with good conductors that resulted in award-winning symphonic cycles. CPO in Georgsmarienhütte, Germany, pursued neglected modern symphonists. These family firms were not competitive with the mainstream record companies but complementary to them. By placing music first and artists second, they restored some common sense to a glamour industry that had lost sight of its priorities. In suburban, often unremarkable, ways they lighted a path into the gathering darkness.

As the strains mounted on great ensembles, and the media future turned imponderable, smallness was a virtue to be admired. The music world was inexorably contracting. At bottom, each western nation might be left with one state opera house and two symphony orchestras for each ten million heads of population. Suppressed by trivia, indifference and its own deadly sins, music cried out for a crumb of comfort. Against a dreaded end, it was modest ventures like Musica Viva, Marlboro, Mikkeli and Hyperion, that gave classical music a glimpse of post-millennial reconstruction.

NOTES

1 copy of letter in author's possession
2 comment to the author
3 Incorporated Society of Musicians, 'Careers With Music', London (ISM) 1995, p. 2
4 source: *Business Age* magazine, May 1994
5 Ken Jones, *Independent*, 10 August 1992, p. 28
6 *The Times*, 26 September 1995, p. 40
7 *The European*, 13–16 May 1993, p. 32
8 source: *Daily Telegraph*, 29 June 1993, p. 31
9 *Daily Telegraph*, 21 July 1994
10 *Sunday Times*, 22 May 1994, p. 5
11 *The Times*, 6 July 1993, p. 42
12 *The Times*, nd
13 comments to the author
14 author's interview, November 1995
15 comments to the author
16 interview with the *Independent*, 22 September 1995

FINALE

CORONER'S REPORT

EXHIBIT A:

THE TOP CLASSICAL RECORD LABELS[1]
1 PolyGram (Deutsche Grammophon, Decca, Philips)
2 EMI (Angel, Virgin, Classics for Pleasure)
3 Warner (Teldec, Erato, Nonesuch, Finlandia)
4 Sony (ex-CBS)
5 BMG (ex-RCA, plus Melodiya, Deutsche Harmonia Mundi, Conifer)
6 Naxos

These semi-official figures, collated in 1992, are the most reliable available at time of publication. In the subsequent four years, however, Naxos has overtaken all other labels in the UK, Scandinavia and parts of Asia. By 1996, it was challenging for third place. BMG rose slightly to outstrip Sony, while Warner performed strongly with *Three Tenors II*.

1 MMC, p. 87: the most recent reliable assessment

EXHIBIT B:

THE TOP ARTISTS' AGENCIES, 1996

1 CAMI (Columbia Artists Management, Inc.)   US
2 IMG (International Management Group)   US/UK
3 ICM (International Creative Management)   US
4 Harrison/Parrott   UK
5 Kajimoto Concert Management Co. Ltd   Japan
6 Stage Door Management (Adua Pavarotti)   Italy

CAMI has a predominance of top conductors, ICM of violinists. IMG is strengthening in singers and instrumentalists. Parrott is the largest independent agency in Europe. Kajimoto is the biggest Asian importer and representative of classical musicians, closely and constantly challenged by Tadatsugu Sasaki of the Japan Performing Arts Foundation. Adua Pavarotti's place in this select company is owed to her tenor husband's phenomenal earnings and to the strength of her representation in Italian opera houses.

EXHIBIT C:

THE TOP 100 CLASSICAL EARNERS AND THEIR AGENTS, 1996

sopranos

Cecilia Bartoli	Mastroianni
Kathleen Battle	CAMI/RW[2]
Barbara Bonney	IMG=CAMI
Maria Ewing	(IMG)[3]
Angela Gheorgiu	CAMI
Galina Gorchakova	Mastroianni
Barbara Hendricks	Engstrom (IMG)
Sumi Jo	IMG
Kiri Te Kanawa	(IMG, Parrott)
Catherine Malfitano	
Jessye Norman	CAMI
Elena Prokina	Mastroianni, Allied
Katia Ricciarelli	CAMI
Cheryl Studer	CAMI
Dawn Upshaw	IMG
Carol Vaness	CAMI=IMG

2 Ronald Wilford's personal clients at CAMI are marked 'RW'
3 brackets indicate a secondary agency, or an agency used by the artist on an ad hoc basis

mezzos/contraltos
Agnes Baltsa   CAMI/RW
Anne Sofie von Otter   CAMI/IMG

tenors
Roberto Alagna   Jean-Marie Poilvé, Paris
José Carreras   (IMG, CAMI)
Placido Domingo
Siegfried Jerusalem   (Anders)
Luciano Pavarotti   Herbert Breslin, Adua Pavarotti

basses/baritones
Paata Burchuladze   Askonas
Simon Estes   CAMI/RW
Thomas Hampson   IMG
Dmitri Hvorostovsky   Askonas
Sergei Leiferkus   Mastroianni/Allied
James Morris   Colbert/Askonas
Ruggero Raimondi   CAMI
Samuel Ramey   CAMI (IMG)
Bryn Terfel   O'Neill
John Tomlinson   CAMI

violinists
Joshua Bell   IMG
Sarah Chang   ICM
Kyung-Wha Chung   CAMI
Gidon Kremer   ICM
Cho Liang-Lin   ICM
Midori   ICM
Viktoria Mullova   CAMI/RW
Anne-Sophie Mutter   CAMI
Itzhak Perlman   IMG
Isaac Stern   ICM
Maxim Vengerov   Askonas

pianists
Martha Argerich   CAMI/RW
Alfred Brendel   Ingpen

Yefim Bronfman	ICM
Evgeny Kissin	IMG (Holt)
Murray Perahia	IMG
Ivo Pogorelich	CAMI/RW
Maurizio Pollini	CAMI/RW
Sviatoslav Richter	(Hochhauser)
András Schiff	
Mitsuko Uchida	Van Walsum
Krystian Zimerman	CAMI

other instrumentalists

Yuri Bashmet	Van Walsum
Emerson string quartet	IMG
James Galway	IMG
Kronos quartet	
Yo-Yo Ma	ICM
Wynton Marsalis	ICM
Mstislav Rostropovich	CAMI/RW

conductors

Claudio Abbado	(CAMI/RW)
Vladimir Ashkenazy	Parrott
Daniel Barenboim	(Holt)
Pierre Boulez	(Ingpen)
Riccardo Chailly	(IMG)
Myung-Whun Chung	Parrott
James Conlon	CAMI
Colin Davis	CAMI/RW
Christoph von Dohnányi	Parrott
Charles Dutoit	
Christoph Eschenbach	CAMI/RW
John Eliot Gardiner	IMG
Valery Gergiev	(CAMI)
Bernard Haitink	Holt (CAMI)
Nikolaus Harnoncourt	
Mariss Jansons	IMG (ICM)
Neeme Järvi	CAMI
Carlos Kleiber	(CAMI/RW)
James Levine	CAMI/RW
Lorin Maazel	

Neville Marriner	IMG
Kurt Masur	CAMI/RW
Zubin Mehta	
Yehudi Menuhin	(IMG)
Riccardo Muti	(CAMI/RW)
Mikhail Pletnev	CAMI/RW
André Previn	CAMI/RW
Seiji Ozawa	CAMI/RW
Simon Rattle	Holt (Salomon)
Esa-Pekka Salonen	Van Walsum
Giuseppe Sinopoli	CAMI/RW
Leonard Slatkin	ICM
Sir Georg Solti	(Ingpen)
Yuri Temirkanov	IMG
Michael Tilson Thomas	CAMI
Edo de Waart	Parrott
Franz Welser-Möst	IMG

EXHIBIT D:

THE MILLION-A-YEAR MUSICIANS

Estimating the exact income of classical artists is an imprecise art, but the following table calculates who made most in the 1995–6 season. Three tenors take the top places with exceptional revenue from their World Cup concert and related spin-offs. The three have topped the annual charts since their first football concert in 1990, which coincided with the deaths of the previous top earners, conductors Herbert von Karajan and Leonard Bernstein. It has been a good era, too, for the tenors' favourite maestro, Zubin Mehta.

1 Luciano Pavarotti   **$16–18 million per annum**
Including share of Three Tenors and arena concerts

2 Placido Domingo   **$10 million**

3 José Carreras   **$10 million**

4 Zubin Mehta   **$6 million**
Including Three Tenors share, new contract at Bavarian State Opera
and guest conducting fee of $15,000 (UK) to $40,000 (Japan)

5 Itzhak Perlman   **$5.5 million**
One hundred 50th-birthday year concerts at $45,000 each, plus recordings

6 Lorin Maazel   **$4.5 million**

$1m from Pittsburgh, $2.7 million from Bavarian Radio,
plus guest concerts and recordings

7 Daniel Barenboim   **$3 million**

$2+ million from Chicago and Berlin, plus guesting and records

8 Vladimir Ashkenazy   **$2.7 million**

Deutsche Sinfonie Orchester job, plus exceptionally busy calendar
as pianist and conductor and huge record catalogue royalties

9 Anne-Sophie Mutter   **$2.5 million**

Highest paid female artist, huge seller in Germany, where she is paid DM
100,000 per concert

= Claudio Abbado

Berlin Philharmonic post, plus heavy tours and big record backlist

11 Jessye Norman   **$2 million**

Biggest in Japan and Salzburg

= Cecilia Bartoli

One Mozart recital disc sold half a million this year,
but her fees in Italy are a modest IL15m (£7,000)

= Seiji Ozawa

Income sheltered in havens, but Boston and
Japan salaries plus records easily top $2m

14 Kurt Masur   **$1.8 million**

NY Philharmonic salary doubled this year to $1.4m,
plus guest dates, records and Leipzig Gewandhaus post

15 Mstislav Rostropovich   **$1.5 million**

Globally conducting and cello-playing,
with huge EMI deal for his Bach suites

= James Levine

The Metropolitan Opera chief was chosen to
conduct the Three Tenors Roadshow from June 1996

17 Kiri Te Kanawa   **$1 million to $1.5 million**

Outdoors with IMG, very high concert fee, lots of records

= John Eliot Gardiner

Top-selling conductor on the DG list, slower in concert hall

= Carlos Kleiber

Turned down $1m for five concerts in Japan;
appearances so rare he can name own price

= Cheryl Studer

Recording most major soprano roles for DG

= **Esa-Pekka Salonen**

$700,000 salary at Los Angeles Philharmonic,
plus Helsinki Festival headship, Sony recordings and guest conducting

. . . and still selling after all these years:

The late Leonard Bernstein   **$2 million**

Bernstein recordings and memorabilia were moving twice as fast after
his death. His composer and author copyrights were snapped up in
1995 by PolyGram; the $2.5m is an estimate of his record
royalties only as a conductor and pianist.

The late Herbert von Karajan   **$1.5m**

Royalties from 900 records pouring in at all price levels,
reissued and personally promoted by widow, Eliette.

EXHIBIT E:

SOME CLOSELY GUARDED, BUT CERTIFIABLY ACCURATE CONCERT FEES

The following fees were paid by London orchestras in two recent seasons.
They reveal the precise market value of major artists, often at some
divergence to their music-biz hype. Nevertheless, arm-wrestling by powerful agents distorted the value of certain performers. Few would imagine that
the world-weary André Previn warranted the top fee in Britain, seven times
the wage of the penetrative and experienced Sir Charles Mackerras, and
fourfold the hire of local lion Simon Rattle. Few would expect the ageing
flautist James Galway and violinist Pinchas Zukerman to take the top solo
fees, outstripped only by the piano stars Perahia and Pollini. At twelve
thousand pounds, Pollini earned £600 for every minute of a Beethoven
concerto.

Exploiting inter-orchestral rivalry, agents were able to sell the same artist
at different prices. Pollini in 1991–2 was paid £11,000 by one London
orchestra and £12,000 by another; Alexeev got £1,800 and £2,100;
Mackerras received £2,000 and £2,750.

The influence of record companies is prevalent but less visible. Wolfgang
Sawallisch was not a box-office draw, but the possibility of EMI sessions
persuaded one orchestra to pay him way over the odds. The Japanese
conductor Kazuhiro Koizumi was barely a household name, but the recording
work he brought to the orchestra earned him four high-profile London
concerts and twice the fee of the rising British conductor, Mark Wiggles-
worth. In serpentine ways such as these do market forces govern the selection

and promotion of artists. Whether merit is ever justly rewarded is up to the music lover to judge.

	1991–2	1992–3
Dmitri Alexeev	£2,100	
Vladimir Ashkenazy (cond)	£7,000	£8,000
Olaf Baer	£3,000	
Kathleen Battle	£6,500	
Hildegard Behrens		£8,500
Joshua Bell		£2,100
Paavo Berglund		£3,000
Kyung-Wha Chung	£4,000	
Brigitte Fassbaender	£4,000	
James Galway		£8,500
Sir Charles Groves	£1,900	
Bernard Haitink	£9,500	£9,500
Ofra Harnoy	£1,100	
Barbara Hendricks		£5,000
Günther Herbig		£3,000
Peter Jablonski	£850	
King's College Choir		£1,353
Kazuhiro Koizumi	£1,750	
Gidon Kremer	£5,000	
Mariss Jansons	£3,500	£4,800
Nigel Kennedy		£4,500
René Kollo	£8,200	
Sergei Leiferkus		£3,000
Radu Lupu		£5,000
Sir Charles Mackerras	£2,000	£3,000
Sir Peter Maxwell Davies		£2,500
Zubin Mehta	£9,500	£10,000
Lord Menuhin (cond)	£5,000	£5,250
Midori	£3,250	£3,500
Shlomo Mintz	£4,000	
Viktoria Mullova	£3,125	
Anne-Sophie Mutter		£7,750
Anne-Sofie von Otter	£3,500	
Murray Perahia	£10,000	
Maurizio Pollini	£12,000	£12,500
Lucia Popp		£6,500

André Previn	£14,000	
Simon Rattle	£4,000	
Carlo Rizzi		£2,000
Gennady Rozhdestvensky		£9,000
Wolfgang Sawallisch	£8,500	
András Schiff		£6,000
Gil Shaham	£1,500	
Kathryn Stott	£975	£1,200
Yuri Temirkanov	£5,000	£5,500
Klaus Tennstedt	£10,000	£10,000
John Tomlinson	£2,500	
Mitsuko Uchida		£3,500
Maxim Vengerov	£2,500	
Hans Vonk		£3,500
Julian Lloyd Webber	£1,867	
Franz Welser-Möst	£5,500	£6,500
Mark Wigglesworth	£900	
Pinchas Zukerman		£8,500

BIBLIOGRAPHY

A. *Principal interviews*
Antonio de Almeida, Provence
Mathias Bamert, London
Lady (Evelyn) Barbirolli, London
Daniel Barenboim, Paris and Munich
Deborah Borda, New York
Pierre Boulez, Paris and London
Schuyler G. Chapin, New York
Myung-Whun Chung, Paris
Peter Diamand, London
Placido Domingo, Salzburg
David Drew, London
Ernest Fleischmann, Los Angeles
Justus Frantz, Hamburg
Daniele Gatti, Rome
Valery Gergiev, St Petersburg

Louis Gilis, Brussels
Clive Gillinson, London
Michael Haas, Hamburg
Bernard Haitink, London
Philip Hart, Santa Fe, New Mexico
Seppo Heikinheimo, Helsinki
Klaus Heymann, Hong Kong and Sydney
Sir Ian Hunter, London
Mariss Jansons, St Petersburg
Hans Landesmann, Salzburg
Masa Kajimoto, Tokyo
Nigel Kennedy, Malvern
Lotte Klemperer, Zurich
Jacques Leiser, London
György Ligeti, Hamburg
John F. Mastroianni, London
Mark H. McCormack, London
Jessye Norman, London
Michael Nyman, London
Norio Ohga, Tokyo
Jasper Parrott, London
Itzhak Perlman, Amsterdam
Janice Roberts Wilford, New Canaan, Ct.
Frank Salomon, New York
Marvin Schofer, New York
Belle Schulhof, London
Rita Schütz, Zurich
Noam Sheriff, Savyon
Michael Shmith, Melbourne
Ed Smith, Birmingham
Isaac Stern, Paris
Wilfred Stiff, London
Wolfgang Stresemann, Berlin
Virgil Thomson, New York
Joeske Van Walsum, London
Elmar Weingarten, Berlin
Ronald A. Wilford, New York
Roger Wright, Hamburg

B. Reports, dissertations, ephemera and unpublished manuscripts

ASOL–92 American Symphony Orchestra League conference proceedings, containing Wolf Organisation report on 'The Financial Condition of Symphony Orchestras', Washington DC, 1992

ASOL–93 Americanizing the American Orchestra: Report of the National Task Force for the American Orchestra: An Initiative for Change, 1993

BACA 92–4 Proceedings of the international conference of the British Association of Concert Agents, London, April 1992, 1993, 1994

CARLESS Richard Carless and Patricia Brewster, 'Patronage and the Arts'. Conservative Political Centre on behalf of the Bow Group, London, 1959

DOUBLE Leila Doubleday, 'Letter to my Grandchildren', 2 typescript vols, unpublished, 1963

ED–56 A Review of the first ten years of the Edinburgh International Festival, its aims and its origins, its achievements and its hopes for the future, Edinburgh (Festival Society Ltd) 1956

GER Olga Geroulanos, 'Music Culture in the Age of Mechanical Reproduction', Master of Philosophy Thesis, Cambridge University, 1993

GLY–34–95 Glyndebourne Festival programmes

HOLT–76 Harold Holt centenary concert programme book, Royal Albert Hall, 1 July 1976

MMC Monopolies and Mergers Commission, 'The Supply of Recorded Music', presented to Parliament, London, June 1994

PH–77 The Philharmonia Orchestra, 1977–8

PLATTE *Musik und Gesellschaft: Technik, Wirtschaft und Ästhetik der Schalplatte. Symposion aus der 'hifi 68 Düsseldorf'* (Braun, Karlsruhe) 1970

POLY–100 *100 Jahre Schallplatte, 1887–1987, von Hannover in die Welt*, PolyGram exhibition catalogue, Hanover, 1987

PSI–ARTS Heather Rolfe, 'Arts Festivals in the UK', Policy Studies Institute, 1992

UE–75 *75 Jahre Universal Edition*, Vienna 1976

ULLMANN Lawrence Morton Lerner, 'The Rise of the Impresario: Bernard Ullmann and the transformation of musical culture in America', Dissertation, University of Wisconsin, 1970

C. Principal books consulted

Arditi, Luigi, *My Reminiscences* (Skeffington & Son, London) 1896

Astruc, Gabriel, *Le pavillon des fantômes*. (Bernard Grasset, Paris) 1929

Attali, Jacques, *Noise: The Political Economy of Music* (transl. Brian Massumi) (MUP, Manchester) 1985

Bachmann, Robert C., *Karajan: Notes on a Career* (transl. Shaun Whiteside) (Quartet Books, London) 1990

Barnum, Phineas T., *Struggles and Triumphs; or, Forty Years Recollections of P. T. Barnum, Written by Himself* (J. B. Burr, Hartford, Conn.) 1869

Batten, Joe, *The Story of Sound Recording* (Rockliff, London) 1956

Bing, Rudolf, *5000 Nights at the Opera* (Hamish Hamilton, London) 1972

Blom, Eric, *Music in England* (Pelican, rev. edn, London) 1947

Boyd, Malcolm, *Bach* (Dent, London) 1983

Breslin, Herbert H. (ed.), The Tenors (Macmillan, New York) 1973

Buckle, Richard, *Diaghilev* (Weidenfeld & Nicolson, London) 1979

Busch, Max, and Peter Dannenberg, *Die Hamburgische Staatsoper, 1678–1988* (Musik und Theater Verlag, Zürich) 1990

Caplat, Moran, *Dinghies to Divas* (Collins, London) 1985

Cardus, Neville, *Autobiography* (Collins, London) 1947

Carpenter, Paul S., *Music: an Art and a Business* (University of Oklahoma Press, Norman) 1950

Chapin, Schuyler G., *Musical Chairs* (Putnams, New York) 1977

Chasins, Abram, *Leopold Stokowski* (Dutton, New York) 1979

Copinger and Skone James on the Law of Copyright, 9th edition (Sweet & Maxwell Ltd, London) 1958

Craft, Robert, *Small Craft Advisories* (Thames & Hudson, London) 1989

Cron, Theodore O., and Burt Goldblatt, *Portrait of Carnegie Hall* (Macmillan, New York) 1966

Culshaw, John, *Ring Resounding* (Secker & Warburg, London) 1967

——, *Putting the Record Straight* (Secker & Warburg, London) 1981

Damrosch, Walter, *My Musical Life* (Scribners, New York) 1926

Daniel, Oliver, *Stokowski: A Counterpoint of View* (Dodd, Mead & Co., New York) 1982

Dannen, Frederic, *The Hit Men* (Muller, London) 1990

Donaldson, Frances, *The Royal Opera House in the 20th Century* (Weidenfeld & Nicolson, London) 1988

Ehrlich, Cyril, *The Music Profession in Britain since the Eighteenth Century* (Clarendon Press, Oxford) 1985

Finck, Henry T., *Success in Music and How it is Won* (John Murray, London) 1890

Fingleton, David, *Kiri* (Collins, London) 1982

Flesch, Carl, *Memoirs* (transl. Hans Keller) (Rockliff, London) 1957

Foss, Hubert, and Noel Goodwin, *London Symphony* (Naldrett Press, London) 1954

Franklin, David, *Basso Cantante, an autobiography* (Duckworth, London) 1969

Frohnmayer, John, *Leaving Town Alive: Confessions of an Arts Warrior* (Houghton Mifflin, New York) 1993

Gallup, Stephen, *A History of the Salzburg Festival* (Weidenfeld & Nicolson, London) 1987

Ganz, Wilhelm, *Memories of a Musician* (John Murray, London) 1913

Gelatt, Roland, *The Fabulous Phonograph, 1877–1977* (Cassell, 2nd rev. edn, London) 1977

Gillis, Daniel, *Furtwängler and America* (Manyland Books, New York) 1970

Glover, J. M., *Jimmy Glover – His Book* (Methuen, London) 1911

Goldin, Milton, *The Music Merchants* (Macmillan, New York) 1969

Graffman, Gary, *I Really Should Be Practising* (Doubleday, New York) 1981

Letters of Percy Grainger, 1901–1914, (ed. Kay Dreyfus) (Macmillan, London) 1985

van Gruithuijsen, Erik, and Peter Junge, *De Revolutie Van Jan Timmer* (Strengholt, Amsterdam–Antwerp) 1992

Gutmann, Albert, *Aus dem Wiener Konzertleben* (Gutmann, Vienna) 1914

Haeusserman, Ernst, *Herbert von Karajan, eine Biographie* (Wilhelm Goldmann Verlag, neubearbeitete auflage, Munich) 1983

Haltrecht, Montague, *The Quiet Showman: Sir David Webster and the Royal Opera House* (Collins, London) 1975

Hambourg, Mark, *From Piano to Forte* (Cassell, London) 1931

——, *The Eighth Octave* (Williams & Norgate, London) 1951

Harewood, Lord, *The Tongs and the Bones* (Weidenfeld & Nicolson, London) 1981

Hart, Philip, *Orpheus in the New World* (Norton, New York) 1973

Heinsheimer, Hans W., *Give my Regards to Aida* (Knopf, New York) 1968

Hellsberg, Clemens, *Demokratie der Könige: Die Geschichte der Wiener Philharmoniker* (M&T Verlag, Zürich) 1992

Hiller, Ferdinand, *Mendelssohn: letters and recollections* (Vienna House, New York) 1972

(HOR), *The Golden Horseshoe: The life and Times of the Metropolitan Opera House*, by the editors of *Opera News* (Viking, New York) 1965

Hughes, Adela Prentiss, *Music is My Life* (World, Cleveland) 1947

Inghelbrecht, D. E., *The Conductor's World* (transl. G. Prerauer and S. Malcolm Kirk. (Peter Nevill, London) 1953

——, *Mouvement contraire; souvenirs d'un musicien* (Editions Domat, Paris) 1947

Jaklitsch, Hans, *Die Salzburger Festspiele, Band III: Verzeichnis der Werke und der Künstler 1920–1990* (Residenz Verlag, Salzburg) 1991

Jefferson, Alan, *Sir Thomas Beecham, a centenary tribute* (Macdonald & Janes, London) 1979

———, *Schwarzkopf* (Gollancz, London) 1996

Joel, John, *I Paid the Piper* (Howard Baker, London) 1970

Kennedy, Michael, *Barbirolli, conductor laureate: the authorised biography* (Macgibbon & Kee, London) 1971

Kesting, Jürgen, *Maria Callas* (transl. John Hunt) (Quartet, London) 1992

Klein, Herman, *The Age of Patti* (T. Fisher Unwin, London) 1920

Knepler, Hugo, *O Diese Künstler* (Fiba-Verlag, Vienna) 1931

Laszlo, Zsigmond, and Béla Mateka, *Franz Liszt, a biography in pictures* (Corvina, Budapest) 1968

Lebrecht, Norman, *The Maestro Myth* (Simon & Schuster, London) 1991

Lee, Edward, *Folksong and Music Hall* (RKP, London) 1982

Lehmann, Lilli, *Mein Weg* (S. Hirtel, Leipzig) 1920

Levi, Erik, *Music in the Third Reich* (Macmillan Press, Basingstoke) 1994

Lipman, Samuel, *Music and More* (Northwestern University Press, Evanston, Illinois) 1992

Loesser, Arthur, *Men, Women and Pianos* (Gollancz, London) 1955

Lynes, Russell, *The Lively Audience; A social history of the visual and performing arts in America, 1890–1950* (Harper & Row, New York) 1985

Mayer, Martin, *The Met: 100 Years of Grand Opera* (Thames & Hudson, London) 1983

Mayer, Martin (with Gerald Fitzgerald), *Grandissimo Pavarotti* (Robert Hale, London) 1986

(MHM) McCormack, Mark Hume, *What They Don't Teach You at Harvard Business School* (Collins, London) 1984

Mapleson, James H. *The Mapleson Memoirs; the career of an operatic impresario, 1858–1888* (ed. Harold Rosenthal) (Putnam, London) 1966

Maretzek, Max, *Crotchets and Quavers* (S. French, New York) 1855

———, *Sharps and Flats* (American Music Pub. Co., New York) 1890

Martin, Ben, *Marcel Marceau: Master of Mime,* (Paddington Press, London) 1978

Melba, Nellie, *Melodies and Memories* (Hamish Hamilton, reprint, London) 1980

Metz, Robert, *CBS: Reflections in a Bloodshot Eye* (Playboy Press, Chicago) 1975

Milstein, Nathan, and Solomon Volkov, *From Russia to the West* (Barrie & Jenkins, London) 1990

Moore, Gerald, *Am I Too Loud? memories of a piano accompanist* (Hamish Hamilton, London) 1962

Moore, Jerrold Northrop, *A Voice in Time: the gramophone of Fred Gaisberg, 1873–1951* (Hamish Hamilton, London) 1976

Nichols, Roger (transl. and ed.), *Debussy Letters* (Faber & Faber, London) 1987

O'Connor, Charles, *The Other Side of the Record* (Alfred A. Knopf, New York) 1947

Paderewski, Ignace Jan, and Mary Lawton, *The Paderewski Memoirs* (Collins, London) 1939

Page, Tim, and Vanessa Weeks Page, *Selected Letters of Virgil Thomson* (Summit Books, New York) 1988

Paley, William S., *As it Happended: A Memoir* (Doubleday, Garden City, NY) 1979

Pavarotti, Adua, *Life with Luciano* (Weidenfeld & Nicolson, London) 1992

Pavarotti, Luciano (with William Wright), *My Own Story* (Sidgwick & Jackson, London) 1981

——, *My World* (Chatto & Windus, London) 1995

Peacock, Alan and Ronald Weir, *The Composer in the Marketplace* (Faber & Faber, London) 1971

Pearton, Maurice, *The LSO at 70, a history of the orchestra* (Gollancz, London) 1974

Pettit, Stephen J., *Philharmonia Orchestra* (Hale, London) 1986

Prieberg, Fred K., *Trial of Strength: Wilhelm Furtwängler and the Third Reich* (transl. Christopher Dolan) (Quartet, London) 1991

Prokofiev, Oleg (transl. and ed.), *Sergei Prokofiev: Soviet Diary 1927 and other writings* (Faber & Faber, London) 1991

Pulver, Jeffrey, *Paganini, the Romantic Virtuoso* (Herbert Joseph, London) 1936

Ratcliffe, Ronald V., *Steinway & Sons* (Chronicle Books, San Francisco) 1989

Rathkolb, Oliver, *Führertre und Gottbegnaber: Künstlereliten im Dritten Reich*, (ÖBV, Vienna) 1991

Riess, Curt, *Rolf Liebermann: Nennen Sie mich einfach Musiker* (Glöss, Hamburg) 1977

Robinson, Harlow, *The Last Impresario, the life, times and legacy of Sol Hurok* (Viking, New York) 1994

Rodzinski, Halina, *Our Two Lives* (Charles Scribner's Sons, New York) 1976

Rohozinski, L., (dir.), *Cinquante ans de musique française, 1875–1925* (Editions Musicales de la Librairie de France, Paris) 1925

Rosen, Carole, *The Goossens, A Musical Century* (André Deutsch Ltd, London) 1993

Rosselli, John, *Singers of Italian Opera; the history of a profession* (CUP, Cambridge) 1992

Roth, Ernst, *The Business of Music* (Cassell, London) 1969

——, *Von Prag bis London* (Atlantis, Zurich) 1974

Rubinstein, Anton, *Autobiography* (Little, Brown, Boston) 1890

——, *My Young Years* (Cape, London) 1973

——, *My Many Years* (Cape, London) 1980

Sachs, Harvey, *Toscanini* (Weidenfeld & Nicolson, London) 1978

Sanjek, Russell and David, *The American Popular Music Business in the Twentieth Century* (OUP, New York) 1991

Saxon, A. H., *P. T. Barnum, The Legend and the Man*, (Columbia University Press, New York) 1989

Saylor, Oliver, *Max Reinhardt and his theatre* New York, 1923

Schonberg, Harold, *Horowitz* (Simon & Schuster, London) 1993

Schuh, Willi, *Richard Strauss, a Chronicle of the early years* (CUP, Cambridge) 1982

Schwarz, Boris, *Great Masters of the Violin* (Hale, London) 1984

Schwarzkopf, Elisabeth, *On and Off the Record: A memoir of Walter Legge* (Faber & Faber, London) 1982

Scott, Michael, *The Great Caruso* (Hamish Hamilton, London) 1988

Shanet, Howard, *Philharmonic: A History of New York's Orchestra* (Doubleday, New York) 1975

Sheean, Vincent, *The Amazing Oscar Hammerstein* (Weidenfeld & Nicolson, London) 1956

Shirakawa, Sam H., *The Devil's Music Master* (OUP, New York) 1992

Smith, Cecil, *Worlds of Music* (Lippincott, Philadelphia) 1952

Stargardt-Wolff, Edith, *Wegbereiter grosser Musiker* (Bote & Bock, Berlin) 1954

Stokowski, Olga Samaroff, *An American Musician's Story* (W. W. Norton, New York) 1939

Storr, Anthony, *Music and the Mind* (The Free Press, New York) 1992

Strakosch, Maurice, *Souvenirs d'un impresario*, Paris, 1887

Stravinsky, Igor, *Selected Correspondence* (edited and selected by Robert Craft) (Faber & Faber, 3 vols, London) 1982–5

Stresemann, Wolfgang, *The Berlin Philharmonic from Karajan to Bülow* (Stapp Verlag, Berlin) 1979

——, *. . . und Abends in die Philharmonie* (Kristall bei Langen Müller, Munich) 1981

——, *Zeiten und Klänge* (Ullstein, Frankfurt) 1994

Stuckenschmidt, H. H., *Zum Hören geboren* (Piper, Munich) 1979

Swoboda, Henry (ed.), *The American Symphony Orchestra* (Basic Books, New York) 1967

Szeps, Berta, *My Life and History* (Cassell, London) 1938

Taubman, Howard, *Music on my Beat* (Simon & Schuster, New York) 1943

Temianka, Henri, *Facing the Music* (Alfred Publishing Co., Sherman Oaks, California) 1980

Virgil Thomson by Virgil Thomson (Weidenfeld & Nicolson, London) 1967

Toobin, Jerome, *Agitato, a Trek through the Musical Jungle* (Viking, New York) 1975

Truman, Margaret, *Harry S. Truman* (Hamish Hamilton, London) 1973

Umbach, Klaus, *Geldschein-Sonate: das Millionenspiel mit der Klassik* (Ullstein, Frankfurt) 1990

Vaughan, Roger, *Herbert von Karajan: The Conductor as Idol* (Weidenfeld & Nicolson, London) 1985

Vishnevskaya, Galina, *Galina* (Hodder & Stoughton, London) 1984

Wagner, Richard, *My Life* (Constable, London) 1911

Walker, Alan, *Franz Liszt, The Virtuoso Years, 1811–47* (Faber & Faber, London) 1983

——, *Franz Liszt, The Weimar Years, 1848–61* (Faber & Faber, London) 1989

Walter, Bruno, *Theme and Variations* (transl. James A. Galston) (Hamish Hamilton, London) 1947

——, *Briefe 1894–1962* (Fischer Verlag, Frankfurt), 1969

Weber, William, *Music and the Middle Classes* (Croom Helm, London) 1975

White, Eric Walter, *The Rise of English Opera* (John Lehmann, London) 1951

Wulf, Josef, *Musik im Dritten Reich* (Sigbert Mohn Verlag, Gütersloh) 1963

Ysaÿe, Antoine, and Bertram Ratcliffe, *Ysaÿe: his life, work and influence* (William Heinemann, London) 1947

A NOTE ON CURRENCIES

Through most of the nineteenth century, the French franc was the most readily exchangeable currency in Europe and the British pound was elsewhere. In the latter part of the twentieth century, their roles were supplanted by the German Mark and the American dollar. The following guide to values is approximate.

1850–1914
£1 = $4.8 = Ffr25 = DM21 = IL27
($1 = Ffr5 = DM 4)

1914–1945
£1 = $4

1948–1980
£1 = $2.8/2.4

1980s
£1 = $1.9/1.2 = DM3.5/3 = Ffr11/10

1995
£1 = $1.5 = DM2.2 = Ffr8

AUTHOR'S ACKNOWLEDGEMENTS

A great many people who helped me with this book specifically asked not to be named. I very much hope none of the following will take offence at this modest expression of my gratitude for their support, advice and hospitality in what was often a wilderness of buried information.

Australia: Lin Bender, Sonia Chalmers, Sandra Keane, Michael Shmith (Melbourne), Kenneth Tribe (Sydney)
Austria: Nicole Bachmann, Wolfgang Herles, Hans Landesmann
Canada: Helen Montagna, Alan Walker
Czech Republic: Jitka Slavikova
Finland: Seppo Heikinheimo
France: Antonio de Almeida, Aviva Cohen, Vincent Meyer
Germany: Anke Grosser, Hellmut Stern (Berlin), Attila Csampai (Munich), Renate Herklotz (Leipzig), Sonia Simmenauer, Vera van Hazebrouck, Michael Haas (Hamburg), Medi Gasteiner (Darmstadt), Fred K. Prieberg (Rheinau)
Israel: Hanoch Ron, Ela and Noam Sherriff
Italy: Margherita Grossi, Marina Mahler

Japan: Masa Kajimoto, Tsutomu Sugiyama

Netherlands: Sytze Smit

Russia: Valery Gergiev, Katarina Sirakanian, Irina Veletskaya, Alexander Yures

Switzerland: Lotte Klemperer, Rita Schütz

UK: Peter Andry, Ewen Balfour, Richard Bebb, Victor Borovsky, Irina Brown, Marius Carboni, Jilly Cooper, William Colleran, Didier de Cottignies, Sarah Crompton, Peter Diamand, Paul Findlay, Massimo Freccia, Berthold Goldschmidt, Judy Grahame, Andrew Green, Margaret Hartog, Louise Honeyman, Martin Huber, Joan Ingpen, Ruth Jordan, Graeme Kay, Ernest Keeling, John Lucas, James Mallet, John McMurray, Sarah Miller, Jerrold Northrop Moore, Michael Poole, Carol O'Brien, Christopher Raeburn, Nigel Reynolds, Zsuzsi Robosz, Carole Rosen, Albi Rosenthal, Tim Rostron, David Sigall, Daniel Snowman, Sam Sylvester, Basil Tschaikov, Christel Wallbaum, Caroline Whyte, John Willan

USA: Deborah Borda, Margaret Carson, Schuyler G. Chapin, David V. Foster, Daniella and Rafi Grunfeld, Gilbert E. Kaplan, Alan Kozinn, Lawrence Morton Lerner, Tim Page, David W. Rubin, Belle Schulhof (New York), Richard Rodzinski (Fla), Naomi Graffman, Jonathan and Ursula Sternberg (Philadelphia), Gideon Toeplitz (Pittsburgh), Meryle Secrest (Washington), Jacques Leiser (San Diego), William Malloch (Los Angeles)

INDEX

Acronyms precede the full name, eg EMI (Electrical and Musical Industries)

POCKET
B O O K S

THE MAESTRO MYTH

Norman Lebrecht

Where have all the great conductors gone? In this
provocative and penetrating history of their profession,
Norman Lebrecht argues that the lust for power and
wealth has brought the maestro breed to the brink of
extinction. *The Maestro Myth* is a refreshingly vigorous,
iconoclastic investigation of a profession which has too
often been the object of sycophantic reverence. No music
lover who enjoys having his opinions and prejudices
challenged will want to be without it.

PRICE £7.99

ISBN 0 671 01045 X

Also by Norman Lebrecht

THE COMPANION TO 20TH CENTURY MUSIC

Price £12.99

ISBN 0 684 82129 X